Richard Lalor Sheil, Thomas MacNevin

The Speeches of the Right Honourable Richard Lalor Sheil

Second Edition

Richard Lalor Sheil, Thomas MacNevin

The Speeches of the Right Honourable Richard Lalor Sheil
Second Edition

ISBN/EAN: 9783744713870

Printed in Europe, USA, Canada, Australia, Japan

Cover: Foto ©ninafisch / pixelio.de

More available books at **www.hansebooks.com**

THE SPEECHES

OF

THE RIGHT HONOURABLE

RICHARD LALOR SHEIL

WITH MEMOIR

BY THOMAS MACNEVIN, ESQ.

AUTHOR OF "THE CONFISCATION OF ULSTER," "THE VOLUNTEERS OF 1782," &c.

Second Edition.

DUBLIN:
JAMES DUFFY, SONS AND CO.,
15, WELLINGTON QUAY;
AND 22, PATERNOSTER ROW, LONDON.
1872.

CONTENTS

	PAGE
Memoir of Richard Lalor Sheil	v
Wolfe Tone's Memoirs	25
Informations against Æneas M'Donnell, May 8, 1827	31
Clare Election, September, 1828	46
Clonmel Aggregate Meeting	71
Repeal of the Union, April 25, 1834	95
Russian and Turkish Treaties, March 17, 1834	111
Orange Lodges, August 11, 1835	120
Church of Ireland, July 23, 1835	126
Irish Municipal Reform Bill, March 28, 1836	139
Tithes, June 2, 1836	145
The Irish Church, August 2, 1836	153
Irish Municipal Bill, February, 22, 1837	160
Civil War in Spain, April 18, 1837	170
Lord Normanby's Government in Ireland, April 19, 1839	176
Lord Stanley's Irish Registration Bill, June 10, 1840	189
The Sugar Duties, May 18, 1841	196
Corn Laws, March 9, 1842	204
Income Tax, April 18, 1842	210
Factory Bill, May 18, 1843	219
Irish Arms Bill, May 19, 1843	226
Vote by Ballot, June 21, 1843	236
Irish State Trials (Queen's Bench)	245
Irish State Trials, February 22, 1844	286
France and Morocco, July 22, 1844	313
Adjournment of the House, August 9, 1844	321
Income Tax, February 19, 1845	325
Post Office Espionage, April 1, 1845	330
College of Maynooth, April 4, 1845	334

CONTENTS

	PAGE
Meeting at Penenden Heath	344
The "Elect"	353
Reply to Mr. M'Clintock	356
Meath Catholic Meeting	365
Connaught Provincial Meeting	372
The Orangemen of Armagh	378
The Bishop of Waterford	385
Vote of Thanks to the Bishop of Waterford	391
Prayer for Emancipation	394
The Duke of York	397
The New Reformation	403
The Forty-Shilling Freeholders	410
Wealth of the Established Church	417
Hibernian Bible Society	421
Prosecution of Mr. O'Connell	427
Course to be Adopted by Catholics	431
Catholic Emancipation	436
Resolutions on the Prosecution of Mr. O'Connell	441
Increase of Power	444
Violence of the Association	448
Simultaneous Meetings	458
Adjournment of the Association	460
Vote of Thanks to Mr. Conway	464
Plato and Dr. Magee	467

MEMOIR

OF

THE RIGHT HONOURABLE
RICHARD LALOR SHEIL M.P.

THE RIGHT HONOURABLE RICHARD LALOR SHEIL was born on the 16th of August, 1791, at the residence of his father, Edward Sheil, Esq., in the county of Kilkenny. That gentleman had acquired a considerable fortune in Cadiz, and invested it in the purchase of Bellevue, near Waterford. Soon after his return from Spain he married Miss Catherine Mac Carthy, of Spring House, in the county of Tipperary, a near relative of Count Mac Carthy of Toulouse, who sold his large property in Ireland, and settled in France during the operation of the penal code.

Mr. Sheil received his first instructions in literature from a French clergyman who had fled from his country during the Revolution, and resided at Bellevue, the house of Mr. Sheil's father, as tutor to his family. Soon after the peace of Amiens the Abbé returned to Toulouse, his native city, and Mr. Sheil was sent to a school established at Kensington, by the Prince de Broglio, the son of the celebrated French general, and a near relation of the present Duke. The following account of his school days, written by Mr. Sheil, is extracted from a periodical work :

" As if it were yesterday, though 'tis now many years ago, (*eheu fugaces !*) I recollect the beautiful evening when I left my home, upon the banks of the river Suir, and sailed from the harbour of Waterford for Bristol, on my way to school. It is scarcely germane to the matter, yet I cannot help reverting to a scene.

which has impressed itself deeply in my recollection, and to which I oftentimes in those visions of the memory, to which I suppose every body is more or less subject, find it a pleasure, though a melancholy one, to return. There are few rivers more picturesque than the Suir, (a favourite with Spenser,) in its passage from Waterford to the sea. It is ample and deep, capable of floating vessels of any tonnage, and is encompassed with lofty ridges of rich verdure, on which magnificent mansions, encompassed with deep groves of trees, give evidence of the rapid increase of opulence and of civilization in that part of Ireland. How often have I stood upon its banks, when the bells in the city, the smoke of which was turned into a cloud of gold by a Claude Lorrain sunset, tolled the death of the departing day! How often have I fixed my gaze upon the glittering expanse of the full and overflowing water, crowded with ships, whose white sails were filled with just wind enough to carry them on to the sea; by the slowness of their equable and majestic movement, giving leave to the eye to contemplate at its leisure their tall and stately beauty, and to watch them long in their progress amidst the calm through which they made their gentle and forbearing way. The murmurs of the city were heard upon the right, and the lofty spire of its church rose up straight and arrowy into the sky. The sullen and dull roar of the ocean used to come over the opposite hills from the Bay of Tramore. Immediately before me were the fine woods of Faithleg, and the noble seat of the Bolton family, (Protestants, who have since that time made way for the Catholic wealthy Powers;) on the left was the magnificent seat of another branch of the same opulent tribe—Snowhill; and in the distance, were the three rivers, the Suir, the Nore, and the Barrow, met in a deep and splendid conflux; the ruins of the old abbey of Dunbrody threw the solemnity of religion and of antiquity over the whole prospect, and by the exquisite beauty of the site, afforded a proof that the old Franciscans, who had made a selection of this lovely spot for their monastery, and who have lain for centuries in the mould of its green and luxuriant churchyards, were the lovers of nature, and that when they left the noise and turmoil of the world, they had not relinquished those enjoyments which are not only innocent, but may be accounted holy. I had many a time looked with admiration upon the noble landscape, in the midst of which I was born, but I never felt and appreciated its beauty so well as when the consciousness that I was leaving it, not to return for years to it again, endeared to me the spot of my birth, and set off the beauty of the romantic place in which my infancy was passed, and in which I once hoped (I have since abandoned the expectation) that my old age should decline. It is not in the midst of its woods that I shall fall into the sere and yellow leaf!

"'Something too much of this.'—The ship sailed, I landed at Bristol, and with a French clergyman, the Abbé de Grimeau who had been my tutor, I proceeded to London. The Abbé informed me that I was to be sent to Kensington House, (a college established by the Pères de la Foi, for so the French Jesuits settled in England at that time called themselves,) and that he had directions to leave me there, upon his way to Languedoc, from whence he had been exiled in the Revolution, and to which he had been driven by the *maladie de pays* to return. Accordingly we set off for Kensington House, which is situated exactly opposite the avenue leading to the Palace, and has the beautiful garden attached to it in front. A large iron gate, wrought into rusty flowers, and other fantastic forms, showed that the Jesuit school had once been the residence of some person of distinction; and I afterwards understood that a mistress of Charles the Second lived in the spot which was now converted into one of the sanctuaries of Ignatius. It was a large old-fashioned house, with many remains of decayed splendour. In a beautiful walk of trees, which ran down from the rear of the building through the playground, I saw several French boys playing at swing-swang; and the moment I entered, my ears were filled with the shrill vociferations of some hundreds of little emigrants, who were engaged in their various amusements, and babbled, screamed, laughed, and shouted in all the velocity of their rapid and joyous language. I did not hear a word of English, and at once perceived that I was as much amongst Frenchmen as if I had been suddenly transferred to a Parisian college. Having got this peep at the gaiety of the school into which I was to be introduced, I was led, with my companion, to a chamber covered with faded gilding, and which had once been richly tapestried, where I found the head of the establishment, in the person of a French nobleman, Monsieur le Prince de Broglio. Young as I was, I could not help being struck at once with the contrast which was presented between the occupations of this gentleman and his name. I saw in him a little, slender, and gracefully-constructed abbé, with a sloping forehead, on which the few hairs that were left him were nicely arranged, and well-powdered and pomatum'd. He had a gentle smile, full of a suavity which was made up of guile and of weakness, but which deserved the designation of *aimable*, in the best sense of the word. His clothes were adapted with a peculiar nicety to his symmetrical person, and his silk waistcoat and black silk stockings, with his small shoes buckled with silver, gave him altogether a glossy aspect. This was the son of the celebrated Marshal Broglio, who was now at the head of a school, and notwithstanding his humble pursuits, was designated by every body as 'Monsieur le Prince.'

"Monsieur le Prince had all the manners and attitudes of the court, and by his demeanour put me at once in mind of the old *regime*. He welcomed my French companion with tenderness, and having heard that he was about to return to France, the poor gentleman exclaimed 'Helas !' while the tears came into his eyes at the recollection of 'cette belle France,' which he was never, as he then thought, to see again. He bade me welcome. These preliminaries of introduction having been gone through, my French tutor took his farewell; and, as he embraced me for the last time, I well remember that he was deeply affected by the sorrow which I felt in my separation from him, and turning to Monsieur le Prince, recommended me to his care with an emphatic tenderness. The latter led me into the school-room, where I had a desk assigned to me beside the son of the Count Décar, who has since, I understand, risen to offices of very high rank in the French Court. His father belonged to the nobility of the first class. In the son, it would have been at that time difficult to detect his patrician derivation. He was a huge, lubberly fellow, with thick matted hair, which he never combed. His complexion was greasy and sudorific, and to soap and water he seemed to have such a repugnance, that he did not above once a week go through any process of ablution. He was surly, dogged, and silent, and spent his time in the study of mathematics, for which he had a good deal of talent. I have heard that he is now one of the most fashionable and accomplished men about the court, and that this Gorgonius, smells now of the pastiles of Rufillus. On the other side of me was a young French West Indian, from the colony of Martinique, whose name was Devarieux. The school was full of the children of the French planters, who had been sent over to learn English among the refugees from the Revolution. He was an exceedingly fine young fellow, the exact reverse in all his habits to Monsieur le Compte Décar, on my left hand, and expended a good deal of his hours of study in surveying a small pocket-mirror, and in arranging the curls of his rich black hair, the ambrosial plenty of which was festooned about his temples, and fell profusely behind his head. Almost

all the French West Indians were vain, foppish, generous, brave
and passionate. They exhibited many of the qualities which
we ascribe to the natives of our own islands in the American
archipelago; they were a sort of Gallican Belcours in little; for
with the national attributes of their forefathers, they united
much of that vehemence and habit of domination, which a hot
sun and West India overseership are calculated to produce. In
general, the children of the French exiles amalgamated readily
with these creoles :—there were, to be sure, some points of substantial difference; the French West Indians being all rich *roturiers*, and the little emigrants having their veins full of the best
blood of France, without a groat in their pockets. But there
was one point of reconciliation between them—they all concurred
in hating England and its government. This detestation was
not very surprising in the West Indian French; but it was not
a little singular, that the boys, whose fathers had been expelled
from France by the Revolution, and to whom England had afforded shelter, and given bread, should manifest the ancient national antipathy, as strongly as if they had never been nursed at
her bosom, and obtained their aliment from her bounty. Whenever news arrived of a victory won by Bonaparte, the whole
school was thrown into a ferment; and I cannot, even at this
distance of time, forget the exultation with which the sons of
the decapitated or the exiled hailed the triumph of the French
arms, the humiliation of England, and the glory of the nation
whose greatness they had learned to lisp. There was one boy
I recollect more especially. I do not now remember his name,
but his face and figure I cannot dismiss from my remembrance.
He was a little effeminate creature, with a countenance that
seemed to have been compounded of the materials with which
waxen babies are made; his fine flaxen hair fell in girlish ringlets about his face, and the exquisite symmetry of his features
would have rendered him a fit model for a sculptor who wished
to throw the *beau ideal* of pretty boyhood into stone. He had
upon him a sickly expression, which was not sufficiently pronounced to excite any disagreeable emotion, but cast over him a
mournful look, which was seconded by the calamities of his family, and added to the lustre of misfortune which attended him.
He was the child of a nobleman who had perished in the Revolution. His mother, a widow, who resided in a miserable lodging in London, had sent him to Kensington House, but it was
well known that he was received there by the Prince de Broglio
from charity; and I should add that his eleemosynary depen-

dence, so far from exciting towards him any of that pity which is akin to contempt, contributed to augment the feeling of sympathy which the disasters of his family had created in his regard. This unfortunate little boy was a Frenchman to his heart's core, and whenever the country which was wet with his father's blood had added a new conquest to her possessions, or put Austria or Prussia to flight, his pale cheek used to flush into a hectic of exultation. and he would break into joyfulness at the achievements by which France was exalted and the pride and power of England were brought down. This feeling, which was conspicuous in this little fellow, ran through the whole body of Frenchmen, who afforded very unequivocal proof of the sentiments by which their parents were influenced. The latter I used occasionally to see. Old gentlemen, the neatness of whose attire was accompanied by indications of indigence, used occasionally to visit at Kensington House. Their elasticity of back, the frequency and gracefulness of their well-regulated bows, and the perpetual smile upon their wrinkled and emaciated faces, showed that they had something to do with the 'vieille cour;' and this conjecture used to be confirmed by the embrace with which they folded the little marquises and counts whom they came to visit.

"Kensington House was frequented by emigrants of very high rank. The father of the present Duke de Grammont, who was at this school, and was then Duke de Guische, often came to see his son. I recollect upon one occasion having been witness to a very remarkable scene. Monsieur, as he was then called, the present King of France, waited one day, with a large retinue of French nobility, upon the Prince de Broglio. The whole body of the schoolboys was assembled to receive them. We were gathered in a circle at the bottom of a flight of stone stairs, that led from the principal room into the playground. The future king of France appeared with his *cortége* of illustrious exiles, at the glass folding-doors which were at the top of the stairs, and the moment he was seen, we all exclaimed, with a shrill shout of beardless loyalty, 'Vive le Roi!' Monsieur seemed greatly gratified by this spectacle, and in a very gracious and condescending manner went down amongst the little boys, who were at first awed a good deal by his presence, but were afterwards speedily familiarized to him by the natural benignity of Charles the Tenth. He asked the names of those who were about him, and when he heard them, and saw in the boys by whom he was encompassed, the descendants of some of the noblest families o France, he seemed to be sensibly affected. One or two names which were associated with peculiarly melancholy recollections, made him thrill. 'Helas ! mon enfant !' he used to say, as some orphan was brought up to him ; and he would then lean down to caress the child of a friend who had perished on the scaffolds of the Revolution."

Mr. Sheil, after mentioning that he was placed at Kensington under the tuition of a Genoese, of the name of Molinari and that Molinari was suddenly ordered to proceed to Siberia, with instructions, if possible, to find his way as a missionary into China, states that he was himself removed to the College of Stonyhurst, of which he gives the following account :—

"The College of Stonyhurst is situated in Lancashire, at the foot of the high hill of Pendel, which, as it was formerly the favourite resort of sorcerers, has, in the opinion of a neighbouring parson, afforded, by a natural succession, a residence to the mysterious ecclesiastics who are adepts in the witchcraft of Ignatius. The scenery by which it is surrounded is of a solemn and almost dreary character. Immediately before the great entrance, which opens into a considerable square, and is surmounted by two very lofty towers, an avenue, in the old English fashion, rises between two large basins of artificial water, whose stagnant tranquillity gives to the approach a dismal aspect. This avenue leads, on the right-hand, to a very extensive deer-park, the neglected walls of which indicate that the spirit of the chase has long since departed from the spot where learning and religion have fixed their abode. A rookery spreads behind the castle (for such it may be justly designated), of ancient and venerable trees. The remains of a noble garden occupy the front; and although its terraces are now dilapidated, and the playground which is used by the students has usurped upon its fine parterres, a noble walk of thickly interwoven yew-trees, which is called the Wilderness, has been spared. and still offers the memorials of magnificence in its long and melancholy vistas. It was originally intended that the building should consist of two wings ; only one, however, was completed, as the expense exceeded the fortune of the projector. The portion of the edifice which is finished, is of great extent. It is of a Gothic character, in the exterior ; but its apartments, and especially the splendid hall, which is flagged with white and polished marble, are of far greater dimensions than the rooms which are generally found in buildings of a similar style. As you look from the great central window of massive stone, you see the ridge of Pendel stretched out in a long line of black and dismal barrenness. The rivers Odder and Ripple, whose banks are lined with fine woods, flow in the valley beneath. The town of Clitheroe is seen on the left, where the plains of Yorkshire present a rich contrast of cultivation in their wide and distant reaches. Ripchester lies on the right; and behind, a line of heathy hills, called Longridge Fell, extends itself for several miles. This fine old mansion was the property of the Sherbourne family, and was afterwards occupied for a period by one of the Dukes of Norfolk. It came by purchase into the hands of the late Mr. Weld, of Ludlow Castle. He had been educated at St. Omer's, among the Jesuits; and after they had been successively obliged to fly from their seminary there, and from Bruges and Liege, they were received by their old pupil at Stonyhurst. During his life, they held the house itself, free from all charges, paying a moderate rent for a considerable tract of ground; and, on his death, (he had first become an ecclesiastic, though he had very large family,) he devised the lands to that sacred corporation, to which he was indebted for his instructions in piety, and for which, as a religionist, he had always entertained a warm predilection. His obsequies were performed with great pomp in the college chapel, and a funeral oration was pronounced upon his merits, amongst which his bequest to the followers of Loyola was not the least conspicuous.

"When I arrived at Stonyhurst College, the principals, and the more eminent teachers, were gentlemen who had held similar situations in the Jesuit establishment at Liege. After they had settled in Lancashire, there were some new recruits added to their numbers; but, generally speaking, the members of the Society had been educated out of England, according to the system adopted in the institutions under the management of that literary order. They were about twenty-five in number, and were, in every respect, superior to the Pères de la Foi, with whom I had sojourned at Kensington, and who merely passed themselves as Jesuits. They were almost all gentlemen by birth, some of them belonging to the best Catholic families in England. Their manners were also distinguished by an urbanity, which it is one of the maxims of their order that they should assiduously cultivate, and which their love of elegant literature had tended to heighten. There were, of course, a few amongst them who were a little uncouth, but these were chiefly persons who had been enrolled in the body since its establishment in Lancashire. Those who had been brought up at St. Omer's, or at Liege, were greatly superior in address to the generality of persons to whom the education of boys is confided. Of the Jesuits whom

I found at Stonyhurst, by far the greater number had become members of the Society of Jesus from motives which were entirely free from all mercenary consideration. They were, as far as I could form a judgment of them, actuated by a sincere piety, and a deep conviction of the truths of their religion, and a zealous solicitude for the welfare of others, which they conceived that they should best promote by dedicating themselves to the education of youth. At the head of the college was the Rector of the English province, the Rev. Dr. Stone. He was a man whom neither his long vigils, nor his habits of abstinence, could reduce into the meagritude of sanctity; and who by his portly belly and his rosy countenance, seemed to bid defiance to the power of fasting, and to the devotion of prayer. Nothing could subdue his goodly corpulency, or invest his features with the emaciation which ordinarily attends the habits of mortification and of self-denial which he practised. He was the most uninterruptedly devout person I have ever seen, and verified those descriptions of lofty holiness with which the writings of Alban Butler (the uncle of the celebrated conveyancer) had rendered me familiar. The students were accustomed to the perusal of the Lives of the Saints, and found in Dr. Stone (except in his external configuration, in which Guido would certainly not have selected a model,) a realization of those pictures of exalted piety which occur in the pages of that learned compiler. He seemed to be in a perpetual commerce with heaven; for even in his ordinary occupations, at his meals, or while he took the exercise necessary for the purposes of health, his eyes were constantly raised, and ejaculations broke from his lips. At first view, one might have taken him for an enacter of piety; and, indeed, his swelling cheeks, and the abdominal rotundity of his person, gave him an exceedingly sublunary aspect; but, after a little while, it was difficult not to feel convinced that his enthusiasm was unaffected, and that his whole heart was devoted in the spirit of the most exalted Chrisanity to God. The reader will think it strange that such a person should have been intrusted with the direction of so great an establishment as this extensive college, the conduct of whose finances would alone have been sufficient to engross the mind, and would have been so utterly alien to the spiritual addictions of Dr. Stone. The Jesuits, however, were too shrewd to leave their money to the care of a person who spent so little of his time in this world. The care of their souls was, by a just division of labour, committed to this great master of spirituality; but they did not molest him with any pecuniary considerations;

these fell to the exclusive province of the Rev. Father Wright, a brother of the Catholic banker in Henrietta-street. * * *

"I have stated that there was a minute allocation of different pursuits according to their respective talents, to the members of the fraternity. The selection of Father Wright to preside over the finances, was not more appropriate than the choice of the remarkable individual who was at the head of what was called the Noviceship. About two miles from the college there stood upon a hill, on the banks of the river Odder, a small house which was dedicated to the residence of the young men who, desiring to become Jesuits, were, according to the rules of the company, obliged to go through a probation for two years of continued meditation and prayer. During that space of time, a candidate for admission to the society must remain entirely secluded from the world, and occupied exclusively in the work of religious perfection. The novices are not allowed to read out of any profane book more than ten lines a day. The college itself was considered to be too worldly and full of turmoil for such a process of complete purification; and in order that their sequestration might be more complete, a little edifice was raised upon a slight elevation which overhung the river Odder. Here no other sounds but the murmurs of the stream as it gurgled over its pebbly bed through the deep groves that hung on either side of it, were heard by the votaries of silence and of solitude, who were embowered in this beautiful abode. How often have I paused to look upon it, in the walks which we were occasionally allowed to take in the vicinity of this pious and lonely spot! On the opposite side of the river was a wood, in which we used to go either to gather nuts or to hunt squirrels. Many a time I have left the pastimes in which my companions were engaged, and, descending to the banks of the stream, have fixed my eyes upon 'the Noviceship' upon the other side; and as I heard the voices of its inmates rising in their evening hymn through the trees which surrounded it, I have felt myself thrilled with all those sensations which belong to the elevation of piety, and what the profane would designate as the romance of religion. In this probationary hermitage the novices were secluded, and over them there presided a man the most remarkable for what I may call the chivalry of Jesuitism whom I have ever seen. Father Plowden was the younger brother of a very ancient Catholic family, and was, I believe, descended from the great lawyer of that name. He had been originally educated in Rome, and was from thence, after spending many years in Italy transferred to

St. Omer's. He was a perfect Jesuit of the old school: his mind was stored with classical knowledge; his manners were highly polished; he had great eloquence, which was alternately vehement and persuasive, as the occasion put his talents into requisition; and with his various accomplishments he combined the loftiest enthusiasm for the advancement of religion, and an utter immolation of himself to the glory of the order, of which he was unquestionably a great ornament. Though greatly advanced in years, he stood erect and tall, with all the evidences of strong and inextinguishable vitality about him. His cheek, though worn, had the hues of health upon it: and though his head was quite bald, the vivacity of his eyes, that shot their light from beneath their broad and shaggy brows, exhibited a mind whose faculties it did not seem to be in the power of time to impair. His powers as a preacher were of a very high class. Students at a public school listen to religious instruction as if it were only a part of the mere routine of their ordinary occupations. When, however, Mr. Plowden ascended the pulpit, every eye and every ear were fixed in attention. His command of lofty diction; his zealous and forcible delivery; the noble port which he assumed as the herald of intelligence from Heaven; and, more than any thing else, the profound conviction which he manifestly entertained of the truth of the doctrines which he interpreted, and the strenuousness of his adjuration in calling men's hearts to God, gave him every title to be considered an orator of the first class. Certainly, the belief that he was altogether devoted to the spiritual welfare of those whom Providence, had in his opinion, assigned to his tutelage, greatly enhanced the impressiveness of his exhortations. He was looked upon as a model of exalted virtue. It was not to the College of Stonyhurst that he confined his labours; he was also busy in the conversion of the population in the vicinity. It not unfrequently happened that he was informed in the midst of a winter's night, that some person at a considerable distance from the college was on the point of death, and stood in need of his spiritual aid. The old man, who did not seem to know what hardship was, would leap from his hard bed, and having hurried on his clothes, he would go forth with a lantern, attended by a lay-brother of the order, and, making his way over the fens and morasses by which the college was surrounded, hasten to the door of the expiring sinner, and arrive at his bed-side in time, as he conceived, to speed his soul to Heaven. This truly zealous and exalted Christian was the President of the Noviceship; and certainly no man could be better calculated to infuse into the minds of others that heroical self-abnegation, and that surrender of all the passions to the advancement of the society, which constitute the perfection of a Jesuit. If he could have contributed to the saving of the soul of a sinner, or to the promotion of the glory of St. Ignatius, by laying his head upon the block, he would, I am sure, have knelt down to it at the warning of an instant, and cried 'strike!' Yet, with all this extraordinary energy of zeal, and though he carried his enthusiasm to the highest point to which it could reach, he was, notwithstanding, wholly free from those weaknesses and credulities which are sometimes found in minds deeply imbued with religious feeling. He was a firm believer in the tenets of his church; but he did not himself practise, nor did he encourage in others, those usages which, in truth, do not belong to the general plan of Catholicity, but have grown out of individual fantasy, and ought not, in fairness, to be regarded as component parts of the general system. It is but doing justice to the Stonyhurst Jesuits to say, that they were by no means given to the inculcation of those opinions, or to the observance of those forms, which have chiefly contributed to create a disrelish for the Roman Catholic religion amongst persons who dissent from its doctrines. * * * * * * *

"There were about one hundred and fifty boys in the college, who were divided into six classes. Each class had a separate master, who at the termination of a year became the head of the next class, into which all the students under his superintendence were transferred; so that in general the same instructor for six years carried on the same boys through their successive gradations of tuition. This plan is the more deserving of remark, because it prevailed through all the Jesuit schools upon the Continent. The lowest class was called the Abecedarians, from their being initiated into the elements of knowledge; the next was called Figures, and afterwards came the classes of grammar, syntax, poetry, and rhetoric. It is obvious that much of a boy's acquirements, and a good deal of the character of his taste, must have depended upon the individual to whose instructions he was thus almost exclusively confined. It was my good fortune to be placed at first in the class of the Rev. Father Laurenson, who was an excellent Latin scholar, and had besides a strong relish for English composition. He was an excellent man, with an exceedingly good heart, with generous and honourable feelings, and entirely free from the suppleness which has been attributed, but in my mind erroneously, to the body to which he belonged. The

Jesuits who were employed in courts to influence the minds of ministers, and to sway the decisions of cabinets, might have been addicted to habits of duplicity, which are almost inseparable from such pursuits; but in their colleges, I apprehend that they were little more than ardent instructors in classical learning; and, as far as my experience goes, I can aver that I never observed the least tendency upon their part to inculcate any doctrine, or to hold up any personal example of that false dexterity which has been so long regarded as their attribute. The Rev. Mr. Laurenson was a great gaunt man, with a deep sonorous voice, and a countenance in which it was easy to discover his vigorous intellect, his open and manly nature, and an irascibility which, with all his efforts, and with the discipline of Loyola, he found it impossible to conquer. Father Laurenson was obliged, from, I believe, ill-health, to give up the class; and was succeeded by a gentleman who is at present at the head of the college, the Rev. Mr. Brooks. He lately attracted some notice in Rome, having attended as deputy from the English Province for the election of a general of the society, upon the death of Alagrius Fortis. having travelled in his own carriage, which excited the comments of his Continental brethren, who thought that a Jesuit might travel in his neighbour's carriage, but was forbidden by his vow of poverty from lolling in his own. If, however, they attributed the selection of this conveyance to any spirit of ostentation in the English deputy, they mistook Mr. Brooks. He was, when he became the teacher of the class to which I belonged, a young man of manners which were pushed, perhaps, to the utmost limit of refinement. His taste in literature was highly cultivated, and his mind was full of examples from the best authors, and of precepts from the best ancient and modern critics. He took exceedingly great pains in exciting an admiration for the beauties of the classical writers which it was his office to explain; and in rendering them into English, he enforced the necessity of preserving the strength and the colour of the Greek or the Latin phrase."

Mr. Sheil, after enlarging on the many advantages incidental to a Stonyhurst education, says:—

"I am at a loss to discover any evil to society, and much more surprised to hear it suggested that any danger can accrue to the state, from the extension of a body which is far more a literary, than a political confederacy in these countries. In France, indeed, where there is a large party of men whose personal interest attaches them to servile habits, it may be justifiable to use the strongest measures, in order to counteract the opinions which the French Jesuits are supposed to inculcate. But in these free islands, where liberty is of long growth, and has struck its roots so deeply into the public mind, even if the Jesuits were disposed to use their utmost efforts to eradicate its principles, they would prove utterly unavailing. The intellect of the country is too powerful to be subdued by their proverbial dexterities. But the greatest injustice is, in my judgment, done to the British and Irish Jesuits, by attributing to them any opinions which are in the least degree hostile to true liberty. The rule of the Order is, that a Jesuit should entertain and teach no political tenets which are not in conformity with the institutions under which he lives. In America, the Jesuits are republicans. Two of them lately visited Rome. On being heard to express some strong democratic sentiments, they were reprehended by the General of the Order; but the Council of Five, to whom they appealed, and to whom the General himself is responsible, declared, that as the form of government in the United States was republican, it was the duty of an American Jesuit to feel as an American citizen, and rescinded the decision of the Superior.

"I should, however, limit myself to the results of my own personal experience; and I can safely appeal to every person who has been educated at Stonyhurst, when I assert, as I most emphatically do, that a base political sentiment was never made a matter of either immediate or indirect inculcation. The Jesuits there were strongly attached to the constitution and liberties of their country. For the glory of England, notwithstanding political disqualifications which affected the Roman Catholics, they felt a deep and enthusiastic interest : of this I recollect a remarkable instance. The students were assembled in order to witness some experiments in galvinism, which a gentleman, who brought to the college a philosophical apparatus, had been employed to perform. In the midst of profound attention, a person rushed in, and exclaimed that Nelson had won a great victory. There was an immediate cheer given by the Jesuits, and echoed by the boys. Presently a newspaper was received, and the whole college gathered round the reader with avidity; and when the details of the battle of Trafalgar were heard, there were repeated acclamations at almost every sentence ; and when the narrative had been concluded, continued shouts for 'old England' were sent up, and every cap was thrown into the air, in celebration of the great event by which the navy of France was annihilated, and our masterdom of the ocean was confirmed. Several days for rejoicing were given to the students, and a poem, which I then, at least, considered a fine one, in honour of the battle, was composed by one of the Jesuits, and admirably recited in the great hall, which was appropriated to such exhibitions.

"I found amongst the Jesuits great kindness, a generous and most disinterested zeal for the advancement in learning of the persons whose minds they had in charge; and to their purity of life, their sincere piety, and their spirit of wise toleration, I am only discharging a duty which I owe to truth, in bearing my warmest attestation. The general policy of the Order may have been found injurious to the well-being of states, in which they acquired an illegitimate ascendancy; their diplomatists and politicians may have accommodated their morality with too ready a flexibility to the inclinations of kings and of women; they may have placed the confessional too near the cabinets of the one, and the boudoirs of the other; but as instructors of youth, when far from courts, and from a pernicious contact with those vices which the danger of infection renders it perilous to cure, they were, I believe, in the main, what my own personal experience has taught me to consider the individuals of their Order whom I had any personal opportunity of observing; and I confess, that I give my full assent to the sentiments which were expressed in their regard by Gresset, in the beautiful poem which he wrote on leaving them for ever, entitled 'Adieux aux Jesuites!'"

Mr. Sheil, soon after leaving Stonyhurst, entered Trinity College, Dublin, where his attention was almost exclusively devoted to classical literature. He became a member of the Historical Society, in which, however, he did not obtain any celebrity. His defects were prominent and obvious—the shrillness of his voice and the singularity of his gesture struck the ordinary observer, and it was only by those who knew that these peculiarities could be countervailed by attributes, which can never be developed except in great assemblies heated by real emotion, that it was foreseen that Mr. Sheil would produce a very considerable effect. The Rev. Mr. James Maghee, who has since obtained so much notice as a polemical disputant, was by far the most distinguished member of the Historical Society, during Mr. Sheil s time; in voice, figure, and gesture, and in all the physical qualifications requisite for success, that gentleman possesses very signal advantages; but those who are most disposed to admire him, must acknowledge that his composition does not exhibit any faculty of a very superior order. It may be questioned whether the habit of speeching in a debating society, where no real business is to be performed, and where the excitement of the puerile orator must be entirely factitious, is not prejudicial. The late Mr. North, was a man of great endowment, diversified acquisition, and with a mind richly embellished by literature of all kinds, but it is believed by many who were well acquainted with him, that he had contracted at a very early period an artificial style of speaking, which at the bar and in the House of Commons failed to produce results corresponding with his high reputation, and with his indisputable talents. It was a matter of some surprise to those who had witnessed Mr. Sheil's very imperfect exhibitions in the Historical Society, to find that in the great Catholic meetings, in which, when a boy, he adventurously took a part, that a sensation was produced by him. Animated at a very early period by a vehement indignation at the wrongs inflicted upon the great community to which he belonged, he had the boldness, and many thought the indiscretion to address vast concourse of Catholics, in Fishamble-street theatre. His speech was full of exaggerations—it was indeed a continued series of hyperbole, but it was delivered with a strange energy of elevation, and so much ardour of temperament, that his auditors, although at first surprised, and startled, and almost disposed to laugh, gradually became excited, and when the beardless patriot sat down, the entire assembly joined in loud and enthusiastic acclamation. Mr. Maurice Fitzgerald, the knight of Kerry, happened to be present at the meeting, and told Mr. Sheil, that he had no doubt that he would one day make a figure in the House of Commons. The speech, when published, was considered to be full of offences against good taste, but great praise was given to it, by men who were less disposed to detect faults, than to discover the indications of future merit. Among the persons of note in Dublin, who were struck by Mr. Sheil's speech, was the late Alexander Knox, generally known by the name of "Spectacle Knox," a man remarkable for his eloquence in common discourse, and whose fluency of fine expression was almost unsurpassed. He requested that Mr. Sheil should be presented to him, and frankly told him what he considered to be his imperfections, but led him to expect that by labour and perseverance his faults would be overcome.

Mr. Sheil having served his term at Lincolns Inn returned to Ireland in 1813. He had been born to considerable expectations, and was the eldest son of a gentleman, whose income exceeded two thousand a year; but his father having engaged in a mercantile partnership in Dublin, whose speculations were disastrous, lost the entire of his property. Mr. Sheil determined not to put his father to any cost connected with his call to the bar and for the purpose of defraying the necessary expense, wrote a tragedy which he entitled "Adelaide ;" it is totally destitute of plot—the style is affected, and in Mr. Sheil's own opinion had no merit. But Miss O'Neil the celebrated actress performed the principal character, on the first appearance of the play in Crow-street, and by her wonderful power produced its temporary success. Mr. Sheil obtained his object, and dedicated the play to Miss O'Neil, whose acting he described in a citation of some verses of Voltaire, peculiarly applicative to that enchanting actress.

In 1816 Mr. Sheil married Miss O'Halloran, a young lady of great personal beauty but without fortune ; and as his progress at the bar was not considerable, he was obliged again to have recourse to the stage. He produced "The Apostate," and "Bellamira," which yielded him by their success considerable emoluments, but were written with so much precipitation, and with such an exclusive view to scenic effect, that it must be acknowledged that they will not fully repay perusal. Having more leisure, and feeling that he could do something better, Mr. Sheil determined to take more pains, and produced the play of "Evadne" in 1819, which had a great run, and in which Miss O'Neil astonished London. The plot of the play is taken in a great measure from Shirley's Traitor, but the scenes and the language are exclusively the creation of Mr. Sheil.

The statue scene produced very great effect : it is entirely original, and attracted the notice of Mr. Villemaine, the celebrated French writer, who told Mr. Sheil that he was greatly struck with it.

Mr. Sheil received for the entire of the plays which were produced by him a sum of not less than £2000. The occupations of a dramatist are so alien from those of a barrister, that it was impossible that he should have made any way in his profession, as long as he continued to write for the stage ; and having obtained by his writings, the means of devoting his attention to the bar, he abandoned those dramatic pursuits in which he had originally engaged, from the motives which have been already assigned. Mr. Sheil's progress at the bar, however, was always impeded by the impression, a not unnatural one, that his mind had been dedicated to an intellectual employment, which amounted almost to a disqualification for signal forensic success. However, after some years, he got into considerable business upon his circuit, and was not without practice in Dublin. It must, however, be acknowledged, that he never obtained eminence in his profession, for although he occasionally delivered speeches which attracted public attention, in no ordinary degree, at the bar, he had not that promptitude in the discharge of the ordinary business of the profession, which is of far greater importance than the higher rhetorical attainments which Mr. Sheil so constantly displayed. He had sufficient leisure to engage in light literary occupations, and wrote several articles in the *New Monthly Magazine*, for which he received large remuneration. Mr. Sheil and Mr. William Henry Curran, the son of the great orator, and who now holds the office of Commissioner of the Insolvent Court, of which he performs the duties in a manner above all praise, undertook the publication of a series of papers entitled, " Sketches of the Irish Bar." These sketches attracted a good deal of notice, both in London and in Dublin.

" The Calamities of the Bar" was written by Mr. Sheil, and was accounted one of the most striking of those which were produced by him.

Mr. Sheil did not, indeed, bestow much pains on anything which he wrote in periodical publications, his chief attention being devoted to politics, in which, from the first establishment of the Catholic Association, he took a very active part. That celebrated body was founded by Mr. O'Connell, in 1822, soon after the visit of the King to Ireland. Mr. Sheil happened to meet Mr. O'Connell at the house of Mr. O'Meara, in the county of Wicklow, and expressed his deep regret that an unfortunate apathy prevailed in the Catholic body. He told Mr. O'Connell that he was convinced that it was in Mr. O'Connell's power to raise the public mind from the prostration into which it was sunken, and that he knew that it was only by his gigantic arm that Ireland could be raised up. Mr. O'Connell had been revolving a great project in his mind, and finding that Mr. Sheil concurred with him in the view which he had taken, he asked Mr. Sheil whether he would co-operate, by taking an active part in the advancement of the Catholic cause? Mr. Sheil agreed to do so, and Mr. O'Connell immediately drew up an appeal to the Irish Catholics, to which he requested Mr. Sheil to attach his name. Mr. Sheil did so, and the document was put into circulation. It was at first attended with little effect, and some Roman Catholic gentlemen affected to consider it an undue assumption of authority, to have summoned them to assemble. A very inconsiderable meeting was got together, at the house of Mr.

Fitzpatrick, in Capel-street; but Mr. O'Connell attended, and expressed his determination never to relinquish the great object, of which the attainment has given him an everlasting renown. The speeches of Mr. O'Connell were distinguished by that combination of eloquence and of reasoning in which he is unequalled; while the declamations of Mr. Sheil were calculated to inflame the public mind. His harangues were regarded in England as characterised by many of the faults of what is called "Irish eloquence;" but Mr. Sheil's speeches in the Catholic Association bear a much closer resemblance to the oratory of the French Revolution, which, however hyperbolical, was of a very exciting quality. His early familiarity with the French language, and his constant perusal of the most eminent French writers, had influenced his style, and contributed perhaps to create a certain mannerism in his composition. In the order of his delivery, and the vehemence with which he invited his countrymen to combine for the enfranchisement of Ireland, his exaggerations were overlooked; he became exceedingly popular, and was accounted one of the most efficient of the men by whom Mr. O'Connell was aided in his great achievement. Such, indeed, was the impression produced by Mr. Sheil, that he was selected in 1825, conjointly with Mr. O'Connell, to attend at the bar of the House of Commons, to plead against the Bill for the suppression of the Catholic Association. Mr. O'Connell and Mr. Sheil, together with other deputies, proceeded to London, and heard the remarkable debate which took place in the House of Commons regarding the right of the Catholic Association to be heard by their Counsel, of which Mr. Sheil wrote an account. He thus describes the effect of an encounter between Mr. Brougham and Mr. Peel. "The latter," he says, " could not resist the tempta"tion of dragging Hamilton Rowan into the debate—a man
" whose white hair should hide his imperfections. Putting aside
" all consideration of any want of generosity in the selection of
" such a topic, it must be acknowledged that he pronounced a
" severe invective with great and very successful force. He be"came heated with victory, and cheered as he was with vehement
" reiteration by his heated multitudinous partizans, he turned
" suddenly towards that part of the house where the deputies were
" seated, and looking triumphantly at Mr. O'Connell, with whom
" he forgot for an instant that he had been, when Secretary for
" Ireland, involved in a personal quarrel, shook his hand with
" scornful exultation, and asked whether the house required any
better evidence of the real character of the Association than

"their address to 'an attainted traitor.' The effect in oratory
"was powerful, and, but for the want of moral dignity, I should
"say that the whole passage was very finely executed. We
"quailed for a moment under the consciousness of discomfiture.
"But the success of Mr. Peel was transitory. Mr. Brougham
"was supplied with several facts of great importance on the in-
"stant, and inflicted on Mr. Peel a terrible retribution. He
"shewed that the government had granted to Hamilton Rowan
"a complete amnesty, and reproached Mr. Peel with his want o
"noble-mindedness in opening a wound which had been closed
"so long, and in turning the misfortunes of an honourable man,
"after the lapse of so much time, into a rhetorical resource
"He got hold of the good feeling of the house—their virtuous
"emotions, and the good feelings which the spirit of party can-
"not entirely suppress, were at once marshalled upon his side.
"Conscious of his advantage, he rushed on his antagonist with
"an irresistible impetuosity, and laid him prostrate. The noblest
"qualities of his eloquence were displayed by him—fierce sar-
"casm, indignant denunciation, exalted sentiment, and solemn,
"but most ardent elocution. He brought his powerful memory
"to his aid, and sustained his defence of Hamilton Rowan by a
'most apposite quotation from Cicero, in which the orator ex-
"tenuates the errors of those who were engaged in Pompey's
"cause."

The deputies were received in London with great cordiality by the leaders of the Whig party. Mr. O'Connell and Mr. Sheil dined at Mr. Brougham's house. There were four Dukes at table. Mr. O'Connell sat between the Dukes of Devonshire and Leinster. The deputies dined at several other houses where they were magnificently entertained. Mr. Sheil says : " I had
" now become more habituated to the display of patrician opulence ;
" I saw the exhibition of its gorgeousness without surprise ; yet,
" I acknowledge that at Norfolk House, where the Duke did me
" O'Connell, Lord Killeen, myself and others, the honor to invite
" us, and brought together an assemblage of men of the highest
" rank in England, I was dazzled with the splendour of an enter-
" tainment to which I had seen nothing to be compared. Norfolk
" House is one of the finest in London. It was occupied at one
" period by members of the royal family, and the Duke mentioned
" that George the Third was born in the room in which we
' dined. I passed through a long series of magnificent apart-
" ments in crimson and gold. There was no glare of excessive
" light in this vast mansion. The massive lamps suspended

"from the embossed and gilded ceilings, diffused a chequered
"illumination, and left the deep distance in the dusk. The
"transition to the chamber where the company were assembled
"and which was glaring with light, presented a brilliant con-
"trast. Among the guests were the Dukes of Sussex, Devon-
"shire, and Leinster; Lords Grey, Fitzwilliam, Shrewsbury
"Donoughmore, Stourton, Clifford, Arundel, Sir Francis Bur-
"dett, Mr. Butler of Lincoln's Inn, Mr. Abercrombie, and Mr.
"Denman were also there. The Duke of Norfolk came forward
"to meet us, and received us in the most cordial manner. Lord
"Fitzwilliam was the person with whom I was most disposed to
"be pleased. It was impossible to look on this nobleman of the
"olden stamp, without a feeling of affectionate admiration. His
"warm love of Ireland lives under the ashes of age, and requires
"to be but stirred to emit its former fire. Speak to him of Ire-
"land, and through the dimness of his eyes a sudden illumina-
"tion sheds forth. He reverted with a Nestorian pride to the
"period of his own government, and stated that he had preserved
"the addresses presented to him by the Catholics of Ireland as
"the best memorials of his life : that he would live long enough
"to witness their emancipation seemed to be the wish nearest to
"his heart. It does one good : it is useful in a moral view to
"approach a nobleman like Lord Fitzwilliam, and to feel that
"there are politicians, animated by a disinterested solicitude for
"the benefit of mankind. Lord Grey was, I have mentioned,
"there : he was silent and reserved. There is something uncom-
"promising, and even stern in his aspect. He has a tone of
"sadness which a placeman would interpret into discontent, but
"his expression is not atrabilious or morose. He has survived
"the death, and, let me add, the virtue of several illustrious
"men, and looks like the solitary column of a fabric, which he
"had long sustained, and which fell at last, and is strewed in
"ruin round him."

It will be seen that Mr. Sheil, some years after this interview
saw Lord Grey in a different position and in a very different
light. The deputation to London was not attended with success:
at one moment Lord Liverpool is supposed to have hesitated, and
in order to counteract the impression that he had given way
delivered what was called his "ether speech." He was in the
habit of taking ether on important occasions, and in declaring
that his mind was unaltered, used a larger dose than usual. t:
which some of his vehemence was ascribed; others attributed i
o his communication with the Duke of York, who took his oath

in the House of Lords, that he never would consent to Catholic Emancipation, in the event of his succession to the throne. That celebrated invocation was afterwards the cause of Mr. Sheil's committing what he had reason to regard as worse than an ordinary mistake. Great indignation was naturally produced in the entire Catholic body; and in that sentiment Mr. Sheil largely shared. On his return to Ireland, he took at the Catholic Association a bolder and a more denunciatory tone; but he did not, in the first instance, employ any expressions which the outrage offered to the Catholics of Ireland did not fully warrant. Having, however, attended at a public dinner at Mullingar, and the health of the Duke of York having been proposed, exasperated by what he regarded as a most unworthy proceeding in a Roman Catholic assembly, he gave utterance to phrases, as unjustifiable as Canning's unfortunate alliteration, "The revered and ruptured Ogden." Mr. Sheil's fierce assault on the Duke of York was very prejudicial to himself, but it afforded a strong evidence of the violent resentment which the conduct of the Duke of York had created in Ireland, and was, so far, of public use. When, however, the death of the Duke was hourly expected, Mr. Sheil made a speech at the Association, in which he expressed his sorrow that he had been betrayed into the use of language so reprehensible as that which he had employed: "My " soul," he exclaimed, in the language of the Lamentations, "was " filled with bitterness, and I was drunk with wormwood. But, " now that we hear that a Prince is dying, and expect every in- " stant that a voice will come upon us, to tell 'that a Prince is " dead'—now that death, who, while he levels the great, subdues " the animosities of the humble, and while he resolves the hearts " of princes into dust, softens the hearts of the lowly into com- " miseration—now that the bell of that lofty temple that towers over the great city, and whose knell is reserved for royalty, has " begun to toll..............It is not with affectation that I speak, " when I declare, that so far from experiencing any feeling of " truculent hilarity, every emotion of anger, every vindictive " and acrimonious sentiment passes away, and the passions by " which I confess that I was recently actuated, expire within me. " It is right that the offence which the Duke of York committed " against our country should be committed to forgetfulness. In- " deed it is almost unnecessary to express a desire, which the " natural oblivion, that must befal the greatest as well as the " humblest of mankind, cannot fail to accomplish. In a month " hence the Duke of York will be forgotten. The pomp of death

" will for a few nights fill the gilded apartments in which his
" body will lie in state. The artist will endeavour to avert that
" decay to which even princes are doomed, and embalm him with
" odours, which may resist the cadaverous scent for a while. He
" will be laid in a winding sheet fringed with silver and with gold
" —he will be enclosed in spicy wood, and his illustrious descent
" and withered hopes will be inscribed upon his glittering coffin.
" The bell of St. Paul's will toll, and London—rich, luxurious,
" Babylonic London—will start at the recollection that even
" kings must die. The day of his solemn obsequies will arrive—
" the gorgeous procession will go forth in its funeral glory—the
" ancient chapel of Windsor Castle will be thrown open, and its
" aisle will be thronged with the array of kindred Royalty—the
" emblazoned windows will be illuminated—the notes of holy
" melody will arise—the beautiful service of the dead will be re-
" peated by the heads of the Church, of which he will be the
" cold and senseless champion—the vaults of the dead will be
" unclosed—the nobles, and the ladies, and the High Priests of
" the land, will look down into those deep depositories of the
" ambition and the vanities of the world. They will behold the
" heir to a great empire taking possession, not of the palace,
" which was raised at such an enormous and unavailing cost,
" but of that 'house which lasts till doomsday.' The coffin will
" go sadly and slowly down; its ponderous mass will strike on
" the remains of its regal kindred; the chant will be resumed, a
" moment's awful pause will take place—the marble vault, of
" which none but the Archangel shall disturb the slumbers, will
" be closed—the songs of death will cease—the procession will
' wind through the aisles again, and restore them to their lone-
' liness. The torches will fade again in the open daylight—the
' multitude of the great will gradually disperse; they will roll
' back in their gilded chariots, into the din and tumult of the
' great metropolis; the business, and the pursuits, and the frivo-
lities of life will be resumed, and the heir to the three kingdoms
will be in a week forgotten. We, too, shall forget; but let us,
before we forget, forgive him!"

Mr. Sheil proceeded to expatiate upon the circumstances to
tenuation, which ought ever, in the mind of an Irish Catholic,
be taken into account in extenuating the extent of the great
ult committed by the Duke of York, in calling God to witness
at he would never assent to the enfranchisement of the Irish
ople. The apology however, if apology it could be called,
d not abate the feeling of deep resentment which had been

created among those in high quarters against Mr. Sheil, and it was decided by the government that the Attorney-General should avail himself of the first opportunity which Mr. Sheil should furnish to institute a prosecution against him. A series of vehement harangues were delivered by Mr. Sheil, which were considered to be of a very exciting nature, but it was not until he selected the memoirs of Theobald Wolfe Tone, as the subject of speech, which the government considered to be fully as minatious as it was admonitory, that it was deemed judicious to institute proceedings against Mr. Sheil in a criminal court. There can be no doubt that the Attorney-General (the present Lord Plunket,) prepared an indictment against Mr. Sheil with great reluctance. It was understood that he took this step by the express directions of the English government :—But in the cabinet itself there were doubts entertained regarding the justice of this proceeding, and Lord Melbourne many years afterwards told Mr. Sheil, at the table of the late Lord Sydenham that Mr. Canning had declared that there was not a sentence of the speech, which would have produced a call of "order" in the House of Commons. Informations having been sworn, Mr Sheil gave bail :—his bail were Mr. O'Connell, and the late Chief Baron Wolfe, between whom and Mr. Sheil there existed a strict friendship from the period in which they first met in Trinity College, to the day on which the country was deprived of that eminent man, in whom a great understanding and a most tender nature were united :—in the interval between the taking of informations, and sending up the indictment, Mr. Sheil made the course pursued by Mr. Plunket the subject of animadversion, and instead of shrinking, declared that he would meet Mr. Plunket face to face in court, and prove that there was nothing in his speech on Wolfe Tone, (of whom Mr. Plunket had been an intimate friend,) so seditious as several speeches delivered by Mr. Plunket himself. It was felt by the law-officers that Mr. Sheil might perhaps make a great impression on the jury by pressing topics of this kind, and in order to ensure a conviction, it was of great moment to give in evidence another speech of Mr. Sheil, delivered before that on Wolfe Tone's memoirs, and published in Carrick's Morning Post, by Mr. Shei. himself. Mr. Sheil when in Paris, in the year 1826, had become acquainted with the Abbé de Genoude, the proprietor of the Etoile, which is now published under the name of the "Gazette de France." Mr. Sheil's facility in writing French struck the Abbé, and at his suggestion Mr. Sheil wrote several articles on

Ireland, which were read with a great deal of interest in Paris and attracted the notice of the English government. Mr. Sheil had referred to these publications in a speech at the Catholic Association, and although it could not separately afford ground for a prosecution, it was considered by the Crown Counsel, that it would, if given in evidence, have a great effect in ensuring a conviction. Mr. Lonergan, the proprietor of Carrick's Morning Post, was called on by the Crown Solicitor for Mr. Sheil's manuscript, but that gentleman peremptorily declared that he would not produce it at the trial. The Crown Counsel then recommended that proof should be given of the words spoken by Mr. Sheil, and accordingly, Mr. Christopher Hughes, who reported at the Association, was applied to by the Crown, but that gentleman, although wholly unknown to Mr. Sheil, and notwithstanding that intimations were given by the Crown that his services would be remembered, gave it to be understood in a manner most honourable to himself, that from him no co-operation in effecting Mr. Sheil's conviction was to be expected. The Crown was thus baffled, and the success of the prosecution became problematical. Bills of indictment were sent up to the Sessions' grand jury. Mr. Plunket attended the court in Green-street, and was accompanied by his friend, Mr. Peter Burrowes. That gentleman seemed anxious to sustain the Attorney-General, whose spirits appeared to droop, or rather to shrink from the performance of a most distasteful office—the prosecution of a man whose language was at most indiscreet, and had been uttered in a cause in which Mr. Plunket himself had spoken so often, with much glowing eloquence, and much indignant elocution. He looked at Mr. Sheil with a countenance expressive of mournfulness, in which sympathy for Mr. Sheil was not unassociated with self-reproach, and when the bills were found, turned his eyes towards Mr. Sheil's counsel with an earnest anxiety to learn what they would do. Mr. Sheil was not himself anxious for postponement, but thought it better that his fate should be at once determined :—but his counsel, Mr. O'Connell, Mr. Holmes, and the present Judge Perrin, suggested on legal grounds that the trial ought to be postponed. The Attorney-General instead of objecting, which he might have done, at once acceded to the proposition, and appeared as if a great weight had been taken off his heart. The event proved the wisdom of procrastination; it was not conjectured at the time that the trial was deferred that it could be postponed beyond a few weeks ; but in the interval between the finding of the bills, and the law term to which the trial had been delayed, Lord Liverpool was struck with apoplexy. Mr. Canning became Prime Minister, and the prosecution was abandoned.

Mr. Canning's administration having within a few months terminated with a life, which sunk under the great aristocratic combination which was leagued against him, and the Goderich cabinet having been found incapable, the Duke of Wellington was placed at the head of affairs, under circumstances most inauspicious to Ireland. The energies of Mr. O'Connell were only augmented by the impediments thrown in his progress, and Mr. Sheil continued to assist him with all the resources of excitement at his command. The public mind was prepared by the Catholic Association and its great leader for a tremendous struggle, and at the Clare election, the whole prowess of Catholic Ireland was put forth. Mr. Sheil attended that election: his speech at the close is inserted in this volume, with an account written by him of the remarkable incidents of which he was a witness when that great victory was won, which led to the immediate settlement of the Catholic Question.

After Mr. Vesey Fitzgerald, a cabinet minister, the attached friend of Mr. Peel, had been defeated, it was known in the political circles, that some great measure connected with the Catholics of Ireland was in discussion in the cabinet. Alarm was taken by the popular fanaticism, of which the county of Kent offers perhaps a more remarkable example than any other district in England, and a great meeting was announced to be held at Penenden Heath on the 24th of October, 1828. This meeting Mr. Sheil determined to attend. He proceeded to London, purchased a freehold, in order to entitle him to speak, and went to the meeting. An account of that remarkable assembly was published at the time, from which the following extract is taken:—

At twelve o'clock the chair was taken by the High Sheriff, and at this moment we turned our eyes to contemplate this amazing assembly, and we do not exaggerate when we say that, with much experience, we have never witnessed a spectacle at all comparable to it. Upwards of 20,000 men stood gathered together in profound silence, but in that momentary hush it was easy to perceive the deep solicitude and the anxious passions by which the two great parties, thus marshalled against each other were equally agitated. Round the Sheriff were assembled what we conjectured to be a class of persons that affected to occupy a neutral station between the two parties, and, indeed, we observed from this small knot, that scarcely any expression, either of approbation or dissent, during the whole course of the day proceeded. The whole mass upon the left, deep and dense, presented at once the evidence of the strength of the Protestant party, and of their inflexible determination. On the right hand, the opposers of the objects of the meeting were assembled in an immense body, in which, unquestionably, much of the wealth and rank of the country were collected. In the waggon next to the Sheriff, on the right, which was that of the Earl of Radnor, stood his lordship with a number of his friends. We remarked that Lord Camden had no waggon. That venerable, mild, and dignified individual, occupied a place on the hustings next the Sheriff, and we thought that the selection of that peculiar locality was intended by him as an indication, that however opposed to the objects of the meeting, he did not enter into it with the feelings of a partizan. Adjoining the waggon of Lord Radnor was that of the Earl of Darnley; next came that of Lord Sondes.

In an adjoining waggon two gentlemen took their station, who, notwithstanding the mourning ordinances of the *Gazette*, were habited in an attire very little suited to the melancholy mood. The first of these gentlemen, tall, strong, healthy, and agricultural, with an aspect and demeanour in which rusticity and intellect were happily blended, though his head was grey, had a cheek fresh and ruddy. His blue eye seemed to glitter with flashes of strong thinking, whilst a latent expression of severity and derision was perceivable, by an attentive observer, under the aspect of jocularity which was spread over his features. This was Mr. Cobbett. Immediately near him was Mr. Hunt. Under these two champions there was gathered a large assemblage of their friends, who gazed with admiration upon them. A succession of other waggons closed the right wing, which were occupied by a numerous body of the Kentish yeomanry. Between the two wings was a large cavalcade of farmers drawn up like troops of horse. Behind them was an immense quantity of vehicles, consisting of private and public carriages, with clusters of freeholders hanging about them. Within the circle which was formed by the waggons, stood upon the ground a dense body of the peasantry, who arranged themselves on the left or the right wing according to their respective political predilections. The whole scene presented a most extraordinary and impressive exhibition. Before beginning the description of the proceedings, it may be necessary to notice a little preliminary address by Mr. Cobbett to the people shortly after his arrival on the ground. He was accompanied thither by Mr. Hunt, with banners; both were greeted with applause as soon as they presented themselves in front of the waggons.

Mr. COBBETT.—My friends, you will hear a great deal of talk here to-day—no doubt you will—about the Pope and the devil.—(A laugh). Do you take care to have nothing to do with either—take care of yourselves—pay attention to the things that belong to you, and you will do that if you attend to me.

After Mr. Plumtree, the member for the county; Lord Camden, Lord Darnley, Lord Winchilsea, Mr. Shee, and Lord Teynham had spoken, Mr. Sheil addressed the meeting in a speech that was repeatedly interrupted *

* See page 344.

In consequence of the loud uproar with which Mr. Sheil was almost incessantly assailed; Mr. Sheil published it in the *Times* and *Sun* newspapers, and it attracted very general notice. The famous Jeremy Bentham was greatly struck by it, and wrote the following letter, which appeared in the *Morning Chronicle* of November 6, 1828. It was addressed by the great philosopher to Mr. Galloway, in reference to a public dinner which was afterwards given to Mr. Sheil at the London Tavern, at which Mr. Smith of Norwich presided.

"Queen-Square-Place, October 31, 1828.

"MY DEAR GALLOWAY,—So masterly an union of logic and rhetoric as Mr. Sheil's speech, scarcely have I ever beheld. I have just received the circular inviting my attendance at the dinner. You know I labour under complaints which prevent my stirring from home, cases of absolute necessity excepted. For years upon years it has been out of the question with me.

"The dinner good—printing and diffusion of the speech still better 'his surely will not be omitted In the *Herald* of this day are two or three abominable letters against Sheil. What say you to adding them, together with the exculpatory statement in the *Sun*, to the reprint of his speech? Might it not be of use in the way of contrast, and as an exemplification of impartiality, in particular, that signed " Verus ?"

"Yours ever,
"JEREMY BENTHAM.

" Alexander Galloway, Esq."

After this adventurous undertaking, Mr. Sheil returned to Ireland, and was cordially received by his countrymen, who conceived that good service had been rendered by him to the great cause in which he had been so strenuously engaged. But at the very time that the meeting at Penendon Heath was held, the Duke of Wellington and Sir Robert Peel were giving way to the enormous pressure of the Catholic Association and its great leader, Mr. O'Connell, and alarmed at the organised disaffection of which Ireland had exhibited the evidence, had determined on the enfranchisement of the Irish people. The resolution of the government was, however, kept secret for several months previous to the meeting of parliament. Parliament met on the 6th of February, 1829, and the speech from the throne recommended "a final, equitable, and satisfactory adjustment of the Catholic claims." It was believed that a voluntary dissolution of the Association would assist the ministry in carrying the great measure which they had announced, and Mr. Sheil moved the dissolution of that body, which was almost unanimously carried.

The Catholic Question having been settled, a great change took place in the fortunes of Mr. Sheil. He was made a king's counsel through Lord Francis Egerton. The Duke of Northumberland paid him marked attention; and Sir Henry Hardinge having been appointed Secretary for Ireland, exhibited towards Mr. Sheil a strong predilection, which continued long after Mr. Sheil became vehemently opposed to the party of which Sir H. Hardinge was one of the chief. Sir H. Hardinge told Mr. Sheil that he had been intrusted to award one-third of the patronage at his disposal to Roman Catholics. He did not continue in office sufficiently long to carry this resolution into effect. The Tories were sent out of office upon Sir Henry Parnell's motion, in November, 1830, and Mr. Sheil dined at the Castle on the day on which the news of their defeat arrived in Dublin. It was an exceedingly dismal festivity: a profound depression was spread over the countenances of almost all the functionaries, who were to meet no more in their official gatherings—the Duke of Northumberland himself did not appear to consider his liberation from the Irish royalty of the Castle as a fortunate incident in his life; and so lugubrious was the feeling which diffused itself over this final conviviality, that with all his fine wit, his admirable humour, and mirthful narrative, Sir Philip Crampton, who was there, failed to produce the ordinary results with which his delightful hilarity is attended.

Upon the change of administration, Mr. Sheil proceeded to London, and received from Lord Anglesea, the new Lord Lieutenant of Ireland, an intimation of his desire to see him. He had been presented to Lord Anglesea in Ireland, and already enjoyed his favourable opinion. Mr. Sheil had always done justice to the earnest solicitude of Lord Anglesea for the happiness of Ireland, and Lord Anglesea was anxious in every way to promote the wishes of Mr. Sheil. Having learned that he wished to obtain a seat in the House of Commons, he told him with that fascinating smile by which all are charmed, by whom Lord Anglesea is approached, that he would do his utmost to introduce Mr. Sheil into the House of Commons.

Mr. Sheil has always expressed the highest admiration for the many noble qualities by which Lord Anglesea is adorned. He regards him as the most chivalrous and high-minded of all the great aristocracy with whom he has ever had any intercourse, and has never failed to say, that the faults committed during his viceroyalty of Ireland were to be imputed to the predominance of Lord Stanley, by whom the generous policy of Lord Anglesea was uniformly thwarted and counteracted.

Lord Anglesea brought Mr. Sheil into parliament in March, 1831, for the borough of Milbourne Port, for which he sat for three months. Mr. Sheil made his first speech in the House of Commons on the 21st of March, on the Reform Bill. A great deal of curiosity was excited by his first appearance on a stage so great and so new. Notwithstanding that prejudices had existed against him, in consequence of the extreme violence of his popular harangues, he was kindly received, and a favourable hearing was given him. Mr. Sheil's voice, his small figure, his angular action, and the restless inquietude of his countenance, were observed with surprise : the efflorescence of his style, too, which is in contrast with his manner, was soon noted, and occasioned some unpropitious conjectures regarding his ultimate success as a parliamentary speaker—he committed one or two mistakes in the use of artificial embellishments, which had well nigh occasioned his failure. But at the conclusion of his speech, in which he spoke with a more natural fervour, and warned his hearers against committing the great error, which had attended the Catholic Question, by a delay of justice ; he, at last, excited the house, and was considered to have succeeded. Sir Robert Peel spoke of the speech in the terms of liberal encomium, and Lord Grey, a few nights afterwards, told Mr. Sheil at his house, that he had made " an excellent speech." The critics in the newspapers differed—some condemned the speech as a total failure—others observed that, with many imperfections, there were evidences of ability to do much more than Mr. Sheil had effected. The following is the criticism in Blackwood, (August, 1831,) in the *Noctes Ambrosianæ*, which are attributed to a celebrated writer. After an exceedingly unfavourable portraiture of Mr. Sheil's exterior, Tickler says : " But never mind—wait a little— and this vile machinery will do wonders.

" NORTH.—We can wait—fill your glass.

" TICKLER.—To make some amends for her carelessness in all other external affairs, nature has given him as fine a pair of eyes as ever graced human head—large, deeply set, dark, liquid, flashing like gems, and these fix you presently, like a basilisk, so that you forget every thing else about him ; and though it would be impossible to conceive anything more absurdly ungraceful than his action, sharp, sudden jolts, and shuffles, and right-about twists and leaps, all set to a running discord of grunts and moans, yet, before he has spoken ten minutes, you forget all this too, and give yourself up to what I have always considered a pleasant sensation—the feeling, I mean, that you are in the presence of a man of genius !"

Parliament having been dissolved in consequence of General Gascoign's motion having been carried, by a majority of eight, Mr. Sheil was returned again for Milbourne Port; but having been informed by the present Judge Crampton, the then Solicitor-General for Ireland, that Lord Anglesea was anxious, provided Mr. Sheil could obtain a seat in Ireland, that he should leave Milbourne Port at his disposal, Mr. Sheil stood for the county of Louth, and was returned with the concurrence of Sir Patrick Bellew, and his brother, Mr. Richard Montesquieu Bellew, the present member for the county. Mr. Sheil stated distinctly at the hustings at Louth, that being returned by a great popular constituency, he should regard the interests of the Irish people as paramount to every other consideration ; and that he would never support the government at their expense. There arose a speedy and unfortunate occasion for electing between the Irish people and the ministry. The latter had determined to maintain the abuses of the Irish Church—the people of Ireland insisted on a measure of large and sweeping retrenchment. The excitement in Ireland on the Church Question was as great as that of England on the question of Parliamentary Reform. In a very short time, O'Connell and almost the entire body of the Irish liberal representatives were placed in virtual opposition. They remonstrated with the minister, but the influence of Mr. Stanley, who was devoted to the Irish Church, was predominant. He had exhibited great ability in debate, and his utter incapacity for government had not yet been signally proved. But his services as a public speaker were more than counterbalanced by the hostility which his demeanour had produced. Abrupt, peremptory, jeering, sardonic, alternately scolding and mocking, heedless of giving pain, reducing every man by whom he was addressed in his own estimation, and giving way, in the midst of the most important discussions, to a kind of harsh puerility, Mr. Stanley contrived to centralize in himself the antipathies of almost every Irishman to whom the Whig government should naturally have looked for support. It was determined by a large body of Irish members to remonstrate with Lord Grey on his Irish policy, and a document, signed by upwards of thirty members, was laid before the Prime Minister, in which a strong expostulation on the course which his government were pursuing was contained. Lord Grey appointed a meeting in Downing-street, at the close of the session of 1832, almost immediately before the dissolution of parliament, with the Irish members by whom he had been addressed. More than thirty attended. The scene was remarkable. The Irish members entered in a body, and bowed to Lord Grey with great and unaffected respect. Mr. O'Connell was not only polite, but deferential in his deportment. No intention was entertained of giving offence to the eminent person whom they had approached and Mr. O'Connell took care to convey that assurance before a word was uttered by him. Lord Grey was cold, lofty, and austere. He drew himself up to his full height, and stood, at first, erect before the Irishmen who were gathered before him. In his fine countenance, displeasure and sorrow were associated; and his voice quivered as he desired the great agitator and his retinue, afterwards known by a more ignominious appellation, to sit down. Lord Grey also sat down, and still holding himself in as much altitude as his position would permit, stated that he had read the address of the Irish members with great pain, and that he was surprised that after all he had done and sacrificed for Ireland, he should have been so ungenerously used. He adverted, with a good deal of genuine emotion, to his long labours in the cause of Irish liberty, and complained of the manner in which he had been requited. Mr. O'Connell said, with great submission in his manner, but with a voice, of which the intentions were not in accordance with his deportment, that the Irish members were fully sensible of the services of Lord Grey, and that nothing but a sense of duty could have induced them to expostulate with so eminent a man, upon what they conceived to be the principles of his government in reference to Ireland. Lord Grey, after hearing Mr. O'Connell for a short time, intimated some impatience, and said that the Irish Catholics were taking such a course, that they would drive the government to the necessity of adopting measures of severity for their suppression. He added, however, this remarkable declaration—" that he would never be the minister by whom those measures, however necessary, should be proposed." The meeting almost immediately after broke up. The first Reform parliament was called, and the first measure proposed was the Coercion Bill. His engagement with himself was not kept by Lord Grey.

Parliament having been dissolved in 1832, and Mr. Sheil having by his marriage with the daughter of Mr. John Lalor of Crenagh, in the county of Tipperary, the widow of Mr. Edward Power, of Gurteen, become connected by property with the county of Tipperary, he stood for that great county, and was returned the first parliament held after the Reform Bill, with the Honourable Cornelius O'Callaghan, the eldest son of Lord Lismore. The Coercion Bill was brought forward at the commencement of the first session. It was vehemently opposed by Mr. Sheil, by whom several of the ministers were more deeply galled than by any other of the antagonists of that odious measure. He quoted passages from the speeches of almost every one of them, reprobatory of the policy on which they were proceeding to govern Ireland. Great hostility was created by this course, and an incident occured which proved how much animosity was entertained towards Mr. Sheil. Mr. Matthew Devonshire Hill stated at Hull, that an Irish member who had denounced the Coercion Bill in the House of Commons, had himself recommended the government to bring it in. It was mentioned in several newspapers that it was to Mr. Sheil that Mr. Hill alluded. Suggestions were made to Mr. Sheil that he ought to send "a friend" to Mr. Hill, who had declared that he would answer the interrogatory of any Irish member to inquire whether it was to him that Mr. Hill referred. Mr. Sheil feeling that a formal encounter with Mr. Hill would not confute Mr. Hill, determined that the matter should be brought before the House of Commons, and to compel Mr. Hill to prefer and prove his charge. Mr. Hill did make the charge against Mr. Sheil in a very full and excited house, and Lord Althorp declared that Mr. Sheil spoke in one way in the house, and in another out of it, Mr. Sheil said, that he should make no observation on what Lord Althorp had said ; but the Speaker having declared that he collected from Mr. Sheil's manner that he meant to send a challenge to Lord Althorp, Mr. Sheil and Lord Althorp were called on to promise that no hostile meeting would take place. With this requisition Lord Althorp and Mr. Sheil refused to comply, and both were committed to the custody of the Sergeant-at-arms. Lord Althorp, after a few hours of imprisonment, being pressed by his friends, agreed to give the undertaking which had been demanded, and he and Mr. Sheil were discharged. Mr. Sheil insisted that he was entitled to a committee, to ascertain the truth of the accusation ; and Sir Robert Peel strenuously contended that the greatest injustice would be done, if it were refused. A committee was moved—Sir Robert Peel and Sir Henry Hardinge attended the committee. Mr. Devonshire Hill was examined by Mr. O'Connell—after stating that his informant was Mr. Silk Buckingham, who now denied that he had ever meant to convey such an impression to Mr. Sheil, and an-

other person whom he would not name, he declared, in a state
of great excitement, bursting into tears, that he not only could
not prove his charge, but that he was now convinced that it was
wholly unfounded. He begged Mr. Sheil to pardon him, and
added that, if Mr. Sheil required it, he would make a public apo
.ogy to him in the House of Commons, but hoped that such an
humiliation would not be inflicted upon him. Mr. Sheil said
that he freely pardoned him, and would not require anything
beyond the report of the committee. The committee reported—
"Your committee, in entering on the delicate and embarrassing duty imposed upon them, ascertained from Mr. Hill, that though he could not admit the entire accuracy of the above paragraph, as a report of what he had publicly spoken at Hull, he, nevertheless, recollected to have publicly charged an Irish member of parliament with conduct similar in substance to that which the paragraph describes. The Irish member, so alluded to, was Richard Lalor Sheil, Esq., member of parliament for the county of Tipperary; and Mr. Hill states the charge, to the best of his belief, to have been substantially as follows :—That Mr Sheil made communications respecting the Irish Coercion Bill to persons connected with the government and others, with the intention thereby of promoting the passing of the Coercion Bill, and having a direct tendency to produce that effect, whilst his speeches and votes in the house were directed to the defeat of the Coercion Bill ;—such was the substance of the allegation into which your committee proceeded to inquire. Two witnesses were called before them at the suggestion of Mr. Hill, and others were about to be examined, when Mr. Hill himself, finding the testimony already heard very different from what he had expected, freely and spontaneously made the following communication to the committee—that he had come to the conviction that his charge against Mr. Sheil of having directly or indirectly communicated, or intended to communicate, to the government, any private opinions in opposition to those which he expressed in the House of Commons, had no foundation in fact ;—that such charge was not merely incapable of formal proof, but was, in his present sincere belief, totally and absolutely unfounded—that he had originally been induced to make mention of it in a hasty and unpremeditated speech, under a firm persuasion that he had received it on undeniable evidence ; but that being now satisfied of the mistake into which he had fallen, and convinced that the charge was wholly untrue, he came forward to express his deep and unfeigned sorrow for having ever contributed to give it cir

:ulation. Mr. Hill added, that if there were any way, consistent with honour, by which he could make reparation to Mr. Sheil, he should deem no sacrifice too great to heal the wound which his erroneous statement had inflicted. It is with the highest gratification that your committee find themselves enabled thus to exonerate an accused member of parliament from imputations alike painful and undeserved. The voluntary avowal of an erroneous statement on the part of Mr. Hill, now puts it in their power to pronounce a decided opinion, and to close the present inquiry. Neither of the witnesses who appeared before the committee deposed to any facts calculated to bear out the allegation against Mr. Sheil; nor did their testimony go to impeach his character and honour in any way, or as to any matter whatever The committee have no hesitation in declaring their deliberate conviction, that the innocence of Mr. Sheil, in respect of the whole matter of complaint referred to their investigation, is entire and unquestionable."

This report having been made,

Mr. SHEIL rose amidst loud cries of "hear" from all parts of the house, which were succeeded by profound silence. After a short pause, he said :—" I stood a few nights ago before this house with no other sustainment than the consciousness of my innocence ; I now stand before it with that innocence announced, in the clearest and most unequivocal language by a committee, composed of men themselves above all suspicion, to the world. I do feel my heart swell within me at this instant, and almost impede my utterance. Justice has been done me. It has been done not only by my judges but by my accuser—he preferred his charges in the house, he reiterated them before the committee, and having gone into his evidence and failed, he then offered me the only reparation in his power, and with a frankness of contrition, which mitigates the wrong he did me, he came forward and announced that not only could he not prove his charge, but believed it to be utterly destitute of foundation. That gentleman having made this acknowledgment, then turned, and addressing himself to me in the tone, and with the aspect of deep emotion, asked me to forgive him ; I had, I own, much to forgive ; he had wounded me, to my heart's core ; he had injured me, and given agony to mine ; he had committed a havoc of the feelings of those who are dearer to me than my life ; and to whom my honour is more precious than my existence, he had furnished to the Secretary for the Colonies, the occasion of addressing me in the language, and with the gesture of solemn admonition, and of pointing out the results of an inquiry, in the tone of prophetic warning. I had indeed much to forgive, and yet I forgive him; because as he protested his innocence of all malevolent intentions, and said that he had been deluded, and acknowledged me innocent of his accusation, I felt that he had done all in his power to repair the wrong, and heavy as it was, when he asked my pardon, I could not withhold it. It would have been unworthy of me, to have availed myself of the occasion thus presented to me, to have cast reproaches on my accuser, or to have been betrayed into vindictive emotion. I did not manifest it then—I shall not exhibit it now. I stood at the verge of a tremendous peril, of the depth of which I was conscious, without dismay—I have trodden the edge of the precipice, in calm security, and it remains that having passed it, I should indulge in no exultation as I betray no fear. The noble lord, for I turn to him, has tendered me an apology—I am to presume that it is not accompanied with any miserable inuendos, and that he cannot purpose to convey any injurious hint. He says that as I have denied his charge—he believes me, and tenders his recantation and his regret—whatever is offered in a fair and ingenuous spirit, I am bound in the same spirit to accept; but let the noble lord look back at the exact state of facts between us. The government having been charged with obtaining votes by alleging that an Irish member had been guilty of an act of perfidy, was interrogated on that head We had a right to put him the question — we had a right to learn two things—first, whether the government had resorted to secret machinery—next whether any communication was made to the government by an Irish member. The noble lord answered the question in the negative, but did not stop there, he went on, and founded a charge of inconsistency, grounded on private conversations. We have heard much denunciation from ministers respecting the disclosures of private discourse, and yet the Chancellor of the Exchequer, the representative of the government, who entertains such a horror of a practice detested by all honourable men, is the very first to make reference to the babble of clubs, to declare his belief of information, to which he gratuitously attaches an injurious importance, and to announce that he would not give up his author, but would take upon himself the responsibility. This defiance having been given, the house interposed : no resource was left me, but to protest that I never expressed myself in favour of the Coercion Bill, and to demand inquiry. I insisted on it—the Secretary for the Colonies, out of regard no doubt for my repuation, pointed out the possible results. His suggestions had no other effect than to confirm me in my purpose, and to make me call more loudly for trial; that trial has proceeded. My private conversation at a club-house has been given in evidence, and the committee declared me innocent of every charge, which has been preferred against me. Did I shrink from the ordeal? did I resort to chicane—did I make my honour a matter of casuistry and special pleading? No, Sir, I invited, I demanded investigation—and my private conversation at the Athenæum Club having been detailed, a conversation after dinner, never recollected even by the narrator for eight months, the accuser declared that his charge is totally destitute of foundation, and the committee at once resolve on my unqualified acquittal. One of the informants of the noble lord was produced—why were they not all brought forward? My accusers were welcome to have got together every loose phrase, every casual and giddy expression uttered in the moments of thoughtlessness and of exhilaration; they were welcome to have collected and collated every sentence uttered by me in convivial gatherings, and to have raked and gathered the sweepings of club-houses, in order to have made up a mass of sordid testimony, and to have cast it into the balance against me. They were welcome to have put me through an ordeal—such as not one of the ministers themselves could encounter—which of you all would dare to stand the test? which of you would have the veil of his privacy rent to pieces, and all his thoughts uttered in the familiarity of common life divulged? But they were welcome to have got together all the whisperers and eavesdroppers of all their clubs against me; I should have defied them, I was prepared with proof to be given by my most intimate and confidential friends, the men with whom I have lived on terms of familiarity and of trust, for upwards of twenty years—the companions of my early life, who knew me as I do myself, and to whom all my thoughts and feelings are almost as well known as their own. I should have been prepared with their evidence, and have established that wherever the Coercion Bill was glanced at, I condemned it in terms of unmitigated detestation, I denounced it as a violation of every one of those principles of liberty of which the Whigs were once the devoted, but not unalterable champions. I did not once, but one hundred times express my horror of the atrocities perpetrated, in parts of the North of Ireland. I did say that to put ruffianism down something ought to be done; I referred to the suggestions made by the committee which sat in 1832 in the Queen's County, and which was composed of men of all parties—but never. I repeat with an emphasis, into which all my heart and soul are thrown. never did I express myself favourable to a bill, which I reprobated in this house, which I denounced elsewhere, in terms of equally vehement censure; and if in place of standing here, I were lying on my death-bed, and about to appear in the presence of my God, I should not dread with the utterance of these words, if they were to be my last, to appear before him."

This speech was received with loud and reiterated acclamation, and Mr. Sheil was placed in a far higher position than he had ever occupied in the House of Commons.

In May, 1834, Mr. Stanley, Sir James Graham, the Duke of Richmond, and Lord Ripon retired from the cabinet. Lord Grey soon afterwards resigned, and Lord Melbourne became Prime Minister. He was dismissed by William the Fourth on the death of Lord Spencer, and Sir Robert Peel was charged with the formation of a government. The Whigs and the Irish members met at Lichfield House soon after Sir Robert had formed his cabinet; Mr. O'Connell and Mr. Sheil concurred in recommending an amnesty—a reconciliation took place, and the Irish members formed what Mr. Sheil called "a compact alliance" with the men who had intimated a determination to redress the grievances of Ireland. This phrase was afterwards misrepresented, and "compact" was substituted for "compact alliance." Sir Robert Peel was defeated on the appropriation question, and went out. Lord Melbourne formed a new government, and Mr. Sheil, in a series of speeches, rendered, what Lord Melbourne admitted to be, essential services to his administration. The most striking speech made by Mr. Sheil, was one during which Lord Lyndhurst happened to be present. Mr. Sheil, in adverting to Lord Lyndhurst's famous assault on the Irish people, turned towards the learned lord with great vehemence of manner, and delivered a denunciation, which was followed by a most remarkable and almost unprecedented excitement. So highly estimated were the exertions of Mr. Sheil by Lord Normanby and Lord Morpeth, that a vacancy having occurred in the office of Solicitor-General for Ireland, both those noblemen recommended that Mr. Sheil should be appointed to fill it; but Lord Melbourne announced to Mr. Sheil himself, that on his coming into office, the King had expressed a strong desire that Mr. Sheil should not be employed; and Lord Melbourne stated that, although he had not made any promise to that effect, he was convinced that the existence of the govern ment would be put to hazard. Mr. Sheil acquiesced, but saw that he must relinquish all hopes of ever obtaining preferment in his profession. He continued his efforts in parliament in favour of the government, without any hope of remuneration. Soon after the death of William the Fourth, however, the obstacle to his advancement having been removed, he was offered the office of Chief Clerk of the Ordnance, but preferred that of Commissioner of Greenwich Hospital, which became vacant by the death of Mr. Crevey, having been led to think that the office was permanent. After having held it for a year, having been warned that it was practically as well as legally held at pleasure, he resigned an office which, indeed, he ought never to have selected, and, in the year 1839, was named Vice-President of the Board of Trade, and was the first Catholic commoner who was raised to the dignity of a Privy Counsellor in England, since the repeal of the Penal Code. His advancement to this important station created a great clamour, and was made the subject of vehement censure at several public meetings, in which the religion of Mr. Sheil was represented as a practical disqualification; but after a few weeks the matter was forgotten. Mr. Sheil continued Vice-President of the Board of Trade for two years, and a few months before the resignation of the Whig ministers, in 1841, was made Judge Advocate-General, in place of Sir George Grey.

On the dissolution of Parliament, in 1841, Mr. Sheil was returned for the borough of Dungarvan. The large expenditure connected with the repeated contests for the county of Tipperary, which he had undergone, induced him to retire from the costly honour of representing that fine district of Ireland. Mr. Sheil continued to attend parliament as assiduously when out of office, as he had previously done, and took part in most of the important debates which arose upon the measures proposed by Sir Robert Peel. His speech upon the Income Tax was regarded as eminently successful. The impression produced by it was so great, that Lord Stanley having risen to reply to it, Sir Robert Peel pulled him back, and insisted on his right of taking the lead.

When Peel retired from office, bearing with him the contempt of the nation, Sheil was nominated to the Mastership of the Mint. After this appointment he seldom took part in the debates in the House of Commons, as his health was very much shaken by his former close attention, and he was harrassed by repeated attacks of gout.

"In 1851 Mr. Sheil was appointed her Majesty's Plenipotentiary at the Court of Tuscany. He died at Florence of a sudden attack of gout, on Sunday, 25th of May, and was interred on Wednesday the 28th in the Church of San Michele. He left no family; his son by his first wife died a few years ago. The managing committee of Glasnevin Cemetery proposed to Sheil's friends to place his remains beside those of O'Connell; the offer was not accepted, as Mrs. Sheil wished that his grave might be where she could in death sleep beside him."*

* Irish Quarterly Review, vol. 1., p. 407

SELECT SPEECHES

OF THE

RIGHT HONOURABLE

RICHARD LALOR SHEIL.

SPEECH UPON THE MEMOIRS OF THEOBALD WOLFE TONE, MADE AT THE
CATHOLIC ASSOCIATION.

THIS book—the life of Theobald Wolfe Tone, who was guilty of a
distempered love of Ireland (he had great talents, and with an adventurous spirit combined an undaunted determination)—contains much
matter, in which a Catholic can find instruction, from which a British
minister ought to derive a warning, while to a Protestant proprietor it
cannot fail to afford a theme, on which, if he shall often reflect, his frequent meditation will not be misapplied. I introduce the subject with
some abruptness; but it is as well that any preliminary expatiation
should be avoided, and that I should proceed at once to the topics to
which it is my intention to direct your notice. I shall advert in the
first instance to the observations made by Wolfe Tone upon the policy
which he conceived it to be wise, on the part of the Catholics of Ireland,
to pursue. He states in a diary kept by him in Paris, that General
Clarke, the son of an Irishman, and who was afterwards created Duke
de Feltre, expressed to him an opinion, that the system which was
called Chouannerie in France, and which is analogous in many respects
to the Rockism of this country, might be usefully resorted to in Ireland,
and that the people, through such means, might be familiarised with
arms, and prepared for a general co-operation, with an invading force.
This suggestion was indignantly repudiated by Wolfe Tone, who justly
observes, that agrarian combinations lead to crimes as unavailing for

any political purpose as they are morally odious, and produce a barbarous and irregular disturbance, which the government regard without alarm, and which affords an opportunity for the enactment of coercive laws, whenever it suits their purpose to resort to them. Tone alludes to another important topic, the disunion of the Catholics amongst themselves, and the secession of the Catholic gentry from the people. He laments these unfortunate incidents, and inveighs against the unhappy spirit of pusillanimous compliance, which characterized the Catholic leaders in the bargain which they were induced to strike with the government in 1793. He states himself to be fully convinced that if, in the midst of the embarrassments of the ministry, with war without, and disaffection within, the men who negotiated on the part of the Catholics of Ireland had adopted the peremptory tone which the condition of the country would have enabled them to assume, the minister would have been compelled to yield, and a measure of complete and unqualified enfranchisement would have been extorted from him. This remark is well founded; I am sure that our interests as well as our honour will be always most effectually consulted by a bold, uncompromising course; that the men at the head of the people must rely upon the people, and nothing but the people, for the accomplishment of every national purpose, and that whenever they shall be weak enough to listen to the false blandishments of power, they will discover that a sacrifice of principle is sure to be followed by a relinquishment of their real interests, and that of their own unwise cunning, as well as of the craft of their antagonists, they will infallibly prove the victims. So much for that portion of this book, which relates more immediately to the course which it befitted the leaders of the Irish Catholics in 1793, in the opinion of Theobald Wolfe Tone, to have adopted. I turn to a topic of deeper interest—to a portion of the narrative contained in these memoirs, calculated to awaken in the mind of an English statesman reflections of a very serious kind, and in which I ventured to say, that practical admonition was to be found. In 1795, Theobald Wolfe Tone was compelled to retire from Ireland to the United States, where he had at first an intention of settling; there in the bosom of his family, with a wife whom he adored, and children who shared in his idolatry for their incomparable mother, he might have led a long and prosperous life, if he knew how to form a just estimate of felicity, and could have appreciated the opportunities of happiness with which he was encompassed. But ambition, or perverted patriotism, was among many passions paramount to every other: he was pursued by the recollections of Ireland: the memory of his country became a malady of his heart: and in the idealism of exile the scenes of oppression which he had witnessed, and at which his blood had boiled, rose with all the distinctness of unimpaired reality before him. The phantasms with which men condemned to leave their country are disastrously haunted, are, to men like Tone, prompters of great enterprise. There gradually grew up in his mind a design as adventurous as any of which the romance of history has left us an example. He formed the determination to strike a blow at England, where he knew that she was most vulnerable, and to invite the French republic to become his auxiliary in an enterprise which should put the British empire to hazard. Full of a purpose, which at first view appeared to be as extravagant as it was criminal, he set sail from America, and arrived at Havre on the first of February, 1796 Having reached Paris, he found himself in a state which men less ardent, and with less fixedness of intent would have looked upon as desperate: he failed for a considerable time in obtaining access to any man in authority, and the little money in his possession was almost expended. He was without friends, without resources of any kind, and could scarcely express himself in the language of the country. It is, indeed, difficult to conjecture a state more utterly hopeless than that to which he was reduced. Yet, in the desolation of a great metropolis, he was upheld by that unalterable purpose, from which the aliment of his soul was derived. At last he obtained an interview with the minister of war His chief credentials, the documents on which he grounded his claim to the confidence of Charles Lecroix, were two votes of thanks, which he had received as their secretary from the Catholics of Ireland. Although Lecroix had never heard of him before, he was struck by his project, and sent him to General Clarke, whose family was connected with Ireland; but Clarke entertained such strange notions about the country from which his father had emigrated, that he inquired from him, whether Lord Clare was likely to co-operate with the French, and whether the Duke of York would accept the sovereignty of Ireland, in the event of its conquest by the French republic. Tone perceived that little could be effected with Clarke, and determined to go directly to the President of the Directory, who was no other than the celebrated Carnot, to whose genius the marvellous successes of France were in a great measure to be ascribed. An interview was obtained, in which the victorious mathematician listened to the enthusiastic Irishman, with a not very unnatural distrust in the feasibility of his project. He slowly acceded to it, and it was proposed by the French Government to send two thousand men to Ireland.. This suggestion Tone treated as an absurdity. His reasoning was so cogent, that he prevailed upon the Directory to resolve upon an expedition of eight thousand men, with fifty thousand stand of arms; but Hoche, who enjoyed the highest military reputation, having been named to the chief command of the invading army, insisted on its being increased from eight to fifteen thousand men, with a large park of artillery, and arms sufficient to supply the insurgent population. The French Directory acceded to this requisition, and that large force, conveyed by seventeen ships of the line, sailed from Brest. While every good citizen must concur in the unqualified condemnation of the man, at whose instance the French Government embarked in an undertaking which, if it had been successful, would have entailed irretrievable calamity upon his country, yet when we look back at the circumstances in which Wolfe Tone was placed, and consider the difficulties with which he had to struggle, that his achievement was a most extraordinary one, must be acknowledged. How must his heart have beaten when he beheld that great armament, with its vast sails dilated in some sort by his own aspiring spirit, steering its course to the island where his cradle was rocked, where the bones of his fathers were deposited, on whose green hills his eyes had first rested, and on whose lofty peaks, against which the Atlantic breaks in thunder, he felt assured that his triumphant standard would be unfurled. Happily for England, these visions of victory, when almost embodied in a fatal realization, were dispelled by the winds, called so justly "the only unsubsidized allies of England;" and by those auxiliaries, on which England cannot rely for ever, the want of wisdom and of foresight in the Government, and the want of an army to defend the country, when it was left wholly unprotected, was supplied. The French fleet was dispersed by a storm;—Hoche was blown out of his course with seven ships of the line; but ten sail of the line, with six thousand troops, reached the Irish coast. Wolfe Tone says that they were so near that he could have pitched a biscuit on shore. A landing might have been at once effected, but the Directory had given orders that the fleet should proceed to Bantry Bay. Ten ships of the line did proceed there, with a force which might have marched to Dublin, and lay for five days in a harbour on the Irish coast. It is a most remarkable circumstance that in the absence of Hoche, the command of the army should have devolved upon Grouchy, in reference to whom these words are set down in the diary kept by Wolfe Tone: "all now depends upon Grouchy." After the lapse of nineteen years, upon the 18th of June, 1815, in what an agony of hope the great emperor directed his glass to the horizon in search of those battalions which he had confided to the same questionable soldier, expecting, to the last, that in the distance he should behold his eagles upon the wing to his rescue. That Grouchy was an instrument of Providence it may not be irrational to think, but that such implements of safety will always be provided it is not an article of faith to believe. Grouchy did not land; and Ireland was preserved. I have done with the incidents in the Memoirs of Wolfe Tone. His subsequent history, the two expeditions which he afterwards planned, and the last scene in his eventful life, in which he resorted to what Edmond Burke has called "the sharp antidote against disgrace,' to avoid the doom which, for those who are guilty of having failed, is proverbially destined,—are full of painful interest; but for the purpose which has induced me to advert to this book what I have said of it is sufficient. That purpose is different from that which may, perhaps, be imputed to me. But what I deeply deprecate, I may be permitted honestly to apprehend, and I own that the perusal of this book has excited in my mind an alarm, to which I think myself justified in giving expression. The voice of admonition is grating to the ear, but the reflections suggested by this volume ought not to be suppressed, however disinclined a minister may be to listen to them. I believe this country to be exposed to the most serious risks, in consequence of the fatal policy which the government are pursuing; I consider their security to be false, and believe them to be treading on the edge of a fearful peril. Who that sees the sleep walker advancing to the precipice, would heed how rudely he might awaken him, if by boldly grasping him he can drag him from the gulf?

In the year 1796, the Catholic population of this country did not exceed three millions; it amounts to double that number. In 1796, the French republic had not recanted its profession of infidelity, and was deeply stained with the blood of martyred priests and pontiffs. The throne of France is occupied by a sovereign anointed with legitimacy the altar has been rebuilt, and the ancient Catholic Church lifts up its mitred and apostolic head. Attractive relations have arisen, where an intercept was created by many repulsive circumstances. The application of steam in naval warfare deserves to be taken into account, and more especially by Mr. Canning, who recently told us that modern science had "taken from the winds their proverbial fickleness." To that eminent man I would more peculiarly commend the memoirs of Wolfe Tone. He cannot fail to recollect, that not very long ago, when he made it his boast that from the recesses in which they were immured, he could let loose the popular passions, and sweep the French monarchy in a hurricane away, Monsieur de Chateaubriand, and Monsieur Hyde de Neuville, and Monsieur de Beaumont, indignant at this presumptuous intimation, pointed to Ireland with a fierce and retaliatory menace, and warned him and his colleagues to beware, lest France should be provoked to do what it was so obvious that it was in her power to accomplish. Mr. Canning must have been stung to the soul by this formidable retort: he acted wisely in not having noticed it in Parliament; but I do think that it is his duty to tell his associates, to whose fatal obstinacy the perils of this country are to be referred, that from the foes of England this disastrous advantage should be taken away, and that by an act of wise and timely justice a country exposed to imminent peril should be impregnably secured. He ought to go with this book in his hand into the cabinet, and plead for the emancipation of Ireland, with the memoirs of Wolfe Tone. There are men among his colleagues by whom he will be told that the Protestants of Ireland are a match for traitors, and that upon them, as the faithful and incorruptible garrison of the country, an unfaltering reliance may be placed. No man entertains a higher estimate of the courage, of the union, of the high and daring spirit of the Protestants of Ireland than I do. Their military qualities are inversely as their numbers. If England be sustained by that powerful body of adherents the likelihood is, that no matter how strongly seconded, France would be ultimately vanquished; but, to what a condition would Ireland be reduced, when the domination of England had been restored in its despotic plenitude, and the penal code in all its baneful vigour had been renewed. Torrents of blood would have been shed, millions of treasure would have been lavished, civil war raging in its worst and most frightful form would have left behind a desolation, to which, by those who made it, the name of peace would be assigned. In six months of a warfare, more than civil, Ireland would recede more than half a century, and from that retrogradation to barbarism, the Protestants of Ireland would not most assuredly derive any advantage equivalent to the calamity which would have been inflicted upon their country. In the Cromwelian spoliation the misfortunes of Ireland were turned by the soldiers of the slaughterer of Drogheda to account. Conquest was followed by confiscation; but Protestantism is now seised in fee of the island, and of the national calamity nothing substantial could be made. The Protestant proprietors of Ireland are as much interested in the pacification of the country (which can be only effected by the redress of the national grievances) as we are. There is, indeed, a class of political sectaries whose livelihood is derived from their religion. The fouler as well as smaller birds of prey croak and flutter in the fear that the receptacles of ascendancy, in which their loathsome nests are built, should be disturbed. But a Protestant gentleman of rank and fortune, who cannot be swayed by the same sordid considerations, should consider the permanent establishment of order, the reconciliation of the people to the government, the abandonment of all revolutionary purpose, the security of the country from all foreign danger, and from all intestine commotion, as objects which, at the sacrifice of his bad predominance, would be cheaply purchased. A Cromwellian proprietor views the tract of woods and lawns with which the piety of his puritanical forefather was rewarded, in all the pride with which the consciousness of long transmitted property is attended. The hope of transmitting his estate to his descendants is one of the most pleasurable of his emotions. He devises his property in strict settlement, and, by complicated limitations endeavours to impart a feudal perpetuity to his possessions; and yet, an admonition, solemn as the warning of Lochiel, might, perhaps, be appropriately given him, that the time might come, when, amidst the shouts of insurgent onslaught, his mansion should be given to the flames; those dearer than his life-blood should lie slaughtered or dishonoured in that home in which they could no longer find a sanctuary, and horrors should be enacted, at the contemplation of which religion trembles and humanity recoils. That the daring intimations, to which I have been sufficiently venturesome to give this impassioned utterance, will be read by those to whom they are intended to be addressed with feelings of resentment, I do not doubt; but by the insensibility of Protestant Ireland to the perils which impend upon us all, a fearless adjuration is required. If I thought that by a reference to such topics, no useful purpose could be accomplished, I should not warn men of a peril which it is not in their power to avert. In the city of lava, with a burning mountain above, and with Herculaneum buried beneath, what would it avail to bid men listen to the roll of the subterranean thunder? wherefore speak of an eruption to those by whom Vesuvius cannot be extinguished? but it is in the power of those to whom I have addressed this intrepid invocation, to save themselves from the peril that overhangs them, and to put the volcano out.

COURT OF KING'S BENCH—Tuesday, May 8, 1827

SPEECH, IN SHOWING CAUSE WHY A CRIMINAL INFORMATION SHOULD NOT BE FILED AGAINST MR. ÆNEAS M'DONNELL, AT THE PROSECUTION OF THE HONOURABLE AND VENERABLE CHARLES LE POER TRENCH, ARCHDEACON OF ARDAGH

Mr. SHEIL, after reading the affidavits, said : I have stated, at very considerable, I hope not at any unnecessary length, the affidavits of the prosecutor and of the defendant, together with the matter contained in the affidavits which have been filed in sustainment of the defendant's case. It remains that I should submit to your Lordships such observations as appear to me to arise out of the facts, and which in my judgment, ought to induce the court to refuse a criminal information. It is right to state, in the first place, the principles on which this court exercises its discretionary power in allowing criminal informations. That they are entirely in the option of the court, will not be disputed. Still this court does not act in an uncertain and capricious spirit, but applies to the circumstances of every case a fixed standard of decision. In the case of the King against Robinson, Lord Mansfield laid it down that the court will not grant a criminal information where the prosecutor is himself to blame, or where considerations of public policy render it inexpedient. The question was connected with an election, and involved much popular passion. The words used by Lord Mansfield are remarkable. "There is," he said, "bad blood enough already." For that, among other reasons (but it was not the least cogent one), he refused the motion. In the present case, the political and religious animosities of two powerful classes of the community are involved, and I cannot refrain from asking, even at the outset, whether there is not already between the parties themselves, and the bodies which they respectively represent, a sufficiency of "bad blood?" The grounds on which I am instructed to rely are threefold :—the prosecutor is himself to blame, and does not come into court (to use the technical expression) with clean hands—the charges brought against him by the defendant are substantially established—and the subject out of which the differences between the parties has arisen is of such a nature, that the court will be loath to interfere. Who is the prosecutor? What are his merits in the transaction? Is he entitled to any special interposition in his favour? These are questions which offer themselves at once to the court. He is the member of a powerful family, with an earl and and an archbishop at its head, which has devoted itself, with a very ardent zeal, to the scriptural education of the Irish peasantry. Among the remarkable, Doctor Trench has rendered himself conspicuous. He was once a soldier, and belonged to a profession whose habits are essentially different from those which are supposed to belong to his present occupation. His life, according to his own description of himself, does not appear to have been immaculate, and if he brought no other qualification to the performance of his sacred duties, he seems at least to have possessed that adaptation to virtue which ought to arise from the fatigue, if not the satiety of those indulgences to which he appears to have been addicted. He was not only a soldier, but an adjutant, and I hope I shall be pardoned for suggesting that the man, who admits that he beheld a woman tortured under his auspices in the barrack-yard of Cork, and to have presided in his official capacity over her sufferings, must have acquired certain peculiarities of character not in very ostensible conformity with that vocation to which, by some very special interference of Providence, must have called him in the midst of wanderings of no ordinary kind. The gallant and reverend plaintiff became a very enthusiastic Christian, so far as mere strenuousness of belief is concerned, and in the year 1818 entered into a compact with the Roman Catholic parish priest, to educate the children of Catholics and Protestants, without distinction of religion. They agreed that no book or usage should be introduced at variance with the creed of either sect. The priest, the Rev. Mr. Larkin, however, discovered that Dr. Trench had introduced a manuscript catechism of his own composition, and proceeded to the school, in order to remonstrate. He went accompanied by two friars, and met the prosecutor at the entrance of the school. The latter advanced with outstretched arms, and exclaimed, "Welcome, Garret, Garret (for Garret was Mr. Larkin's christian name), welcome, Garret. The flock is numerous, but the shepherds are few." The result of the discussion between the priest, the friars, and the archdeacon was, that the children of Catholic parents withdrew from the school, and the archdeacon caused the priest of the parish to be distrained for a hanging gale of rent; but he was not deterred from the prosecution of his favourite scheme, for he published a notice, which was posted up in his own hand-writing, that none of the tenants over whom he had any control had any favour to expect who did not send their children to his school, and procure certificates from two devout ladies who were mentioned in the notice. He carried this menace into effect, for the tenants who obeyed his directions were liberally rewarded, while upon many a wretched serf sentence was pronounced and executed, with a rigour which would have done credit to any court-martial of which the archdeacon ever was a member. Religion, grafted upon the military genius of the archdeacon, does not appear to have been very successfully inoculated. A great deal of misery was the result of that vitiated enthusiasm, which considers the means, no matter how severe, as justified by the sanctity of the object which they are intended to attain. The labourers who declined to follow the ordinances of Archdeacon Trench were dismissed, and the houses of such of the occupiers of Lord Clancarty's lands as manifested any conscientious contumacy were thrown down; their families were cast upon the world. It is needless to state that this somewhat anomalous, though not very uncommon mode of disseminating the tenets of the Gospel, occasioned much affliction. The peasantry were placed in a condition truly pitiable. The archdeacon threatened them with the terrors of this world, and the priest with the retribution that awaited them in the next. The gentry took part in the contest, and while the peasantry were persecuted and oppressed, the county, which had hitherto been remarkable for the concord which prevailed among all classes, presented the most painful scenes of religious discord. It was in this state of things that Mr. M'Donnell arrived in the county of Galway—thither he proceeded to visit his family. Dr. Coen, the Roman Catholic bishop of the diocese, knowing that Mr. M'Donnell was employed by the Roman Catholic body as their agent, requested him to attend a meeting at Loughrea, which was convened in order to petition Lord Clancarty to put some check on the doctor's injudicious zeal. The bishop, deeply afflicted by the sufferings of his flock, had himself previously applied to Lord Clancarty, but in vain. A public meeting was called, in the hope that a supplication to his lordship, proceeding from a numerous and respectable assembly, on behalf of his tenantry, would be attended with better results. Mr. M'Donnell states that the strongest evidences of distress were displayed among the people, many of whom were moved to tears. Mr. M'Donnell was affected by what he saw and heard, and it was under the influence of the impressions which were produced upon him on the occasion, that he attended the meeting of the London Hibernian Bible Society, held upon the 16th of October, at Ballinasloe. The object of this institution is stated by the prosecutor to be the dissemination of the Scriptures without note or comment. None of its regulations were inserted in the notice, nor was any prohibition introduced into it against the attendance, speaking or voting of any individuals who were not members of the society. It does not appear that Lord Dunlo, the chairman, or even Doctor Trench himself, or any one individual who attended, with the exception of Mr. Pope and Captain Gordon, belonged to the institution. Doctor Trench states, indeed, that it was one of its rules that none but members should be permitted to speak; but that rule was not only not adhered to, but was not even noticed in the course of the proceeding. Mr. M'Donnell moved an amendment; he was not prevented from so doing; on the contrary, the chairman actually put the amendment from the chair on the second day of the meeting. The assembly was adjourned from the 10th to the succeeding day, when Captain Gordon opened the discussion. Mr. M'Donnell replied, and, as I have already intimated, moved an amendment, and pressed the chairman to put the question. Lord Dunlo observed that new matter had been introduced, and that Mr. Pope should be permitted to reply. To this proposition Mr. M'Donnell assented, provided that, in case Mr. Pope was permitted to make any further observations, he should be allowed to exercise the right which he derived from established usage, of making the final reply. On this understanding the meeting adjourned to the next day. During the first two days it cannot be pretended that there was any impropriety committed by Mr. M'Donnell, either in speaking or in moving an amendment, for his right to speak and vote were distinctly recognized by the chairman, who was the organ of the meeting. It appears, therefore that Mr. M'Donnell did not commit any original deviation from propriety. During the first two days there were only two policemen stationed in the meeting, and Dr. Trench did not actively interfere but on the morning of the 12th the aspect of affairs underwent a material alteration. The moment the doors were opened, Dr. Trench placed himself at the entrance, and, under his direction, a number of Protestants of the lower class, with, as it is alleged, arms under their greatcoats, were specially admitted, and stationed, by the doctor's orders, in the assembly. He felt the importance of carrying the day, and brought to the meeting the powers of a magistrate, the habits of a soldier, and the passions of a priest. His favourite project was to be promoted; it was of the greatest consequence, in his mind, that it should appear that in a great assembly, held in what may be called a Roman Catholic county, the circulation of the Scriptures, without note or comment, had been publicly approved. To gain this object an effort was required, and it was deemed advisable to put Mr. M'Donnell down. For this purpose the room was filled with police, who appeared to be under the doctor's orders, and a large body of these Irish gens-d'armes were stationed outside the place of meeting. The archdeacon, who was well accustomed to military operations, posted himself beside my Lord Dunlo, and stood with an attitude, looked with an air, and spoke with an intonation of command. The debate was opened by Mr. Pope, when Mr. M'Donnell recalled to the chairman the reservation of his right to reply. Lord Dunlo, who during the two preceding days had permitted Mr. M'Donnell not only to speak but to propose an amendment, and had actually put that amendment from the chair, having received a whisper from Dr. Trench, now, for the first time, informed Mr. M'Donnell that he had no right to open his lips, and in place of putting the amendment, proposed a series of resolutions favourable to the objects of the society, which he declared to be carried, and left the chair. Mr. M'Donnell moved that the Hon. Gonville Ffrench should take it. He was a magistrate, the son of a peer, and the person next in rank to Lord Dunlo. He advanced to take the chair, when Doctor Trench, turning to the police, exclaimed, "do your duty." The police were not slow in obeying his orders, and rushed, with fixed bayonets, upon the people! I stop here in the narration of the facts, and call again the attention of the court to the principles upon which criminal informations are granted or refused. I have already referred the court to the authority of Lord Mansfield; and although it was merely in the course of argument that Lord Erskine pronounced what may be called a commentary upon the law, still, as the court decided in his client's favour, in Captain Bayley's case, and as the positions he lays down are indisputable, it may not be improper to quote what was said by that great advocate, not, indeed, as an authority, but because the doctrine which he lays down is clearly and succinctly expressed:—" This is not a complaint in the ordinary course of law, but an application to the court to exert an eccentric, extraordinary, voluntary jurisdiction, beyond the ordinary course of justice:—a jurisdiction which I am authorized, from the best authority to say, this court will not exercise, unless the prosecutors come pure and unspotted; deny, upon oath, the truth of every word and sentence which they complain as injurious; for, although in common sense, the matter may not be the less libellous, because true, yet the court will not interfere by information, for guilty or even equivocal characters, but will leave them to its ordinary process. If the court does not see palpable malice and falsehood on the part of the defendant, and clear innocence on the part of the prosecutor, it will not stir; it will say, this may be a libel; this may deserve punishment; but go to a grand jury, or bring your action; all men are equally entitled to the protection of the laws, but all men are not equally entitled to an extraordinary interposition and protection beyond the common distributive forms of justice." That what I have read is law will scarcely be disputed. The court will inquire whether the prosecutor is himself deserving of condemnation, and will look to the inception of the proceedings, without attending minutely to subsequent details. The principle applied every day to cases of duelling, may, without any violence, be extended to cases of libel. If an individual gives the first offence, no matter by what outrages he may be subsequently provoked, this court will leave him to proceed by indictment. If Dr. Trench was originally in the wrong—if, when under the influence of his religious passions, he acted in such a manner as to deserve reproof, the court will not inquire whether it was excessive and disproportioned to the fault committed by the prosecutor, no more than it will ask whether a challenge was warranted by the offence, but will simply inquire whether the doctor was not guilty of a very signal transgression of propriety in his conduct at Ballinasloe. I am indisposed to use any coarse or contumelious phrase in his regard—I will not accuse him of any directly sanguinary intent—I will not say that he went armed with the Riot Act, and attended by the police, in order to avail himself of the first opportunity of letting them loose upon a defenceless body of his fellow-citizens. But it is one question, whether a purpose so detestable entered distinctly into his contemplation, and another, whether he did not, while under the operation of those fanatical opinions, which obscure the understanding, while they indurate the heart, perpetrate a flagitious outrage—an act inconsistent with the character of a clergyman, the principles of a Christian, and the good feelings of a man. Without charging him with a deliberate depravity, I accuse him of a wild fanaticism, which is analogous to ferocity in its results—and I collect from his previous habits, the motives and the passions by which he was instigated in the incident which is more directly before the court. The man who, in the prosecution of his object, had crushed the miserable peasantry subject to his dominion; who had prostrated their hovels, and, unmoved by tears, by cries, and by supplications, had, in the name of God and of his Gospel, scattered desolation and despair about him— the man who combined with his religious habits the habits of courts-martial, was, of all others, the most likely to be hurried into the perpetration of what, in an archdeacon, may be called an error, but, in a less venerable person, would be accounted a crime. Your lordships will scarcely permit yourselves to approve (and if you grant the information, you must approve) of the introduction of a military force into the midst of an assembly, convened for the propagation of the Word of God? A meeting of the Hibernian London Society is convened—their object is to circulate the Scriptures—they assemble to listen to two itinerant

delegates from the parent branch—the people are invited to attend—
Mr. M'Donnell urges his arguments against a scheme offensive to the
feelings, and incompatible with the religion of the people—during two
days his right to take a share in the proceedings is not disputed—Lord
Dunlo leaves the chair—a magistrate, a gentleman of family and of fortune, and in every way respectable, is called to it—there was no riot—
no blow was struck—no injurious exclamation was employed—no violence, nor symptom of violence, appeared. The object of the meeting
—the rank and character of the persons assembled—every thing forbade
the expedient to which Dr. Trench resorted ; and yet notwithstanding
the combination of circumstances which inhibited the use of a military
force, a dignitary of the Established Church rushes forth, in the frenzy
of fanaticism, and calling on the police " to do their duty," precipitately
reads the Riot Act, the preliminary to the effusion of blood. I see
nothing in the whole transaction which can afford a palliation for his
conduct ; and notwithstanding his own protestations, it appears manifest
that he had determined to disperse the meeting at the point of that
instrument of persuasion with which he was, in his younger years, professionally familiar. He carries the Riot Act to the meeting—he fills it
with police—admits his own peculiar supporters to the meeting, and
arrays them in a body—superintends the proceedings—gives the signal
—calls upon the police to advance—bids them rush upon the multitude,
and a scene takes place calculated to excite the indignation of the
people, and that of every honest man who hears the details of the proceedings in this court. The police, who were stationed in the meeting,
precipitated themselves upon the people. Another body rushed up
stairs, with their swords drawn and their bayonets fixed. They drove
the Catholics before them, and mingled invectives against their religion
with their ferocious exclamations. The people fled; the open windows
afforded refuge to many of them, and women threw themselves for
safety upon the adjoining roofs. If the people had resisted—if, fired
with a natural resentment, they had turned upon the men by whom they
were so wantonly assailed—if they had merged the duty of citizens in
the feelings of outraged human nature, what would have been the result?
The lives of hundreds might have been lost—the public streets might
have ran with blood—a general carnage might have ensued, and the
Honourable and Rev. Charles Le Poer Trench, instead of having the
presumption to come, with hands so defiled, for a criminal information
into this court, would appear at the bar of justice, and stand a trial for
his life. I come now to the circumstances under which the speech was
spoken, of which Dr. Trench complains. Mr. M'Donnell, after the
assembly had been broken up, used every exertion to tranquillize the people. A public meeting was called upon the 16th, in order to consider the
propriety of presenting a memorial to the Lord Lieutenant. In the
interval, Dr. Trench did not procure informations to be lodged against
any one individual for a riot. He read the Riot Act—he caused the
police to charge the people, and yet no single individual was accused by
the doctor of having taken part in the tumult. The Roman Catholic
assembled upon the 16th, and at that meeting Mr. M'Donnell spoke in

the language of strong censure of Dr. Trench. Independent of the actual outrage committed upon him, the newspapers in the interest of the doctor had represented Mr. M'Donnell's conduct in the most odious light. In his speech he charged Dr. Trench with the insertion of an attack upon him, and that allegation is not denied. But compared with the affront offered to him, and to every Roman Catholic, such aspersions are of no account. This court will not grant an information against a man, who, provoked by a single offensive phrase, sends a challenge Will the court grant an information against an individual who was provoked—not by a contumelious expression—not by a contemptuous look —but by an outrage, as exasperating as it is possible to conceive? It is said that his retaliation was disproportionate to the injury which he had received, and that the charges brought against Dr. Trench were unfounded. I will admit, for the sake of argument, that the charges preferred against him by Mr. M'Donnell are unfounded, that he never presided over the torture of a miserable female—that he never applied to a sub-sheriff for liberty to play the part of an executioner, and inflict a frightful torment with his own hands—that he never prostrated houses, expelled their wretched occupiers, and filled the hearts of parents with despair and sorrow—but while, for a moment and no more, I admit all this, I appeal to the principle upon which this court regulates its decisions, and put this question—" Does not the man who sends a hostile message act against the laws of God, and the ordinances of society?" —yet, if he has received an affront—if he has been designated by some ignominious appellation, no information will be granted against him. Is duelling an excepted case—and will this court consider the individual who seeks to take away human life, as sheltered from a criminal information by the offence which he has sustained, and shall the mere utterer of words be the object of the sternest judicial rigour? Shall he who levels a pistol at my heart escape with impunity—and shall the man whose pen drops gall, be deprived of the benefit of the same extenuation? This court tells many a prosecutor, "although your life has been aimed at—although the defendant sought to wipe out the offence which you have offered to him with your blood—yet, as you were originally to blame, you are not entitled to favour; other remedies are open to you, and we leave you to seek them." Consider then the nature and extent of the provocation which Mr. M'Donnell had received, in order that you may judge whether he was originally to blame. He went to a public meeting at Ballinasloe, to discuss a subject in which he felt a profound interest. The proceedings of the Hibernian Bible Society are not exempt from the cognizance of public opinion, and are liable to the strictures to which even the measures of government are exposed. Whether right or wrong he acted under the influence of strong impressions. He thought it absurd to put a book, upon the construction of which the wisest and best men have differed, into indiscriminate circulation, amongst those whose minds are as obtuse as their hands are hard. He was at a loss to discover the benefits that could result from a medley of religions, and a miscellany of creeds. He conceived that it would be wiser to allow the humble peasant to continue in the exercise of that form of worship in which he was born, in which he had lived, and in which it is his best hope to die. He was convinced, that he had the authority of the clergy of his own church to warrant him in that conviction, that the system of which Dr. Trench is the advocate, is incompatible with the essential spirit of the Catholic religion. He looked upon the itinerant hawkers of a new-fangled Christianity as the emissaries of dissension, and he saw that religious rancour, and all the fury of theological detestation, marked the steps of these vagabond apostles wherever they appeared. With these impressions he attended the meeting at Ballinasloe. He spoke, and his right to speak was not disputed. He was guilty of no greater offence than that of vindicating the Roman Catholic clergy from the accusations which Mr. Pope and Mr. Gordon had cast upon them. He avoided all angry recrimination. He did not, in answer to the charges brought against the Catholic clergy, lift the veil from the abuses of the Establishment—he did not, when the Catholic priesthood were charged with profligacy, say one word about Dr. Trench. When the calumniators of his church went back to the distance of centuries for instances of depravity in Catholic bishops, Mr. M'Donnell did not allude to the execrable misdeeds of no very remote occurrence, on which Protestants should reflect before they bring their charges against the poor and unendowed clergy of the Catholic church. He did not, in discussing the propriety of circulating the Scriptures among all classes, without distinction, inquire whether some details contained in the history of a sensual people, were fit for the perusal of boyhood and a virgin's meditations. He did not put any one argument, or make an observation which would excite the prejudices, or alarm the sensitiveness of the most enthusiastic of his hearers. He was contented with the vindication of the Catholic hierarchy and clergy from the most foul and false aspersions, and remonstrated, in the language of subdued expostulation, on the evil effects of the system which the London Hibernian Society employed its emissaries to promote; and yet, for this, for no more than this, a body of infuriated police are let loose upon the people. They are halloed on by this regimental divine. The Roman Catholics are assailed with every species of insult and of outrage, and Mr. M'Donnell himself is thrust out of the assembly, amidst the shouts of Dr. Trench's myrmidons, with the grasp of ruffianism on his neck, the sabre over his head, and the bayonet at his back; and shall I be told that Mr. M'Donnell received no provocation? There is not a man with a drop of manly blood in his veins, who would not be fired, and almost maddened by it. The doctor, indeed, swears there was a riot. True it is that he did himself engender and create a frightful tumult. But what evidence is there that before he drew the Riot Act out of his pocket, there was any, the least symptom of disturbance? Was a blow given? Was a menacious gesture used? Was there a threat in attitude or in words? He does not venture to suggest it. This court ought not to be satisfied with general allegations that a riot existed, without having the precise facts and circumstances before it, which are the ingredients of the offence, and which constitute its legal essence. I impeach the doctor's affidavit upon two grounds.

First, that he does not state any one fact which goes to establish that there was a riot, and secondly. that he did not afterwards take any proceedings against any one of the alleged rioters. Was a single person arrested? Were there informations lodged? Was any step taken by this enraged magistrate to punish the offence which had induced him to uncage all the ferocious passions of the police and set them upon the people? I have argued this case as if the charges brought against the doctor were wholly unfounded, and insist that the impropriety of his conduct disentitled him to a criminal information. But, my Lords, Mr. M'Donnell has in his affidavit justified the accusations which he has preferred, and it was my duty to comply with his instructions, and read not only his own affidavit, but those of the numerous witnesses by whom he is corroborated. I will not go so far as to say, that truth affords a complete defence, but I do say, that there is a manifest distinction between an indictment and an information. In the former, truth is no defence—but as an information is entirely in the discretion of the court, the truth of the charges will be taken into consideration, and will be thrown into the balance in order to adjust it. I am free to admit, that if the accusations are unfounded, Dr. Trench is most aggrieved, and justice ought to rise up in indignation in his defence. I do not say that the charges are well founded—it is not my province to decide that question—but if they are, (and your lordships will weigh all the probabilities) you will pause before you grant a favour to Dr. Trench, and decide whether he is the best qualified person to superintend the morals of Ballinasloe. What, then, are the charges against him? They are threefold It is alleged that he is not a fit person to preside over the education of youth—first, because he was a man of licentious habits—secondly, because he has inflicted the greatest misery upon the unfortunate peasantry under his dominion—and thirdly, that he is a man of the cruel propensities, which created for him an appellation with which the most shocking images of horror are associated. With respect to the first charge, (and I again repeat that I am only arguing hypothetically, and in obedience to my client's positive instructions) Mr. M'Donnell has sworn that the doctor, since he became a clergyman has led a most immoral life. His miscellaneous amours are set forth with minuteness—and the progeny of his indulgences are also specified. Mr. M'Donnell has, indeed, given as particular details of the reverend gentleman's sacerdotal frailties as your lordships could require every thing has been done by him to remove any disposition to incredulity with which charges against an archdeacon ought to be received. It may be objected that these statements are made upon belief. Mr. M'Donnell, however, has encountered this objection; but when I was about to read the affidavit of an unfortunate female, containing some particulars calculated to satisfy your lordships, if you entertained any doubt of the fidelity of Mr. M'Donnell's delineations of debauchery, the counsel for the archdeacon stopped me, and insisted that the affidavit was filed too late, and was not admissible. The court decided that it was not, and therefore I shall not even state what that affidavit set forth. But I shall be permitted to say, that it does strike me as extraordinary that the clergyman who comes into this court with such ostentatious claims to sanctity, and who demands a reparation for the injury done to his character, should seek a shelter from investigation in mere forms of law, and rely upon the tardiness with which the affidavit has come in, as a ground for withholding the facts from the court. If the charges are untrue, why not meet them with the scorn with which conscious virtue should always encounter the accusations of malignity? The doctor enters the temple of justice as proudly as he would mount the steps of his own church, and with a lofty demeanour demands redress; but the moment proof is offered of the charge, he shrinks into the first dark hiding-place of the law where he can find a refuge. Having said thus much upon this suppression of a most material affidavit, I think it an act of justice to Dr. Trench to say, that the charge to which I have adverted relates to his former life; but, that although for many years after he entered the church he persevered in those addictions which he had acquired in a less ascetic profession, he has lately reformed his conduct, and allowed time to apply its moralising influence to a fiery and impassioned temperament. But men of vehement characters engage in the pursuit of virtue with the same excessive ardour with which they obey the allurements of pleasure, and the transition in excesses is not uncommon. The doctor's letters to the parish priest, asking his leave to preach in the Catholic chapel, afford evidence of this. It is not easy to imagine a more extraordinary composition than the following.—" Dear Garret, dear fellow-servant, have we not the same Master over us—oh, how long and how often have I perverted his gifts, abandoned his works, and done despite to the spirit of his grace, and truly it is high time to awake out of sleep. Let us cast away the works of darkness and put upon us the armour of light. I have a long account to settle—an account of twenty years' standing, at which time, as his ministering servant, he delivered to me his goods. Gracious God! what an awful prospect is before me, and if he hath in mercy snatched me as a brand from the burning, am I still to continue the same wilful, disobedient, rebellious, slothful servant as before." This letter is accompanied by others in the same strain, and in one he applies to the aforesaid Garret Larkin, to allow him to usurp his functions in the chapel, and from the altar to denounce the errors of his religion. This proposition might only excite a smile, if we did not recollect that the very man who indulged in these effusions, was invested with the power of inflicting dreadful oppression. It is positively stated, that the doctor posted up a notice, in his own hand-writing, and signed with his name, denouncing vengeance on all those who should not obey his fanatical injunctions, and send their children through that process of apostacy which he had devised. He carried his menaces with a frightful fidelity into execution. Look at the example of Catherine Heney, for instance, who swears, that having, in obedience to the parish priest, refused to send her five children to the anti-Catholic school kept by the doctor, she was turned out of her cabin, with her starving and shivering orphans, and when her house had been thrown down, was obliged to seek refuge in a pig-stye, where she lay upon heaps of filth in a fever, surrounded by the miserable offspring for whom she was no longer able to procure nourishment. It may be urged that she is not deserving of belief, because her evidence is tainted by her poverty—but let it not be forgotten that the parish priest swears, that he attended her when she was driven from her house, and gives his confirmation to her statement. Your lordships will not say, that the affidavit of a Catholic clergyman of respectability is to be discredited, for no other reason than that it contains imputations upon a Protestant archdeacon. The affidavit of Catherine Heney is sustained by a vast number of other depositions to similar instances of oppression. Dr. Coen, the Roman Catholic bishop of the diocess, has made an affidavit, in which the general conduct of the archdeacon is described. He represents Dr Trench as managing and directing a barbarous and most heart-rending persecution. The next charge against him is expressed in the alleged libel in the following words : " I never was charged with bringing a female to the triangle." In answer he states, that he never exercised any power vested in him with cruelty, and that he never did bring a female to the triangle, and he proceeds to put your lordships in possession of the circumstances under which he admitted that he did preside over the public military torture of a female in the barracks at Cork.—He states that he was adjutant of the Galway militia, from the year 1797 to the year 1799, and that he was present, in his official capacity, when the sentence of a court-martial was executed upon a woman, who had been detected in stealing some articles belonging to the soldiers of the regiment, to the best of his recollection. To the best of his recollection ! I do not think that he should have any very obscure or imperfect remembrance of such an incident in his life as this. It ought to have been burned into his memory in colours of blood, which the years, which have made his head white, ought never to have effaced. At that time it appears there was a great tendency to pilfering, and this female propensity in the regiment it was deemed advisable to scourge out. The doctor tells us, that so efficacious was the example given by the flogging of a woman in the barracks, that the crime was, to the best of his recollection, suppressed. She was sentenced to twenty-five lashes, he says, but very few were applied. What does he call a "few ?" It would have been condescending of him to have stated his notions of number, but he does not enter into that trivial particular, nor does he mention the name of the commanding officer, nor that of a single member of the court-martial; he does, indeed, say that General Lake approved of the sentence, and proceeds to pronounce a gratuitous encomium upon the general's humanity, which, I suppose, includes a latent panegyric upon his own. The woman was flogged in his presence. His narration does not precisely correspond with that of an eye-witness to the scene. Patrick Muldoon, a soldier of the 13th regiment, states, " that he was in it for twenty-five years, and was sergeant for seven years, and has now a pension of £35 for his service ; that before he went into the line he was in the Galway militia, and remembers that a woman was flogged in the barrack, when Archdeacon Trench was adjutant; that the archdeacon was the only officer that was present—that the woman was flogged for having stolen a brass candlestick—that he saw the woman stripped down to the waist, and flogged in the usual way between the shoulders." This affidavit is corroborated by that of Edmund Melody, who says, " That Winifred Hynes, the wife of a private in the regiment, was accused by Richard Marmion, of having pledged two candlesticks, his property, whereupon the said adjutant, the Hon. Charles Le Poer Trench, ordered her to be put into the guard-house, where she remained the whole night, and on the next morning, when the regiment was on parade, said Winifred was, by order of said adjutant, brought out, guarded by a file of soldiers, and in the presence of the regiment, which was formed into a hollow square to witness her punishment, the said Winifred Hynes was tied up hands and feet to the triangles, and the said Winifred Hynes having made vehement struggles to avoid being stripped naked, for the purpose of punishment, the said adjutant went up to the drum-major, cursed and damned him for not tearing off her clothes, and in a great passion, giving him a blow with a stick, ordered the said drum-major to tear and cut them off, upon which the said drum-major, with a knife, cut open said Winifred's gown, and then tore her other covering from her shoulders, down to the waist, after which she received fifty lashes, on the bare back from two drummers, in the usual way of flogging soldiers. That during said horrid exhibition, a Mr. Davis, an officer in said regiment, went up to the said adjutant and told him, in the hearing of deponent, that Peter Hynes, the husband of the said Winifred, was absolutely fainting in the ranks, at seeing his wife exposed in such a manner, and begged of said adjutant to allow Peter Hynes to retire to his room, upon which the said adjutant answered, he might go where he pleased, and he did not care if the devil had him. Saith that after said flogging, the said Winifred, with her back still bleeding, was publicly drummed out of the barrack-yard, to the tune of the 'rogue's march.' Saith he never heard, nor does he believe, that said Winifred Hynes was tried by any court-martial, but was punished, as aforesaid, by the sole order and authority of the said adjutant, the Honourable and now the Rev. Charles Le Poer Trench, who, on account of his many severities, and particularly of the said flogging of said Winifred Hynes, was called in the regiment by the name of ' skin him alive.'" I make no comment for the present on the facts stated in this affidavit, except that they completely bear out the allegation of Mr. M'Donnell, and merely submit it to your consideration, whether that gentleman has, in this transaction, at least, very greatly misrepresented this merciful teacher of the word of God. But it may be said, that the conduct of Doctor Trench was very essentially and amiably different, after entering into holy orders—that notwithstanding the identity of person, no identity of character existed between the adjutant and the archdeacon, and that the doctor presented, in his subsequent demeanour, a christian and interesting contrast. The following incident in the doctor's ecclesiastical life, which is stated by Mr. M'Donnell in his affidavit, throws some light upon his disposition, and will enable the court to judge how far he is right in his conceptions of himself, for he intimates that he never was guilty of cruelty, and that he is a man of a very sensitive and tender heart. Mr. M'Donnell states that he was informed by the sub-sheriff of the county of Galway, that in the absence of the common executioner, when the sentence of whipping was to be executed in the town of Loughrea upon two culprits, the archdeacon proposed that he should take the lash into his own hands, and whip the malefactors through the principal streets in the town. It may, perhaps, be said that the thing is incredible—that it is impossible that any minister of religion should gratuitously offer to perform such an office. Perhaps it will be said that I have no right to state any thing upon the mere hearsay of Mr. M'Donnell. Well, be it so; but Mr. M'Nevin has made an affidavit. I repeat it—the sub-sheriff of the county of Galway has sworn an affidavit in the following words:—

"Daniel M'Nevin, of Middle Gardiner-street, in the county of Dublin, Esquire, maketh oath, and saith, that in the year one thousand eight hundred and ten, deponent was acting sub-sheriff to Peter Blake of Corbally Castle, in the county of Galway, Esquire, who was high-sheriff of said county, for said year; saith, that at the quarter sessions of Loughrea, in the summer of said year, as deponent best recollects, two tenants of the late Lord Clonbrock's were convicted of stealing a small quantity of wool, and sentenced to be whipped, on a market-day, in the town of Ballinasloe, from one extremity of said town to the other; saith, on the day previous to the one appointed for putting the said sentence into execution, deponent sent a man, accompanied by a military party, for the purpose of executing said sentence to Ballinasloe aforesaid, from Loughrea, in said county, where deponent then resided, but said man absconded in the course of the night out of the guard-house, where he was with the prisoners, and when deponent arrived at Ballinasloe, on the morning of the day on which the sentence was to be carried into execution as aforesaid, deponent was much alarmed at finding that he had not any person to perform the duty; deponent saith, he thereupon informed the prosecutor in the cause, of the man's having so absconded, inasmuch as deponent saith the said prosecutor had presided with the barrister on the bench, at the sessions at which the man had been so convicted and sentenced; deponent saith, the said prosecutor was very much displeased at deponent having informed him that deponent had not then any person to flog the said prisoners, and said prosecutor threatened this deponent with the consequences, alleging, that the said prosecutor would bring deponent's conduct in that instance before the Court of King's Bench, and have deponent fined five hundred pounds; deponent saith, that thereupon deponent informed said prosecutor he was ready and willing to pay any sum that could in reason be demanded by any person for performing such duty, provided he, said prosecutor, who had influence in the town of Ballinasloe, could procure a person to do it, on which the said prosecutor proposed to deponent to accompany him to the colonel of a regiment of cavalry, then quartered at Ballinasloe, who, prosecutor said, he had no doubt would give a man for the purpose; deponent saith, that accordingly deponent did accompany the said prosecutor, to the colonel, when the prosecutor made the application, which said colonel indignantly refused to comply with; deponent saith, that thereupon the said prosecutor was more provoked than before, and he again threatened deponent with the court of King's Bench, and the utmost rigour of the law, and deponent being really afraid that said prosecutor would carry his threats into execution, asked him what he could do to extricate himself from the difficult situation in which deponent was then placed, and that deponent was willing to do any thing that could in reason be expected from him, to which deponent positively saith, the said prosecutor distinctly replied to deponent in the words, ' we will do the duty between us ; I will flog them from Cuff's down to Custom-house-gap, if you will flog them from that to Dr. Kelly's house;' deponent saith, deponent indignantly rejected the proposal so made to him; deponent, with the assistance of a friend, afterwards fortunately procured a person to execute said sentence ; saith, the prosecutor accompanied this deponent, and walked after the car to which the criminals were tied, between two files of soldiers, and deponent and said prosecutor had proceeded a very few yards, when prosecutor found fault with the man, for not inflicting the punishment with sufficient severity; and at length said prosecutor became so abusive to deponent on the same account, that deponent was obliged to call in the officer commanding the military attending on said occasion, to put said prosecutor out of the ranks; deponent further saith, that deponent having been at the Earl of Clancarty's some time previous to the day on which the aforesaid sentence was to be put into execution, that deponent was invited by him, the said earl, to dine at Garbally on said day, but deponent, in consequence of the conduct of the prosecutor, declined going to Garbally on that day, as deponent could not think of dining in company with a man who could treat him as the prosecutor had done."

Such is the affidavit of Mr. M'Nevin, and such is the Hon and Rev. Charles Le Poer Trench, Archdeacon of Ardagh, who solicits a special favour at your hands, and complains that the defendant upon whom he caused an outrage to be perpetrated, has represented him as a ruthless man, whose character and whose conduct stand in frightful contrast with the precepts of that gospel, of which he violates the first ordinances, while he preaches its propagation. He was either serious in the proposition made by him to Mr. M'Nevin or he was not. If he intended to perform the part of a public executioner—if it was, indeed, his purpose to take the cat-o'-nine-tails into that hand with which he distributes the sacramental bread, and circulates the consecrated chalice, and to go through the process of bloody laceration, what sort of heart must he carry in his bosom ? And if he spoke in jest, what a subject for merriment in a minister of Christ ! Two wretched men were to be flogged— they were to undergo a frightful punishment, and upon their anticipated tortures, this teacher of the gospel indulges in the spirit of truculent hilarity and of sanguinary jest. But why should it be imagined that he was not serious in the proposition, made to the sub-sheriff of Galway, who swears to the fact ? He gave proof of his sincerity in this tender of his services for the accommodation of the sheriff, for he followed the cart, walked in the procession of agony, gazed on the convulsions of the writhing culprits, gloated on their tortures, and refreshed himself with their groans. Nor should we marvel at the part which was enacted by him: he was the relapsed adjutant—covered with the surplice, while his mind was in regimentals; there was, after all, in this transaction little more than "a revival" of the emotions with which he had presided over the tortures of a woman—had ordered her to be brought forth, guarded by a file of soldiers, and in the presence of the whole regiment, caused her raiment to be torn from her back, and woman as she was ordered her shift to be dragged off, until she stood naked to the waist; saw her bound to the triangle—the scourge laid upon her quivering flesh—beheld her writhing and convulsive motions—heard her shrieks and did not cry out "hold, hold!" and now, with his hands yet stained with the indelible and "damned spot" which the blood spattered by the scourge has left upon them, he comes into this court and asks for a criminal information.

My lords, you may condemn the defendant, for having, under the influence of the resentful feelings, produced by the monstrous outrage which was offered to him by the prosecutor, reverted to these incidents in the life of Archdeacon Trench, but you are not to determine merely whether the defendant is to be blamed, but whether the prosecutor has purged himself of the offences imputed to him. I submit to you that in the entire of the transactions out of which this prosecution has arisen, Archdeacon Trench has acted in such a way, that to the special interference of the King's Bench he is without a claim. There is another consideration which I venture to present to you. As it is entirely matter of discretion with your lordships to grant or to withhold the remedy for which the prosecutor has applied: the public interests are not to be excluded from your regard. Is it judicious of your lordships to interfere in the contest which is now waging, not only between these parties, but between two great religious factions in this country You do no wrong to the prosecutor by refusing him relief in a specific form. He has still a remedy by indictment or by action. On grounds of public policy, it is unwise that you should intermingle in this angry contention, especially where the interposition of your lordships, instead of allaying the popular passions, is calculated to excite them. Let it not be said (as it will be said if you grant the information) that the Court of King's Bench deliberately approved of the dispersion of an assembly convened for the purposes of religion, by a military force— that your lordships unnecessarily interfered in the fierce controversy which is carried on with all the proverbial rancour of theological detestation, and that justice left her lofty seat to rush into the midst of a polemical affray, not in order to separate the disputants, but to renovate the combat.

[The Court made the conditional rule absolute, and afterwards sentenced Mr. M'Donnell to twelve months' imprisonment. He was, however, discharged from prison by order of government some months before the expiration of the term of his sentence.

CLARE ELECTION.

SPEECH MADE AT THE CLARE ELECTION—PRECEDED BY AN ACCOUNT OF THAT EVENT, WRITTEN BY MR. SHEIL IN SEPTEMBER, 1828.

THE Catholics had passed a resolution to oppose the election of every candidate who should not pledge himself against the Duke of Wellington's administration. This measure lay for some time a dead letter in the registry of the Association, and was gradually passing into oblivion, when an incident occurred which gave it an importance far greater than had originally belonged to it. Lord John Russell, flushed with the victory which had been achieved in the repeal of the Test and Corporation Acts, and grateful to the Duke of Wellington for the part which he had taken, wrote a letter to Mr. O'Connell, in which he suggested that the conduct of his Grace had been so fair and manly towards the Dissenters, as to entitle him to their gratitude; and that they would consider the reversal of the resolution which had been passed against his government, as evidence of the interest which was felt in Ireland, not only in the great question peculiarly applicable to that country, but in the assertion of religious freedom through the empire. The authority of Lord John Russell is considerable, and Mr. O'Connell, under the influence of his advice, proposed that the anti-Wellington resolution should be withdrawn. This motion was violently opposed, and Mr. O'Connell perceived that the antipathy to the Great Captain was more deeply rooted than he had originally imagined. After a long and tempestuous debate, he suggested an amendment, in which the principle of his original motion was given up, and the Catholics remained pledged to their hostility to the Duke of Wellington's administration. Mr. O'Connell has reason to rejoice at his failure in carrying this proposition; for if he had succeeded, no ground for opposing the return of Mr. Vesey Fitzgerald would have existed.

The promotion of that gentleman to a seat in the cabinet created a vacancy in the representation of the county of Clare; and an opportunity was afforded to the Roman Catholic body of proving, that the resolution which had been passed against the Duke of Wellington's government was not an idle vaunt, but that it could be carried in a striking instance into effect. It was determined that all the power of the people should be put forth. The Association looked round for a candidate, and without having previously consulted him, selected Major M'Namara. He is a Protestant in religion, a Catholic in politics, and a Milesian in descent. He was called upon to stand. Some days elapsed and no answer was returned by him. The public mind was thrown into suspense, and various conjectures went abroad as to the cause of this singular omission. Some alleged that he was gone to an island off the coast of Clare, where the proceedings of the Association had not reached him; while others suggested that he was only waiting until the clergy of the county should declare themselves more unequivocally favourable to him. The latter, it was said, had evinced much apathy, and it was rumoured that Dean O'Shaughnessy, who is a distant relative of Mr. Fitzgerald, had intimated a determination not to support any anti-ministerial candidate. The major's silence, and the doubts which were entertained with regard to the allegiance of the priests, created a sort of panic at the Association. A meeting was called, and various opinions were delivered as to the propriety of engaging in a contest, the issue of which was considered exceedingly doubtful, and in which, failure would be attended with such disastrous consequences. Mr. O'Connell himself did not appear exceedingly sanguine; and Mr. Purcell O'Gorman, a native of Clare, and who had a minute knowledge of the feelings of the people, expressed apprehensions. There were, however, two gentlemen, (O'Gorman Mahon and Mr. Steele,) who strongly insisted that the people might be roused, and that the priests were not as lukewarm as was imagined. Upon the zeal of Dean O'Shaughnessy, however, a good deal of question was thrown. By a singular coincidence, just as his name was uttered, a gentleman entered, who, but for the peculiar locality, might have been readily mistaken for a clergyman of the Established Church. Between the priesthood of the two religions there are, in aspect and demeanour, as well as in creed and discipline, several points of affinity, and the abstract sacerdotal character is readily perceptible in both. The parson, however, in his attitude and attire, presents the evidences of superiority, and carries the mannerism of ascendancy upon him. A broad-brimmed hat, composed of the smoothest and blackest material, and drawn by two silken threads into a fire-shovel configuration, a felicitous adaptation of his jerkin to the symmetries of his chest and shoulder, stockings of glossy silk, which displayed the happy proportions of a swelling leg, a ruddy cheek, and a bright authoritative eye, suggested, at first view, that the gentleman who had entered the room while the merits of Dean O'Shaughnessy were under discussion, must be a minister of the prosperous Christianity of the Established Church. It was, however, no other than Dean O'Shaughnessy himself. He was received with a burst of applause, which indicated that, whatever surmises with respect to his fidelity had previously gone out, his appearance before that tribunal was considered by the assembly as a proof of his devotion to the public interest. The dean, however, made a very scholastic sort of oration, the gist of which it was by no means easy to arrive at. He denied that he had enlisted himself under Mr. Fitzgerald's banners, but at the same time studiously avoided giving any sort of pledge. He did not state distinctly what his opinion was with respect to the co-operation of the priests with the Association; and when he was pressed, begged to be allowed to withhold his sentiments on the subject. The Association were not, however, dismayed; and it having been conjectured that the chief reason for Major M'Namara having omitted to return an answer was connected with pecuniary considerations, it was decided that so large a sum as five thousand pounds of the Catholic rent should be allocated to the expenses of his election. O'Gorman Mahon and Mr. Steele were directed to proceed at once to Clare, in order that they might have a personal interview with him · and they immediately set off. After an absence of two days, O'Gorman Mahon returned, having left his colleague behind in order to arouse the people; and he at length conveyed certain intelligence with respect to the Major's determination. The obligations under which his family lay to Mr. Fitzgerald were such, that he was bound in honour not to oppose him. This information produced a feeling of deep disappointment among the Catholic body, while the Protestant party exulted in his apparent desertion of the cause, and boasted that no gentleman of the county would stoop so low as to accept of the patronage of the Association. In this emergency, and when it was universally regarded as an utterly hopeless attempt to oppose the cabinet minister, the public were astonished by an address from Mr. O'Connell to the freeholders of Clare, in which he offered himself as a candidate, and solicited their support.

Nothing but his subsequent success could exceed the sensation which was produced by this address, and all eyes were turned towards the field in which so remarkable a contest was to be waged. The two candidates entered the lists with signal advantages upon both sides. Mr. O'Connell had an unparalleled popularity, which the services of thirty years had secured to him. Upon the other hand, Mr. Vesey Fitzgerald presented a combination of favourable circumstances, which rendered the issue exceedingly difficult to calculate. His father had held the office of prime sergeant at the Irish bar; and, although indebted to the government for his promotion, had the virtuous intrepidity to vote against the Union. This example of independence had rendered him a great favourite with the people. From the moment that his son had obtained access to power, he had employed his extensive influence in doing acts of kindness to the gentry of the county of Clare. He had inundated it with the overflowings of ministerial bounty. The eldest sons of the poorer gentlemen, and the younger branches of the aristocracy, had been provided for through his means; and in the army, the navy, the treasury, the Four Courts, and the Custom House, the proofs of his political friendship were everywhere to be found. Independently of any act of his which could be referred to his personal interest, and his anxiety to keep up his influence in the county, Mr. Fitzgerald, who is a man of very amiable disposition, had conferred many services upon his Clare constituents. Nor was it to Protestants that these manifestations of favour were confined. He had laid not only the Catholic proprietors, but the Catholic priesthood, under obligation. The bishop of the diocess himself, (a respectable old gentleman who drives about in a gig with a mitre upon it,) is supposed not to have escaped from his bounties; and it is more than insinuated that some droppings of ministerial manna had fallen upon him. The consequence of this systematized and uniform plan of benefaction is obvious. The sense of favour was heightened by the manners of this extensive distributor of the favours of the crown, and converted the ordinary feeling of thankfulness into one of personal regard. To this array of very favourable circumstances, Mr. Fitzgerald brought the additional influence arising from his recent promotion to the cabinet; which, to those who had former benefits to return, afforded an opportunity for the exercise of that kind of prospective gratitude which has been described to consist of a lively sense of services to come. These were the comparative advantages with which the ministerial and the popular candidate engaged in this celebrated contest; and Ireland stood by to witness the encounter.

Mr. O'Connell did not immediately set off from Dublin, but before his departure several gentlemen were despatched from the Association in order to excite the minds of the people, and to prepare the way for him. The most active and useful of the persons who were employed upon this occasion, were the two gentlemen to whom I have already referred, Mr. Steele and O'Gorman Mahon. They are both deserving of special commendation. The former is a Protestant of a respectable fortune in the county of Clare, and who has all his life been devoted to the assertion of liberal principles. In Trinity College he was amongst the foremost of the advocates of emancipation, and at that early period became the intimate associate of many Roman Catholic gentlemen who have since distinguished themselves in the proceedings of their body. Being a man of independent circumstances, Mr. Steele did not devote himself to any profession, and having a zealous and active mind, looked round for occupation. The Spanish war afforded him a field for the display of that generous enthusiasm by which he is distinguished. He joined the patriot army, and fought with desperate valour upon the batteries of the Trocadero. It was only when Cadiz had surrendered, and the cause of Spain became utterly hopeless, that Mr. Steele relinquished this noble undertaking. He returned to England, surrounded by exiles from the unfortunate country, for the liberation of which he had repeatedly exposed his life. It was impossible for a man of so much energy of character to remain in torpor; and on his arrival in Ireland, faithful to the principles by which he had been uniformly swayed, he joined the Catholic Association. There he delivered several enthusiastic declamations in favour of religious liberty. Such a man, however, was fitted for action as well as for harangue; and the moment the contest in Clare began, he threw himself into the combat with the same alacrity with which he had rushed upon the French bayonets at Cadiz. He was serviceable in various ways. He opened the political campaign by intimating his readiness to fight any landlord who should conceive himself to be aggrieved by an interference with his tenants. This was a very impressive exordium. He then proceeded to canvass for votes; and, assisted by his intimate friend, O'Gorman Mahon, travelled through the country, and, both by day and night, addressed the people from the altars round which they were assembled to hear him. It is no exaggeration to say, that to him, and to his intrepid and indefatigable confederate, the success of Mr. O'Connell is greatly to be ascribed. O'Gorman Mahon is introduced into this article as one amongst many figures. He would deserve to stand apart in a portrait. Nature has been peculiarly favourable to him. He has a very striking physiognomy, of the Corsair character, which the Protestant Gulnares, and the Catholic Medoras, find it equally difficult to resist. His figure is tall, and he is peculiarly free and *dégagé* in all his attitudes and movements. In any other his attire would appear singularly fantastical. His manners are exceedingly frank and natural, and have a character of kindliness as well as of self-reliance imprinted upon them. He is wholly free from embarrassment, and carries a well-founded consciousness of his personal merit; which is, however, so well united with urbanity, that it is not in the slightest degree offensive. His talents as a popular speaker are considerable. He derives from external qualifications an influence over the multitude, which men of diminutive stature are somewhat slow in obtaining. A small man is at first view regarded by the great body of spectators with disrelish; and it is only by force of phrase, and by the charm of speech, that he can at length succeed in inducing his auditors to overlook any infelicity of configuration; but when O'Gorman Mahon throws himself out before the people, and, touching his whiskers with one hand, brandishes the other, an enthusiasm is at once produced, to which the fair portion of the spectators lend their tender contribution. Such a man was exactly adapted to the excitement of the people of Clare; and it must be admitted that, by his indefatigable exertions, his unremitting activity, and his devoted zeal, he most materially assisted in the election of Mr. O'Connell. While Mr. Steele and O'Gorman Mahon harangued the people in one district, Mr. Lawless, who was also despatched upon a similar mission, applied his faculties of excitation in another. This gentleman has obtained deserved celebrity by his being almost the only individual among the Irish deputies who remonstrated against the sacrifice of the rights of the forty-shilling freeholders. Ever since that period he has been eminently popular; and although he may occasionally, by ebullitions of ill-regulated but generous enthusiasm, create a little merriment amongst those whose minds are not as susceptible of patriotic and disinterested emotion as his own, yet the conviction which is entertained of his honesty of purpose, confers upon him a considerable influence. "Honest Jack Lawless" is the designation by which he has been known since the "wings" were in discussion. He has many distinguished qualities as a public speaker. His voice is deep, round, and mellow, and is diversified by a great variety of rich and harmonious intonation. His action is exceedingly graceful and appropriate: he has a good figure, which, by a purposed swell and dilation of the shoulders, and an elaborate erectness, he turns to good account; and by dint of an easy fluency of good diction, a solemn visage, an aquiline nose of no vulgar dimension, eyes glaring underneath a shaggy brow with a certain fierceness of expression, a quizzing-glass, which is gracefully dangled in any pauses of thought or suspensions of utterance, and, above all, by a certain attitude of dignity, which he assumes in the crisis of eloquence, accompanied with a flinging back of his coat, which sets his periods beautifully off, "Honest Jack" has become one of the most popular and efficient speakers at the Association. Shortly after Mr. Lawless had been despatched, a great reinforcement to the oratorical corps was sent down in the person of the celebrated Father Maguire, or, as he is habitually designated, "Father Tom." This gentleman had been for some time a parish priest in the county of Leitrim. He lived in a remote parish, where his talents were unappreciated. Some accident brought Mr. Pope, the itinerant controversialist, into contact with him. A challenge to defend the doctrines of his religion was tendered by the wandering disputant to the priest, and the latter at once accepted it. Maguire had given no previous proof of his abilities, and the Catholic body regretted the encounter. The parties met in this strange duel of theology. The interest created by their encounter was prodigious. Not only the room where their debates were carried on was crowded, but the whole of Sackville-street, where it was situated, was thronged with population. Pope brought to the combat great fluency, and a powerful declamation. Maguire was a master of scholastic logic. After several days of controversy, Pope was overthrown, and "Father Tom," as the champion of orthodoxy, became the object of popular adoration. A base conspiracy was got up to destroy his moral character, and by its failure raised him in the affection of the multitude. He had been under great obligations to Mr. O'Connell, for his exertions upon his trial; and from a just sentiment of gratitude, he tendered his services in Clare. His name alone was of great value; and when his coming was announced, the people everywhere rushed forward to hail the vindicator of the national religion. He threw fresh ingredients into the caldron, and contributed to impart to the contest that strong religious character which it is not the fault of the Association, but of the government, that every contest of the kind must assume. "Father Tom" was employed upon a remarkable exploit. Mr. Augustine Butler, the lineal descendant of the celebrated Sir Toby Butler, is a proprietor in Clare : he is a liberal Protestant, but supported Mr. Vesey Fitzgerald. "Father Tom" proceeded from the town of Ennis to the county chapel where Mr. Butler's freeholders were assembled, in order to address them ; and Mr. Butler, with an intrepidity which did him credit, went forward to meet him. It was a singular encounter in the house of God. The Protestant landlord called upon his freeholders not to desert him.— "Father Tom" rose to address them in behalf of Mr. O'Connell. He is not greatly gifted with a command of decorated phraseology; but he is master of vigorous language, and has a power of strong and simple reasoning, which is equally intelligible to all classes. He employs the syllogism of the schools as his chief weapon in argument; but uses it with such dexterity, that his auditors of the humblest class can follow him without being aware of the technical expedient by which he masters the understanding. His manner is peculiar: it is not flowery, nor declamatory, but is short, somewhat abrupt, and, to use the French phrase, is "tranchant." His countenance is adapted to his mind, and is expressive of the reasoning and controversial faculties. A quick blue eye, a nose slightly turned up, a strong brow, a complexion of mountain ruddiness, and thick lips, which are better formed for rude disdain than for polished sarcasm, are his characteristics. He assailed Mr. Butler with all his powers, and overthrew him. The topic to which he addressed himself, was one which was not only calculated to move the tenants of Mr. Butler, but to stir Mr. Butler himself. He appealed to the memory of his celebrated Catholic ancestor, of which Mr. Butler is justly proud. He stated, that what Sir Toby Butler had been, Mr. O'Connell was ; and he adjured him not to stand up in opposition to an individual whom he was bound to sustain by a sort of hereditary obligation. His appeal carried the freeholders away, and one hundred and fifty votes were secured to Mr. O'Connell. Mr. Maguire was seconded in this achievement by Mr. Dominick Rouayne, a barrister of the Association, of considerable talents, and who not only speaks the English language with eloquence, but is master of the Irish tongue; and throwing an educated mind into the powerful idiom of the country, wrought with uncommon power upon the passions of the people.

Mr. Sheil was employed as counsel for Mr. O'Connell before the assessor; but proceeded to the county Clare the day before the election commenced. On his arrival, he understood that an exertion was required in the parish of Corofin, which is situate upon the estate of Sir Edward O'Brien, who had given all his interest to Mr. Vesey Fitzgerald. Sir Edward is the most opulent resident landlord in the county. In the parish of Corofin he had no less than three hundred votes; and it was supposed that his freeholders would go with him. Mr. Sheil determined to assail him in the citadel of his strength, and proceeded upon the Sunday before the poll commenced to the chapel of Corofin. Sir Edward O'Brien having learned that this agitator intended this trespass upon his authority, resolved to anticipate him, and set off in his splendid equipage, drawn by four horses, to the mountains in which Corofin is situated. The whole population came down from their residences in the rocks, which are in the vicinity of the town of Ennis, and advanced in large bands, waving green boughs, and preceded by fifes and pipers, upon the road. Their landlord was met by them on his way. They passed him by in silence, while they hailed his antagonist with shouts of applause, and attended him in triumph to the chapel. Sir Edward O'Brien lost his resolution at this spectacle; and, feeling that he could have no influence in such a state of excitation, instead of going to the house of Catholic worship, proceeded to the church of Corofin. He left his carriage exactly opposite the doors of the chapel, which is immediately contiguous, and thus reminded the people of his Protestantism, by a circumstance, of which, of course, advantage was instantaneously taken. Mr. Sheil arrived with a vast multitude of attendants at the chapel, which was crowded with a people, who had flocked from all quarters; there a singular scene took place. Father Murphy, the parish priest, came to the entrance of the chapel, dressed in his surplice. When he appeared, the multitude fell back at his command, and arranged themselves on either side, so as to form a lane for the reception of the agitator. Deep silence was imposed upon the people by the priest, who had a voice of subterraneous thunder, and appeared to hold them in absolute dominion. When Mr. Sheil had reached the threshold of the chapel, Father Murphy stretched forth his hand, and welcomed him to the performance of the good work. The figure and attitude of the priest were remarkable. My English reader draws his ordinary notion of a Catholic clergyman from the caricatures which are contained in novels, or represented in comedies upon the stage; but the Irish priest, who has lately become a politician and a scholar, has not a touch of Foigardism about him; and an artist would have found in Father Murphy rather a study for the enthusiastic Macbriar, who is so powerfully delineated in "Old Mortality," than a realization of the familiar notions of a clergyman of the Church of Rome. Surrounded by a dense multitude, whom he had hushed into profound silence, he presented a most imposing object. His form is tall, slender, and emaciated; but was enveloped in his long robes, that gave him a peculiarly sacerdotal aspect. The hand which he stretched forth was ample, but worn to a skinny meagritude. His face was long, sunken, and cadaverous, but was illuminated by eyes blazing with all the fire of genius and the enthusiasm of religion. His lank black hair fell down his temples, and eyebrows of the same colour stretched in thick straight lines along a lofty forehead, and threw over the whole countenance a deep shadow. The sun was shining with brilliancy, and rendered his figure, attired as it was in white garments, more conspicuous. The scenery about him was in harmony; it was wild and desolate, and crags, with scarce a blade of verdure shooting through their crevices, rose everywhere around him. The interior of the chapel, at the entrance of which he stood, was visible. It was a large pile of building, consisting of bare walls, rudely thrown up, with a floor of clay, and at the extremity stood an altar made of a few boards clumsily put together.

It was on the threshold of this mountain temple that the envoy of the Association was hailed with a solemn greeting. The priest proceeded to the altar, and commanded the people to abstain, during the divine ceremony, from all political thinking or occupation. He recited the mass with great fervency and simplicity of manner, and with all the evidences of unaffected piety. However familiar from daily repetition with the ritual, he pronounced it with a just emphasis, and went through the various forms which are incidental to it with singular propriety and grace. The people were deeply attentive; and it was observable that most of them could read, for they had prayer-books in their hands, which they read with a quiet devotion. Mass being finished, Father Murphy threw his vestments off, and, without laying down the priest, assumed the politician. He addressed the people in Irish, and called upon them to vote for O'Connell in the name of their country and of their religion.

It was a most extraordinary and powerful display of the externals of eloquence, and as far as a person unacquainted with the language could form an estimate of the matter by the effects produced upon the auditory, must have been pregnant with genuine oratory. It will be supposed that this singular priest addressed his parishioners in tones and gestures as rude as the wild dialect to which he was giving utterance. His actions and attitudes were as graceful as those of an accomplished actor, and his intonations were soft, pathetic, denunciatory, and conjuring, according as his theme varied, and as he had recourse to different expedients to influence the people. The general character of this strange harangue was impassioned and solemn, but he occasionally had recourse to ridicule, and his countenance at once adapted itself with a happy readiness to derision. The finest spirit of sarcasm gleamed over his features, and shouts of laughter attended his description of a miserable Catholic who should prove recreant to the great cause, by making a sacrifice of his country to his landlord. The close of his speech was peculiarly effective. He became inflamed by the power of his emotions, and while he raised himself into the loftiest attitude to which he could ascend, he laid one hand on the altar, and shook the other in the spirit of almost prophetic admonition, and while his eyes blazed and seemed to start from his forehead, thick drops fell down his face, and his voice rolled through lips livid with passion and covered with foam. It is almost unnecessary to say that such an appeal was irresistible. The multitude burst into shouts of acclamation, and would have been ready to mount a battery roaring with cannon at his command. Two days after the results were felt at the hustings; and while Sir Edward O'Brien stood aghast, Father Murphy marched into Ennis at the head of his tenantry, and polled them to a man in favour of Daniel O'Connell. But I am anticipating.

The notion which had gone abroad in Dublin that the priests were lukewarm, was utterly unfounded. With the exception of Dean O'Shaughnessy, who is a relative of Mr. Fitzgerald (and for whom there is perhaps much excuse), and a Father Coffey, who has since been deserted by his congregation, there was scarcely a clergyman in the county who did not use his utmost influence over the peasantry. On the day on which Mr. O'Connell arrived, you met a priest in every street, who assured you that the battle should be won, and pledged himself that "the man of the people" should be returned. "The man of the people" arrived in the midst of the loudest acclamations. Near thirty thousand people were crowded into the streets of Ennis, and were unceasing in their shouts. Banners were suspended from every window; and women of great beauty were everywhere seen waving handkerchiefs, with the figure of the patriot stamped upon them. Processions of freeholders, with their parish priests at their head, marched like troops to different quarters of the city; and it was remarkable that not a single individual was intoxicated. The most perfect order and regularity prevailed; and the large bodies of police which had been collected in the town stood without occupation. These were evidences of organization, from which it was easy to conjecture the result.

The election opened, and the court-house in which the sheriff read the writ presented a new and striking scene. On the left hand of the sheriff stood a cabinet minister, attended by the whole body of the aristocracy of the county of Clare. Their appearance indicated at once their superior rank and their profound mortification. An expression of bitterness and of wounded pride was stamped in various modifications of resentment upon their countenances; while others who were in the interest of Mr. Fitzgerald, and who were small Protestant proprietors, affected to look big and important, and swelled themselves into gentry upon the credit of voting for the minister. On the right hand of the sheriff stood Mr. O'Connell, with scarcely a single gentleman by his side; for most even of the Catholic proprietors had abandoned him, and joined the ministerial candidate. But the body of the court presented the power of Mr. O'Connell in a mass of determined peasants, amongst whom black coats and sacerdotal visages were seen felicitously intermixed, outside the balustrade of the gallery on the left hand of the sheriff. Before the business began, a gentleman was observed on whom every eye was turned. He had indeed chosen a most singular position; for instead of sitting like the other auditors on the seats in the gallery, he leaped over it, and, suspending himself above the crowd, afforded what was an object of wonder to the great body of the spectators, and of indignation to the high sheriff. The attire of the individual who was thus perched in this dangerous position was sufficiently strange. He had a coat of Irish tabinet, with glossy trowsers of the same national material; he wore no waistcoat; a blue shirt lined with streaks of white was open at his neck; a broad green sash, with a medal of "the order of Liberators" at the end of it, hung conspicuously over his breast; and a profusion of black curls curiously festooned about his temples, shadowed a very handsome and expressive countenance, a great part of which was occupied by whiskers of a bushy amplitude. "Who, Sir, are you?" exclaimed the high sheriff, in a tone of imperious solemnity, which he had acquired at Canton, where he had long resided in the service of the East India Company. But I must pause here—and even at the hazard of breaking the regular thread of the narration, I cannot resist the temptation of describing the high sheriff. When he stood up with his wand of office, the contrast between him and the aerial gentleman whom he was addressing was to the highest degree ludicrous. Of the latter some conception has already been given. He looked a chivalrous dandy, who, under the most fantastical apparel, carried the spirit and intrepidity of an exceedingly fine fellow. Mr. high sheriff had, at an early period of his life, left his native county of Clare, and had migrated to China, where, if I may judge from his manners and demeanour, he must have been in immediate communication with a mandarin of the first class, and made a Chinese functionary his favourite model. I should conjecture that he must long have presided over the packing of Bohea, and that some tincture of that agreeable vegetable had been infused into his complexion. An oriental sedateness and gravity are spread over a countenance upon which a smile seldom presumes to trespass. He gives utterance to intonations which were originally contracted in the East, but have been since melodized by his religious habits into a puritanical chant in Ireland. The Chinese language is monosyllabic, and Mr. Molony has extended its character to the English tongue; for he breaks all his words into separate and elaborate divisions, to each of which he bestows a due quantity of deliberate intonation. Upon arriving in Ireland he addicted himself to godliness, having previously made great gains in China, and he has so contrived as to impart the cadences of Wesley to the accentuation of Confucius.

Such was the aspect of the great public functionary, who, rising with peculiar magisteriality of altitude, and stretching forth the emblem of his power, inquired of the gentleman who was suspended from the gallery who he was.—"My name is O'Gorman Mahon," was the reply delivered with a firmness which clearly showed that the person who I conveyed this piece of intelligence thought very little of a high sheriff and a great deal of O'Gorman Mahon. The sheriff had been offended by the general appearance of Mr. Mahon, who had distracted the public attention from his own contemplation; but he was particularly irritated by observing the insurgent symbol of "the order of Liberators" dangling at his breast. "I tell that gentleman," said Mr. Molony, ' to take off that badge." There was a moment's pause, and then the following answer was slowly and articulately pronounced :—" This gentleman (laying his hand on his breast) tells that gentleman (pointing with the other to the sheriff), that if that gentleman presumes to touch this gentleman, that this gentleman will defend himself against that gentleman, or any other gentleman, while he has got the arm of a gentleman to protect him." This extraordinary sentence was followed by a loud burst of applause from all parts of the court-house. The high sheriff looked aghast. The expression of self-satisfaction and magisterial complacency passed off of his visage, and he looked utterly blank and dejected. After an interval of irresolution down he sat. "The soul" of O'Gorman Mahon (to use Curran's expression) "walked forth in its own majesty;" he looked "redeemed, regenerated, and disenthralled." The medal of "the order of Liberators" was pressed to his heart. O'Connell surveyed him with gratitude and admiration; and the first blow was struck, which sent dismay into the heart of the party of which the sheriff was considered to be an adherent.

This was the opening incident of this novel drama. When the sensation which it had created had in some degree subsided, the business of the day went on. Sir Edward O'Brien proposed Mr. Vesey Fitzgerald as a proper person to serve in parliament. Sir Edward had upon former occasions been the vehement antagonist of Mr. Fitzgerald, and in one instance a regular battle had been fought between the tenantry of both parties. It was supposed that this feud had left some acrimonious feelings which were not quite extinct behind, and many conjectured that the zeal of Sir Edward in favour of his competitor was a little feigned. This notion was confirmed by the circumstance that Sir Edward O Brien's son (the member for Ennis)* had subscribed to the Catholic rent, was a member of the Association, and had recently made a vigorous speech in parliament in defence of that body. It is, however, probable that the feudal pride of Sir Edward O'Brien, which was deeply mortified by the defection of his vassals, absorbed every other feeling, and that, however indifferent he might have been on Mr. Fitzgerald's account, yet that he was exceedingly irritated upon his own. He appeared at least to be profoundly moved, and had not spoken above a few minutes when tears fell from his eyes. He has a strong Irish character impressed upon him. It is said that he is lineally descended from Brian Boiruinhe. He is squat, bluff, and impassioned. An expression of good nature, rather than of good humour, is mixed up with a certain rough consciousness of his own dignity, which in his most familiar moments he never lays aside, for the Milesian predominates in his demeanour, and his royal recollections wait perpetually upon him. He

---
* William Smith O'Brien, late member for Limerick, one of the traversers indicted for in 1848, and sentenced to transportation.

is a great favourite with the people, who are attached to the descendants of the ancient indigenous families of the county, and who see in Sir Edward O'Brien a good landlord, as well as the representative of Brian Boirumhe. I was not a little astonished at seeing him weep upon the hustings. It was, however, observed to me, that he is given to the "melting mood," although his tears do not fall like the gum of "the Arabian tree." In the House of Commons he once produced a great effect by bursting into tears, while he described the misery of the people of Clare, although, at the same time, his granaries were full. It was said that his hustings' pathos was of the same quality, and arose from the peculiar susceptibility of the lacrymatory nerves, and not from any very nice fibres about the heart: still I am convinced that his emotion was genuine, and that he was profoundly touched. He complained that he had been deserted by his tenants, although he had deserved well at their hands; and exclaimed that the country was not one fit for a gentleman to reside in, when property lost all its influence, and things were brought to such a pass. The motion was seconded by Sir A. Fitzgerald in a few words. Mr. Gore, a gentleman of very large estate, took occasion to deliver his opinions in favour of Mr. Fitzgerald; and O'Gorman Mahon and Mr. Steele proposed Mr. O'Connell. It then fell to the rival candidates to speak, and Mr. Vesey Fitzgerald, having been first put in nomination, first addressed the freeholders. He seemed to me to be about five and forty years of age, his hair being slightly marked with a little edging of scarcely perceptible silver, but the care with which it was distributed and arranged, showed that the cabinet minister had not yet entirely dismissed his Lothario recollections. I had heard, before I had even seen Mr. Fitzgerald, that he was in great favour with the Calistas at Almack's; and I was not surprised at it, on a minute inspection of his aspect and deportment. It is not that he is a handsome man, (though he is far from being the reverse), but that there is an air of blended sweetness and assurance, of easy intrepidity and gentle gracefulness about him, which are considered to be eminently winning. His countenance, though too fully circular, and a little tinctured with vermillion, is agreeable. The eyes are of bright hazel, and have an expression of ever earnest frankness, which an acute observer might suspect, while his mouth is full of a strenuous solicitude to please. The moment he rose, I perceived that he was an accomplished gentleman; and when I had heard him utter a few sentences, I was satisfied that he is a most accomplished speaker. He delivered one of the most effective and dexterous speeches which it has ever been my good fortune to hear. There were evident marks of deep pain and of fear to be traced in his features, which were not free from the haggardness of many an anxious vigil; but though he was manifestly mortified in the extreme, studiously refrained from all exasperating sentiment or expression, spoke at first with a graceful melancholy, rather than a tone of passioned adjuration. He intimated that it was rather a measure of rous, if not unjustifiable policy, to display the power of the Association in throwing an individual out of parliament who had been the warm uniform advocate of the Catholic cause during his whole political life. He enumerated the instances in which he had exerted himself in behalf of that body which were now dealing with him with such severity, and referred to his services with regard to the college of Maynooth. The part of his speech which was most powerful, related to his father. The latter had opposed the Union, and had many claims upon the national gratitude. The topic was one which required to be most delicately touched, and no orator could treat it with a more exquisite nicety than Mr. Fitzgerald. He became, as he advanced, and the recollection of his father pressed itself more immediately upon his mind, more impassioned. At the moment he was speaking, his father, to whom he is most tenderly attached, and by whom he is most beloved, was lying upon a bed from whence it was believed that he would never rise, and efforts had been made to conceal from the old man the contest in which his son was involved. It was impossible to mistake genuine grief, and when Mr. Fitzgerald paused for an instant, and turning away, wiped off the tears that came gushing into his eyes, he won the sympathies of every one about him. There were few who did not give the same evidence of emotion: and when he sat down, although the great majority of the audience were strongly opposed to him, and were enthusiasts in favour of the rival candidate, a loud and unanimous burst of acclamation shook the court-house.

Mr. O'Connell rose to address the people in reply. It was manifest that he considered a great exertion to be requisite in order to do away the impression which his antagonist had produced. It was clear that he was collecting all his might, to those who were acquainted with the workings of his physiognomy. Mr. O'Connell bore Mr. Fitzgerald no sort of personal aversion, but he determined, in this exigency, to have little mercy on his feelings, and to employ all the power of vituperation of which he was possessed, against him. This was absolutely necessary; for if mere dexterous fencing had been resorted to by Mr. O'Connell, many might have gone away with the opinion that, after all, Mr. Fitzgerald had been thanklessly treated by the Catholic body. It was therefore disagreeably requisite to render him, for the moment, odious. Mr. O'Connell began by awakening the passions of the multitude in an attack on Mr. Fitzgerald's allies. Mr. Gore had lauded him highly. This Mr. Gore is of Cromwellian descent, and the people detest the memory of the protector to this day. There is a tradition (I know not whether it has the least foundation) that the ancestor of this gentleman's family was a nailor by trade in the Puritan army. Mr. O'Connell, without any direct reference to the fact, used a set of metaphors, such as "striking the nail on the head,"—" putting a nail into a coffin," which at once recalled the associations which were attached to the name of Mr. Gore; and roars of laughter assailed that gentleman on every side. Mr. Gore has the character of being not only very opulent, but of bearing regard to his possessions proportioned to their extent. Nothing is so unpopular as prudence in Ireland; and Mr. O'Connell rallied Mr. Gore to such a point upon this head, and that of his supposed origin, that the latter completely sunk under the attack. He next proceeded to Mr. Fitzgerald, and having drawn a picture of the late Mr. Perceval, he turned round and asked of the rival candidate, with what face he could call himself their friend, when the first act of his political life was to enlist himself under the banners of "the bloody Perceval." This epithet (whether it be well or ill deserved is not the question) was sent into the hearts of the people with a force of expression, and a furious vehemence of voice, that created a great sensation amongst the crowd, and turned the tide against Mr. Fitzgerald. "This too," said Mr. O'Connell, "is the friend of Peel— the bloody Perceval, and the candid and manly Mr. Peel—and he is our friend! and he is every body's friend! The friend of the Catholic was the friend of the bloody Perceval, and is the friend of the candid and manly Mr. Peel!"

It is unnecessary to go through Mr. O'Connell's speech. It was stamped with all his powerful characteristics, and galled Mr. Fitzgerald to the core. That gentleman frequently muttered an interrogatory, "Is this fair?" when Mr. O'Connell was using some legitimate sophistication against him. He seemed particularly offended when his adversary said, "I never shed tears in public," which was intended as a mockery of Mr. Fitzgerald's references to his father. It will be thought by some sensitive persons that Mr. O'Connell was not quite warranted in this harsh dealing, but he had no alternative. Mr. Fitzgerald had made a very powerful speech, and the effect was to be got rid of. In such a warfare a man must not pause in the selection of his weapons, and Mr O'Connell is not the man to hesitate in the use of the rhetorical sabre. Nothing of any peculiar interest occurred after Mr. O'Connell's speech upon the first day. On the second the polling commenced; and on that day, in consequence of an expedient adopted by Mr. Fitzgerald's committee, the parties were nearly equal. A Catholic freeholder cannot, in strictness, vote at an election without making a certain declaration upon oath respecting his religious opinions, and obtaining a certificate of his having done so from a magistrate.—It is usual for candidates to agree to dispense with the necessity of taking this oath. It was, however, of importance to Mr. Fitzgerald to delay the election; and with that view his committee required that the declaration should be taken. Mr. O'Connell's committee were unprepared for this form, and it was with the utmost difficulty that magistrates could be procured to attend to receive the oath. It was therefore impossible, on the first day, for Mr. O'Connell to bring his forces into the field, and thus the parties appeared early equal. To those who did not know the real cause of this circumstance, it appeared ominous, and the O'Connellites looked sufficiently ank; but the next day every thing was remedied. The freeholders ere sworn *en masse*. They were brought into a yard inclosed within ur walls. Twenty-five were placed against each wall, and they simultaneously repeated the oath. When one batch of swearers had been posed of, the person who administered the declaration, turned to the joining division, and despatched them. Thus he went through the adrangle, and in the course of a few minutes was able to discharge a hundred patriots upon Mr. Fitzgerald. It may be said that an oath ght to be more solemnly administered. In reply it is only necessary

to observe, that the declaration in question related principally to "the Pretender," and when "the legislature persevere in compelling the name of God to be thus taken in vain," the ritual becomes appropriately farcical, and the manner of the thing is only adapted to the ludicrous matter upon which it is legally requisite that Heaven should be attested! The oath which is imposed upon a Roman Catholic is a violation of the first precept of the decalogue! This species of machinery having been thus applied to the art of swearing, the effects upon the poll soon became manifest, and Mr. O'Connell ascended to a triumphant majority. It became clear that the landlords had lost all their power, and that their struggles were utterly hopeless. Still they persevered in dragging the few serfs whom they had under their control to the hustings, and in protracting the election. It was Mr. Fitzgerald's own wish, I believe, to abandon the contest, when its ultimate issue was already certain; but his friends insisted that the last man whom they could command should be polled out. Thus the election was procrastinated. In ordinary cases, the interval between the first and the last day of polling is monotonous and dull; but during the Clare election so many ludicrous and extraordinary incidents were every moment occurring, as to relieve any attentive observer from every influence of ennui. The writer of these pages was under the necessity of remaining during the day in the sheriff's booth, where questions of law were chiefly discussed, but even here there was much matter for entertainment. The sheriff afforded a perpetual fund of amusement. He sat with his wand of office leaning against his shoulder, and always ready for his grasp. When there was no actual business going forward, he still preserved a magisterial dignity of deportment, and with half-closed eyelids, and throwing back his head, and forming with his chin an obtuse angle with the horizon, reproved any indulgence in illicit mirth which might chance to pass amongst the bar. The gentlemen who were professionally engaged having discovered the chief foible of the sheriff, which consisted in the most fantastical notions of himself, vied with each other in playing upon this weakness. "I feel that I address myself to the first man of the county," was the usual exordium with which every legal argument was opened. The sheriff, instead of perceiving the sneer which involuntarily played round the lips of the mocking sycophant, smiled with an air of Malvolio condescension, and bowed his head. Then came some noise from the adjoining booths, upon which the sheriff used to start up and exclaim, I declare I do not think that I am treated with proper respect—verily I'll go forth and quell this tumult—I'll show them I am the first man in the county, and I'll commit somebody." With that "the first man in the county," with a step slightly accelerated by his resentment at a supposed indignity to himself, used to proceed in quest of a riot, but generally returned with a good-humoured expression of face, observing:—
"It was only Mr. O'Connell, and I must say, when I remonstrated with him he paid me proper respect. He is quite a different person from what I had heard. But let nobody imagine that I was afraid of him. I'd commit him, or Mr. Vesey Fitzgerald, if I was not treated with proper respect; for by virtue of my office I am the first man in the county

A young gentleman (Mr. Whyte) turned his talent in mimicry to a very pleasant and useful account. He acted as agent to Mr. O'Connell, in a booth of which the chief officer, or sheriff's deputy, as he is called, was believed to be a partizan of Mr. Fitzgerald, and used to delay Mr. O'Connell's tallies. A tumult would then ensue, and the deputy would raise his voice in a menacing tone against the friends of Mr. O'Connell. The high sheriff himself had been accustomed to go to the entrance of the different booths and to command silence with his long-drawn and dismal ejaculations. When the deputy was bearing it with a high hand, Mr. Whyte would sometimes leave the booth, and standing at the outward edge of the crowd, just at the moment that the deputy was about to commit some partizan of Mr. O'Connell, the mimic would exclaim in a death-bell voice, " Silence, Mr. Deputy, you are exceedingly disorderly —silence." The deputy being enveloped by the multitude, could not see the individual who thus addressed him, and believing it to be the sheriff, sat down confounded at the admonition, while Mr. O'Connell's tally went rapidly on, and the disputed vote was allowed. These vagaries enlivened occupations which in their nature were sufficiently dull. But the sheriff's booth afforded matter more deserving of note than his singularities. Charges of undue influence were occasionally brought forward, which exhibited the character of the election in its strongest colours. One incident I particularly remember. An attorney employed by Mr. Fitzgerald rushed in and exclaimed that a priest was terrifying the voters. This accusation produced a powerful effect. The counsel for Mr. O'Connell defied the attorney to make out his charge. The assessor very properly required that the priest should attend; and behold Father Murphy of Corofin! His solemn and spectral aspect struck every body. He advanced with fearlessness to the bar, behind which the sheriff was seated, and inquired what the charge was which had been preferred against him, with a smile of ghastly derision. " You were looking at my voters," cries the attorney. " But I said nothing," replied the priest, " and I suppose that I am to be permitted to look at my parishioners." " Not with such a face as that!" cried Mr. Dogherty, one of Mr. Fitzgerald's counsel. This produced a loud laugh ; for, certainly, the countenance of Father Murphy was fraught with no ordinary terrors. " And this, then," exclaimed Mr. O'Connell's counsel, " is the charge you bring against the priests. Let us see if there be an act of parliament which prescribes that a Jesuit shall wear a mask." At this instant, one of the agents of Mr. O'Connell precipitated himself into the room, and cried out, " Mr. Sheriff, we have no fair play—Mr. Singleton is frightening his tenants—he caught hold of one of them just now, and threatened vengeance against him." This accusation came admirably apropos. " What!" exclaimed the advocate of Mr. O'Connell, " is this to be endured? Do we live in a free country, and under a constitution? Is a landlord to commit a battery with impunity, and is a priest to be indicted for his physiognomy, and to be found guilty of a look?" Thus a valuable set-off against Father Murphy's eyebrows was obtained. After a long debate, the assessor decided that, either a priest or a landlord actually interrupted the poll, they should he indiscriminately committed; but thought the present a case only for admonition. Father Murphy was accordingly restored to his physiognomical functions. The matter had been scarcely disposed of, when a loud shout was heard from the multitude outside the court-house, which had gathered in thousands, and yet generally preserved a profound tranquillity. The large window in the sheriff's booth gave an opportunity of observing whatever took place in the square below; and, attracted by the tremendous uproar, every body ran to see what was going on amongst the crowd. The tumult was produced by the arrival of some hundred freeholders from Kilrush, with their landlord, Mr. Vandeleur, at their head. He stood behind a carriage, and, with his hat off, was seen vehemently addressing the tenants who followed him. It was impossible to hear a word which he uttered; but his gesture was sufficiently significant: he stamped, and waved his hat, and shook his clenched hand. While he thus adjured them, the crowd through which they were passing, assailed them with cries, "Vote for your country, boys! Vote for the old religion!—Three cheers for liberty!—Down with Vesey, and hurrah for O'Connell!" These were the exclamations which rent the air, as they proceeded.—They followed their landlord until they had reached a part of the square where Mr. O'Connell lodged, and before which a large platform had been erected, which communicated with the window of his apartment, and to which he could advance whenever it was necessary to address the people. When Mr. Vandeleur's freeholders had attained this spot, Mr. O'Connell rushed forward on the platform, and lifted up his arm. A tremendous shout succeeded, and in an instant Mr. Vandeleur was deserted by his tenants. This platform exhibited some of the most remarkable scenes which were enacted in this strange drama of "The Clare Election." It was sustained by pillars of wood, and stretched out several feet from the wall to which it was attached. Some twenty or thirty persons could stand upon it at the same time. A large quantity of green boughs were turned about it; and from the sort of bower which they formed, occasional orators addressed the people during the day. Father Sheehan, a clergyman from Waterford, who had been mainly instrumental in the overthrow of the Beresfords, displayed from this spot his popular abilities. Dr. Kenny, a Waterford surgeon, thinking that "the times were out of joint," came "to set them right." Father Maguire, Mr. Lawless, indeed, the whole company of orators, performed on this theatre with indefatigable energy. Mirth and declamation, and anecdote and grotesque delineation, and mimicry, were all blended together for the public entertainment. One of the most amusing and attractive topics was drawn from the adherence of Father Coffey to Mr. Fitzgerald. His manners, his habits, his dress, were all selected as materials for ridicule and invective; and puns, not the less effective because they were obvious, were heaped upon his name. The scorn and detestation with which he was treated by the mob, clearly proved that a priest has no influence over them when he attempts to run counter to their political passions. He can hurry them on in the career into which their own feelings impel them, but he cannot turn them into another course,

Many incidents occurred about this rostrum, which, if matter did not crowd too fast upon me, I should stop to detail. I have not room for a minute narration of all that was interesting at this election, which would occupy a volume, and must limit myself to one, but that a very striking circumstance. The generality of the orators were heard with loud and clamorous approbation; but, at a late hour one evening, and when it was growing rapidly dark, a priest came forward on the platform, who addressed the multitude in Irish. There was not a word uttered by the people. Ten thousand peasants were assembled before the speaker, and a profound stillness hung over the living, but almost breathless mass. For minutes they continued thus deeply attentive, and seemed to be struck with awe as he proceeded. Suddenly, I saw the whole multitude kneel down, in one concurrent genuflection. They were engaged in silent prayer, and when the priest arose (for he too had knelt down on the platform), they also stood up together from their orison. The movement was performed with the facility of a regimental evolution. I asked (being unacquainted with the language) what it was that had occasioned this extraordinary spectacle? and was informed that the orator had stated to the people that one of his own parishioners, who had voted for Mr. Fitzgerald, had just died; and he called upon the multitude to pray to God for the repose of his soul, and the forgiveness of the offence which he had committed in taking the bribery oath. Money had been his inducement to give his suffrage against Mr. O'Connell. Thus it was the day passed, and it was not until nearly nine o'clock that those who were actively engaged in the election went to dinner. There a new scene was opened. In a small room in a mean tavern, the whole body of leading patriots, counsellors, attorneys, and agents, with divers interloping partakers of election hospitality, were crammed and piled upon one another, while Mr. O'Connell sat at the head of the feast almost overcome with fatigue, but yet sustained by that vitality which success produces. Enormous masses were strewed upon the deal boards, at which the hungry masticators proceeded to their operations. The more intellectual season of potations succeeded. Toasts were then proposed and speeches pronounced, and the usual "hip, hip, hurra!" with unusual accompaniments of exultation, followed. The feats of the day were then narrated:—the blank looks of Mr. Hickman, (Mr. Fitzgerald's confidential solicitor and conducting agent,) whose face had lost all its natural hilarity, and looked at the election like a full moon in a storm; and the tears of Sir Edward O'Brien, were alternately the subjects of merriment. Mr. Whyte was called upon for an imitation of the sheriff, when he used to ride upon an elephant at Calcutta. But in the midst of this conviviality, which was heightened by the consciousness that there was no bill to be paid by gentlemen who were the guests of their country, and long before any inebriating effect was observable, a solemn and spectral figure used to stride in, and the same deep church-yard voice which had previously startled my ears, raised its awful peal, while it exclaimed "The wolf, the wolf is on the walk. Shepherds of the people, what do you here? is it meet that you should sit in joyance, while the freeholders remain unprovided, and temptation, in the shape of famine, is amongst them? Arise, I say, arise—the wolf, the wolf is on the walk."

Such was the disturbing adjuration of Father Murphy of Corofin, whose enthusiastic sense of duty never deserted him, and who, when the feast was unfinished, entered like the figure of death in an Egyptian banquet. He walked round the room with a measured pace, chasing the revellers before him, and repeating the same dismal warning—" The wolf, the wolf is upon the walk!" Nothing was comparable to the aspect of Father Murphy upon these occasions, except the physiognomy of Mr. Lawless. This gentleman, who had been usefully exerting himself during the whole day, somewhat reasonably expected that he should be permitted to enjoy the just rewards of patriotism for a few hours without any nocturnal molestation. It was about the time that the exhilarating influence of his eloquent chalices was beginning to display itself, that the dismal cry was wont to come upon him. The look of despair with which he surveyed this unrelenting foe to conviviality, was almost as ghastly as that of his merciless disturber; and as, like another Tantalus, he saw the draughts of pleasantness hurried away, a schoolmaster, who sat by him, and who " was abroad" during the election, used to exclaim—

———"A labris sitiens fugientia captat
Flumina."———

It was in vain to remonstrate against Father Murphy, who insisted that the whole company should go forth to meet " the wolf upon the walk." Upon going down stairs, the lower apartments were found thronged with freeholders and priests. To the latter had been assigned the office of providing food for such of the peasants as lived at too great distance from the town to return immediately home; and each clergyman was empowered to give an order to the victuallers and tavern-keepers to furnish the bearer with a certain quantity of meat and beer. The use of whiskey was forbidden. There were two remarkable features observable in the discharge of this office. The peasant who had not tasted food perhaps for twenty-four hours, remained in perfect patience and tranquillity until his turn arrived to speak " to his reverence;" and the Catholic clergy continued with unwearied assiduity, and the most amiable solicitude, though themselves quite exhausted with fatigue, in the performance of this necessary labour. There they stayed until a late hour in the morning, and until every claimant had been contented. It is not wonderful that such men, animated by such zeal, and operating upon so grateful and so energetic a peasantry, should have affected what they succeeded in accomplishing. The poll at length closed; and, after an excellent argument delivered by the assessor, Mr. Richard Keatinge, he instructed the sheriff to return Mr. O'Connell as duly elected. The court-house was again crowded, as upon the first day, and Mr. Fitzgerald appeared at the head of the defeated aristocracy. They looked profoundly melancholy. Mr. Fitzgerald himself did not affect to disguise the deep pain which he felt; but preserved that gracefulness and perfect good temper which had characterized him during the contest, and which, at its close, disarmed hostility of all its rancour. Mr. O'Con

..ell made a speech distinguished by just feeling and good taste, and begged that Mr. Fitzgerald would forgive him, if he had upon the first day given him any sort of offence. Mr. Fitzgerald came forward, and unaffectedly assured him, that whatever was said should be forgotten He was again hailed with universal acclamation, and delivered a speech which could not surpass, in good judgment and persuasiveness, that with which he had opened the contest, but was not inferior to it. He left an impression, which hereafter will, in all probability, render his return for the county of Clare a matter of certainty ; and, upon the other hand, I feel convinced that he has himself carried away from the scene of that contention, in which he sustained a defeat, but lost no honour, a conviction that not only the interests of Ireland, but the safety of the empire, require that the claims of seven millions of his fellow-citizens should be conceded Mr. Fitzgerald, during the progress of the election, could not refrain from repeatedly intimating his astonishment at what he saw, and from indulging in melancholy forebodings of the events, of which these incidents are perhaps but the heralds. To do him justice, he appeared at moments utterly to forget himself, and to be absorbed in the melancholy presages which pressed themselves upon him. "Where is all this to end?" was a question frequently put in his presence, and from which he seemed to shrink.

At the close of the poll, Mr. Sheil spoke in the following terms:—

I am anxious to avail myself of this opportunity to make a reparation to Mr. Fitzgerald. Before I had the honour of hearing that gentleman, and of witnessing the conciliatory demeanour by which he is distinguished, I had in another place expressed myself with regard to his political conduct, in language to which I believe that Mr. Fitzgerald referred upon the first day of the election, and which was, perhaps, too deeply tinctured with that animosity which is almost inseparable from the passions by which this country is so unhappily divided. It is but an act of justice to Mr. Fitzgerald to say, that, however we may be under the necessity of opposing him as a member of an administration hostile to our body, it is impossible to entertain towards him a sentiment of individual hostility; and I confess, that, after having observed the admirable temper with which he encountered his antagonists, I cannot but regret that, before I had the means of forming a just estimate of his personal character, I should have indulged in remarks, in which too much acidity may have been infused. The situation in which Mr. Fitzgerald was placed, was peculiarly trying to his feelings He had been long in possession of this county. Though we considered him as an inefficient friend, we were not entitled to account him an opponent. Under these circumstances it may have appeared harsh, and perhaps unkind, that we should have selected him as the first object for the manifestation of our power ; another would have found it difficult not to give way to the language of resentment and of reproach, but so far from doing so, his defence of himself was as strongly marked by forbearance as it was by ability. I thought it, however, not altogether impossible that before the fate of this election was decided, Mr. Fitzgerald might have been merely practising an expedient of why concilation, and that when he appeared so meek and self-controlled in the midst of a contest which would have provoked the passions of any ordinary man, he was only stifling his resentment, in the hope that he might succeed in appeasing the violence of the opposition with which he had to contend. But Mr. Fitzgerald, in the demeanour which he has preserved to-day, after the election has concluded with his defeat, has given proof that his gentleness of deportment was not affected and artificial: and, now that he has no object to gain, we cannot but give him as ample credit for his sincerity, as we must give him for that persuasive gracefulness by which his manners are distinguished. Justly has he said that he has not lost a friend in this country; and he might have added that, so far from having incurred any diminution of regard among those who were attached to him, he has appeased to a great extent the vehemence of that political enmity in which the associate of Mr. Peel was not very unnaturally held. But, Sir, while I have thus made the acknowledgment which was due to Mr. Fitzgerald, let me not disguise my own feelings of legitimate, but not I hope offensive exultation at the result of this great contest, that has attracted the attention of the English people beyond all example. I am not mean enough to indulge in any contumelious vaunting over one who has sustained his defeat with so honourable a magnanimity. The victory which has been achieved, has been obtained not so much over Mr. Fitzgerald, as over the faction with which I excuse him to a great extent for having been allied. A great display of power has been made by the Catholic Association, and that manifestation of its influence over the national mind, I regard as not only a very remarkable, but a very momentous incident. Let us consider what has taken place, in order that we may see this singular political phenomenon in its just light. It is right that we attentively survey the extraordinary facts before us, in order that we may derive from them the moral admonitions which they are calculated to supply. What then has happened? Mr. Fitzgerald was promoted to a place in the Duke of Wellington's councils, and the representation of this great county became vacant. The Catholic Association determined to oppose him, and at first view the undertaking seemed to be desperate. Not a single Protestant gentleman could be procured to enter the lists, and in the want of any other candidate, Mr. O'Connell stood forward in behalf of the people. Mr. Vesey Fitzgerald came into the field encompassed with the most signal advantages. His father is a gentleman of large estate, and had been long and deservedly popular in Ireland. Mr. Fitzgerald himself, inheriting a portion of the popular favour with a favourite name, had for twenty years been placed in such immediate contiguity to power, that he was enabled to circulate a large portion of the influence of government through this fortunate district. There is scarcely a single family of any significance among you, which does not labour under Mr. Fitzgerald's obligations. At this moment it is only necessary to look at him, with the array of aristocracy beside him, in order to perceive upon what a high position for victory he was placed. He stands encompassed by the whole gentry of the county of Clare, who, as they stood by him in the hour of battle, come here to cover his retreat. Almost every gentleman of rank and fortune appears as his auxiliary, and the gentry, by their aspect at this instant, as well as by their devotedness during the election, furnish evidence that in his person their own cause was to be asserted. To this combination of favourable circumstances—to the political friend, to the accomplished gentleman, to the eloquent advocate, at the head of all the patrician opulence of the county, what did we oppose? We opposed the power of the Catholic Association, and with that tremendous engine we have beaten the cabinet minister, and the phalanx of aristocracy by which he is surrounded, to the ground. Why do I mention these things? Is it for the purpose (God forbid that it should!) of wounding the feelings or exasperating the passions of any man? No, but in order to exhibit the almost marvellous incidents which have taken place, in the light in which they ought to be regarded, and to present them in all their appalling magnitude. Protestants who hear me, gentlemen of the county Clare, you whom I address with boldness, perhaps, but certainly not with any purpose to give you offence, let me entreat your attention. A baronet of rank and fortune, Sir Edward O'Brien, has asked whether this was a condition of things to be endured he has expatiated upon the extraordinary influence which has been exercised in order to effect these signal results; and, after dwelling upon many other grounds of complaint, he has with great force inveighed against the severance which we have created between the landlord and tenant. Let it not be imagined that I mean to deny that we have had recourse to the expedients attributed to us; on the contrary, I avow it. We have put a great engine into action, and applied the entire force of that powerful machinery which the law has placed under our control. We are masters of the passions of the people, and we have employed our dominion with a terrible effect. But, Sir, do you, or does any man here, imagine that we could have acquired this formidable ability to sunder the strongest ties by which the different classes of society are fastened, unless we found the materials of excitement in the state of society itself? Do you think that Daniel O'Connell has himself, and by the single powers of his own mind, unaided by any external co-operation, brought the country to this great crisis of agitation? Mr. O'Connell, with all his talents for excitation, would have been utterly powerless and incapable, unless he had been allied with a great conspirator against the public peace: and I will tell you who that confederate is—it is the law of the land itself that has been Mr. O'Connell's main associate, and that ought to be denounced as the mighty agitator of Ireland. The rod of oppression is the wand of this enchanter, and the book of his spells is the penal code. Break the wand of this political Prospero, and take from him the volume of his magic, and he will evoke the spirits which are now under his control no longer. But why should I have recourse to illustration which may be accounted fantastical, in order to elucidate what is in itself so plain and obvious? Protestant gentlemen, who do me the honour to listen to me, look, I pray you, a little dispassionately at the real causes of the events which have taken place amongst you. I beg of you to put aside

your angry feelings for an instant, and believe me that I am far from
thinking that you have no good ground for resentment. It must be
most painful to the proprietors of this county to be stripped in an
instant of all their influence; to be left destitute of all sort of sway over
their dependants, and to see a few demagogues and priests usurping
their natural authority. This feeling of resentment must be aggravated
by the consciousness that they have not deserved such a return from
their tenants; and as I know Sir Edward O'Brien, to be a truly benevolent landlord, I can well conceive that the apparent ingratitude with
which he was treated, has added to the pain which every landlord must
experience; and I own that I was not surprised to see tears upon his
eyelids, while his face was inflamed with the emotions to which it was not
in human nature that he should not give way. But let Sir Edward
O'Brien, and his fellow-proprietors, who are gathered about him, recollect, that the facility and promptitude with which the peasantry have
thrown off their allegiance, are owing not so much to any want of just
moral feeling on the part of the people, as to the operation of causes
for which the people are not to blame. In no other country, except in
this, would such a revolution have been effected. Wherefore? Because
in no other country are the people divided by the law from their superiors, and cast into the hands of a set of men, who are supplied with the
means of national excitement by the system of government under which
we live. Surely no man can believe that such an anomalous body as
the Catholic Association could exist, excepting in a community which
had been alienated from the state by the state itself. The discontent
and the resentment of seven millions of the population have generated
that domestic government, which sways public opinion, and uses the
national passions as the instruments of its will. It would be utterly
impossible, if there were no exasperating distinctions amongst us, to
create any artificial causes of discontent. Let men declaim for a century, and if they have no real grievance their harangues will be empty
sound and idle air. But when what they tell the people is true—when
they are sustained by substantial facts, effects are produced, of which
what has taken place at this election is only an example. The whole
body of the people having been previously excited, the moment any
incident, such as this election, occurs, all the popular passions start
simultaneously up, and bear down every obstacle before them. Do not,
therefore, be surprised that the peasantry should throw off their allegiance, when they are under the operation of emotions which it would
be wonderful if they could resist. The feeling by which they are actuated, would make them not only vote against their landlord, but would
make them scale the batteries of a fortress, and mount the breach; and
gentlemen, give me leave to ask you, whether, after a due reflection
upon the motives by which your vassals (for so they are accounted) are
governed, you will be disposed to exercise any measure of severity in
their regard. I hear it said, that before many days go by, there will
be many tears shed in the hovels of your slaves, and that you will take
a terrible vengeance. I trust that you will not, when your own passions shall have subsided, and your blood has had time to cool, persevere

In such a cruel, and let me add, such an unjustifiable determination.
Consider whether a great allowance should not be made for the offence
which they have committed. If they are under the influence of fanaticism, such an influence affords many circumstances of extenuation:—
you should forgive them, "for they know not what they do." They
have followed their priests to the hustings, and they would follow them
to the scaffold. You will ask, wherefore they should prefer their priests
to their landlords, and have a higher reverence for the altars of their
religion, than for the counter in which you calculate your rents? Consider a little the relation in which the priest stands towards the peasant.
I will take for my example an excellent landlord and an excellent
priest. The landlord shall be Sir Edward O'Brien, and the priest shall
be Mr. Murphy of Corofin. Who is Sir Edward O'Brien? A gentleman who from the windows of a palace, looks upon possessions almost
as wide as those which his ancestors beheld from the summit of their
feudal towers. His tenants pay him their rent twice a-year, and have
their land at a moderate rate. But what are his claims, when put into
comparison with those of Mr. Murphy of Corofin, to the confidence, to
the affection, and to the fidelity of the peasants who are committed to
his care? He is not only the minister of that humble altar at which
their forefathers and themselves were taught to kneel, but he is their
kind, their familiar, yet most respected friend. In their difficulties and
distresses they have no one else to look to; he never fails when consulted by them, to associate his sympathy with his admonition; for their
sake he is ready to encounter every hazard, and, in the performance of
the perilous duties incident to his sacerdotal office, he never hesitates
to expose his life. In a stormy night, a knocking is heard at the door
of the priest of Corofin. He is told that at the foot of the mountain a
man of guilt and blood has scarcely more than an hour to live. Will
the teacher of the gospel tarry because of the rain and of the wind, and
wait until the day shall break, when the soul of an expiring sinner can
be saved, and the demons that are impatient for him can still be scared
away? He goes forth in the blackness of the tempestuous midnight—
he ascends the hill, he traverses the morass—and faint, and cold, and
dripping, finds his way to the hovel where his coming is awaited;—with
what a gasping of inarticulate gratitude—with what a smile of agony
he welcomed! No fear of contagion, no dread of the exhalations of
mortality, reeking from the bed of the pestilential man can appal him,
but kneeling down at the side of the departing culprit, and sustaining
him in his arms, he receives from lips impregnated with death, the
whisper with which the heart is unloaded of its mysteries, and, raising
his eyes to heaven, pronounces the ritual of absolution in the name
Him of whose commission of mercy he is the befitting bearer, and
whose precepts he illustrates in his life and inculcates in his example.
And can you feel wonder and resentment that under the influence of
such a man as I have described to you, your dependants should have
ventured upon a violation of your mandates? Forgive me if I venture to supplicate, on behalf of your tenants, for forbearance. Pardon
them, in the name of one who will forgive you your offences in the

same measure of compassion which you will show to the trespasses of those who have sinned against yourselves. Do not persecute these poor people: don't throw their children upon the public road, and send them forth to starve, to shiver, and to die. For God's sake, Mr. Fitzgerald, as you are a gentleman and a man of honour, interpose your influence with your friends, and redeem your pledge. I address myself personally to you. On the first day of the election you declared that you would deprecate persecution, and that you were the last to wish that vindictive measures should be employed. I believe you—and I call upon you to redeem that pledge of mercy, to perform that great moral promise. You will cover yourself with honour by so doing, in the same way that you will share in the ignominy that will attend upon any expedients of rigour. Before you leave this country to assume your high functions, enjoin your friends with that eloquence of which you are the master, to refrain from cruelty and not to oppress their tenants. Tell them, Sir, that instead of busying themselves in the worthless occupation of revenge, it is much fitter that they should take the political condition of their country into their deep consideration. Tell them that they should address themselves to the legislature, and implore a remedy for these frightful evils. Tell them to call upon the men, in whose hands the destiny of this great empire is placed to adopt a system of peace, and to apply to Ireland the great canon of political morality—*pacis imponere morem*. Let it not be imagined that any measure of disfranchisement, that any additional penalty, will afford a remedy. Things have been permitted to advance to a height from which they cannot recede. Protestants, awake to a sense of your condition. What have you seen during this election? Enough to make you feel that it is not a mere local excitation, but that seven millions of Irish people are completely arrayed and organized. That which you behold in Clare, you would behold, under similar circumstances, in every county in the kingdom. Did you mark our discipline, our subordination, our good order, and that tranquillity, which is formidable indeed? You have seen sixty thousand men under our command, and not a hand was raised, and not a forbidden word was uttered in that amazing multitude. You have beheld an example of our power in the almost miraculous sobriety of the people. Their lips have not touched that infuriating beverage to which they are so much attached, and their habitual propensity vanished at our command. Is it meet and wise to leave us armed with such a dominion? Trust us not with it; strip us of this appalling power; disarray us by equality; instead of angry slaves make us contented citizens; if you do not, tremble for the result.

CLONMEL AGGREGATE MEETING.

SPEECH MADE AT AN AGGREGATE MEETING IN CLONMEL DURING THE ASSIZES.

THE assizes held for this, the great county of Tipperary, exhibit a deplorable spectacle of turbulence and of guilt. I consider it to be my duty to address to this immense assembly, composed of several thousands, and comprehending a vast body of the peasantry, some well-meant advice. You are well aware that in the course which I have adopted, I have not displayed a pusillanimous spirit, and that I am deeply sensible of the wrongs which are inflicted upon my country. What I shall say, therefore, in the shape of strong reproof, will be taken in good part. I tell you undisguisedly, that although I consider the government to have adopted unavailing and inapplicable means for the restoration of tranquillity, yet that I look upon the crimes committed amongst you with dismay. What have I not witnessed in the course of the few days which the assizes have occupied! What a stain have those crimes left upon the character of your country! Look at the murder of the Sheas—look at the midnight conflagration in which eighteen of your fellow-creatures perished, and tell me if there be anything in the records of horror by which that accursed deed has been excelled! In that night which stands without a parallel—a child was born in fire—transferred from the womb to flames, kindled by fiends, who exulted round the furnace with whose roaring the shrieks of agony were mingled! What must have been the pains of that delivery in which a mother felt the infant that was clasped against her bosom consumed by the fires with which she was surrounded! The mother was found dead near a tub of water, in which she had plunged her infant, and the child was discovered with its skull burned off, while the rest of the limbs were preserved by the water in which the expiring parent had striven in the united pains of death and child-birth to preserve it. With what exclamation shall we give vent to the emotions which are awakened by the recital of that which you tremble to hear, and which here were human beings found who were not afraid to do! We can but lift up our hands to the God of justice, and ask him why he has invested us with the same forms as the wretches who did that unexampled murder. Although accompanied by circumstances of inferior terror, the recent assassination of Barry belongs to the same class of guilt. A body of men, at the close of day, enter a peaceful habitation, on the Sabbath, and regardless of the cries of a frantic woman, who, grasping one of the murderers, desired him "to think of God, and of the blessed night, and to spare the father of her eight children," dragged him forth, and when he "offered to give up the ground tilled and untilled, if they spared him his life," answered with a yell of ferocious fury, and telling him "he should have ground enough," plunged their bayonets into his heart! An awful spectacle was presented on the trial of the wretched individuals who were convicted of the assassination. At one extremity of the bar stood a boy, with a blooming face, and with down on his cheek, and at the other an old man, in the close of life, with a haggard look, and a deeply furrowed countenance, with his head covered with hoary and dishevelled hair. However remote the periods of their birth, they met not, indeed, in the same grave, (for they are without a tomb,) but on the same scaffold together. In describing the frightful scene, it is consoling to find that you share with me in the unqualified detestation which I have expressed; and I am convinced that it is unnecessary to address to you any further observation on the subject. But I must call your attention to another trial —that of the Hogans, which affords a melancholy lesson. The trial was connected with the baneful practice of avenging the affronts offered to individuals, by enlisting whole clans, who wage an actual war, and light sanguinary battles whenever they encounter. I am very far from saying that the deaths which occur in these barbarous combats are to be compared with the guilt of preconcerted assassination, but that they are accompanied with deep criminality, there can be no question, and the system which produces them is as much marked with absurdity as it is deserving of condemnation. In this country a man who chances to receive a blow, instead of going to a magistrate to swear informations, lodges a complaint with his clan, who enter into a compact to avenge the insult—a reaction is produced, and an equally extensive confederacy is formed on the other side. All this results from an indisposition to resort to the law for protection, for amongst you it is a point of honour not to have recourse to any of the legitimate means provided for your redress. The battle waged between the Hickeys and the Hogans, in which not less than five hundred men were engaged, presents in a strong light the consequences of this most strange and absurd system. Some of the Hickey party were slain in the field, and four of the Hogans were tried for the murder; they were found guilty of manslaughter, and are to be immediately transported; three of them are married and have families, and from their wives and children are condemned to separate for ever. In my mind these unhappy men have been doomed to a fate still more disastrous than those who have perished on the scaffold. In the calamity which has befallen Matthew Hogan, of whom most of you have heard, every man in court felt a sympathy. With the exception of his having made himself a party in the feuds of his clan, he has always conducted himself with propriety. His landlord felt for him a strong regard, and exerted himself to the utmost in his behalf. He never took part in deeds of nocturnal atrocity—honest, industrious, mild, and kindly-natured, he was seconded by the good-will of every man who was acquainted with him. His circumstances were not only comparatively good, but, when taken in reference to his condition in society, were almost opulent. He rather resembled an English yeoman than an Irish peasant. His appearance at the bar was in a high degree impressive—tall, athletic, with a face finely formed, and wholly free from any ferocity of expression, he attracted every eye, and excited even among his prosecutors a feeling of commiseration. He formed a remarkable contrast with the ordinary class of culprits who

ɔur public tribunals. So far from having guilt and
with want upon his countenance, its prevailing cha-
tive of gentleness. This man was convicted of man-
hen he heard the sentence of transportation for life,
rom his cheek—his lips were dry and ashy—his hand
es became incapable of tears. Most of you consider
ight evil, and it may be so to those who have no ties
their country. I can well imagine that a deportation
which, for most of its inhabitants, is a miserable one,
ge greatly for the better. Although the Irish people
attachments, and are fond of their father's graves—
nd the genial climate of New Holland afford many
But there can be none for Matthew Hogan; he is in
—is a prosperous farmer—yet he must leave his coun-
nust part from all that he loves, and from all by whom
is heart will burst in the separation. What a victim
that unfortunate man of the spirit that rages amongst
Hogan will feel his calamity with more deep intensity,
irally sensitive and kindly natured. He was proved
life of one of his antagonists in the fury of the com-
of generous commiseration. One of his own kindred,
of his fate, said he would feel it the more, because
man's vernacular pronunciation) "he was so tinder."
f nature will produce a more painful laceration of the
ids his family farewell for ever. The prison of this
, on Monday next, a very afflicting spectacle. Before
ehicle which is to convey him for transportation to
illowed to take leave of his wife and children. She
osom; and while her arms are folded round his neck
in the agony of anguish, on his breast—his children,
his knees in playful emulation for his caresses * * *
with this distressing picture—your own emotions will
e pains of this poor man will not end at the threshold
e will be conveyed in a vessel, freighted with affliction,
and will be set on the lonely and distant land from
part no more; the thoughts of home will haunt him,
deadly tenacity to his heart. He will mope about in
l sorrow—he will have no incentive to exertion, for he
farewell to hope. The instruments of labour will hang
—he will go through his task without a consciousness
ing. Thus every day will go by, and at its close, his
ill be to stand on the shore, and fixing his eyes in that
n he will have been taught that his country lies, if not
he will, at least, exclaim, in the sentiments which have
id so pathetically expressed in the song of exile:—

" Erin, my country, tho' sad and forsaken,
　In dreams I revisit thy sea-beaten shore;
But, alas! in far foreign lands I awaken,
　And sigh for the friends that can meet me no more.

CLONMEL ASSIZES.

> "Where is my cabin door, fast by the wild wood,
> Sisters and sire did you weep for its fall?
> Where is the mother that looked on my childhood,
> And where is the bosom-friend dearer than all?"

I have dwelt, perhaps, longer than I ought to have done, upon the details of this poor man's misfortunes; but my time has not been misspent, nor have I abused your patience, if I have, in any degree, succeeded in making you sensible of the extent of calamity which follows the indulgence of that disastrous predilection for tumult which characterises the mass of the population. Let not what has taken place at these assizes be thrown away upon you! I implore you for your country's sake, for your own sake, to take warning from the melancholy examples which have been presented to you—give up those guilty feuds which lead to savage bloodshed, and end in everlasting exile. You will not blame me for the advice which I have offered you, and you may rest assured, that I have nothing but your interest at heart, and am actuated towards you by just and honourable motives. I thought it my duty to avail myself of this opportunity, to lay before you a summary of the chief incidents of which I have been a mournful witness at these assizes, and to conjure you, in the name of the highest and holiest obligations, to co-operate together in the repression and the denunciation of the previous habits, which cast such deep dishonour upon the population of this unfortunate and guilty county.

To this speech, as immediately connected with it, is annexed an account of a trial which took place at Clonmel, at the Spring Assizes, 1828, written by Mr. Sheil, and published by him, in the "Sketches of the Irish Bar."

I propose to myself the useful end of fixing the general attention upon a state of things, which ought to lead all wise and good men to the consideration of the only effectual means by which the evils which result from the moral condition of the country may be remedied.

In the month of April, 1827, a gentleman of the name of Chadwick was murdered in the open day, at a place called Rath Cannon, in the immediate vicinity of the old Abbey of Holycross. Mr. Chadwick was the member of an influential family, and was employed as land agent in collecting their rents. The person who fills this office in England is called "a steward;" but in Ireland it is designated by the more honourable name of a land agency. The discharge of the duties of this situation must be always more or less obnoxious. In times of public distress, the landlord, who is himself urged by his own creditors, urges his agent on, and the latter inflicts upon the tenants the necessities of his employer. I have heard that Mr. Chadwick was not peculiarly rigorous in the exaction of rent, but he was singularly injudicious in his demeanour towards the lower orders. He believed that they detested him; and possessing personal courage, bade them defiance. He was not a man of a bad heart; but was despotic, and contumelious in his manners to those whose hatred he returned with contempt. It is said that he used to stand amongst a body of the peasantry, and, observing that his corpulency was on the increase, was accustomed to exclaim, " I think I am fattening upon your curses!" In answer to these taunts, the peasants who surrounded him, and who were well habituated to the concealment of their fierce and terrible passions, affected to laugh, and said, " that his honour was mighty pleasant; and sure, his honour, God bless him, was always fond of his joke!" But while they indulged in the sycophancy, which is but a mask under which they are wont to hide their sanguinary detestations, they were lying in wait for the occasion of revenge. Perhaps, however, they would not have proceeded to the extremities to which they had recourse, but for a determination evinced by Mr. Chadwick to take effectual means for keeping them in awe. He set about building a police barrack at Rath Cannon. It was resolved that Mr. Chadwick should die. This decision was not the result of individual vengeance. The wide confederacy into which the lower orders are organized in Tipperary held council upon him, and the village areopagus pronounced his sentence. It remained to find an executioner. Patrick Grace, who was almost a boy, but was distinguished by various feats of guilty courage, offered himself as a volunteer in what was regarded by him as an honourable cause. He had set up in the county as a sort of knight-errant against landlords; and, in the spirit of a barbarous chivalry, proffered his gratuitous services wherever what he conceived to be a wrong was to be redressed. He proceeded to Rath Cannon; and without adopting any sort of precaution, and while the public road was traversed by numerous passengers, in the broad daylight, and ust beside the barrack, in the construction of which Mr. Chadwick was ngaged, shot that unfortunate gentleman, who fell instantly dead.— This dreadful crime produced a great sensation, not only in the county where it was perpetrated, but through the whole of Ireland. When it was announced in Dublin, it created a sort of dismay, as it evinced the irit of atrocious intrepidity to which the peasantry had been aroused. was justly accounted, by those who looked upon this savage assassition with most horror, as furnishing evidence of the moral condition the people, and as intimating the consequences which might be antipated from the ferocity of the peasantry, if ever they should be let se. Patrick Grace calculated on impunity; but his confidence in e power and terrors of the confederacy with which he was associated mistaken. A brave, and a religious man, whose name was Philip ra, was present at the murder. He was standing beside his employer, . Chadwick, and saw Grace put him deliberately to death. Grace was ll aware that Mara had seen him, but did not believe that he would e to give evidence against him. It is probable, too, that he conjected that Mara coincided with him in his ethics of assassination, and lauded the proceeding. Mara, however, was horror-struck by what ad beheld; and under the influence of conscientious feelings, gave ediate information to a magistrate. Patrick Grace was arrested. tried at the summer assizes of 1827. I was not present at his trial,

but have heard from good authority that he displayed a fearless demea
nour; and that when he was convicted upon the evidence of Philip Mara,
he declared that before a year should go by he should have vengeance
in the grave. He was ordered to be executed near the spot where his
misdeed had been perpetrated. This was a mistake, and produced an
effect exactly the reverse of what was contemplated. The lower orders
looked upon him as a martyr; and his deportment, personal beauty, and
undaunted courage, rendered him an object of deep interest and sympathy upon the scaffold. He was attended by a body of troops to the
old Abbey of Holycross, where not less than fifteen thousand people
assembled to behold him. The site of the execution rendered the spectacle a most striking one. The Abbey of Holycross is one of the finest
and most venerable monastic ruins in Ireland. Most travellers turn
from their way to survey it, and leave it with a deep impression of its
solemnity and grandeur. A vast multitude was assembled round the
scaffold. The prisoner was brought forward in the midst of the profound
silence of the people. He ascended and surveyed them; and looked
upon the ruins of the edifice which had once been dedicated to the worship of his religion, and to the sepulchres of the dead which were strewed
among its aisles, and had been for ages as he was in a few minutes
about to be. It was not known whether he would call for vengeance
from his survivors, or for mercy from Heaven. His kindred, his close
friends, his early companions, all that he loved and all to whom he
was dear, were around him, and no sound, except an universal sob from
his female relatives, disturbed the awful taciturnity that prevailed. At
the side of Patrick Grace stood the priest—the mild admonitor of the
heart, the soother of affliction, and the preceptor of forgiveness, who
attended him in the last office of humanity, and who proved by the result
how well he had performed it. To the disappointment of the people,
Patrick Grace expressed himself profoundly contrite; and, although he
evinced no fear of death, at the instance of the Roman Catholic clergyman who attended him, implored the people to take warning by his
example. In a few moments after, he left this life. But the effect of
his execution will be estimated by this remarkable incident. His gloves
were handed by one of his relations to an old man of the name of John
Russell, as a keepsake. Russell drew them on, and declared at the
same time, that he should wear them "till Paddy Grace was revenged:"
and revenged he soon afterwards was, within the time which he had
himself prescribed for retribution, and in a manner which is as much
calculated to excite astonishment at the strangeness, as detestation for
the atrocity of the crime, of which I proceed to narrate the details.

Philip Mara was removed by government from the country. It was
perfectly obvious, that if he had continued to sojourn in Tipperary, his
life would have been taken speedily, and at all hazards, away. It was
decided that all his kindred should be exterminated. He had three
brothers; and the bare consanguinity with a traitor (for his crime was
treason in the eyes of the associates) was regarded as a sufficient offence
to justify their immolation. If they could not procure his own blood
for the purposes of sacrifice, it was however something to make libation

of that which flowed from the same source. The crimes of the Irish are derived from the same origin as their virtues. They have powerful domestic attachments. Their love and devotion to their kindred instruct them in the worst expedients of atrocity. Knowing the affection which Mara had for his brothers, they found the way to his heart in the kindest instincts of humanity; and from the consciousness of the pain which the murder of "his mother's children" would inflict, determined that he should endure it. It must be owned, that there is a dreadful policy in this system. The government may withdraw their witnesses from the country and afford them protection; but their wives, their offsprings, their parents, their brothers, sisters, nay, their remotest relatives, cannot be secure, and the vengeance of the ferocious peasantry, if defrauded of its more immediate and natural object, will satiate itself with some other victim. It was in conformity with these atrocious principles of revenge that the murder of the brothers of Philip Mara was resolved upon. Strange to tell, the whole body of the peasantry in the neighbourhood of Rath Cannon, and far beyond it, entered into a league, for the perpetration of this abominable crime; and while the individuals who were marked out for massacre were unconscious of what was going forward, scarcely a man, woman, or child looked them in the face, who did not know that they were marked out for death. They were masons by trade, and were employed in building the barrack at Rath Cannon, on the spot where Chadwick had been assassinated, and where the funeral of Patrick Grace (for so his execution was called) had been performed. The peasantry looked in an probability with an evil eye upon every man who had put his hand to this obnoxious work; but their main object was the extermination of Philip Mara's brothers. They were three in number—Daniel, Laurence, and Timothy. On the 1st of October they were at work, with an apprentice in the mason trade, at the barrack at Rath Cannon. The name of this apprentice was Hickey. In the evening, about five o'clock, they left off their work, and were returning homewards, when eight men with arms rushed upon them. They were fired at; but the fire-arms of the assassins were in such bad condition, that the discharge of their rude musketry had no effect. Laurence, Timothy, and the apprentice, fled in different directions, and escaped. Daniel Mara lost his presence of mind, and instead of taking the same route as the others, ran into the house of a poor widow. He was pursued by the murderers, one of whom got in by a small window, while the others burst through the door, and with circumstances of great savageness put him to death. The intelligence of this event produced still greater sensation than the murder of Chadwick; and was as much the subject of comment as some great political incident, fraught with national consequences in the metropolis. The government lost no time in issuing proclamations, offering a reward of £2000 for information which should bring the assassins to justice. The magnitude of the sum induced a hope that its temptation would be found irresistible to poverty and destitution so great as that which prevails among the class of ordinary malefactors. It was well known that hundreds had cognizance of the offence; and it was concluded that, amongst so numerous a body, the tender of so large a reward could not fail to offer an effectual allurement. Weeks, however, passed over without the communication of intelligence of any kind. Several persons were arrested on suspicion, but were afterwards discharged, as no more than mere conjecture could be adduced against them. Mr. Doherty, the Solicitor-General, proceeded to the county of Tipperary, in order to investigate the transaction; but for a considerable time all his scrutiny was without avail. At length, however, an individual of the name of Thomas Fitzgerald, was committed to gaol upon a charge of highway robbery, and in order to save his life, furnished evidence upon which the government was enabled to pierce into the mysteries of delinquency. The moment Fitzgerald unsealed his lips, a numerous horde of malefactors were taken up, and farther revealments were made under the influence which the love of life, and not of money, exercised over their minds. The assizes came on; and on Monday, the 31st of March, Patrick Lacy and John Walsh were placed at the bar, and to the indictment for the murder of Daniel Mara pleaded not guilty.

The court presented a very imposing spectacle. The whole body of the gentry of Tipperary were assembled in order to witness a trial, on which the security of life and property was to depend. The box which is devoted to the grand jury was thronged with the aristocracy of the county, who manifested an anxiety far stronger than the trial of an ordinary culprit is accustomed to produce. An immense crowd of the peasantry was gathered around the dock. All appeared to feel a deep interest in what was to take place; but it was easy to perceive in the diversity of solicitude which was expressed upon their faces, the degrees of sympathy which connected them with the prisoners at the bar. The more immediate kindred of the malefactors were distinguishable by their profound but still emotion, from those who were engaged in the same extensive organization, and were actuated by a selfish sense that their personal interests were at stake, without having their more tender affections involved in the result. But besides the relatives and confederates of the prisoners, there was a third class amongst the spectators, in which another shade of sympathy was observable. These were the mass of the peasantry, who had no direct concern with the transaction, but whose principles and habits made them well-wishers to the men who had put their lives in peril for what was regarded as the common cause. Through the crowd were dispersed a number of policemen, whose green regimentals, high caps, and glittering bayonets, made them conspicuous, and brought them into contrast with the peasants, by whom they were surrounded. On the table stood the governor of the gaol, with his ponderous keys, which designated his office, and presented to the mind associations which aided the effect of the scene. Mr. Justice Moore appeared in his red robes lined with black, and intimated by his aspect that he anticipated the discharge of a dreadful duty. Beside him was placed the Earl of Kingston, who had come from the neighbouring county of Cork to witness the trial, and whose great possessions gave him a peculiar concern in tracing to their sources the disturbances, which had already a formidable character, and intimated still more ter-able results. His dark and massive countenance, with a shaggy and wild profusion of hair, his bold imperious lip, and large and deeply set eye, and his huge and vigorous frame, rendered him a remarkable objec : without reference to his high rank and station, and to the political part which he had played in the political convulsion of which it is not impossible that he may witness, although he should desire to avert, the return. The prisoners at the bar stood composed and firm. Lacy, the youngest, was dressed with extreme care and neatness. He was a tall handsome young man, with a soft and healthful colour, and a bright and tranquil eye. I was struck by the unusual whiteness of his hands, which were loosely attached to each other. Walsh, his fellow-prisoner and his brother in crime, was a stout, short, and square-built man, with a sturdy look, in which there was more fierceness than in Lacy's countenance; yet the latter was a far more guilty malefactor, and had been engaged in numerous achievements of the kind, whereas Walsh bore an excellent reputation, and obtained from his landlord, Mr. Creagh, the highest testimony to his character. The Solicitor-General, Mr. Doherty, rose to state the case. He appeared more deeply impressed than I have ever seen any public officer, with the responsibility which had devolved upon him; and by his solemn and emphatic manner rendered a narration, which was pregnant with awful facts, so impressive, that during a speech of several hours' continuance he kept attention upon the watch, and scarcely a noise was heard, except when some piece of evidence was announced which surprised the prisoners, and made them give a slight start, in which their astonishment and alarm at the extent of the information of the government were expressed. They preserved their composure while Mr. Doherty was detailing the evidence of Fitzgerald, for they well knew that he had become what is technically called "a stag," and turned informer. Neither were they greatly moved at learning that another traitor of the name of Ryan was to be produced, for rumours had gone abroad that he was to corroborate Fitzgerald. They were well aware that the jury would require more evidence than the coincidence of swearing between two accomplices could supply. It is, indeed, held that one accomplice can sustain another for the purposes of conviction, and that their concurrence is sufficient to warrant a verdict of guilty; still juries are in the habit of demanding some better foundation for their findings, and, before they take life away, exact a confirmation from some pure and unquestionable source. The counsel for the prisoners participated with them in the belief that the crown would not be able to produce any witnesses except accomplices, and listened, therefore, to the details of the murder of Daniel Mara, however minute, without much apprehension for their clients, until Mr. Doherty, turning towards the dock, and lifting up and shaking his hand, pronounced the name of "Kate Costello." It smote the prisoners with dismay. At the time, however, that Mr. Doherty made this announcement, he was himself uncertain, I believe, whether Kate Costello would consent to give the necessary evidence; and there was reason to calculate upon her reluctance to make any disclosure by which the lives of "other people," as the lower orders call their kindred, shou'd be affected.

The statement of Mr. Doherty, which was afterwards fully made out in proof, showed that a wide conspiracy had been framed in order to murder Philip Mara's brothers. Fitzgerald and Lacy, who did not reside in the neighbourhood of Rath Cannon, were sent for by the relatives of Patrick Grace, as it was well known that they were ready for the undertaking of "the job." They received their instructions, and were joined by other assassins. The band proceeded to Rath Cannon in order to execute their purpose, but an accident prevented their victims from coming to the place where they were expected, and the assassination was, in consequence, adjourned for another week. In the interval, however, they did not relent, but, on the contrary, a new supply of murderers was collected, and on Sunday, the 30th of September, the day preceding the murder, they met again in the house of a farmer, of the name of Jack Keogh, who lived beside the barrack where the Maras were at work. Here they were attended by Kate Costello, the fatal witness, by whom their destiny was to be sealed. In the morning of Monday, the 1st of October, they proceeded to an elevation called "the Grove," a hill covered with trees, in which arms had been deposited. This hill overlooked the barrack where the Maras were at work. A party of conspirators joined the chief assassins on this spot; and Kate Costello a servant and near relative of the Keoghs (who were engaged in the murder), again attended them. She brought them food and spirits. From this ambush they remained watching their prey until five o'clock in the afternoon, when it was announced that the Maras were coming down from the scaffolding on which they were raising the barrack. It appeared that the murderers did not know the persons whose lives they were to take away, and that their dress was mentioned as the means of recognition. They advanced to the number of eight; and, as I have already intimated, succeeded in slaying one only of the three brothers. But the most illustrative incident in the whole transaction was not what took place at the murder, but a circumstance which immediately succeeded it. The assassins, with their hands red with blood, proceeded to the house of John Russell. He was a man of a decent aspect and demeanour, above the lower class of peasants in station and habits, was not destitute of education, spoke and reasoned well, and was accounted very orderly and well conducted. One would suppose that he would have closed his doors against the wretches who came reeking from their crime. He gave them welcome, tendered them hospitality, and provided them with food. In the room where they were received by this hoary delinquent, there were two individuals of a very different character and aspect from each other. The one was a girl, Mary Russell, daughter of the proprietor of the house. She was young, and of an exceedingly interesting appearance. Her manners were greatly superior to those of persons of her class, and she was delicate and gentle in her habitual conduct and demeanour. Near her there sat an old woman, in the most advanced stage of life, a kind of Elspeth, who from her age and relationship was an object of respect. The moment the assassins entered, Mary Russell rushed up to them, and with a vehement earnestness exclaimed, "Did you do any good?" They stated, in reply, that one of the Maras was shot; when Peg Russell (the withered hag) who sat moping in the reverie of old age, till her attention was aroused by the sanguinary intelligence, lifted her shrivelled hand, and cried out with a shrill and vehement bitterness, "You might as well not have killed any, since you did not kill them all." Strange and dreadful condition of Ireland! The witness to a murder denounces it. He flies the country. His brothers, for his crime, are doomed to die. The whole population confederate in their death. For weeks the conspiracy is planned, and no relenting spirit interposes in their slaughterous deliberations. The appointed day arrives, and the murder of an innocent man is effected, while the light is still shining, and with the eye of man, which is as little feared as that of God, upon them. The murderers leave the spot where their fellow-creature lies weltering; and instead of being regarded as objects of execration and of horror, are chid by women for their remissness in the work of death, and for the scantiness of the blood which they had poured out. Thus it is that in this unfortunate country not only men are made barbarous, but women are unsexed, and filled

―――― "From the crown to the toe, top-full
Of direst cruelty."

These were the facts which Mr. Doherty stated, and they were established by the evidence. The first witness was Fitzgerald. When he was called, he did not appear on the instant, for he was kept in a room adjoining the court, in order that he might not avail himself of the statement and fit his evidence to it. His testimony was of such importance, and it was known that so much depended upon it, that his arrival was waited for with strong expectation; and in the interval before his appearance on the table, the mind had leisure to form some conjectural picture of what he in all likelihood was. I imagined that he must be some fierce-looking, savage wretch, with baseness and perfidy, intermingled with atrocity, in his brow, and whose meanness would bespeak the informer, as his ferocity would proclaim the assassin. I was deceived. His coming was announced—way was made for him—and I saw leap upon the table, with an air of easy indifference and manly familiarity, a tall, athletic young man, about two or three and twenty, with a countenance as intelligent in expression and symmetrical in feature, as his limbs were vigorous and well-proportioned. His head was perfectly shaped, and surmounted a neck of singular strength and breadth, which lay open and rose out of a chest of unusual massiveness and dilation. His eyes were of deep and brilliant black, full of fire and energy, intermixed with an expression of craft and sagacity. They had a peculiarly watchful look, and indicated a vehemence of character, checked and tempered by a cautious and observant spirit. In his mouth, which disclosed a range of teeth of the finest form and colour, firmness and intrepidity were strongly marked. His hair was short and thick, but his cheek was so fresh and fair, that he scarcely seemed to have ever had any beard. The fellow's dress was calculated to set off his figure. It left his breast almost bare, and the knees of his breeches being open, a great part of his muscular legs appeared without covering, as his stockings did not reach to the knee. He was placed upon the chair appropriated to witnesses, and turned at once to the counsel for the crown, in order to narrate his own achievements as well as those of his associates in depravity. I have never seen a cooler, more precise, methodical and consistent witness. He detailed every circumstance to the minutest point, which had happened during a month's time, with a singular accuracy. So far from manifesting any anxiety to conceal or to excuse his own guilt, he on the contrary set it forth in the blackest colours. He made himself a prominent actor in the business of blood. The life which he led was as strange as it was atrocious. He spent his time in committing outrages at night, and during the day in exacting homage from the peasantry, whom he had inspired with a deep dread of him. He walked through the county in arms, and compelled every peasant to give him bed and board wherever he appeared. In the caprices of his tyranny, he would make persons who chanced to pass him, kneel down and offer him reverence, while he presented his musket at their heads. Yet he was a favourite with the populace, who pardoned the outrages committed on themselves, on account of his readiness to avenge the affronts or the injuries which they suffered from others. Villain as the fellow was, it was not the reward which tempted him to betray his associates. Though £2000 had been offered by government, he gave no information for several months; and when he did give it, it was to save his life, which he had forfeited by a highway robbery, for which he had been arrested. He seemed exceedingly anxious to impress upon the crowd, that though he was a "stag," it was not for gold that he had sold the cause. Life itself was the only bribe that could seduce him from "honour," and even the temptation which the instinctive passion for existence held out to him, was for a long while resisted. Mr. Hatchell cross-examined this formidable witness with extraordinary skill and dexterity, but he was still unable to shake his evidence. It was perfectly consistent and compact, smooth and round, without any point of discrepancy on which the most dexterous practitioner could lay a strong hold. The most unfavourable circumstance to his cross-examiner was his openness and candour. He had an ingenuousness in his atrocity which defied all the ordinary expedients of counsel. Most informers allege that they are influenced by the pure love of justice to betray their accomplices. This statement goes to shake their credit, because they are manifestly perjured in the declaration. Fitzgerald, however, took a very different course. He disclaimed all interest in the cause of justice, and repeatedly stated that he would not have informed, except to rescue himself from the halter which was fastened round his neck. When he left the table, he impressed every man who heard him with a conviction of not only his great criminality, but his extraordinary talents. He was followed by another accomplice, of the name of Ryan, who was less remarkable than Fitzgerald, but whose statement was equally consistent and its parts a adhesive to each other as the more important informer's. They had been left in separate gaols, and had not had any communication, so that t could not be suggested that their evidence was the result of a comparison of notes, and of a conspiracy against the prisoners. This Ryan also alleged that he had informed merely to save his life. These witnesses were succeeded by several, who deposed to minute incidents which went to corroborate the informers; but, notwithstanding that a strong case had been made out by the crown, still the testimony of some untainted witness to the leading fact was requisite, and the counsel for the prosecution felt that on Kate Costello the conviction must still depend. She had not taken any participation in the murder. She could not be regarded as a member of the conspiracy; she was a servant in the house of old John Keogh, but not an agent in the business; and if she confirmed what the witnesses had deposed to, it was obvious that a conviction would ensue; while, upon the other hand, if she was not brought forward, the want of her testimony would produce a directly opposite result. She was called, and a suspense far deeper than the expectation which had preceded the evidence of Fitzgerald was apparent in every face. She did not come, and was again summoned into court. Still Kate Costello did not appear. Repeated requisitions were sent by the Solicitor-General, but without effect; at length every one began to conjecture that she would disappoint and foil the crown; and the friends of the prisoners murmured " that Kate Costello would not turn against her people;" an obvious feeling of satisfaction pervaded the crowd, and the prisoners exhibited a proportionate solicitude in which hope seemed to predominate. Suddenly, however, the chamber door communicating with the room where the witnesses were kept was opened, and one of the most extraordinary figures that ever appeared in that strange theatre, an Irish court of justice, was produced. A withered, diminutive woman, who was unable to support herself, and whose feet gave way at every step, to which she was impelled by her attendants, was seen entering the court, and tottering towards the table. Her face was covered, and it was impossible, for some time after she had been placed on the table, to trace her features; but her hands, which were as white and clammy as a corpse's, and seemed to have undergone the first process of decomposition, shook and shuddered, and a thrill ran through the whole of her miserable and worn-out frame. A few minutes elapsed before her veil was removed; and, when it was, the most ghastly face which I have ever observed was disclosed. Her eyes were quite closed, and the eyelids shrunken as if by the touch of death. The lips were like ashes, and remained open and without movement. Her breathing was scarcely perceptible, and as her head lay on her shoulder, her long black hair all dishevelled, and added to the general character of disordered horror which was expressed in her demeanour. Now that she was produced, she seemed little calculated to be of any use. Mr. Doherty repeatedly addressed himself to her, and entreated her to answer. She seemed unconscious even of the sound of his voice. At length, however, with the aid of water, which was applied to her mouth, and thrown in repeated aspersions over her face, she was in some degree restored, and was able to breathe a few words. An interval of minutes elapsed between every question and answer. Her voice was so low as to be scarcely audible, and was rather an inarticulate whisper, than the utterance of any connected sentence. She was, with a great deal to do, conducted by the examiner through some of the preliminary incidents, and at last was brought to the scene in the Grove where the murderers were assembled. It remained that she should recognise the prisoners. Unless this were done nothing would have been accomplished. The rod with which culprits are identified was put into her hand, and she was desired to stand up, to turn to the dock, and to declare whether she saw in court any of the men whom she had seen in the Grove on the day of the murder. For a considerable time she could not be got to rise from her seat; and when she did, and stood up after a great effort over herself, before she had turned round, but while the rod was trembling in her hand, another extraordinary incident took place. Walsh, one of the prisoners at the bar, cried out with the most vehement gesture,—" O God! you are going to murder me! I'll not stand here to be murdered, for I'm downright murdered, God help me!" This cry, uttered by a man almost frenzied with excitation, drew the attention of the whole court to the prisoner; and the judge inquired of him of what he complained. Walsh then stated with more composure, that it was unfair, while there was nobody in the dock but Lacy and himself, to desire Kate Costello to look at him, for that he was marked out to her where he stood. This was a very just observation, and Judge Moore immediately ordered that other prisoners should be brought from the gaol into the dock, and that Walsh should be shown to Kate Costello in the midst of a crowd. The gaol was at a considerable distance, and a good deal of time was consumed in complying with the directions of the judge. Kate Costello sank down again upon her chair, and in the interval before the arrival of the other prisoners we engaged in conjectures as to the likelihood of Walsh being identified. She had never seen him, except at the Grove, and it was possible that she might not remember him. In that event his life was safe. At last the other prisoners were introduced into the dock. The sound of their fetters as they entered the court, and the grounding of the soldiers' muskets on the pavement, echoed through the court. It was now four o'clock in the morning; the candles were almost wasted to their sockets, and a dim and uncertain light was diffused through the court. Haggardness sat upon the spectators, and yet no weariness or exhaustion appeared. The frightful interest of the scene preserved the mind from fatigue. The dock was crowded with malefactors, and brought as they were in order that guilt of all kinds should be confused and blended, they exhibited a most singular spectacle. This assemblage of human beings laden with chains was, perhaps, more melancholy from the contrast which they presented between their condition and their aspect. Even the pale light which glimmered through the court did not prevent their cheeks from looking ruddy and healthful. They had been awakened in their lonely cells in order to be produced, and, as they were not aware of the object of arraying them together, there was some surprise mixed with fear in their looks. I could not help whispering to myself as I surveyed them, "what a noble and fine race of men are here, and how much have they to answer for, who, by degrading, have demorafised such a people!" The desire of Walsh having been complied with, the witness was called upon a second time to place the rod upon his head. She rose again, and turned round, holding the fatal wand. There was a deep silence through the court; the face of Walsh exhibited the most intense anxiety, as the eyes of Kate Costello rested upon the place where he stood. She appeared at first not to recognise him, and the rod hung loosely in her hand. I thought, as I saw her eyes traversing the assemblage of malefactors, that she either did not know him, or would affect not to remember him. At last, however, she raised the rod, and stretched it forth, but before it was laid on the devoted head, a female voice exclaimed, "Oh, Kate!" This cry, which issued from the crowd, and was probably the exclamation of some relative of the Keoghs, whose destiny depended on that of Walsh, thrilled the witness to the core. She felt the adjuration in the recesses of her being. After a shudder, she collected herself again, and advanced towards the dock. She raised the rod a second time, and having laid it on the head of Walsh, who gave himself up as lost the moment it touched him, she sank back into her chair. The feeling which had filled the heart of every spectator here found a vent, and a deep murmur was heard through the whole court, mingled with sounds of stifled execration from the mass of the people in the back-ground. Lacy also was dentified; and here it may be said that the trial closed. Walsh, who, while he entertained any hope, had been almost convulsed with agitaion, resumed his original composure. He took no farther interest in he proceeding, except when his landlord gave him a high character for ntegrity and good conduct; and this commendation he seemed rather o consider as a sort of bequest which he should leave to his kindred, han as the means of saving his life. It is unnecessary almost to add, hat the prisoners were found guilty.

Kate Costello, whose evidence was of such importance to the crown, ad acted as a species of menial in the house of old John Keogh, but as a near relation of her master. It is not uncommon among the ower orders to introduce some dependant relative into the family, who oes through tasks of usefulness which are quite free from degradation, id is at the same time treated, to a great extent, as an equal. Kate ostello sat down with old Jack Keogh and his sons at their meals, and as accounted one of themselves. The most implicit trust was placed her; and on one of the assassins observing "that Kate Costello could ing them all," another observed, "that there was no fear of Kate." or would Kate ever have betrayed the men who had placed their con- 'ence in her from any mercenary motives. Fitzgerald had stated that e had been at "the Grove" in the morning of the day on which the irder was committed, and that she could confirm his testimony. She s in consequence arrested, and was told that she should be hanged less she disclosed the truth. Terror extorted from her the reveal- nts which were turned to such account. When examined as a wit- s on the trial of Lacy and of Walsh, her agitation did not arise from regard for them, but from her consciousness that if they were con- ted her own relatives and benefactors must share in their fate. The

H

trial of Patrick and John Keogh came on upon Saturday, the 5th of April, some days after the conviction of Lacy and of Walsh, who had been executed in the interval. The trial of the Keoghs was postponed at the instance of the prisoners, but it was understood that the crown had no objection to the delay, as great difficulty was supposed to have arisen in persuading Kate Costello to give completion to the useful work in which she had engaged. It was said that the friends of the Keoghs had got access to her, and that she had refused to come forward against "her people." It was also rumoured that she had entertained an attachment for John Keogh, and although he had wronged her, and she had suffered severe detriment from their criminal connexion, that she loved him still, and would not take his life away. There was, therefore, enough of doubt incidental to the trial of the Keoghs to give it the interest of uncertainty; and, however fatal the omen which the conviction of their brother conspirators held out, still it was supposed that Kate Costello would recoil from her terrible task. The court was as much crowded as it had been on the first trial, upon the morning on which the two Keoghs were put at the bar. They were more immediate agents in the assassination. It had been in a great measure planned, as well as executed by them; and there was a farther circumstance of aggravation in their having been in habits of intimacy with the deceased. Their appearance struck every spectator as in strange anomaly with their misdeeds. They both seemed to be farmers of the most respectable class. Patrick, the younger, was perfectly well clad. He had a blue coat and white waistcoat, of the best materials used by the peasantry; a black silk handkerchief was carefully knotted on his neck. He was lower in stature, and of less athletic proportions than his brother John, but had a more determined and resolute physiognomy. He looked alert, quick, and active. The other was of gigantic stature, and of immense width of shoulder and strength of limb. He rose beyond every man in court, and towered in the dock. His dress was not as neatly arranged as his brother's, and his neck was without covering, which served to exhibit the hugeness of his proportions. He looked in the vigour of powerful manhood. His face was ruddy and blooming, and was quite destitute of all darkness and malevolence of expression. There was perhaps too much fulness about the lips, and some traces of savageness, as well as of voluptuousness, might have been detected by a minute physiognomist in their exuberance; but the bright blue of his mild and intelligent eyes counterbalanced this evil indication. The aspect of these two young men was greatly calculated to excite interest; but there was another object in court which was even more deserving of attention. On the left hand of his two sons, and just near the youngest of them, sat an old man, whose head was covered with a profusion of gray hairs, and who, although evidently greatly advanced in years, was of a hale and healthful aspect. I did not notice him at first, but in the course of the trial, the glare which his eye gradually acquired, and the passing of all colour from his cheek, as the fate of his sons grew to certainty, attracted my observation, and I learned on inquiry, what I had readily conjectured, that he was the father of the prisoners at the bar

ord during the fifteen or sixteen hours that he
ce upon the dreadful scene which was going on
pearance of Kate Costello herself, whom he had
rished, scarcely seemed to move him from his ter-
he was, as on the former occasion, the pivot of the
cipations that she would not give evidence "against
od" were wholly groundless, for on her second
is she enacted her part with much more firmness
She had before kept her eyes almost closed, but
ixed them upon the counsel, and exhibited great
ness in their expression, and watched the cross-
at wariness and dexterity. I was greatly surprised
can only refer it to the spirit of determination
the first difficulty on the former trial had pro-
pery step in blood had been taken, and she trod
the second. Whatever may have been the cause,
d little compunction in bringing her cousins to
od on the head of her relative and supposed para-
:. At an early hour on Sunday morning the ver-
ught in. The prisoners at the bar received it
turned deadly pale. The change in John Keogh
a in the morning of Saturday he stood blooming
·, and was now as white as a shroud. The judge
as the morning of Easter Sunday, (which is com-
surrection of the dead,) he should not then pro-
them. They cried out, " A long day, a long day,
: same time begged that their bodies might be
This prayer was uttered with a sound resembling
meral, and accompanied with a most pathetic ges-
ing themselves with a sort of oscillation up and
s thrown back, striking their hands, with the fin-
inst their breasts, in the manner which Roman
g "The Confiteor." The reference which they
Irew my attention to the miserable old man. Two
i, had attended him in court, and when his sons,
nd guilty, were about to be removed, he was lifted
i he was with difficulty sustained, and was brought
e wanted to embrace John Keogh, and stretched
him. The latter, whose manliness now forsook
ron spikes to his full length, got the old man into
his tears ran down his face, pressed him long and
They were, at length, separated, and the sons
cells appointed for the condemned. The judge
e court was gradually cleared. Still the father of
ed between his two attendants nearly insensible.
it to depart. I followed him out. It was a dark
he wind beat full against him, and made him tot-
His attendants addressed to him some words of
with religion, (for these people are, with all their

crimes, not destitute of religious impressions,) but the old man only answered them with his moans. He said nothing articulate, but during all the way to the obscure cellar into which they led him, continued moaning as he went. It was not, I trust, a mere love of the excitement which arises from the contemplation of scenes in which the passions are brought out, that made me watch this scene of human misery. I may say, without affectation, that I was (as who would not have been?) profoundly moved by what I saw; and when I beheld this forlorn and desolate man descend into a cellar, which was lighted by a feeble candle, and saw him fall upon his knees in helplessness, while his attendants gave way to sorrow, I could not restrain my own tears.

The scenes of misery did not stop here. Old John Russell pleaded guilty. He had two sons, lads of fifteen or sixteen, and, in the hope of saving them, acknowledged his crime at the bar; " Let them," he said, in the gaol where I saw him, " let them put me on the trap if they like, but let them spare the boys."

I shall not proceed farther in the detail of these dreadful incidents. There were many other trials at the assizes, in which terrible disclosures of barbarity took place. For three weeks the two judges were unremittingly employed in trying cases of dreadful atrocity, and in almost every instance the perpetrators of crimes the most detestable, were persons whose general moral conduct stood in a wonderful contrast with their isolated acts of depravity. Almost every offence was connected with the great agrarian organization which prevails through the county. It must be acknowledged that, terrible as the misdeeds of the Tipperary peasantry must upon all hands be admitted to be, yet, in general, there was none of the meanness and turpitude observable in their enormities which characterise the crimes that are disclosed at an English assize. There were scarcely any examples of murder committed for mere gain. It seemed to be a point of honour with the malefactors to take blood, and to spurn at money. Almost every offence was committed in carrying a system into effect, and the victims who were sacrificed were considered by their immolators as offered up, upon a justifiable principle of necessary extermination. These are assuredly important facts, and after having contemplated these moral phenomena, it becomes a duty to inquire into the causes from which these marvellous atrocities derive their origin. But before I proceed to suggest what I conceive to be the sources of a condition so disastrous, it is not inappropriate to inquire how long the lower orders in Ireland have been habituated to these terrible practices, and to look back to the period at which they may be considered to have had their origin. If these crimes were of a novel character, and had a recent existence, that circumstance would afford strong grounds for concluding that temporary expedients, and the vigorous administration of the law applied to the suppression of local and ephemeral disturbances, would be of avail. But if we find that it is not now, or within these few years, that these symptoms of demoralisation have appeared, it is then reasonable to conclude that there must be some essential vice, some radical imperfection in the general system by which the country is governed, and it is necessary to ascertain what the extent and root of the evil is, before any effectual remedy can be discovered for its cure. This is a subject of paramount interest, and its importance will justify the writer of this article, after a detail of the extraordinary incidents which he has narrated, in taking a rapid retrospect of antecedent events, of which recent transactions may be reasonably accounted the sequel. The first and leading feature in the disturbances and atrocities of Tipperary is, that they are of an old date, and have been, for much more than half a century, of uninterrupted continuance. Arthur Young travelled in Ireland in the years 1776, 1777, and 1778. His excellent book is entitled, " A Tour in Ireland, with general Observations on the Present State of that Kingdom." Although the professed object of Arthur Young in visiting Ireland was to ascertain the condition of its agriculture, and a great portion of his work turns upon that subject, yet he has also investigated its political condition, and pointed out what he conceived to be the chief evils by which the country was afflicted, and the mode of removing them. He adverts particularly to the state of the peasantry in the South of Ireland, and it is well worthy of remark that the outrages which are now in daily commission, were of exactly the same character as the atrocities which were perpetrated by the Whiteboys (as the insurgents were called) in 1760. "The Whiteboys," says Arthur Young, in page 75 of the quarto edition, "began in Tipperary. It was a common practice with them to go in parties about the country, swearing many to be true to them, and forcing them to join by menaces which they very often carried into execution. At last they set up to be general redressers of grievances—punished all obnoxious persons who advanced the value of lands, or held farms over their head; and, having taken the administration of justice into their own hands, were not very exact in the distribution of it. They forced masters to release their apprentices, carried off the daughters of rich farmers, ravished them into marriages, they levied sums of money on the middling and lower farmers, in order to support their cause in defending prosecutions against them, and many of them subsisted without work, supported by these prosecutions. Sometimes they committed considerable robberies, breaking into houses and taking money under pretence of redressing grievances. In the course of these outrages they burned several houses, and destroyed the whole substance of those obnoxious to them. The barbarities they committed were shocking. One of their usual punishments, and by no means the most severe, was taking people out of their beds, carrying them naked in winter on horseback for some distance, and burying them up to their chin in a hole with briers, not forgetting to cut off one of their ears." Arthur Young goes on to say that the government had not succeeded in discovering any radical cure. It will scarcely be disputed that the Whiteboyism of 1760 corresponds with that of 1828; and if, when Arthur Young wrote his valuable book, the government had not discovered any "radical cure," it will scarcely be suggested that any remedy has since that time been devised. From the period at which these outrages commenced, the evil has continued in rapid augmentation. Every expedient which legislative ingenuity could

invent has been tried. All that the terrors of the law could accomplish
has been put into experiment without avail. Special commissioners and
special delegations of counsel have been almost annually despatched into
the disturbed districts, and crime appears to have only undergone a
pruning, while its roots remained untouched. Mr. Doherty is not the first
Solicitor-General who has been despatched by government for the purpose of awing the peasantry into their duty. The present Chief Justice
of the King's Bench (Charles Kendal Bushe), when filling Mr. Doherty's
office, was sent upon the same painful errand, and after having been
equally successful in procuring the conviction of malefactors, and having brandished the naked sword of justice with as puissant an arm, new
atrocities have almost immediately afterwards broken forth, and furnished new occasions for the exercise of his commanding eloquence. It
is reasonable to presume that the recent executions at Clonmel will not
be attended with any more permanently useful consequences, and symptoms are already beginning to re-appear, which may well induce an
apprehension that before much time shall go by, the law officers of the
crown will have to go through the same terrible routine of prosecution.
It is said, indeed, that now something effectual has been done, and that
the gaol and the gibbet there have given a lesson that will not be speedily
forgotten. How often has the same thing been said when the scaffold
was strewed with the same heaps of the dead! How often have the
prophets of tranquillity been falsified by the event! If the crimes which,
ever since the year 1760, have been uninterruptedly committed, and
have followed in such a rapid and tumultuous succession, had been only
of occasional occurrence, it would be reasonable to conclude that the
terrors of the law could repress them. But it is manifest that the
system of atrocity does not depend upon causes merely ephemeral, and
cannot, therefore, be under the operation of temporary checks. We
have not merely witnessed sudden inundations which, after a rapid desolation, have suddenly subsided; we behold a stream as deep as it is dark,
which indicates, by its continuous current, that it is derived from an
unfailing fountain, and which, however augmented by the contribution
of other springs of bitterness, must be indebted for its main supply to
some abundant and distant source. Where then is the well-head to be
found ? Where are we to seek the origin of the evils, which are of such
a character that they carry with them the clearest evidence that their
causes must be as enduring as themselves? It may at first view, and
to any man who is not well acquainted with the moral feelings and
habits of the great body of the population of Ireland, seem a paradoxical
proposition that the laws which affect the Roman Catholics furnish a
clue, by which, however complicated the mazes may be which constitute
the labyrinth of calamity, it will not be difficult to trace our way. It
may be asked, with a great appearance of plausibility (and indeed it is
often inquired), what possible effect the exclusion of a few Roman
Catholic gentlemen from parliament, and of still fewer Roman Catholic
barristers from the bench, can produce in deteriorating the moral habits
of the people? This, however, is not the true view of the matter. The

exclusion of Roman Catholics from office is one of the results of the penal code, but it is a sophism to suggest that it is the sum total of the law itself, and that the whole of it might be resolved into that single proposition. The just mode of presenting the question would be this: " What effect does the penal code produce by separating the higher and the lower orders from each other? Before I suggest any reasons of my own, it may be judicious to refer to the same writer, from whom I have extracted a description of the state of the peasantry, with which its present condition singularly corresponds. The authority of Arthur Young is of great value, because his opinions were not in the least degree influenced by those passions which are almost inseparable from every native of Ireland. He was an Englishman—had no share in the factious animosities by which this country is divided—he had a cool, deliberate, and scientific mind—was a sober thinker, and a deep scrutinizer into the frame and constitution of society, and was entirely free from all tendency to extravagance in speculation, either political or religious. Arthur Young's book consists of two parts. In the first he gives a minute account of what he saw in Ireland, and in the second, under a series of chapters, one of which is appropriately entitled " Oppression," he states what he conceives to be the causes of the lamentable condition of the people. Having prefixed this title of " oppression" to the 29th page of the second part of his book, he says, " The landlord of an Irish estate inhabited by Roman Catholics, is a sort of despot, who yields obedience in whatever concerns the poor to no law, but his own will. To discover what the liberty of a people is, we must live amongst them, and not look for it in the statutes of the realm: the language of written law may be that of liberty, but the situation of the poor may speak no language but that of slavery. There is too much of this contradiction in Ireland; a long series of oppression, aided by many very ill-judged laws, has brought landlords into a habit of exerting a very lofty superiority, and their vassals into that of a most unlimited submission— speaking a language that is despised, professing a religion that is abhorred, and being disarmed, the poor find themselves, in many cases, slaves, even in the bosom of written liberty. * * * * The abominable distinction of religion, united with the oppressive conduct of the little country gentlemen, or rather vermin of the kingdom, who were never out of it, altogether bear still very heavy on the poor people, and subject them to situations more mortifying than we ever behold in England." In the next page after these preliminary observations, this same writer (who said in vain fifty years ago, what since that time so many eminent men have been in vain repeating) points out more immediately the causes of the crimes committed by the peasantry, which he distinctly refers to the distinctions of religion. " The proper distinction in all the discontents of the people is into Protestant and Catholic. The Whiteboys being labouring Catholics, met with all those oppressions I have described, and would probably have continued in full submission, had not very severe treatment blown up the flame of resistance. The atrocious acts they were guilty of made them the objects of general indignation: acts were passed for their punishment, which seemed calculated for the meridian of Barbary: it is manifest that the gentlemen of Ireland never thought of a radical cure, from overlooking the real cause of the disease, which, in fact, lay in themselves, and not in the wretches they doomed to the gallows. Let them change their own conduct entirely, and the poor will not long riot. Treat them like men, who ought to be free as yourselves: put an end to that system of religious persecution, which for seventy years has divided the kingdom against itself. In these two things lies the cure of insurrection—perform them completely, and you will have an affectionate poor, instead of oppressed and discontented vassals; a better treatment of the poor in Ireland is a very material point to the welfare of the whole British empire. Events may happen which may convince us fatally of this truth. If not, oppression would have broken all the spirit and resentment of men. By what policy the government of England can, for so many years, have permitted such an absurd system to be matured in Ireland, is beyond the power of plain sense to discover." Arthur Young may be wrong in his inference, (I do not think that he is,) but, be he right or wrong, I have succeeded in establishing that he, whose evidence was most dispassionate and impartial, referred the agrarian barbarities of the lower orders to the oppression of the Roman Catholics. But the passage which I have cited is not the strongest. The seventh section of his work is entitled "Religion." After saying that "the domineering aristocracy of five hundred thousand Protestants, feel the sweets of having two millions of slaves," (the Roman Catholic body was then not one-third of what the penal code has since made it,) he observes, "the disturbances of the Whiteboys which lasted ten years, (what would he now say of their duration?) in spite of every exertion of legal power, were, in many circumstances, very remarkable, and in none more so than in the surprising intelligence among the insurgents, wherever found. It was universal, and almost instantaneous. The numerous bodies of them, at whatever distance from each other, seemed animated by one zeal, and not a single instance was known, in that long course of time, of a single individual betraying the cause. The severest threats and the most splendid promises of reward had no other effect than to draw closer the bonds which cemented a multitude to all appearance so desultory. It was then evident that the iron hand of oppression had been far enough from securing the obedience, or crushing the spirit of the people; and all reflecting men, who consider the value of religious liberty, will wish it may never have that effect—will trust in the wisdom of Almighty God, for teaching man to respect even those prejudices of his brethren, that are imbibed as sacred rights, even from earliest infancy; that by dear-bought experience of the futility and ruin of the attempt, the persecuting spirit may cease, and toleration establish that harmony and security which five score years' experience has told us, is not to be purchased at the expense of humanity."

This is strong language, and was used by a man who had no connecting sympathy of interest, of religion, or of nationality with Ireland. So unequivocal an opinion, expressed by a person of such authority, and whose credit is not affected by any imaginable circumstance, must be admitted to have great weight, even if there was a difficulty in perceiving the grounds on which that opinion rested. But there is little or none. The law divides the Protestant proprietor from the Catholic tiller of the soil, and generates a feeling of tyrannical domination in the one, and of hatred and distrust in the other. The Irish peasant is not separated from his landlord by the ordinary demarcations of society. Another barrier is erected, and, as if the poor and the rich were not already sufficiently apart, religion is raised as an additional boundary between them. The operation of the feelings, consequent on this division, is stronger in the county of Tipperary than elsewhere. It is a peculiarly Cromwellian district, or, in other words, the holy warriors of the Protector chose it as their land of peculiar promise, and selected it as a favourite object of confiscation. The lower orders have good memories. There is scarce a peasant, who, as he passes the road, will not point to the splendid mansions of the aristocracy, embowered in groves, or rising upon fertile elevations, and tell you the name of the pious Corporal, from whom the present proprietors derive a title which, even at this day, appears to be of a modern origin. These reminiscences are of a most injurious tendency. But, after all, it is the system of religious separation which nurtures the passions of the peasantry with these pernicious recollections. They are not permitted to forget that Protestantism is stamped upon every institution in the country, and their own sunderance from the privileged class is perpetually brought to their minds. Judges, sheriffs, magistrates, crown counsel, law officers,—all are Protestant. The very sight of a court of justice reminds them of the degradations attached to their religion, by presenting them with the ocular proof of the advantages and honours which belong to the legal creed. It is not, therefore, wonderful that they should feel themselves a branded cast; that they should have a consciousness that they belong to a debased and inferior community ; and having no confidence in the upper classes, and no reliance in the sectarian administration of the law, that they should establish a code of barbarous legislation among themselves, and have recourse to what Lord Bacon calls " the wild justice" of revenge. A change of system would not perhaps produce immediate effects upon the character of the people : but I believe that its results would be much more speedy than is generally imagined. At all events, the experiment of conciliation is worth the trial. Every other expedient has been resorted to, and has wholly failed. It remains that the legislature, after exhausting all other means of tranquillising Ireland, should, upon a mere chance of success, adopt the remedy which has at least the sanction of illustrious names for its recommendation. The union of the two great classes of the people in Ireland, in other words, the emancipation of the Roman Catholics, is in this view not only recommended by motives of policy, but of humanity ; for who that has witnessed the scenes which I have (perhaps at too much length) detailed in these pages, can fail to feel that, if the demoralization of the people arises from bad government, the men who from feelings of partisanship persevere in that system of misrule, will have to render a terrible account?

Note.—These observations were published a year before Catholic emancipation was carried; but the system of practical ascendancy was long continued. Lord Normanby, the benefactor of Ireland, introduced a system of government, whose object was to give effect to a measure of which the principle had not been carried out. An almost total cessation of crime ensued. Unfortunately, the people have relapsed into the commission of outrages whose cause it is not difficult to surmise.]

REPEAL OF THE UNION.

SPEECH IN THE HOUSE OF COMMONS ON THE 25TH OF APRIL, 1834.

The speech just spoken by the member for the county of Wexford has been received with acclamations, and if it were less able, the acclamation would not, perhaps, have been less enthusiastic, or less loud. Fortunate advocate, whose success depends as much at least on the predilections of the tribunal, as upon the merits of the cause! I have heard my honourable friend when he exhibited fully as much eloquence as upon this occasion, but never saw him received with such cordiality at the outset, or such rapture at the termination of any of his former harangues. With what clearness of exposition, with what irresistible force, for example, did he demand justice for the Irish people after the massacre of Newtownbarry! He presented a picture of that atrocious transaction, compared to which, his accounts of the fatal effects of agitation are weak and inefficient indeed. The incidents which he described, and the picturesque diction in which his narrative was conveyed, ought to have produced a great impression upon his auditory yet how coldly did all that he then urged fall upon his hearers. You were then frigid and apathetic; you are now, in the highest degree, susceptible and alive to the accomplishments of the member for the county of Wexford. My honourable friend is now a devoted and unqualified antagonist of repeal. Was it always thus? Did he not say—that if justice was not done to Ireland on the tithe question, he should, however reluctantly, become an advocate for repeal.

Mr. LAMBERT.—I do not recollect having ever said so.

Mr. SHEIL.—At all events, he declared that the denial of justice with respect to the Irish Church, would have the effect of inducing the great mass of the population to embrace repeal. Whether he spoke of himself, or of the country, putting personal considerations out of view, the inference is nearly the same. He expressed a desire when he began, that the member for Dublin should be in attendance while he reviewed his conduct. The wish was gratified. The member for Dublin entered the house, (which the honourable member for the county of Wexford never would have entered but for the member for Dublin,) and I own that I did not think that he had any cause to wince under the chastisement applied to him by the hon. member. But how, after all, are the real merits of this great question affected by these resentful references to incidents which have taken place outside this house? Is this the proper field for encounter between two honourable gentlemen? The member for the county of Wexford may have been wronged;—language may have been applied to him by the member for Dublin with regard to his conduct on the Coercion Bill, which deserves condemnation. I regret it; but let him bear in mind that the obligation conferred upon him by the member for Dublin, ought to outweigh every jury. Though he has been smitten in the face, let him remember at the hand that struck him, struck his fetters off. The honourable member for Wexford has adverted to the remuneration, which the people of Ireland have bestowed upon the member for Dublin. He should have considered the extent of the service, before he derided the reward. For thirty years the member for Dublin has toiled in the cause of Ireland : he has been mainly instrumental in achieving the liberty of his fellow-countrymen ; he has relinquished great emoluments by abstracting himself from his profession, and by making a dedication of his faculties to the interests of his country :—Ireland felt that it behove her to prove her gratitude for that freedom, which is above all price.

I turn from these painful topics to the subject presented to our deliberation. Not a word has as yet been said upon the amendment Many may conceive that the original proposition ought to be rejected, and yet will, I hope, pause before they adopt the sentiments contained in the address. The question before the house is, not merely whether a committee should be granted for the purpose of investigating a question on which the Secretary for the Treasury thought it not inexpedient to deliver an harangue, of which the length must be admitted to be unsurpassed, but whether we shall vote an address, which not only contains an approval of the Union, but states besides, that the policy adopted with respect to Ireland has been judicious, wise, and just. Observe what it is you are called upon to place on record ; mark the following paragraph :—

" We humbly represent to your Majesty that the Imperial Parliament have taken the affairs of Ireland into their most serious consideration, and that various salutary laws have been enacted since the Union for the advancement of the most important interests of Ireland, and of the empire at large."

What other object can there be for this assertion, but to declare that the course pursued by parliament has been such, as not to make it requisite that any change should be adopted. Suppose that in the year 1827, when Mr. Canning was Prime Minister, and so many members of the present cabinet were associated with him, the noble lord, the Paymaster of the Forces had introduced the question of parliamentary reform, which Mr. Canning declared he would resist,—not "to the death," but to the last moment of his life, and that the Conservative party had introduced an address against reform similar to this address against repeal, would not all the arguments advanced in support of this address have applied as forcibly to that which I have hypothetically suggested ? The Conservative address against reform might have run thus :—" We, your Majesty's most dutiful and loyal subjects, the Commons in parliament assembled, feel it our duty humbly to approach your Majesty's throne, to record, in the most solemn manner, our fixed determination to maintain, unimpaired and undisturbed, the constitution of parliament—(I substitute it for ' legislative union'), which we consider to be essential to the strength and stability of the empire, to the continuance of the connexion between the two countries, and to the peace, and security and happiness of all classes of your Majesty's subjects. In expressing to your Majesty our resolution to maintain the constitution inviolate, we humbly beg leave to assure your Majesty, that we shall persevere in applying our best attention to the removal of all just causes of complaint, and to the promotion of all well-considered measures of improvement."

Had such an address been proposed, how would it have been denounced? Would it not have been considered as amounting to a sanction of all the policy pursued by the boroughmongering administrations? In that light it would, beyond doubt, have been represented by that Whig party, which, after having passed their political lives in reprobating the conduct of their opponents while they were in power, call on the house to pronounce upon the measures of the last thirty-four years an unqualified panegyric. I shall, in the course of the observations I mean to make, revert to this view of the amendment, which I have only suggested, in order that the house might see exactly what it was called on to do, and the extent of the proposition which has been made by the government. I return to the original motion. The member for Dublin demands a committee to inquire into the results of the Union, and the probable consequences of its continuance. I should at once grapple with the argument derived from the alleged likelihood of separation, but that it belongs to the prophetic part of the case ;—it is better to deal with facts before we indulge in predictions ; and, before we look forward, to look back. Before the year 1782, Ireland lay prostrate. The foot of England was upon her neck, and was applied with the pressure which, in such an attitude, is habitually employed. Why do I revert to a period so remote? I call up your ancestors in order to show you that you have preserved a resemblance to them—in the pictures of your predecessors a national likeness may be traced. Between an Irish Parliament under the direct control of an English, and an Imperial Parliament, in which Irish members are overwhelmed by English majorities, there is some distinction, but not much difference to be found. Was Ireland justified in demanding her independence? Few will deny it. Yet its advocates were aspersed with contumelies as foul as is now poured from high places on the champions of repeal.

The tract of Molyneux was burned by order of the British House of Commons, and the office was performed by an appropriate representative of the feelings of Englishmen towards the sister country. This proposition was treated as a wretched absurdity, or a base expedient. It was denounced as impracticable, events converted the impossibility into fact. When the Irish Parliament had achieved its independence, how did it employ the noble instrument which it had so gloriously won? Free trade, the independence of the judges, the Habeas Corpus Act, concessions to the Roman Catholics, were the measures associated with independence. The Secretary to the Treasury, Mr. Spring Rice, has cited the authority of Mr. Grattan, for the purpose of showing that Mr. Grattan condemned the proceedings of the Irish Parliament from the year 1782, up to the time of the Union. I could cite the authority of Mr. Grattan on the other side ; but I will not occupy the time of the house with prolixities of this sort, nor refer to a multitude of authorities. To me, however, I cannot refrain from adverting, that of Edmund Burke, because it must weigh beyond every other, in the mind of the Secretary for the Treasury, as Edmund Burke considered England his adopted, and (he had good cause to do so) his dearer country. It is not wonderful that Edmund Burke should have given a preference to England; " where a man hath his treasure, there also he hath his heart." I shall not molest the house with long extracts; it is enough to refer to Edmund Burke's speech on conciliation with America, and to his letter to Sir Hercules Langrishe, for glowing descriptions of the rapid and wide advances made by Ireland after 1782. The course adopted by the government is singular,—they tell us in the first place, that all reference to events before the Union is inapplicable, and that our encomiums on the Irish Parliament are out of place, and afterwards they themselves resort to every petty anecdote connected with our parliament, and disinter from oblivion every derogatory circumstance, to make out a case against us. The argument is this:—the Irish Parliament was often under the influence of the populace—its proceedings were interrupted and controlled, and therefore it ought not to exist. Might I not say, Cromwell broke into this house, bade a rude soldier take away " this bauble" on which I now lay my hand, therefore there ought not to be a House of Commons! The reasoning against the Irish Parliament is the same. The Secretary for the Treasury has quoted every bad act passed by the Irish—he has quoted every good one passed by an Imperial Parliament. Why did he omit any the least mention of any one of the beneficial measures enacted by the parliament of his country? I should be justified in opening the Irish Statutes, and going through the entire of its legislation. But this would be a tedious process. To one part only of the legislation of the Irish Parliament shall I call the attention of the house. Many a time has it been said that the Irish Parliament, left to itself, would never carry the Roman Catholic Question. Let us not judge by idle conjectures of what it was probable it would have done, but by a reference to what it actually did do. What was the conduct with respect to the Roman Catholics of the Irish and the English Parliaments at the same time? The English Parliament made some concessions, but excluded Roman Catholics from the Universities, from corporations, from the bench of magisterial justice, from grand juries, from petty juries, and from the hustings. What, on the other hand, was the conduct of the Irish Parliament? It admitted Roman Catholics to the Universities, to corporations, to the magisterial bench, to the grand jury box, to the petty jury, and, above and gloriously paramount to all, it conferred upon them the elective franchise —furnished the fulcrum by which Ireland placed a mighty lever— gave the weapon with which the victory of peace was achieved—gave that which, being conceded, the noble residue of freedom could not be withheld. I shall, by and by, have occasion to compare the conduct of the Imperial Parliament with that of the Irish Parliament, with regard to the Catholic Question.

We are told that an Irish Parliament would be favourable to separation. The object of the rebellion was separation. How did the Irish Parliament act? If it co-operated with the conspirators, or connived at their project, there would be some plausibility in the suggestion. But not only was there no party with a leaning to the insurgents, but there was not a man in that assembly who did not concur in the suppression of the revolt; and it was remarkable that the men who were most devoted to Irish independence, were equally attached to connexion with this country. Never did there exist a body which displayed a mo.e genuine and enthusiastic loyalty; and shall that great fact be held in no account? France saw in the Irish Parliament a representative of the intelligence of Ireland, whose moral influence co-operated with military power, and who rallied the nation round the standard of the King, by inculcating the great principle, that allegiance is but a modification of patriotism, and fidelity to our institutions a part of the love of country. Pass to the Union. Of the infamy of the means by which it was carried, it is unnecessary to say much, because the fact is undisputed. But it is said—"of what consequence are the means? *Factum valet."* Convenient aphorism! By a judicious application of this canon in the Machiavelian casuistry, there is no atrocity which may not be turned to account. Lord Grey would not—God forbid!—have ever robbed Ireland of her legislature, but he has no objection to become receiver of her spoliated rights. But let us put the ethics of the question, except so far as they are connected with expediency, out of the case; yet have they no connexion with expediency? The means have mingled with the effects, because they have generated the feelings which would more than vitiate any good which the Union could produce. From a source so foul, the Irish people think that nothing pure can be derived. They think that no matter over what time it may pass, the current can never run clear. They look back with detestation to the venality and the turpitude by which their legislature was bartered—that which is an object of national abhorrence must be prolific of many evils, and barren of all good. Some one said that a fault was worse than a crime; a crime seldom fails to be a fault. The memory of the delinquency makes it a mistake. The consideration of the instrumentality by which the Union was accomplished is not irrelevant; but let us consider the more direct and palpable effects of the measure. They are divisible into two heads, —the fiscal and political. The Secretary for the Treasury has appealed to a great number of financial facts, to sustain the proposition that the Union has produced the prosperity of Ireland. In 1796 Edmund Burke published his letters on the Regicide Peace. In one of them, like the Secretary for the Treasury, he combines rhetoric and arithmetic together. He refers to the exports and imports, to the official returns respecting the revenue, the customs, taxes, excise, manufactures, and tonnage, and all the other materials of fiscal calculation. He concludes that nothing is so useful as war, and calls on England to fight on. But if the inference of Edmund Burke were wrong, is the inference of the member for Cambridge right? Look at Canada. Its prosperity may be demonstrated. Why should not Ireland prosper with a local government as well as Canada? If you effected a Union with Canada, would you not lose the country—would you keep it for three years? The Secretary for the Treasury says, that Ireland prospers because she enjoys a free trade. In the event of repeal would there not be a free trade? Is it not the interest of both countries that there should not be any commercial restrictions? Ireland consumes £7,000,000 of your manufactures—you consume several millions of her produce. How would it be your interest to restrict her trade, when she affords you your best, nearest, and safest market? Are not the people of England clamouring for a free trade with France? Would they refuse it to Ireland? I deny—(and I know it is the sentiment of the great body of my countrymen)—that a repeal of the Union would produce an abolition of the free trade between the two countries. Will the Vice-President of the Board of Trade assert that repeal ought to lead to a cessation of free trade between Ireland and England, when he maintains the utility of free trade with all the world. But, then, it is said that, in consequence of the Union, Ireland has the exclusive market of England. If that has hitherto been the case, how long will you pledge yourselves that this advantage shall continue? Will you pledge yourselves that the present corn laws shall stand? Will the English manufacturer concur in such a pledge? and if he will not, what becomes of this argument? Place the integrity of the empire in one scale, and a quartern loaf in the other, and on which side, in the mind of a political economist, will the preponderancy be found? But after all, is it here, in a debate like this, that questions so complicated are to be determined?

Give me leave to ask of those who have heard the honourable member for Dublin, and who have listened to the member for Cambridge, whether the arithmetic of both parties is not a much fitter subject for investigation in a committee, than for discussion, or rather retorts, and derisions, and invective, and acclamation here? Was Ireland prosperous before the Union? Mr. Pitt, Mr. Burke, and a crowd of other authorities, have been cited to establish it. But it may be said that the antecedent prosperity of Ireland does not touch the main question. If so, why did the right honourable gentleman think it necessary to advert to it? He has taken from it every quality of impertinence, and given it relevancy and value. To one prominent point in this part of the case I shall apply myself. Indeed, with respect to finance, there is but one observation which I desire to make, and in that I believe myself to be well founded, for I am borne out in it by the authority of a gentleman who was once Chancellor of the Exchequer for Ireland—Sir John Newport; and this opinion is sustained by that of Lord Plunket. I will not trouble the house by quoting their opinions at length, but I will give the substance of them; and if any one doubts the accuracy of my statement, I can produce the passages to which I refer. Ireland, at the time of the Union, was charged with the contribution of two-seventeenths to the general expenditure of the two kingdoms. Was that fair? Sir John Newport pronounced it to be most unjust—so did Lord Plunket; but the fact goes further than their authority, for it turned out that Ireland was unable to pay the share she had contracted to contribute. What was the consequence? It was necessary to make up the deficiency by successive loans. Where was the money borrowed? In England; and the revenue of Ireland was applied to paying the interest on these loans. How many millions were paid by Ireland in con-

sequence of that injustice? Between £4,000,000 and £5,000,000 a
year up to 1816. You have got so much, then, of the revenue of Ireland, which you ought never to have received. Has no injustice been
done to Ireland in this respect? But you will tell me that you have
cured all this by the consolidation of the exchequers of the two countries. You have not; because, at the time of the Union, you agreed
that the surplus revenue of Ireland should be spent in Ireland: there
would have been a surplus, but for the charge of two-seventeenths
You consolidated the exchequers on account of the excessive charge,
and now the whole of our revenue comes to your exchequer. By the
returns, a clear surplus beyond our expenditure appears; that surplus
you receive.

You talk of British capital flowing into Ireland—you might as well
talk of infusing blood into the veins, while you were opening the arteries. The Secretary for Ireland says absenteeism existed before the
Union. Yes; but you have aggravated the disease, and taken away
the cure. Do you deny that the evil has been augmented? The Secretary for the Treasury tells us that Dublin is more prosperous. Hear
the report of a committee of this house, in 1825:—

" Your committee feel an earnest hope that the peculiar situation in
which the city of Dublin has been placed by the Union will not be lost
sight of by this house. Prior to that event, ninety-eight Peers and a
proportionate number of wealthy Commoners inhabited the same. At
present the number of resident Peers does not exceed twelve."

At the present moment there are not more than two. Ninety-eight
resident Peers before the Union—at present two! The report of the
committee contains these additional words:—

" Thus the effect of the Union has been to withdraw from Dublin
many of those who were likely to contribute most effectually to its opulence and prosperity."

The same opinion was expressed by Sir John Newport, on the 22nd
April, 1822, in a debate in this house, in which the Right Honourable Secretary to the Treasury took part.

" Before the Union (said Sir John) the progress of taxation in Ireland had been comparatively moderate, and I am perfectly convinced
that had parliament, since the Union, pursued the course which wisdom
stated with respect to this object, it would have been precisely the
verse of that which they have adopted. It is manifest that one of the
ills of Ireland, confessedly prominent in the list of those under which
he suffers, is the magnitude and number of her absentee proprietors.
By their absence the people are deprived of those to whom they could
with confidence look up."

Is the absence of the nobility and chief gentry of that country of no
account? I admit that some noblemen, like the Duke of Devonshire,
Lords Hertford, Lansdowne, Camdem, Fitzwilliam, Essex, and others,
must remain residents in this country. Some arrangement might be
made by an Irish Parliament in their regard; but the necessity of
attending the two houses here has caused the absence of others, who
otherwise would live in Ireland. An Irish Parliament would tax absen-

teeism. The Secretary for Ireland, the member for Staffordshire, between whom and the honourable member for Belfast, there last night passed an interchange of parliamentary endearments, spoke of a tax upon the property of absentees as amounting to confiscation. Are the acts of the Irish Parliament void? You would resent a hint touching the invalidity of the Act of Union: extend to other acts the benefit of your doctrine. We have acts of the Irish Parliament (Richard II. and Henry VIII.), by which the proprietors of estates were subject to a heavy forfeiture during their absence. This principle of taxation was adopted by an English Parliament when the kings of England had dominions in France, and their subjects preferred residence on their estates in that country. Look at the inconvenience of the tax on the one hand, and the misery of the people of Ireland on the other, and then tell me which ought to weigh most in the consideration of the legislature.

When you expatiate on the increased prosperity of the country as proved by its exports, do you forget that when converted into money, it is in the palaces, the banquets and saloons of this metropolis, that the fruits of Irish labour are expended? What is the condition of the mass of the people? The population of Ireland has doubled since the Union. Has her capital increased in the same proportion—and is there not a far greater mass of misery than there was before? "The greater happiness of the greater number" being applied as a test, in what light shall we see the results of the Union to the people, the state of the people? The exports of Ireland, forsooth—go—let the right honourable gentleman take his stand on the quay of the city which he once represented—let him look on whole fleets upon the Shannon, freighted to the water's edge with grain, the produce of myriads of acres, and with flocks and herds innumerable, depastured upon the land on which heaven has rained fertility, and after he shall have contemplated the spectacle on which it does the heart of an economist good to rest, let him turn round and look on the starving peasantry by whom all these materials for absentee splendour have been created—behold the famine the wretchedness, and the pestilence of the Irish hovel, and if he have the heart to do so, let him mock at the calamities of his country, and proceed in his demonstration of the prosperity of Ireland. The mass of the people are in a condition more wretched than that of any nati‹ in Europe; they are worse housed, worse covered, worse fed than t! basest boors in the provinces of Russia; they dwell in habitations which your swine would not be committed; they are covered with rags which your beggars would disdain to wear; and not only do they never taste the flesh of the animals which crowd into your markets, and while the sweat drops from their brows, they never touch the bread into which their harvests are converted. For you they toil—for you they delve—they reclaim the bog—and drive the plough to the mountain's top for you. And where does all this misery exist? In a country teeming with fertility, and stamped with the beneficent intents of God. When the famine of Ireland prevailed—when her cries crossed the Channel, and pierced your ears, and reached your hearts the granaries of Ireland were bursting with their contents, and while a people knew down, and stretched out their hands for food, the business of deportation, the absentee tribute was going on. Talk of the prosperity of Ireland! Talk of the external magnificence of a poorhouse, gorged with misery within. I am glad that I have recollected the poor laws. Wherefore are half this house favourable to an Irish poor law? Is it not because the people are reduced to straits at which humanity recoils? And how does your sympathy with the Irish poor at one moment accord with your expatiations on Irish prosperity at another. But let me be just. I do not accuse the Secretary for the Treasury of being favourable to poor laws. He sees the poor laws from the Shannon, as he sees repeal from the Thames. He takes a treasury view of the one, and a Mount Trenchard view of the other. We propose repeal—others propose poor laws. What does he suggest? What nostrum will he produce from the Downing-street dispensary of political empiricism? All that Ireland requires is good government? Has she been well governed? " Yes," says the Secretary of the Treasury. I proceed to the political head of this great question.

The right honourable gentleman, on this part of the case, has spoken with more than his usual talent—which is saying much ; and with more than his usual earnestness—which is saying a good deal. He designates himself as a West Briton. He does himself injustice, for he is more than English. It was said of the English colonist, that he was *Hibernis Hibernior*. He improved upon our indigenous barbarism. British civilization has produced an opposite result, in a proportionate degree of refinement on the mind of the right honourable gentleman. All the mud of his native Shannon has not only been washed off by his ablutions in the Cam, but he comes more fresh and glossy from the academic water, than those who at their birth were immersed in the classic stream. But did the right honourable gentleman always see the government of Ireland in the same light—or does the configuration, and do the colours of objects, depend on the position from which they are seen? There was a time when the right honourable gentleman saw nothing but gloom in the political horizon ; but now every cloud is filled with the radiance of his imagination, and he beholds nothing but brightness, gorgeousness, and gold. He has represented the conduct of the Imperial Parliament towards his native country as wise and generous. I shall be able to prove, from the uniform tenor of the right honourable gentleman's speeches in opposition, that until he came into office he regarded the system by which Ireland was governed as fraught with injustice. He is picked from the speeches delivered by the member for Dublin every ose expression, every careless phrase which he could apply to his purses. Blame us not if in this, as in other particulars, we presume to low your example. Since you rely upon the ebullitions of popular citement at public meetings, and upon those thoughtless and inconsiderate declamations which are thrown off in utter recklessness amidst nual gatherings of the people—since you quote after-dinner orators, I rely upon the rhetoric of the Corn Exchange ; permit us, on the er hand, to refer to your own solemn and reiterated declarations made in your legislative capacity in this house, and to exhibit the enormity of the contradiction that exists between your conduct in office and that which you adopted before you arrived at power. How has Ireland been governed since the Union? Whigs of 1834—how have the forebodings of the Whigs of 1799 been fulfilled? They foretold the result of that vile exchange, that base swap by which Ireland was forced to give up the entirety of her legislature for a miserable sixth in that imperial co-partnership, and became dependant upon majorities composed of men who care little about the welfare, sympathize less with the feelings, and know nothing of the interests of Ireland. Let us see the evidences of British magnanimity, British generosity, and British justice? The Secretary for the Treasury has gone through a variety of details to establish the undeviating beneficence of an Imperial Legislature. Hear the language (let him listen to it) uttered by himself on the 22nd of April, 1822. Thus speaks the member for Limerick :—

"What was the first tribute which the mperial Parliament of 1801 tendered to Ireland in their first - otice of the situation of that country after the Union? Their first statute was the Irish Martial Law Bill."

On Wednesday the right honourable gentleman recapitulated the acts which the Imperial Parliament had passed for Ireland. He went through acts for lighting and paving the streets—he enlarged on the achievements of pure legislation—he recounted the provisions of various statutes on small subjects—but never once alluded to the questions which touch the heart of the country to the core ; and entirely forgot that, in 1822, he had exclaimed that the renewal of martial law in 1801, was the first piece of legislation adopted by the Imperial Parliament with respect to Ireland. But I will not do him the injustice of suppressing the rest of his observations in that remarkable declaration. The right honourable gentleman went on, and said that the spirit in which the British Parliam ent legislated for Ireland had been in accordance with the principle on which the act establishing martial law was founded. He added—

In tracing the history of Irish legislation, both before and since the Union, there appeared as it were, two streams passing through the channel of Parliament In one flowed acts of strenuous finance, or equally strong coercion—the one with great malice, the other with great power. In the other channel the struggle was made, but made in vain, to procure an examination into the state and condition of the people, in the hope of discovering and applying some remedy for their evils."

Will the right honourable gentleman give us a committee to examine into them now?

"It was curious (he continued), in tracing these proceedings, to observe with what a singularly felicitous uniformity the channel of coercion always flowed, and that of inquiry was always resisted and impeded."

Thus spoke the right honourable gentleman in 1822. Now hear his amendment of 1834. See what a metamorphosis the right honourable gentleman has undergone? Peruse the address in which he sets forth the wisdom of British legislation, and reconcile the member for Limrick with the Secretary for the Treasury if you can. I could quote fifty speeches of the right honourable gentleman of the same character, but I have not time; let us turn from him, and in a rapid retrospect, look at the policy pursued by the Imperial Parliament since the Union. Not a mere hint, not an insinuation whispered by a secretary into the ear of a Catholic peer at the Castle, but a pledge was given (the more obligatory because it rested upon honour for its fulfilment), that the Union should be followed by emancipation. How was that pledge redeemed? What evidence was afforded of the liberal and enlightened spirit of the Imperial Legislature? Panegyrists of the Union try it by its fruits, and look to historical notorieties, as well as to treasury calculations. Mr. Pitt could not carry the question—he was compelled to resign. 1801, 1802, 1803 and 1804 passed by. The question was not even introduced; it would have been treated as repeal is to-night. Henry Grattan himself did not, until 1805, venture to raise his voice in the cause of his country. At length Mr. Fox, in 1805, moved for a committee. The proposition was spurned at: the Whigs came in. The "no popery" howl is raised—the Catholic question is left to the umpirage of a ferocious multitude, and the rights of millions of your fellow-subjects are trampled under foot by the infuriated populace which Protestantism has summoned to its aid. The Whigs are driven from office —not for having proposed emancipation, but for having made the humble suggestion that men who shed their blood for England, should be capable of honour. The new parliament assembles. Ireland asked for freedom, and she received the Insurrection Act. In 1812 an ordinance issues, signed "Wellesley Pole," from the Castle, and the Catholic committee is dispersed. Mr. Saurin tries the Catholic delegates and fails. He mends his hand, packs a jury, and procures a conviction. The jury was packed—the panel was sent marked and dotted from the Castle. Who were the loudest to proclaim, and to reprobate the practice by which justice was polluted to its source?- The very men who now see nothing in the government of Ireland but matter for admiration, and persevere in the very course which they had formerly held up to the execration of the country. In 1814, the Insurrection Act is renewed: the Whigs hurled the thunders of their eloquence against it. Would that I could here make some pause, in order to lay before the house some of those masterpieces of eloquence in which they held up to indignation the outrage committed on the constitution. But I must hurry on; seven years go by; nothing is done for Ireland, and yet all this while there has been a vast majority of Irish members in favour of Catholic emancipation. Their remonstrances, their entreaties for justice were spurned and derided. By whom was Ireland oppressed and degraded? By whom was the penal system (the parent of such a brood of evil) maintained? Englishmen, by you! and yet, in the face of these facts, an Irishman asks you to pronounce a retrospective panegyric upon the fanaticism by which the measures of thirty years were distinguished. In 1821, George the Fourth goes to Ireland; in our loyalty he finds evidence of our felicity. In 1822, Lord Wellesley (the present viceroy) recommends the renewal of the Insurrection Act. It was consistent to send him to administer the coercive bill. No one was more prominent than the Secretary for the Treasury in reprobating the principles on which that unconstitutional proceeding was founded. In 1824, the Insurrection Act was again renewed, and again the Whigs declaimed and stormed. In the interval the Catholic Association was created. By whom? Not by the Catholic gentry—not by the men who denounce repeal and repealers—but, with the aid of the people, by a man who, whatever estimate may be formed of this question in this house, has done great things; has written his name in ineffaceable permanence in the records of his country, and built himself on the liberty of Ireland a monument which will never fall. The agitation and organization of Ireland proceeded. In 1825, the Catholic delegates arrived in London. How many of the evils that have since arisen might have been prevented if the terms which were tendered by Ireland had not been rejected. Mr. Canning comes into office; gives up Catholic emancipation, and is denounced for apostacy by Lord Grey. Why did Mr. Canning give up that measure? Was it from any renegade spirit? It was because he knew it was hopeless to attempt to carry the question in the Imperial Parliament, " which has passed," according to the Secretary of the Treasury, " so many salutary and beneficial measures for the people of Ireland." We were as much at your mercy then as we were before 1782. The prejudices of England were insuperable. The Goderich Administration, Lansdowne, Herries and Co., succeeded Canning. It died in its cradle. At length—(there was one Arthur Wellesley, member for Trim, in the Irish House of Commons, who asserted the necessity of emancipation in 1793)—at length the Duke of Wellington consummated in the cabinet that renown which he had obtained in the field, and, with the aid of a man who did incalculable services by inestimable sacrifices, gave freedom to 7,000,000 of his fellow-citizens; but with what injustice was it accompanied? The Irish Parliament bestowed upon the forty-shilling freeholders of Ireland the elective franchise. It remained for the Imperial Parliament to deprive them of the right. This proceeding was denounced as spoliation. By whom? By Lord Brougham—by Lord Grey—the men who would not commit the robbery, but who, when the Reform Bill came on, refused restitution. Are not these facts? Have I said a word that is not the fact? And to all this what does the Secretary for the Treasury reply? At the end of almost every fourth sentence in one part of his speech—(I was surprised, knowing his command of language, and the copiousness of his vocabulary)—the right honourable gentleman exclaimed " nonsense," then he cried out " trash," and afterwards " stuff." Ah, Sir, there is, in this melancholy detail. truth, dismal, disastrous truth. Your delay of emancipation was fatal. If you had passed the Catholic Relief Bill years before, none of the results which you so much lament would have been produced. You were wrong; you know it, and yet I scarce condemn you for it. I blame the Union, which left the people of Ireland at the mercy of the fanatical passions, by which the legislature was controlled. But the Secretary for the Treasury exclaims, " If the agitators would but let us alone, and allow Ireland to be tranquil." The agitators, for-south! Does he venture—has he the intrepidity to speak thus? Agitators! Against deep potations let the drunkard rail;—at Crockford's let there be homilies against the dice box;—let every libertine lament the progress of licentiousness, when his Majesty's ministers deplore the influence of demagogues, and Whigs complain of agitation.

How did you carry Reform? Was it not by impelling the people almost to the verge of revolution? Was there a stimulant for their passions—was there a provocative for their excitement, to which you did not resort? If you have forgotten, do you think that we shall fail to remember your meetings at Edinburgh, at Paisley, at Manchester, at Birmingham? Did not 300,000 men assemble? Did they not pass resolutions against taxes? Did they not threaten to march on London? Did not two of the cabinet ministers indite to them epistles of gratitude and of admiration? and do they now dare—have they the audacity to speak of agitation? Have we not as good a title to demand the restitution of our parliament, as the ministers to insist on the reform of this house? Wherefore should we not adopt the same means to effect it? The member for the county of Wexford has had the imprudence to talk of Catholic bishops being treated with disrespect, and of excesses committed by the populace. Bishops! What, is it only in Ireland that it is a crime to assail a bishop? And have the flames of Bristol left no reflection behind?

I have demonstrated that at least for twenty-nine years Ireland was misgoverned. Twenty-nine years of agitation, and at length justice was extorted from an Imperial Parliament? But since emancipation, since the Whigs have come into office, has all gone well? Let us pass over some smaller details—the Arms Bill, the jury packing, the exclusion of Catholics on tithe questions, the infusion of theology into the police; let us go to great and essential incidents. I shall dwell on no more than three. In your Reform Bill you adopted population as a standard here; you did not employ it in Ireland. You gave Wales, with 800,000 people, three additional representatives, eight to Scotland with 2,500,000, and five to Ireland with her 8,000,000. You did not restore the forty-shilling freeholders. You have left towns in Ireland with 12,000 people without a representative; and you have left your paltry boroughs here. It was either necessary, or it was not, to pass our Coercion Bill. It was either necessary, or it was not, for the opponents of the Insurrection Act to put upon the statute-book a precedent for tyranny, and to supersede the tribunals of the country with the legislation of the Horse-Guards, and the judicature of the barrack-yard. If it was unnecessary, it was detestable and atrocious; and if it was necessary for Lord Grey to introduce a bill which passed without assent in the Lords, and which there were men who support ministers who declared that they would rather die than support it in that shape; that was necessary, by whom was the necessity created? You have had Ireland for thirty-three years under your rule—you have been his absolute and undisputed masters; and if her condition be deplorable—atrocities have been perpetrated which call for rigorous laws, are you not responsible for this disastrous state of things—and to you, and to your Union, which armed you with power unlimited for good or evil, is it not to be referred? So much for your coercive measure; but for its severity you made up (did you not?) by your Tithe and Church Bills, your 147th clause, and those absurd and cruel experiments—absurd in theory and cruel in result—with which you have endeavoured to reconcile that most monstrous of all anomalies—a Church of one religion, and almost an entire nation of another.

I turn to the member for Paisley, and other Scotchmen who appeal to the results of the Scotch Union. Was such an article, as the fifth article of the Act of Union, giving eternity to the Protestant Church, among the terms on which Scotland gave up her legislature? If any attempt had been made to establish episcopacy by her Union—if a mitred pontificate had been inflicted upon her, what would have been the consequences? She would not have for a moment endured it. Her people would have risen almost to a man against such a Union—to the death they would have resisted it—the country would have been deluged in blood. And if at last England and episcopacy had prevailed, they must have reared their altars in a desert, for Scotland would have left them nothing but a wilderness for their worship.

I cannot sit down without adverting to two points: first, the probable constitution of an Irish Parliament; secondly, the likelihood of separation. As to the first, let the Whigs recollect that, on the Reform Question, it was urged that this house would be filled by men of an inferior station. It was answered, property must prevail; wherefore should it not prevail in Ireland as well as here? Is it not manifest that, in a little while after the repeal had been carried, the Irish nation would follow the example of all other nations, and select men of influence, from fortune or talents (which give a higher title to respect), as the depositaries of the legislative trust? The qualification of the Irish voter (£10 a-year rent), ought surely to secure a highly respectable representation. Besides, observe that if the evil is to take place after repeal, it must take place without it. If Ireland would then return 300 unworthy men, she will return 105 of the same character; and thus you entail on yourselves as great an evil as that which you apprehend as a consequence of repeal. The arguments which are urged against repeal, were the very same as those which were pressed by Conservatives against reform. They said that a collision would take place between Lords and Commons, and saw as many calamities in that collision, as you foresee in the anticipated disagreements of the Irish and English Parliaments. No man pointed out these consequences with more force than Mr. Canning—an authority which the noble lo. d the Secretary for Foreign Affairs, and the President of the Board of Control, once held in some regard. But was Lord Grey terrified by the phantom of revolution? Why should he expect that we should be dismayed by another spectre, which was as huge and hideous im 1800 when he looked at it without dismay. Is the argument more valid now than it was then? It is built on this abstract proposition; two parliaments cannot amicably co-exist. He then said they could. He was not a beardless politician at that epoch; he had already proposed his grea plan of Reform—he was about the age of the Secretary for the Colonies—had reached the age of discretion, and had passed the period at which men might be led away by a juvenile enthusiasm—when the understanding may be obscured by the mists which arise from the boiling emotions of the heart. Lord Grey's assertion is as valid as it was thirty-four years ago: it is one of those propositions which time cannot impair.

What was then a sophism cannot grow into a reason, as into a sophism a reason cannot degenerate. Let it be borne in your minds that although some of the arguments against a union were founded on temporary and transient circumstances, yet others (like that grounded on the fear of separation), were permanent, and are now just as good as they were a quarter of a century ago. The authority of Plunket and Bushe, and Saurin, and, above all, the authority of Grattan, is as powerful as it ever was. The Secretary for the Treasury insists that Grattan had changed his mind. His son has proved the contrary. He read his answer in 1810, declaring that he desired the restoration of the Irish Parliament. To what document was that answer a response? To an address from the grand juries of Dublin, in which they describe the evils of the Union, and call on Mr. Grattan to employ his great faculties in accomplishing its repeal. Mr. Grattan did not change his mind. But what is the crime of the repealers? This—that they consider Lord Grey a good statesman, when he is old—but a better prophet, when he was young. I blame him not for having altered his opinion; but I own myself to be surprised that he should lavish in the speeches, for the utterance of which he avails himself of the royal enunciation, such unqualified and almost contumelious condemnation of those with whom he strenuously coincided when he was upwards of thirty years of age. But have we no better argument than that which Lord Grey so often urged against Mr. Pitt, when he reproached him with a desertion of his former opinions. How stands history? It is asked, when did two parliaments long co-exist in friendship? Show me an instance in which 8,000,000 of people in one island submitted to a parliament held in another, and containing such proportions as exist in this assembly. The case of America is obvious; but look to two strong instances—Sweden and Norway have one King and two parliaments. Since the year 1815, there has been no quarrel between the legislatures. Turn to Belgium. Does not the example bear us out? Hear an extract from the declaration of Belgian independence. After alleging that the Union was obtained by fraud, the document goes on and states that—

"An enormous debt and expenditure, the only portion which Holland brought to us at the time of our deplorable Union—taxes overwhelming by their amount—laws always voted by the Dutch for Holland only (and always against Belgium), represented so unequally in the States-General—the seat of all important establishments fixed in Holland—the most offensive partialities in the distribution of civil and military employments—in a word, Belgium treated as a conquered province, as a colony: everything rendered a revolution inevitable."

Do you mark this? You were instrumental in affecting the Union of Belgium and Holland. Lord Castlereagh, who carried the Irish

Union, represented you at the Congress in which the different arrangements with respect to Belgium and Holland were made. You have yourselves recently been parties to that separation which Belgium demanded, and you assented to the grounds on which it was required. All the public establishments removed to Holland! What has become of our Custom House, of our Stamp Office? Our Royal Hospital too, built by a contribution made among the Irish soldiers, raised out of a sixpence which they joyfully gave to provide for them an asylum, that institution, connected with our national pride, associated with our best feelings of country, you, for the sake of some miserable saving, have determined to annihilate. Take warning—you have made experiments enough. Be taught not by the failures of others, but by your own. Go on as you have hitherto proceeded, and you will soon find the entire of Ireland united for repeal. A reference has been made to the small number of signatures to petitions. If there shall be a million next year, what will you say? We are told that the Irish people do not desire repeal. Are thirty-eight Irish members out of one hundred and five nothing? What other test do you demand? The last election ought to exhibit the truth. That last election verified the prediction which I made to the Chancellor of the Exchequer: I went to him when the Tithe Bill was pending in 1832.—I told him what would happen. I exclaimed, "You are on the eve of a general election; you are driving the Irish to fury by your tithe measures, and the result will be, that on every hustings in the south, the standard of repeal will be planted." It is said that the gentry are against repeal. How fast do the gentry of every country fall into the mass of the people! They desert one by one, and the moment it is their interest, they combine with the class once designated as the multitude. How soon the populace becomes the people! Let a few years go by, Catholic and Protestant will be reconciled—the national mind will become one mass of hot emotion—the same disregard for the interests and feelings of Ireland will be displayed in this assembly; and, if there should be an outbreak of popular commotion here—if the prediction of the Conservatives should be fulfilled—and if your alliance with France, which is as unstable as its dynasty, should give way, you may have cause to lament, when lamentation will be unavailing, that to seven millions of Irishmen justice was refused.

RUSSIAN AND TURKISH TREATIES.

SPEECH IN THE HOUSE OF COMMONS, MARCH 17, 1834.

endeavour, in discharging the duty I have undertaken, to avoid
of partisanship, which, in a question of this kind, would be
[out of place, and simply to present to the house the facts
conceive should induce the noble lord at the head of the foreign
nt, to furnish the house and the public with the documents I
ave produced. The motion I have risen to make is this :—
1 humble address be presented to his majesty, that he will be
y pleased to give directions that there be laid before this house,
any treaty or treaties which have been concluded between
ian and Turkish governments, since the 1st of January, 1833,
h have been officially communicated to the British govern-
gether with copies of any correspondence between his majes-
rnment and the Russian and Turkish governments, relative to
reaties."
eed at once to the statement of the facts, the incidents, and
nents, on which I rely. I shall not take any remote period,
nence at the autumn of the year 1831. In the autumn of that
forces of the Pacha of Egypt began their march ; on the 3rd
nber, 1831, the siege of Acre was commenced ; in May, 1832,
; Ibrahim proceeded on his march, and advanced into Syria;
4th of June, Damascus was taken. In July, 1832, another
tle was fought, and Ibrahim advanced upon Taurus ; he passed
one who will give the slightest examination to the relative
of the two armies, must see that the success of Ibrahim was
. This was the state of affairs in July, 1832. What was
e adopted by Turkey? She applied for aid to England. The
mitted, in a speech made by the noble lord in this house on
of July, 1833. It was further admitted by the noble lord,
is country had then thought proper to interfere, its interference
ve been effectual.
'ALMERSTON.—No.
IEIL.—It is so stated. It has also been stated, but I know not
)n good authority, that the application of Turkey to this count. 7
ance was sustained by Russia, which power is said to have inti
r wish, or solicited, that the aid asked by Turkey should be given
refused her assistance. That fact will not be questioned ; it
o be explained. It was asked at the time, why assistance was
1 to our ancient ally? But the events which subsequently
, gave retrospective force to the interrogatory ; for it is
e not to ask, with a sentiment stronger than mere curiosity,
is that Turkey, when she sought our assistance, was thrown
sia as her only resource? The refusal having been given, is
nost extraordinary circumstance that England sent no ambas-
Constantinople? The war began in October, 1831 ; Acre fel

in May, 1832; Damascus, in June, 1832: the Taurus was passed; aid was asked from and refused by England; and yet no ambassador was sent from England! Let the noble lord, if he will have the goodness to note the questions I ask in the course of my statement, tell us how it happened that the war had been concluded two months before the English minister arrived at Constantinople? The battle of Koniah was fought on the 21st of September, 1832; and although this progress of Ibrahim attracted the attention of Europe, it does not seem to have induced the English cabinet to give any acceleration to the movements of my Lord Ponsonby. He was appointed, I believe, in December, 1832; but he did not arrive in Constantinople till May, 1833, after the battle of Koniah had been fought, and application had been made by Turkey to Russia; and, indeed, after—as it is stated upon authority, I believe, worthy of credit, and which it will remain for the noble lord to confirm or contradict—Russia had written to the sultan in the language of fraternal or diplomatic endearment, making him a tender of the assistance of Russia, whether that assistance was required by sea or by land. On the 17th of February, the French admiral, Roussin, arrived at Constantinople, and this leads me to remark upon a circumstance deserving of notice. It is this;—that not only England, but France, had no ambassador at Constantinople during the progress of the events I have mentioned. The reason of France being thus situated, is said to be, that General Guilleminot, who had been there as ambassador, having suggested to the Porte, on the breaking out of the Polish insurrection, that that was a good opportunity to repair the disasters and injuries of the war which terminated in the treaty of Adrianople, Prince Pozzo di Borgo applied to the French minister, Sebastiani, to have him removed. I mention this as a kind of excuse for England, because France, having only a *charge d'affaires*, it may be said that we were not called upon to have more than a secretary of legation Admiral Roussin having arrived on the 17th of February, he, on the 19th of February, remonstrated with the divan, on the fatal effects to the Turkish empire which must result from calling in Russia as an auxiliary. On the very next day the Russian fleet appeared in the Bosphorus. There was, however, no immediate disembarkation. The French admiral remonstrated, but the English ambassador was not there to remonstrate, for Lord Ponsonby was relieving himself at Naples from the fatigues of his diplomatic negociations in Belgium. An effort was made by him, however, to induce Ibrahim to retreat, but all it led to was the raising a question respecting the possession of Armenia. In that question, admiral Roussin said he would not interfere, not wishing to concern himself in the domestic quarrels of the parties. He accordingly retired, and 20,000 Russians encamped on the Asiatic shore of the Bosphorus. Complete possession having been taken of Constantinople, Count Orloff arrived, if not before Lord Ponsonby, to much better purpose; for, whilst he seemed to be engaged in the show and festivities of the capital, on the illuminations of their seraglio, he was all the while effecting a clandestine treaty with the sultan, not only without the intervention, but without the knowledge of the English or French embassies. That was the treaty of the 8th of July, the production of which I seek from the noble lord. I have now, by a succinct narrative, brought down my statement to that important period, the 8th of July, 1833, the date of the subjugation of Turkey; not I hope, of the dishonour of England. When was that treaty known by the noble lord? I may mention, by the way, a remarkable circumstance which took place in the House of Commons on the 11th of July.

My honourable friend who sits beside me (the member for Coventry) moved for certain papers respecting the recent transactions between Russia, Turkey, and Mchemct Ali. On that occasion the noble lord opposite pronounced a speech, reflecting the highest credit on his diplomatic abilities. The noble lord stated, as a reason for not producing the papers, that the events to which they related could hardly be said to be brought to a close, and that the documents asked for ought not to be produced, till a diplomatic wind-up had been arrived at. But he expressed sentiments worthy of a proselyte of Mr. Canning, observing, that it was quite a mistake to suppose that England was not prepared to go to war if honour and dignity required it: mentioning, at the same time, that assistance had been refused to Turkey. This being on the 11th of July, the noble lord, of course, was not aware of the treaty on the 8th of July. How did the English public become acquainted with that treaty? Or, perhaps, the more proper question would be—how did the noble lord become acquainted with it? The noble lord obtained his first information touching, I will not say, the details and particulars, but the substance of that treaty, from a letter which appeared in the *Morning Herald*, on the 21st of August, 1833, from its correspondent at Constantinople. In this letter it was stated that Count Orloff had succeeded completely in throwing dust into the eyes of the English and French ambassadors; for that, whilst he appeared to be absorbed in all the gaieties of the Turkish metropolis, he was in reality prosecuting the deep and dark designs which Russia had so long entertained; and that on the 8th of July he had induced the sultan to conclude an offensive and defensive treaty, admitting the virtual surrender to Russian dominion of all the rights of Turkey.

The particulars of that treaty, beyond three articles, the writer did not pretend to know; but he added, that the next day Count Orloff set off for St. Petersburgh; that the greatest confusion and dismay prevailed among the other diplomatic bodies; and, that they had despatched couriers to their respective courts. This letter was brought under the attention of the House of Commons on the 24th of August, by the honourable and gallant member for Westminster; on which occasion the noble lord stated in his place, that of the treaty of the 8th of July he officially knew nothing whatever; the only information he had upon the subject being through the medium of the public journals, on whose activity he passed a just panegyric—an activity which mainly, on that occasion, much surpassed that of the agents of the government. The noble lord, on that occasion, admitted a second that Turkey had asked for assistance from England before applying for it to Russia. I have now brought myself down to the 24th of August, 1833. On the 29th of August, the King delivered his speech from the throne on the prorogation of parliament. With these facts, or these rumours which, at all events, ultimately turned out fatal facts —with all these circumstances before it—the cabinet advised his Majesty to declare in his speech from the throne—and that speech must constitutionally be considered the speech of his Majesty's ministers—that the relation between Turkey and England remained undisturbed.

Let the house bear in mind that the noble lord, if he had not received the despatch, forwarded to him on the 9th of July, certainly had had his attention called to the treaty of the 8th of July or the 14th of August; and yet persuades his colleagues to advise his Majesty to say on the 29th of August—

"The hostilities which had disturbed the peace of Turkey have been terminated; and you may be assured that my attention will be carefully directed to any events which may affect the present state or the future independence of that empire."

I now pass at once to the month of October in the same year. In October, M. La Grenée, the French *chargé d'affaires*, addressed a letter to Count Nesselrode of a most remarkable kind. Considering the close junction which subsisted between the courts of St. James's and the Tuilleries—a junction which I hope still continues—considering the fidelity of that alliance to be mutual—it is hardly too much to look upon this note as if it came from the noble lord himself, sitting in Downing-street. This note of M. La Grenée was written in October, but was not published in Paris till the 23rd of December, 1833, when it came before the whole of the European public. I pray the particular attention of the house to this note. Our attention has lately been directed to matters of domestic interest and immediate pressure; but be it remembered, that events are now going on which are fraught with consequences that may affect our domestic interests as much as others which only appear larger because more near. The note of M. La Grenée to Count Nesselrode runs thus:—

"The undersigned Chargé d'Affaires of his Majesty the King of the French, has received orders to express to the cabinet of St. Petersburgh the profound affliction felt by the French government, on learning the conclusion of the treaty of the 8th of July last, between his Majesty the Emperor of Russia and the Grand Signior. In the opinion of the King's government, this treaty assigns to the mutual relations existing between the Ottoman empire and Russia a new character, against which the powers of Europe have a right to protest."

To this note, Count Nesselrode replied in the following cant, offensive, and almost contumelious language:—

"It is true that this act changes the nature of the relations between Russia and the Porte, for in the room of long-continued hostilities it substitutes that friendship and that confidence, in which the Turkish government will henceforth find a guarantee for its stability and necessary means of defence, calculated to ensure its preservation. In this conviction, and guided by the purest and most disinterested intentions, his Majesty the Emperor is resolved, in case of necessity, to discharge faithfully the obligations imposed on him by the treaty of the 8th of July, thus acting as if the declaration contained in the note of Monsieur La Grenée had no existence.

"St. Petersburgh, Oct. 1833."

This note is taken from the *Augsburgh Gazette*, to which it purports to have been transmitted in a letter from Paris on the 23rd of December. Here let one remark be made, which will not trench on the distinct classification of facts. If the French government remonstrated, it is to be presumed that the noble lord did not remain silent. Where is his correspondence? Was a note as affronting written in reply, or was it even couched in more caustic phraseology, and in the same style of contemptuous repudiation as the article in the *St. Petersburgh Gazette*, on the presumption of our interference in the affairs of Poland? To return to dates and facts—on the 1st of January, Pozzo di Borgo addressed the King of the French, and on that occasion the accomplished Corsican pronounced on Louis Philip an eulogium, accompanied with protestations, characteristic of both—of the party who indulged in, and the party who was graciously pleased to accept the hollow panegyric. Six days after, in bringing up the address, M. Bignon delivered a speech, which was received with equal surprise and acclamation. He denounced the conduct of Russia towards Poland, and held out the aggressions upon Turkey as indicative of that deep and settled purpose, of which he had, in his official capacity, a perfect cognizance. In 1807, he said, Alexander had tendered all Southern Europe to Napoleon, provided Napoleon would give him what he called at once a homely, but powerful diction—the key of his own house—Constantinople. That offer was refused; the consequences were foreseen by Napoleon. M. Bignon then warned France to beware of the advances of Russian power in the east, and denounced, while he revealed her policy, and invoked his countrymen to awaken to a sense of the insults offered to the dignity of France, and the violation offered to her rights. To this speech, the Duke de Broglie made an answer conspicuous in itself, and which his subsequent conduct rendered still more remarkable. He expressed his unqualified concurrence in all that had been said, and thanked M. Bignon for having given expression to the sentiments which he and his colleagues entertained. On the very next day, this very man went down to the chamber, and made a speech which was received with astonishment by both countries. He contended that no violation of treaty had taken place, expressed satisfaction with Russian policy, and stated that there had been no material alteration made respecting the passage of the Dardanelles. M. Thiers, in reply to M. Mauguin, said nearly the same thing; and, although La Grenée's note was yet fresh in every memory, and the Duke of Broglie's approval of Bignon's speech was ringing in every ear, expressed no sort of discontent at any of the incidents which had taken place. M. Thiers, however, incidentally acknowledged that it was a part of the treaty, that all vessels of powers at war with Russia should be excluded from the passage of the

Dardanelles. Our own parliament did not meet until the 5th of February; but before it assembled an accident occurred which remains to be explained. The French and English fleets united, proceeded to the Dardanelles, which Russia had spared no expense to fortify; and, having displayed the tricolour, and " the meteor flag of England," as it has been nobly called, near the spot where Sir George Duckworth, when Lord Grey was Secretary for Foreign Affairs, expended a good deal of powder without much avail, both fleets sailed away, and instead of proceeding to Smyrna, gave a preference to a more distant and less commodious harbour, where, however, Russian influence was not quite so predominant as in that celebrated haven. The glory of this expedition belongs to the First Lord of the Admiralty; but it is to be conjectured that the achievement was suggested by the genius of the Secretary for Foreign Affairs. But in what did it result? That remains to be told; and, for the satisfaction of that curiosity, I, this night, afford an opportunity.—Parliament met on the 5th. The King's speech informed us that the integrity of the Porte was, for the future, to be preserved (the sultan having been first stripped, and then manacled,) and that his Majesty continued to receive assurances which did not disturb his confidence that peace would be preserved. The Duke of Wellington, in another place, adverted to the treaty of Constantinople, and Lord Grey retorted Adrianople upon his Grace. But in the treaty of Adrianople there was, at all events, nothing that infringed upon our rights as to the navigation of the Black Sea; and it is to be recollected that whatever the First Lord of the Treasury might have said, the Secretary for Foreign Affairs declared that—" while he desired peace, of war he was not in the least afraid." In this house no interrogatories were put. On the 24th of February the following paragraph appeared in *The Globe*, which, from its being the supposed organ of government, deserves great attention, the more especially as we are left to the newspapers for our intelligence. That article stated—

" Another treaty between Russia and Turkey has been concluded at St. Petersburgh, which was signed by Achmet Pacha on the 29th of last month............Enough has transpired to satisfy the most jealous that its spirit is pacific, and indeed advantageous to the Turkish empire. The Porte is relieved from the pressure of the engagements imposed upon her at Adrianople; and we understand that the principalities, with the exception of Silistria, will shortly be evacuated, and the sum exacted by the former treaty reduced one-third. Such relaxations of positive engagements are proofs either of the moderation and good sense of Russia, or of the influence which the union of England and France, and the firm and concerted language of those two powers, have acquired in the councils of St. Petersburgh."

Is it not reasonable that this treaty should be laid before the house? It is to be observed, that in any account of it, either in our journals or in the *Algemeine Zeitung*, not one word is said of the passage of the Dardanelles. The principalities of Wallachia and Moldavia, indeed, are to be evacuated. That circumstance is a mere delusion; for Wallachia and Moldavia are as much dependent on Russia as if they had actually been transferred. Their hospodars are virtually nominated by Russia; no Turk can reside in the country; and every appointment, down to that of the humblest officer, is affected through Russian dictation. Silistria is retained—the key of the lower Danube, commanding all Bulgaria, and a place so important, that the Greek emperors constructed a wall there to protect their frontier, and guard against the incursions of the barbarians. As to the remission of money, that concession is made to an insolvent debtor; it is not the first time that Russia has adopted the same course; the payment of a tribute is of little moment from a country which is almost incorporated in her dominions, and will soon meet the fate of so many of the Turkish provinces. But how does this treaty modify or affect that of the 8th of July? It does not at all relate to it. It concerns the treaty of Adrianople; and as long as we have nothing else on this question, the house is entitled to receive adequate information from the government. With respect to the Dardanelles, a matter of signal importance to England—affecting her commerce—affecting not only the navigation of the Euxine, but giving Russia a control over Greece and the entire Archipelago,—it may be as well to state with brevity the treaties that existed between England and Turkey, and those that existed between Russia and Turkey, previous to that regarding which information is demanded. I will not go back to the reign of Elizabeth. By the treaty of 1675, concluded by Sir John Finch, the navigation of all the Turkish seas was secured to England. In 1809, a little time after our rupture with the Porte, produced by he attack on the Dardanelles, a new treaty was executed, by which the passage of the Dardanelles, and the canal of Constantinople, was secured o England. The 11th article provided, that in time of peace no ship f war should pass, no matter to what country it might belong. In 774, by the treaty of Kaynadgi, the passage of the Dardanelles was rst secured to Russian merchant vessels. In 1780, a quarrel took lace respecting an armed vessel. In 1783, a new treaty was entered ito, and another in 1792 (that treaty by which the Crimea, just like reece, was declared independent, and then absorbed in Russian dominion), and by both treaties the passage was secured to merchant vessels only.

In 1800, Russia having obtained the protectorship of the Ionian lands (their importance we felt in 1815, not so much because we sired to acquire, as to take them from a power that aimed at predominance in the Mediterranean), entered into a treaty, securing the ssage to the merchant vessels of the islands. In 1812, the treaty of charest was signed, by which Bessarabia was given up to Russia, d all former treaties respecting the Dardanelles were confirmed. In 29, the treaty of Adrianople was signed, and with respect to the rdanelles, contained the following passage:—

'7th Article. The sublime Porte declares the passage of the Canal Constantinople completely free and open to Russian merchant vessels ler merchant flags, from the Black Sea to the Mediterranean, and n the Mediterranean to the Black Sea; upon the same principle the age is declared free and open to all merchant vessels belonging to powers at peace with the Porte. The Porte declares, that under no pretence whatsoever will it throw any obstacle in the way of the exercise of this right, and engages, above all, never hereafter to stop or detain vessels, either with cargo or in ballast, whether Russian, or belonging to nations with which the Porte shall not be in a state of declared war."

In the manifesto, published by the Emperor Nicholas, on the 1st of October, 1829, he says:—

"The passage of the Dardanelles and the Bosphorus is henceforth free and open to the commerce of all the nations of the world."

Thus the stipulation was, that all nations at peace (not, be it observed, with Russia, but with the Porte), should enjoy the right of unimpeded passage; but how has that been affected by the treaty of the 8th of July? Will it be said, that nothing was accomplished by the Autocrat by that treaty? If so, why was it signed without the knowledge of our ambassador, and in a clandestine and surreptitious way? What are its provisions? Do the public journals give a just account of it? Is it true, that it provides that no vessels belonging to a power at war with Russia shall enjoy that right? If so, the alteration is palpable; and if there be no express declaration to this effect, let there be an alliance, offensive and defensive, and the Porte is bound to consider every enemy of Russia as its own; the consequence is precisely the same as if the Porte surrendered to Russia the possession of the Dardanelles, and the last of the Sultans is the first satrap of Nicholas the Great.

There does not appear to be any sound reason for withholding this treaty. It has been the subject of remonstrance by France—of debate in the French Chamber—of diversified commentary in the public journals. Why withhold it? There must be a strange inconsistency in publishing all the enormous answers to protocols respecting Belgium, where the transaction is as yet incomplete, and in refusing to furnish anything but materials for surmise on this treaty. Ponderous folios of fruitless negociations on the affairs of Belgium have been given to the world. Let the government act upon the principle adopted in that case, and give the English people the means of forming a judgment of the policy which his Majesty's ministers have adopted in a question where the national honour and interest are so deeply involved. It may be said, " Trust in the minister, be sure that he will not desert his duty, or acquiesce in any measure incompatible with the honour of England." I should be disposed to do so, when I take into account that the Secretary for Foreign Affairs was a political follower of Mr. Canning, who considered the interests and the honour of England as so closely blended, and although the noble lord may have abandoned the opinions on domestic policy which were entertained by Mr. Canning where he was in the wrong, it is to be presumed that he adhered with a closer tenacity to those opinions in foreign policy where Mr Canning was in the right. But this ground of confidence in the noble lord is modified, if not countervailed, by the recollection, that in many recent transactions he has been baffled by that power which has gathered all the profligate nobility of Europe together, in order to compound a cabinet of Machiavellian mercenaries to maintain the cause of slavery through the world. Look at Belgium—look at the Russian-Dutch loan. The noble lord, although guided by the prince of Benevento, has lost his way in the labyrinth which Russia has prepared for him and Poland. "We shall," he exclaimed, "remonstrate." We did remonstrate, and despatched Lord Durham to St. Petersburgh (why was not Sir Stratford Canning there?) and what has been the result? If confidence be to be entertained in the noble lord, it must be built on some firmer basis than his entertainment of the treaty of Vienna. Instead of calling on the people of England to confide in him, let him build his confidence in the English people. They are attached to peace, but they are not afraid of war. Our fleet could blow the Russian navy from the ocean. England is yet match for the Northern Autocrat, and there is might enough left in her arm to shatter the colossus that bestrides the sea by which Europe is divided from Asia, and which has been accounted from time beyond record one of the demarcations of the world.

ORANGE LODGES

SPEECH IN THE HOUSE OF COMMONS, AUGUST 11, 1835.

It is remarkable that the gallant colonel (Verner), the Deputy Grand Master of Ireland and Viceroy to the Duke of Cumberland, has not stated that ne was ignorant of the existence of Orange lodges in the army. This omission is the more deserving of notice, because he was colonel of the 7th dragoons—because he was examined twice before the committee—and because the several other functionaries of the Orange body have declared their utter ignorance of that which they ought to have known so well. Independently of these considerations, it appears by a report of the proceedings of the English Grand Lodge, that the gallant colonel was present when (the Duke of Cumberland being in the chair) a resolution respecting the establishment of Orange lodges in the army was moved. Is it true that he was present?

Colonel VERNER.—I was never asked, in the committee, whether I knew of the existence of Orange lodges in the army. I now declare that I was utterly ignorant of the fact; and I do not remember whether I was or was not present when the resolution, to which the honourable gentleman adverts, was carried in the English Grand Lodge.

Mr. SHEIL.—How far the answer fits the question let the house judge It appears that the gallant colonel did attend the English Grand Lodge, on what occasion he does not distinctly recollect—his memory is misty —but it would be important that he should state how far the impression is correct, that Orange lodges have been established in the army with the sanction of the Duke of Cumberland, and by virtue of resolutions, passed when the Orange Grand Lodge was graced by the presence of his Royal Highness! I turn from the gallant colonel to the general question. At the commencement of the session I charged the Conservative government with having advanced Orangemen to places of high station, and having given to Orange lodges answers amounting to a recognition of their public usefulness. This motion was not unattended with a salutary effect; immediately after, the member for Kilkenny,* to whom the country is greatly indebted for the disclosures which he has been instrumental in producing, moved the appointment of the committee. On that committee the leading functionaries of the Orange body were placed. And yet it is said that the committee was packed; but let us see who were the members of it:—the honourable members for Sligo and for Cavan were upon it; and there were also Mr. Jackson, Mr. Wilson Patten—I suppose that he is a Conservative—Colonel Wood, Lord Castlereagh, Mr. Nicholl, Sir James Graham—(I really do not know with which party to class him)—Colonel Conolly, and Colonel Perceval. I do not think that this selection can be said to be an unfair one, but it is alleged that the mode in which the witnesses were examined was unjust. The Grand Master, and the Grand Treasurer, and the

e examined—(they are all Grand)—the order of
gether inverted, and the Orange party were allowed
nselves, and for a number of days none but Orange
ined. Colonel Verner was twice examined—first
1835, and again on the 9th of April. Then came
ner O'Sullivan—certainly a very competent witness
1 respect to both religions, for with regard to one
the "Pleasures of Memory," and to the other, he,
th the "Pleasures of Hope;" Mr. M. O'Sullivan,
, was produced, and was examined on the 13th of
id 26th of May, and again on the 27th of May: so
upon theology and the Reverend Mortimer O'Sul-
Mr. Swan, the Deputy Grand Secretary; next came
, the Assistant Grand Treasurer, who was examined
;h, and 13th of June; next Mr. W. Ward, the soli-
body, who was produced to show that they never
d with the administration of justice; then again,
came Mr. Mortimer O'Sullivan—*ecce iterum Cris-*
came Mr. Hugh Baker. Yet it is alleged that
ealing in the examination of witnesses, although
esolutions of the honourable member for Middlesex
n the testimony of a party adverse to Orangeism,
iony of Orangemen supported by the journals and
mselves produced. What appears to be the state of
e to the Orange institution, from the evidence
nen themselves? A confederacy exists, exclusively
its of 150,000 men; the members are initiated with
rious ritual—they enter into a compact of religious
hood—signs and pass-words are employed by them
:landestine recognition—their proceedings are regu-
ws, the most specific and the most minute—they are
representative assembly called the Grand Lodge of
if delegates from every part of Ireland—the whole
nto departments, in which lodges affiliated and cor-
other are established—and this enormous mass of
itism is in arms, while a Prince of the Blood, not
rone, is at its head!
aralleled institution worked? Let us inquire what
ith respect to the administration of justice and the
ry, and ask how has it been employed as a political
)ose of persecution, and under what circumstances
iizance it has extended itself into the army? The
ge have defended a series of prosecutions instituted
rs of this turbulent fraternity, by the crown. An
streets of Dundalk, strikes a Roman Catholic dead;
the crown, convicted of manslaughter, and sentenced
:onment. His defence was conducted by the Orange
ge lodges came to a resolution to support him. Cer-
at Newry were sentenced to sixteen months' impri-

▸nment by a Protestant magistrate; to these malefactors the Grand Orange Lodge extended their pecuniary aid, and they conducted their defence. They not only defended but prosecuted. Three magistrates in Cavan dispersed an Orange procession; the Grand Orange Lodge determined to institute a prosecution against the civil authorities who had the audacity to interfere with them; they sent down to Cavan their solicitor, and the grand jury threw out the bills. At the last Meath election a body of 200 Orangemen, gathered from the adjacent counties, entered the town of Trim. They fill the Court-house; a dagger is seized in the hand of one of them by the High Sheriff; they spread confusion and dismay, and after having enacted their part, return to the town of Kells. Here they meet a Roman Catholic, and put him to death; they are prosecuted, and the Grand Orange Lodge, by a specific resolution, advances money to conduct the defence. An Orangeman is indicted; in the jurors' box twelve Orangemen are placed; the magistrates, if the case be tried at quarter sessions, are members of this fatal fraternity; under these circumstances, what a mockery is the administration of justice! Sir Frederick Stovin speaks of it as a subject of public ridicule and contempt. But facts are better than opinions. Take the following:—In a prayer-book a notice of Orange assassination is written; Sir Frederick Stovin and his subordinate, Duff, who was employed in the police, had incurred the displeasure of the Orangemen of Tyrone, and in the prayer-book belonging to the wife of Mr. Duff— left in the church that she had been in the habit of attending—an Orange notice, threatening death to Sir Frederick Stovin and to her husband, is written. Almost immediately after, a meeting is called at Dungannon at which the Lord Lieutenant of the county Tyrone attends, and the Orangemen appear in considerable force, with military music, and invested with their factious decorations. A scene of excitement ensues —shots are discharged—a musket is levelled at Sir Frederick Stovin, and the ball whistles at his ear; and all this occurs in the pacific province of Ulster.

What, the house will ask—atrocious as the circumstances may appear —what has all this to do with the administration of justice? At that meeting, attended with so many incidents of a revolting character, Lord Claude Hamilton was made an Orangeman—he was initiated at the house of a publican of the name of Lilburne; and immediately afterwards he was made a magistrate. In this state of things, what other feeling but one of dismay amongst Roman Catholics, and one of impunity can exist amongst the Orange population of the country? I appeal to a fact again: At the last spring assizes for the county of Armagh, three Orangemen were prosecuted for marching in a procession. Baron Pennefather suggested to them, with a view to a mitigation of their sentence, that they ought to express regret for having violated the law. Did they intimate their contrition? Did they declare their determination never to commit a similar outrage on the public peace again? In open court, and in the face of the judge, these audacious confederates whistled an air, called "The Protestant Boys." And what was the course taken by indignant justice?—what, do you conjecture, was their sentence? Not two years' imprisonment—not one year—not six months. The learned judge tempers justice with mercy, and sentences these presumptuous delinquents to an imprisonment of three weeks. The Dorchester labourers were sentenced to transportation for seven years, and the Orange malefactors to an imprisonment for three weeks. But how has the Orange Society affected the peace of the country? We are told that Ulster is in a state of profound and prosperous repose; but by the evidence, what appears? In the broad day, on the 17th of January last, a body of Orange incendiaries enter a Roman Catholic village, called Anagagh, and, in the face of the noon-tide sun, set fire to the houses of the Roman Catholic inhabitants; they then retire to a hill called Pinigo, to the number of near 200, form themselves in military array—Sir Frederick Stovin advances at the head of the military, with a piece of artillery, in order to disperse them—the magistrate, by whom he is attended, declines giving an order to fire—and the Orangemen, in martial order, and with martial music, bidding and looking defiance, march away. And how are they armed? With yeomanry muskets. The entire yeomanry force of Ireland is, in fact, enrolled in the Orange associations, and when a conflict ensues with the people the consequences are easily foreseen: witness the slaughters of which they have been guilty, the blood in which they have waded, the horrors which they have perpetrated: witness Newtownbarry! How has the Orange institution been employed as a political engine? To their declaration of allegiance a condition is attached. They engage to maintain the throne, so long as by the throne Protestant ascendancy is supported. They expel from their society every member who does not comply with their ordinances at elections. They issue proclamations, commanding every Orangeman to petition parliament for or against specific measures —and they are armed with what must be considered formidable instruments of supplication. At the close of the last year it was determined y a cabal that Lord Melbourne should be driven from office. At Hillsorough 75,000 Orangemen are assembled to sustain the Conservative dventurers in their daring and desperate enterprise, and to prove that iey are not the remnant of a despicable faction. But will it be said, Had they not a right to all this? Had they not the advice of the ing to speak out? Had they not a right to petition parliament, and ldress the crown at Hillsborough?" Be it so. Granting them their erogative at Hillsborough, what have they to do with Quebec? The, use seems startled with the question. It is readily explained. The rangemen of Ireland have passed resolutions for the extension of their iety into Upper and Lower Canada. The Grand Lodge of England ve appointed a Grand Secretary to visit the British colonies of North uerica, with directions to communicate with the Grand Master. Why his? Upon what pretence? For what purpose? Is their object ensive? What, in God's name have the Irish or English Orangemen do with Lower Canada, whose religion is Catholic, whose established urch is Catholic, whose legislature is Catholic—for eighteen out of nty of the inhabitants are Catholics? Are they not contented with king the baneful roots of their confederacy into the heart of the

British empire, but they must extend ramifications across the Atlantic, in order to supply the North American colonies with their poisoned fruits?

I come to the army, the most important topic. This loyal brotherhood, the guardian of peace, the promoter of tranquillity, despite of the notorious rules of the Horse Guards, and in violation of every principle of military discipline, have introduced into the army its secret, its factious, and mutinous organization? The fact is beyond all dispute; but there are circumstances connected with it, which are not a little remarkable. There is, in the code of Orange legislation, an ordinance that all regiments in the army shall be considered as districts. It is the 15th rule of 1824. So late as this very year in the Grand Orange Lodge of Ireland, a warrant was granted to create a lodge in the army; and who was in the chair? Mr. Cromelin, the Grand Master of the county of Down. This resolution and the presidency of Mr. Cromelin on the occasion, appear in the appendix to the report. But let the house mark the following resolution, "That the next warrant should be granted to the 66th Regiment." Who was it moved that resolution? No ordinary individual—a man, holding, in the Orange body, the highest position, but who began his political life as a Fellow of Trinity College, Dublin, (of which the Duke of Cumberland is chancellor), who has since figured in Brunswick clubs, and has exhibited, on various occasions, at public meetings in England,—the Rev. Charles Boyton, the associate of Mr. Mortimer O'Sullivan, the Grand Chaplain of the Orange Grand Lodges, and—mark it!—the Chaplain to the Earl of Haddington, the late Lord Lieutenant. But all the functionaries of the Orange body, despite all this, were ignorant of what was going on in the army. The knowledge of some people is wonderful; but not half so marvellous as the ignorance of others. The next time the honourable gentleman opposite, the Grand Treasurer, late Treasurer to the Ordnance, who was admitted, with the Duke of Wellington, a doctor of common law at Oxford, visits that learned and loyal establishment, I pray of him to revive the old college play of "Ignoramus;" the principal characters to be performed by Alexander Perceval, Henry Maxwell, and his Royal Highness the Duke of Cumberland. His Royal Highness has written a letter. He never heard of Orange lodges in the army—never heard of the orders of 1822 and 1829,—of the rule of the Orange body, that every regiment should be considered a district—of the majority of the Grand Lodge having carried a resolution, on a division, to establish Orange lodges in the army—of the printed book of warrants, in which the list of military warrants is contained;—neither does his Royal Highness recollect having been present when, in 1831, 1832, 1833, and 1835, warrants were granted, whilst he was in the chair, to military men, and actually a soldier attended as representative of his regiment. His Royal Highness does not bear all this in mind, and is utterly ignorant of the introduction, into the army, of the lodges, of which he is the Grand Master. Heaven forbid that I should question the truth of his Royal Highness's allegation; I fly in the midst of difficulties, which might startle the belief of men of less accommodating credulity than mine.

Credo, quia impossibile est. But, Sir, there is a consideration of infinite importance connected with his Royal Highness, and independent of his knowledge or his ignorance. Is it befitting that any British subject should possess the power of which he has made himself the master? Is it safe, that a prince of the blood should be invested with this portentous authority? He is declared, by the rules of the English Grand Lodge, to be absolute and uncontrollable: he is addressed with a species of prophetic greeting—" Hail, that shalt be king hereafter !" an aphorism of theology. If that prediction shall be verified ; if by some fatality, England shall be deprived of the princess who is the object of her affection and of her hope—that princess who, if maternal virtues be hereditary, must be wise, and gentle, and good—if, Sir, the Imperial Grand Master be fated to be the Sovereign of this vast empire, I trust that by 100,000 Irish Janissaries the throne of Ernest the First will never be surrounded!

One, and the most important, of all questions, remains. What are the house and the government to do under the existing facts of the case? That something must be done, is manifest. You cannot tolerate this institution. If you do what will be the result? How will the Roman Catholic soldiers feel, with whom your army is filled, who have fought your battles, participated in your glory, and furnished the raw material out of which the standard of victory has been wrought? If, by your connivance, you convert this confederacy into a pattern, and if a counter organization shall be formed—if we, the Irish millions, shall enrol ourselves in some analogous organization—if its members shall be admitted with a solemn religious ceremony—if the obligation of a political fraternity shall be inculcated—if signs, and tests, and pass-words shall be employed—if a representative assembly, consisting of deputies from every Irish county shall be held in the metropolis, and subordinate lodges shall be held in every department into which the country shall be subdivided, what will befal? To the vanquished, and to the victors, —woe! The gulf of civil warfare will yawn beneath the feet of Ireland, and in the abyss all her hopes will be swallowed. Avert, avert the calamity, which, if I have anticipated, it is only to shudder at its prospects. Save us from these terrible possibilities ! Adopt a measure which, by a timely application, may prevent these terrific results from coming to pass. If I relied upon them less, I should warn them more. I will not tell them that I expect—I know—that they will do their duty.

CHURCH OF IRELAND.

SPEECH IN THE HOUSE OF COMMONS, JULY 23, 1835.

THE honourable baronet (Sir R. Bateson) who spoke last, and who designates himself as one of the representatives of the intellect of Ireland (intellect appears to be an item of Protestant monopoly), contradicted in his peroration the bold assertion with which he began. At the outset, he talked of those Irish members who dissent from him, and coincide with the government, as persons of very small account; at the conclusion, he describes their great and baneful power. The honourable baronet, indeed, and those with whom he is in the habit of acting, have had an ample experience of the efficiency, the energy, the vigilance, and the union of that body, which he affects to treat with disregard, but to which, in his arguments, he offers the acknowledgment of his involuntary respect. We are the majority—the great majority of the Irish members. Among us are men of as high station, and as large possessions, as the honourable baronet: we speak the sentiments of the great mass of the Irish people on a question that most nearly touches the interests of Ireland. If, for a series of years, the majority of Scotch representatives had, upon a Scotch question, declared a strong and unvarying opinion, there are few who would suggest that, to their opinions no attention ought to be paid; and when, by the majority of Irish members, it is insisted that justice and expediency require that a particular policy should be adopted in reference to a subject by which Ireland and her tranquillity are so immediately affected, it is strange that any individual should speak with disparagement of those by whom millions of his countrymen are represented. I have thought it right to advert to a topic on which the honourable gentleman has indulged in insinuations by which our hostility may be imbittered, but our real influence never can be impaired.

The measure which the government has brought forward, is founded upon that principle for the adoption of which those who know Ireland best have uniformly contended, as affording the only basis on which a salutary system of corrective legislation can be founded. That principle is now, for the first time, proposed to be embodied with distinctness in a legislative enactment. Its germ was indeed to be found in the Church Temporalities Bill, which is commonly known by the name of Stanley's Act. The noble lord opposite, in the suspension clause, had the merit of furnishing a most valuable precedent, and indeed (although unconscious of it) laid down the principle upon which this bill in a great measure rests—

Lord STANLEY.—No! No!

Mr. SHEIL.—That bill contained a clause providing for the suspension of benefices.

Lord STANLEY.—For what purpose?

Mr. SHEIL.—I take not the will for the deed, but the deed for the will. I care little about the p rpose contemplated by the noble lord, but look to the results to which his measure must lead. He provided that, in certain cases, whole districts might be left without a Protestant clergyman, and that in those districts the church should have no external, visible sign. No spiritual consolation, as it is called, was to be administered to Protestant parishioners in the localities which were to fall within the provisions of the noble lord's celebrated measure; no opportunity for conversion was to be given to the Roman Catholic inhabitants. That bill went much farther than the present project: because, by the latter, a Protestant traveller, wnose itinerant orthodoxy chances to stand in need of spiritual aid, is to find a Protestant clergyman at hand, bound to administer to his religious need; a stipend is to that end provided: but by the bill of the noble lord all trace of Protestantism was to be swept away, and unmolested Popery was to be left in complete and undisputed possession of the ground from which, under the auspices of the noble lord, its competitor was to be driven. It concerns the house little what object the noble lord might have had in view; the inference from his measures is irresistible. Such premises are supplied by his expedients, as to afford an irresistible conclusion against the policy to which he still inconsistently and obstinately adheres. Did not the right honourable baronet, the member for Cumberland,* on a former occasion, admit the force of these observations, when he expressed his regret that he had ever given his assent to that clause in the Church Temporalities Bill? I wish that he were here, in order that he might give upon this subject some more satisfactory explanation than his noble confederate can furnish. On ordinary occasions, it is, perhaps, sufficient that the noble lord should be present as representative of his right honourable friend; there is such a unity of sentiment, such a singleness of object, on the part of both those distinguished associates, that the opinions of the one always afford an adequate intimation of the views of the other; but, in the present instance, it is not unreasonable to desire that the right honourable baronet should have condescended to be present. His speech was of such a character —he has assailed his opponents in terms so unqualified—that, after the delivery of a vituperative harangue, he ought to have attended the house, and encounter the men on whose character he has committed an assault.

I own that I was anxious the right honourable baronet should be present, when to his historical references from Clarendon, an answer, which he might have anticipated, was to be given. That right honourable baronet, not satisfied with invoking the religious prejudices of the English people, has resorted to citations, of which the object appears to be to awaken a feeling of alarm in the mind of the highest personage in the realm. Was it to produce an impression at Windsor that the right honourable baronet, last night, assigned as a cause of the fall of the monarchy, the abandonment, by Charles the First, of the interests of the church? It was not a little amusing to hear the right honourable baronet avail himself of the same expedients which were employed

* Sir J Graham.

by Mr. Croker, in his speech against reform. To what a pass has an ex-reformer arrived, when from Mr. Croker he borrows, without acknowledgment, the arguments employed by the literary leader of Conservatism, against the measure in which the right honourable baronet and the noble lord bore so conspicuous a part! But did he not forget, when he was quoting Clarendon, and describing the steps which led Charles to the fatal window in Whitehall, that the noble lord opposite had given of those events a very different account; and, in taking Mr. Croker to task, had uttered the following striking and fervid passage? This was Lord Stanley's language on the occasion to which I refer:—

"At length, when Charles wanted to force episcopacy upon Scotland, &c., he was forced to call together that parliament which he had for so many years endeavoured to dispense with. But they knew him too well to put any trust in him. When they spoke of grievances, he spoke of subsidies; and when they properly refused them, without better security than promises, the insincerity of which they were convinced of, he had recourse to a prompt and abrupt dissolution, and thus added wanton insult to continued injury. He was soon again compelled to call them together. Again he thought to temporize, and again he met the same resistance; and his tyranny ended, as I hope tyranny ever will end, in base, and timid, and degrading concession."

Such is the account given by the noble lord opposite of transactions which his colleague in opposition has endeavoured to apply, in a manner so different, in order to awaken apprehensions where, I trust, that no susceptibility of impressions so erroneous will be found. But in the crisis of their political fortunes, the opponents of this bill resort to every means by which, in any quarter, excitement may be generated. Here all the opponents (the strangely-combined opponents of the government) are resolved to try their strength. No stand was made on the Corporation Bill—the Conservatives had the virtue not to resist what they had not the courage to propose. But on the Irish Church, prejudice may be roused, fanaticism may be kindled, misrepresentation may be circulated; accordingly, round the standard of sinecurism a rally is made, and an alliance—a holy one—formed between the Conservative party, whom no one can fairly blame, and the ex-Reformers, the antagonists of their old friends, and the friends of their old antagonists—dealers in pious philippics and religious intrigue. To popular excitement, connected with the old horror of Popery, it is manifest, that these united forces look; but they will find that they mistake the echo of their own delusions for the confirmation of public opinion. Where are the petitions of the people? Have even the Cumberland yeomen stirred? We have heard of a declaration from a fanatical Scotch synod; but from the mass of the Scotch people has any remonstrance been preferred? How did the majority of Scotch members vote on the resolution on which this bill is founded? The people of that country look to this government with a confidence which appeals to antiquated theology cannot disturb. They see that, in the short period during which they held office, they have carried through this house one of the most important measures of reform which has ever yet been propounded · that they have carried it without the aid of the members for Cumberland or Lancashire—without whom it now appears possible that a government really can go on;—and seeing such practical benefits already effected, they will listen with incredulity to those whose zeal for religion is not a little heightened by their emotions as partisans. Out of the house their policy will fail; and in the house the stratagem to which they have had recourse, in moving an instruction, would be of little avail The course pursued is remarkable. After the second reading they oppose the principle; and before the house goes into committee, they criticise the details. In the last session they resisted the Tithe Bill in the second reading, although it did not include any new appropriation this bill, besides the appropriation clause, contains much that is condemned, and contains nothing which is approved; yet the second reading passes, not only without division, but without comment. You desire to divide the bill into two parts: having done so, which will you select? You disapprove of the entire in its aggregate form; which of the fractions will you approve, if your instruction should be carried? There is not a principle, there is not a detail in this bill which has not been the subject of condemnation. The men who would subtract £25 per cent. from the revenues of the clergy by the Tory bill, (which fell still-born, and whose authors died in childbed), cry out against any diminution of their incomes; and the great author of the metallic currency, who has reduced rents £50 per cent. insists that the church ought not to be affected by the revolutions of Mark-lane. Will the renowned Cumberland political economist, who would have subtracted £30 per cent. from the demands of every mortgagee in the country—give to the opinion of the eminent transmuter of paper into gold, the benefit of his disinterested coincidence on this head? Talk indeed of not reducing the compositions! If there had not been any compositions, tithes would have fallen one-half. How do they stand in this country? A gentleman, a considerable proprietor in Warwickshire (whose name I will mention to any body who desires it), told me that for his lay tithes, not very long ago, he received upwards of £2000 a-year, and that they have since fallen to £800.

It is insisted that there will be no surplus. If there be not, no practical harm will be done to the church; but the recognition of the rinciple will be a just and conciliatory tribute to the reasonable feelıgs of the Irish people. But how do you make out that there will be o surplus? You expatiate on the poverty of the Irish church. Why id you always refuse a committee on the subject? It was repeatedly roposed by the honourable member for Middlesex. You state that ıe revenues of the church have been exaggerated; but what test will ıu employ to ascertain them? What is the amount of the bishops ·venues? You tell us that they do not exceed £130,000 a year; but .eir amount really is £150,000 as returned by the dignitaries themlves. Whether this ought to be conclusive I will not determine; but is I do know, that in calculating the net income, the bishops have deducted ;ents' fees, and all expenses incidental to the collection of their for nes. The income of the Archbishop of Armagh, which is now

£17,000 a year, will rise to £23,000 a year, by his own return; and observe, that neither this increase nor any other is included in the £150,000. It is stated that the glebe lands of Ireland are worth only £17,000 a year. Even the right honourable member for Tamworth has stated that Lord Althorp has underrated the value of the glebe lands: there are 85,000 Irish acres. Most glebes have good houses on them, and £120,000 a-year is not an exaggerated estimate. But why has not a return of their value been obtained? Again, on what authority is the amount of ministers' money set forth? I come to a most important item, ministers' money (a tax raised on every house), which illustrates the spirit of depreciation with which the wealth of the church is reduced by its advocates. I hold a return of the amount of the property of the minor ecclesiastical corporations: it is stated, by the return, to be £57,000 a-year. At what sum did Lord Althorp, before that return was made, estimate this portion of the ecclesiastical possessions? At £2,000 a-year. But it is alleged a large portion of that sum is applicable to the reparation of cathedrals. Granted: but still is it not church property? and is it not most unfair to exclude it from the account? Why are the surplice fees never mentioned? They are not fixed permanent property: true ;—but in estimating the means of livelihood of the clergy, we must take this detail of sustenance into consideration. Thus it is manifest that there never has been a just and full account of church property; and if there be not—the blame lies with those who have refused committees, and never given us access to the true sources of information. I venture to say, that if to-morrow a committee were moved for on the Irish church, it would be opposed by the Conservatives and their associates. But the real object of the opponents of the bill, in the course which they have adopted is, by running into collateral topics, to lead away the attention of parliament from the simple question—whether the resolution passed deliberately by the house should be rescinded. That resolution has nothing to do with details. It affirmed a great principle; and the Conservatives having been flung by that resolution out of power, endeavour, by indirect means, to nullify and render it of no avail. But to that resolution the house will adhere; and if the bill shall return from the Lords mutilated in that essential particular, this house will repudiate the wretched fragment. That resolution was passed without the report. The report gave it the strongest corroboration. It has changed the opinions of the honourable member for Berkshire, who has made a great sacrifice of his personal feelings and his parliamentary attachments to his duty. To the leading features in the report, and to no other, I shall refer. What has become of the 3,000,000 of Protestants, of which the member for the University of Oxford has so often said so much? There appear to be only 852,000 Episcopal Protestants in Ireland, and even they include the Methodists, who are attached by so slender a tie to the church; they have no episcopal ordination—no imposition of hands;—(I cannot understand by what medium their clergy receive the Divine Spirit.) They may have the same faith, but they have not the same discipline nor the same government; and an alien priesthood will soon become a hostile one.

But look to the Presbyterians. In the province of Armagh (the North of Ireland), the fortress of orthodoxy, there are upwards of 600,000 Presbyterians, and there are not 600,000 Episcopal Protestants. What inference do I draw from thence? This: that the allegation that the church is the tie between England and Ireland is fallacious. The Presbyterians are attached to England; they are hostile to the church, so says the moderator of Ulster Synod, Mr. Montgomery. The conclusion is obvious: you do not need the church treasure to supply the chest out of which the garrison of Ireland, the Irish Protestants, are to be remunerated for their mercenary allegiance. Thus far for the North: descend to other districts. I shall take only one—the province of Tuam. What is its ecclesiastical wealth? The returns show, that the episcopal revenue in that province amounts to £22,000 a-year at the least. The glebe lands, prebendary revenue, and tithes, amount to at least £100,000 including the first item. I believe that it is much more. This is a large sum. Now comes the question—"How many Protestants are there in the province?" There are 1,100,000 Catholics; and, what will the house think?—300,000 Protestants?—No; 200,000?— No; one?—No, no; only 45,000. Gracious God! £100,000 a-year for the "spiritual consolation" of 45,000 Protestants! This is in itself most gross; but contrast makes it monstrous. Turn from Tuam to a neighbouring country—not France, because there is a foolish notion that the French are all infidels, and therefore no analogy can be derived from their example: turn to a country just near you, where there is a great zeal for religion; a zeal which Protestants might regard as almost equivalent to fanaticism—turn to Belgium, your ally, for which you have sacrificed so much—the Catholic country with a Protestant king; —turn to Belgium, and what state of things do you find there?— 1,000,000 of Catholics. What hierarchy suffices for that number? One archbishop and four bishops. How much money do they receive? £17,000 a-year, by which the seminaries attached to their sees, as well s their own dignities, are sustained. The Irish Primate with 23,000 -year, and the whole Belgium hierarchy, and all their establishments, ith only £17,000! Pass to the priesthood. Here is the Belgium udget. I have the official document. The entire church establishent of Belgium does not cost more than the sum devoted to the salation of 45,000 Protestants in the province of Tuam; and mark, the uties of the Catholic clergy are infinitely more laborious. The prace of confession is alone sufficient to render the functions of the atholic priest far more onerous than those of the Protestant pastor t with this small sum religion thrives in Belgium—(religion never es except of pecuniary repletion); while the Protestant church in eland, with all its wealth, makes, in conversion, no sort of way. How uch more rational it is to appeal to the example of the Belgian people an to the doctrines of a Belgian professor, and to try the Catholic ligion by the practice of a great body of its professors, than to deterne it by ponderous volumes of exploded theology, which give aliment prejudices viler than the worms by which those tomes of virulent inity are consumed. In Belgium the Protestant clergy are supported by grants made by a Catholic parliament, and not only is not the allowance a narrow one, but in consideration of the charges attendant on the Protestant pastor, he receives a larger stipend than the Roman Catholic rector. The statesmen of Exeter Hall, however, shutting out these facts, would blow the dust that covers the works of Dens into the eyes of the British people. Because there are abominable opinions in Dens, there are to be abominable sinecures in Ireland; because priests are charged with a disposition to propagate religion with the sword, parsons are to levy tithes with the bayonet? Are you to have your Rathcormacs, because we have had our *autos-da-fé?* Look, I say it again, to the Belgian Catholic church—its tolerance, its small cost to the state, its humble and apostolic circumstances—a priesthood without wealth, a hierarchy without pomp. Turn from thence to your Irish church, and with the spirit of the gospel let both be compared.

I may be told that I ought not to seek in a foreign country for illustration—be it so. I appeal to Scotland. The right honourable baronet, the member for Cumberland, has invited me to cross the border. He tells me that some Scotch synod or other has interfered in Irish affairs. I stop not to inquire into their discretion; I stop not to ask whether they, whose ancestors revolted against episcopacy, and won the enjoyment of their religion with their broad swords, and established the great principle, that the church of the minority should not live at the cost of the majority of the people, are justified in taking part with 800,000 against 7,000,000, including 600,000 Presbyterians, who bear to the Irish Church as great a disrelish as the Roman Catholic Irish people. Putting these considerations aside, I ask this plain question —How much does the Scotch church cost? Not, certainly, £300,000 a-year. There are nearly 2,000,000 churchmen in Scotland; they have less than £300,000 a-year (I really believe less) for their spiritual wants. There are in Ireland not half the number, and three times as much money is dedicated to their salvation. If the religion of 2,000,000 churchmen in Scotland costs so much, how much ought the religion of 800,000 to cost in Ireland? By what rule of proportion is that problem to be solved? But it is said that each individual Scotch clergyman receives a comfortable stipend. Compare the thousands a-year payable to an Irish sinecurist with the few hundreds payable to a Scotch working clergyman, and what inference will be deduced? When did this compassion for the poor Irish curates with large families arise? To their Conservative sensibilities when did honourable gentlemen first begin to give way? We never heard a word against pluralities, and the wretched dependence of the lower class of the Protestant priesthood upon the gorged and pampered dignitaries of the Establishment, until the Agitators, as they are called, denounced the enormous wealth of the church, and called for retrenchment. Of new distribution not a syllable was said, until the new appropriation was demanded, and it is only to escape from the one, that in the other you now seek a tardy refuge. Curates and their children might stand starving at the bishop's gates, if the opulence of the Establishment had never been assailed: it is only when that opulence is held out to public condemnation that the

bler clergy is made a topic for the excitation of
lemen, habitually satirical upon the rights of the
etic upon the privileges of the church. Not con-
ce to Scotland, the advocates of the Irish Church,
int which ought to be paid to a Protestant clergy-
advert to the sum voluntarily paid to the Catholic
ands to whom he stands in the relation of pastor,
otector, friend. You have no right to compare
f sickness—beside the straw where agony is laid,
rom morning to night, and from night to morning,
ill of the meanest of his flock ; and, through storm
h glens and morasses, to the expiring peasant he
s way ; nor business nor pleasure ever can supply
for an omission in his laborious and exhausting
i soul, his entire existence are devoted to those
lly and tenderly calls " his people." Turn from
sinecurist of your religion, without congregation
ministering occasionally, if at all, at a deserted
nely walls the diatribes against the creed of the
manner of effective occupation but that of eating
i, and begetting others to do the same after him ;
, draw from the livelihood paid of their own accord
the priest, the standard by which the parson ought
stained. Out of what resources—from what fund
om you venture to assimilate the sinecurists of the
hed with the means of life ? One would imagine,
ou, that they were maintained at the national
liamentary grant—by some sort of *regium donum*,
lence is it that these revenues, on which you expa-
The treasury is in the nation's heart :—out of their
erality, unassisted by any contribution from the
f Ireland have maintained their church—affording
intary over the compulsory principle—proving the
ood, the gratitude of the country, and supplying
qualities that belong to the character of the Irish
lp giving way to an emotion of pride when I con-
idst of poverty, of circumstances the most unto-
ic most deterring, we have accomplished. There
the state, supported by galling imposts, with enor-
iues, with wealth exceeding that of any establish-
ind there, beside it, stands the unaided church of
intain our priesthood in comfort, and our hierarchy
Christian mediocrity that, between their precepts
revents all offensive contrast ; while to our clergy
l that becomes them. To the worship of our God
temples, worthy of the lofty recollections associated
ie sight of which fills the traveller with admiration,
the artist, and to the poor man's heart imparts
ousness that he has assisted the splendid edifice in

its ascent by his humble contribution. And when, out of our own resources, we do all this—when, paupers as we are represented to be, we have thus not only given sustainment but a just elevation to our ancient church, how paltry it is of Protestantism, with its enormous revenues—boasting, as it does, that all the aristocracy belong to it— to come here, making a poor face, and with its coffers replenished with the public gold, whining and whimpering about the wretched destitution to which it is about to be reduced.

I own to you that, in considering this subject, with a view to speak upon it, I had collected a great deal of materials connected with topics which are not unfrequently introduced, such as the distinction between individual and corporate property—the old division into four parts of the church property—and I was prepared to cite various authorities to establish a proposition on which schoolmen might dissertate, but with which politicians have little concern. After reflecting, however, on this vast question, it struck me that the interests involved were really too important to be discussed with the subtlety of scholastic disputation, or the musty pedantry of antiquarian research; and that where interests of such incalculable importance are at stake, it is our duty to discuss them upon the grounds of public expediency, or, I should rather say, of public exigency, alone, in a spirit becoming men in whose hands the destinies of an empire are placed, and by whom, in such an emergency, all regards independent of public usefulness ought to be dismissed.— Abandoning all metaphysical disquisitions, I proceed not to a consideration of mere expediency, but of paramount and dire necessity; and I lay down a very plain proposition, and it is this—however harsh the truth, it must be told—it is this:—Whatever may be your inclination, you have not the ability to maintain the Irish establishment. Why? because the power of the Irish people has risen to such a pitch, that to the mistaken interests of an impuissant minority, the rights undoubted, although not undisputed, of the erroneous majority, cannot any longer be sacrificed with impunity. What is the great question into which all these matters of incidental consideration really resolve themselves?— The policy upon which Ireland must be governed. At first view, the subject seems to be a wretched dispute between Catholic and Protestant —a miserable sectarian controversy. It is no such thing; it is the very self-same question by which cabinet after cabinet has been annihilated —of which the Catholic question was but one shape;—it is the struggle for complete political equality on the part of the overwhelming majority upon the one hand, and for political ascendancy on the part of the minority upon the other. Can that ascendancy be maintained? Look at Ireland, and at the circumstances by which the existing state of things has been produced? I should be justified in going back half a century, and in tracing the growth of the popular power from its small beginnings, to the elevation and the extent to which it has spread and ascended. There are men now living, who recollect the time when the great bulk of the Irish people were reduced to a state to which serfship and helotism might be justly applied. We had no property, and we could not by law acquire it; we had no intelligence, and all access to the sources of edu

: we were not only excluded from every political
it from every honourable profession. The mass of
ared to be a dull, inert heap of senseless matter;
iciples of vitality were contained. Those principles
great events. America was freed; the Irish Pro-
sserted its independence; then came that resusci-
ugh an appalling process of conjuration, the Revo-
) all this I pass rapidly by, and come to events much
ie time, which is within the remembrance of us all
en in this house, who, of the power of the Irish
most painful, the most dear-bought experience—
iworth* and for Lancashire.† Both entered official
r Ireland—both devoted themselves to ascendancy
its victims. In 1813 the member for Tamworth
itary to the Lord Lieutenant; and as he united
great anxiety to do good, had circumstances been
d had he had just laws to administer, how different
i government? But he was attached to a party
s talents, and frustrated his purposes. He could
the evil; and although he now expresses a strong
tical abuses, of that disrelish while he was in office
equivocal evidence, and allowed sinecures (those
us abhorrence) to remain undisturbed. He had,
except in measures of repression; the Insurrection
id on the 3rd of June, 1814, a proclamation was
ces, to prevent the assemblages of the people. The
put down; not so the spirit of the people; it was
'er can be dead. It was raised again in that cele-
hich embraced an entire people, and made such a
of strength, that in 1825 it was deemed requisite
'hich the right honourable baronet was a member,
i and idle effort! We laughed it to scorn. We
n, where we had agreed to connect the church by
, provided that by liberty the state should connect
e. The offer was repudiated:—we invoked the
were armed with the elective franchise; those gal
iss men rushed to the hustings with the courage
nich Irish soldiers, led by you (pointing to Sir IL
the breach: the holds of ascendancy were carried;
annihilated in Waterford; the aristocracy was
in Louth: these were, however, but the preludes
iter. In two years after, Mr. Vesey Fitzgerald,
at as member of the cabinet, stood for Clare: he
ader of the Irish people; he was discomfited; the
led with exultation; the national sympathy became
ers shouted, and threw up their caps for joy upon
y surveyed the popular ovation. Astonished by
lled by what they anticipated—the Duke and his

obert Peel. † Lord Stanley.

distinguished colleague gave way to the power of which they beheld these marvellous manifestations. But all had not been accomplished; it remained that, having won emancipation for ourselves, we should secure reform for you. There was a majority of English, and a majority of Scotch members against reform; it was achieved by the men whom the Irish people had poured, in a noble exercise of their privileges, into this house. "We did the state some service, and they know it;" and the first to acknowledge it was the noble lord the member for Lancashire! Strange! that, with that confession upon his lips, he should not have felt deeply conscious that the power to which he had resorted as an auxiliary, might be converted into an irresistible antagonist; and that when, with that incendiary eloquence of which he is the master, he was setting the passions of England on fire—strange, that it should never have occurred to him that we should avail ourselves of his example, and that in as strong and peremptory a tone as that in which he had demanded the reform of the parliament, the reform of the church would be required. But he had a great abhorrence for rotten boroughs, while for rotten livings he entertained an equally vehement, and not very unnatural predilection. He set up as the champion of the church, and entered into a struggle with the Irish people. It was not long before he alienated the whole Irish party, not only from himself, but from those colleagues who have since been released from the incumbrance of his co-operation, and between whom and Ireland, an honest, sincere, and permanent reconciliation, founded upon wise measures, and upon a just sense of the honourable motives from whence they have originated, has been effected.

The first proceeding on the part of the noble lord, which indeed affords tolerable evidence of his genius for government, was the Stanley "Arms' Bill:" this even his associates scouted from the cabinet. He then proceeded with his church reform, and in order to conciliate the Irish Catholics, excluded every Roman Catholic member from the Tithe Committee. In 1831, he gave £60,000 to the clergy, and passed a bill by which he transferred certain arrears to the Attorney-General, and commenced in the inferior courts a scene of unexampled litigation.— The profuse shedding of human blood ensued. In 1832, his Tithe Bill, by which a final adjustment was to be accomplished, was produced. It was instantly denounced as pregnant with the most baneful consequences. Mark, Englishmen! mark this:—at the period when that bill was brought forward, the Irish Catholics did not demand a reduction of tithes; there was no £1,000,000 then due; no sacrifice from the clergy, no sacrifice from the country, was required. All we asked was—a recognition of the principle which is, at last, expressed in this bill; and if that principle had been recognised in time, how much misfortune to

andard of Repeal was planted upon every hustings. The Coercion ill is passed—£1,000,000 is given to the Irish clergy—the church Temporalities Bill is introduced, with a great but latent principle of improvement—the influence of the noble lord prevails, and the 147th clause is truck out; meanwhile the clergy starve. The session of 1834 is opened. The letter of Lord Anglesey—(whose heart was full of the love of Ireland, but whose good intentions were marred by his coadjutor in the Irish government)—is produced: it calls for a new appropriation. Mr. Ward brings his motion forward—the church commission is issued by Lord Grey: the noble lord—(who affects to consider Lord Grey as opposed to Irish church reform, when the commission stares the noble lord in the face)—retires from office, lets go a Parthian and envenomed shaft at his associates—and there he now is, facing his former friends and in juxta-position with his former antagonists. How far he has descended or has risen in public estimation, I leave to be determined by his own judgment and that of the party of which he is the leader, which has been rapidly diminishing in numbers, and has undergone, to use the mathemetical phrase of the member for Tamworth, " a process of diminution." The government, in 1834, having been relieved from the assistance of the noble lord, brings a Tithe Bill forward, which would have given the clergy bread, and have gone a considerable way towards an adjustment of the question. It receives the approbation of a large body of the Irish representatives; it is thrown out, and the clergy are left to perish by those sinister auxiliaries who support the church by making martyrs of its ministers—parliament is prorogued—Lord Melbourne is dismissed from the cabinet with as little ceremony as a menial would be discharged from the palace. Suddenly, and to himself, I believe, unexpectedly, the right honourable baronet is raised to the premiership; the fortunes of this great country are placed by his sovereign in his hands; he arrives, declares himself the champion of the church, dissolves the parliament, strains every treasury nerve to return a Conservative house of Commons; the parliament of his own calling meets; he is beaten on the speakership, and does not resign; he is defeated on the amendment, and still retains his office; he is discomfited upon the Irish church, and he no longer considers it compatible with his dignity, his duty, or his honour, to remain in place; he surrenders the trust reposed in him by his Sovereign, and retires with disaster, but without humiliation—for he fell in a contest with millions; he had chosen a nation for antagonist, and it was impossible that he should not be overthrown. Far be it from me to dispute the talents, the skill, the various attributes of government, which he displayed; the greater the talents, the more consummate the skill, the more various the attributes for government of which he gave the proof—the more unquestionable the evidence of that power against which he sought to make battle, and by which he was struck down. Of that power I have traced the progress—that power, vested in millions, deputed to the great majority of Irish representatives, developed, not created by emancipation, confirmed by reform —which, so far from being attended with any likelihood of decrease, accompanied by the splendid certainty of augmentation: 3,000,000 have swollen since the Union to 7 000 000—they return the majority of the representatives of the country—they are led on by men of unalterable determination—in intelligence and in property they are making rapid advances—with Roman Catholics of high ability the bar is crowded —by them the highest law offices are filled—they are within a step of the bench of justice—if there were no further change by the legislature, the advance of the people would be still inevitable—the Corporation Bill (for you cannot legislate for one country on different principles from those which you apply to the other) is at hand. Can you wish, and if you wish, can you hope, that this unnatural, galling, exasperating ascendancy should be maintained? Things cannot remain as they are—it is impossible that they should retrograde—what expedient are you prepared to adopt? Would you re-enact the penal code, let loose Orangeism from its den? Would you drive the country into insurrection—cut down the people—avail yourselves of the most horrible instrumentality that a faction, panting for new confiscations, can apply—and bid the yeomanry draw forth the swords, clotted with the blood of 1798, that they may be brandished in massacre, and sheathed in the nation's heart. From so horrible a conception you instinctively and virtuously recoil. But, shrinking as you do from such a purpose, to what expedient will you fly? Will you dissolve the parliament What!—after you have already had recourse to that perilous expedient? You thought that you could manage the house of your own calling—you declared it at Tamworth. Have you not too deep a stake in fame, in fortune, in property, and in renown, to renew these terrible experiments? If a Conservative parliament should be assembled, its duration must be brief —its existence will be stormy and agitated while it lasts; but if the excited people should infuse an undue proportion of the democratic element into the representation, you will have raised a spirit which you will have no spell to lay, exposed an institution more valuable than the church to peril; and put, perhaps, what is more precious than the mitre, to a tremendous hazard—and all for what? For what are all these risks to be incurred?—for what are all these appalling hazards to be run ?— for what stake is this awful die to be cast? For what are cabinets after cabinets to be dissolved, appeals after appeals to be made to the people—the public credit to be annihilated—the lords brought into collision with the master power of the state—the royal prerogative, by its repeated exercise, abridged of the reverence which is due to it—the palace shaken to its foundations—and the empire itself brought to the verge of that gulf to which, by causes of less pressure, so many countries have been irresistibly and fatally driven? For what, into all these affrighting perils are we to rush? For what, into those terrific possibilites are we madly, desperately, impiously to plunge? For the Irish church!—the church of the minority, long the church of the state, never the church of the people—the church on which a faction fattens, by which a nation starves—the church from which no imaginable good can flow, but evil after evil in such black and continuous abundance has been for centuries, and is to this day, poured out—the church by which religion has been retarded, morality has been vitiated, atrocity has been engendered; which standing armies are requisite to sustain, which has cost England millions of her treasure, and Ireland torrents of her blood!

IRISH MUNICIPAL REFORM BILL.

SPEECH IN THE HOUSE OF COMMONS, MARCH 28, 1836.

THE speech of the honourable and learned gentleman (Sir W. Follett) would have been an exceedingly powerful one against Catholic emancipation, or against the extension to Ireland of parliamentary reform but those measures having been carried, it is preposterous to rely upon a policy utterly at variance with the principles on which they were founded. The honourable and learned member has relied upon a concession made by the government respecting the administration of justice. The appointment of the sheriffs has been transferred to the crown. This, said the honourable and learned member for Exeter, established a distinction between England and Ireland;—wherefore, since you have made this distinction, not abolish corporations altogether? I answer, that the appointment of sheriffs is an incident to the existence of corporate bodies, and not one of its elements,—that Ireland does not require an exact identity in every particular, but a general assimilation —that she does not ask that all the details shall be the same, but that the principles shall be analogous;—change the elevation of the edifice, but let the foundation of popular control remain untouched. Although an influence will cease to be exercised by corporations over courts of justice, yet over corporations a safe and salutary influence will still be exercised by the people. The nomination of sheriffs is taken away, but much is left behind ; the care of many local concerns, the guardianship of the public peace, the security and convenience of public ways, the imposition of taxes, their allocation and collection, and the management of corporate property. Is the latter of no consequence ? Try it by his test ; the Drapers' Company have estates in Londonderry ; suppose that it were proposed to that company to transfer their estates to the town, how would such a suggestion be received ? How offensive, then, the project to leave to English corporations their Irish estates, and to strip Irish corporations of their possessions ? I acknowledge that I regard the transfer of the right to nominate sheriffs as not only a concession but a sacrifice ; and I, for one, would not acquiesce in it, if I did not feel that something, nay, that much, ought to be yielded, in order to adjust those questions, without the settlement of which peace in Ireland is impossible and prosperity hopeless ; and if, after this step towards a compromise has been taken by the government, the bill be elsewhere rejected, or there shall be substituted for it what Ireland shall repudiate,—and if, by this expedient, the abuses of corporations, the distortion of justice, the plunder of corporate revenues, and political procuracy shall be perpetuated,—the people of England will know where the blame of that scandalous continuance ought to attach, and will determine between the men who are anxious, as far as it is practicable, to extend the benefit of British institutions, and those who, having had so long and minute a cognizance of those abuses, never applied a remedy ; and who, at last, when they can no longer be palliated with impunity, have recourse to a mock demolition, and send up to the House or Lord a project to which the Commons of England, Ireland, and Scotland never can accede.

All that has been said against this bill—all that has been insidiously insinuated, boldly stated, ingeniously inferred, and against "old friends and colleagues" contumeliously quoted, can, into a very short and unfortunately, familiar phrase "No Popery," be appropriately condensed. It is said that if we are once armed with power, we shall become unjust, arbitrary, and oppressive; that we shall follow the example given us, and that, by a Catholic combination, Protestants will be excluded from corporations. It is not a little remarkable that two noble lords, the members for Lancashire (North* and South†) who have touched on this topic, should, at the last election, have been proposed by Catholics to their constituents. But it will be suggested that Catholics in England and Ireland are very different. In Ireland you fear a sacerdotal ascendancy, which in England you have no reason to apprehend.

No man has enlarged more eloquently and pathetically upon this topic than the honourable member for Cumberland.‡ This night the right honourable baronet, relieved from those nautical occupations from which the illustrations of his eloquence were once derived, has suddenly taken to the consolations of religion, and there is reason to apprehend that this quondam Whig functionary—this ex-Lord of the Admiralty, has laid aside the Naval Almanac for "Fox's Martyrs." I do not believe that the speeches of the Catholic priests to which he has referred, are accurately reported ; and if I did, I should consider them as affording grounds for increasing the estimates, and for establishing a higher class of rhetoric at Maynooth. But mark the inconsistency between Conservative reasoning and assertion. We are told that there is no connexion between parliamentary and municipal reform ; yet all the arguments against municipal elections are derived from the conduct of the Catholic clergy on parliamentary elections. Now, if the argument were good for anything, it would lead to the abolition of parliamentary, not of municipal institutions. For my part, I avow the interference of priests at elections, if it gratifies the noble lord, the member for Lancashire, and the right honourable member for Cumberland ; and, I will add, that in no instance did the Catholic clergy interfere with more effect than in 1831, in order to carry the Reform Bill, when those honourable gentlemen were in office ; I do not, I own, recollect that on that occasion those distinguished individuals deprecated the sinister assistance to which the government, of which they formed a part, were indebted. But how does it come to pass that the Catholic priests enjoy a monopoly of their moral anger ? Have not the landlords some claim to their virtuous indignation ? They denounce what they call the tyranny of the priesthood ; but when they see families turned out in hundreds from their hovels—women without covering, and children without food ;— for these droves of human wretchedness, have they no commiseration ?

* Lord Stanley   † Lord Egerton.   ‡ Sir James Graham.

What connexion is there between tithes and borough-rates—between the corporation fund and the exsanguined treasure of the church? On a municipal election, I cannot conceive any one question by possibility to arise on which the priesthood can take the least political, personal, or any other imaginable concern. But in parliamentary elections what is at stake? The abolition of that detestable impost which has drenched Ireland in blood—which has produced atrocities from which every feeling of humanity, and every sentiment of religion are abhorrent, and which ought to make certain religious men whom I see before me, kneel down and pray to God every night, before they sleep, that for Rathcormac they may be forgiven. Interfere at elections! Yes:—the priests achieved emancipation, and broke down the power of the Beresfords in Waterford, annihilated the Fosters in Louth, and triumphantly carried the Clare election. Led on by them, the intrepid peasantry rushed to the hustings with the fearlessness with which Irish soldiers precipitate themselves into the breach, drove Toryism' from its holds, and of the emancipation of their country planted the immovable standard. In the same noble cause they devotedly persevere. Never, until the tithe question shall be justly adjusted, will the clergy of Ireland intermit their efforts to achieve the redress of those grievances to which the disturbed state of that country may be referred. But you that talk of the Irish clergy, have you no cause to look at home? Do your priesthood never interpose in political questions? I ask the honourable member for Exeter, who has read a letter from a Catholic bishop of Carlow, whether of the Bishop of Exeter, he has ever, peradventure, chanced to hear? He has referred to the Popish Doctor Nolan—has he no reason to recollect the Protestant Doctor Phillpotts? That learned prelate I admire for his talents; but surely they do not surpass the political zeal, with which his religious emotions are associated. All allowance should be made for the Catholic bishop, by those whose cause is so materially promoted by the Protestant prelate upon the other. But turn from Exeter to Ireland. Has this house never heard of the Reverend Mr. Boyton? He is the founder of the Brunswick Clubs, and it was proved n evidence, before the Orange committee, that he actually moved the rection of an Orange lodge in one of his Majesty's regiments. This vas the individual whom my Lord Haddington selected to officiate as me of the chaplains at the Castle. Talk, indeed, of the Catholic clergy: n November, 1834, a meeting of the Orange Society was held in Dublin, at which the Lord Mayor of the city of Dublin presided, and at which the Reverend Mr. M'Crea recited a poem, the burden of which vas—

  Then, put your trust in God, my boys,
  And keep your powder dry.

never heard the poetry of this belligerent predestinarian made the ibject of censure by those who condemn the political interposition of e Catholic priesthood. Sir, I think that I can demonstrate that every jection on a religious ground, so far as the church is involved, to unicipal reform in Ireland, was just as applicable to municipal reform England. It is said that corporations were established in Ireland maintain the Protestant interest. For what purpose were the Test and Corporation Acts passed in this country? They were enacted in order to protect the episcopal interest in England, against the influence of the Dissenters. They were regarded as the great bulwarks of the establishment; yet those bulwarks you surrendered in 1828 to the myriads of sectaries by which your church was encompassed; to Baptists, Quakers, Socinians, Independents, Presbyterians, Methodists—you threw open the fortresses of the establishment to all the hordes, who, with the voluntary principle, are battering your church to the earth; and when we who are akin to you (for your religion is only Popery cut down)—when we, from whose ecclesiastical escutcheon, your own, with a bar sinister, might be appropriately borrowed—when we, I say, demand the benefit of British institutions, you affront us with a proposition which to the Dissenters of this country—when the Test and Corporation Acts were at stake, and when corporate reform was in question—not one of you, not even in the House of Lords ever dared to make. The Duke of Wellington had not the boldness, my Lord Lyndhurst had not the dexterity, my Lord Winchilsea was not sufficiently excited, nor my Lord Roden sufficiently inspired;—it was reserved for us—it was reserved for colonial dependent Ireland—for us, on whom a faction trampled, but on whom, with God's blessing, and the aid of our determination, they shall tread no more—for us it was reserved, that we should be told, when to the interests of the thousand few the rights of the million many can no longer, with common decency, be sacrificed—that both from the few and from the many their national institutions should be taken away, and out of the ruins of the corporations Dublin Castle should be enlarged. Of the Act of Union, is not this a manifest infringement? When it is proposed in this house to reduce the sinecures of the Established Church, men cry out and say that the Union is violated; if the entire of the Irish corporations be swept away, and that against the will of the majority of the Irish members, will not the Union be trampled under foot? But it may be said,—so, indeed, it was observed by the learned member for Exeter,—that before the Union, corporations were Protestant. He forgets that by the Act of 1793, Roman Catholics were made admissible to corporations by law; but that from 1793 to 1829 not a single Roman Catholic was received into the Dublin corporation. In 1829 the member for Tamworth declared, in his emancipation speech, that Roman Catholics should be admitted to all corporate offices, and should be invested with all municipal privileges; there are accordingly two sections in his Emancipation Act to that effect. From that day to this, not a single Roman Catholic has had the benefit of those clauses in the act of parliament. By passive resistance, a Protestant passive resistance, the law has been frustrated and baffled. The right honourable baronet gave us a key that would not turn the lock; and when British justice is about to burst open the doors, he would level these institutions to the earth, and bury our rights, his own act of emancipation—God forbid! that I should add, his own dignity and honour—under the ruins. Sir, the right honourable gentleman appears to me to adhere to his old Irish policy; and although he carried emancipation, in obedience to his reason, he is acting on emancipation, in compliance with those religious instincts which he ought to get under his control. In the course of the last session I ventured to address myself to him in the language of strenuous, but most unaffectedly respectful expostulation; I presumed to entreat of him to take a retrospect of his Irish policy, and to inquire from him whether of every failing, and every failure, he did not in his Irish policy find the cause? I told him that Ireland had a grave ready for his administration—and that grave soon closed upon it.

I should not venture to advert to what I then said, but what has since befallen has given to those observations a remarkable confirmation. The moment the session of parliament terminated, the subordinates of the right honourable baronet commenced the "No Popery" cry. The result of that pious enterprise has corresponded with its deserts. The parliament assembles, and at the very outset the right honourable baronet tries his fortune on Irish grounds again, by moving an amendment, and he is at once and signally defeated. A few days elapse and he sustains a still more conspicuous discomfiture. Not in order to give way to a feeling of inglorious exultation do I refer to the dissolution of the Orange Society, but for the purpose of showing the "sweet uses" of which adversity is susceptible, and leaving out the offensive epithets in the citation to point to the "precious jewel" it contains. It was a vast incorporation, including 100,000 armed men, with individuals of the highest station among its leaders, and a prince of the blood at its head. Where is it now? Can you not derive admonition from its fall? You have seen administration after administration dissolved by the power of the Irish people; by the power of the Irish people you have seen your own cabinet dashed in an instant to pieces; and now, struck to the heart, you behold your own gigantic auxiliary laid low. Taught so long, but uninstructed still, wherefore, in the same fatal policy, with an infatuated pertinacity, do you disastrously persevere? You think, perhaps, that emancipation has failed. Six years in a nation's life are less than as many minutes of individual duration. You have not given it (what you asked for yourself) a fair trial, and have yourself, to a certain extent, counteracted its operation. At the very outset you entered into a struggle with the son of the earth, who has rebounded with fresh vigour from every fall; and, notwithstanding all our experience—although injustice carries with it the principle of self-frustration—although the poisoned chalice is sure, in its inevitable circulation, to return to the lips of those by whom it is commended—still, adhering to your fatal policy, and haunted by your anti-O'Connellism—still, instead of rising to the height of the great argument, and ascending to a point of moral and political elevation, from which you could see wide and far—you behold nothing but objects which, by their closeness, become magnified, and have nothing but the fear of O'Connell before your eyes. You do not legislate for a people, but against a man. Even if I were to admit that he had been occasionally hurried to excesses, for which your impolicy should in reality be responsible. ,e me still leave to ask whether millions of his fellow-countrymen and your fellow-citizens (for such, thank God! we are) and generations yet unborn, must pay the penalty? Granting him a life as long as Ireland can pray for, and his adversaries can deprecate, will he not be survived by the statute book? Have you made him immortal as well as omnipotent? Is your legislation to be built on considerations as transitory as the breath with which he speaks; and are structures that should last for ages, to have no other basis than the miserable antipathies by which we are distracted? Let us remember, in the discharge of the great judiciary functions that are imposed upon us, that we are not the trustees of contemporary interests only, but of the welfare of those by whom we are to be succeeded; that our measures are in some sort testamentary, and that we bequeath to posterity a blessing or a bane; and, impressed with that high,—and I do not exaggerate when I call it that holy—consciousness, let us have a care lest to a sentiment of miserable partisanship we should give way. To distinctions between Catholic and Protestant let there be an end. Let there be an end to national animosities as well as to sectarian detestations. Perish the bad theology, which, with an impious converse, makes God according to man's image, and with infernal passions fills the heart of man! Perish the bad, the narrow, the pernicious sentiments, which for the genuine love of country, institutes a feeling of despotic domination upon your part, and of provincial turbulence upon ours;—and while upon pseudo religion and pseudo patriotism I pronounce my denunciation, live (let me be permitted to pray) the spirit of philanthropic, forbearing, forgiving Christianity amongst us! and, combined with it, live the lofty love of country, which associates the welfare of both islands with the glory of this majestic empire—which, superior to the small passions that ought to be as ephemeral as the incidents of which they were born, acts in conformity with the imperial policy of William Pitt, and the marvellous discovery of James Watt—sees the legislation of the one ratified by the science of the other, and of the project of the son of Chatham, in the invention of the mighty mechanist, beholds the consummation.

TITHES.

SPEECH IN THE HOUSE OF COMMONS, JUNE 2, 1836.

THE right honourable baronet (Sir James Graham) has concluded a speech in favour of religion and of liberty, by a citation from an Atheist and a Tory. He has indulged in a dissertation upon property, which it is to be lamented that the Cumberland yeomen did not hear, in order that he may henceforth correct erroneous notions on that subject. The right honourable baronet has also quoted Paley; but he has forgotten to state that Paley is of opinion that the members of a government have no right to determine what is, or is not, the true religion, but should abide by the opinion of the majority of the people. He ought also to have remembered an authority better than Paley—the Scotch Parliament—which, in the act abolishing prelacy, laid down, as the great reason for that celebrated proceeding, that that institution was opposed to the feelings of the majority of the Scotch people. These are great principles, and are worth far more consideration than the details of the measure before the house; it is not a question of vulgar arithmetic, but of vast policy, involving those regards by which Ireland ought in future to be permanently and uniformly governed. Two measures have been proposed, the one by a noble lord, the Secretary for Ireland,* who has won our confidence, attachment, and respect; the other by a noble lord who was Secretary for Ireland,† and whose biography constitutes a calamitous portion of the history of Ireland. The one proposes appropriation; the other distribution. Between which should we elect? The plan to which appropriation is an incident provides a surplus; the plan which has distribution in view, leaves no surplus to be applied. It is evident that the latter is framed so as to avoid the creation of the surplus. But is there one? Let the statistics of the country be consulted. There are 600,000 Presbyterians, 850,000 Episcopal Protestants, and 3,600,000 Roman Catholics. In one archdiocese there are only 40,000 Protestants, and there are 1,800,000 Roman Catholics. What more need be stated, in order to prove that a surplus exists, and that the existing system cannot be maintained?

It has been suggested by the noble lord that the inferior Protestant clergy are now paid in a manner disproportioned to their merits; for my part, wherever real services are to be performed, I am not only willing, but anxious that a clergyman should be adequately rewarded; but where there is no congregation, I do not desire to see an useless ecclesiastic, no matter to what religion he may be attached. But when did the noble lord, who now advocates new distribution, first bethink himself of the poverty of the Protestant clergy? When did he first give way to these feelings of commiseration in favour of the wretched curate and the family depending on him for sustainment? He never proposed any measure for their relief, until the demands of millions had urged

* Lord Morpeth. † Lord Stanley.

this great question to the issue to which it has advanced. He says he never can or will consent to it. I never expected, indeed, that he would divest himself of the fatal pertinacity which characterizes him, and which has been the source of so much calamity to the country that was so long abandoned to his control. The man who can, without remorse, witness the fatal results of his miserable legislation, must indeed be incapable of penitence; but he is mistaken in supposing that his consent is necessary to the achievement of this great measure. This house, rested as it is with a power which is sure to prevail at last, sustained by the great body of the nation, has means of persuasion which have not been tried on former occasions in vain. Does the noble lord recollect by what expedient the cabinet of which he was a member carried the Reform Bill?—and as that measure was accomplished, its results, its inevitable results, of which this is one, will by the same instrumentality be achieved. It is sufficient to trace the progress of this question, in order to see that its advances to success are beyond all doubt, and that although it may be retarded, it cannot be stopped. There is a class of questions which cannot retrograde, which cannot continue stationary, and which must needs go on. Of this character were the Slave question, the Catholic question, and the Reform question. Of this class is that which the Irish millions, returning to this house a vast majority of the representatives of Ireland, never will relinquish. In the year 1824, this question was first pressed to a division by the member for Middlesex. In the minority the names of Hobhouse, of Rice, of Russell are to be found. They saw, even then, that the concession of this right to Ireland was indispensable for her peace.

The member for Cumberland has quoted a speech of the Secretary of the Home Department in 1833, to prove that he was opposed to the new appropriation; but that speech referred to the 147th clause, and to a contingent and improbable surplus, in the Church Temporalities Bill, and not to a surplus definite, substantial, palpable, like that which will result from the contemplated measure. It may be said that the noble lord, as well as the Secretary for the Home Department, has been consistent. He has been, indeed, obstinate in his adherence to a detail, but his general policy has been most incongruous. The instant the reform of the parliament was proposed in England, the reform of the church was with the same loud voice imperatively required in Ireland. The excitement which arose in one country on the question by which it was most deeply interested, soon extended itself to the other, on the grievance by which it was most sensibly and painfully affected. "Down," cried England, "with nomination in the parliament;" "down," cried Ireland, "with sinecurism in the church;"—"perish Gatton and Old Sarum," cried the people of this country; "perish the abuses," answered the Irish millions, "which nothing but Old Sarum and Gatton can maintain." How, indeed, was it possible that the popular agitation which pervaded one country, should not have been communicated to the other? How could Ireland remain in apathetic contemplation of the great scenes which were passing in this country? Yet the noble lord, who himself administered to the provocation of the popular passions in England, and he right honourable baronet, conceived that they could play the Gracchi of parliamentary reform, and complain of sedition, when Ireland demanded. in the same right, the reform of the church.

When the Tithe Bill was introduced in 1832, the Irish members remonstrated in vain; the measure was passed into a law. The people assembled in thousands and tens of thousands to petition against it They were dispersed at the point of the bayonet, and their leaders arrested, convicted by packed juries, and imprisoned. The parliament was dissolved; and provoked by these despotic proceedings, the shout for repeal arose from every hustings. The Coercion Bill was introduced, and even that melancholy measure, although intended to repress the display of the popular power, contributed to advance this question: for the English members who had consented to severity, determined that that severity should have justice for its companion. The Church Temporalities Bill was introduced; it swept ten bishops away; it abolished church-cess; it provided that certain vacant benefices need not be filled up (thus letting a great principle, indirectly, in); but unfortunately the 147th clause, which did not, indeed, expressly assert appropriation, but intimated its adoption, was rejected; and so, from the measure, no tranquillizing consequences ensued. At the opening of the session in 1834, a most important discussion took place. It was proved that the Marquess of Anglesey had, so far back as 1832, written a despatch to the cabinet, insisting on appropriation, as indispensable for the settlement of Ireland; and thus, while the Irish Secretary was exclaiming against all concession, that distinguished nobleman was bearing to the necessity of this great measure his incalculably important attestation; the question thus every day gained ground. The member for St. Alban's at length gave his celebrated notice. The matter was brought to issue between the parties in the cabinet, as it is at this moment between the two branches of the legislature, and the celebrated church commission went forth. The noble lord (Lord Stanley) perceived, that if the people were counted, the days of ecclesiastical abuse would be numbered. He saw that appropriation was involved in the inquiry that must lead to t, and he resigned. He left Lord Grey behind him. What inference is thence to be deduced? If the noble lord's resignation was founded in one principle, Lord Grey's retention of office must have rested upon he exact reverse. Why did the noble lord refer so repeatedly, last ight, to Lord Grey? What did he desire to intimate? Against any insinuation, which he meant to convey, let the church commission issued y Lord Grey be appealed to. The Melbourne cabinet is formed—and issolved in a moment of royal misapprehension of the state of Ireland he right honourable member for Tamworth comes in, announces the on-appropriation as the basis of his policy, is struck down by the resolution moved by the noble lord, and out of the ruins of his administration irnishes a new proof of the necessity of making this great and paramount concession to the power by which that administration was laid ostrate. The Melbourne cabinet send up their bill to the Lords—it lost; but are the government shaken, or in the least degree affected it? No; a resolution of the Commons annihilates a ministry in an instant; and to the Lords the cabinet bid defiance. Who, then, will deem it matter of doubt by whom the victory will be won, if, indeed, the two houses should unhappily be driven to an encounter. Take that single fact; do not go to remote periods or questionable examples; look at the event within your immediate recollection, at that which is passing this moment before our eyes—and away with all fear on the part of the people, and with all confidence on the part of their antagonists!

The session of 1835 closes, and in Ireland events arise which exhibit the fatal impolicy of the Lords in a new and remarkable light. The tithe question which had before been so productive of disaster, generates a series of new evils. The lay association is formed in order to enforce the payment of the obnoxious impost; the heads of the Orange body are among the chief directors of its proceedings. The names of Roden, Farnham, and Lorton, stand conspicuous in the committee.— I pronounce no opinion on their motives, no censure on their proceedings, nor do I, indeed, know to what extent the lay association has interposed; but this I do know, that never in the annals of litigation, was such a scene as the court of Exchequer now presents, exhibited. The writ of rebellion is issued; the law officers appear before the Chief Baron and his brethren, to oppose the employment of the police in the execution of these writs; the executive is discomfited by the court, and the Chief Baron becomes virtually the master of the whole constabulary force. The execution of writs of rebellion is confided of necessity, in many cases, to commissioners of the lowest class, and of the most desperate character. These miscreants enforce the attendance of the police at the dead of night, break open the doors of nominal rebels, whose treason consists in non-payment of tithes, and incarcerate the delinquents. Is this state of things to continue? As yet, indeed, there has been no violent outrage, because the people look to the settlement of the question, and entertain the strongest confidence in the government; but if the question continues unadjusted, and there shall appear but one mode of effecting it, I shrink, I own, from the contemplation of the consequences. It is monstrous, Sir, that this condition of things should be allowed to continue, and that, for the sake of an abstraction, the Conservative party should allow Ireland to be exposed to the disasters which may befal us. There is not a Protestant state in Europe excepting this, in which a proposition so preposterous as that church property is inalienable is asserted. The right honourable baronet referred to the condition of the Lutheran and Protestant Church in Prussia, adding that the cases did not apply. Why, the opponents of popular privileges continually resort to foreign example for arguments against innovation; but when we appeal to the same source, when we point to Germany, in proof that Catholics and Protestants can live in perfect amity, that the Lutheran Church is paid exactly in proportion to the labours of its clergy, and that the income is regulated by the congregation;—when we show them there is nothing in the two religions to create hostility if it be not hastened by the law, we are told that the case does not apply, and that if an example is to be produced it is not from the Continent that it is to be imported. Be it so. Let us turn to Scotland. The house will permit me to read some extracts from Spottiswood's History of the Scotch Church, which will set in a conspicuous light the principles upon which the great ecclesiastical appropriation was settled. Spottiswood says:—

"In the convention kept at Edinburgh in January preceding (1560) a form of church policy was presented and desired to be ratified.—Because this will fall to be often mentioned, and serveth to the clearing of many questions which were afterwards agitated in the church, I thought meet, word by word, here to insert the same, that the reader may see what were the grounds laid down at first for the government of the church."

After stating four other heads, the document proceeds to set forth the fifth, which is entitled—"Concerning the provision of ministers and distribution of the rents and possessions justly pertaining to the church." Under this head the following passage occurs:—

"That two sorts of people must be provided for out of that which is called the patrimony of the church—to wit, the poor, and teachers of youth. The poor must be provided for in every parish—the poor widows, the fatherless, the impotent maimed person, the aged, and every one that cannot work, or such persons as are fallen by the course of nature into decay, ought to be provided for."

(Page 160)—"It is necessary that care be had of the virtuous and godly education of youth, therefore we judge that in every parish there should be a schoolmaster, such a one as is able at least to teach the grammar and Latin tongue."

Again, in page 289 of the same work, we find that in the year 78—

"Mr. Andrew Melvil held the church busied with the matter of policy, which was put in form, and presented to the parliament at their sitting at Striveling."

This form of church policy is entitled—"Heads and Conclusions of the Church." Chapter the 9th is entitled—"Of the Patrimony of the Church, and Distribution thereof;" and the 9th section runs thus:—

The canons make mention of a fourfold distribution of the patrimony of the church; whereof one part was applied to the pastor, or for his sustentation and hospitality; another to the elders and deacons and the whole clergy; the third to the poor sick persons and strangers; and the fourth to uphold the edifice of the church, and other officers specially extraordinary. We add hereunto schools and schoolmasters, who ought well may be sustained of the same goods."

Chapter the 13th has the following heading:—

The conclusion, showing the utility that shall flow from this reformation in all estates."

The 5th section runs thus:—

Finally, to the King's Majesty and estate this profit shall redound, the officers of the church being sufficiently provided, according to the aforesaid distribution, the surplus may be liberally bestowed for the supporting of the prince's estate and the affairs of the common-wealth."

At the time this form of church policy was presented, episcopacy had not been abolished, but the assembly of the church passed an ordinance, that—

"Bishops should not take up, for maintaining their ambition, the rents, which might maintain many pastors, schools, and poor; but content themselves with a reasonable portion for discharging their office." —Spottiswood, p. 303.

The efforts which were made to force upon Scotland an establishment at variance with the feelings of the people, are too familiar for expatiation they terminated as we all know; and in 1689 that famous act was passed, which in a few words does such great things. The act is this—mark it, Englishmen, mark it; it is full of wisdom, and in the briefest compass includes the largest policy:—

"Act abolishing prelacy, July 22, 1689. Whereas the estates of this kingdom, in their claim of right, declared that prelacy—(I leave out mere verbiage) is and hath been a great and insupportable grievance to the nation, and contrary to the inclinations of the people, &c.; and the King and Queen's Majesties do declare that they will settle that church government in this kingdom which is most agreeable to the inclinations of the people," &c.

"Most agreeable to the inclinations of the people!" In those words a solution of the happiness of Scotland is to be found. Noble and enviable country! She has won victories in civilisation. Her agriculture has climbed to the summit of those hills whose heather was once red with her martyrs' blood; the palaces of her industry ascend on the banks of every frith; her estuaries are covered with native-owned vessels, which bear the produce of her labour to the remotest marts; in every science that exalts and expands the mind, in every art that cheers and embellishes existence, Scotland has made the most important contributions to the happiness of mankind. But, alas! when from the contemplation of the splendid spectacle which Scotland exhibits, I turn to my own unfortunate country, my heart sinks, I confess, within me, under a melancholy consciousness in which every Irishman, no matter what may be his creed, ought to participate. But if Ireland do exhibit this fatal contrast—if, in a country that ought to teem with abundance, there prevails wretchedness without example—if millions of paupers are there without employment, and often without food or raiment—where is the fault? Is it in the sky, which showers verdure? —is it in the soil, which is surprisingly fertile?—or is it in the fatal course which you, the arbiters of her destiny, have adopted? She has for centuries belonged to England; England has used her for centuries as she has pleased. How has she used her, and what has been the result? A code of laws was in the first place established, to which in the annals of legislative atrocity there is not a parallel; and of that code—those institutes of unnatural ascendancy—the Irish Church is a remnant. But although that detestable policy was then without example, it has since been chosen as a model. Well did Nicholas exclaim, when he perused the debates (as I have heard) in this house, on his own frightful tyranny to Poland—well did he exclaim, "Poland is Russia's Ireland." He confiscates, as your fathers did; he banishes as they did; he debases, as they did; he violates the instincts of human nature, and from the parent tears the child, as they did; and he inflicts upon a atholic people a church alien to their national habits, feelings, and elief, as you do. And think you not that there are men to be found in the senate of St. Petersburgh, who exclaim that the Greek Church must be maintained in all its ascendancy in Poland—that it is the bond of connexion between Poland and Russia—that a Greek priest dispensing hospitality, and holding out a salutary example by the excellence of his moral conduct, must in every Polish village be the source of improvement?* And can you doubt that some Tartar secretary for Poland is sufficiently prompt to furnish the materials for a Warsaw speech, and to exclaim that a lesson must be given to Poland, and that she must be taught to fear, before she can learn how to love? You all exclaim, the Russian policy is not only wicked but insane. Is English policy commendable and wise? In Heaven's name what useful purpose has your gorgeous establishment ever promoted? Last night the member for Weymouth, who represents and expresses the feeling of so large a portion of the religious and moral community of this country—who does not love Popery, but who abhors tyranny—told you that his conviction was that the abuses of the Protestant Church had been the greatest impediment to the progress of the Protestant religion. You cannot hope to proselytise us through the means of the establishment. You have put the experiment to the test of three centuries. If the truth be with you it may be great, but in this instance it does not sustain the aphorism—for it does not prevail. You have tried everything. Penal codes, foundling hospitals, charter schools (those nurseries for corporations), Kildare-street societies; but these you have abandoned; and even the noble lord opposite, with all his scriptural addictions—and although he be the author of a work on the parables (I wonder what he says about the Pharisee)—still, so convinced was he of the futility of all attempts at our conversion, that he himself introduced that system which is so erroneously designated by his present auxiliaries, as the "mutilation" of the Word of God. But who that reflects on the subject for a moment can believe that the abuses of the church can have any other effect than to array the country against the system with which it is connected? How can religion advance—with police, process servers, and commissioners of rebellion for its missionaries? Recollect what arguments, or, if you please, what sophisms these abuses supply to its opponents. Have not the rival clergy an opportunity of asking whether it is in an Aceldama that the vineyard of the Lord should be planted? Whether they are indeed the ministers of Christ who, while they inculcate the reading of his Word, enter the field of massacre with the Gospel, as an implement for swearing a distracted mother over the body of her child that

* This alludes to an expression used by Lord Stanley with regard to Ireland

lies dead and stark before her.* But if in a religious point of view the establishment cannot conduce to the interests of religion—in a political view, what purpose does it answer? It is said that it cements the Union—cements the Union! It furnishes the great argument against the Union—it is the most degrading incident of all the incidents of degradation by which that measure was accompanied—it is the yoke, the brand, the shame, and the exasperation of Ireland—it arrays millions of Irishmen against you, and marshals them in opposition to the measure, of which you avail yourselves for the sustainment of a monstrous army, and which you plead in bar to that requisition for redress, which, it is not wise, because it will not be safe to withhold.

* This alludes to an incident in one of the tithe massacres in Ireland.

THE IRISH CHURCH

SPEECH IN THE HOUSE OF COMMONS, AUGUST 2, 1836

How few there are who look beyond to-day and have a political to-morrow, who believe it possible that the abuses of the Irish Church can be long maintained? The right honourable baronet, the member for Tamworth, does not labour under so signal a delusion. His speech to-night was an intimation of despair: he said that if the blow must be struck, it should not be struck by him; he spoke of the prostration of those pillars, which he declared that he, for one, would not contribute to overthrow. What did he mean but to tell us, that upon this question he would not play the part which, in reference to the great measure of Catholic aggrandizement, he was driven by that high necessity which results from a sense of duty to perform?—that he would leave it to others to do what he foresees to be ultimately inevitable—that he had already made sufficient sacrifices, and that a second martyrdom to fame could not be endured! A man endowed with the sagacity of the right honourable gentleman must needs feel that the continued sustainment of the church in the enjoyment of its gorgeous superfluities is impossible. The only chance of preserving whatever there is of any value in the church, infinitesimal as it may be, is the speedy application of a bold process of reform. In time—take down in time the splendid pinnacles which the right honourable baronet mistakes for "the pillars" of the church—take down the golden dome, which has become too ponderous and has begun to totter—take down that gorgeous mass which does not belong to the Christian order, if you would serve the edifice, which it endangers far more than it adorns:—in the first political concussion, it will not only fall, but overwhelm the altar in its ruins.

The proposition which I mean briefly to assume in this debate is as simple as it is bold. Instead of entering into half-forensic and demi-scholastic disquisitions upon the nature of church property, I frankly and fearlessly tell you, that with the power which Catholic Ireland has acquired, and is rapidly acquiring, your sacerdotal predominance is incompatible. Have you observed the development of Catholic Ireland? It is the fashion to say that the property of Ireland is almost exclusively Protestant, and I acknowledge that, when you revert to the military spoliations inflicted on us by your ancestors, you should arrive at the conclusion that you have left us bare. It was a biting sarcasm of him who said that the history of Ireland was a continuation of rapine.* But while I admit that the fee-simple of Ireland is in a great measure Cromwellian, I asseverate that the mass of property to which political influence is attached is in the hands of the Catholic middle classes.—The Reform Bill has been attended in Ireland with one most important result, which has not been the subject of as much attention as it deserves.

---

* Sir Hercules Langrishe was asked where was the best history of Ireland to be found; said: 'In the continuation of *Rapin*.'—ED.

Before that event the close boroughs of Ireland were in the hands of a few Protestant nominators, who deputed their representatives, the guardians of ecclesiastical opulence to this house; a large transfer of power in this essential particular has taken place: it is now vested in the Roman Catholic inhabitants of the towns of Ireland which send members here. I do not think that I can present the extraordinary change which has taken place in this most essential regard, in a more striking light, than by giving a kind of ocular demonstration, and bidding you fix your eyes on two very remarkable and exceedingly interesting gentlemen, who are sitting this moment immediately opposite to each other —the one is the member for the University of Oxford, and the other the member for Dundalk. But although the member for Dundalk (Mr. Sharman Crawford) never was and never will be member for the University of Oxford, the other (Sir Robert Inglis), the member for the University of Oxford was once member for Dundalk. My Lord Roden, influenced of course by no sublunary considerations, the patron before the Reform Bill of the borough of Dundalk, selected the honourable baronet as the most appropriate representative of his own ecclesiastical attachments in the house. Since the Reform Bill my honourable friend behind me has been chosen by the people of Dundalk as the sentinel of their interests, and as the mirror in which their feelings and opinions will be most faithfully reflected. Look at them both—Look at the incarnation of plenteous Toryism upon one side, and the exemplification of somewhat spare and stern Republicanism on the other, and of the effects of the Reform Bill you will behold the most striking illustration. The house, I perceive, find in the contrast of the two honourable gentlemen a subject of merriment, which they, who themselves participate in it, do not take in bad part: but though there may be matter for mirth in the outward and visible signs of the old system and of the new, you will see, upon reflection, that from the type of Conservatism and the symbol of Democracy thus offered to you in this exhibition of the honourable gentlemen, most important inferences are to be deduced. The boroughs of Ireland have been delivered to the majority of the people;—the influence exercised a few years ago by individual Protestant patricians has been handed over to the merchants, and traders, and mechanics, located in the towns, by whom their representatives are delegated to the House of Commons. You must be sensible that the consequences of this great alteration are most prejudicial to the ecclesiastical establishment of Ireland, and that in the particular to which I have alluded, Catholic power has gained an extraordinary augmentation.

In the Irish counties again a great preponderance of Catholic influence will be found, and it may be stated, without dread of contradiction that the very great majority of the representatives of Ireland are returned by that community which not very long since was considered to be destitute of parliamentary influence. It is worth your while to look a little further into the circumstances which ought to convince you that every day the Church of Ireland—that structure of ascendancy which cannot long survive its parent—is becoming more and more enfeebled, and losing the sustainment on which it formerly relied. The greater the advances of Ireland in prosperity, the greater the expansion of trade, and the improvement in agriculture: the more Ireland sells and buys, the more ships enter her harbours; the greater the wealth the earth throws up from her bosom, the greater must be the progress of the people, as contra-distinguished to the aristocracy of Ireland, and the more formidable the array of those millions by whom the abatement of the great anomaly is required. Note an incident to the state of Ireland, which may at first view escape your notice. A small sect once enjoyed a monopoly of the patronage of the crown—Protestantism supplied the channel beyond which the royal bounty, issuing from the Castle, was never permitted to flow:—but now, under a government, by which the principle of emancipation is carried out, an indiscriminate participation takes place in the dignities and in the emoluments connected with the chief departments of the state In the year 1812, the Catholics of Ireland were denounced as "miscreants" by a Protestant Attorney-General for Ireland, and one of the "miscreants" is now Attorney-General for Ireland. My learned friend, the member for Cashel (Mr. Sergeant Woulfe), who occupies the highest place in his profession, is one of his Majesty's law-officers; and my friend, the member for Clonmel (Mr. Ball), for talents and erudition is unsurpassed at the Irish bar: these eminent men are advancing to the bench. In a country so situated, of whose condition these facts are striking illustrations, can the Irish Church be long maintained? If we were seven millions of unintellectual degraded serfs—a heap of helotism—of our seven millions little account should be made. If the physical aspect of Ireland has undergone a great change, a still more conspicuous moral alteration has taken place. Not only has cultivation made its way into the morass, but the mind of Ireland has been reclaimed. With the education of the people the permanence of unnatural and anti-national institutions is irreconcilable. But if education has done much, agitation, the apprenticeship to liberty, has done more; although in your judgment it may have been productive of many mischiefs, they are outweighed by the preponderant and countervailing good. Public opinion and public feeling have been created in Ireland. Men of all classes have been instructed in the principles on which the rights of nations depend. The humblest peasant, midst destitution the most abject, has learned to respect himself. I remember when if you struck him he cowered beneath the blow; but now lift up your hand, the spirit of insulted manhood will start up in a bosom covered with rags, his Celtic blood will boil, as yours would do, and he will feel, and he will act, as if he had been born in this noble land of yours, where the person of every citizen is sacred from affronts, and from his birth he had breathed the moral atmosphere which Britons are accustomed to inhale. Englishmen, we are too like you to give you leave to do us wrong, and, in the name of millions of my countrymen, assimilated to yourselves, I demand the reduction of a great abuse—the retrenchment of a monstrous sinecure—or, in other words, I demand justice at your hands. "Justice to Ireland" is a phrase which has been, I am well aware, treated as a topic for derision, but the time will come, or is it, perhaps, remote, when you will not be able to extract much matter for ridicule in those trite but not trivial words. "Do justice to America, exclaimed the father of that man by whom the Irish Union was accomplished, "do it to-night—do it before you sleep." In your National Gallery is a picture on which Lord Lyndhurst should look: it was painted by Copley, and represents the death of Chatham, who did not live long after that celebrated invocation was pronounced. "Do justice to America—do it to-night—do it before you sleep." There were men by whom that warning was heard who laughed when it was uttered. Have a care lest injustice to Ireland and to America may not be followed by the same results—lest mournfulness may not succeed to mirth, and another page in the history of England may not be writ in her heart's blood.

IRISH MUNICIPAL BILL.

SPEECH IN THE HOUSE OF COMMONS, FEBRUARY 22, 1837.

THE right honourable baronet (Sir James Graham) began the speech, in many particulars remarkable, which he has just concluded amidst the applauses of those, whose approbation, at one period of his political life, he would have blushed to incur—by intimating that he was regarded as a "bigot" on this side of the house. Whether he deserves the appellation by which he has informed us that he is designated, his speech to-night affords some means of determining. I will not call him a bigot—I am not disposed to use an expression in any degree offensive to the right honourable baronet, but I will presume to call him a convert, who exhibits all the zeal for which conversion is proverbially conspicuous. Of that zeal we have manifestations in his references to pamphlets about Spain, in his allusions to the mother of Cabrera, in his remarks on the Spanish clergy, and the practice of confession in the Catholic Church. I own that, when he takes in such bad part the strong expressions employed in reference to the Irish Church (expressions employed by Protestants, and not by Roman Catholics), I am surprised that he should not himself abstain from observations offensive to the religious feelings of Roman Catholic members of this house. The right honourable baronet has done me the honour to produce an extract from a speech of mine, delivered nearly two years ago at the Coburg Gardens; and at the same time expressed himself in terms of praise of the humble individual who now addresses you. I can assure the right honourable baronet that I feel at least as much pleasure in listening to him, as he has the goodness to say that he derives from hearing me.

He has many of the accomplishments attributed by Milton to a distinguished speaker in a celebrated council. He is "in act most graceful and humane—his tongue drops manna." I cannot but feel pride that he should entertain so high an opinion of me, as to induce him to peruse and collect all that I say even beyond these walls. He has spent the recess, it appears, in the diligent selection of such passages as he has read to-night, and which I little thought, when they were uttered, that the right honourable baronet would think worthy of his comments. However, he owes me the return of an obligation. The last time I spoke in this house, I referred to a celebrated speech of his at Cockermouth, in which he pronounced an eloquent invective against "a recreant Whig;" and as he found that I was a diligent student of those models of eloquence which the right honourable baronet used formerly to supply, in advocating the popular rights, he thought himself bound, I suppose, to repay me by the citation, which has, I believe, produced less effect than he had anticipated. The right honourable baronet also adverted to what he calls " the Lichfield House compact." It is not worth while to go over the same ground, after I have already proved, by reading in the house the speech which has been the subject of so much remark—how much I have been misrepresented; I never said that there was a " compact ;" I did say, and I repeat it, that there was " a compact alliance." Was that the first occasion on which an alliance was entered into ? Was Lichfield House the only spot ever dedicated to political reconciliations ? Has the right honourable baronet forgotten, or has the noble lord (Stanley) who sits beside him, succeeded in dismissing from his recollection, a meeting at Brookes's Club at which the Irish and English reformers assembled, and, in the emergency which had taken place, agreed to relinquish their differences and make a united stand against the common foe ? Does the noble lord forget an admirable speech (it was the best post-prandial oration it was ever my good fortune to have heard) delivered by a right honourable gentleman who was not then a noble lord, and was accompanied by a vehemence of gesture and a force of intonation not a little illustrative of the emotions of the orator, on his anticipated ejectment from office ? That eloquent individual, whom I now see on the Tory side of the house, got up on a table, and with vehement and almost appalling gesture, pronounced an invective against the Duke of Wellington, to which, in the records of vituperation, few parallels can be found. I shall not repeat what the noble lord then said.

Lord STANLEY.—You may.

Mr. SHEIL.—No; my object is not to excite personal animosities among new, but ardent friends. I have no malevolent motive in adverting to that remarkable occasion. If I have at all referred to it, it is because the right honourable baronet has been sufficiently indiscreet to talk of Lichfield House :—let him, for the future, confine himself to the recollections of Brookes's, instead of selecting as the subject of his sarcasms the meeting in which that reconciliation took place to which Ireland is indebted for the exclusion of the noble lord opposite, and his associates, from power. The right honourable baronet has been guilty of another imprudence: he has charged Lord Mulgrave with the promotion of Mr. Pigot to a forensic office in Dublin Castle. Mr. Pigot's offence, it seems, consists in his having been a member of the Precursor Association. Does the right honourable baronet recollect where he sits in this house—with whom he is co-operating—with what party he and the noble lord opposite have entered into confederacy—when he makes matters of this kind the groundwork of imputation? Who were the first men selected for promotion by the Tories? To what association did they belong? Let the right-honourable baronet look back, and behind him he will see the treasurer, the grand treasurer, of the Orange Association, whom the member for Tamworth appointed Treasurer of the Ordnance—when his Sovereign placed him at the head of the government of his country. What are the offences of the National Association, when compared with the proceedings of the Orange Institution? Are our proceedings clandestine? Are figures and symbols resorted to by us? Have we tampered with the army, as the Orange Society has been convicted by a committee of this house of having done?

Colonel PERCEVAL.—I deny that the Orange Society tampered with the army. I admit that such warrants were issued.

Mr. SHEIL.—I will not dispute with the gallant colonel about a word. If the phrase "tampered" be objected to, I will adopt any word the gallant colonel will do me the favour to suggest, in order to express a notorious and indisputable fact. It was proved beyond all doubt, and even beyond all controversy, that the Orange Society made the utmost efforts to extend itself into the army; that a number of regimental warrants were issued, and that resolutions were actually passed, at meetings of the society, upon the subject. From this society, the gallant officer, who was one of its functionaries, was selected, in order to place him in the Ordnance; and, by a curious coincidence, having been treasurer to the Orange Institution, he was appointed to the same fiscal office in the Ordnance, to whose treasureship he was raised. How, then, can gentlemen be guilty of the imprudence of talking of Mr. Pigot's appointment—(he is a gentleman conspicuous for his talents and high personal character)—when their own party made, within a period so recent, such an appointment as that to which I have reluctantly but unavoidably adverted. But, Sir, can we not discuss the great measure of municipal reform without descending to such small and transitory considerations as the selection of this or that man for office? Talk of Lord Mulgrave's government as you will, you cannot deny that his administration has been, beyond all example, successful. He has acted on the wise and obvious policy of adapting the spirit of his government to the feelings of the numerous majority of that Irish nation by whom he is respected and beloved. His measures have been founded on the determination to regard the rights of the many, instead of consulting the factious interests of the few; and, by the just and wise system on which he has acted, he has effected a complete reconciliation between the government and the people. You speak of his liberating prisoners from gaols:—I disdain even to advert, in reply, to the comments which have been made on this act of clemency by men who are naturally the advocates of incarceration. I meet these gentlemen with the broad fact, that the country has, under Lord Mulgrave's government, made a great progress towards that pacification which I make no doubt that, under his auspices, Ireland will attain. Look to the county which I have the honour to represent, and which has been unhappily conspicuous for the disturbances of which it was once the scene. Mr. Howley, the assistant-barrister for that county—a gentleman whose authority is unimpeachable, and who, by his impartial conduct, his admirable temper, his knowledge, and his talents, has won the applause of all parties—states, in his charge delivered at Nenagh, that there is an end to the savage combats at fairs; and, in a return made by the clerk of the crown for the county, it appears that, in every class of crime, there has been, within the last year, a most extraordinary diminution. This surely is better evidence than the assertions made in Tory journals, and adopted by gentlemen whose political interests are at variance with their amiable aspirations for the establishment of order in their country. But, Sir, the most remarkable incident to the administration of my Lord Mulgrave has been, its effect upon the great political question which, not very long ago, produced so much excitement in one country, and not a little apprehension in the other. Without having recourse to coercive bills—without resorting to a single measure of severity—by impressing the people of Ireland with a conviction that he was determined to do them justice, Lord Mulgrave has laid the Repeal question at rest. It is, if not dead, at least deeply dormant; and, although such a policy as that of the noble lord opposite would soon awaken or resuscitate it again, as long as the principles on which the government of Lord Mulgrave and of the noble lord the member for Yorkshire* is carried on, are adhered to, so long you will find that the people of Ireland will remain in a relation not only of amity, but of attachment to the administration. It may be asked, how the good results of the policy I have been describing can affect the question before the house? Thus:—the executive has, by its judicious measures, by adapting itself to the political condition of the country, and by its preference of the nation to a faction completely succeeded. It has held out a model which the legislature ought to imitate. Let the parliament enact laws in the spirit in which the laws, even as they stand, have been carried into effect in Ireland. Let the good of the country, instead of the monopoly of a party, supply the standard by which parliament shall regulate its legislation; and to what the Irish government has so nobly commenced, a perfect and glorious completion will one day be given.

I turn from the consideration of those topics connected with the existing condition of affairs in Ireland, to the discussion of the broader ground on which the question ought to be debated. I ask you to do justice to Ireland. Every man in this house will probably say, that he is anxious to do Ireland justice; but what is justice to Ireland? It will assist us, in investigating that question, to determine, in the first

* Lord Morpeth.

place, wnat is justice to England? In this country the Corporation and Test Acts were always regarded as the muniments of the church and corporations, through their effects, as its chief bulwarks. Mr. Canning was so strongly persuaded of this, that in 1827, while he declared himself the advocate of emancipation, he announced his firm resolve to stand by the Protestant corporations, and not to consent to the repeal of the law which gave them their peculiar character, and connected them with the establishment. Those laws were, however, repealed by the member for Tamworth; he could not help repealing them; he then began to undergo that process of soft compulsion, in submitting to which he afterwards acquired those habits of useful complaisance—in which we shall furnish him with the strongest motives to persevere. The Test and Corporation Acts having been repealed, still, through the machinery of self-election, the body of the people were deprived of the practical advantages which ought to have resulted from that repeal. The reformed House of Commons determined to place corporations under popular control. The Lords thought it imprudent to resist. No one was found bold enough to state that because a transfer of power would take place from the Tories to the Reformers, therefore corporations should be abolished. Take Liverpool as an example. A transfer of influence has taken place there, to such an extent that, very much to the noble lord's astonishment, his plan for the mutilation of the Word of God has been adopted in the schools under the superintendence ot the corporations. Let us now pass to Ireland. I will admit for the sake of argument, that corporations were established to protect the Protestant Church; they would thus rest on the same ground as the Test and Corporation Acts: the latter having been abandoned in England, and having been followed by corporate reform, the same reasons apply to the relinquishment of the principle of exclusion in Ireland, which is utterly incompatible with the ground on which Catholic Emancipation was acknowledged to have been conceded. What took place when emancipation was carried? Was it intimated that we should be excluded from corporations? The direct contrary was asserted. "Roman Catholics (said the right honourable member for Tamworth, in the admirable speech in which he acknowledged the gentle violence by which the rights of Ireland were ravished from his reluctant coyness), Roman Catholics shall be admitted to all corporate offices in Ireland." This was strong; but he did more. In the bill framed under his superintendence, two clauses were introduced providing for the admission of Catholics into corporations. Was the right honourable gentleman sincere? Did he intend that to the heart of Ireland, beating as it was with hope, the word of promise should be kept? Who can doubt it? Who can believe that the right honourable baronet would be capable of practising a delusion? What he did, he did unwillingly; but he did with honesty whatever he did. His act of enfranchisement was baffled in this regard, and, by a combination among corporators, Catholics were excluded. From that day to this, not a single Roman Catholic—not one—has been admitted into the corporations attached to the metropolis of our country. I boldly ask the right honourable baronet whether he approves of this exclusion, and of the means by which it was effected? Was it not a fraud upon us, and upon the law, by which, clearly and inequivocally, admission into corporations was secured to us? If it was intended that we should not have the benefit of Catholic Emancipation in this particular, it ought, in common candour, to have been told us; but to pass an act making us admissible—to allow seven years to pass, and permit the law to be frustrated in that interval—and then when a measure is brought forward in order to give us the advantage of that law, to destroy corporations lest we should be admitted—is not consistent with English fairness, with that honest dealing for which you are conspicuous, nor, let me add, with the personal character of the right honourable baronet. Ay, but the church may be injured. Why did you not think of that when emancipation was being carried? Why make your argument in favour of the church posterior to your legislation against it? I call on the right honourable baronet, not only in the name of justice to us, but in the name of his own dignity, as he would preserve that amity with himself which results from the consciousness of honest and noble dealing—I call on him to abandon his party, in adherence to his pledge; and if, between his politics and his integrity, he must make a choice, I know that he will not hesitate, for a moment, in making his election.

He fears an injury to the church. This church, by which a single object contemplated in a national establishment has never yet been attained—this church of yours is made the burden of every speech by which the cause of Toryism is sought to be maintained; and to every project for the improvement of the country, and the assertion of the people's rights, is presented as an insuperable obstacle. When we call on you to abolish the fatal impost which keeps the country in a paroxysm of excitement, you cry out, "the Church!" When we bid you rescue the country from the frightful litigation which turns our courts of justice into an arena for the combat of the political passions, you cry out, 'the Church!" And when we implore you to fulfil your contract at the Union, to redeem your pledge, given with emancipation, to extend to us British privileges, and grant us British institutions, you cry out, 'the Church!" The two countries must have the same church, and for that purpose the two countries must not have the same corporations! They are incompatible; we must then elect between them; which shall we prefer—the church of one million, or the corporations of seven; What an argument do the auxiliaries of the establishment advance, when they admit that the sacrifice of the national rights is necessary for its sustainment. But if this position be founded, wherefore was parliamentary reform ever conceded to us? Are we qualified to elect members of the House of Commons, but unfit to elect members of the Common Council? Are we unworthy of being the managers of our own local concerns—while here, in this great Imperial assembly, with the legislators of the British empire, with the arbiters of the destiny of the noblest nation in the world, we stand on a lofty level? Never was there any inconsistency comparable to this! I have a right to rise here, and to demand justice for my country, as representative of the second county in Ireland; and I am unworthy of being a corporator of Cashel or of Clonmel. I may be told that the Tories resisted the extension of parliamentary reform to Ireland, and on the very grounds on which they oppose the application of corporate reform. I must acknowledge it: they did insist that the close boroughs of Ireland were intended as the bulwarks of the Protestant interest; they did contend that a Catholic ascendancy would be the result of a parliamentary reform; and they urged with great zeal and strenuousness, that the demolition of the Established Church would be its inevitable consequence. In what a burst of lofty eloquence did the noble lord, who now sits opposite, refute them! "What!" he exclaimed, "deny to Ireland the benefits of the reform you give to England—withhold from Ireland the advantages which, at the Union, you pledged yourselves to grant her! deny her a community in your privileges, and an equal participation in your rights! Then you may repeal the Union at once, for you will render it a degrading and dishonourable compact." But I do injustice to that admirable passage; and as the noble lord may have forgotten it, as his recollections may be as evanescent as his opinions, I think it better to read what, from memory, I have imperfectly referred to. The passage will be found in the 17th volume of *The Mirror of Parliament*, page 2288. He begins with a panegyric on the Irish members. We were agitators then, just as much as we now are; we held and professed exactly the same opinions; we had an association at full work, just as we now have; but the noble lord did not, at that time, think it judicious to appeal to passages to which he has since addressed himself. The passage runs thus:—

"We have been told that the English bill does not in any case apply to Ireland, and that the circumstances of the two countries are different: but I am sure that honourable gentlemen will find that the principle of reform is the same, whether it is applied to England or Ireland; and if it be just here, so it must be just there. I would entreat those who advocate the Conservative interests, and who consider themselves the supporters of Protestant institutions, to look to the danger to which these institutions will be exposed in Ireland by withholding the privileges which this bill is to confer. If they wish to give Ireland a real, solid, substantial grievance—if they wish to give some handle to excitement, and to present a solid argument for the repeal of the Union—they need only show that, in the British House of Commons, English interests are treated in one way, and Irish interests in another, that in England the government rule by free representation, and by the voice of the people—while in Ireland that voice is stifled, and the people are shut out from a fair share in the choice of their representatives. I fear that, if we do not concede in a spirit of fairness and justice, agitation will break out, in a manner which it has never done before. I cannot conceive anything more clear than that the present measure is only the extension of the principle of the English bill to Ireland. I cannot conceive upon what principle we can refuse to place both countries on an equality, and make the same principle applicable to the election of all members of the united Legislature of the British empire."

The house has heard this passage with surprise; and although every sentence that I have read has produced a sensation, there is not, in the entire, a sentiment which has called forth more astonishment than the reference made to the repeal of the Union, as a result of the denial o equal privileges to the English and to the Irish people. And here let me turn to the right honourable member for Cumberland, and ask him, what he now thinks of his expostulation with the Irish Attorney-General, on his assertion that injustice would furnish an argument for repeal: Did not his noble friend, when in office, when Secretary for Ireland, solemnly assert the same thing? I will read the passage again—" If they wish to give Ireland a real, solid, substantial grievance—if they wish to give some handle to excitement, and to present a solid argument for the repeal of the Union—they need only show that, in the British House of Commons, English interests are treated in one way, and Irish interests in another." This is nobly expressed; but, in the midst of our admiration of such fine sentiments, founded on such lofty principles, and conveyed in language at once so beautiful and so perspicuous, what melancholy feelings, what mournful reflections arise! Alas! that the man who uttered what I have just read, who was capable of feeling and of expressing himself thus, in whom such a union of wisdom and eloquence was then exhibited—alas! that he should now be separated from his old associates, and that, united to his former antagonists, he should not only act on principles diametrically the reverse, but denounce his colleagues, and enter with the men whom he formerly represented as the worst enemies of his country into a derogatory league. But, not contented with joining them, in the transports of his enthusiasm he has gone beyond them; and on the first night of this debate, taking up the part of a prophet, when he had ceased to perform that of a statesman, he told the people of Ireland, in a burst of intemperate prediction, that never—no, never—should the municipal privileges, granted to the people of England, be extended to them.

Lord STANLEY.—I never said so.

Mr. SHEIL.—Then the noble lord has been grievously misrepresented. I acknowledge that I was not present when he spoke, but I was told by several persons that he had stated that this measure never should be carried.

Lord STANLEY.—I did not state that the measure never should be carried. I did state that the people of England would not yield to alarm and intimidation, and that the advocates of this measure were taking the worst means to effect their object. The honourable and learned gentleman confesses that he was not present when I spoke, and he should therefore be cautious in attributing to me the opinions which he has ascribed to me, in this attack which he has been making, knowing, as he does, that it is out of my power to reply.

Mr. SHEIL.—When the noble lord denies the use of certain expressions, and disclaims the sentiment conveyed by them, I at once accede to his interpretation of what he said, or rather meant to say. The noble lord observes that I am making an attack on him, knowing that he has to reply. The noble lord is well aware, from experience, that whether he has a right to reply or not, I never have the least dread of him, and that on no occasion in this house, have I ever, in the performance of my duty to my country, shrunk from an encounter with him. He calls my speech an attack on him. I am not pronouncing a personal invective against the noble lord. I am not exceeding the limits of fair discussion, or violating either the ordinances of good breeding or the rules of this house. I am exhibiting the inconsistencies and incongruities of the noble lord, and stripping his opinions of any value which they may possess, by proving him, at a period not remote, to have acted on, and to have enforced, principles directly opposite to those of which he is now the intolerant advocate. This is the extent of my attack on him. He will, however, pardon me for suggesting to him, that, if I did assail him with far more acrimony than I am disposed to do, he is the last man in this house who ought to complain. Who is there that shows less mercy to a political adversary? Who is so relentless in the infliction of his sarcasms, even on his old friends and associates? However, I ought not to feel much surprise that he should be so sensitive as he shows himself to be: no man fears an operation so much as a surgeon, and the drummer of a regiment trembles at the lash. But the noble lord mistakes: it is not any attack from me which he has cause to apprehend;—he bears that within his own bosom which reproaches him far more than I do. But, from his emotions, from his resentments, and from his consciousness, let us turn to something more deserving of regard, and consider how far it is probable that this measure can be successfully resisted. I wish to avoid all minacious intimations, and, therefore, I will not say that it must and shall be carried; but, adopting the calmer tone of deliberation, I entreat the noble lord opposite, and the house, to consider what the probabilities are which are connected with this question, and whether it is likely that the demand made by Ireland for justice can be long treated by any branch of the legislature with disregard?

I assert that Ireland, sustained as she is by the sympathies of a very large portion of the people of this country, must prevail in the cause in which her feelings are so deeply engaged, and on whose prosecution she is firmly and unalterably determined. I undertake to prove this proposition, and it will certainly be felt to be most important to consider whether it be just; for if men are once persuaded that this measure must ultimately be carried, they will feel that it is better to do, at once, what must be done at last, and that discussion ought to cease where necessity has begun to operate. I put the case of Ireland thus:— if the Catholic millions, by their union, by their organisation, by their associated power, carried their emancipation, what is the likelihood of their success in the pursuit of their present objects? If we forced the right honourable member for Tamworth to yield to us (a man not only of as great eloquence in debate, but of great discretion, of great influence, free from ebullitions of intemperance, and whose personal character entitles him to the confidence of his party), shall we not now overcome any obstacles which the noble lord may present to our progress? Let him remember that our power is more than trebled, and if, contending with such disadvantages as we had to struggle with, we prevailed,—where are the impediments by which our career in the pursuit of what remains to be achieved for the honour of our country, shall be even long retarded? It behoves the noble lord to look attentively at Ireland. Wherever we turn our eyes, we see the national power dilating, expanding, and ascending:—never did a liberated nation spring on in the career that freedom throws open towards improvement with such a bound as we have—in wealth, in intelligence, in high feeling, in all the great constituents of a state, we have made in a few years an astonishing progress. The character of our country is completely changed: we are free, and we feel as if we never had been slaves. Ireland stands as erect as if she had never stooped;. although she once bowed her forehead to the earth, every mark and trace of her prostration have been effaced. But these are generalities—these are vague and abstract vauntings, without detail. Well—if you stand in need of specification, it shall be rapidly, but not inconclusively, given. But told:—I was going to point to the first law offices in the country, filled by Roman Catholics—I was going to point to the second judicial office in Ireland filled by a Roman Catholic—I was going to point to the crowds of Roman Catholics who, in every profession and walk of life, are winning their way to eminence in the walks that lead to affluence or to honour. But one single fact suffices for my purpose: emancipation was followed by reform, and reform has thrown sixty men, devoted to the interests of Ireland, into the House of Commons. If the Clare election was a great incident,—if the Clare election afforded evidence that emancipation could not be resisted,—look at sixty of us (what are Longford and Carlow but a realisation of the splendid intimations that Clare held out?)—look, I say, at sixty of us,—the majority, the great majority of the representatives of Ireland,—leagued and confederated by an obligation and a pledge as sacred as any with which men, associated for the interests of their country, were ever bound together. Thank God, we are here! I remember the time when the body to which I belong were excluded from all participation in the great legislative rights which we are now in the possession. I remember to have felt humiliated at the tone in which I heard the cause of Ireland pleaded, when was occasionally admitted under the gallery of the House of Commons. I felt pain at hearing us represented as humble suppliants for liberty, and as asking freedom as if it were alms that we were soliciting. Perhaps that tone was unavoidable: thank God, it is no longer necessary' appropriate. Here we are, in all regards your equals, and demanding our rights as the representatives of Britons would demand their own. We have less eloquence, less skill, less astuteness than the great men to whom, of old, the interests of Ireland were confided; but we make up for these imperfections by the moral port and rational bearing that become us. In mastery of diction we may be defective; in resources of argument we may be wanting; we may not be gifted with the accomplishments by which persuasion is produced: but in energy, in strenuousness, in union, in fidelity to our country and to each other, and above all in the undaunted and dauntless determination to enforce equality for Ireland, we stand unsurpassed. This, then, is the power with which the noble lord courts an encounter, foretels his own victories, and triumphs in their anticipation in the House of Commons. Where are his means of discomfiting us? To what resources does he look for the accomplishment of the wonders which he is to perform? Does he rely upon the excitement of the religious and national prejudices of England; and does he find it in his heart to resort to the "no Popery" cry?— Instead of telling him what he is doing, I'll tell the country what, thirty years ago, was done. In 1807, the Whigs were in possession of Downing-street, and the Tories were in possession of St. James's Palace, but, without the people, the possession of St. James's was of no avail. The Whigs proposed that Roman Catholics should be admitted to the higher grades in the army and navy. The Tories saw that their opportunity was come, and the "no Popery" cry was raised. There existed, at that time, a great mass of prejudice in England. You had conquered Ireland and enslaved her; you hated her for the wrongs that you had done her, and despised her, and perhaps justly, for her endurance: the victim of oppression naturally becomes the object of scorn: you loathed our country, and you abhorred our creed. Of this feeling, the Tories took advantage; the tocsin of fanaticism was rung; the war-whoop of religious discord, the savage yell of infuriated ignorance, resounded through the country. Events, that ought to have been allowed to remain buried in the oblivion of centuries, were disinterred; every misdeed of Catholics, when Catholics and Protestants imbrued their hands alternately in blood, was recalled;—the ashes of the Smithfield fires were stirred, for sparks with which the popular passions might be ignited. The re-establishment of Popery,—the downfal of every Protestant institution,—the annihilation of all liberty, civil or religious, these were the topics with which crafty men, without remorse of conscience, worked on the popular delusion. At public assemblies, senators, more remarkable for Protestant piety than Christian charity, delivered themselves of ferocious effusions amidst credulous and enthusiastic multitudes :—then came public abuses, at which libations to the worst passions of human nature were prodigally poured out. "Rally round the King, rally round the church, rally round the religion of your forefathers,"—these were the invocations with which the English people were wrought into frenzy; and having, by these expedients, driven their antagonists from office, the Tories passed, themselves, the very measure for which they made their competitors the objects of their denunciation. Are you playing the same game? If you are, then shame, shame upon you! I won't pronounce upon your motives: let the facts be their interpreters. What is the reason that a new edition of Fox's Martyrs, with hundreds of subscribers, and with the name of the Duke of Cumberland at their head has been announced? Wherefore, from one extremity of the country to the other, in every city, town, and hamlet, is a perverse ingenuity employed, in order to inspire the people of this country with a detestation of the religion of millions of their fellow-citizens. Why Popery, with her racks, her tortures, and her faggots, conjured up in order to appal the imagination of the English people? Why is perjury to our God—treason to our Sovereign—a disregard of every obligation divine and human, attributed to us? I leave you to answer those questions. and to give your answers, not only to the interrogatories which thus vehemently, and, I will own, indignantly I put to you, but to reply to those which must be administered to you, in your moments of meditation, by your own hearts. But, whatever be your purpose in the religious excitement which you are endeavouring to get up in this country, of this I am convinced,—that the result of your expedients will correspond with their deserts, and that as we have prevailed over you before, we shall again and again discomfit you. Yes, we, the Irish millions, led on by men like those that plead the cause of those millions in this house, must (it is impossible that we should not) prevail; and I am convinced that the people of England, so far from being disposed to array themselves against us, despite any remains of the prejudices which are fast passing away in this country, feel that we are entitled to the same privileges, and extend to us their sympathies in this good and glorious cause.

What is that cause? I shall rapidly tell you. You took away our parliament—you took from us that parliament which, like the House of Commons of this country, must have been under the control of the great majority of the people of Ireland, and would not, and could not, have withheld what you so long refused us. Is there a man here who doubts that if the Union had not been conceded, we should have extorted emancipation and reform from our own House of Commons? That House of Commons you bought, and paid for your bargain in gold; ay, and paid for it in the most palpable and sordid form in which gold can be paid down. But, while this transaction was pending, you told us that all distinctions should be abolished between us, and that we should become like unto yourselves. The great minister of the time, by whom that unexampled sale of our legislature was negotiated, held out equality with England as the splendid equivalent for the loss of our national representation; and, with classical references, elucidated the nobleness of the compact into which he had persuaded the depositants of the rights of their countrymen to enter. The act of Union was passed, and twenty-nine years elapsed before any effectual measure was taken to carry its real and substantial terms into effect. At last, our enfranchisement was won by our own energy and determination; and, when it was in progress, we received assurances that, in every respect, we should be placed on a footing with our fellow-citizens; and it was more specially announced to us, that to corporations, and to all offices connected with them, we should be at once admissible. Pending this engagement, a bill is passed for the reform of the corporatio of this country; and in every important municipal locality in England, councillors are selected by the people as their representatives. This important measure having been carried here, the Irish people claim an extension of the same advantages; and ground their title on the Union, on Emancipation, on Reform, and on the great principle of perfect equality between the two countries, on. which the security of one country and the prosperity of both must depend. This demand, on the part of Ireland, is rejected; and that, which to England no one was bold enough to deny, from Ireland you are determined, and you announce it, to withhold. Is this justice? You will say that it is, and I should be surprised if you did not say so. I should be surprised, indeed, if, while you are doing us wrong, you did not profess your solicitude to do us justice. From the day on which Strongbow set his foot upon the shore of Ireland, Englishmen were never wanting in protestations of their deep anxiety to do us justice:— even Strafford, the deserter of the people's cause—the renegade Wentworth, who gave evidence in Ireland of the spirit of instinctive tyranny which predominated in his character—even Strafford, while he trampled upon our rights, and trod upon the heart of the country, protested his solicitude to do justice to Ireland. What marvel is it, then, that gentlemen opposite should deal in such vehement protestations? There is, however, one man, of great abilities, not a member of this house, but whose talents and whose boldness have placed him in the topmost place in his party—who, disdaining all imposture, and thinking it the best course to appeal directly to the religious and national antipathies of the people of this country—abandoning all reserve, and flinging off the slender veil by which his political associates affect to cover, although they cannot hide, their motives—distinctly and audaciously tells the Irish people that they are not entitled to the same privileges as Englishmen ; and pronounces them, in any particular which could enter his minute enumeration of the circumstances by which fellow-citizenship is created, in race, identity, and religion—to be aliens—to be aliens in race—to be aliens in country—to be aliens in religion.* Aliens! good God! was Arthur, Duke of Wellington, in the House of Lords, and did he not start up and exclaim, "Hold! I have seen the aliens do their duty?" The Duke of Wellington is not a man of an excitable temperament. His mind is of a cast too martial to be easily moved; but notwithstanding his habitual inflexibility, I cannot help thinking that when he heard his Roman Catholic countrymen (for we are his countrymen) designated by a phrase as offensive as the abundant vocabulary of his eloquent confederate could supply—I cannot help thinking that he ought to have recollected the many fields of fight in which we have been contributors to his renown. " The battles, sieges, fortunes that he has passed," ought to have come back upon him. He ought to have remembered that, from the earliest achievement in which he displayed that military genius which has placed him foremost in the annals of modern warfare, down to that last and surpassing combat which has made his name imperishable—from Assaye to Waterloo—the Irish soldiers, with whom your armies are filled, were the inseparable auxiliaries to the glory with which his unparalleled successes have been crowned. Whose

Lord Lyndhurst was sitting under the gallery during Mr. Shell's speech. Mr. Shel' looked and shook his head indignantly at him at this part of his speech. The effect produced was remarkable. The whole house turned towards Lord Lyndhurst, and the shouts of the ministerialists, encountered by the vehement outcries of the Conservatives, continued for minutes.
The *Times* next morning observed: " A scene of the Corn-Exchange character occurred in the course of Mr. Shell's speech, when referring to the expressions said to have been used by Lord Lyndhurst with respect to ' aliens.' The honourable member for Tipperary turned towards the benches allotted to the peers, where Lord Lyndhurst was sitting. This was the signal for the most infuriate yelling from the ministerial benches."—*Times*, February 29, 1837

were the arms that drove your bayonets at Vimiera through the phalanxes that never reeled in the shock of war before? What desperate valour climbed the steeps and filled the moats at Badajos? All his victories should have rushed and crowded back upon his memory—Vimiera, Badajos, Salamanca, Albuera, Toulouse, and, last of all, the greatest——. Tell me, for you were there—I appeal to the gallant soldier before me (Sir Henry Hardinge,) from whose opinions I differ, but who bears, I know, a generous heart in an intrepid breast;—tell me, for you must needs remember—on that day when the destinies of mankind were trembling in the balance—while death fell in showers—when the artillery of France was levelled with a precision of the most deadly science —when her legions, incited by the voice, and inspired by the example of their mighty leader, rushed again and again to the onset—tell me if, for an instant, when, to hesitate for an instant was to be lost, the "aliens" blenched? And when at length the moment for the last and decisive movement had arrived, and the valour which had so long been wisely checked, was at last let loose—when, with words familiar, but immortal, the great captain commanded the great assault—tell me, if Catholic Ireland, with less heroic valour than the natives of this your own glorious country, precipitated herself upon the foe? The blood of England, Scotland, and of Ireland, flowed in the same stream, and drenched the same field. When the chill morning dawned, their dead lay cold and stark together;—in the same deep pit their bodies were deposited—the green corn of spring is now breaking from their commingled dust—the dew falls from heaven upon their union in the grave. Partakers in every peril—in the glory shall we not be permitted to participate; and shall we be told, as a requital, that we are estranged from the noble country for whose salvation our life-blood was poured out?

CIVIL WAR IN SPAIN.

SPEECH IN THE HOUSE OF COMMONS, APRIL 18, 1837.

IF the learned member (Mr. Grove Price) had been born in Spain, he ought to have been returned to the Cortes, as representative of La Mancha! What a strange anomaly will enthusiasm produce in even an accomplished mind! Despite his habitual horror for Popery, I question whether he does not regard the Inquisition as a venerable Con servative institution; and whether, in the event of the triumph of Don Carlos, he would not gladly journey across the Pyrenees, in order to witness the burning of the Quadruple Treaty at an *auto-da-fe*.

The military and political character of the gallant member by whom this motion was brought forward gives it a peculiar interest. As a soldier, his opinions, when unbiassed, are of the highest value. And the part he plays as a politician is so conspicuous, that it is not unreasonable to conjecture that this motion is part of a combined plan of operations, by which a very important position is to be carried by the gallant officer. But an additional interest is given to this question by the admixture of military with civil accomplishments. The motion was seconded by a profound, but unemployed diplomast, Sir T. Canning; an eminent negociator, once in the confidence of the Whigs, and now not undeserving Tory trust. There is a practical antithesis in the right honourable gentleman; for while for the Emperor Nicholas he has no strong personal relish, he is not without some propensity to the adoption of a Sclavonic policy at Madrid. I like to do justice; and I trust the right honourable gentleman will forgive me if I say, having heard him designate the noble lord (Lord Palmerston) as his "noble friend," I should think that the right honourable gentleman must have laboured under a very strong and painful sense of public duty, when he took a part so prominent in assailing the measures of his noble—and I believe he has found him his faithful—friend. If that speech had been made under ordinary circumstances, perhaps no great consequence might have attached to it. But there is yet another view in which this motion is most important; it is an announcement of the policy intended to be pursued by the Tories upon their anticipated advent to power The right honourable member for Tamworth has recently intimated that he will, although with great reluctance, submit to the infliction of power; and he has also intimated that he would endeavour to manage a House of Commons better than Lord Melbourne (he says) can manage the House o Peers—and give this house an opportunity of atoning for that parricidal blow by which his official existence was suddenly abridged. It is as well that we should be apprised that the victory of Conservatism in St. James's will be followed by the triumph of Carlism at Madrid.

I pass to the Quadruple Treaty. The decision of the house, upon this subject, must turn upon the general construction of the treaty, and the course pursued by the government. Let me examine both. What standard shall we adopt in interpreting the treaty? Not a mere literal one—we are to consider the circumstances under which the treaty was entered into, its objects, and the means by which they are to be accomplished. What was the object of that Quadruple Alliance? The pacification of the Peninsula; the expulsion of Carlos from Spain, and of Miguel from Portugal; the securing free institutions to the one, and the permanent ejection of Carlos from the throne of the other. Any fair man, who looks at the events which took place at that period, must come to this conclusion. It may be asked, what concern have we with Spain? I answer by asking, what concern has Russia with Spain? What have Austria and Prussia to do with Spain? And if despots feel their interests so deeply involved in the form of government which she assumes, shall it be said that the people of this country ought to be indifferent to the extension of the principles from which England derives her power and her virtue? But, putting considerations aside which may be regarded as vague and indefinite, look back a little at events which have happened within a few years, and we shall see how material it is to sustain British interests in the Peninsula, in order to countervail the great northern confederacy which is leagued against us. We shall see the consequences of neglecting liberty in Spain. In 1820 the constitution was proclaimed—at the council of the Congress at Verona, it was determined by Russia that it should be crushed. In 1823, under he influence, and swayed by the councils, of the autocrat, the Duke l'Angouleme marched into Spain. It is notorious that he obtained possession of Spain as the trustee for Alexander, and was a mere instrument in the hands of the Czar. The ascendancy of Russia was established, and she took advantage of her predominance over France: being ure that her dependant, bribed by the gift of Spain into acquiescence, would not join us, she fell on Turkey, crossed the Balkan, in 1829, xtorted the Treaty of Adrianople, and laid the Sultan so utterly prostrate, that England, in 1830, could not lift him into independence and ignity again. This is the simple narrative of incidents of which we t feel the results: the transactions in the East were, beyond doubt, fluenced by our original supineness; and it is the duty of British ministers to endeavour to repair these errors, and to regain an influence rough liberal institutions in the Peninsula.

Thus I account for the policy by which the Quadruple Treaty was stated, and with a view to which it ought to be interpreted and forced. Look now at the more immediate circumstances under which was framed. Don Carlos and Don Miguel were both in Portugal in pril, 1834. If Don Carlos should recover the throne of Spain, it was vious that Don Miguel would recover that of Portugal. We were und, under treaties, to protect Portugal, and thus the entire Peninsula was embraced in the treaty. Instead, then, of wasting time in ils about particular passages in the treaty, let us see what was doing l what ought to have been done under the treaty. The Duke of llington gave it a complete ratification. He ordered 50,000 muskets e sent to the Basque provinces. For what purpose? I call on the tlemen opposite, who cry out so vehemently for justice to Navarre

—I call on those who tell us that the Basques are fighting for thei immemorial rights, and who protest that we ought not to interfere in the struggle, to tell me for what purpose the Duke of Wellington sent 50,000 bayonets to Spain? And if it was no violation of the treaty, nor inconsistent with our political obligations, to employ bayonets against the Basques, how have the government offended against the principles by which British statesmen ought to be swayed, in allowing British subjects to use the weapons which it is admitted the Duke of Wellingte transmitted to the Peninsula? There is no distinction between the transmission of arms and the authorization of British subjects to enter the service of Spain; and they indulge in mere factitious sensibility who contend that the Basques, after having associated their cause with an avowed despot, are engaged in a struggle which entitles them to the sympathies of Great Britain. The constitution gives the Basques the same privileges as are awarded to other Spaniards: it places all Spaniards upon a level; and the Basques are not contending for a participation in the rights of citizens, but for an exemption from their liabilities.

I come to the order in council. Let it not be supposed that our government volunteered in granting permission to British subjects to enter into the Spanish service. On the 7th of May, the Spanish ministry applied to us for co-operation. It was feared that direct intervention would alarm the sensitiveness of Castilian pride. In 1819, the the Foreign Enlistment Act was passed; but a power was reserved to the crown to suspend its operation. It was clear that circumstances were anticipated under which it might be deemed judicious that foreign enlistment should be allowed. It was thought, in 1823, by the Whigs, that though circumstances had arisen at that juncture, and that a good moral effect would be produced by repealing the act, and thus signifying the interest we took in the liberties of Spain—(I may incidentally observe that the noble lord the member for Lancashire voted for the repeal of the act; how he will vote to-night it is not for me to anticipate)—the application to which I have referred having been made to the Whig government for assistance, it was thought that the wisest course would be to issue the order in council. Let us see how far that proceeding, which was, beyond all doubt, in conformity with the spirit of the treaty, has been justified, in point of policy, by events. Three charges have been brought against the Legion; and insubordination, inhumanity, and want of disciplined intrepidity in action, have been attributed to them. With respect to disorganization, it existed to a considerable extent; but it ought to be recollected that, even in the best armies, it will, under peculiar circumstances, unfortunately arise. Was not the retreat of the Duke of Wellington, after his defeat at Burgos, attended with a lamentable loss of discipline, for which the Duke of Wellington is not in the slightest degree responsible? And how can it be wondered at, that such levies as composed the Auxiliary Legion should in the midst of hardships, certainly not occasioned by themselves, have been deficient in subordination?

With respect to the excesses into which the Legion had been betrayed, let it be remembered that, although they were not justifiable they were not unprovoked. They gave no quarter, and they received none; to the merciless they showed no mercy; and I question whether the gallant officer opposite, at the head of the best troops in the service, could, notwithstanding all his habits of control, restrain his men from vengeance, if they saw their fellow-soldiers lying butchered and mutilated with every incident of the most degrading ignominy before them. But from every participation in these offences against humanity, General Evans is entirely free. No order of a vindictive character was ever issued by him. And if a single officer, under the influence of excited passion, let his feelings burst forth in an ebullition of reprehensible resentment, and that fact is stated in an anonymous publication, how unjust it is to charge the entire British Legion with that want o. humanity which has been imputed to them. But while the gallant officer is thus at once vehement and pathetic in reprobating the excesses of retaliation, what will he say of the atrocious Durango decree, by which murder in cold blood was enjoined by Don Carlos? The Tories will of course condemn him; but, while they condemn him, they recommend measures of which the effect will be to plant the crown of Spain upon his head. With respect to the last charge—the want of valour—it cannot be denied that a portion of our troops gave way. But I believe that most troops, excepting those which have acquired a veteran stability, are occasionally subject, in a moment of surprise, to such moral disasters as, in the instance referred to, befel the Auxiliary Legion. Having admitted the occurrence of this deplorable incident, give me leave to ask whether it is not, in some degree, countervailed by those examples of high courage which, in many other instances, the Legion have furnished? Was it quite legitimate to expatiate with so much force upon a single calamity, and to omit the mention of those achievements for which the Legion deserve no ordinary praise? The Spanish Cortes and Government thanked General Evans after the battle of St. Sebastian; the French general expressed his warmest commendations; and I shall, I hope, be pardoned for suggesting that an incident which, to a French soldier, afforded matter for congratulation, ought, in the mind of the gallant officer opposite, to have, in some sort, counterbalanced the unfortunate transaction upon which the gallant officer has so strongly dilated.

I pass to the second branch of the motion of the gallant officer.— Nothing can be worse, it seems, than the failure of the Legion, excepting the success of the marines. The gallant officer would withdraw the Legion because, as he erroneously conceives, they have failed; and would withhold the assistance of the marines because they have succeeded! This is exceedingly anomalous. Let it be observed that '' is not upon any large ground of public policy that he recommends that the marines should be removed from the field in which they have won laurels that have borne precious fruit. He dwells entirely upon the nature of the service to which he conceives that these fine troops ought to be confined, and insists that it is only upon the ocean they should be permitted to serve their country. I answer the gallant officer by a reference to their motto. "*Per mare, per terram*" sets all discussion upon this part of the question at rest. Read the treaty with a view to the interests of your country, and not to the speculations of your party, and you will rid yourselves of miserable dissertations on mere words and phrases, and arrive at the just and lofty sense of this great quadruple compact.

It is alleged that the measures of the government have not produced any good results. Try that allegation by this test. If those measures had not been adopted—if the Auxiliary Legion and the marines had not given their co-operation, what would have befallen the Spanish people? Do you not know, on Major Richardson's authority, that Bilboa would have been taken by assault? and would not the British seamen have seen from afar upon the main the Durango standard of Don Carlos floating from the castle of St. Sebastian? Take another test, if you please it. Let me suppose this motion carried. If you carry the present motion—if you prevent any acknowledgment of the Legion—if you break the character of this force—if you withdraw the marines from the north coast of Spain (the importance and efficiency of whose services you cannot deny)—what will be the result? The courier who will convey the intelligence will convey tidings of great joy to St. Petersburg, to Vienna, and to Berlin; and he will convey tidings of great dismay wherever men value the possession of freedom or pant for its enjoyment. It will palsy the arm of liberty in Spain. It will fill her heart with despair. A terrible revulsion will be produced; from Calpe to the Pyrenees the cry, "We are betrayed by England!" will be heard, and over that nation which you will indeed have betrayed, Don Carlos will march, without an obstacle, to Madrid.

You cheer me in mockery—do you? Who are you that cheer me? Not your leaders—not the men who are placed conspicuously before me. They know, they feel, the impolicy of these rash manifestations. They profess horror at the atrocities of Don Carlos, and deprecate his triumph; but you that cheer me, disclose your hearts, and exhibit the wishes by which your political conduct is determined. Cheer on—exult in the anticipated victories of despotism in Spain, and with your purpose let the people of England be made well acquainted. But, turning from you, I call upon the rest of the house, and to the British people beyond the house, to reflect upon the events which must follow the triumph of Don Carlos. Do you not know him? Do you stand in need of any illustrations of his character? What was it that befel Spain when the constitution was suppressed in 1823? Do you not think that Don Carlos will improve upon Ferdinand's example, and recollect what model was held out to him? Have we forgotten the massacre at Cadiz? Is Riego's blood effaced from our memories? Do you doubt that the same terrible career of remorseless, relentless vengeance will be pursued by the marble-hearted despot by whom such horrors have been already perpetrated? With whom, attended with what companionship, encompassed by what councillors, did Don Carlos land in England? Did he not dare to set his foot upon our shores with Moreno, the murderer of Boyd and Torrijos beside him? But what further evidence of his character and his propensities do we want, than his terrible Durango ordinance? I have heard it asked whether it be befitting that in Spain, the theatre of so many of those exploits whose memory will be everlasting, the British flag should be lowered in discomfiture, and before mountain peasants British soldiers should give way? I feel the force of that question; but there is another which I venture to put to every man who hears me, and, among all those that hear me—above all—to the gallant officer by whom this motion has been made. I invoke the same recoilections—I appeal to the same glorious remembrances; and in the name of those scenes of which he was not only a witness, but in which he bore a part, of which he carries the honourable attestation about him, I ask whether it be befitting that in Spain—that in the country whose freedom was achieved by such prodigies of English valour, where so many of your fellow-soldiers, who fell beside you, lie buried—is it, I ask, befitting that in that land, consecrated, as it is, in the annals of England's glory, a terrible, remorseless, relentless despotism should be established, and that the throne which England saved should be filled by the purple tyrant whose arms have been steeped to the shoulders in the blood of your countrymen—not slain in the field of honourable combat, but when the heat of battle had passed, and its sweat had been wiped away—savagely and deliberately murdered? Their bones are bleaching on the Pyrenean snows—their blood cries out; and shall we, intrusted as we are by the British people with the honour, and the just vengeance of our country—shall we, instead of flying to arms, facilitate the ascent to the throne of Spain of the guilty man by whom these outrages upon every law, divine and human, have been committed? Never! The people of this country are averse to wanton war; but where the honour of England is at stake, there is no consequence which they are not prepared to meet—no treasure which they are not ready to lavish—no hazard which they will not be found prompt to encounter.

LORD NORMANBY'S GOVERNMENT OF IRELAND.

SPEECH IN THE HOUSE OF COMMONS, APRIL 19, 1839.

In one opinion expressed by the learned member for Bandon (Mr. Sergeant Jackson) I entirely concur. It would be difficult, indeed, to dissent from him, when he declared his speech to be "no joke." That speech may be distinguished by ability; but, among its multifarious merits, we should look for originality in vain. I will not say that it was, so far as its topics were concerned, " tedious as a twice-told tale ;" but I may venture, without any departure from good breeding, to suggest, that its principal materials were of a nature to ensure, among the gentlemen behind him, untired applause for the untiring reiteration of the same charges in nearly the same form of phrase. It is fortunate for the learned gentleman that he may indulge in such repetitions without the hazard of incurring any expression of weariness from his admirers. I pass from the learned gentleman to the speech of my honourable friend, the member for Finsbury,* who announced, at the opening of this evening's discussion, that he intended to move an additional amendment connected with the extension of parliamentary reform. I shall content myself with making two observations on the course which he, and some gentlemen who act with him, are disposed to take. Let me be permitted to advise them to take care lest they fall into the very signal error which was committed by the Tories in 1830. By the effects of that mistake they are still pursued, for their reconciliation, however strenuous the professions of its sincerity, is not yet complete. Let me be allowed, in the second place, to remark, that when the member for Finsbury and his associates condemn the conduct of the present ministers, with the exception of the policy pursued by them in reference to Ireland, they make a very large exception indeed. That exception includes a great segment of the empire—one-third of the population of these islands—a country whose government has been attended with almost incalculable difficulties—which, to preceding administrations, has been the constant occasion of embarrassment, and has shaken cabinet after cabinet to their foundations—which, as it has already exercised a great influence over the councils of England, is likely to exercise an influence at least as great over her future fortunes—which, after having occupied the attention of the legislature for many years, is, at this moment, of an importance so paramount, as to exclude all other subjects from our thoughts, and to engross the solicitude of every man who takes the slightest concern in the events by which the destinies of this great nation are to be determined. When, therefore, it is observed, that the Whigs deserve no praise except for the government of Ireland—unconciously, perhaps, but most certainly, the highest encomium is passed upon the present administration, and a merit is admitted to belong to them, by which a multitude of errors, in the eyes of true reformers

* Mr. T. Duncombe.

should be covered. But I turn to the amendment proposed by the member for Tamworth (Sir R. Peel). Between that exceedingly temperate amendment, and the declamation by which it has been sustained, there is a good deal of contrast. I do not advert to the speech of the right honourable baronet by whom it has been moved. That was a truly previous question speech (the amendment is the "previous question" in a periphrase): it was a speech of a precursor character, in the better sense of that significant expression. But what a discrepancy was exhibited between it and the effusions by which it was succeeded! The right honourable baronet, who can command their votes, ought to put some check on the insubordinate spirit by which the eloquence of his followers is occasionally distinguished. He ought to silence that piece of Sligo ordnance (Colonel Perceval), which is formidable in its recoil. The Recorder for Dublin, himself, exhibits in his oratory some rant of discipline. The right honourable baronet, however, may rely on the votes of the learned gentlemen, and the other forensic statesmen with whom he is associated. But there is a class of stanch old Tories, at whose support of the previous question I shall be surprised. I allude to the forty gentlemen, who, upon the second reading of the Irish Corporation Bill, rose against the member for Tamworth in a conscientious mutiny, and, disclaiming the control of that distinguished person, voted in direct opposition to the pledges given by him and the Duke of Wellington upon that momentous question. Will they—will the men who made themselves so conspicuous by their impracticable honesty, upon an occasion so remarkable and so recent, forego all the praise which they have lately earned from the Orangemen of Ireland, and support an amendment which, instead of negativing the original motion, eludes the question really at issue between us, and upon which the government have called for the opinion of the House of Commons? I do not think that the ministers could with propriety have taken any other course. Look at the facts. The amendment commences by referring to a most important one, from which an irresistible argument in favour of the original motion may be deduced. The Recorder for Dublin moved for a return of certain papers connected with the commission of crime in Ireland. He did not venture to move for an inquiry. Why, if an inquiry is, as alleged, of absolute necessity, was it not demanded in the House of Commons? Why do the Tories move for papers in one house, and for committee in the other? The Recorder for Dublin did not dare to make a motion by which the sense of the House of Commons should be taken: he thought it far more prudent to get up a debate, made up of unsupported asseverations against the Irish government, and with this view, speeches infinite in length, and infinitesimal in detail, were delivered by himself and the honourable and learned member for Bandon, who, with their auxiliaries, failed, however, in imparting any interest to a motion, which was to terminate without a division; many hours were expended in discussions perfectly useless, until some gentleman had compassion on the speaker, and, in the midst of the performance of what I may designate by an expression of Swift's, "a Newgate Pastoral," interrupted the proceeding, by taking notice that there were not forty members present, and then counted out the house. Thus lamely and impotently concluded this grand performance in the House of Commons. Not so in the House of Lords. There Lord Roden moves for censure in the guise of inquiry, for who can doubt that inquiry to be equivalent to censure, which originates with my Lord Roden, and which is to be conducted by Dr. Phillpotts—which has its source in the mercy of his gracious Majesty the King of Hanover, and to the direction of which the inquisitorial genius of the meek and apostolic pontiff, who keeps a small Vatican at Exeter, is to be applied? The character of the parties by whom the motion for a committee was brought forward and supported, and the constitution of the committee itself, ought to set at rest all doubt as to its objects and effect; but if any doubt could be entertained upon the subject, the limitation of the inquiry to the four years, during which Lord Normanby was chief governor of Ireland, must at once remove it. Why are the Lords' Committee to confine their investigation to the last four years? Last night the member for Pembroke told us, that an inquiry was, for many reasons, to be desired: and among others, he informed us, that he conceived that we should consider how it came to pass, that spade husbandry had succeeded in Belgium and had not succeeded in Ireland. On these grounds he, somewhat fantastically, justifies an inquiry into crime, in the House of Lords, since 1835. How miserable are the subterfuges by which gentlemen endeavour to escape from the effect of that specific limitation to the extent of the inquiry which was defined and marked out with so much care in Lord Roden's motion? The right honourable member for Tamworth cited several examples of inquiry to prove that inquiry did not imply condemnation; but did he show an instance of one founded on charges against a minister, and limited to the period during which that minister was in office? Suppose that, after he had left Ireland in 1818, a member of the House of Commons had stated all the atrocities that were perpetrated when he was Secretary to the Lord Lieutenant—had described the system pursued for many years by a government unequivocally Tory—had expatiated upon the exclusion of all Catholics from the places to which they were admissible—upon the mode in which justice was administered—upon the construction of the jury under Mr. Saurin's auspices, on Sheridan's trial, and other details of a kindred character, and had then moved for an inquiry into the state of crime since the year 1812 (when his government commenced), would the right honourable baronet have called it a mere inquiry, and designated it, as he now designates that proceeding in the other House of Parliament? But it has been said, there will be a collision with the House of Lords if the original motion is carried; we have been referred to a precedent so far back as the year 1703; and the right honourable baronet read a passage from Burnet, which I admit was most effective.

Lord STANLEY.—Hear, hear, hear!

Mr. SHEIL.—The noble lord (Lord Stanley) cries "Hear, hear!" Does the noble lord, who cries "Hear, hear!" when I say that the passage from Burnet was most effective, forget the transaction to which he himself was a party in 1833? The object of Lord Roden's motion is the inculpation of Lord Normanby; just as, in 1833, the object of the Duke of Wellington was the inculpation of the Whig Secretary for Foreign Affairs, when he moved for an address, praying that the crown would enforce our neutrality with Portugal. What did the Whig cabinet do? It called for a counter vote from this house, and the ministers acknowledged that a collision with the Lords was implied. Why did not the member for Tamworth touch on that proceeding? Was it because he remembered how the cabinet was composed? or did he leave it to the noble lord opposite, and the right honourable baronet, to explain the matter as well as the swamping of the House of Lords agreed to by the cabinet of 1831? But the noble lord, the member for Stroud* did not rely on the precedent as emphatically as he might have done: perhaps he wished to spare the feelings of the member for Lancashire, his noble and exceedingly inveterate friend. I perceive that the noble lord the member for Lancashire and the member for Pembroke are exchanging looks and whispers across the member for Tamworth, who is placed between them, and seem not to recollect the fact to which I am alluding. With the pleasures, of which memory is the source, I shall feel very great gratification in supplying them. On the 3rd of June, 1833, the Duke of Wellington moved and carried an address, praying the crown to enforce neutrality with Portugal. On the 6th of June, a motion was made in this house, declaratory of confidence in his Majesty's ministers in respect to their foreign policy. The government called on this house for a counter vote, and acknowledged, that a collision with the Lords was implied in the proceeding, to the adoption of which they had invited the House of Commons. All that has been said in reference to collision in this debate was insisted upon with as much strenuousness as is now employed in deprecating a collision with the other House of Parliament. The motion was carried by a very large majority, and was supported by every member of the cabinet in the House of Commons. Who were the members of the cabinet in 1833? I was, I own, not a little surprised when I saw the noble lord, the member for North Lancashire, immediately before the debate commenced, advance to the table with some solemnity of deportment, and heard him read with good emphasis, but, by no means, good discretion, a petition from Rochdale, touching the evils of collision with the House of Lords. The noble lord was himself a member of the cabinet, when, in 1833, this house, at the instance of the government, pronounced a virtual condemnation of the proceeding uggested by the Duke of Wellington, and adopted by the other House of Parliament. To the censure of one house the confidence of the other was opposed. But I ought not, perhaps, to dwell on this instance of inconsistency, on the part of the noble lord, when I recollect a fact far more important, which was revealed by the Secretary of the Home Department, who ought to write a history of the Grey administration. The disclosure is calculated to throw a strong light upon the character of some of the leading public men in this country. Few could have onjectured that such a measure could have been seriously contemplated,

Lord J. Russell.

when we consider the language now habitually employed by them in reference to the House of Lords. What! the whole cabinet, in 1831, with one exception, agreed to swamp (that was the phrase)—yes, to wamp the House of Lords. I like the word "swamp;" it is nautical. You laugh, because it is associated with Greenwich; you ought to laugh because it is connected with the Admiralty, and revives all the recollections of a celebrated image, derived by one of the right honourable swampers opposite, from the sinking of the Royal George. Having disposed of the argument grounded on the evils which, it is alleged, are likely to result from a collision between the two Houses of Parliament, I come to the consideration of the substantial merits of the proposition made by the noble member for Stroud, in which we are called upon to express our distinct approval of the policy upon which Lord Normanby's government was carried on. How should that question be discussed? How will history hereafter treat it? When the time for impartial adjudication shall have arrived, and the historian shall revert to the events on which we are now about to pronounce a judgment, from which our own feelings, interests, and passions, cannot be wholly excluded, what are the chief incidents in Lord Normanby's administration, on which the sentence of those by whom we shall be succeeded will be founded? I do not think that, in the opinion expressed by the many gentlemen upon the other side of the house, history will concur; I am convinced that history will not dwell on the topics which they have selected, for the purpose of vituperative expatiation. Will history—will "the philosophy which teaches by example" consider it to be consistent with the dignity or the usefulness of its lofty purpose to descend to the minute particulars of elaborate investigation, into which the antagonists of my Lord Normanby have not thought it unworthy to enter? The appointment of constables of police; the entrance, by a back door, effected by the Lord Lieutenant into the court-house at Sligo; the adventures of Tom Gallagher, or of Nora Creina, on which the learned sergeant who spoke last has dwelt so pathetically, will not be deemed fitting matter for commemoration, when the principles on which Lord Normanby carried on the government of Ireland, and the results to which his policy must inevitably lead, shall be discussed by those who will hereafter have to find upon those momentous subjects their final and unbiassed verdict. Condemn Lord Normanby, if you choose; but when you condemn him, let your sentence rest upon some nobler ground of imputation than, in this debate, has been urged against him. From such details as they have chosen to establish their case, his worst adversaries should have turned away, and should have disdained, against such a man, in such a cause, and before such a tribunal, to prefer the charges which, of the accusers and of the accused, were equally unworthy. Charge Lord Normanby, if you please, with an abandonment of that policy by which Ireland was ruled so long, by the men who regarded that policy as the only means of preserving what is called British connexion and Protestant interests; charge him with having preferred the conciliation of an entire people to the mercenary sustainment of a decayed and impuissant faction: charge him with having grounded his administration upon a scheme of government subversive of that party which was held so long to be the garrison of the country. These are accusations worthy of him, and of you : but you should not stoop to a miserable criticism upon the appointment of subordinate officers in the police, and of stipendiary magistrates, whose only offence is to be found in their consanguinity with the member for Dublin ; upon the alleged liberation of men charged with larcenies and assaults, without a strict compliance with technical formalities ; upon the absence from levees of discontented barristers ; upon the invitations of Agitators to the vice-regal convivialities, and other matters of an analogous character, which the impugners of Lord Normanby's government ought to have felt it unbecoming of them to have made the subject of their acrimonious but frivolous inculpation. No, Sir ; it is not thus that they ought to have sustained their virtual impeachment of the man who, having completely succeeded in Jamaica, and discomfited the planter faction, in preparing the way for the enfranchisement of his fellow-men, undertook the government of Ireland with a determination to carry the emancipation of his fellow-citizens into full effect ;—who, by adhering to that noble and salutary determination, secured the confidence and the attachment of the immense majority of the people whom his sovereign, with a special expression of her just reliance, had recommitted to his care ;—who, although the entire suppression of all political excitement was rendered impracticable, by the obstinate adherence of his antagonists to a policy no longer applicable to the condition of the country, succeeded in divesting it of its most formidable characteristics ; who won for the government with which he was connected the undeviating support of two-thirds of the members who are delegated by Ireland to this house ;—and who, after four years of unparalleled popularity, having been transferred to the government of those colonies for whose pacification he has displayed the highest aptitude, carries away with him the noblest of all rewards, in the proud and thrilling consciousness of having most assuredly deserved, as he has, beyond all doubt, obtained, the lasting gratitude of the Irish people.

These, Sir, appear to me to be the most conspicuous incidents in the government of Lord Normanby, and I think them far more worthy of consideration than the details into which the opponents of the motion before the house have thought proper to enter ; yet, to such of those details as are of any moment, I deem it right to advert. First, let me refer to the patronage of the crown. With respect to the church, the right honourable member for Tamworth confesses that Lord Normanby deserves unqualified praise. But, in this acknowledgment, does he not make a most signal and large admission ? Lord Normanby and the whigs were charged with aiming at the total subversion of the church. Had they entertained such a purpose, would they not have betrayed it to its enemies, and garrisoned it with traitors to its cause ? But what did Lord Normanby do ? He selected men of the highest character, of the most unexceptionable conduct, to fill every ecclesiastical dignity at his disposal. It is enough to refer to his last appointment, that of . Tonson, who, in his address to his clergy, informs them that it is to Lord Normanby, alone, that he is indebted for his elevation. Hear another fact. Lord Normanby promoted thirty-seven curates· they had no other claim but that which their piety and their poverty gave them to his consideration. But on the use of this branch of Lord Normanby's patronage it is unnecessary that I should say more, because the member for Tamworth, in moving the amendment, distinctly and unequivocally declared that Lord Normanby deserved great praise for the course which he had followed in reference to the church. What a contrast did the right honourable member for Pembroke afford to the right honourable member for Tamworth! The latter, who during his whole life has been opposed to the men now in power, frankly and generously bestowed upon Lord Normanby his warm panegyric in one essential department of his administration; while the member for Pembroke, who told us, last night, that he had for years been associated with the present ministers, and bound to them by the ties of personal regard, pronounced upon them one continuous invective, unrelieved by a single sentiment or expression in which a lingering kindness to his former colleagues were evinced.

But if the right honourable baronet withheld praise where it was due, his censure ought, at least, to have been fair. Was that censure fair, when, last night, he spoke of the appointments in the police? He said much of the resignation of Colonel Shaw Kennedy. But why did he not, at the same time, mention that Colonel Macgregor, who, if he has any politics, is a Conservative, was named to succeed him; and why did it not occur to him to state that, out of the four provincial inspectors, three were Protestants, selected for their personal qualifications, without the slightest regard to party objects? I will not waste time by going through the various instances in which Lord Normanby is accused of having misapplied his patronage. The truth is, that the men who call themselves "the Protestants of Ireland," considered an exclusive enjoyment of the patronage of the crown as a sort of ancient Protestant prerogative; and when they saw an office of any kind given away to an emancipated Catholic, they charged Lord Normanby with a violation of their vested rights. So little sympathy, however, will, I am sure, be felt in this house for the party to whom Lord Normanby did not give the opportunity of being ungrateful, that I pass over everything that has been said upon this subject, with the exception of what has been urged with regard to the appointment of that present Irish Solicitor-General, when he was promoted, two years ago, to the office of counsel to the Castle. It is objected, that he belonged to a society formed for the advancement of corporate reform. The society was not a secret one—it was not exclusive—it resorted to no signs of mysterious recognition—no declaration of conditional allegiance to the Sovereign and of unconditional allegiance to the Grand Master, was imposed upon the initiated; and I do not believe, whatever may have been its other demerits, that by that society, warrants to the army, signed with the name of "Ernest," were ever issued. The member for Tamworth read a long extract from a newspaper, called the *Sligo Champion*, describing Lord Normanby's progress in Sligo, and his entrance by a postern door, into the court-house. As he has read a Whig newspaper, I shall read an extract from a Tory one—not a provincial newspaper, but the gazette of Toryism in Ireland—the *Evening Mail*. The *Evening Mail*, of the 31st of December, 1835, contains the following article:—

"When the new administration conferred upon Lord Roden the high and distinguished office of Steward of his Majesty's Household, they offered a compliment to private worth, and paid a deference to public integrity; and it was fitting that from such a cabinet, and to such a man, the one should be tendered and the other yielded. But, independently of everything due to the noble individual—and no one is entitled to higher honour or greater consideration—there was a party in this country, at whose head Lord Roden had been placed, who had reason to expect, if not a right to claim, that the personage so honoured by them should not be forgotten or neglected by a ministry which has been placed in its present position through their agency and instrumentality. That party is composed of the Protestants of Ireland. Sir Robert Peel has done his duty. He has recognised the claim by a nomination of our acknowledged leader to the very highest situation in his Majesty's household."

Go, after this, and complain of Lord Headfort, and Mr. Pigot! Of the very remarkable appointment to which the paragraph which I have just read refers, I could say much, but that I have no desire to expatiate upon it in the spirit of acrimonious amplification. I excuse the member for Tamworth: indeed, I believe that he could not avoid the course which he adopted. He could not help promoting the men who had sustained him, although they were exceedingly obnoxious to the great majority of the Irish people; but if he comes into office to-morrow, will he not have the same painful necessities imposed upon him? He will not be able to escape from the difficulties resulting from the support with which he is encumbered; he must make appointments of a character similar to that to which I have just referred. Let him not, however, blame us if, in these appointments, we see evidence of the spirit in which his Irish government must be conducted. He may speak as he will of an impartial administration of justice, and an impartial system of government; but through what instrumentality is it to be carried on? No man has ever more strenuously asserted, that between men and measures no distinction should be made. The fact is, every man is a measure—every appointment is an indication of policy. Who are to be our men? We know who they were before, and we know into what excesses, in their exultation, the Orange party were betrayed? And an you be surprised, that we should look with dismay at the restoration o power of a party, of whose spirit we have had an experience so unhappy? Accordingly, through all Ireland there prevails an excitement almost unparalleled, not because we bear an antipathy to the member for Tamworth, but because we know that our country will be the victim of the exigencies to which he will be reduced.

The next charge to which I shall refer, relates to the administration f justice. Sir Michael O'Loghlen, when Irish Attorney-General, made vo important changes; he ordered that juries should not be packed. id he appointed local solicitors. Sir Michael O'Loghlen is an admirable judge; all parties concur in his praise; he is not likely to have been guilty of any very reprehensible proceeding as Attorney-General. Do English gentlemen think that juries ought to be packed, and that men should be set aside on account of their politics or their religion? An itinerant crown solicitor goes down twice a year to the assizes of a county, in which he does not reside; the panel is called; and is he, from mere whim, or in a freak of authoritative caprice, to order respectable men, who have come, pursuant to a summons, a distance, perhaps, of forty miles, to be put aside? Why, Sir, the member for Tamworth ought to be the last man in this house to advocate such a practice; for his Juries Bill in this country was introduced, among other purposes, to prevent the packing of juries in criminal cases in this country. Sir Michael O'Loghlen did no more than act in conformity with its spirit in Ireland. With respect to the appointment of local crown solicitors at sessions, no measure has been more useful; and if Mr. Howley, the assistant-barrister of Tipperary, has won from men of all sides the most unqualified encomium—if his talents, his temper, his discrimination, his patience, and every other judicial quality, have been the theme of panegyric; and if he has put down, as he has done, the class of crime falling within his jurisdiction in Tipperary; it is right that I should add, that he told me, and authorised me to state, that he derived the most essential assistance from the local solicitor, Mr. Cahill, a gentleman of great abilities and of the highest character, who was appointed under Lord Normanby's government. Sir, the reference to the state of Tipperary leads me to a painful and melancholy topic. I must admit, it is impossible, indeed, to deny that great crimes have been committed in many parts of Ireland. But are they to be attributed to Lord Normanby's government? Throughout the whole country, at every Tory gathering, at every festival—which, of rancour and bad feeling and anti-Christian hatred are indeed Conservative, but to all kindly sentiment and all charity are fatal indeed—in every Tory newspaper and periodical in the country, it has been studiously and perseveringly insisted, that to Lord Normanby's government every crime in Ireland is to be referred; and although it is notorious that, under Tory governments, when a policy, diametrically the reverse of Lord Normanby's, was adopted, crimes as appalling were perpetrated—witness Wild Goose Lodge—witness the murder of the Sheas—(to a cottage in which eighteen human beings were assembled, fire was applied in the dead of the night, and before the day had dawned, men, women, children—all had perished!)—still, the people of this country have been, to a certain extent, persuaded that to the government of Lord Normanby every atrocity is to be attributed, and to think that there exists a design to murder every Protestant proprietor—nay, that there has been established a sort of " secret tribunal," of which the peasants are the executioners, the priests the judges, and that the representative of his Sovereign presided in that " red land" over the judicature of blood. To the propagation of this belief, men have lent themselves, who should have known better; and the inquiry in the House of Lords, limited to Lord Normanby's government, and founded upon attacks directed against him, is calculated to strengthen an impression which is of all others the most unfounded, and which has party objects, beyond all doubt, in view. Sir, it is the duty of this house to counteract an impression so injurious, and which is likely to lead to consequences the most pernicious. It is not my intention to enter into any inquiry, founded on the numerous authorities which might be cited on the subject, of the causes of the long-continued perpetration of crime in Ireland. I shall content myself with one; and I refer to it solely because it exhibits a singular coincidence of opinion, at the distance of three hundred years, between two Englishmen, officially employed in Ireland. Repeated allusion has been made, in the course of this debate, to the letter addressed by Mr. Drummond to the magistrates of the county of Tipperary. I hold in my hand a volume of the State Papers of the year 1535. Brabazon, writing to Cromwell in that year, says, that the crimes of the lower orders arise exclusively from the cruelty and extortion of the proprietors of the soil. He adds, that a just government would soon raise Ireland to a level in civilisation with this country. From that remote time, it would be easy to present to the house a series of authorities reaching down to the present day, in which a singular concurrence in that sentiment would be found; but citations in this house are not calculated to excite much attention; and, indeed, upon the causes of our calamitous criminality, such citations are superfluous. Instead of its being wonderful that, in Ireland, disastrous outrage should have prevailed so long, it would be astonishing if it had been otherwise If any other country had been governed as you have governed us, would not the results have been the same as are presented to you by the island which has been so long subject to your dominion, and for whose guilt, as well as for whose misfortunes, it ought to occur to you that you should be held responsible? Take any country you please—take the country, for example, of the honourable gentleman opposite, the member for Kilmarnock, who is taking notes of what I am uttering, with a view, I suppose, to reply to me. I will furnish him with materials for a reply, by inquiring from him, and every other Scotch gentleman who does me the honour to attend to me, what would have been the fate of their country, if the same policy had been pursued in its regard as was adopted towards the unfortunate island whose condition, social, moral, and political, affords you so much ground for lamentation. If Scotland (which has made a progress so signal in prosperity of all kinds—and which, with so many claims to praise, possesses, in that Burns has nobly called her "virtuous populace," the chief title to admiration)—if Scotland, I say, had been portioned out by the sword of military rapine among merciless adventurers—if, after the work of robbery was done, a code for the debasement of the Presbyterian population had been enacted—if the Presbyterians of Scotland had not only been despoiled of property, but deprived of all power to acquire it—if they had been shut out of every honourable employment, and debarred from every creditable pursuit—if they had been spoliated of every political franchise, deprived of education, and reduced to a state of vassalage, compared to which feudal serfship would be one of dignity and of honour—and if all these legislative atrocities had been perpetrated under the pretence of maintaining an Episcopal establishment amongst a degraded Calvinistic people, have you a doubt—has any Scotchman a doubt—has the member for Kilmarnock (he is the only representative of a Scotch burgh who takes part against us)—has even the member for Kilmarnock a doubt that, even long after that system had been partially abolished, Scotland would present the same spectacle as Ireland now exhibits, and to Tory orators would afford as wide and desolate a field for their mournful expatiation. Inquire, forsooth, into the state of Ireland since 1835! Since 1835! No, Sir; but from the day on which, to rapacity, to cruelty, to degradation, to the oppression by which the wise are maddened, our wretched island was surrendered. From that day to this hour let your inquiry be extended; and, when that inquiry shall have terminated, you will learn that it is not at the door of Lord Normanby that Irish atrocities are to be laid, but that they should be deposited at your fathers' graves; and that their guilt, in a long inheritance of sin, should descend upon you. It is in the history—in every page of the history—of Ireland, that the causes of her excesses are to be sought; and, whoever shall read that history, with the spirit in which it ought to be perused, will cry " Shame !" upon the men who avail themselves of the crimes inevitably incidental to the condition of the people, in order to raise a clamour against the government, to rouse the religious passions of this country, and to turn the old "No Popery" cry to a political account. But that they should resort to it, I should not feel surprise. No! I, when I bear in mind how often the detestation which Englishmen are taught to bear to the religion of England, in some of its best and noblest times, has been converted to a depraved instrumentality—how often the wildest fanaticism has been the auxillary of the foulest faction—that, many and many a year ago, upon the murder of Godfrey, the Popish plot was got up—that, upon the attestation of villains the most worthless of mankind, the people of England were persuaded that the Irish Protestants were to be massacred, and that the Irish Papists were to invade this country, in order to establish Popery in England—that, under the influence of a sanguinary panic, your forefathers were hurried into excesses the most frightful—that the courts of justice were turned into arenas of human butchery, in which jurors and judges vied with each other in their appetite for blood—that wretched priests, to whom the murder of every Protestant was attributed, were dragged from the hiding holes where they cowered for safety, and savagely disembowelled—that the best and noblest of all the land perished with protestations of their innocence, to which posterity has done a tardy justice, quivering upon their dying lips—and that all these atrocities were perpetrated under the excitement created by that base cabal, of which Ashley Cooper, who had been Lord Chancellor (an Atheist, affecting to be a bigot), played so prominent a part—when I bear in mind, that again at a period less remote, when the first repeal of the worst part of the penal code was proposed, the same base cry was raised, and an association called the "Protestant" was formed, which Edmund Burke represents to have been composed of as unprincipled impostors as ever in the degraded name of religion trafficked on the credulity of mankind; when I remember, that, at a period more proximate, in the memory of most of us, in 1807, when the Whigs proposed that your Catholic fellow-countrymen should be eligible to places of honour in the naval and military professions, again for factious purposes, that same cry was raised—that when there was no Lord Normanby—when there was in Ireland no political agitation—when of O'Connell nothing had been heard—yet, upon Ireland, and upon the religion of her people, and the ministers of that religion, the same odious calumnies were cast, and we were held up, as a nation of idolaters, of blasphemers, and of perjurers, to the execration of the English people—and that all this was done by the very party who, in eight years afterwards, themselves proposed and carried the very measure, which has been made the instrument of all this abominable excitement; how, when I remember all this, can I feel surprise that for the same bad purposes, men should be found capable of resorting to the same base expedients; and that, to the same execrable passions, they should address the same infernal invocation? And what was the state of England, when, to recover possession of office, the Tories of 1807 raised their "No Popery" cry? You stood upon the verge of a tremendous peril: the great conqueror was in his full career of victory; and, had he landed an army on the Irish shore, little short of miracle could have saved us. But now, we are at profound peace; now, nothing is to be apprehended; now, the Orangemen of Ireland can trample on us with impunity, and on the neck of the Irish people the foot of Rodenism may with impunity be planted. Ha! be not too sure of that! And, that you may not be too sure of it, let us, for a moment, consider who are the Irish people? The noble lord the member for Stroud, on the first night of this debate, read a passage from Edmund Burke, in which it is stated, that the Irish Catholics had been reduced to a mere populace, without property, education, or power. And, if we were still what we once were, then, indeed, to our old Orange masters we might again with impunity be given up. But a prodigious change has befallen in our condition—a change greater, perhaps, than any of which in the annals of any people any example can be found. Who, then, are the Irish people? They are those mighty masses, who, gradually recovering and emerging from the effects of conquest, of rapine, and of oppression, brought to bear against the tyranny, once deemed as irresistible as it was remorseless, the resources, which nothing but a cause just beyond all others in the sight of Heaven, and the deepest consciousness of the heart of man, could supply; and after a struggle, of which the fame should be as imperishable as the results are everlasting, by dint of indefatigable energy, of indissoluble union, and of undaunted and indomitable determination, won from their antagonists their irrevocable freedom; who, following up that noble event in a spirit not unworthy of it, became the auxiliaries of their British fellow-citizens, in another great achievement—and now, demanding equality or its only alternative, and putting in for that equality a justly operative requisition, stand before you in one vast array, in which, with increasing numbers, increasing wealth, increasing intelligence, and increasing and consolidated power, are associated and offer to your most solemn thoughts, a series of reflections, which should teach you to beware of collision with the Irish people. . You talk to us of collision with the Lords ; of collision with millions of your fellow-citizens beware ; beware of collision with those millions, to whom a power has been imparted, which in your hearts you know you can never recal. If the member for Tamworth, on the first night of this debate, cautioned us with any truth to beware of " entrance in a quarrel," with how much more justice should he himself be warned to avoid a contention with those of whose prowess he has already had an experience so instructive! Such a contention would not be wise. What do I say, wise? it would not be safe, and its consequences might be disastrous beyond what it may be prudential to point out. It is not to Ireland alone that those consequences would be confined ; they would extend far beyond her ; and every British interest would be affected by them. " We are at war," exclaims the Duke of Wellington, " in America and in Asia." If we are at war in America, this is not the time to hand Ireland over to the rule of that party, who, between Catholics and Protestants, between Irishmen and Englishmen would draw the " boundary line." We are indeed at war in Asia, and disclosures have recently been made respecting the views and feelings of Russia in regard to this country, which must convince us that the peace of Europe is more than insecure. With respect to France, is it not manifest that, if the Tories had been in office two months ago, and had acted on the principles which they profess in opposition, we should have been hurried into a war with France by the blockade of Mexico ? Algiers remains as a ground of difference ; and, independently of these considerations, France itself is in a state so volcanic—a concussion, and an eruption are so probable—that upon any permanent alliance with that country it would be rashness to rely.

This, then, is not the time—this is not the befitting time—in the heart of the British empire, amidst two-thirds of the population of these islands—in place of that sentiment of impassioned allegiance which Lord Normanby succeeded in creating, to substitute a feeling of deep, resentful, and perilous discontent ; to convert Ireland into a source of your weakness, from a bulwark of your strength; to make her an item in the calculations of your antagonists, and to the external risks by which we are encompassed, to superadd this fearful domestic hazard. These are reflections which will not be lightly dismissed by you, if to the modern name, by which your party desires to be designated, you have any claim ; if, to the real interests of this country, to the integrity of this vast dominion, and to the safety of Ireland, a principle truly Conservative is to be applied ; but if it shall be otherwise—if, blinded by party—if, of everything, except the gratification of factious passions, and of antipathies national and religious, you shall be regardless, and you shall give no heed to the dangers consequent upon their indulgence—it only remains for me to pray (and in the deepest sincerity of my heart that prayer is offered up) that you may not live to lament, that to the admonitory intimations given you, by the events which are passing around you, you were insensible, when your regrets will be embittered by the consciousness, that repentance will have become useless, and remorse will be without avail.

LORD STANLEY'S IRISH REGISTRATION BILL.

SPEECH IN THE HOUSE OF COMMONS, JUNE 10, 1840.

THE argument of the noble lord is at variance with the statement with which he commenced his speech. He began by stating, that the first clause in his bill would not operate as a disfranchisement of voters already registered, but he afterwards proceeded to advocate the principle of disfranchisement, from the consciousness that the first clause was founded upon it. He insisted, that a multitude of claimants had found their way by illegitimate means upon the registry, and that by a process of re-investigation, introduced into this bill, those claimants ought to be deprived of the privilege which the registry had conferred. This is disfranchisement to all intents and purposes. The clause proposed by my noble friend, the Secretary for Ireland, is, I admit, at utter variance with the clause so strenuously supported by the noble lord, and which, indeed, constitutes the essence of his bill. The noble lord disfranchises upon grounds antecedent to the registry, while the Secretary for Ireland confines the revision to matter which has arisen subsequent to the registry. For the imperfections incidental to the Irish system of registration—and to what system of registration are not imperfections incidental?—the amendment proposed by the Secretary for Ireland affords a commensurate remedy. Vested rights—rights obtained through the means provided by the law for their acquisition, and which are therefore vested, are secured by the amendment, while, at the same time, care is taken, that where those rights in point of fact have ceased to exist, the loss of the qualification shall operate as a defeasance, and of the mere form of registry no fraudulent use shall be made. The names of those who have died or become insolvent, or who have parted with their interest, are to be struck off the registry, and as outstanding certificates may be employed as the means of personation, the whole system of certificates is to be abolished. The noble lord calls, by way of retort, the abolition of the certificates a disfranchisement. Certificates are but the evidence of the title to vote. The title itself is not affected by the change of the evidence, and the Solicitor-General's proposition does no more than substitute a different proof less liable to exception, by which, however, the right to be proved is not in the slightest degree affected. This misrepresentation upon the part of the noble lord is very inconsistent with those professions of fairness in which the noble lord so frequently and so strenuously indulges, from a consciousness, I fear, that those professions are not wholly uncalled for upon the part of the noble lord. The clearance of the registry of all those who have forfeited their title since the registry by means of an annual revision, ought to satisfy those who do not look for anything beyond the correction of the abuses which we ought to be solicitous to remove. But it is urged by the noble lord, that crowds who never possessed the qualification have found admission to the registry. If this were true, if their allegations were well founded who to the abuses of the Irish registry are so sensitively alive, but who to the fabrication of fictitious votes, who to the profligacy, the corruption, the bribery, the debauch, the perjury, and its more infamous subornation which prevail at your own elections, are philosophically insensible, and give to Ireland the exclusive advantage of their virtuous, but not wholly disinterested indignation—if, I say, their allegations were well founded, and practices so corrupt had been employed for the purpose of giving an undue preponderance to the popular party, it is obvious that the constituency would be enormous. The country would swarm with spurious voters, and herds of wretched serfs would be driven at every election to the hustings under the terror of what the noble lord, with his usual happiness of conciliatory phrase, was pleased to designate as "excommunication." But what is the state of the constituency of Ireland, and how do the statistical returns laid upon the table of this house sustain the statements of the noble lord, who, not contented with revision, insists upon re-investigation, insists upon an appeal to the judge of assize, and all those complicated impediments to the extension of the elective franchise, which, in the spirit of consistent "obstruction," the noble lord, with an ingenuity so perverse, has so elaborately devised? The noble lord is a proprietor in the county of Tipperary. He corresponds with the agents of Conservative Clubs in that county, and he has been intrusted with several petitions, not indeed very numerously signed, from the county which I have the honour to represent, in which it was stated, that "thousands" had been improperly admitted upon the registry. What then is the constituency of the county of Tipperary? That county is of great extent, remarkable for its fertility; it is studded with large and thriving towns, and its population exceeds 400,000. You will say, you will of course conjecture, that under such circumstances the constituency of the county Tipperary must amount to 10,000. No. Well, to 8000? No. To 6000? No. To 5000? Not 5000. To 4000? Not to 4000. Well, then, to 3000? With the aid of sacredotal anathemas, and secular imprecation, we must needs have, at all events, raised our practical voting constituency. At the last general election, the contest lasted for five days in the county of Tipperary. The county was polled out, and the numbers who voted did not amount to 2400. And here let me advert to a letter stated by the noble lord to have been written to him by the agent of the Tipperary Conservative Association, containing a narrative respecting two tenants of Mr. Faucett. The noble lord does not know Mr. Kernan, his correspondent—never saw him in his life—never heard of him before, and yet he produces a letter written by that gentleman, as a ground for disfranchising the constituency of Ireland. This is indeed a strong proceeding. He would sentence Ireland to a deprivation of her rights on the evidence of a mere letter which would not be received upon the trial of the meanest case in the meanest court of judicature in the kingdom. I have received a letter from a very respectable gentleman, Mr. Michael Meagher, distinctly contradicting the statements of Mr. Kernan. Mr. Meagher says:—

"About a fortnight back my attention was called to a report of a speech purporting to have been delivered by Lord Stanley, in his place in the House of Commons, on the 18th ult., relative to his bill on the Irish elective franchise. In a portion of that speech he is reported to have stated that he received a letter from a Mr. Kernan, registry agent for the Conservatives of North Tipperary, wherein, amongst other things, it was alleged that ' a tenant of Mr. Faucett, over eighty years of age, held a farm, out of which he registered in 1832—that in 1834 he gave up the farm to Mr. Faucett, from his inability to hold the same —that Mr. Faucett gave him an acre of land free to live on—that at the election of 1837, this old man of eighty years of age was dragged to the hustings at Clonmel, and there made to vote for Sheil and Cave, notwithstanding his being warned by his landlord not to do so, as he knew his title was extinct.' Further, he (Lord Stanley) is reported to have stated, from the same information, that ' another tenant of Mr. Faucett, named Roger Meara, registered in 1832—was murdered in 1837—was placed on the list of applicants for registry in January, 1840, and that the agent produced his (Meara's) former certificate of 1832—swore that he received it from said Meara for the purpose of having him re-registered, and actually got him registered on that occasion before Mr. Howley, assistant barrister.' The first statement is false, inasmuch as Mr. Faucett has but four freeholders on his entire estate, and those held a lease before he (Mr. Faucett) purchased the property, which lease is still in existence; the same freeholders still hold the same farm and franchise —none of them are either eighty, seventy, sixty, or fifty years of age— no tenant has surrendered his farm to Mr. Faucett; for, to do that gentleman justice, he does not render any tenant unable to pay rent. As I was one of the persons who conducted the freeholders from this county to Clonmel at the aforesaid election, I solemnly declare that there was no tenant of Mr. Faucett's of that age, who went to the hustings; the only tenants of his that went were the four herein mentioned, and they had, and still have, a *bona fide* interest in their farms to entitle them to the franchise. With regard to Roger Meara, it is true he registered in 1832; it is true he was murdered in 1837; it is also equally true that his name was on the list of applicants for registry in January, 1840, for this reason—the person who is registry agent for the liberals in North Tipperary, being unable to ascertain all the persons who were either dead or disentitled to re-register, served notice for all persons on the former registry list in this division; thereby giving an opportunity to every person legally entitled to come forward and re-register. Roger Meara's name, through that means, appeared on the list of applicants in January, 1840; but as to the agent producing his (Meara's) certificate, that I distinctly deny. I was the only person who held the certificates of the persons from the division where Meara did live. It is untrue that Meara was either registered in 1840, as stated by him, or ttempted to be registered either by me or any other person. I will put the matter at rest by challenging Mr. Kernan to show Roger Meara's name on the new list of registered persons for 1840, or any list but that of 1832."

Here, then, is a direct contradiction of the assertions—the unsupported assertions—of a man whom the noble lord never saw in all his life, of whom he knows nothing but that he is the agent to a Conservative association in the county of Tipperary. It requires some intrepidity to rest such a bill upon testimony of this kind. But since great importance is attached to the letters of Conservative functionaries, what will the noble lord say to the circular issued by the agent to the Conservative club, in the county of Cork, which has been read, and of which the authenticity has not been disputed in this house? That letter enjoins the importance of stripping the tenantry of lay landlords of the elective franchise. But since I am speaking of the county of Cork, what, let me ask, is the constituency of that great county? The population exceeds 700,000; the constituency does not amount to 4000. The same disproportion between the constituency and the representation prevails in every other district in Ireland. Let statistics be compared with the statements of the noble lord; let statistics, in which there is no faction, no baffled ambition, no spirit of rancorous conversion, be compared with the evidence with which the noble lord endeavours to sustain his case. If his assertions be well founded—if the noble lord do not labour under the most egregious misconceptions—the registry of Ireland would present an enormous constituency; but the direct reverse is the fact. The constituency is miserably small; but small as it is, it has been too large for your purposes, small as it is, your projects have been defeated, your aspirations have been thwarted, and the country has been saved by it from your dominion. It must be reduced to dimensions more in conformity with your views, and accordingly. by the very first clause in your bill, one-half of the registered constituency is to be disfranchised by the operation of that clause, thus :—A farmer, call him for the sake of distinctness, John Morrisy, lives forty miles from Cork: on the 1st of October, 1836, John Morissy served notice to register; he attended at the sessions on the 20th; his lease was produced, he underwent a strict scrutiny, and after a full investigation was duly registered his right is vested, and he voted at the last general election in the exercise of that right. The bill of the noble lord with the clause in debate passes. John Morissy's landlord objects to his retention on the registry. He is compelled to go through the same vexatious process as before, and is registered again. His landlord appeals against the registry; for three months no decision can be had, and, in the interval, to the relation of landlord and tenant, that of appellant and respondent is superadded. At length the judges of assize arrive, and John Morissy leaves his fields, his plough, his harrow, and sets off for Cork. He reaches the court-house, after a journey of forty miles, and has the advantage of witnessing the trials of some ejectments for non-payment of rent, from which valuable intimations are derived by him. At length his appeal is called on, counsel are employed against him by Mr. Nettles the agent to the Conservative Club, and the case is powerfully stated by some learned sergeant with a minacious aspect, and ultra-forensic faculties of intimidation. His own landlord is produced as a witness against him, and after a fierce political struggle, the learned judge strikes him off the registry; and availing himself of the power with which he is specially invested by the noble lord, mulcts him in costs, and sends him home without a shilling in his pocket as an example to all refractory tenants, and an exemplification of the advantages which the noble lord, our very peculiar benefactor, is determined to inflict upon the Irish people. It is fortunate, I think, tnat in the first clause of this bill so much of its worst matter is condensed, for an opportunity is given at the outset to those who voted for going into a committee to repair any mistake into which, under a conscientious, but recent sense of duty, they may have been unwittingly betrayed. In the assault committed upon the existing registry they will hardly concur. It was a strong measure to disfranchise the forty-shilling freeholders—to the last it was resisted by Lord Grey; not even for the sake of emancipation would he sacrifice the rights of those by whom the most imperative argument for emancipation had been supplied. But for what purpose is this new infringement upon principle to be perpetrated? For a purpose in reference to which he must indeed be a sceptic, by whom the slightest doubt is entertained. Protestations, indeed, in sufficient abundance are made by the promoters of this measure; that they look to nothing more than the suppression of the abuses at which their moral sense revolts. At abuses their moral sense does not always so readily take alarm; witness the Irish corporations, for whose peculations and whose frauds, by so many shifts and expedients, a discreditable impunity has been so long procured. But it is sufficient to look across that table to estimate the value of the clause which the noble lord has placed in the outset of his bill. If the motives by which this project is dictated were ostensibly the most pure and the most disinterested, by the general policy of the noble lord the specific proposition should still be fairly tried. To the gift, however specious, an apprehension of the donor should be extended; but in this instance, the object of the noble lord is not only undisguised, but a veil of the flimsiest texture is scarce cast upon it. Who, that looks back to the incidents fresh in the recollection of every one of us, can entertain the least question relative to the purposes of this measure? In 1835, it was avowed that the Tory party looked to the divisions that prevailed between the Whigs and the Irish members as a means of carrying on what was termed by a great misnomer a Conservative government. Had those divisions still subsisted, I do not think that so lynx-eyed a vigilance would have been displayed in detecting the abuses of the Irish registry. In 1837, on the accession of her Majesty to the throne, a general election took place, and eight additional members were returned by the Irish popular party. It became indispensable for the purposes of Toryism that the phalanx by which the ministers were supported should be broken up. There existed at that time a tribunal for the trial of election petitions, whose proceedings were of the most censurable character. It did great credit to the member for Tamworth that he contributed to the abolition of that tribunal in 1839; but of that which he contributed to abolish in 1839, the Tory party availed themselves in 1837. The Spottiswood conspiracy was formed, and large sums were levied, in order, through the instrumentality of that profligate tribunal, that the representatives of the people of Ireland should be expelled from the House of Commons. That proceeding, bad as it was, found its most strenuous advocates among the champions of this measure. The men who expatiated so pathetically upon the abuses of the Irish registry, turned that scandalous system of adjudication to account. Who that looks back to that transaction can doubt that the blow which was aimed at the representation, is now directed against the constituency? During the last recess the labours of the Conservative press were devoted to the impeachment of the £10 constituency. On the 19th of December last it was officially announced in the great Conservative journal that this measure would be brought forward. The session commences—the honourable baronet, the member for Devonshire, moves his celebrated resolution. In the debate that ensued, the most offensive distinctions were taken between the English and the Irish members—the spirit, the animus of this project was made manifest. That the men by whom, or on whose behalf such sentiments were uttered, should support a measure of disfranchisement like this, is natural and consistent; but it is most unnatural and most inconsistent that any man calling himself a Reformer should co-operate in such an enterprise, and should become the auxiliary of a man who, upon every Irish question, is utterly destitute of the slightest claim upon the confidence of parliament, who was told by Lord Althorp to his face, in the face of the house and of the country, that his administration of Ireland had been a lamentable failure—who has since that time, by the extent of his political transitions, acquired a new title to the disrelish of one country, and to the distrust of both—who deals for ever in extremes —was ready to swamp the Lords when he was a Whig, and is ready to swamp the people when he has turned a Tory—lauded the Irish members to the skies in 1832, when it suited his purpose, and would now slap the door of the House of Commons in their faces; and of all the traits in the political character of the noble lord, of all the incidents to his political conduct the most to be lamented—who, after having denounced " an expiring faction," and held them up to public scorn, now leagues himself with that bad Irish party which he represented as miserable, and which is not the less deserving of the designation which he thought it not unmeet to employ in their regard, because he has combined with them for the achievement of their pernicious projects, and has so far forgotten the principles which ought to have descended to him as an inheritance, as to prostitute his talents for the atttainment of purposes to which every beating of his heart must at this moment tell him that they ought never to have been applied; and is this the man—is it to such a man that the delicate and difficult, and almost perilous task of legislating for Ireland ought to be confided—is this the man to whom we are to surrender the franchise of the country, upon which he inflicted calamities so fearful, and which was driven almost to insurrection by his misrule? See what in the course of a few weeks he has accomplished. The country was at rest—political excitement had subsided—that wise policy to which last year this house bore an attestation so signal, had produced the most salutary fruits. No public meetings were held, the tithe question had been adjusted, and the very name of a measure, to Englishmen of all others the most obnoxious, was scarcely uttered. A general calm prevailed. Suddenly the noble lord bursts like a hurricane upon us. The elements of confusion are at once let loose, and the country is swept back into that tempestuous agitation from which we deemed ourselves secure. Stop, while there is yet time—stop the noble lord in his career of mischief, or the consequences may be irretrievable. You may gain a temporary triumph; you may rob us of the fruits of that emancipation which the itinerant incendiaries invite you openly and directly to rescind; but your victories will be dearly purchased. Of Ireland—of organized, confederated, discontented Ireland, beware; beware of that country which you ought to have been instructed by experience, fearful, if not humiliating, not to hold in disregard. Twelve months have scarcely passed since the member for Tamworth declared that Ireland presented to him his greatest difficulty. Will that difficulty be diminished by the sinister co-operation of his noble and exceedingly formidable friend? Persevere in that policy by which this measure had been prompted, and Ireland will soon be in a condition more fearful than that which preceded emancipation. You will enter again into an encounter with that gigantic agitation by which you were before discomfited, and by which (for its power is treble) you will be again overthrown; for all the consequences that will ensue from the excitement which you will have wantonly engendered, you will be responsible : you will be responsible for the calamities which will gush in, in abundance so disastrous, from the sources of bitterness which you will have unsealed. If Ireland shall be arrested in the march of improvement in which she has been under a Whig government rapidly advancing—if Ireland shall be thrown back fifty years—if the value of property shall be impaired—it the security of property shall be shaken—if political animosities shall be embittered—if religious detestations shall become more rabid and more envenomed—if the mind of Ireland shall become one heated mass, ready to catch fire at a single spark ; for all this you will be responsible. And do not think that it is to Ireland that the evil effects of your impolicy will be confined. If in this country the fell spirit of democracy which lately appeared amongst you shall be resuscitated, I do not think that to your Irish garrison (for what will your army be but a garrison ?) you can with confidence look for succour. There is reason too, to apprehend that the state of Ireland may affect you in your foreign relations—that England will not maintain the post and dignity that become her—that foreign cabinets may take advantage of our intestine dissensions to exact from us humiliating conditions—and that thus, to the maintenance of Protestant ascendancy in a distracted province, you will sacrifice the ascendancy of England through the world. It is of that ascendancy, that better, nobler, and more exalted ascendancy, that I am the advocate; and it is because I am so, because I am as devoted to the maintenance of her glory, the honour, and the power of this great country, as if I were born among yourselves, and from my birth had breathed no other air than you have—it is for this that I am solicitous that you should not relinquish one of the noblest means of its sustainment, and that I warn you not to hazard the affections, the warm, devoted, enthusiastic affections of millions of high-minded and high-hearted men ; but to preserve;

in a spirit of wise conservation, the great moral bulwark which you find in those affections—which does not form an item in your estimates, which is so cheap that it costs nothing but justice, and which, as long as you shall retain, so long, against every evil that may befal you, your empire will be impregnably secure.

THE SUGAR DUTIES.

SPEECH IN THE HOUSE OF COMMONS, MAY 18, 1841.

THE department with which I have the honour to be connected (the Board of Trade) will afford me a justification for interfering in this debate; it has been protracted beyond the ordinary period of the duration of our debates, but not to a period incommensurate with the importance—the incalculable importance, of a subject upon which, in the exercise of their appellate jurisdiction, the people of England must ultimately decide. I shall not trespass upon the indulgence of those who surround me, or upon the forbearance of those to whom I am opposed, at any inappropriate length. I shall confine myself to the resolution of the noble lord, and do my best to avoid the example of those who have wandered far away from it, and who have indulged in dissertations not more mysterious to their auditors than to themselves. I shall, Sir, in the first instance, address myself to that branch of the question in reference to which, the people of England, the virtuous and humane people of England, feel a deep and a most honourable concern. If, Sir, to the progress of the slave-trade, by an exorbitant differential duty between colonial and foreign sugar, any effectual impediment were interposed—if, notwithstanding that exorbitant differential duty, the slave-trade were not successful to an extent which has been stated, with too much justice, in the course of this debate, to cast a stain upon Christian Europe—if to slave-grown sugar every port upon the Continent were not thrown widely and indiscriminately open—if with the produce of slave-labour in many forms, coffee, cotton, tobacco, our own markets were not glutted—if we were not ourselves the importers, the refiners, and the re-exporters of slave-grown sugar to the Continent, ay, and to our own colonial possessions, to an enormous annual amount, I am free to confess that with regard to the propriety of making a reduction of a differential duty, thus supposed for a moment, for the purposes of humanity as well as of monopoly, to be effectual, I should be disposed to entertain a doubt But, Sir, when I consider that in checking the progress of the slave-trade, the safeguard of monopoly is utterly without avail—when I consider that the differential duty, which keeps the price of sugar up, does not keep the price of human beings down—when I consider that without casting upon a barbarous traffic any, the slightest impediment, the differential duty has the effect of impairing the public revenue, and, by enhancing the cost of one of the necessaries of life, of imposing upon the humbler classes of the community, a grievous charge—when I consider that the differential duty confers no substantial benefit upon any class of the community, excepting upon those benevolent monopolists whose sensibilities are not unprompted by their profits, and who, to the emotions of a lucrative philanthropy, find it as easy, as it is convenient, whenever a purpose, personal or political is to be promoted, to give way —I am at a loss, I own, to discover any just motive for giving sustainment to a monopoly fraught with so much multifarious evil, or for supporting the resolution of the noble lord. That resolution is conceived in a spirit of such obvious partisanship that I cannot withhold the expression of my surprise that my right honourable and most distinguished friend, the member for the Tower Hamlets, should have considered it to be consistent with his unaffected abhorrence of slavery (for his abhorrence of slavery is unaffected) to give it his support. It does not require his sagacity, forensic, judicial, and senatorial, to perceive that this resolution is little else than a sort of previous question in disguise; it contains no pledge against the future introduction of slave-grown sugar—it is transitory and ephemeral; it provides a ready retreat from the high ground which the new, I should rather say, the novel associates of my right honourable friend in the cause of freedom, have so vauntingly taken up, and while it states, that the House of Commons is not prepared (no—not yet prepared) to recognise the introduction of slave-grown sugar, it intimates that under happier auspices, through that preparatory process, the House of Commons may be prevailed upon to pass. How little does this resolution, dexterous, adroit, and almost crafty, accord with the frank, the ingenuous, and, in the cause of virtue, the ardent and impassioned character of my right honourable friend. If any doubt could be entertained regarding the object and the effect of such a resolution, it would be removed by the speech of the noble lord, the member for North Lancashire, who declared again and again, that for the present a great experiment ought not to be disturbed. Surely this ought to convince my right honourable friend, who will forgive me, I feel convinced, if I am bold enough to tell him that in supporting a resolution, couched in such phraseology as this is, he is almost as inconsistent as those incongruous sentimentalists by whom, provided it be not presented in a saccharine form, the produce of slave-labour is unscrupulously consumed. But from personal and innocuous inconsistencies, let me pass to the anomalies, which are incidental to our fiscal system. Last year we imported upwards of twenty-eight million pounds of slave coffee, of which upwards of fourteen millions were slave-grown. The noble lord the member for Lancashire, struggling with this overwhelming fact, suggested that to the supply of the coffee market our colonies were not adequate. The noble lord seems to think that the encou:

ragement of the slave-trade is matter of mercantile expediency, and that on the price-current our philanthropy ought to depend, and our markets should be opened or shut to slave-grown produce as they rose or fell It is quite true that when the duty upon coffee was high—was 1s. 7d. per pound—the consumption was so inconsiderable that the colonies supplied us with all the coffee which we required; but when the duty was lowered, the consumption increased to an extent which, without exaggeration, may be designated as enormous. It is worth while to look with some minuteness into the effect which the diminution of duty produced upon the importation of coffee. The following table is remarkable

COFFEE—TAXATION AND CONSUMPTION.

Years.	Quantity retained for home consumption.	Rate of duty per lb.		Net revenue.
	lbs.	s.	d.	£
1807	1,170,164	1	7⅝	161,245
1812	8,118,734	0	7	255,184
1824	7,993,040	1	0	407,544
1831	21,842,264	0	6	559,431
1840	28,723,735	0	6	922,862

From this table it is manifest, that by the reduction of duty an enormous augmentation in the importation of coffee was produced. In 1807, when the duty was 1s. 7d. no more than 1,170,164 pounds of coffee were imported, the revenue was no more than £161,245; and when the duty was reduced, the importation of coffee rose to the vast amount of 28,723,735 pounds of coffee, and the revenue produced was £922,862. I repeat, that of this vast mass of coffee, more than 14 million pounds were slave-grown. But this anomaly, great as it is, is little when compared with the monstrous incongruity of receiving slave-grown sugar in bond, of refining and exporting it, and at the same time, of excluding it from the home market, where, upon its consumption, a duty might be raised. In 1840 we imported upwards of eight hundred thousand hundred-weight of slave-grown sugar—it was refined and exported. What revenue was raised upon it? Not a single shilling, while all the expenses incidental to the bonding system were incurred in its regard. By no one could such a system be sustained, except by the noble lord the member for North Lancashire, by whom an elaborate vindication of these anomalies was fearlessly undertaken. I shall not attempt to follow the noble lord through the various and exceedingly irrelevant topics with which his speech was made up, but I think it right to disabuse the country of any erroneous impressions which, in reference to the opinions of Mr. Huskisson, the noble lord laboured to produce. The noble lord told us that he was a disciple of Mr. Huskisson, and took upon himself to set his opinions forth. Never was there a more egregious misrepresentation. After hearing the noble lord, I turned to a more authorised source of information—the speeches of Mr. Huskisson—and I found that, in the account given of the sentiments of that illustrious man, his disciple was most singularly mistaken. In the year 1830, in the month of March, Mr. Huskisson made two speeches; one was delivered by him on the 16th of March, in a debate on the state of the country; the other on the 25th of March, upon a motion of Mr. Poulett Thompson. On the 16th of March, Mr. Huskisson said:—

" Our Corn-laws, however expedient to prevent other evils in the present state of the country, are in themselves a burden and a restraint upon its manufacturing and commercial industry. Whilst the products of that industry must descend to a level of the general market of the world, the producers, so far as food is concerned, are debarred from that level."

But, Sir, in a subsequent but proximate debate, Mr. Huskisson expressed himself in a manner still more unequivocal. I shall read his exact words. They are to be found in page 555 of the third volume of his speeches. Those words are these:—

" It was (he said) his unalterable conviction that we could not uphold the Corn-laws now in existence, together with the present system of taxation, and at the same time, increase the national prosperity and preserve public contentment. That those laws might be repealed without affecting the landed interest, whilst, at the same time, the distress of the people might be relieved, he never had any doubt whatever. A general feeling prevailed, that some change must be effected, and that speedily. Nor were there any individuals more thoroughly persuaded of it than one who moved in the humbler walks of life."*

Such was the language of Mr. Huskisson in 1830, language expressive of opinions very different from those which the noble lord, who told us that he was his disciple (who could have conjectured it?) had ascribed him. In 1830 Mr. Huskisson had been liberated from the trammels of the Tory party; he had abandoned that party to which the noble lord is united now, and had thrown off the shackles which the noble lord has now put on. Sir, I pass from the noble lord to the monopoly which he sustains. I support what is commonly called, the West-India interest. There are West-Indians, I rejoice to say, who, of the mode of promoting the prosperity of our colonies, entertain a just appreciation. On the 11th of February last, a meeting was held in Trinidad of the chief proprietors and agriculturists. Mr. Burnley was in the chair. He spoke as follows (I quote from a Trinidad paper):—

' I shall hail with pleasure the day when every monopoly and restriction can, advantageously for the rest of the empire, be done away with. Thank God! we are now emancipated as well as our labourers; and we can walk abroad, bold and erect, and claim the benefit of the freest principles; and if we are honestly and fairly allowed to trade with all the world without restriction, we fear no competition from any quarter the colonial market of the mother-country; and when that is effected,

* See also Hansard, vol. 23 New Series, pp. 602, 816.

the agriculture of Trinidad will successfully compete with that of every other country depending upon slave-labour."

These are wise and liberal opinions, but in these opinions, it is but just to say, that West-Indians, in this country at least, do not generally coincide. For my own part, I should be much disposed to make allowance for the feelings of the West-Indian proprietors, if they did not affect sentiment, if they did not talk of slavery and of its horrors (what right have they to talk of it?) and if they contented themselves with stating the circumstances which constitute the alleged hardship of their case. Their case is this—their slaves were emancipated in 1833, and for the loss which they sustained, they consider themselves to be entitled, in the shape of exclusive privileges, to compensation. This is a plain statement, and the answer is also plain—England paid a ransom, which almost dazzles the imagination, and she is entitled to a receipt in full. No, answers the member for Newark, whose motion is insatiable, and who cries out, like the horse-leech's daughter, "More, more." The member for Newark insists that the West-India planters were entitled not only to twenty millions, but to countless millions beyond that sum. He acknowledged, that since 1833, in addition to the twenty millions, the West-Indians had received, at least, ten millions, in the form of a protective duty. This admission is most important. But the member for Newark is mistaken in supposing the sum paid to the West-Indies, in the form of protection, to be so small as ten millions, in addition to the twenty which was paid them. I inquired of my friend Mr. M'Gregor, the Secretary of the Board of Trade, how far the member for Newark was correct, and he, who is distinguished for accuracy as well as for surpassing talent, told me that the West-Indies had received upwards of nineteen millions, in addition to the twenty millions already paid them. He gave me the following table:—

Years.	Quantity consumed.	Difference of price.	Amount of tax or premium to West-India Interest.
		£ s. d.	£
1834	4,154,411	0 6 2	1,280,943
1835	4,421,145	0 6 0	1,326,343
1836	3,922,901	0 13 0	2,549,885
1837	4,349,053	0 13 4	2,679,934
1838	4,418,334	0 12 5	2,743,048
1839	4,171,938	0 17 1	3,471,151
1840	3,764,710	1 7 7	5,192,161
Total tax since abolition		. . . .	19,243,465

The house hates vulgarities of all kinds, and of all vulgar things, hates vulgar arithmetic the most; but on this occasion some indulgence for figures ought to be manifested, and the table which I have produced ought to be examined, when to the West-India planters we are invoked to extend our commiseration. But mark, these West-Indians are not contented with that they have already got; they insist upon a permanent tax upon the English people. I contend, Sir, that a perpetuation of monopoly was no part of the contract made with the West-India planters. The noble lord the member for Lancashire, who told us, that as he organ of the Whig government (the organ of the Whig government!!) he introduced the Emancipation Act, has not suggested that the continuance of monopoly was any part of the contract. If it were, upon what principle could the equalisation of the duties on East and West-Indian sugar and rum have been sustained? When that equalisation was proposed, the unfortunate West-Indians made out precisely the same case as they make out at present. They told us that the West-Indies were in a state of transition, that a great experiment ought not to be disturbed, that East-India sugar was the produce of slave-labour, that it was produced from dates at a very inferior cost. With what scorn were these expostulations received by the representatives of the East-Indian interest in the House of Commons! How indignant they were at the remotest, and the most delicate reference to Hill Coolies and to slaves; and with what impassioned force my honourable friend, the member for Beverley, denounced the effrontery of the men, who, with twenty millions in their coffers, to a continuance of their monopoly had the audacity to put in a claim; but now—now, Sir, that these East-Indians have got a share in the privileges against which they inveighed so vehemently: now that they are embraced in the monopoly which they represented as so detestable, they who have made no sacrifice, whom no loss of any kind has been sustained, whose slaves have not been emancipated; they, forsooth, have the unparalleled intrepidity to turn round, and, uniting themselves with those very West-Indians of whom they were before the fierce antagonists, talk to us of the expediency of sustaining the colonial interests, while of the interests of the people of England they are utterly forgetful, and think nothing of the sacrifice which an exorbitant protection, even upon their own admission, of necessity involves. The resolution adverts to sacrifices: yes, much has indeed been sacrificed, but you are not contented; you require that an annual tribute shall be offered to monopoly, and to ensure its punctual payment, you insist that, instead of recruiting the revenue by a just apportionment of existing duties, new burdens shall be imposed upon the people. This proceeding will, most assuredly, be attended with evils far greater than any which can by possibility arise from reducing the duties upon sugar, from introducing it into a larger consumption, and thus producing that accession to the revenue which, if we may judge from the parallel case of coffee, must necessarily ensue. If such consequences followed from the reduction of the duty upon coffee as I have loved to have been derived from it; from the reduction of the duty on sugar, whose admixture with coffee is indispensable, and of which the use is so multifarious, analogous results must follow. Independently of his fiscal advantage, a two-fold benefit must accrue to the great mass of the community. In the first place, we cheapen one of the necessaries of life; and in the next place, it is obvious that if we take more of the produce of other countries, other countries must take more of the produce of our own; to that extent the manufacturers of England must be promoted, and to that extent the employment of our operatives must be encouraged. To their sufferings, the Tories everywhere I hope, at the hustings I am sure, are alive; but when the obvious means of alleviation are proposed, they sacrifice the interests of that vast class of the community for which so much commiseration is possessed by them, to the maintenance of that too narrow commercial system, by which, if we adhere to it, consequences the most pernicious will be entailed upon us. We are met upon the Continent by retaliatory tariffs. Of our discoveries in mechanics, of our finest and most powerful machines, of the advantages of which we were once in the exclusive enjoyment, our foreign competitors are now possessed; to other markets, to markets in the countries in which manufactures do not exist, and in which it will be our fault if they shall arise, the eyes of every British statesman ought to be intently turned: and, above all, to that splendid mart which is opened to us, in the young and prosperous empire of Brazil. I am astonished that any man should speak of our commercial relations with that rapidly progressing country in the language of depreciation. Before his constituents, such language would not be adopted by the noble lord, the member for Liverpool; he would not, before his constituents venture to insinuate that he considered the renewal of the treaty with Brazil as a matter of small amount; or if he did, and looked from the hustings to the harbour of that great city which he has the honour to represent, in many a noble ship, of all his fallacies he would behold the refutation. But how can we reasonably expect that the Brazilians will make concessions to us, if to them we refuse to make any concessions; and if the Parliament of England is not prepared (to adopt the phraseology of your resolution) to take the produce of Brazil, have we not reason to apprehend that the Parliament of Brazil will be unprepared to take the produce of England? And, even with reference to the slave-trade, is it not likely that we shall accomplish far more by treaty, enforced as treaties ought to be, than by any fiscal regulations which it is possible to devise? One of the evils resulting from these fiscal regulations is this:—the people of England are taught to rely upon them as the means of restraining the slave-trade, instead of adopting the measures by which that important object might be obtained. Meetings are held, harangues are delivered, admirable resolutions are passed, and the work of abomination all the while goes on. Of a great and powerful country, expedients, so unavailing as our differential duties have been proved to be, are unworthy, and when England stands forward in the cause of humanity, it is not from the Custom-house that her weapons should be supplied. Despite your differential duty, the slave-trade is infamously prosperous—the monster consumes his thousand victims a day. There is not a creek upon the slave-coast in which the barks engaged in that atrocious traffic do not lie in wait; and even while I speak—while we sit in council here—across that ocean which Englishmen are accustomed to call their own—across that ocean which has been most nobly called 'your home upon the deep"—how many a slave-bark, freighted with woe, despite your differential duty, holds on with impunity her swift and unimpeded way, while you, with the evidence, the incontrovertible evidence before you, of the futility—the utter and most scandalous futility of your differential duty for the accomplishment of any one purpose by which the interests of humanity, as distinct from those of monopoly, can be promoted—instead of calling upon England, to put forth her might, and invoking her to employ the only efficient means by which this horrible traffic in our fellow-creatures can be put down, expatiate upon the blesssings of monopoly; descant upon 63s., and 36s., and 24s., and propound resolutions for the sustainment of that fiscal anomaly, by which (and you know it,) to the atrocities of the slave-trade not the slightest obstacle is presented, while to our revenues the deepest detriment is done. The embarrassments with which every minister of this country, whether he be Whig or Tory, will have to contend for many a day, will be augmented, by which a deprivation of one of the commonest commodities of life will be inflicted upon the lower classes, by which industry will be paralysed, the employment of our suffering and pining operatives will be abridged, our commercial relations with one of our best allies will be endangered, and we shall run the risk of closing, perhaps for ever, a field of almost boundless enterprise upon the commercial genius of the English people

CORN LAWS.

SPEECH IN THE HOUSE OF COMMONS, MARCH 9, 1842.

I CERTAINLY am surprised that the right honourable gentleman who has just sat down, and who is so remarkable for perspicuity, should have mistaken the observation of the noble lord (Viscount Howick,) who is so remarkable for his perspicuity. The right honourable baronet has misconceived what the noble lord advanced, and he seems to me to have omitted that part of the speech which is most deserving of attention. Among the observations of the noble lord, I was struck with one which appeared to me particularly deserving of attention. The noble lord designated the measure of the right honourable baronet as the precursor of ulterior measures. The noble lord stated it was obvious that the right honourable baronet cannot stop here, and that either he or some other minister must ultimately abandon this protection. To that observation no remark has been made by the right honourable gentleman. Whether he agrees in that remark, or did not agree, it is not for me to determine. I think that the observation of the noble lord deserves the most serious consideration. The right honourable baronet is about to tamper with the law which regulates the price of provisions. It has been well said by Edmund Burke, in his excellent thoughts on scarcity, "that to tamper with the laws regulating the price of provisions, is at all times dangerous," but when you do tamper with these laws—when you do more—when you do yield to public opinion, you ought, at least, to see that you are acting satisfactorily to some great party. You are about to take the first step, and that an important step, in the course of innovation. You are about to take a step which does not satisfy all parties, even on your own side. The Duke of Buckingham, at least, feels a strong objection to it. When that change is proposed, he, who was not in the cabinet of 1839, ceased to be in the cabinet of 1842. Might he venture to say, "*Honi soit qui mal y pense?*" When you are about to make a change which is thought material by your own supporters, it is a matter of much regret and of some surprise, that you do not at once that which you or some one else must do at last. You still adhere to the vicious principle of the present system, of which perpetual uncertainty is the conspicuous essence. You still adhere to the sliding-scale. You adhere to the principle that affords incentives, and that affords opportunities for fraudulent combinations. You still adhere to the principle which substitutes the spirit of rash adventure for the spirit of legitimate commercial speculation You apply the principle of a sliding-scale to corn alone—you apply it to no other article of human food. Colonial coffee and colonial sugar are protected by fixed duties. It is said that the sugar duties are about to undergo a change. It is rumoured that the apprehensions which were so lately entertained as to the indirect sanction you would give to the slave-trade begins to subside. Do you mean to apply the principle of the sliding-scale to coffee and to sugar? If you did so, if you passed a law declaring that the duty upon

Brazilian sugar and upon Havannah sugar. shall depend upon the average price of East India and of West India sugar, I will ask the right honourable gentleman, the Vice-President of the Board of Trade, whose peculiar care this would be, whether such a law would not inflict a great practical injury on the growers of coffee and the growers of sugar in the Brazils? I do not feel surprised that the agriculturists of this country do not adopt the opinions—the extreme opinions as they are considered by many—of Mr. Adam Smith, and Mr. Huskisson in his latter days, that the very measures intended for the protection of the agricultural interests are in fact deleterious to them; but it does appear to me strange that the advice of so decided a friend of protection as Mr. M'Cullogh, should not have more weight with the agriculturists. Mr. M'Cullogh says that a fluctuating scale of duty adds an artificial variation to the inevitable natural variations of the seasons, and inflicts as much injury upon the farmers as upon the traders. Is this a sound principle? Let us examine how the sliding-scale works now, to see how it will work under the proposed changes. The sliding-scale in one single year, in the year 1835, shifted thirty-five times—it underwent thirty-five different changes. On the 19th of July, in 1838, the duty was 20s. 8d.; on the 13th of September, the duty was 1s. ; in the week ending October 11th, it was again 20s. 8d.; and, before the end of December, it again descended to 1s. In the year 1840, the lowest duty was 2s. 8d.; it remained so for one week, and in five weeks afterwards it was 20s. 8d. In the year 1840, on the 17th September, it was only 1s.; in the next week, it was 2s. 8d.; it rose to 16s. 8d. the next week; to 20s. 8d.; and on the 14th October it reached 22s. 8d. It appears to me that this system, or anything like this system, must produce injury to the agriculturists, and that the farmers suffer equally with other classes, from that which they believe to be their safeguard. But, says the right honourable baronet, "the new plan which I propose, and the machinery which I introduce, will obviate many of the objections of the present law. I introduce rests, which will baffle the fraudulent working of the averages." It is true that you lower the duty, but you leave a duty ranging between 20s. and 1s. You therefore leave ample opportunity for working the averages—you leave every chance for having a glut of corn at a time when it can be contemplated this long duty will arrive. It has been urged, and I admit the force of the objection, that in times of scarcity it will be very difficult to maintain a fixed duty. I will meet that objection, and I will answer it by a reference to Mr. M'Cullogh. He says that if the ports are constantly open, if there is a regular trade in corn at a fixed duty, the supply would be perpetual; and that if there be a fixed duty we shall take away the chance of a great scarcity. I admit the force of the objection; but where there is a choice of evils—where we have to make our election between difficulties, I would confide in a fixed duty to be brought under the consideration of parliament, rather than surrender the averages to the jobbers of Mark-lane. Whatever may be the opinions as to a fixed duty or the effect upon the commercial and manufacturing interests of this country, there is no doubt during the last four years millions of quarters of corn

have been imported, and yet we have no trade. Trade is barter—trade is the exchange of one commodity for another. When our demand for corn is desultory, the demand for our manufactures cannot be permanent. If there were a free trade in corn, foreign countries would not pass laws intended to exclude our manufactures; they would not do as they now did—they would not pass retaliatory tariffs to protect their own domestic manufactures. It is not the agriculturists of this country, it is not the independent yeoman, it is not the farmer who expends his capital upon his land, it is not the man who dreads competition from foreign markets, but it is those in possession of the secrets of our mechanism—it is those who emulate us in industry and begin to rival us in skill, that your corn laws afford protection. It will hardly be contended, that the countries from which during the last four years we have drawn our supplies of corn, have taken the manufactures of this country in return in anything like a commensurate quantity. It appears, from a return laid upon the table of the house, that the number of English vessels which entered the Baltic in ballast in the year 1839 was 1100—not laden with your manufactures, but wholly in ballast. Look at the returns also before the house of the number of vessels which entered the port of Dantzic in 1838, distinguishing those which were laden and those in ballast. In 1838 there were 413 English vessels entering the port of Dantzic in ballast; and in the same year 417 vessels left the port of Dantzic laden with corn. This proves undeniably that when you now take corn from foreign countries your own manufactures are not taken in return. What effect has this system upon your currency— upon that metallic currency which the right honourable gentleman had established, and over which he ought to watch with peculiar care? It seems to me to be impossible to establish a metallic currency, and to continue a system of laws such as those which exist. Corn must be paid for in bullion; the exchange is against us; the circulation is checked, and the inevitable result is a panic. I beg to call the attention of the house to the language of Mr. Huskisson in 1821, with reference to this view of the subject. In the famous report of 1821, the words which I shall read were applied by him to the existing system of corn laws—that of 1815. The words of Mr. Huskisson are as applicable to the existing system of the right honourable baronet as if they were yesterday specifically composed to meet it. These are the words of Mr. Huskisson:—
' " The inconvenient operation of the present corn laws, which appears to be less the consequence of the foreign corn brought into the country in the average of years than the manner in which the grain is introduced, is not confined to great fluctuation in price, and consequent embarrassment both to the grower and consumer, for the occasional prohibition has also a direct tendency to contract the extent of our commercial dealings with other states, and to excite in the rulers of those states a spirit of permanent exclusion against the manufactures of this country. In this conflict, the exclusion is injurious to both. The two parties, however, are not upon an equal footing. On our part, the prohibition must yield to the wants of the people; on the other side, there

is no such overruling necessity, and inasmuch as the reciprocity of demand is the foundation of all means of payment, a large and sudden influx of corn might, under these circumstances, create a temporary derangement in the course of exchange, the effect of which, after the resumption of cash payments, might lead to a drain of specie from the bank, the contraction of the circulation, a panic among the public banks, and a public dearth, as experienced in former years of scarcity."

That was written by Mr. Huskisson in 1821, two years after the bill was passed, which is rendered memorable by the association with it of the name of the right honourable baronet at the head of her majesty's government. I am not one of those who are disposed to quarrel with the measure of the right honourable baronet. I think that it evinced the possession of great moral courage in the right honourable baronet to effect and carry out such a measure. But it is said, do not make such a change in the relation of the agriculturist of this country as the alteration of the corn law would effect; do not rush upon a step which will occasion such a revolution in the position of the property of the agricultural interests of England. But, by the measure of 1819, the right honourable baronet changed every contract in the kingdom—he altered the relation of landlord and tenant, the relation of debtor and creditor, and of every class in the country; he instituted a new order of things, to the results of which, the celebrated and learned author of "Corn and Currency" has so well alluded. But the right honourable baronet was not then a minister of the crown; his solicitude for the interests of his country were unbiassed by any anxiety for the maintenance of his party. I wish he could now act with the same moral intrepidity, and heedless of all intimations given to him in another place, and would make the amendment which the country demands, in a spirit worthy of an Englishman, and would afford relief to the operatives of the country more effectual than any to be found in an acknowledgment, however eloquent, of their wretchedness, or in any unprofitable commiseration. It is said that the corn laws are not connected with the distress of the country—the existence of any distress is denied.— The existence of it has been proved, and now I come to this part of the case. For my own part, when I find the corn laws affect the trade of this country—when I find the corn laws affect the manufactures of this country—the employment of the people—I find in them an adequate cause of that public distress which exists, and an adequate cause of that legitimate effect is, I think, fairly ascertained. If something effectual is not done in parliament—in a parliament in which the landed interests are said to have such an influence—I am afraid that the people of this country will be disposed to turn with resentful importunity from the mere expression of our sympathy, and will adopt a more stringent mode of proceeding; and as they have been led to believe that the poor law was not enacted from any profound solicitude for the poor, so they will think that the corn laws are retained from an exclusive regard to the feelings and interests of the rich. And I must say that it would be hard indeed for this house to turn from the supplications for relief; it would be hard if, while we by our legislation affect the employment of the people, and induce the operatives of this country to ask for an asylum in those domiciles of woe which are provided for them, we refuse to afford them the means of supporting themselves in a manner becoming their ancient character and position. If charity is to be withheld, let not work, at all events, be refused. The people of England do not ask for charity, they do not go on their knees to ask any eleemosynary contributions; they ask for bread to produce work; for work to produce bread; they ask not for cheap bread, indeed, but for more—they ask for the means of earning bread, whether it be cheap or costly.— They call on us to strike off those fetters which cramp the industry of the country, and in doing so they wish us to consult, not merely their interest, but our own. I entirely agree in the sentiments which I have heard expressed by an honourable and learned member to-night, that the agricultural and commercial interests of the country are not distinct. So far from their being distinct—so far from their being at variance and conflicting with each other, they are the same. Trade depends upon agriculture, agriculture depends upon trade. I am sure my honourable friend the member for Stockport, when he looks upon the splendid picture which the rural scenery of England presents, would draw from its contemplation one of the highest pleasures. I am sure the right honourable gentleman the member for Kent, a native English gentleman, must see in the very smoke with which our cities are enveloped from their furnaces, intimations of the means by which the agricultural interest is advanced, and the greatness of the country is achieved. No, Sir, the commercial and agricultural interests of England are not distinct. But if they were—if it was necessary to make a distinction between them—if in giving sustainment to both it is necessary to make a sacrifice of either, I should be disposed to say that the maintenance of the commerce of England ought, in the mind of every Englishman deserving the name, to be the object of paramount consideration. It is not, after all, by agriculture that this country is so distinguished; for what is this but a speck upon the scene? It is not to agriculture—it is not to the extent or fertility of our soil—it is not to any rare skill in calling forth the products of the earth. No; it is the spirit of commercial enterprise by which Englishmen are distinguished from any other nation on the face of the earth. It is the indomitable perseverance in the glorious pursuit of our boundless traffic, by which every difficulty has been overcome, and every obstacle surmounted. It is to the unwearied energies of the country, to its amazing industry, to its untiring zeal, to the marvellous skill with which it has filled the earth with the products of its labour—it is this commerce which has extended its influence to the boundaries of the earth—it is to these glorious causes that England is indebted for its prominence among the nations of the earth. Against our trade it was that our mighty adversary directed his principal attempts. He, however, failed. Let us have a care lest we effect by our policy what Napoleon was unable to accomplish; let us have a care lest by an obstinate adherence to a system which so many enlightened men, men not more enlightened than impartial, have condemned as the source of so much mischief; which has already produced so much calamity, and threatens us with, perhaps, still greater injury which contracts our commerce, which exposes our monetary system to perpetual disturbance, which reduces our operatives to a state of the most unhappy destitution; let us, too, have a care lest, by a pernicious adherence to that fatal system, we do not entail evils upon our country for which your talents, if you were the brightest, your wisdom if you were the wisest, and your virtues if you were the most high-minded minister to whom the care of England was ever intrusted, would be unable to find a cure.

INCOME TAX.

SPEECH ON THE INCOME TAX, APRIL 8, 1842.

IF for the sustainment of the honour and the interests of England an income tax were required, I make no doubt that the people of this country would at once submit to it, and follow with promptitude, the example which our gracious Sovereign has spontaneously and magnanimously given; but of this generous example, the minister should be slow to take advantage, and should avoid with peculiar care, any exaggerated description of the perils or of the embarrassments of the country, in order to produce an acquiesence in a tax of all others the most convenient to the minister, but the most harassing and vexatious to the people. Does the condition of England, does the state of her finances, do existing difficulties, do impending perils, make the imposition of a tax so odious, matter of inevitable need? That question will be put ere many months shall have passed, by that portion of the community in which political power is deposited, and upon the answer to that question, the stability of the government will depend, when the merits of the minister shall be tried by some better test than the acclamations of heated partisans, and shall be determined by the results to which his legislation will conduct us. The right honourable baronet has little to apprehend, during the passage of his bill through the parliament. He told us, that he was ready to take the course which he had adopted in 1835. But I cannot help thinking that his magnanimity is misplaced; his public virtue will not be put to a trial so severe. Although it may seem paradoxical to say so, his difficulties will be the result of his success, and his will be one of those victories, which it requires less ability to win than to follow up. When the income-tax shall have been in actual operation—when a theory in the parliament shall have become a burden upon the people—when schedule D shall have been made fearfully intelligible—when this tax shall have been charged, to use a phrase familiar in debates on the Irish Registration Bill, upon the "beneficial interest" which a man has in all his earnings, and no allowance shall have been made as against this impost, for food, for fire, for raiment, for the roof over an English tradesman's head—when the privacy of so many Englishmen shall have been invaded by the inquisitors, who are to be attached to your new fiscal tribunal—when a scrutiny shall have been instituted into the affairs of every man, whom your commissioners, original, additional, or special, shall conjecture to have gained £150 in a single year—when all the pain and all the humiliation incidental to this tax shall have been felt, then, I feel persuaded that the people of this country will inquire whether this tax would not have been avoided, or whether the right honourable baronet did not take advantage of a majority, hot from the struggle of recent election, to inflict a tax, for which neither the present condition, nor the future prospects of England, afforded a justification. I have little doubt, that the people of England will think that the right honourable baronet was mistaken in his view of the public embarrassments, that he over-rated the exigencies of the hour, and that for the imposition of a tax so unjust, so inquisitorial and so immoral, he should have forfeited the confidence of the country. It is alleged by the right honourable baronet, that an income tax is indispensable for the purpose of repairing a two-fold deficiency—that which already exists, and that which a great commercial experiment will involve. To create an additional deficiency in order to repair it by an income tax, to inflict a new wound in order to apply a favourite cure, is more than tentative, and if my right honourable friend, the late Chancellor of the Exchequer, had made a proposition like this, he would have been regarded as an empiric of the most adventurous kind. But it is the good fortune of the right honourable baronet, that his supporters entertain in his regard that sort of confidence, which Waller has happily described in his celebrated address to a great projector:—

"Still as you rise, the state, exalted too,
Feels no disorder, when 'tis changed by *you*."

I am one of those, however, who do not think that the experiment of the right honourable baronet is of such value, that for the sake of indulging him in it, the country should submit to the calamity of an income tax. The tariff, by which the deficiency of £1,200,000 is to be at once created, is not such a masterpiece, as to induce us to acquiesce in such an imposition as he declares to be necessary for his great undertaking. He begins by sacrificing £600,000 of the timber duties. Why should he abolish the duties on Canadian timber? Sir Henry Parnell, whose authority he quotes, and for whom he entertains great respect, ever since his celebrated motion on the civil-list in 1830, does not suggest that the duties on Canadian timber should be given up. Mr. M'Gregor, the Secretary to the Board of Trade, a man of great talent, knowledge, and experience, whose evidence was so important before the Import Duty Committee; who resided a considerable time in Canada, and who has written a valuable work on the subject, does not recommend that the duty on Canadian timber should be wholly relinquished, but that it should be reduced from 10s. to 7s. 6d. It is known to everybody that there is a species of Canadian timber, which we cannot dispense with, yellow pine for example, which is employed for a variety of purposes, to which Baltic timber is not applicable. It must come into this country, and to relinquish the revenue that would be derived from it, is a most imprudent proceeding. The course adopted with regard to the sugar duties is most censurable. When the enormous sum of £20,000,000, was given to the West-India planters, there was no stipulation that their monopoly should be preserved, and accordingly the duties on East-India and West-India sugar were soon after equalized. The duties on East-India and West-India rum were recently placed on a level. The present Chancellor of the Exchequer, the champion of the West-India interest, expostulated in vain. His eloquence appears to be more influential in the cabinet, than it was last year in the House of Commons. As long as there existed an inequality of duty in East-India and West-India produce, the East and West-Indians were strong antagonists; but the duties having been equalized, they formed a junction in favour of mono-

only; the government here entered into their views, and have consulted their interests at the expense of the whole British community. The Import Duties Committee entered into a very minute and most important consideration of the effects that would follow from a reduction of the duties on foreign sugar. Those duties are enormous; they amount to the sum of 63s. per cwt., while the duty on colonial sugar is only 24s. It was proved before the Import Duty Committee, by witnesses, whose judgment is unimpeachable, that as the reduction of the duty on coffee produced a great increase of consumption and of revenue, the reduction of the duty on sugar would have the same effect; that to cheapen one of the necessaries of life would be of essential utility to the humbler classes; that sugar would be employed in various ways in which on account of its cost, it is not now used; that our commercial relation with the Brazils would be most advantageously extended and confirmed; and that the demand for our manufactures would be considerably increased, and that an impulse would be given to the operative industry of the country. Mr. M'Gregor stated, that the revenue might be increased by so large a sum as £3,000,000, by a judicious alteration of the sugar duties. To that alteration the right honourable baronet prefers an income tax; and, among other objections to a change in the sugar duties, informs us that he does not desire to give an impulse to slave labour. Yet, by a strange contradiction, he reduces the duty on foreign coffee, the produce of slave labour, and he permits Brazilian and Cuba sugar to be refined in England, and to be exported for consumption in those very colonies in which slavery has been suppressed. His tariff is in these particulars most essentially imperfect. In the case of such a tariff, the evils of an income tax ought not to be inflicted, and if any substantial argument can be adduced in favour of so odious a measure, it is in the existing deficiency that we must endeavour to discover it. That a deficiency exists must be admitted and deplored, but those who are disposed to pronounce an unmeasured censure upon the Whig government, as the occasion of that deficiency, ought to bear in mind, that from 1830 to 1836, the Whigs reduced taxes to the amount of £6,000,000, and that notwithstanding that great reduction, there was a surplus of revenue in that time of upwards of £6,000,000, so that no actual augmentation of the national debt has taken place under the Whig ministry. It was imagined, that the Tories had reduced the taxes to such an extent, before the accession of the Whigs, that no opportunity would be afforded to their successors of diminishing the public burdens. I am very far from denying that the Tories deserve great praise for having, independently of the income tax, abolished seventeen or eighteen millions of other taxes, but it seems extraordinary that when his predecessors began by repealing the income tax, and then proceeded to remit other taxes to a vast amount, the right honourable baronet should invert the order of proceeding, and as if the income tax were of all taxes the least onerous, the most popular and the most just, he should make it the object of predilection, and select it as the basis of his whole system of finance. What is the history of this income tax, which the right honourable baronet prefers to every other impost? It was proposed by Mr.

Pitt, in whose gigantic footsteps the right honourable baronet, so far as taxation is concerned, seems disposed to tread, in the midst of a great emergency. The rights, liberties, institutions of England—the existence, the life of England, were at stake. But Mr. Pitt did not, in enforcing the necessity of having recourse to an income tax, deliver a speech so elaborate as the right honourable gentleman to the patriotism of Englishmen, he did not address any enthusiastic adjunction No wonder the funds at fifty-two, the mutiny at the Nore, a rebellion in Ireland, disaster abroad, treason at home, the armies of the French republic everywhere victorious—these topics did not require any eloquence to set them off. Accordingly the income tax was adopted in 1798 without a dissentient voice, but four years after, as soon as the peace of Amiens had been concluded, Mr. Addington went down to the House of Commons, and declared that, as the income tax was a war tax, and ought to be reserved for the greatest emergencies, it gave him the utmost satisfaction to be able to announce that it should be forthwith repealed. But Sir Francis Burdett was not contented with this intimation, for on the 12th of April in the same year, he said, that he was not satisfied that that tax should merely be repealed, but that some declaration should be placed on the records of parliament with respect to it, that should ever afterwards stigmatise it as an infamous measure. The honourable baronet added,

"The income tax has created an inquisitorial power of the most partial, offensive, and cruel nature. The whole transactions of a life may be inquired into; family affairs laid open, and an Englishman, like a culprit, summoned to attend commissioners, compelled to wait like a lacquey in their anti-chamber from day to day until they are ready to institute their inquisition into his property; put to his oath, after all perhaps disbelieved, surcharged, and stigmatised as perjured, without any redress from, or appeal to a jury of his country. And it is worth remarking, too, that a little before the introduction of this unprincipled scheme of plunder, the law of perjury was altered, and the punishment made transportation to Botany Bay. Sir, the repeal of this tax is not a sufficient remedy for its infamy; its principle must be stigmatised and branded."

I do not quote this language because I attach any particular value to the opinions of the honourable baronet, but because this language is expressive of the public sentiment in 1802, of which at that time the honourable baronet was a vindicator. Hostilities having been recommenced, it became necessary to resort again to this calamitous impost. Disaster followed upon disaster, and in 1806, when in the battle of Austerlitz, Austria had been struck down, when Prussia and Russia had been humbled to the dust, when to the progress of the great conqueror no obstacle seemed to be interposed—let the condition of England in 1806 and in 1842 be compared—it became necessary to exact the income tax with still greater rigour, and that machinery was framed which the right honourable baronet has selected as his model. The right honourable baronet has adverted to some of the provisions in the bill introduced

by Lord Henry Petty, but he omitted any reference to the concluding, and, in my mind, conclusive clause:—
"And be it further enacted, that this act shall commence and take effect from and after the 5th day of April, 1806, and together with the duties therein contained, shall continue in force during the present war, and until the 6th day of April next after the ratification of a definitive treaty of peace, and no longer."

During ten years England had ample experience of the fearful evils of this most obnoxious impost—of those evils the right honourable baronet spoke somewhat lightly; and such language was employed in reference to this tax, that it seems sufficiently clear that if once the blister is applied it will become perpetual, and the more it draws the more closely it will adhere. We have been told that there is no tax, indeed which is not attended with inconvenience; that no fair man can reasonably object to a disclosure of his circumstances, and that the people of this country are too moral to yield to the pernicious influences with which it is supposed that an income tax will be attended. With such showy plausibilities is the medicament, the bitter medicament, gilded by the adroit experimentalist by whom it is compounded. The impressions connected with the income tax are not so vivid as they were twenty-six years ago; but there remains on record, and set forth in the history of parliament, sufficient evidence to prove with what feelings of deep loathing the income tax was regarded by the great mass of the English people. Is it mere imagination to suggest that this tax is unjust, inquisitorial, and immoral? Did it not, while in operation, teem with evil? Was it not fertile of falsehood and of fraud? Was not the scrutiny which is inseparable from it an object of execration, and through the length and breadth of the land was not a cry raised for its repeal, as if it were one of the greatest calamities which could be inflicted on the country? Are the statements set forth in the remarkable petition of the bankers, merchants, and traders of London, in 1816, against this tax, mere invention? That petition was presented by Sir William Curtis, a man devoted to the Tory party, but who denounced the income tax, and said that it was a monstrous breach of faith to continue it after the war had ceased. Sir James Shaw stated that he had attended the meeting, at which 22,000 of the citizens of London had assembled, and that the income tax had been unanimously reprobated. Mr. Baring, the greatest merchant in the greatest mercantile country in the world (you have lately given evidence of your reliance on his judgment and his sagacity), concurred in the unqualified condemnation of the income tax. Mr. Wilberforce, who had the morals of England so much at heart, pronounced a strong censure on this baneful impost. But in reading the speeches delivered in 1816, against the income tax, I was not struck by any one of them more than by that of a man well acquainted with the interests of all classes of Englishmen, and to whom the right honourable baronet must look back with a feeling of affectionate veneration—I allude to the late Sir Robert Peel. He said that it was utterly absurd to imagine that the income tax, which pressed upon the middle classes, did not affect the humbler classes of the community; and he added, that an income tax, in his judgment, was the very worst—ay, the very worst, which could be proposed. Such were the men by whom the continuance of the income tax was opposed. By whom was it supported? By Mr. Vansittart and Lord Castlereagh. But Lord Castlereagh had a far more powerful case than the right honourable baronet. England had borrowed one hundred millions in the two preceding years; the repeal of the income tax would necessitate a loan of twelve millions for the then current year, and eight millions after. The country had not recovered from the fearful struggle from which it had come exhausted and breathless—the effects of the war had not passed away, and under these circumstances Lord Castlereagh appealed to the country, to make a sacrifice for two years longer, and to make one last effort for the sustainment of the public credit. To his invocation the House of Commons were insensible, and it will be strange indeed, if in a reformed parliament—in a parliament whose reform he to the last opposed—the member for Tamworth should achieve that which in an unreformed parliament, with all his influence, and all his plausibility, Lord Castlereagh was not able to accomplish. The motion for a continuance of the income tax was lost by a majority of thirty-seven. It was repealed, and in the succeeding years, up to the present period—independently of the income tax—twenty-three millions of taxes were remitted. In that enormous mass cannot the right honourable baronet find some means of recruiting the finances of his country, without resorting to so fatal an expedient? He does not choose, it is said, to renew those taxes which would press upon the comforts of the poor, whose "ignorant impatience of taxation" it is no longer judicious to provoke. It is almost unnecessary to suggest that, as the late Sir Robert Peel observed, the tax which presses upon the middle classes must affect all those below them; but how does the right honourable baronet reconcile with his sympathy for the poor the maintenance of the great colonial interests, while so many thousand of poor operatives, cutters of corks, makers of shoes, gloves, bonnets, are sacrificed to the genius of free trade with so relentless a rigour? Let the interests of the poor be consulted, but by some means less inequitable than an income tax. What can be more unjust than to lay the same tax upon the intellect of one man, and upon the acres of another? Look at the proprietor of great territorial possessions, encompassed with every advantage by which existence can be cheered, and life can be prolonged, in the daily enjoyment of the most healthful exercise, free from all mental pain, and exempt from every discomfort, excepting that which arises (to use a phrase of Edmund Burke) "from the laborious lassitude of having nothing to do," secure of the permanent retention of his estates, and of transmitting to his progeny the splendid mansion and extensive domains, which through a long succession have come down to him. Turn from him to the professional man, who is engaged from morning till night, and from night almost till the break of day, in the exhausting occupations from which his precarious subsistence is derived: mark, not only the toil, the incesant toil which it is his destiny to suffer, but the wear and tear of the feelings, and of the faculties which he must needs undergo, the despondency, the faintness of heart which at the approach of the slightest ailment must come upon him, the sense of insecurity by which he must perpetually be haunted, the apprehension, the consuming solicitude that must beset him, lest by the gradual decay of his faculties, or the sudden loss of health, he may be deprived of the means of earning his livelihood, and those who are inestimably dearer to him than himself, may be reduced to destitution. Look, I say, at these two men, of whom I have presented to you no exaggerated delineation, and then do you—you, who are yourselves the inheritors of large possessions—you, who are born to affluence—you, who have never known a care of to-morrow—do you who live at home at ease," and know so little of dangers and the storms of adversity—do you, I say, declare whether it be just, whether it be fair, whether it be humane, that upon both these men, and in the same proportion, the same impost should be inflicted. Shall we levy the same contribution on a man with £10,000 a-year, and upon officers in the army and navy, poor clergymen who endeavour to educate their children as the children of gentlemen should be brought up, widows with miserable jointures, tradesmen, artisans, small retailers who eke out a subsistence from the petty business to which, for sixteen or seventeen hours out of the four-and-twenty, they are devoted? Is it right to tax them as you do the great patricians of the land, and to force them to discover upon oath what perhaps it most deeply concerns their just and legitimate pride that they should conceal? What can be more fearful, more humiliating, than to make a confession of adversity—to let a set of heartless functionaries into the secrets of calamity, and to lay misfortune bare? The commissioners are empowered to examine upon oath, and to repudiate the testimony which a man gives in his own favour. To what immoral results must this practice lead? It has been suggested, that under our existing system, oaths must frequently be administered, and that there is a good deal of swearing in the Excise. True; but is it judicious to extend through every ramification of society the spirit of the Excise, and to get up a struggle between the interests and the conscience of every man who is to be charged with this baneful impost? The people of England are moral, but they have cause to pray, that into temptation they may not be led. This tax is an immoral one; and, as I have heard in this house, when the rights and franchises of my countrymen were in question, a vehement denunciation against "villanous perjury," I trust that to the Irish hustings your abhorrence of perjury will not be confined; that to its perpetration you will not supply incentives; that as you are not, I hope, Pharisees in religion, you will not prove remorseless Publicans in finance; and that you will not send forth a band of tax-gatherers through the kingdom, and arm them with the Gospel, that they may put the conscience of every honest man to the question; while to every prevaricator, every shuffler, every equivocator, every perjurer, an impunity, proportioned to his utter destitution of all principle, is scandalously secured. I am not in speaking thus, guilty of any the least exaggeration of the evils of the income tax, be— I find a warrant for every word that I have uttered in the reiterated statements contained in hundreds of petitions which in 1816 were piled upon the table of the House of Commons, and of these statements no contradiction was ever yet attempted. The evils of the income tax are so monstrous, that it is almost impossible to heighten them—they set hyperbole at defiance. But, at all events, of no exaggeration could any man in inveighing against the evils of the income tax be possibly guilty comparable to the exaggeration into which the right honourable baronet allowed himself to be betrayed, when he indulged in a description so eloquent, but so highly coloured, of the disasters of his country.— Remarkable as his speech was for a surplus of ability, it was not more conspicuous for talent than for the very exaggerated terms in which he permitted himself to describe the difficulties and dangers of England. If, Sir, at the close of that speech, some one who had lived in sequestration from the world, and for the last five or six years had not heard of the events which have passed within that period, had chanced to have entered this house, he would, I think, have been tempted to exclaim — appalled by the right honourable baronet's magnificent peroration— " Good God, what has happened! Is England brought to the verge of ruin? Has one greater than Napoleon—of whom Napoleon was but the precursor—appeared? Is the world in arms against England?— Have her fleets been sunk in the ocean, and, with Wellington at their head, have those legions that were once deemed invincible, at last given way?" What would be his surprise at hearing that the repose of Europe was undisturbed, that her Majesty had declared that she continued to receive assurances of the most friendly dispositions from all princes and states, that all the great powers had signed a common treaty for the preservation of the dominions of the Porte, and for the maintenance of peace; and that not very long ago another right honourable baronet, the Secretary for the Home Department, had taken upon himself to state, as evidence of the influence of a Conservative government in promoting peace, that the French minister had agreed to reduce the navy of France, and that wherever our eyes were turned prospects of cloudless felicity were disclosed. What! when a purpose is to be gained, shall one minister announce that, under Tory auspices, the peace of Europe is secure; and when money is to be got, is another minister, or rather the master of the ministers, to talk of the cannon, whose sound has not yet reached our ears, and to strike terror into the heart of the country with vague and appalling intimations! Contrast the speech of the right honourable baronet on the income tax with that which he delivered on the corn laws: The distresses of the country were then, forsooth, transitory and evanescent—they arose from bad harvests, and the temporary difficulties of America; and in the resources of England, in her energy and elastic power, his confidence was unabated. I concur with him, and thank God that we are not come to such a pass, that the right honourable baronet is justified in insisting upon the adoption of an impost, which hitherto (except in the midst of the most disastrous warfare) no minister of England, except himself, has had the boldness to propose—which is fraught with such multifarious mischiefs, that the instant her great adversary had been subdued, England declared that she would no longer bear it—which, in its working, is admitted by its advocates to be most cruelly unjust—which establishes an inquisition almost as abominable as a religious one—which multiplies oaths—makes as familiar as mere household words that awful attestation by which, as we speak the truth, we call on God to help us—converts the Gospel into a mere implement of finance—prostitutes to purposes the most vilifying that sacred book, which it is your boast that beyond all Christian nations you hold in reverence—which awards a premium to falsehood, and inflicts a penalty on truth—from which honesty cannot escape, and by which fraud cannot be caught, and which, of all the imposts which it is possible for a perverse ingenuity to devise, is the most prejudicial to the interests, offensive to the feelings, abhorrent to the religious sentiments, and revolting to the moral sense of the English people.

FACTORY BILL.

SPEECH IN THE HOUSE OF COMMONS ON THE EDUCATION CLAUSE MAY 18, 1843.

THE Roman Catholic population of this country is already so considerable, the Irish immigration into the factory districts is so great, that being a member of that Church, to which there exists in this country a tendency to revert, I think myself not unauthorised to take part in a discussion, with which the merits of the Factory Bill are so intimately connected. I frankly acknowledge, that considering the difficulties with which the government have to contend in reference to all questions relating to the Roman Catholic religion, a concession by no means unimportant has been made to us. It is not rendered imperative on Catholic children to read and to learn the authorised version of the Scriptures, as we entertain the opinion that the sacred writings ought not to be used as a school book, that the rudiments of literature ought not to be taught through its intervention, that an irreverent familiarity with holy writ may lead to its degradation; that the perusal of the Bible, unaccompanied with that interpretation which our Church has from the earliest foundation of Christianity, as we conceive, put upon passages which are either obscure or doubtful, is not judicious, and that the unqualified exercise of the right of private judgment must conduce to error; as we hold besides, that facts are recorded in the history of an exceedingly carnal people, which it can answer no useful purpose to bring within the cognizance of childhood, and from which modesty should instinctively turn away—these, I say, being our sentiments upon a question of much controversy, though differing from our view, you have been sufficiently just to make allowance for what you consider to be our mistake in this regard; and notwithstanding that in this country there prevails a very opposite opinion, although it has been made a point of Protestant honour, that without distinction of age, of sex, or circumstance, the sacred writings shall every where, and by every body, be indiscriminately perused, you have taken our conscientious difficulties into account, and have not insisted that against the will of Roman Catholic parents, their children shall be subjected to the compulsory acquisition of elementary knowledge through the medium of holy writ. That concession having been made, I own, that bearing in mind the incalculable importance of applying a remedy to the evils which result from the ignorance which is submitted to prevail in the factory districts, I felt that the measure proposed by her Majesty's government ought not to be resisted on any light and trivial ground, that it ought not to be made the subject of a mere political or sectarian struggle, and that a perverse ingenuity in devising arguments against it ought not to be indulged. I asked myself whether there was any real practical evil to be apprehended by those who are not in communion with the establishment, and I was anxious, if possible, that my own judgment should yield an acquiescence to the reasons which were urged in favour of the scheme propounded in its ameliorated form, by the right honourable baronet. It is matter to me of unaffected regret, that after giving the plan the best consideration in my power, I have not been able to arrive at a conclusion favourable to the measure; for while I am aware that the professors of my religion are exempt from the necessity of receiving instruction, in the sacred writings, in a form to which they object, I feel, in the first place, that an unnecessary and therefore illegitimate predominance was given to the church, and that it was my duty to look to the government plan, not merely with reference to the manner in which my own individual religion was affected, but to the general usefulness of the scheme, to its compatibility with the principles of religious liberty, the maintenance of which is as important as the diffusion of knowledge. Not only is the board constituted in such a way as to deprive Dissenters, although a majority of the rate-payers, of their just share of influence, but the master of the school, by whom the Scriptures are to be taught, must be, *ex necessitate*, a member of the church. Now, if it be right that Catholics should be exempted from the necessity of reading the Scriptures at all, it is just that Dissenters should be exempted from instruction through the medium of an episcopal delegate, in the Scriptures, of which the exposition is confided to him. The right honourable baronet took a distinction between expounding and interpreting, but it is of a character so subtile that no ordinary casuist could have struck upon it. Not only is an ascendancy given to the church against which a not unnatural pride on the part of Dissenters revolts, but opportunities of proselytism, the more dangerous because the better disguised, are afforded. The more accomplished, the more skilful, the more zealous the churchman is, the more likely he will be to avail himself of the facilities with which he will be obviously supplied. Would the right honourable baronet permit an adroit, persuasive Catholic to teach the Scriptures to a child in whose orthodoxy he felt a concern? I very much doubt it. He should, therefore, excuse Dissenters for objecting to the influence with which men will be endowed in public schools, whose dogmas are almost as much at variance with those of Dissenters as the doctrines of the Church of Rome. Putting all considerations of the progress which has been made by the dogmas of men who, to the honour of Dr. Pusey, are designated by a reference to his name, there is so signal a difference between the opinions of Dissenters and those of genuine churchmen upon the doctrine of succession, and the power of the priesthood founded on the Scriptures, that if there were nothing else, it would afford a reason for objection. The Bishop of Exeter, who is not, I believe, as yet attached to the Oxonian school of Theology, has, in his charge, claimed prerogatives and powers as great as any to which the most absolute prelate of the ancient church could put in his title. If even to the assumptions of that conspicuous Pontiff a Dissenter might reasonably object, the spread of Puseyism must awaken an *a fortiori* fear. It is notorious that although the external aspect of the church remains superficially the same, it has undergone a great internal change. Men of distinguished talent, of exemplary lives, of great learning and piety, have from motives the best and purest, made an eloquent announcement of opinions, in more strict conformity with the tenets of the Catholic Church than with the principles of the Reformation. Those opinions have been adopted by laymen highly born and bred, remarkable for their proficiency in literature, for the gracefulness of their minds, and their persuasive manners. The new, or rather the revived doctrines have made great way among the clergy, who have begun to display the zeal, the energy, the devotedness and enthusiasm by which the missionaries of that church to which they have approximated, are distinguished. As yet these tenets have perhaps made no considerable progress among the mass of the people, but for the people those tenets possess great allurements. If Protestantism, says Madame de Staël, appeals to the understanding, Catholicism addresses itself to the heart. How largely have the Puseyites borrowed from that portion of our religious system, whose truth exalts, consoles—which raises us above the sphere of ordinary thinking, chases despair from anguish, restores to us "the loved, the lost, the distant and the dead," pours into minds the most deeply hurt the most healing balm, ministers to the loftiest hope, and awakens those imaginings, which, to use the Miltonian phrase, "brings all heaven before our eyes." Aware of the attractiveness of our tenets, those who regard them as a delusion, not unnaturally conceive that against these allurements, more than ordinary caution is necessary, and tremble at the influence which may be exercised with so much facility at a period of life when the first and the most permanent impressions are confessedly made in the inculcation of doctrines for which they conceive that no scriptural sanction can be adduced. It may be said that their apprehensions are ill founded, and that care will be taken by the Prime Minister that no heterodox ecclesiastic shall be raised to the episcopal dignity; but, Sir, we must bear in mind that proof is almost every day afforded us of the appositeness of Lord North's remark, that "the first thing a bishop does is to forget his maker." Witness Dr. Daly, who was named a bishop in Ireland the other day, and immediately after poured out an anathema against the government scheme of education in Ireland. But even with regard to the prime minister's nomination, what security have the Dissenters got, beyond such intimations as a cheer affords? Among the supporters of the right honourable baronet, are there not men distinguished by their talents, with more than a leaning to the new theology? Nay, was not Lord Morpeth himself sternly reproved on one remarkable occasion for railing at the Oxonian Professors, by a distinguished gentleman, who is favourable to freedom in trade, but a monopolist of truth? And if it be thought that I ought not to refer to an incident so remote, and before the honourable gentleman was in office, let me be permitted to ask, whether not many nights ago, there were not remonstrances addressed to the member for Kent of a very significant sort, by gentlemen whom the cheering of the Prime Minister did not deter from a confession of their creed? The fact is, it is hard to know who is, or who is not a Puseyite. I have even heard it made a question whether the representative of Oxford himself does not to a certain extent, and more especially on the eve of a dissolution sympathise with the divines, by whom so great and just an influence is enjoyed in the learned localities where their talents and their devotion are pre-eminently displayed. I have heard it said that he must have a most difficult card, which few but himself could play; for my part, I do not believe that he is a Protestant in one college, and a pseudo-Catholic in another; I do not believe that he adopts any of those amenities for which a celebrated order in the Catholic Church, distinguished by their genius and erudition, are supposed to have had recourse for the advancement of truth: my opinion is, that while he adheres to the principles of genuine Protestantism, he is forgiven on his canvass for the sake of certain associations with Popery, which are irresistibly suggested by the honourable baronet. But whatever may be the religious predilections of the representative of Oxford, of the inclinations of Oxford itself there can be little doubt. Can we wonder then that the Dissenters should object to a surrender of their schools to the church, when the church itself derives its own instruction from what Dissenters consider a contaminated source? It is from these considerations that the fears of the Dissenters originate, and to those considerations we must ascribe the extraordinary excitement which has been manifested through the country, and the enormous mass of petitions with which your table has been loaded. The church-rate agitation was not comparable in its fervour, to that which we have lately witnessed. The Dissenters were far more disposed to give you up their money than their creed. Besides the payment of church-rates is an abuse which the law has long sanctioned, which time has consecrated, and which, if not venerable, is at all events hoary: but in the present instance you propose an innovation against the liberty of conscience, and utterly at variance with the spirit of modern legislation. This is a relapse into intolerance. Before the repeal of the Test and Corporation Acts, it might have been reasonable enough—no it would never have been reasonable,—but it would have been consistent enough to have claimed this exclusiveness for the church:—but now it is anomalous indeed. The Tory party resisted the repeal of the Test and Corporation Act as long as they could: at length in 1828 the right honourable baronet at the head of her Majesty's government gave way, and passed a measure which was the precursor of emancipation. Having passed that measure, why does he upon a collateral question adhere to a policy wholly inconsistent with it? But on the part of the Home Secretary, the incongruity is still more glaring. He was not driven into the repeal of the Test and Corporation Acts: he supported the noble lord on his first introduction of the bill. You will tell me, perhaps, that the Test and Corporation Act has nothing to do with this bill. I answer that the great principle on which it was founded, of removing every obstruction which religious differences had created, is in direct antagonism to the basis of your scheme, and that it is most absurd that Dissenters should be admissible to this house, to every office of dignity and of influence under the crown, to the highest place in the cabinet itself, and yet should be excluded from all influence in those schools which are to be sustained by rates raised from those very Dissenters, upon whom this most offensive disqualification is to be inflicted. The schools are local, are to be supported by a local rate and not a national fund—the district, not the state, is to be taxed for their maintenance; is it not monstrous, then, that in those localities where these Dissenters constitute a majority, they should be made the object of this wanton legislative affront? You don't pursue this course in Ireland— why? Because the majority of the people are Catholic. But in the districts where local schools are to be supported with local imposts, the majority are, in many instances, Dissenters. The church, therefore, cannot insist that in right of their general tutelage of the national mind, they are entitled to the control which is given them by this bill; and I am at a loss to discover what they conceive it will profit them to exercise a power so invidious as that which they are now seeking to obtain. What have they to dread from the imaginary influence of dissent in the schools which it is proposed to establish? Let them consider the bulwarks by which the church, in reference to national instruction, is already sustained, and let them dismiss their fears of any evil effect which these schools can have on its stability. Is not Cambridge, is not Oxford theirs? In Durham have they not gained an university? Are not all the great seminaries in which the gentry of this aristocratic country are educated, in their keeping? Have they not a direct masterdom over almost every place of public instruction, where the men, who are to will the destinies of England receive the elements of instruction? Do not a vast body of the middle classes draw their first intellectual nutriment from the bosom of the church, and can you turn your eyes to any part of this great kingdom, in which you do not find the church already exercising an influence over education, which it is impossible to distrust? With these vast advantages is not the church contented, but must she needs, after having herself most reprehensibly neglected the education of the poor, when a measure is proposed to rescue the infant operative from the degradation and the depravity of ignorance, is she to come forward with her pretensions, and claim, as a matter of ecclesiastical prerogative, the instruction of the factory infants, on whom she never cast a thought away before? What has the church to dread? Has she reason to tremble at the influence of dissent among the lower classes of the manufacturing population? If in the possession of the truth, wherefore does she not manifest the security which the consciousness of its possession should inspire? If built upon a rock, why should she dread that the gates of Gehenna shall prevail against her, and as she has retained so much of the old religion (the Americans call England the old country, you should call the Catholic, the old religion), as she has retained so much of its doctrines, and prefers the title of Anglo-Catholic to any other designation, why does she not copy her great predecessor in that attribute, which a convert from your establishment, and one of the greatest ornaments of your literature, so well ascribed to her?—

"Without unspotted, innocent within,
She feared no danger, for she knew no sin."

If there be any danger which she has cause to apprehend, it is that which must result from the hostility which she will produce among all classes of Dissenters by the unjust assumption of authority, who will, beyond all question, be arrayed against her, if she has the misfortune to succeed in her unjustifiable pretensions. She will embody and array together all those sects which have now no common bond of union, and even among the Wesleyans, who are supposed to adhere to her by some sort of ligament or other, she will produce an antipathy which it is most unwise to create. I have often heard the Wesleyan Methodists made the theme of Conservative panegyric. The most distinguished Tories, especially at the eve of a general election, have been lavish in their encomiums on this powerful body: what a mistake it is to enter into a quarrel with them upon what is a mere point of punctilio with the church? Instead of trespassing upon their rights, why does not the church follow their example, and become their honourable competitor in the work of education? If it be of importance that the lower orders should cling to the church, has not the church some better expedient for the retention of its adherents than the invasion of religious freedom? Monopolies in religion are like all other monopolies—they retard improvement. It will do no harm to put the Church upon the necessity of exertion, and teach her that instead of relying on any unjust predominance, she should resort to more legitimate endeavours, to secure an honourable influence among the humbler classes of the people. It is by piety, by benevolence, by zeal, by meekness, and by humility, by the association in the primitive doctrine of primitive practice, that an influence most useful to the country and most honourable to the establishment will be extended. Let the church herself with the opportunities, incalculably great, which her affluence affords her—let her prelates—be distinguished for munificence: let them look on the noble structures which the bishops of the olden time have left as monuments of their pious disinterestedness through the length and width of all the land; let them in raising many a great moral edifice emulate that generous example; let her priests become the associates, the friends, the auxiliaries, the protectors, the consolers of the afflicted, the humble, and the poor; let them not only by their persuasiveness, allure to brighter worlds, but let them by their example "lead the way." Let religion be recommended by the practice of the church, and in the Christian assemblage of persuasive virtues let the Protestant Propaganda be found; but let not the church, from a sacerdotal passion for ascendancy, from a love of clerical predominance, thwart the great work of education, and incur the awful responsibility of becoming instrumental in the propagation of all the vices, which ignorance has spawned upon the country. At the conclusion of the very remarkable speech in which the Secretary for the Home Department introduced the measure which was so ably propounded by him, he called on us to "raise up our hearts," and to rise above all lowly prejudice in the achievement of a great moral purpose. It is to the church itself that this "*sursum corda*," this invocation, taken from the ancient ritual of Catholicism, should be addressed; he should abjure the body over which he exercises so great and natural an influence, and for which he has made great sacrifices, to ascend above every inferior consideration, and to regard the instruction of the people as paramount to every other object. The right honourable baronet has again and again protested his strong anxiety to render his measure acceptable to the great mass of the community, and to introduce such modifications as should meet all just objections. I trust that his professions may be realized, and as he told us that he would send forth his bill in the hope that it would receive the public sanction and indicate that the "waters of strife had subsided," let me be permitted to hope that he will associate with that image another incident connected with the primeval history of mankind, and bear in mind that every colour was united in distinctness without predominance, that token of peace which God set in the cloud, as a covenant of his reconciliation with the world.

IRISH ARMS BILL.

SPEECH IN THE HOUSE OF COMMONS, MAY 19, 1843

If I were convinced that the Arms Bill, even in its present most obnoxious shape, was necessary for the repression of crime, I should reluctantly indeed, but strenuously, sustain it; but of its utter inefficiency for the attainment of that legitimate purpose, in which it is obligatory upon us all to concur, I am thoroughly persuaded. It is not to the want of an Arms Bill, such as this, it is to the imperfect, I am almost justified in calling it the impotent administration of justice, that the atrocities, by which certain districts in Ireland are unfortunately characterized, are to be ascribed. In the county of Tipperary the prosecutions at the assizes are begun, conducted, and terminated in such a manner as to secure impunity to crime. How has it come to pass, that the offences which fall within the jurisdiction of the assistant-barrister, and are prosecuted by the local solicitor, have so signally diminished? I attribute that remarkable decrease to two causes; first, to the high judicial qualities, the talent, the firmness, the impartiality which has won the confidence of all parties, by which Mr. Howley, the assistant-barrister, is distinguished; and in the next place, to the signal usefulness of the local solicitor for the crown (Mr. Cahill) who unites with great ability a perfect knowledge of the country; has the best opportunities of ascertaining every incident connected with the cases in which he is concerned; is well acquainted with the character of every witness for the prosecution and the defence; never puts innocence in peril; and never permits ruffianism to escape. But while minor violations of the law are prosecuted with so much effect, what course is taken at the assizes? I beg most distinctly to state that nothing can be more remote from my intention than to speak in the language of personal depreciation of Mr. Kemmis, the crown solicitor for the Leinster circuit, or to suggest that a local solicitor should be employed in his place, without adding, that he should receive for any loss he may sustain the most ample compensation. But granting him to possess the highest professional qualifications, I have no hesitation at the same time in stating that the business of the crown cannot be efficiently carried on by a legal absentee, who knows nothing of the county, is utterly ignorant of the witnesses produced for or against the crown, is utterly unable, not from any want of capacity, but from his position, to suggest or advise the means by which truth can be substantiated, and falsehood can be confuted, is hurried from one assize town to another, and must get up his briefs with inevitable precipitation for the information of counsel, who are opposed by the most skilful advocates, aided by a local solicitor for the defence, by whom every imaginable expedient for the frustration of the crown is employed. It is obvious that, under this system, you give to crime advantages incalculably great. Another suggestion I shall, from a sense of duty—from my solicitude for the public tranquillity—venture to make. You resort to informers, and you pay them largely for their corrupt contribution to

...e enforcement of the law, but to honest witnesses adequate protection is not given. Some years ago the house of a person of the name of Crawford was attacked, and he was beaten almost to death. He was afraid to prosecute. He lived in my neighbourhood. I obtained from the government an undertaking that he and his family should be sent to one of the colonies, and should be provided for. He was prevailed on to prosecute, and justice was done, and a most useful example made. If you will pledge yourselves to protect the witnesses for the crown, by enabling them to emigrate, and by compensating them for the loss of their country, you will effect much more than by the unconstitutional proceeding which I am aware your high partisans invite you to adopt. It would be far more befitting in the landed proprietors to attend at the assizes, and perform their duty on criminal trials, than to call for a violation of a great public right. If there is a special commission got up with parade, and attended by the Attorney-General, with a retinue of counsel, the chief gentlemen of the county do not think it inconsistent with their dignity to act on the petty jury ; but at the assizes, though the crimes to be prosecuted are of the same class, the juries are wholly different. The petty jury is considered an ungenteel and low concern the balance in which human life is trembling is committed to coarser and less aristocratic sustainments, and complaints are afterwards made of the constituion of juries by the very men who vote it, what they call, in their familiar parlance, " a bore" to attend. There is nothing which I more strongly deprecate than the setting aside of juries by the crown, except for the clearest and most indisputable reasons, but, on the other hand, I do think that the attendance of Roman Catholics and Protestants, of station and influence, on the criminal jury, should be enforced; and that, if necessary, fines of £500 or £600 should be imposed upon them. The utmost care should of course be taken that the juries should not be exclusive, and that no ground for imputation should be afforded ; but that precaution being adopted, it is clear that the verdicts found by that class of men, whether of acquittal or of condemnation, would meet the general sanction. I am very well aware that the gentry of the country will be very adverse to this proposition ; but they should bear in mind how large a stake they have in the tranquillity of the country, which will be far better promoted by these means than by an Arms Bill, which will take from honest men the means of defence, and will not deprive the turbulent and the lawless of the means of aggression. When murder becomes lucrative, it is not easy to deprive the assassin of the tools of his profitable trade. If you could succeed in depriving him of his more noisy implements of death, you would but teach him to substitute a more silent but not less efficacious weapon : but you cannot frame a law which he will not readily evade. The wretch who is not appalled at murder, will not tremble at an Arms Bill —your penalties of ten or twenty pounds will be scorned by men who put existence into habitual peril. These are among my reasons for thinking that the Arms Bill will not be in any degree conducive to the purpose it has ostensibly in view, while by its enactment, without obtaining any countervailing benefit, you commit   anifest trespass upon one of the chief constitutional rights which the bill, deriving its designation from those rights, has received. But my main objection to this bill is founded upon the distinction which it establishes between England and Ireland. "Repeal the Union—restore the Heptarchy!" Thus exclaimed George Canning, and stamped on the floor of this house as he gave utterance to a comparison in absurdity, which has been often cited. But that exclamation may be turned to an account, different from that to which it is applied. Restore the heptarchy—repeal the union. Good. But take up the map of England, and mark the subdivisions into which this your noble island was once distributed, and then suppose that in this assembly of wise men—this Imperial Parliament—you were to ordain that there should be one law in what once was the kingdom of Kent, and another in what once was the kingdom of Mercia—that in Essex there should be one municipal franchise, and in Sussex there should be another; that among the East Angles there should be one parliamentary franchise, and in Wessex there should be another; and that while through the rest of the island the Bill of Rights should be regarded as the inviolate and inviolable charter of British liberty, in the kingdom of Northumberland, an Arms Bill, by which the elementary principles of British freedom should be set at nought, should be enacted—would you not say that the restoration of the heptarchy could scarcely be more preposterous? What a mockery it is, what an offence it is to our feelings, what an insult to the understanding it is to expatiate upon the advantages of the union, and bid us rejoice that we are admitted to the great imperial co-partnership in power, while you are every day making the most odious distinctions between the two countries, establishing discriminating rights which are infinitely worse than discriminating duties, and furnishing the champions of repeal with pretences more than plausible, for insisting that if for England and for Ireland different laws are requisite, for Ireland and for England different lawgivers are required. My chief, my great objection to this measure is, that it is founded upon the fatal policy to which Englishmen have so long adhered, and from which it is so difficult to detach them, of treating Ireland as a mere provincial appurtenance, instead of regarding her as part and parcel of the realm. You are influenced by a kind of instinct of domination, which it requires no ordinary effort of your reason to overcome. I do not think that by Englishmen an Arms Bill like this would be endured. That observation does not rest on mere conjecture; in the year 1819 this country was in a most perilous condition. It appeared from a report made by a secret committee of which the present Lord Derby was the chairman, that large bodies of men were trained to the use of arms in the dead of the night, in sequestered places; that revolutionary movement, to be accomplished by disciplined insurrection, was contemplated, and that revolt was organized for war. In this state of things an English Arms Bill, one of the Six Acts, was proposed. Lord Castlereagh was then leader of the House of Commons, but although he had served his apprenticeship in Ireland—although he had dissected in Ireland before he attempted to operate in England; and although his hand was peculiarly steady, and he was admitted on all hands not to be destitute of determination, still he did not think it prudent to propose for England such a bill as for Ireland you have thought it judicious to introduce. There is the English Arms Bill of 1819. It is comprised in a single page, look at it; the ocular comparison will not be inappropriate; here is the Irish Arms Bill, a whole volume of coercion, in which tyranny is elaborated in every possible diversity of form which it was possible to impart to it. In the English Arms Bill no penalty whatever was inflicted for the possession of arms: in your Arms Bill, an Irishman can be transported for seven years for having arms in his possession. But although the English Arms Bill was moderate when compared with the Irish, yet Lord Grey denounced it in the House of Lords.* In the House of Commons, Mr. Henry Brougham exclaimed: "Am I an Englishman? for I begin to doubt it, when measures so utterly abhorrent from the first principles of British liberty are audaciously propounded to us?" That great orator then proceeded to offer up an aspiration that the people would rise up in a simultaneous revolt and sweep away the government by which a great sacrilege upon the constitution had been perpetrated. What would he have said—how would Lord Castlereagh have been blasted by the lightning and appalled by the thunder of his eloquence if a bill had been brought forward, under which the blacksmiths of England should be licensed, under which the registry of arms was made dependent on a bench of capricious magisterial partisans, under which an Englishman might be transported for seven years, for exercising the privilege secured to him by the Bill of Rights; and every pistol, gun, and blunderbuss was to be put through that process of branding, the very motion of which, in 1831, made by the noble lord opposite, the Secretary for the Colonies, the then Secretary for Ireland, produced an outburst of indignation. It is said that this bill has nothing new. That is a mistake—it contains many novelties in despotism, many curiosities in domination. My friend the member for Rochdale has pointed them out. But supposing that everything was old in this bill, does not your defence rest on a perseverance in oppression, on that fatal tenacity with which you cling to a system, to which your experience should tell you that it is folly to adhere? This bill, it was observed by the noble lord the Secretary for Ireland, was found, in 1807, in the portfolio of the Whig Secretary. The Whigs had prepared a measure of coercion and of relief. The Tories turned them out on the measure of relief, and of the measure of coercion took a Conservative care. The Secretary for Ireland stated that the first Arms Bill was introduced in 1807 by Sir Arthur Wellesley. Sir Arthur Wellesley! The transition which has taken place from Sir Arthur Wellesley—from the official of Dublin Castle to the warrior, by whose fame the world is filled—is not greater than the transition of the country which gave him birth, from enslaved and degraded to enfranchised and liberated Ireland, who has grown too gigantic for your chains, and dilated to dimensions which your fetters will no longer fit. But although the project of an Arms Bill was unfortunately found in the Whig portfolio, that measure was condemned

---

* Mr. Sheil read Lord Grey's protest against one of the Six Acts in 1819.

at the time by some of the most distinguished members of that great party. Hear what Sir Samuel Romilly says of the measure in his diary. In speaking of the Insurrection Act and the Arms Bill, which he regarded as near akin, he says (vol. 6, p. 214):—

"The measure appeared to me so impolitic, so unjust, and likely to produce so much mischief, that I determined, if any person divided the house, to vote against it. I did not speak against the bill: that it would pass, whatever might be said against it, I could not doubt; and therefore thought that to state my objections against it, could have no other effect, than to increase the mischief, which I wished to prevent. What triumphant arguments will this bill, an! that which is depending in the house for preventing the people having arms, furnish the disaffected with in Ireland? What laws more tyrannical could they have to dread, if the French yoke were imposed on them? To adopt such a measure at a moment like the present, appears to me to be little short of madness. Unfortunately the measure had been in the contemplation of the late ministry. They had left a draft of the bill in the Secretary of State's office, and they were now ashamed to oppose, what some of themselves had thought of proposing. The Attorney and Solicitor of Ireland had approved of the bill, but Pigot and myself had never heard that such a matter was in agitation, till it was brought into the house, by the present ministers."

Such was the opinion of Sir Samuel Romilly: in the judgment of the majority of this house, as it is at present constituted, that opinion may have no weight, but I am able to refer to the authority of a distinguished statesman, who is at this moment in the full fruition of the confidence of parliament. That eminent person stated that—

"The speaker asked what was the melancholy fact? That scarcely one year had at any period elapsed since the Union during which Ireland was governed by the ordinary course of law; that in 1800 we found the Habeas Corpus Act suspended, and an act for the suppression of rebellion in force; that in 1801 it was continued; in 1802 it expired in 1803 disturbances occurred, and Lord Kilwarden was murdered by a savage mob; that in 1804 the act was renewed; in 1806 disorders arose, and the Insurrection Act was introduced in consequence; in 1810 and 1815 the Insurrection Act was renewed; and in 1825 an act was passed for the suppression of dangerous associations, and particularly of the Catholic Association; in 1826 the act was continued, and in 1827 it expired; and after this enumeration of acts of impolicy and injustice he asked, 'Shall this state of things continue without an effort to remedy it?'"

Who was it that spoke these words? Were they spoken by Henry Brougham? Were they spoken by Lord John Russell? No:—the man that gave utterance to these words was no less a person than the First Lord of the Treasury,* the ruler in some sort of this great and majestic empire; it was by him that the policy, with which this very measure is connected, was virtuously and vehemently denounced. The

---

* Sir R. Peel.

speech to which I have referred was spoken in 1829, before Catholic Emancipation was actually passed, it was, indeed, the speech in which the whole plan of emancipation was propounded. But if the policy, thus strenuously condemned by the Prime Minister, was deserving of censure before the great measure of Catholic enfranchisement, is it not in the highest degree incongruous, it is not indeed monstrous on the part of the government, of which that right honourable gentleman is the head, to propound the very measure which had been the object of his almost unqualified condemnation. But I shall be told that the predictions made by the Roman Catholic leaders have been falsified, and that they have themselves done their utmost to prevent the fulfilment of their prophecies. [Hear, hear.] You say "hear, hear ;" but your derisive cheering is inappropriate. If Roman Catholic Emancipation had been carried, when the Catholic clergy could have been connected by what Mr. O'Connell called a golden link, with the state, those predictions would, in all likelihood, have been fulfilled, but when you yourselves permitted emancipation to be, I will not say extorted, but won from you by the means through which it was obtained, what results would you have reasonably anticipated, but those to which you have yourselves most essentially contributed? How could you expect that 7,000,000 of your fellow-citizens could by possibility acquiesce in an institution, against which reason and justice concurrently revolt? How could it be expected that after emancipation, when England was agitated by the Reform question, Ireland should remain passive and apathetic, and should not demand a redress of those grievances, which pressed upon her far more heavily than any abuse connected with your former parliamentary system? And now, when from morn till night, and from night till morn, Englishmen cry out that the Union must be maintained, how can any one of you imagine that we shall not insist that the principles upon which the Union was founded, should be carried into effect, and that all odious distinctions between the two countries shall be abolished? You think that the repealers of Ireland are conspicuously in the wrong ; are you sure that you are yourselves conspicuously in the right? Passing over the questions connected with the Established Church, questions which are dormant, but not dead, and which I have not the slightest doubt that your impolicy will revive, I ask you, whether in the course pursued in the Municipal Bill you have evinced a just desire to place England and Ireland upon a level? Was the language employed by the noble and learned lord, who has the conscience of the Sovereign in his keeping, and which is fresh in the memory of the Irish people, calculated to reconcile us to the legislative dominion of this country? You withheld the Municipal Bill as long as with safety you could deny it to us, and when at last you were forced to yield, you still adhered to your old habit of distinction—you created a different franchise for the two countries, and although you gained nothing whatever for your party in the result, and were completely baffled, as I told you you would beyond all doubt be, you left in the Municipal Bill an envenomed sting behind. But let us turn to the other instances, in which your dispositions towards Ireland are too faithfully exemplified. Let us turn to the registration

of votes, from the registration of arms. Where is your Registration
Bill? I am putting to you the question which, three years ago, was
put again and again, to the Whig Government by their antagonists.
" Where is the Registration Bill ?" cried Mr. Baron Lefroy. " Where
is the Registration Bill ?" cried Mr. Jackson, now a judge of the
Common Pleas. " Where is the Registration Bill ?" cried Mr. Litton,
now a Master in Chancery. But more loudly and more vehemently than
all the rest. " Where, where is the Registration Bill ?" cried the noble
lord, the Secretary for the Colonies. Not a month, not a week, not a
day was to be lost in the judgment of the anxiously impatient lord.
The Whigs brought in a bill, and gave a liberal definition of the franchise; their object was to establish a constituency commensurate with
the wealth, and the intelligence, and in some degree with the numbers
of the Irish people. The measure was defeated; and the noble lord who
was possessed at the time with a passion for legislating for the Irish people. provided a bill at the close of 1841, by which the independence of
the people of Ireland would have been totally unprotected, and of which
the bare proposal has done more to advance the cause of Repeal than
all the speeches which the member for Cork* had ever delivered upon
the subject. Parliament was dissolved, a new parliament was elected,
and a Tory ministry was the result. As soon as the Tories were
fully installed in office, it was but natural to ask them the question
which they had put so often, " Where is the Registration Bill ?"
Some vague intimation was given that the government would bring
forward a measure in the course of the session. In the course of the
session the Longford committee excluded Mr. White from parliament,
but at the same time reported, that the law was so doubtful, had led to
more contrary decisions, and had been the subject of so much contention among the Irish judges, that it was incumbent on the government
to settle the question, and to bring in a declaratory act; still nothing
was done in 1842. At the commencement of the present session, the
Secretary for the Home Department was asked what he meant to do,
in reference to the Registration Bill, the eternal Registration Bill? He
answered, " Oh, we will first proceed with the English Registration
Bill." But for the English Registration Bill there was no urgent
necessity—there was no pretence whatever for giving the English precedence over the Irish measure. Well, the English Registration Bill
is brought in and passed, and then the question is renewed, " Where is
the Irish Registration Bill?" And to that question what reply was
given? Oh, we must first bring in the Irish Arms Bill. Thus, notwithstanding the reiterated demand for the Irish Registration Bill made
by the Tories themselves when out of office, notwithstanding the report
of the Longford Election Committee, notwithstanding the repeated
engagements to bring the measure forward, not only is not that measure produced, but to the Arms Bill, to this outrage upon the just principles of liberty, the bill declaratory of the parliamentary franchise of
the people of Ireland is postponed. And on what ground has this pre-

* Mr. O'Connell

.edence of the Arms Bill been maintained? wherefore is it that everything is to be postponed to an Arms Bill? The Secretary for Ireland tells us, that order must be asserted, before freedom is conferred, that crime must be repressed, and that the " thirst for Arms," that was his expression, must be repressed. The thirst for arms! There is another thirst, for which you have taken care to provide. Have you, who profess yourselves to be guardians of the national morality, manifested an uniform and undeviating solicitude for the virtue of the people over whom you are appointed to watch? Despite of every remoustrance, notwithstanding the most earnest expostulation, did you not persist in the enactment of a financial measure, which has given the strongest stimulant to crime, and has already produced some of the most deleterious effects which, it was foretold, would be inevitably derived from it. You know full well, that the most frightful crimes which have been perpetrated in Ireland, have had their origin in those habits of intoxication, which the Evangelist of Temperance, if I may so call him, had so effectually restrained, until the Chancellor of the Exchequer had determined to counteract his noble efforts. Every private still is a hot-spring, from which atrocity gushes up, and supplies those draughts of fire, with which ferocious men madden themselves to murder, and drive away every sentiment of humanity and of remorse, and surrender themselves to the demon that takes possession of their hearts. And yet you talk to us of the necessity of suppressing crime being paramount to every other consideration, and of the " thirst for arms," and deal in all that false sentimentality, with which the real purpose by which you are actuated, is so thinly and imperfectly disguised. It is not wonderful that when such is the spirit in which you legislate for Ireland, that the people of Ireland, weary of and disgusted with your unfairness and incapacity, should demand the restitution of their parliament, and insist upon the right of governing themselves. And how has the First Lord of the Treasury met the requisition for self-government, which the Irish people had preferred to him? He came down to the house with a well meditated reply to the question put to him by the noble lord (Lord Jocelyn), and referring to the answer of King William the Fourth, in which that monarch expressed himself opposed to the Repeal of the Union, stated her Majesty's coincidence with that opinion ; but omitted the conciliatory assurances with which that opinion was accompanied. I am very far from believing that the right honourable baronet, as has been imputed to him, intended by a reference to his Sovereign, to produce any refrigeration in the feelings of warm attachment which the people of Ireland entertain towards their beloved Sovereign ; I think, that as he appealed in the name of the parliament to their fears, he appealed in the name of their Sovereign to the affections of the Irish people. For my own part, as long as I shall be permitted to refer to a document which has become a part of history, I never shall object to any reference to the opinions of my Sovereign with regard to Ireland. I hold in my hand a letter written by Lord John Russell to Lord Normanby, by the command of his Sovereign. on her accession to the throne That letter is in the following words:—

"Whitehall, July 18, 1837.

"My Lord—In confiding again to your Excellency the important charge of administering the affairs of Ireland in her Majesty's name, the Queen has commanded me to express to your excellency her Majesty's entire approbation of your past conduct, and her desire that you should continue to be guided by the same principles on which you have hitherto acted.

"The Queen willingly recognises in her Irish subjects a spirit of loyalty and devotion to her person and government.

"Her Majesty is desirous to see them in the full enjoyment of that civil and political equality which, by a recent statute, they are fully entitled to, and her Majesty is persuaded that when invidious distinctions are altogether obliterated, her throne will be more secure and her people more truly united.

"The Queen has seen with satisfaction the tranquillity which has lately prevailed in Ireland, and has learned with pleasure that the general habits of the people are in a state of progressive improvement arising from their confidence in the just administration of the power of government.

"I am commanded by her Majesty to express to you her Majesty's cordial wishes for the continued success of your administration; and your Excellency may be assured that your efforts will meet with firm support from her Majesty.

"The Queen further desires that you will assure her Irish subjects of her impartial protection.

"JOHN RUSSELL."

Such was the language dictated by the young Queen of England to her minister. She had read the history of Ireland—she had perused (and in the perusal was not, I am sure, unmoved) the narrative of oppression and woe; she knew that for great wrongs a great compensation was due to us; she felt more than joy at witnessing the blessed fruits which had resulted from the first experiment in justice, and she charged her minister to express her deep solicitude for the welfare of the people of Ireland. Never did a sovereign impose upon a minister a more pleasurable office. With what admiration, with what a sentiment of respectful and reverential admiration must he have looked upon that young and imperial lady, when, in the fine morning of her life, and in the dawn of her resplendent royalty, he beheld her with the most brilliant diadem in the world glittering upon her smooth and unruffled forehead with her countenance beaming with dignified emotion, and heard her, with that voice which seems to have been given to her for the utterance of no other language than that of gentleness and of mercy, giving expression to her affectionate and lofty sympathy for an unfortunate, but a brave, a chivalrous, and for her enthusiastically loyal and unalterably devoted people. How different a spectacle does Ireland now present from that which it then presented to the contemplation of her sovereign! She cannot be insensible to the change. In return for your stern advice to your sovereign, did you not receive a reciprocal admonition; and did she not tell you, or did not your own conscience tell you to look on Ireland, and to compare her condition under a Whig and Conservative administration. But it is not with Whig policy alone that your policy should be compared; your own policy in a country more fortunate than ours furnishes almost an appropriate matter of adjuration. Why do you tell me, in the name of common consistency and plain sense, wherefore do you adopt in Canada a policy so utterly opposite from that which in Ireland it is your and our misfortune that you should pursue? From a system so diametrically opposed, how can the same results be expected to follow? In Canada, under the old colonial rule, there prevailed a strong addiction to democracy, a leaning towards the great republic in their vicinage, a deep hatred of England, and a spirit which broke at last into a sanguinary and exceedingly costly rebellion. You had the sound feeling and the sound sense to open your eyes at last to the series of mistakes, which successive governments had committed with regard to Canada; your policy was not only changed but revolutionized; you abandoned the "family compact;" you placed the government in sympathy with the people, and you raised to office men who had been pursued to the death, and conferred honours upon those to whom decapitation, had they been arrested, would at one period have been awarded. The result has been what all wise men had anticipated and what all good men had desired. In a late debate I heard the Prime Minister expatiate upon the necessity of dealing in reference to Canada, in the most liberal and conciliatory spirit, and when I heard him, I could not refrain from exclaiming: "Oh! that for Ireland, for unhappy Ireland—Oh! that for my country, he would feel as he does towards Canada, and in its regard act the same generous part!" That prayer which rose involuntarily from my lips, I now—yes, I now venture to address to you. The part which in Canada you have had the wisdom and the virtue to act, have in Ireland, (but oh! without a civil war!) have the virtue and the wisdom to follow. Rid, rid yourself in Ireland of "the family compact." Banish Orangeism from the Castle; put yourselves into contact in place of putting yourselves into collision with the people? reform the Protestant Church; conciliate the Catholic priesthood; disarm us, but not of the weapons against which this measure is directed—strip us of that triple panoply with which he who hath his quarrel just is invested—do this, and if you will do this, you will do far-more for the tranquillization of Ireland, for the consolidation of the empire, and for your own renown, than if you were by arms bills and by coercion acts, and by a whole chain of despotic enactments, to succeed in inflicting upon Ireland, that bad, that false, that deceptive, that desolate tranquillity which the history of the world, which all the philosophy that teaches by example, which the experience of every British statesman, which, above all, your own experience should teach you, is sure to be followed by calamities greater than any by which it was preceded.

VOTE BY BALLOT.

SPEECH IN THE HOUSE OF COMMONS, JUNE 21, 1843.

It is more than difficult to give freshness and originality to the subject which has been introduced with so much ability by my honourable friend,* and if it were incumbent on those who take a share in its discussion to impart to it that sort of interest which arises from speculations equally novel and refined, I should not have ventured to interpose; but so far from thinking that the ballot offers an appropriate occasion for a display of that dexterity in disputation, from which, if some entertainment, little instruction can be derived, I feel persuaded that a great and simple cause must be damaged far more than it can be promoted by any subtlety of disquisition which may be indulged in its sustainment. Where manifest abuses exist—abuses not only capable of proof, but of which the evidence amounts to demonstration, and arguments founded on undisputable facts can be so readily adduced, political metaphysics ought to be avoided. It is far wiser, in place of straining for ingenuities in favour of the ballot, to revert to those reasons which long-continued evils have long presented to us, and as it is by repeated appeals to their sense of justice, that the opinion of the people of this country is ultimately influenced, as the ballot is to be carried in the same way in which all the great changes in which we have been the witnesses have been accomplished, and as in those signal instances it was necessary again and again, and session after session, to urge the same obvious motives for the measures which were pressed with a strenuous reiteration upon the parliament and the country; so in this important discussion, the circumstance that an argument has been advanced, or a striking fact has been stated before, furnishes no just reason for not again insisting upon it. I do not, therefore, hesitate to revert in the outset, although it may have been already mentioned, to what took place in reference to the ballot when the Reform Bill was originally propounded. I attach great importance to the facts which ought to put an end to the dispute regarding what is called the finality of the Reform Bill, in reference to the question before the house. The noble lord, the member for London, has been, I think, a good deal misrepresented on this head; for some among his supporters have naturally conjectured that he regarded the Reform Bill as a monument where he should "set up his everlasting rest." But I for one never understood the noble lord to have spoken in the sense ascribed to him. I admit, that if the members of Earl Grey's government had entered into an agreement, that not only no ulterior alteration of the franchise should be ever supported by them, but that, in reference to the mode of exercising it, no change should ever be proposed, that compact, no matter how preposterous, might be plausibly relied upon, against those who were parties to it—against any further movement upon their part, it might be pleaded as an estoppel;

* Mr. Grote.

but it can be proved, by evidence beyond dispute, that as far as the ballot is concerned, no such bargain as has been imputed to the Whig government was ever thought of; the direct contrary of what has been so frequently insinuated is the truth. A committeee of five distinguished men, all of them more or less conspicuous for agitation in the cause of reform, was named by the government to draw up a plan of reform. A scheme was accordingly framed by them, and the vote by ballot formed a part of it. The measure of which the noble lord approved in 1831 cannot be of that immoral and debasing character which its antagonists have sometimes represented it to be. My more immediate purpose, however, in referring to a fact announced by the noble lord himself, is to introduce with greater effect the declaration made by the noble lord on moving to bring in the Reform Bill, in March, 1841. The report in favour of the ballot was not adopted, but it was agreed that upon the question no decision should be formed one way or the other, and that the Reform Bill should be laid before the house without prejudice to the future adoption of the ballot. This was unequivocally declared by the noble lord in his celebrated speech on moving that bill, which, on account of his great services to the cause of freedom, was so appropriately confided to him. I cannot conceive how, after such a declaration, made under such circumstances by the noble lord, in language as clear as the English tongue can supply, there can be any doubt as to the question of fact, namely, that the Reform Bill was not in any way to affect the question of ballot. But in the progress of the bill what befel? When the Chandos clause was proposed, Lord Althorp resisted it, and declared it to be contrary to the spirit of the Reform Bill, and said that it would furnish a strong argument for the ballot. Thus, it appears, that before the Reform Bill was brought forward, the ballot was proposed by certain members of the government. When the Reform Bill was brought forward there was an express reservation in favour of the right of thereafter proposing the ballot, and during the discussion of the measure the leader of the House of Commons deliberately stated that a principle had been grafted on the measure, which altered its character and afforded good grounds for demanding the ballot. Let us follow the bill to the House of Lords. Lord Grey made this most important statement:—He said that the agricultural interest had already been greatly strengthened by the Reform Bill; that the Chandos clause conferred on that interest an accession of influence which was excessive and undue, and that that clause, not originally contemplated by the ministry, would furnish strong reasons for the ballot. Well might Lord Grey have said so He had, in devising the Reform Bill, adhered to his plan of reform brought forward in 1782, and cut the counties of England into sections. This had, it is manifest, the direct tendency to augment the agricultural interest, and to strengthen the influence of individuals in the localities where their property was situated. Lord Grey, however, did not intend that tenants at will, whose subserviency is implied by their designation, should be invested with the franchise; and when he found that this vast addition was made to the local power of the landed gentry in every county in

England, he saw, with his habitual perspicacity, that the abuse of that power, thus unexpectedly augmented, would lead to a demand for that mode of exercising the franchise by which that power should be reduced to its proper limits. Lord Grey foretold that the landed interest would acquire, by the Reform Bill thus altered, an injurious power. Let us turn from the prediction to its fulfilment, and from the most illustrious prophet of the consequences of the Chandos clause, to a most distinguished witness to its effects. If an ordinary man had stated in the House of Commons that the result of the Reform Bill was, that when the opinions of a few great proprietors in the section of an English county were known, it was fortunately easy to foresee the inevitable result of the election—that statement would, from its important truth, have attracted notice; but when one of the leading members of Lord Grey's administration—when one of the men who had been most conspicuous in advocating the cause of reform in the House of Commons, and whose eloquence was only surpassed by his spirit of fearless adventure in going all lengths for its attainment—when the noble lord the member for Lancashire announced with an anomalous triumph, that the counties of England had fallen into the hands of a few nominators, and that, in fact, the spirit of the old close borough system had been extended to the chief agricultural divisions of England, no wonder that an admission made by that eminent person, who thus made an involuntary contribution to the cause of reform, from which he had seceded, should have produced a great and lasting sensation through the entire country. In his address to the electors of London, the noble lord who represents it, referred to that admission of the noble lord the member for Lancashire, and dwelt upon the state of things in the English counties, which he described. I confess that when I read the address of my noble friend, I could not help exclaiming, "Now Lord John must come round to the ballot." Perhaps I was too sanguine, but if to the ballot he has not come round, what remedy is he prepared to apply to the evil, in evidence of which he has thus cited the noble lord? What is to be done? If nothing is to be done, why was the disastrous truth set forth so conspicuously and prominently in the letter of the noble lord? Why exhibit the disease? Why disclose the foul distemper? why conceal the gangrene in the very vitals of our system, unless you are prepared to adopt the only efficient remedy for its cure? I do think that after this admission, to insist upon the fact that there exists an undue influence which it is necessary to control in this country, is almost superfluous. It has been more than once confessed by the right honourable baronet the member for Tamworth, that intimidation was carried to a most criminal extent. I recollect that in 1837 it was imputed to him that he had used coercion over his dependants at Tamworth, and that with a most honourable indignation he repudiated the charge, and demanded a retractation, which he obtained. I have heard him say in this house, and I believe him, that he abhorred intimidation. What will he do for its repression? You are anxious, honestly anxious, to put a stop to bribery; you have given proof of your honourable solicitude in this regard; and in this useful and honourable wish you have incurred the censures of men, who are more anxious to extend the church, than the morality of which the church should furnish the example. But is bribery to be corrected, and is intimidation to be left unchecked and unrestrained? The right honourable baronet observed that his party were not interested in supporting bribery. Passing by the reasons, let me ask, are his party interested in maintaining intimidation? You will answer—. No. Well, will you do something to put a stop to it? You will say, perhaps, that the ballot will not do it. Let us consider whether it will or not, and let us at the same time consider the objections in a social and moral point of view, which are urged against it. The ballot will not secure secrecy. This objection to its inefficiency as a protection, is very much at variance with the allegations of its efficacy, as an instrument of fraud. But by the ballot why should not secrecy be secured? When applied to the purposes of social life, in our clubs, and in various institutions, it gives concealment. I have inquired most particularly into the working of the ballot under Hobhouse's Act, in the parish of St. James, and I am assured that those who desire to conceal their votes can do so if they please. The majority of the householders in that parish give their open parliamentary votes for the Tory candidates, and their secret parochial vote for the Whig candidates; and I this evening presented a most important petition from that parish in favour of the ballot. Pass to other countries—France for example. It is not pretended that the ballot does not meet the object for which it was devised. It is suggested that men who voted by ballot would betray themselves by their rash disclosures; I do not think that secrets, which might well be designated " secrets of the prison-house," from the consequences to which they would lead, would be told. But landlords would act on a conjecture—I cannot think so ill of them. The open vote in defiance of a proprietor is regarded as an insult; the secret vote could hardly be construed into an affront. Under the vote by ballot men would not be stimulated to vengeance by their political associates; they would not be cheered and halloed on in the work of devastation; and I feel convinced, that under our present system, much of the cruelty that is inflicted, arises from the urgency with which men are invoked by their confederates to make examples of the wretches who dare to resist their will—to turn a whole family out upon the road upon a mere guess, would be a frightful proceeding, and one to which few would be sufficiently remorseless to resort. But, Sir, the real, the only substantial objection to the ballot, is grounded on the diminution of the influence which property ought to possess. The legitimate influence of property is one thing, and its despotism is another. I do not think that that rightful influence would be materially impaired. There is in every country, but especially in these countries, where the aristocratic principle prevails so much through all gradations of social life, a natural deference to station and authority, and a tendency in all classes to acquiesce in the wishes of those who stand in a relative superiority in their regard. A man may render himself odious by his misdeeds, and denude himself of the sway which property confers; such a man would have no weight, nor ought he to have it, over his dependants.—

A violation of the duties of property might incur a forfeiture of its rights, but I cannot bring myself to believe that a good man, who sought his own happiness in the diffusion of felicity, would not exercise over the objects of his bounty the influence with which his virtues ought to be attended. His dependants would resort to him for counsel and for guidance; his example would furnish the light by which their way would be directed, and he would himself enjoy from the consciousness of that authority—derived from minds so lofty and so pure—a far higher pleasure than he could find in the exercise of a stern and arbitrary domination. But supposing that the influence of property would be to a certain extent diminished by the ballot, are you sure that the influence of property has not been pushed so far beyond its due limits, as to endanger itself by the excess to which it has already reached? Before the Reform Bill, the nomination system was carried so far, and had created such an oligarchical interest in the state, that to save the state itself a change was indispensable. In the course of the ten years which have elapsed since the Reform Bill, how many boroughs have fallen into the hands of individual proprietors, and what formidable abuses arise from the preponderance of large properties in small divisions of intersected counties! Every day the evil will increase, and every day the demand for a redress of this signal grievance will become more loud and imperative; the feeling of the parliament, elected under peculiar circumstances, and in a moment of re-action, will be at variance with the feeling of the people; the tide, having ebbed to the lowest mark, will flow back again, and sweep away the barriers that were intended to restrain it. If something be not done by those who ought to derive a warning from the past, and beware of the influences of transitory success in producing a vain and self-deceptive exultation, do not in time adopt the measures requisite to correct abuses proved and indisputable, the next requisition for a change, which shall be made, perhaps by an excited people, will be far more formidable than that which we propose, and may lead to consequences by which the worst prognostications may be realised. One, and one only remaining objection to the ballot remains to be noticed. It is said that the morals of the people would be affected by clandestine voting—that it would conduce to the propagation of the most pernicious habits—that falsehood and dissimulation would be its natural results—men would make promises which they had no intention of keeping, and suspicion and mistrust would arise where confidence and reliance now happily prevail. I am persuaded that promises spontaneously made, flowing from a free and unbiassed volition, would be observed under the ballot as faithfully as they now are; and with regard to promises purchased from corruption or wrung from fear, they belong to that class of engagements of whose inchoate depravity the profligate performance is the infamous consummation. I am well aware that, generally speaking, citations from the writers of antiquity are little applicable to our system of government and our code of morality; the opinions of men who lived upward of two thousand years ago have little weight, but there is a passage with reference to the moral of the ballot, in a speech of the great Athenian, which I have never seen quoted, so forcible and so true, that I shall be excused for adverting to it:—

"If," says Demosthenes, in his speech on the false embassy, addressing an assembly of five hundred judges, who were to vote by ballot, "if there be any man here sufficiently unfortunate to have been betrayed into a corrupt engagement to vote against his conscience and his country, let him bear in mind that to the fulfilment of that promise he is not bound—that those with whom he has entered into that profligate undertaking will have no cognizance of its performance, but that there is a divinity above us who will take cognizance of his thoughts, and know whether he shall have fulfilled that duty to his country which is paramount to every other obligation; your vote is secret, you have nothing to apprehend, for safety is secured to you by the wisest regulation which your lawgivers ever yet laid down."

To all times and to all countries, the principle thus powerfully expressed is appropriate. A dishonourable contract is void, and to the discharge of a great trust impunity should be secured. The franchise, you often tell us, is a trust granted, but for whom? If for the proprietor of the soil, if for the benefit of the landlord, if it is in him indeed that the beneficial interest is vested, by all means let the vote be public, and let the real owner of the vote have the fullest opportunity of knowing with what fidelity the offices of servitude have been performed; but if the franchise is a trust for the benefit of the community, and if the publicity of its exercise conduces to its violation, then, in the name of common consistency, do not insist upon our adherence to that system of voting, by which the object you have, or ought to have, most of all at heart, is so manifestly counteracted, nor dwell upon the deception which may be practised through the ballot between those who make these false promises, and those who have no right to demand them, while to the fraud upon the country practised under the system of open voting you seem so reckless. I am a good deal struck with the vast importance which is attached by certain gentlemen to the public morals at one moment, and their comparative indifference at another. When the ballot is in question they exclaim, "Good God! shall we introduce into England a system of voting by which duplicity and dissimulation, and all the base results that follow from them, shall be propagated amongst us?" But let the great Conservative leader propose a measure which he himself acknowledged to be conducive to falsehood and to perjury, and most debasing in its operations, their horror of these immoralities all at once subsides, and they seek a refuge from their own consciousness of the inevitable consequences of their proceedings, in the old sophism of authority, that proverbial plea, to which power has a tendency so irrepressible, whenever it is its convenience to have recourse. But there are political as well as fiscal exigencies, and of the favourite plea of her antagonist, let freedom be permitted to avail herself. The ballot has its evils, but it is justified by necessity, and great as these evils may be, they are more than countervailed by the abuses which are incident to our existing system. I am free to acknowledge, that if the public exercise of the franchise were accompanied by that freedom, of which the noble etymology of the word gives us the intimation, I should infinitely prefer the system of open voting, which is more congenial with your habits. I own that an Englishman, who advances with a firm step and a high independent bearing to the hustings, and in the face of his country, gives his honest independent vote for the man in whose public virtue, in whose personal integrity, in whose capacity to serve the state he places an implicit confidence, and if his confidence by his vote gives the public an honourable proof, does present to me, advocate of the ballot as I am, a fine spectacle. Yes, some statesmen, for example, the hereditary proprietor of some segment of a mountain, reclaimed by the industrious man from whom it has come down to him, exempt from all tribute, and every incident of dependancy, some Cumberland statesman, whose spirit is as free and liberal as the air which he inhales, whose heart beats high with the consciousness of the high trust reposed in him, and of the moral responsibility which attaches to its performance, does present to me, in the uncontrolled and unshackled exercise of the great prerogative of the people, an object to which my admiration is promptly and sincerely given. But turn from Cumberland and its statesmen, to the mournful realities which are offered to you in the land from which I come, and look at the £10 voter who has had the fortune to pass through the registration court, and who receives from his landlord a summons to attend the hustings, and in a contest between a Liberal and a Tory candidate, to give his vote on one side, his feelings (feelings like your own), all his national predilections, all religious emotions, all his personal affections, are enlisted:— on one side he sees a man whom he has long been accustomed to regard as the deliverer of his country—whom he looks upon as the champion of his creed and of his priesthood—of the land in which he was born, and for which, if there were need, he would be prompt to die—his eye fills, and his heart grows big, and prayers break from his lips as he beholds him ; and on the other side—the side on which he is called upon to vote—he beholds some champion of that stern ascendancy by which his country had long been trodden under foot, by whom his religion had long been vilified, its ministers had long been covered with opprobrium, and the class to which he belongs had long been treated with contumely and disdain ; for such a man he is called upon, under a penalty the most fearful, with impending ruin, to give his false and miserable suffrage ; trembling, shrinking, cowering, afraid to look his friends and kinsmen in the face, he ascends the hustings as if it were the scaffold of his conscience, and, with a voice almost inarticulate with emotion, stammers out, when asked for whom he votes— not the name of him whom he loves, and prizes, and honours—but of the man whom he detests, loathes, abhors ; for him it is, it is in his favour, that he exercises the great trust, the sanctity of which requires that it should be exercised in the face of the world ; for him it is, it is in his favour, that he gives utterance to that which, to all intents and purposes, is a rank and odious falsehood ; but perhaps he resists, perhaps, under the influence of some sentiment, half-religious, half-heroic, looking martyrdom in the face, he revolts against the horrible tyranny that you would rivet on him, and he votes, wretch that he is, in conformity with the dictates of his conscience, and what he believes to be the ordinance of his religion. Alas for him! a month or two go by, and all that he has in the world is seized; the beast that gives him milk, the horse that drags his plough, the table of his scanty meal, the bed where anguish, and poverty, and oppression were sometimes forgotten—all, all are taken from him, and with Providence for his guide, but with God. I hope, for his avenger, he goes forth with his wife and children upon the world. And this, this is the system which you, and you, but I hope [...] (turning to Lord John Russell) are prepared to maintain! [...] he system under which what is called a great trust is performed [...] yes of the country; this is the system under which, by the exer- [...] the great prerogative of freemen, open and undisguised, every [...] citizen invested with the franchise should feel himself exalted! [...] upon this mockery! and if I cannot say fie upon them, what [...] say of the men who, with these things of a constant and perpetual [...] ce staring them in the face, tall. to us of the immorality of the [...] nd tell us, forsooth, that it is an un-English proceeding. [...] lish! I know the value of that expressive and powerful word. [...] the great attributes by which the people of this country are dis- [...] ed, and of the phrase which expresses the reverse of these habits, [...] appreciate the full and potent signification. Fraud is indeed [...] lish, and dissimulation, and deception, and duplicity, and double- [...] g, and promise-breaking, all, every vice akin to these vile things [...] deed un-English; but tyranny, base, abominable tyranny, is [...] English; hard-hearted persecution of poor fanatic wretches is [...] -English; crouching fear on one side, and ferocious menace and [...] ess savageness upon the other, are un-English! Of your exist- [...] stem of voting these are the consequences; and to these evils, [...] trous as they are, you owe it to your national character, to truth, [...] tice, to every consideration, political, social, religious, moral, at [...] to provide the cure. What shall it be? Public opinion! Public [...] . We have been hearing of it this long time—this many a day [...] been hearing of public opinion. In the last ten years and [...] henever the ballot has been brought forward, we have been [...] for corruption, for intimidation, for everything, public opinion [...] supply the cure—that marvellous and wonder-working principle, [...] sedative of the passions, that minister to the diseases of the mind. [...] alterative of the heart, was to extinguish cupidity, was to coerce [...] ition, allay the fears of the slave, mitigate the ferocity of the tyrant, and over all the imperfections of our nature to extend its soft and salutary sway. Well, how has it worked? Public opinion, so far as bribery is concerned, is given up; few, except the members for the University of Oxford and the University of Dublin, those amiable gentlemen, among whose virtues a peculiar indulgence for parliamentary frailties are conspicuous, would recommend that Southampton and Belfast, and the rest of the delinquent boroughs, should be consigned to public opinion. But if for bribery public opinion has lost all its sanitive operation, is it, in the name of common consistency, for intimidation, that this specific is to be reserved? Upon bribery, of the two, public opinion would have the greater influence. To bribery there is attached some sort of discredit; but intimidation is not only openly practised, but ostentatiously avowed. Men do not deny, but take pride in it; they applaud themselves, too, for the wholesome severity which they have exercised, and the salutary examples they have made. So far, indeed, is the principle of intimidation carried, that a regular theory of coercion has been established, and the great patricians of the land compress their notions of their privileges into a phrase, to lay down the dogmas of despotism in some trite saying, and, in some familiar sentence, to propound the aphorisms of domination. When these doctrines are unrecanted in language, and in conduct are unrecalled—when such doctrines are defended, vindicated, and applauded —when they are acted upon to an extent so vast that it is almost difficult to suggest where they have not been applied—how long, how much longer, are we to look to public opinion as the corrective of those evils, which, without the application of some more potent remedy, it is almost an imposture to deplore? Show me a remedy beside the ballot, and I will at once accede to it. Show me any other means by which the tenants of your estates and the retailers of your commerce, and all those whose dependence is so multifariously diversified, can be protected —show me any other means by which a few men of property, confederated in the segment of a divided county, shall be frustrated in conspiring to return your fractional county members—show me any other means by which this new scheme of nomination shall be baffled and defeated—show me any other means by which a few leading gentlemen in the vicinage of almost every agricultural borough shall be foiled in their dictation to those small tradesmen whose vote and interest are demanded in all the forms of peremptory solicitation. Show me this, and I give up the ballot. But if you cannot show me this—for the sake of your country, for the sake of your high fame; upon every motive, personal and public; from every consideration, national and individual—pause before you repudiate the means, the only means, by which the spirit of coercion now carried into a system shall be restrained, by which the enjoyment of the franchise shall be associated with the will, by which the country shall be saved from all the suffering, the affliction, and the debasement with which a general election is now attended; and without which, to a state of things most calamitous and most degrading, there is not a glimpse of hope, not a chance the most remote, that the slightest palliative will be applied

THE IRISH STATE TRIALS.

SPEECH IN THE COURT OF QUEEN'S BENCH, IN IRELAND, IN THE CASE OF THE QUEEN *v.* DANIEL O'CONNELL, JOHN O'CONNELL, AND OTHERS, IN DEFENCE OF MR. JOHN O'CONNELL.

I AM counsel for Mr. John O'Connell. The importance of this case is not susceptible of exaggeration, and I do not speak in the language of hyperbole when I say that the attention of the empire is directed to the spot in which we are assembled. How great is the trust reposed in you—how great is the task which I have undertaken to perform? Conscious of its magnitude, I have risen to address you, not unmoved, but undismayed; no—not unmoved—for at this moment how many incidents of my own political life come back upom me, when I look upon my great political benefactor, my deliverer, and my friend; but of the emotion by which I acknowledge myself to be profoundly stirred, although I will not permit myself to be subdued by it, solicitude forms no part. I have great reliance upon you—upon the ascendancy of principle over prejudice in your minds; and I am not entirely without reliance upon myself. I do not speak in the language of vain-glorious self-complacency when I say this. I know that I am surrounded by men infinitely superior to me in every forensic, and in almost every intellectual qualification. My confidence is derived, not from any overweening estimate of my own faculties, but from a thorough conviction of the innocence of my client. I know, and I appear in some sort not only as an advocate but a witness before you. I know him to be innocent of the misdeeds laid to his charge. The same blood flows through their veins—the same feelings circulate through their hearts: the son and the father are in all political regards the same, and with the father I have toiled in no dishonourable companionship for more than half my life in that great work, which it is his chief praise that it was conceived in the spirit of peace—that in the spirit of peace it was carried out—and that in the spirit of peace it was brought by him to its glorious consummation. I am acquainted with every feature of his character, with his thoughts, hopes, fears, aspirations. I have—if I may venture to say—a full cognizance of every pulsation of his heart. I know—I am sure as that I am a living man—that from the sanguinary misdeeds imputed to him, he shrinks with abhorrence. It is this persuasion—profound, impassioned—and I trust that it will prove contagious—which will sustain me in the midst of the exhaustion incidental to this lengthened trial; will enable me to overcome the illness under which I am at this moment labouring; will raise me to the height of this great argument, and lift me to a level with the lofty topics which I shall have occasion to treat in resisting a prosecution, to which in the annals of criminal jurisprudence in this country no parallel can be found. Gentlemen, the Attorney-General, in a statement of eleven or twelve hours' duration, read a long series of extracts from speeches and publications, extending over a period of nearly nine months

S

At the termination of every passage which was cited by him, he gave utterance to expressions of strong resentment against the men by whom sentiments so noxious were circulated, in language most envenomed. If, gentlemen of the jury, his anger was not simulated ; if his indignation was not merely official ; if he spoke as he felt, how does it come to pass that no single step was ever taken by him for the purpose of arresting the progress of an evil represented by him to be so calamitous? He told you that the country was traversed by incendiaries who set fire to the passions of the people ; the whole fabric of society, according to the Attorney-General, for the last nine months has been in a blaze ; wherefore then did he stand with folded arms to gaze at the conflagration ? Where were the Castle fire-engines—where was the indictment —and of *ex officio* information what had become? Is there not too much reason to think that a project was formed, or rather that a plot was concocted, to decoy the traversers, and that a connivance, amounting almost to sanction, was deliberately adopted as a part of the policy of the government, in order to betray the traversers into indiscretions of which advantage was, in due time to be taken ? I have heard it said that it was criminal to tell the people to " bide their time ;"* but is the government to " bide its time," in order to turn popular excitement to account ? The public prosecutor who gives an indirect encouragement to agitation, in order that he may afterwards more effectually fall upon it, bears some moral affinity to the informer, who provokes the crime from whose denunciation his ignominious livelihood is derived. Has the Attorney-General adopted a course worthy of his great office— worthy of the ostensible head of the Irish bar, and the representative of its intellect in the House of Commons? Is it befitting that the successor of Saurin, and of Plunket, who should " keep watch and ward" from his high station over the public safety, should descend to the performance of functions worthy only of a commissary of the French police ; and in place of being the sentinel, should become the " Artful Dodger" of the state ? But what, you may ask, could be the motive of the right honourable gentleman for pursuing the course he has adopted, and for which no explanation has been attempted by him? He could not have obtained any advantage signally serviceable to his party by prosecuting Mr. Duffy or Dr. Gray, for strong articles in their newspapers ; or by prosecuting Mr. Steele or Mr. Tierney, for attending unlawful assemblies. He did fish with lines—if I may avail myself of an illustration derived from the habits of my constituents at Dungarvan—but cast a wide and nicely constructed trammel-net, in order that by a kind of miraculous catch he might take the great agitator leviathan himself, a member of parliament —Mr. Steele, three editors of newspapers, and a pair of priests, in one stupendous haul together. But there was another object still more important to be gained. Had the Attorney-General prosecuted individuals for the use of violent language, or for attending unlawful meetings, each individual would have been held responsible for his own acts; but in a prosecution for conspiracy, which is open to every one of the objec-

* One of the songs of the *Nation* is entitled " Bide your time."

tions applicable to constructive treason, the acts and the speeches of one man are given in evidence against another, although the latter may have been at the distance of a hundred miles when the circumstances used against him as evidence, and of which he had no sort of cognizance, took place. By prosecuting Mr. O'Connell for a conspiracy, the Attorney-General treats him exactly as if he were the editor of the *Nation*, the editor of the *Freeman*, and the editor of the *Pilot*. Indeed, if five or six other editors of newspapers in the country had been joined as traversers, for every line in their newspapers Mr. O'Connell would be held responsible. There is one English gentleman, I believe, upon that jury. If a prosecution for a conspiracy were instituted against the Anti-Corn Law League in England, would he not think it very hard indeed that Mr. Cobden and Mr. Bright should be held answerable for every article in the *Chronicle*, in the *Globe*, and in the *Sun?* How large a portion of the case of the crown depends upon this implication of Mr. O'Connell with three Dublin newspapers? He is accused of conspiring with men who certainly never conspired with each other. For those who know anything of newspapers are aware that they are mercantile speculations — the property in them is held by shares—and that the very circumstance of their being engaged in the same politics alienate the proprietors from each other. They pay their addresses to the same mistress, and cordially detest each other. I remember to have heard Mr. Barnes, the celebrated editor of the *Times* newspaper, once ask Mr. Rogers what manner of man was a Mr. Tomkins? to which Mr. Rogers replied, " he was a dull dog, who read the *Morning Herald*." Let us turn for a moment from the repeal to the anti-repeal party. You would smile, I think, at the suggestion that Mr. Murray Mansfield* and Mr. Remmy Sheehan† should enter into a conspiracy together. Those gentlemen would be themselves astonished at the imputation. Suppose them to be both members of the Conservative Association; would that circumstance be sufficient to sustain, in the judgment of men of plain sense, the charge of conspiracy upon them? Gentlemen, the relation in which Mr. Duffy, Mr. Barrett, and Dr. Gray stood to the Repeal Association, is exactly the same as that in which Mr. Staunton, the proprietor of the *Weekly Register*, stood towards the Catholic Association. He was paid for his advertisements, and his newspaper contained emancipation news, and was sent to those who desired to receive it. Mr. Staunton is now a member of the Repeal Association ; he will tell you that his connexion with that body is precisely of the same character as that which existed with the celebrated body to which I have referred; he will prove to you, that over his paper Mr. O'Connell exercises no sort of control, and that all that is done by him in reference to his paper, is the result of his own free and unbiassed will. The speeches made at the Association and public meetings were reported by him in the same manner as in the other public journals ; he is not a conspirator ; the government have not treated him as such. Why? Because there were no poems in his

* The proprietor of the *Evening Packet*.
† The proprietor of the *Evening Mail*. Both high Conservatives

paper like "The Memory of the Dead,"* which although in direct opposition to the feelings of Mr. O'Connell, and which he had frequently expressed, is now used in evidence against him. Gentlemen, I have said enough to you to show how formidable is this doctrine of conspiracy —of legal conspiracy—which is so far removed from all notions of actual conspiracy, to show you further how cautious you ought to be in finding eight of your fellow-citizens guilty of that charge. The defendants are indicted for conspiracy, and for nothing else. No counts are inserted for attending unlawful assemblies. The Attorney-General wants a conviction for a conspiracy, and nothing else. He has deviated in these particulars from English usage. In indictments for a conspiracy, counts for attending unlawful assemblies are in England uniformly introduced. English juries have almost uniformly manifested an aversion to find men guilty of a conspiracy. Take Henry Hunt's case as an example. When that case was tried England was in a perilous condition. It had been proved before a secret committee of the House of Commons, of which the present Earl of Derby, the father of Lord Stanley, was the chairman, that large bodies of men were disciplined at night in the neighbourhood of Manchester, and made familiar with the use of arms. An extensive organization existed. Vast public assemblies were held, accompanied with every revolutionary incident in furtherance of a revolutionary object—yet, an English jury would not find Henry Hunt guilty of a conspiracy, but found him guilty, on the fourth count of the indictment, for attending an unlawful assembly. Some of the Chartists were not found guilty of a conspiracy, but were found guilty upon counts from which the word "conspiracy" is left out. Gentlemen, the promises of Mr. Pitt, when the Union was carried, have not been fulfilled —the prospects presented by him in his magnificent declamation have not been realized ; but, if in so many other regards we have sustained a most grievous disappointment—if English capital has not adventured here—if Englishmen have preferred sinking their fortunes in the rocks of Mexico rather than embark them in speculations connected with this fine but unfortunate country—yet, from the Union let one advantage be at all events derived: Let English feelings—let English principles— let English love of justice—let English horror of oppression—let English detestation of foul play—let English loathing of constructive crime, find its way amongst us! But, thank God, it is not to England that I am driven exclusively to refer for a salutary example of the aversion of twelve honest men to prosecutions for conspiracy. You remember the prosecution of Forbes, and of Handwich, and other Orangemen of an inferior class, under Lord Wellesley's administration;. they were guilty of a riot in the theatre, but they were charged with having entered into a great political confederacy to upset Lord Wellesley's government, and to associate him with the "exports of Ireland." The Protestant feeling of Ireland, rose—addresses were poured in from almost every district in the country, remonstrating against a proceeding which was represented as hostile to the liberties of the country, and as a great

* This song was set out at full in the indictment.

stretch of the prerogative of the crown. The jury did their duty, and refused to convict the traversers. The Irish Catholics at that time, heated by feelings of partisanship, were rash enough to wish for a conviction. Fatal mistake! A precedent would have been created, which would soon have been converted into practice against themselves. Gentlemen, we are living in times of strange political vicissitude. God forbid that I should ever live to see the time—(for I hate to see ascendancy of every kind)—God forbid that I should ever live to see the time, or that our children should ever live to see the time, when there shall be arrayed four Catholic judges at a trial at bar upon that bench, when the entire of the government bar who shall be engaged in a public prosecution shall be Roman Catholic ; and when a Catholic crown solicitor shall strike eleven Protestants from the special jury list, and leave twelve Roman Catholics in that box. I reassert it, and exclaim again, in all the sincerity of my heart, that I pray that such a spectacle never shall be exhibited in this the first criminal court in the land. I know full well the irrepressible tendency of the power to abuse. We have witnessed strange things, and strange things we may yet behold. It is the duty, the solemn duty—it is the interest, the paramount interest—of every one of us, before and above everything else, to secure the great foundations of liberty—in which we all have an equal concern—from invasion, and to guard against the creation of a precedent which may enable some future Attorney-General to convert the Queen's Bench into a star-chamber, and commit a further inroad upon the principles of the constitution. Gentlemen, it is my intention to show you that my client is not guilty of any of the conspiracies charged in the indictment; and in doing so I shall have occasion to advert to the several proceedings that have been adopted by the government, and to the evidence that has been laid before you. But before I proceed to that head of the division which I have traced out for myself, I shall show you what the object of my client really was ; I shall show you that that object was a legal one, and that it was by legal means that he endeavoured to attain it. The Attorney-General, in a speech of considerable length—but not longer than the greatness of the occasion amply justified—adverted to a great number of diversified topics, quoted the speeches of Sir Robert Peel and of Lord John Russell—adverted to the report of the secret committee of the House of Lords in 1797, and referred to the great era of Irish parliamentary independence, 1782. That he should have been so multifarious and discursive, I do not complain. In a case of this incalculable importance we should look for light wherever it can be found. I shall go somewhat farther than the year 1782 ; but do not imagine that I mean to enter into any lengthened narrative or elaborate expatiation. Long tracts of time may be swiftly traversed. I do not think that any writer has given a more accurate or more interesting account of the first struggle of Ireland for the assertion of her rights than Sir Walter Scott. He was a Tory. He was bred and born, perhaps, in some disrelish for Ireland ; but when he came amongst us, his opinions underwent a material alteration. The man who could speak of Scotland in those noble lines which were cited in the course of this trial, with so much passionate attachment, made a just allowance for those who felt for the land of their birth the same just emotion. In his life of Swift, he says, Molyneux, the friend of Locke and of liberty, published in 1698, "The case of Ireland being bound by act of parliament in England, stated," in which he showed with great force, "that the right of legislation, of which England made so oppressive a use, was neither justifiable by the plea of conquest, purchase, or precedent, and was only submitted to from incapacity of effectual resistance. The temper of the English House of Commons did not brook these remonstrances. It was unanimously voted that these bold and pernicious assertions were calculated to shake the subordination and dependance of Ireland, as united and annexed for ever to the crown of England, and the vote of the house was followed by an address to the Queen, complaining that although the woollen trade was the staple manufacture of England, over which her legislation was accustomed to watch with the utmost care, yet Ireland, which was dependant upon and protected by England, not contented with the linen manufacture, the liberty whereof was indulged to her, presumed also to apply her credit and capital to the weaving of her own wool and woollen cloths, to the great detriment of England. Not a voice was raised in the British House of Commons to contradict maxims equally impolitic and tyrannical. In acting upon these commercial restrictions, wrong was heaped upon wrong, and insult was added to injury—with this advantage on the side of the aggressors, that they could intimidate the people of Ireland into silence by raising, to drown every complaint, the cry of 'rebel,' and 'Jacobite.'" When Swift came to Ireland in 1714, he at first devoted himself to literary occupations; but at length his indignation was aroused by the monstrous wrongs which were inflicted upon his country. He was so excited by the injustice which he abhorred, that he could not forbear exclaiming to his friend Delany, "Do not the villanies of men eat into your flesh?" In 1720 he published a proposal for the use of Irish manufacture, and was charged with having endeavoured to create hostility between different classes of his Majesty's subjects, one of the charges preferred in this very indictment. At that time the judges were dependant upon the crown. They did not possess that "fixity of tenure" which is a security for their public virtue. They are now no longer, thank God, "tenants at will." They may be mistaken—they may be blinded by strong emotions—but corrupt they cannot be. The circumstance detailed in the following passage in the life of Swift could not by possibility occur in modern times. "The storm which Swift had driven was not long in bursting. It was intimated to Lord Chief Justice Whitshed by a person in great office" (this if I remember right, was the expression used by Mr. Ross, in reference to a great unknown, who sent him here), "that Swift's pamphlet was published for the purpose of setting the two kingdoms at variance; and it was recommended that the printer should be prosecuted with the uttermost rigour. Whitshed was not a person to neglect such a hint, and the arguments of government were so successful that the grand juries of the county and city presented the dean's pamphlet as a seditious, factious and virulent libel. Waters, the printer, was seized and forced to give great bail; but, upon his trial, the jury, though some pains had been bestowed in selecting them, brought him in not guilty; and it was not until they were worn out by the Lord Chief Justice, who detained them eleven hours, and sent them nine times to reconsider their verdict, that they, at length, reluctantly left the matter in his hands, by a special verdict; but the measures of Whitshed were too violent to be of service to the government; men's minds revolted against his iniquitous conduct." Sir Walter Scott then proceeds to give an account of the famous Drapier's Letters. After speaking of the first three, Sir Walter Scott says, "It was now obvious, from the temper of Ireland, that the true point of difference between the two countries might safely be brought before the public. In the Drapier's fourth letter, accordingly, Swift boldly treated of the royal prerogative, of the almost exclusive employment of natives of England in places of trust and emolument in Ireland; of the dependence of that kingdom upon England, and the power assumed, contrary to truth, reason, and justice, of binding her by the laws of a parliament in which she had no representation." And, gentlemen, is it a question too bold of me to ask, whether if Ireland have no effective representation—if the wishes and feelings of the representatives of Ireland upon Irish questions are held to be of no account —if the Irish representation is utterly merged in the English, and the minister does not, by a judicious policy, endeavour to counteract it—as he might in the opinion of many men, effectually do—is not the practical result exactly the same as if Ireland had not a single representative in parliament? Gentlemen, Swift addressed the people of Ireland upon this great topic, in language as strong as any that Daniel O'Connell has employed "The remedy," he says, "is wholly in your own hands. * * * By the laws of God, of nations, and of your country, you are, and ought to be, as free a people as your brethren in England." "This tract," says Sir Walter Scott, "pressed at once upon the real merits of the question at issue, and the alarm was instantly taken by the English government, the necessity of supporting whose domination devolved upon Carteret, who was just landed, and accordingly a proclamation was issued offering £300 reward for the discovery of the author of the Drapier's fourth letter, described as a wicked and malicious pamphlet, containing several seditious and scandalous passages, highly reflecting upon his Majesty and his ministers, and tending to alienate the affections of his good subjects in England and Ireland from each other." Sir Walter, after mentioning one or two interesting anecdotes, says— " When the bill against the printer of the Drapier's Letters was about to be presented to the grand jury, Swift addressed to that body a paper entitled ' Seasonable Advice,' exhorting them to remember the story of the Leyone mode by which the wolves were placed with the sheep on condition of parting with their shepherds and mastiffs, after which they ravaged the flock at pleasure." A few spirited verses, addressed to the citizens at large, and enforcing similar topics, are subscribed by the Drapier's initials, and are doubtless Swift's own composition, alluding the charge that I: had gone too far in leaving the discussion of

Wood's project, to treat of the alleged dependance of Ireland. He concludes in these lines—

> "If then, oppression has not quite subdued
> At once your prudence and your gratitude—
> If you yourselves conspire not your undoing—
> And don't deserve, and won't bring down your ruin.—
> If yet to virtue you have some pretence—
> If yet you are not lost to common sense,
> Assist your patriots in your own defence;
> That stupid cant, " he went too far," despise,
> And know that to be brave is to be wise;
> Think how he struggled for your liberty,
> And give him freedom while yourselves are free."

At the same time was circulated the memorable and apt quotation from Scripture, by a Quaker (I do not know, gentlemen, whether his name was Robinson, but it ought to have been)—" And the people said unto Saul, shall Jonathan die who hath wrought thy great salvation in Israel? God forbid! As the Lord liveth there shall not one hair of his head fall to the ground, for he hath wrought with God this day; so the people rescued Jonathan, and he died not." Thus admonished by verse, law, and Scripture, the grand-jury assembled. It was in vain that the Lord Chief Justice Whitshed, who had denounced the dean's former tract as seditious, and procured a verdict against the prisoner, exerted himself upon a similar occasion. The hour for intimidation was passed. Sir Walter Scott, after detailing instances of the violence of Whitshed, and describing the rest of the dean's letters, says—" Thus victoriously terminated the first grand struggle for the independence of Ireland. The eyes of the kingdom were now moved with one consent upon the man by whose unbending fortitude and pre-eminent talent this triumph was accomplished. The Drapier's head became a sign; his portrait was engraved, worn upon handkerchiefs, struck upon medals, and displayed in every possible manner as the *Liberator* of Ireland." Well might that epithet "grand," be applied to the first great struggle of the people of Ireland by that immortal Scotchman, who was himself so " grand of soul," and who of mental loftiness, as well as of the magnificence of external nature, had a perception so fine—and well might our own Grattan, who was so great and so good, in referring to his own achievement in 1782, address to the spirit of Swift and to the spirit of Molyneux his enthusiastic invocation—and may not I, in such a cause as this, without irreverence, offer up my prayer, that of the spirit by which the soul of Henry Grattan was itself inflamed, every remnant in the bosoms of my countrymen may not be extinguished. A prosecution was not instituted against the great conspirators of 1782. The English minister had been taught in the struggles between England and her colonies a lesson from adversity, that school-mistress, the only one from whom ministers ever learn anything —who charges so much blood, so much gold, and such torrents of tears, for her instructions. In reading the history of that time, and in tracing the gradual descent of England from the tone of despotic dictation to the reluctant acknowledgement of disaster, and to the ignominious confession of defeat, how many painful considerations are presented to us! If in time—if the English minister in time had listened to the eloquent warnings of Chatham, or to the still more oracular admonitions of Edmund Burke, what a world of woe would have been avoided! By some fatality, England was first demented, and then was lost. Her repentance followed her perdition. The colonies were lost; but Ireland was saved by the timely recognition of the great principle on which her independence was founded. No Attorney-General was found bold enough to prosecute Flood and Grattan for a conspiracy. With what scorn would twelve Irishmen have repudiated the presumptuous functionary by whom such an enterprise should have been attempted. Irishmen then felt that they had a country; they acted under the influence of that instinct of nationality, which, for his providential purposes, the author of nature has implanted in us. We were then a nation—we were not broken into fragments by those dissensions by which we are at once enfeebled and degraded. If we were eight millions of Protestants (and, heaven forgive me, there are moments when, looking at the wrongs done to my country, I have been betrayed into the guilty desire that we all were); but, if we were eight millions of Protestants, should we be used as we are? Should we see every office of dignity and emolument in this country filled by the natives of the sister island? Should we see the just expenditure requisite for the improvement of our country denied? Should we see the quit and crown rents of Ireland applied to the improvement of Charing-Cross, or of Windsor Castle? Should we submit to the odious distinctions between Englishmen and Irishmen introduced into almost every act of legislation? Should we bear with an Arms Bill, by which the Bill of Rights is set at nought? Should we brook the misapplication of a Poor Law? Should we allow the parliament to proceed as if we had not a voice in the legislature? Should we submit to our present inadequate representation. Should we allow a new tariff to be introduced, without giving us the slightest equivalent for the manifest loss we have sustained? And should we not peremptorily require that the Imperial Parliament should hold a periodical sessions for the transaction of Irish business in the metropolis of a powerful, and, as it then would be, an undivided country? But we are prevented by our wretched religious distinctions from co-operating for a single object, by which the honour and substantial interests of our country can be promoted. Fatal, disastrous, detestable distinctions! Detestable, because they are not only repugnant to the genuine spirit of Christianity, and substitute for the charities of religion the rancorous antipathies of sect; but because they practically reduce us to a colonial dependency, make the Union a name, substitute for a real union a tie of parchment which an event might sunder—convert a nation into an appurtenance, make us the footstool of the minister, the scorn of England, and the commiseration of the world. Ireland is the only country in Europe in which abominable distinctions between Protestant and Catholic are permitted to continue. In Germany, where Luther translated the Scriptures; in France, where Calvin wrote the Institutes; nay, in the land of the Dragonados and the St. Bartholomews; in the land from whence the forefathers of one of the judicial functionaries of this court, and the first ministerial officer of the court were barbarous driven—the mutual wrongs done by Catholic and Protestant are forgiven and forgotten, while we madmen that we are, arrayed by that fell fanaticism which, driven from every other country in Europe, has found a refuge here, precipitate ourselves upon each other in those encounters of sectarian ferocity in which our country, bleeding and lacerated, is trodden under foot. We convert the Island, that ought to be one of the most fortunate in the sea, into a receptacle of degradation and suffering; counteract the designs of Providence, and enter into a conspiracy for the frustration of the beneficent designs of God. (Great applause and clapping of hands in court for some minutes.)

CHIEF JUSTICE. —If public feeling is exhibited again in this manner, or if the proceedings of the court are again interrupted, I must order the galleries to be cleared. (Addressing Mr. Sheil)—I am sure, Mr. Sheil, you do not wish it yourself.

Mr. SHEIL.—There is nothing I deprecate more, my lord; for it is not by such means that the minds of the jury are to be convinced.

CHIEF JUSTICE.—Certainly not.

Mr. SHEIL.—I am much obliged to your lordship for interrupting me, as it has given me a few moments' rest.

CHIEF JUSTICE.—Whenever you feel exhausted, sit down and rest.

The right honourable gentleman thanked his lordship and resumed his address. It is indisputable that Ireland made a progress marvellously rapid in the career of improvement which freedom had thrown open to her; she ran so fast that England was afraid of being overtaken. Mr. Pitt and Mr. Dundas concurred in stating that no country had ever advanced with more rapidity than Ireland. Her commerce and manufactures doubled; the plough climbed to the top of the mountain, and found its way into the centre of the morass. This city grew into one of the noblest capitals of the world—wealth, and rank, and genius, and eloquence, and every intellectual accomplishment, and all the attributes by which men's minds are exalted, refined, and embellished, were gathered here. The memorials of our prosperity remain. Of that prosperity architecture has left us its magnificent attestation. This temple, dedicated to justice, stands among the witnesses, silent and solemn, of the glory of Ireland, to which I may appeal. It is seen from afar off. It rises high above the smoke and din of this populous city; be it the type of that moral elevation, over every contaminating influence, to which every man who is engaged in the sacred administration of justice ought to ascend! The penal laws were enacted by slaves and relaxed by freemen. The Protestants of Ireland had been contented to kneel to England upon the Catholic's neck. They rose to a nobler attitude, and we were permitted to get up. In 1782, the Protestants of Ireland who had acquired political rights, communicated civil privileges to their fellow-subjects. In 1793 they granted us the elective franchise—a word of illustrious etymology. There can be no doubt that the final adjustment of the Catholic question upon terms satisfactory to both parties would have been affected, and without putting the country to that process of fearful agitation through which it has passed, if the rebellion of 1798, so repeatedly and with a sincerity so unaffected denounced by Mr. O'Connell, had not marred the hopes of the country and essentially contributed to the Union. Mr. Pitt borrowed his plan of the Union from that great soldier to whom the gentry of this country are under obligations so essential. It must be acknowledged, however, that they make up by the fervour of their loyalty for the republican origin of their estates. Oliver Cromwell first devised the Union. He returned 400 members for England, 30 for Scotland, and as many for this country ; a report of the debates in that singular assembly was preserved by Thomas Burton, who kept a diary, and is stated in that book, which I hold in my hand, to have been a member of the parliaments of Oliver and Richard Cromwell, from 1656 to 1659. It was published a few years ago from a MS. in the British Museum. The members from Ireland were English soldiers, who had acquired estates in Ireland.— You would suppose that they were cordially welcomed by their English associates, for they were Englishmen, bred and born ; and they had very materially contributed to the tranquillization of Ireland. I hope I use the most delicate and least offensive term. I acknowledge that I had anticipated as much before I read the book. What was my surprise when I found that these deputies from Ireland were considered to be in some sort contaminated by the air which they had breathed in this country, and that they were most uncourteously treated by the English members. A gentleman whose name ought to have been Copley,* says " These men are foreigners." The following is the speech :—" Mr. Gewen said, it is not for the honour of the English nation for foreigners to come and have power in this nation. They are but provinces at best." Doctor Clarges says, on behalf of Ireland, page 114, " They (the Irish) were united with you, and have always had an equal right with you. He that was king of England was king of Ireland, or lord. If you give not a right to sit here, you must in justice let them have a parliament at home. How safe that will be, I question. Those that sit for them are not Irish teagues ; but faithful persons." Mr Gewen again observes—" It were better both for England and for Ireland that they had parliaments of their own. It is neither safe, just, nor honourable to admit them. Let them rather have a parliament of their own.' Mr. Antie observes—" If you speak as to the convenience in relation to England, much more is to be said why those who serve for Scotland should sit here. It is one continent, and elections are easier determined ; but Ireland differs. It is much fitter for them to have parliaments of their own. That was the old constitution. It will be difficult to change it, and dangerous for Ireland. They are under an impossibility of redress. * * * Their grievances can never be redressed. Elections can never be intermixed. Though they were but a province, there were courts of justice and parliaments as free as here. * * * I pray that they may have soon to hear their grievances in their own nation, seeing that they cannot have them heard there." Sir Thomas Stanley observes :—" I am not to speak for Ireland but for the English in Ireland. * * * * The members for Ireland and the

---

* The family name of Lord Lyndhurst.

electors are all Englishmen, who naturally claim to have votes in making laws by which they must be governed; they have fought your battles obtained and preserved your interests, designed by the famous long parliament, obtained by blood, and sought for by prayer solemnly." You may ask of me, wherefore is it I make these references? I answer, because the institutions of a country may change; the government may, in its form, undergo essential modifications; but the basis of the national character, like its language, remains the same, and to this very day there prevails in the feelings of Englishmen towards this country what I have ventured to call elsewhere—the instinct of domination. Towards the Protestants of Ireland, when the Papists were ground to powder, the very same feeling prevailed, of which we see manifestations to this hour. The question is not one between Catholic and Protestant; but is between the greater country and the smaller, which the former country endeavours to keep under an ignominious control. The Union was carried by corruption and by fear. The shrieks of the rebellion still echoed in the nation's ear. The *habeas corpus* act was suspended, and martial law had been proclaimed; the country was in a state of siege; the minister had a rod of steel for the people; and a purse of countless gold for the senator. But in the midst of that parliamentary profligacy, at which even Sir Robert Walpole would have been astonished, the genius of the country remained incorruptible—Grattan, Curran, and the rest of those famous men, whose names cast so bright a light upon this, the brightest part of our history, never for a moment yielded to a sordid or ignoble impulse. All the distinguished men of the bar were faithful to their country. Sir Jonah Barrington, in his History of the Rise and Fall of the Irish Nation, has quoted the speeches of the most eminent men of our profession; amongst which those of Mr. Goold, who argued the question of right with equal eloquence and subtlety, Mr. Joy, Mr. Plunket, Mr. Bushe, and Mr. Saurin, are conspicuous. Lord Plunket denied the right of parliament to destroy itself. Mr. Saurin appealed to the authority of Mr. Locke. The same course was taken by Mr. Bushe, whom we have lost so lately—Bushe, whom it was impossible for those by whom the noblest eloquence was justly prized, not to admire— whom it was impossible for those by whom the purest worth was justly estimated, not to reverence—and whom it was impossible for those by whom a most generous and exalted nature could be appreciated, not to love. The Attorney-General has stated that the opinions of these eminent persons, delivered at the time of the Union, ought to be held in no account. What reason did he give for not attaching any value to the authority of Mr. Saurin? He said Mr. Saurin expressed his opinions in mere debate. So that the most important principles, solemnly laid down in parliamentary debate are to be regarded as little better than mere forensic asseveration. I can now account for some speeches which I heard in the House of Commons regarding the education question. I think, however, that if such doctrines be propounded in the House of Commons itself, they would be listened to with surprise. You have heard, gentlemen, in the course of this trial, something of the morality of war, and also something of the morality of rebellion, which the right honourable gentleman was pleased to substitute as a synonyme for war ; but of the morality of parliament, I trust you will not form an estimate from the specimen presented to you by her Majesty's Attorney-General. But these opinions, Mr. Attorney-General observed, were expressed before the act of parliament was passed. Surely the truth of great principles does not depend upon an act of parliament. They are not for an age, but for all time. They are immutable and imperishable. They are immortal as the mind of man, incapable of decomposition or decay. The question before you is not whether these principles are well or ill founded, but you must take the fact of their having been inculcated into your consideration, where you have to determine the intent of the men upon whose motives you have to adjudicate. The great authority to which the traversers appeal gives them a right to a political toleration upon your part, and should induce you to think that even if they were led astray, they were led astray by the authority of men with whom surely it is no discredit to coincide. But whatever we may think of the abstract validity of the Union, you must bear in mind that Mr. O'Connell has again and again stated, that the Union being law, must, as long as it remains law, be submitted to ; and all his positions regarding the validity of the Union have no other object than the constitutional incitement of the people to adopt the most effectual means through which the law itself may be repealed or modified. The Union was a bargain and sale—as a sale it was profligate, and the bargain was a bad one—for better terms might have been obtained, and may be still obtained, if you do not become the auxiliaries of the Attorney-General. Two-thirds of the Irish Parliament were suppressed. Not a single English member was abstracted ; and there can be no doubt we stood immediately after the Union in such a relation towards the English members, that we became completely nullified in the House of Commons. But, gentlemen, one could, perhaps, be reconciled to the terms of the Union, bad as they were, if the results of the Union had been beneficial to this country. We are told by some that our manufactures and our agricultural produce has greatly augmented ; but what is the condition of the great bulk of the people of the country? which is, after all, the consideration that, with Christian statesmen, ought to weigh the most. The greatest happiness of the greatest number is a Benthamite antithesis ; but there is a great deal of Christianity condensed in it. When travellers from France, from Germany, from America arrive in this country, and contemplate the frightful spectacle presented by the misery of the people, although previously prepared by descriptions of the national misery, they stand aghast at what they see, but what they could not have imagined. Why is this? If we look at other countries and find the people in a miserable condition we attribute the fault to the government. Are we in Ireland to attribute it to the soil, to the climate, or to some evil genius who exercises a sinister influence over our destinies ? The fault, as it appears to me, is entirely in that system of policy which has been pursued by the Imperial Parliament, and for which the Union is to be condemned. Let me see, gentlemen, whether I can make out my case. I shall go through the leading facts with great celerity; but in such a case as this I should not apprehend the imputation of being wantonly prolix. Your time is, indeed, most valuable, but the interests at stake are inestimably precious; and time will be scarce noted by you when you bear in mind that the effects of your verdict will be felt when generations have passed away—when every heart that now throbs in this great assembly shall have ceased to palpitate—when the contentions by which we were once agitated shall touch us no further: and all of us, Catholic and Protestant, Whig and Tory, Radical and Repealer, and Conservative, shall have been gathered where all at last lie down in peace together. The first measures adopted by the Imperial Parliament were a continuation of martial law, and an extended suspension of the *habeas corpus* act. Mr. Pitt was honestly anxious to carry Catholic Emancipation, and to make at the same time a provision for the Roman Catholic clergy. You may—some of you may—perhaps, think that Catholic Emancipation ought never to have been carried; but if it was to be carried, how much wiser would it have been to have settled it forty-four years ago, and without putting the country through that ordeal of excitement through which the Imperial Parliament, by the procrastination of justice, forced it to pass. Mr. Pitt, by transferring the Catholic Question from the Irish to the Imperial Parliament, destroyed his own administration, and furnished a proof that, in place of being able to place Ireland under the protection of his great genius, he placed her under the control of the strong religious prejudices of the English people. Mr. Pitt returned to the first place in the ministry without, however, being able to make any stipulations for the fulfilment of his own engagements, or the realization of the policy which he felt to be indispensable for the peace of Ireland. The Roman Catholic Question was brought forward in 1805, and was lost in an Imperial House of Commons. Mr. Pitt died of the battle of Austerlitz, and was succeeded by the Whigs. They proposed a measure which the Tories, who drove them out on the "No Popery" cry, carried in 1816, and who then introduced the new doctrine, that the usefulness of public measures is to be tried far less by the principles on which they were founded, than by the parties by which they were accomplished. The expulsion of the Whigs from office in 1806, may, in your judgment, have been a fortunate proceeding; but fortunate or unfortunate, it furnishes another proof that the government of Ireland had been made over, not so much to the parliament as to the great mass of the people by whom that parliament is held under control. The Tories found in the portfolio of the Whigs two measures; a draft bill for Catholic Emancipation, which the Duke of Wellington, then Sir Arthur Wellesley, the Secretary for Ireland, flung into the fire; and an Arms Bill, to which clauses have been recently added, which even Mr. Shaw declared were "wantonly severe." You may conceive that an Arms Bill, with all its molestations, may be required; but it is beyond question that, in the year 1819, when England was on the verge of a rebellion, no such bill was ever propounded by the British ministry; and granting, for a moment, for the sake of argument, that some such bill is requisite, how scandalously must a country have been governed for almost half a century, if this outrage upon the Bill of Rights be required! Having passed the Arms Bill and the Insurrection Act, its appropriate adjunct, the Imperial Parliament proceeded to reduce the allowance to Maynooth. There is but one opinion regarding Maynooth, that it should be totally suppressed, or largely and munificently endowed, and that an education should be given to the Roman Catholic clergy, such as a body exercising such vast influence ought to receive. There are some who think that it were better that the Catholic clergy were educated in France. I do not wish to see a Gallo-Hibernian church in Ireland. Parisian manners may be acquired at the cost of Irish morality, and I own that I am too much attached to my Sovereign, and to the connexion of my country with England, to desire that conductors of French ambition, that instruments of French enterprise, that agents of French intrigue, should be located in every parochial sub-division of the country. State to an English Conservative the importance of opening a career for intellectual exertion, by holding out prizes to genius at Maynooth, and he will say it is all true; but the English government are unable to carry the measure. Why? Because the religious objections of the people of England are in the way. Another of the results of the Legislative Union, in 1810, a decade since the Union had elapsed, the country was in a miserable condition—its destitution, its degradation, were universally felt, and by none more than the Protestants of Dublin. A requisition was addressed to the High Sheriff of the city, signed by men of the greatest weight and consideration amongst us. A meeting was called; Sir James Riddle was in the chair. At that meeting Mr. O'Connell attended. He had in 1800 made his first speech against the Union, and in 1810 he came forward to denounce that measure. The speech delivered by him on that occasion was precisely similar to those numerous and most powerful harangues which have been read to you. He is represented in 1844 by her Majesty's Attorney-General as influenced by the most guilty and the most unworthy motives. The people are to be arrayed, in order that at a signal they may rise, and that a sanguinary republic should be established, of which Daniel O'Connell is to be the head. If these are the objects in 1844, what were the objects in 1810? The same arguments, the same topics of declamation, the same vehement adjurations, are employed. Gentlemen of the jury, that speech will be read to you; I entreat of you to take it into your box—to compare it with the speeches read on behalf of the crown, and by that comparison to determine the course which you ought to take when the liberty of your fellow-subject is to depend upon your judgment. I am too wearied at present to read that speech; but with the permission of the court, I will call on Mr. Ford to read it.

CHIEF JUSTICE.—Certainly.

JUDGE PERRIN.—Where did the meeting at which that speech was spoken take place?

Mr. SHEIL.—At the Royal Exchange.

Mr. Ford then read the following speech:—

"Mr. O'Connell declared that he offered himself to the meeting with unfeigned diffidence. He was unable to do justice to his feelings, on the great national subject on which they had met. He felt too much of personal anxiety to allow him to arrange in anything like order, the many topics which rushed upon his mind, now, that after ten years of silence and torpor, Irishmen again began to recollect their enslaved country. It was a melancholy period, those ten years, a period in which Ireland saw her artificers starved—her tradesmen begging—her merchants become bankrupts—her gentry banished—her nobility degraded. Within that period domestic turbulence broke from day to day into open violence and murder. Religious dissensions were aggravated and embittered. Credit and commerce were annihilated—taxation augmented in amount and in vexation. Besides the ' hangings off' of the ordinary assizes, we had been disgraced by the necessity that existed for holding two special commissions of death, and had been degraded by one rebellion—and to crown all, we were at length insulted by being told of our growing prosperity. This was not the painting of imagination—it borrowed nothing from fancy. It was, alas! the plain representation of the facts that had occurred. The picture in sober colours of the real state of his ill-fated country. There was not a man present but must be convinced that he did not exaggerate a single fact. There was not a man present but must know that more misery existed than he had described. Such being the history of the first ten years of the Union, it would not be difficult to convince any unprejudiced man that all those calamities had sprung from that measure; Ireland was favoured by Providence with a fertile soil, an excellent situation for commerce, intersected by navigable rivers, indented at every side with safe and commodious harbours, blessed with a fruitful soil, and with a vigorous, hardy, generous, and brave population: how did it happen, then, that the noble qualities of the Irish people were perverted? that the order of Providence was disturbed, and its blessings worse than neglected? The fatal cause was obvious—it was the Union. That those deplorable effects would follow from that accursed measure was prophesied. Before the Act of Union passed, it had been already proved that the trade of the country and its credit must fail as capital was drawn from it—that turbulence and violence would increase when the gentry were removed to reside in another country—that the taxes should increase in the same proportion as the people became unable to pay them! But neither the arguments nor the prophetic fears have ended with our present evils. It has also been demonstrated, that as long as the Union continues so long must our evils accumulate. The nature of that measure, and the experience of facts which we have now had, leave no doubt of the truth of what has been asserted respecting the future; but, if there be any still uncredulous, he can only be of those who will not submit their reason to authority. To such persons the authority of Mr. Foster, his Majesty's Chancellor of the Exchequer for Ireland, would probably be conclusive, and Mr. Foster has assured us that final ruin to our country must be the consequence of the Union. I will not dwell, Mr. Sheriff, on the miseries of my country; I am disgusted with the wretchedness the Union has produced, and I do not dare to trust myself with the contemplation of the accumulation of sorrow that must over whelm the land if the Union be not repealed. I beg to call the attention of the meeting to another part of the subject. The Union, Sir, was a violation of our national and inherent rights: a flagrant injustice. The representatives whom we had elected for the short period of eight years had no authority to dispose of their country for ever. It cannot be pretended that any direct or express authority to that effect was given to them, and the nature of their delegation excludes all idea of their having any such by implication. They were the servants of the nation, empowered to consult for its good; not its masters to traffic and dispose of it at their fantasy or for their profit. I deny that the nation itself had a right to barter its independence, or to commit political suicide; but when our servants destroyed our existence as a nation, they added to the baseness of assassination all the guilt of high treason. The reasoning upon which those opinions are founded is sufficiently obvious. They require no sanction from the authority of any name; neither do I pretend to give them any weight by declaring them to be conscientiously my own; but if you want authority to induce the conviction that the Union had injustice for its principle, and a crime for its basis, I appeal to that of his Majesty's present Attorney-General, Mr. Saurin, who in his place in the Irish Parliament pledged his character as a lawyer and a statesman, that the Union must be a violation of every moral principle, and that it was, a mere question of prudence whether it should not be resisted by force. I also appeal to the opinions of the late Lord High Chancellor of Ireland, Mr. George Ponsonby, of the present Solicitor-General, Mr. Bushe, and of that splendid lawyer Mr. Plunket. The Union was therefore a manifest injustice; and it continues to be unjust at this day; it was a crime, and must be still criminal, unless it shall be ludicrously stated, that crime, like wine, improves by old age, and that time mollifies injustice into innocence You may smile at the supposition, but in sober sadness you must be convinced that we daily suffer injustice; that every succeeding day adds only another sin to the catalogue of British vice; and that if the Union continues it will only make the crime hereditary and injustice perpetual. We have been robbed, my countrymen, most foully robbed, of our birthright, of our independence; may it not be permitted us mournfully to ask how this consummation of evil was perfected? For it was not in any disastrous battle that our liberties were struck down; no foreign invader had despoiled the land; we have not forfeited our country by any crimes; neither did we lose it by any domestic insurrection; no, the rebellion was completely put down before the Union was accomplished; the Irish militia and the Irish yeomanry had put it down. How, then, have we become enslaved? Alas! England, that ought to have been to us a sister and a friend—England, whom we had loved, and fought and bled for—England, whom we have protected, and whom we do protect—England, at a period when, out of 100,000 of the seamen in her service, 70,000 were Irish, England stole upon us like a thief in the night, and robbed us of the precious gem of our liberty, she stole from us 'that in which nought enriched her, but made us poor indeed.' Reflect then, my friends, on the means employed to effect this disastrous

T

measure. I do not speak of the meaner instruments of bribery and corruption. We all know that everything was put to sale—nothing profane or sacred was omitted in the union mart. Offices in the revenue, commands in the army and navy, the sacred ermine of justice, and the holy altars of God, were all profaned and polluted as the rewards of union services. By a vote in favour of the Union, ignorance, incapacity, and profligacy obtained certain promotion; and our ill-fated, but beloved country was degraded to her utmost limits before she was transfixed in slavery. But I do not intend to detain you in the contemplation of those vulgar means of parliamentary success—they are within the daily routine of official management; neither will I direct your attention to the frightful recollection of that avowed fact, which is now part of history, that the rebellion itself was fomented and encouraged in order to facilitate the Union. Even the rebellion was an accidental and a secondary cause—the real cause of the Union lay deeper, but it is quite obvious— it is to be found at once in the religious dissensions which the enemies of Ireland have created, and continued, and seek to perpetuate amongst themselves, by telling us off, and separating us into wretched sections and miserable sub-divisions; they separated the Protestant from the Catholic, and the Presbyterian from both; they revived every antiquated cause of domestic animosity, and invented new pretexts of rancour; but, above all, my countrymen, they belied and calumniated us to each other; they falsely declared that we hated each other; and they continued to repeat that assertion until we came to believe it; they succeeded in producing all the madness of party and religious distinctions; and whilst we were lost in the stupor of insanity, they plundered us of our country, and left us to recover at our leisure from the horrid delusion into which we had been so artfully conducted. Such then were the means by which the Union was effectuated. It has stripped us of commerce and wealth—it has degraded us, and deprived us not only of our station as a nation, but even of the name of our country— we are governed by foreigners—foreigners make our laws—for were the hundred members who nominally represent Ireland in what is called the Imperial Parliament—were they really our representatives, what influence could they, although unbought and unanimous, have over the 558 English and Scotch members? But what is the fact? Why, that out of the hundred, such as they are, that sit for this country, more than one-fifth know nothing of us, and are unknown to us. What, for example, do we know of Andrew Strahan, printer to the king? What ran Henry Martin, barrister-at-law, care for the rights and liberties of Irishmen? Some of us may, perhaps, for our misfortunes, have been compelled to read a verbose pamphlet of James Stevens, but who knows anything of one Crile, one Hughan, one Cackin, or of a dozen more whose names I could mention, only because I have discovered them for the purpose of speaking to you about them? What sympathy can we, in our sufferings, expect from those men? what solicitude for our interests? what are they to Ireland, or Ireland to them? No Mr. Sheriff, we are not represented; we have no effectual share in the legislation; the thing is a mere mockery; neither is the Imperial Parliament competent to legislate for us: it is too unwieldly a machine to legislate with discernment for England alone; but with respect to Ireland it has all the additional inconveniences that arise from want of interest and total ignorance. Sir, when I talk of the utter ignorance in Irish affairs of the members of the Irish Parliament, I do not exaggerate or misstate; the ministers themselves are in absolute darkness with respect to this country. I undertake to demonstrate it. Sir, they have presumed to speak of the growing prosperity of Ireland; I know them to be vile and profligate; I cannot be suspected of flattering them; yet, vile as they are, I do not believe that they could have had the audacity to insert in the speech, supposed to be spoken by his Majesty, that expression, had they known that, in fact, Ireland was in abject and increasing poverty. Sir, they were content to take their information from a pensioned Frenchman, a being styled Sir Francis D'Ivernois, who, in one of the pamphlets which it is his trade to write, has proved by excellent samples of vulgar arithmetic, that manufactures are flourishing, our commerce extending and our felicity consummate. When you detect the ministers themselves in such gross ignorance as, upon such authority, to place an insulting falsehood as it were in the mouth of our revered sovereign, what think you can be the fitness of the minor imps of legislation to make laws for Ireland? Indeed, the recent plans of taxation sufficiently evince how incompetent the present scheme of parliament is to legislate for Ireland. Had we an Irish parliament, it is impossible to conceive that they would have adopted taxes at once oppressive and unproductive; ruinous to the country, and useless to the crown. No, Sir, an Irish Parliament, acquainted with the state of the country, and individually interested to tax proper objects, would have, even in this season of distress, no difficulty in raising the necessary supplies. The loyalty and good sense of the Irish nation would aid them and we should not, as now, perceive taxation unproductive of money but abundantly fertile in discontent. There is another subject that peculiarly requires the attention of the legislature: but it is one which can be managed only by a resident and domestic parliament—it includes everything that relates to those strange and portentous disturbances which, from time to time, affright and desolate the fairest districts of the island. It is a delicate difficult subject, and one that would require the most minute knowledge of the causes that produce those disturbances and would demand all the attention and care of men, whose individual safety was connected with the discovery of a proper remedy. I do not wish to calculate the extent of evil that may be dreaded from the outrages I allude to, if our country shall continue in the hands of foreign empirics and pretenders; but it is clear to a demonstration that no man can be attached to his King and country who does not avow the necessity of submitting the control of this political evil to the only competent tribunal—an Irish Parliament. The ills of this awful moment are confined to our domestic complaints and calamities. The great enemy of the liberty of the world extends his influence and his power from the Frozen Ocean to the Straits of Gibraltar. He threatens us with invasion from the thousand ports of his vast empire; how is it possible to resist him with an impoverished, divided, and dispirited empire? If then you are loyal to your excellent Monarch—if you are attached to the last relic of political freedom, can you hesitate to join in endeavouring to procure the remedy for all your calamities—the sure protection against all the threats of your enemy—the repeal of the Union. Yes, restore to Irishmen their country, and you may defy the invader's force; give back to Ireland her hardy and brave population, and you have nothing to dread from foreign power. It is useless to detain the meeting longer, in detailing the miseries that the Union has produced, or in pointing out the necessity that exists for its repeal. I have never met any man who did not deplore this fatal measure which had despoiled his country; nor do I believe there is a single individual in the island who could be found even to pretend approbation of that measure. I would be glad to see the face of the man, or rather of the beast, who could dare to say he thought the Union wise or good—for the being who could say so must be devoid of all the feelings that distinguish humanity. With the knowledge that such were the sentiments of the universal Irish nation, how does it happen that the Union has lasted for ten years? The solution of the question is easy—the Union continued only because we despaired of its repeal. Upon this despair alone has it continued—yet what could be more absurd than such despair? If the Irish sentiment be but once known—if the voice of six millions be raised from Cape Clear to the Giant's Causeway—if the men most remarkable for their loyalty to their King and attachment to constitutional liberty will come forward as the leaders of the public voice, the nation would, in an hour, grow too great for the chains that now shackle you, and the Union must be repealed without commotion and without difficulty. Let the most timid amongst us compare the present probability of repealing the Union with the prospect that in the year 1795 existed of that measure being ever brought about. Who in 1795 thought an Union possible? Pitt dared to attempt it, and he succeeded; it only requires the resolution to attempt its repeal; in fact, it requires only to entertain the hope of repealing it, to make it impossible that the Union should continue; but that pleasing hope could never exist, whilst the infernal dissensions on the score of religion were kept up. The Protestant alone could not expect to liberate his country—the Roman Catholic alone could not do it—neither could the Presbyterian—but amalgamate the three into the Irishman, and the Union is repealed. Learn discretion from your enemies—they have crushed your country by fomenting religious discord, serve her by abandoning it for ever. Let each man give up his share of the mischief; let each man forsake every feeling of rancour; I say not this to barter with you, my countrymen. I require no equivalent from you; whatever course you shall take, my mind is fixed. I trample under foot the Catholic claims, if they can interfere with the repeal; I abandon all wish for emancipation, if it delays the repeal. Nay, were Mr. Percival to-morrow to offer me the repeal of the Union upon the terms of re-enacting the penal code, I declare from my heart, and in the presence of my God, that I would most cheerfully embrace his offer. Let us then, my beloved countrymen, sacrifice our wicked and groundless animosities on the altar of our country; let that spirit, which heretofore emanating from Dungannon spread all over the island, and gave light and liberty to the land, be again cherished amongst us—let us rally round the standard of old Ireland, and we shall easily procure that greatest of political blessings, an Irish King, an Irish House of Lords, and an Irish House of Commons."

Mr. SHEIL then continued.—Gentlemen, you have heard that speech read from beginning to end, because that speech conveys the same sentiments, the same feelings, and inculcates the same great principles, almost in the very same language, as we find employed by Mr. O'Connell in 1843 and 1844. That long series of speeches and of writings produced by Mr. O'Connell within the last nine months, are no more than an expansion of the speech of 1810. Was he a conspirator in 1810? If so, he was engaged in a conspiracy with Sir Robert Shaw, who took the chair when the high sheriff left it, and declared that it was the boast of his life that he had opposed the Union, and that he persevered in the same sentiments; and will a man in 1844 be accounted guilty of a crime verging on treason, because he has repeated the opinions which he entertained when the shade of an imputation did not rest upon him? This is a consideration to which, I am sure, you will think that too much importance cannot be attached. At that aggregate meeting, including so large a portion of the Protestant inhabitants of this town, with the high sheriff of the Dublin corporation in the chair, a series of resolutions were passed against the Union. It was determined that petitions should be presented to parliament, and that they should be intrusted to Sir Robert Shaw and to Mr. Grattan. Sir Robert Shaw, in his answer, stated that he had opposed the Union in parliament, and that his opinions were unaltered. The following is the answer of Mr. Grattan, and that answer affords a proof of the falsehood of an allegation often made, that a great change of opinion had taken place in the mind of that illustrious man with respect to the Legislative Union:

" Gentlemen—I have the honour to receive an address presented by your committee, and an expression of their wishes that I should present certain petitions and support the repeal of an act entitled the Act of Union; and your committee adds, that it speaks with the authority of my constituency, the freemen and freeholders of the city of Dublin. I beg to assure your committee, and through them my much-beloved and much-respected constituents, that I shall accede to their proposition. I shall present their petitions, and shall support the Repeal of the Act of Union with that decided attachment to our connexion with Great Britain, and to that harmony between the two countries, without which the connexion cannot last. I do not impair either, as I apprehend, when I assure you I shall support the Repeal of the Act of Union. You will please to observe that a proposition of that sort, in parliament, to be either prudent or possible, must wait till it is called for and backed by the nation. When proposed I shall then—as at all times I hope I shall—prove myself an Irishman, and that Irishman whose first and last passion was his native country." " HENRY GRATTAN."

"Backed by the nation." Mark that phrase. It occurs again and again in the speeches of Mr. O'Connell. Mr. O'Connell again and again declares that unless backed by the nation nothing can be accomplished by him. And if it be a crime to apply all the resources of his intellect, with an indefatigable energy, and an indomitable perseverance to the attainment of that object by the means described by Mr. Grattan in the phrase, " backed by the nation," then is the son of Daniel O'Connell guilty. It will be strange, indeed, if in the opinion of twelve men of plain sense and of sound feeling, it should be deemed a crime to seek the attainment of repeal by the only instrumentality by which Mr. Grattan said it could be effected. What is the meaning of " backed by the nation?" What is the nation? We say, the Irish Catholics, the enormous majority of the people, are the nation You say the Irish Protestants, who have the property of the country, who are in the exclusive enjoyment of great intellectual advantages, and who are united, organised, and determined, are the Irish nation. The Irish Catholics and the Irish Protestants are both in the wrong. Neither constitute the Irish nation. Both do; and it was the sustainment of both that Mr. Grattan considered to be indispensable to make the proposition in parliament either prudent or possible. That just object— the combination of all classes and of all parties in this country—Mr. O'Connell has laboured to attain. You may think that he has laboured, and will labour in vain, to attain it; but you cannot consider it criminal to toil for its accomplishment; and if you conceive that this was his object and the object of his son—or if you have a reasonable doubt upon the subject, you are bound to acquit him. In 1812 Mr. Percival lost his life, and efforts were made to construct a cabinet favourable to emancipation; the project failed, and a state prosecution against the Catholic Board was resolved on. Mr. Burrowes was the counsel for the defendants, and at the outset of his speech he boldly adverted to the fact that not a single Roman Catholic was upon the jury. He said—" I confess, gentlemen, I was astonished to find that no Roman Catholic was suffered to enter the box, when it is well known that they equal, if not exceed, Protestant persons upon other occasions; and when the question relates to privileges of which they claim a participation, and you possess a monopoly. I was astonished to see twenty-two Protestant persons, of the highest respectability, set aside by the arbitrary veto of the crown, without any alleged insufficiency, upon the sole demerit of suspected liberality. I was astonished to find a juror pressed into that box who did not deny that he was a sworn Orangeman, and another who was about to admit, until he was silenced, that he had prejudged the cause. Those occurrences, at the first aspect of them, filled me with unqualified despair. I do not say that the crown lawyers have had any concern in this revolting process, but I will say that they ought to have interfered in counteracting a selection which has insulted some of the most loyal men of this city, and must disparage any verdict which may be thus procured. But, gentlemen, upon a nearer view of the subject, I relinquish the despair by which I was actuated. I rest my hopes upon your known integrity, your deep interest in the welfare of the country, and the very disgust which yourselves must feel at the manner and motive of your array. You did not press forward into that jury box—you did not seek the exclusion, the total exclusion of any Roman Catholic—you, no doubt, would anxiously desire an intermixture of some of those enlightened Roman Catholics whom the Attorney-General declared he was certain he could convince, but whom he has not ventured to address in that box. The painful responsibility cast upon you is not of your own wishing, and I persuade myself you will, on due reflection, feel more indisposed to those who court and influence your prejudices, and would involve you in an act of deep responsibility, without that fair intermixture of opposite feelings and interest, which, by inviting discussion, and balancing affections, would promise a moderate and respected decision, than towards me, who openly attack your prejudices, and strive to arm your consciences against them. You know as well as I do that prejudice is a deadly enemy to fair investigation—that it has neither eyes nor ears for justice—that it hears and sees everything on one side—that to refute it is to exasperate it; and that, when it predominates, accusation is received as evidence, and calumny produces conviction." It might at first appear likely that a Protestant jury would take an address so bold in bad part; but they gave Mr. Burrowes credit for his manly frankness, and they acquitted the traversers. The crown resorted to a second prosecution; means more effectual were adopted, and a conviction was obtained. Mr. Saurin did not deny that the Roman Catholics had been excluded.—He was of opinion that Protestant ascendancy should every where prevail, and not least in those public tribunals which are armed with so much authority, and exercise so much influence over the fortunes of the state. I did not blame Mr. Saurin. He acted, in all likelihood, conscientiously, and whatever were his faults, duplicity was certainly not amongst the number. I saw him in the height of his power and in his fall; he was meek in his prosperity, and in his adverse fortune he was serene. The lustre of adversity shone in his smile; for his faults, such as they were, his name, in an almost inevitable inheritance of antipathy, furnishes an excuse. How much more commendable was his conduct and the conduct of the government of the day, than if they had been profuse of professions they never meant to realize, and had offered an insult to the understanding as well as a gross wrong to the rights of the Irish people; and yet I shall not be surprised if, notwithstanding all that has happened, the same cant of impartiality shall be persevered in, and that we shall hear the same protestations of solicitude to make no distinction between Catholics and Protestants in all departments, but more especially in the administration of the law. The screen falls—" the little French milliner" is disclosed—" by all that is horrible, Lady Teazle ;" yet Joseph preserves his self-possession, and deals in sentiment to the last. But if, after all that has befallen, my Lord Eliot shall continue to deal in sentimentality in the House of Commons, the exclamation of Sir Peter Teazle, " Oh, damn your sentiment!" will break in upon him on every side. The government, as I told you, in 1812, succeeded in their state prosecution. What good for the country was effected by it? Was the

Catholic question put down, or did a verdict facilitate the government
of Mr. Peel, who was soon after appointed Secretary for Ireland. He
was an Irish member. You are surprised at the intimation. He was
returned for the borough of Cashel, where a very small, but a very discriminating constituency, were made sensible of his surpassing merits
It has been remarked that young statesmen who are destined to operate
upon England, are first sent to dissect in this country. Mr. Peel had a
fine head and admirable instruments, and he certainly gave proof that he
would give the least possible pain in any amputations which he might
afterwards have to perform. He was decorus—he avoided the language of wanton insult—endeavoured to give us the advantages of a
mild despotism, and "dwelt in decencies for ever." Yet was his Irish
government, and he must have felt it, an utter failure—he must have
seen, even then, the irresistible arguments in favour of Catholic Eman
cipation; but he had not the moral intrepidity to break from his party
and to do at once what he was compelled to do afterwards. The Insurrection Act was renewed, the disturbances of the country were not
diminished, and Ireland continued to reap the bitter fruits of imperial
legislation. A new policy was tried after Mr. Peel had proceeded to
England, and the notable expedient was adopted of counteracting the
Secretary with the Lord Lieutenant, and the Lord Lieutenant with the
Secretary. We had Grant against Talbot, and Wellesley against Goul
burn. It is almost unnecessary to say, that a government carried on
upon such a principle was incapable of good. The Roman Catholics of
Ireland had been led from time to time to entertain the hope that something
would be done for their relief. Their eyes were opened at last by the
disingenuous dealing of George IV., who only smothered his laughter
with the handkerchief with which he affected to dry his eyes; and Danie.
O'Connell, feeling that liberty could never be achieved by going through
the miserable routine of supplication, founded the celebrated society, by
which results so great were almost immediately produced—the Catholic
Association was created by him. He constructed a gigantic engine by
which public opinion was to be worked—he formed with singular skill
the smallest wheels of his complicated machinery, and he put it into
motion by that continuous current of eloquence which gushed with an
abundance so astonishing, as if from a hot well, from his soul. A vast
organization of the Catholic millions was accomplished; the Catholic
aristocracy—the middle classes—the entire of the clergy were enrolled
in this celebrated confederacy. The government became alarmed, and
in 1825 a bill was brought in for the suppression of this famous league.
Mr. O'Connell proceeded to London and tendered the most extensive
concessions to the government. An offer was made to associate the
Catholic Church with the state. If the Catholic question had been
adjusted in 1825, and upon the terms proposed, it is obvious that the
fearful agitation that disturbed the country during the four succeeding
years would have been avoided. Not only were the offers rejected, but
the bill for the suppression of the Catholic Association was carried. It
was, however, laughed to scorn, and proved utterly inoperative. The
energy of Mr. O'Connell now redoubled. The peasantry were taught to

feel that the elective franchise was not a trust vested in the tenant for the benefit of the landlord. A great agrarian revolt took place, accompanied, beyond all doubt, with great evils, for which, however, those by whom justice was so long delayed, are to be held responsible; the Beresfords were overthrown in Waterford; in Louth the Foresters received a mortal blow; and at length the great Clare election gave demonstration of a moral power, whose existence had scarcely been conjectured. I remember to have seen the late Lord Fitzgerald—an accomplished and enlightened man—looking with astonishment at the vast and living mass which he beheld from a window of a room in the court-house where that extraordinary contest was carried on. There was sixty thousand men beneath him—sober, silent, fierce. He saw that something far more important than his return to parliament was at stake.— Catholic Emancipation was accomplished; and here I shall put two questions. The first is this—Do you think that up to the 13th of April, 1829, the day on which the royal assent was given to the Catholic Relief Bill, the system of government instituted and carried on, under the auspices of an Imperial Parliament, was so wise, so just, so salutary, so fraught with advantages to this country—so conducive to its tranquillization and to the development of its vast resources—that for nine-and-twenty years the Union ought to have been regarded as a great legislative blessing to this country? The second question I shall put to you is this—Does it not occur to you that if the present indictment for a conspiracy can be sustained, an indictment for a conspiracy might have been just as reasonably preferred against the men who had associated themselves for the attainment of Catholic Emancipation? There is not a count in this indictment which, by the substitution of "Catholic Emancipation" for "Repeal," might not have been made applicable to the great struggle of the Irish Catholics in 1828 and 1829. Money was collected by the Catholic Association. In America, and more especially in Canada, strong sympathy for Catholic Ireland was expressed. In the Chamber of Deputies, M. Chateaubriand adverted to the state of Ireland in the language of minacious intimation. Enormous assemblages were held in the south of Ireland, but more especially in the county of Kilkenny. Speeches were delivered by Mr. O'Connell and by others, fully as inflammatory as any which have been read to you. What would have been thought of an indictment for a conspiracy against Mr. O'Connell, against the *Evening Post*, the *Freeman's Journal*, the *Morning Register*, Dr. Doyle, and my friend, Tom Steele who was at that time, as he is now, a knight-errant animated by noble chivalry against oppression in every form? Would it not have been deemed a monstrous thing to have read a very exciting article in three Roman Catholic newspapers, against the men by whom perhaps they never had been perused? Such a thing was never thought of There were, indeed, prosecutions. The individual who now addresses you was prosecuted for a speech on the expedition of Wolfe Tone. The bills were found; but Mr. Canning declared in the cabinet that there was not a single line in the speech, which, if spoken in the House of Commons, would have justified a call for order, and he denounced the prosecution as utterly unjust. The prosecution was accordingly abandoned. But, gentlemen, if I had been prosecuted for a conspiracy, and held responsible, not for my own speeches, but for those of others, in how different and how helpless a position should I have been placed? Have a care how you make a precedent in favour of such an indictment. During the last nine months, the Attorney-General had ample opportunities, if his own statement be well founded, of instituting prosecutions against individuals for what they themselves had written or done. In this proceeding, whose tardiness indicates its intent, you will not I feel confident, become its auxiliaries. A Coercion Bill, if the repeal of the Union is to be put down, would be preferable, for it operates as a temporary suspension of liberty, but the effects of a verdict are permanently deleterious. The doctrine of conspiracy may be applied to every combination of every kind. It is directed against the Repeal Association to-day; it may be levelled against the Corn Law League to-morrow. In one word, every political society, no matter how diversified their objects, or how different their constitution, is within its reach. The Catholic question having been considered, the Tories were put out by a conspiracy formed amongst themselves. The Whigs come in and the Reform Bill is carried—how? A hundred and fifty thousand men assemble at Birmingham, and threaten to advance on London; a resolution not to pay taxes is passed, and applauded by Lord Fitzwilliam. Lord John Russell and Lord Althorpe became the correspondents of the Birmingham Union. Cumber is reduced to ashes; Bristol is on fire; the peers resist, and the Whig cabinet with one voice exclaims, "Swamp the House of Lords!" And who are the men—the bold, audacious men—conspirators, indeed!—who embarked in an enterprise so fearful, and which could be only accomplished by such fearful means? You will answer, Lord Grey. Yes. Lord John Russell? To be sure. Lord Althorpe? No doubt about it. But is our list exhausted? Do you remember Mr. Hatchell asking Mr. Ross, "Pray, Mr. Ross, have you any acquaintance with Sir James Graham?" It is not wonderful that the Attorney-General should have started up and thrown his buckler over the Secretary of the Home Department. Sir James Graham has Ireland under his control. From the Home Office this prosecution directly emanates. Gamblers denounce dice—drunkards denounce debauch—against immoralities let wenchers rail. When Graham indicts for agitation his change of opinion may, for aught I know, be serious, nor have I from motives of partizanship the slightest desire, especially behind his back, to assail him; I will even go so far as to admit that his conversion may have been disinterested; but I do say that he is, of all men, the last under whose auspices a prosecution of this character ought to be carried on. The Reform Bill becomes the law of the land—the parliament is dissolved, and a new parliament is summoned and called together under the Reform Bill—and the very first measure adopted in that reform parliament is a Coercion Bill for Ireland. The Attorney-General read a speech of Lord John Russell's in favour of coercion. He omitted to read the numerous speeches subsequently made by that noble person, in which his mistake with respect to

Ireland is honourably confessed. Gentlemen, I shall not go through the events of the last ten years in detail. It is sufficient to point out to you the various questions by which this unfortunate country has been successively convulsed. The Church Question. The Tithe Question. The Municipal Bill. The Registration Bill. These questions, with their diversified ramifications, have not left us one moment's rest. Cabinets have been destroyed by them. The great parties in the state have fought for them. Ireland has supplied the fatal field for the encounter of contending parties. No single measure for the substantial and permanent amelioration of the country has been adopted; and here we are, at the opening of a new session of parliament, with a poor-rate on our estates, a depreciating tariff in our markets, and a state prosecution in her Majesty's Court of Queen's Bench. Such, gentlemen, are the results of the system of policy adopted in that Imperial Parliament whose wisdom and whose beneficence have been made the theme for such lavish panegyric. Gentlemen, I do not know your political opinions. I do not know that there is any one man among you favourable to the Repeal of the Union; but if every one of you are fearful of that measure becoming ultimately the occasion of a dismemberment of the empire, still its discussion may not be useless. If the councils of the state were governed by no other considerations than those which are founded upon obvious justice; or if measures were to be carried by syllogisms, and government was a mere matter of dialectics, then all great assemblages of the people should, of course, be deprecated, and every exciting adjuration addressed to the passions of the people should be strenuously reproved. But it is not by ratiocination that a redress of grievances can be obtained. The agitator must sometimes follow the example of the diplomatist, who asks for what is impossible, in order that what is possible may be obtained. It must strike the least observant that when the government complains most vehemently of demagogue audacity, their resentment is the precursor of their concessions. Take, as an example, the landlord and tenant commission, which there are some conservatives who think will disturb the foundations of property, and against which Lord Brougham addressed his admonitory deprecation to Sir Robert Peel. For my own part, I think it may lead to results greater than were contemplated; for it appears to me to have been chiefly intended as a means of diverting public attention from the consideration of the other great grievances of the country.* The main source of all these grievances, I am convinced, is to be found in the colonial policy pursued with regard to this country. The Union never has been carried into effect. If it had, Ireland would not be a miserable dependant in the great imperial family. The Attorney-General expressed great indignation at the motto at Mullaghmast—" Nine millions of people cannot be dragged at the tail of any nation on earth " That sentiment is taken from a paragraph in the *Morning Chronicle* newspaper, and I have no hesita-

---

* The apprehensions of the Conservatives and the expectations of the right honourable gentleman are both set at rest by the appearance of the Report of the Commission.—ED.

ion in saying that I at once adopt it. To mere numbers, without intelligence, organization, or public spirit, I for one attach no value. But a great development of the moral powers of Ireland has taken place. Instruction is universally diffused. The elements of literature, through which political sentiment is indirectly circulated, are taught by the state. Ireland has, if I may so speak, undergone a species of transformation. By one who had seen her half a century ago, she would be scarcely recognized. The simultaneous, the miraculous abandonment of those habits to which Irishmen were once fatally addicted, at the exhortation of an humble friar, is a strong indication of what might be done by a good government with so fine a people. Without saying that the temperance movement affords a proof of the facility with which the national enthusiasm can be organised and directed, I think it is one among the many circumstances which should induce us to think that we have come to such a pass in this country that some great measures for its security and for its happiness are required. I perceive the great literary organ of the Whig party has recently suggested many bold measures, which it represents as necessary for Ireland. There are numerous difficulties connected with some of the propositions to which I refer; but there is one which I consider to be as practicable as it is plain and just. It is recommended that the Imperial parliament should sit at certain intervals in this great city.* I cannot see any sound objection in the Imperial Parliament assembling in the month of October, for the discharge of Irish business alone, and that all imperial questions should be reserved until the London session commenced, as it now does in the month of February. The public departments, it is true, are all located in London; but during the Irish session a reference to those departments would not be required. Such a session might be inconvenient to English members; but the Repeal agitation and a state prosecution, like the present, are attended with inconveniences far greater than any which English members in crossing the Irish Channel would encounter. The advantages which would accrue from the realization of this project are of no ordinary kind. The intercourse of the two countries would be augmented to a great extent—their feelings would be identified—national prejudices would be reciprocally laid aside. An English domestication would take place.. Instead of lending money upon Irish mortgages, Englishmen would buy lands in Ireland and live upon them. The absentee drain would be diminished. The value of property would be very nearly doubled. Great public works would be undertaken; and the natural endowments of the country would be turned to account. This city would appear in renovated splendour. Your streets would be shaken by the roll of the gorgeous equipages in which the first nobles of the country would be borne to the senate house, from which the money changers should be driven. The mansions of the aristocracy would blaze with that useful luxury which ministers to the gratification of the affluent, and to the employment and

---

* This proposition was made in the Dublin Corporation by Dr. Maunsell, a Conservative gentleman of considerable acquirements, but the learned doctor's motion was left unseconded.—ED.

the comforts of the poor. The Sovereign herself would not deem the sea of her parliament unworthy of her residence. The frippery of the viceregal court would be swept away. We should look upon royalty tself, and not upon the tinsel image; we should behold the Queen of England, of Ireland, and of Scotland in all the pomp of her imperial regality, with a diadem—the finest diadem in the world—glittering upon her brow, while her countenance beamed with the expression of that sentiment which becomes the throned monarch better than the crown. We should see her accompanied by the prince of whom it is the highest praise to say that he has proved himself to be not unworthy of her. We should see her encompassed by all the circumstances that associate endearment with respect. We should not only behold the Queen, but the mother and the wife, and see her from the highest station, on which a human being could be placed, presenting to her subjects the finest model of every conjugal and maternal virtue. I am not speaking in the language of a factitious enthusiasm when I speak thus. I am sure that this project is not only feasible but easy. If the people of this country were to combine in demanding it, a demand so just and reasonable could not be long refused. It is not subject to any one of the objections which attach to the Repeal Question. No rupture of the two parliaments—no dismemberment of the empire is to be apprehended. Let Irishmen unite in putting forth a requisition for a purpose which the minister would not only find expedient, but inevitable. But if you, gentlemen, shall not only not assist in an undertaking so reasonable and so safe, but shall assist the Attorney-General in crushing the men whc have had the boldness to complain of the grievances of their country, you will lay Ireland prostrate. Every effort for her amelioration will be idle. Every remonstrance will not only be treated with disregard, but with disdain; and, for the next twenty years, we may as well relinquish every hope for our country. Gentlemen, you may strike agitation dumb —you may make millions of mutes; but beware of that dreary silence, whose gloomy taciturnity is only significant of the determination of its fearful purpose. Beware of producing a state of things which may eventuate in those incidents of horror which every good man will pray God to avert, and which will be lamented by those who contribute to their occurrence, when repentance, like that of those who are for ever doomed, shall be unavailing, and contrition shall be in vain. Gentlemen of the jury, I do not deny that strong speeches have been made by my client, and by the rest of the traversers; but I do deny that those speeches, when taken altogether, bear the interpretation put upon them. To this subject I shall revert. At present I entreat you to consider whether the speeches of Mr. John O'Connell are of a more exciting and inflammatory character than those which are spoken in almost every popular assembly, whether it be Whig, Radical, or Conservative. Mr John O'Connell proposed the health of the Queen in language of enthu siastic loyalty at Mullaghmast, and added that the speech delivered by the Queen was the speech of the ministers, and could not be justly considered as the emanation of her own unbiassed mind. This is, beyond all question, constitutional doctrine; although the Attorney-General took a most especial care not to mention this; indeed he made an ultraforensic endeavour to convey to you the impression that the traversers had spoken of her Majesty in the language of personal disrespect. He was hurried away so far by an unfortunate impetuosity as to start up during the trial and say that her Majesty had been spoken of as a fishwoman. For this most gross misrepresentation there is not the slightest shadow of foundation. In every speech in which any allusion to the Queen was made, the most profound deference was expressed for the Sovereign, who enjoys the unaltered and unalterable confidence of her Irish people. Mr. John O'Connell may have used strong expressions, but he is not indicted for them. He is indicted for a conspiracy, and for nothing else And even if he were indicted for these strong expressions, in the uniform habit of Englishmen in their public discussions, he would find a justification. You, probably, have read some of the speeches made at the meetings of the Anti-Corn Law League. They were fully as violent as the Repeal harangues. The aristocracy is denounced as "selfish," "sordid, and "base-hearted." A total overthrow of the existing order of society is foretold; references are made to the French Revolution; and the great proprietors of the country are warned to beware. But the Anti-Corn Law League, it may be said, is a Radical institution. How is it the Tories themselves, when under the influence of partizanship, expressed themselves in reference to the Sovereign herself? You cannot have forgotten the contumelies heaped upon the head of the Queen upon the resignation, in 1839, of Sir Robert Peel I will not, gentlemen, disgust you by a more distinct reference to those traitorous diatribes, in which even clergymen took part. It is better we should inquire how it is that gentlemen connected with these very prosecutions have thought it decorous to comport themselves when their own passions were excited. The name of the Right Honourable Frederick Shaw is attached to the proclamation. I hold in my hand the peroration of a speech delivered by that gentleman, and reported in the *Evening Mail*. —" The government might make what regulation it pleased; but he trusted the people knew their duty too well to submit to its enactments. It might degrade our mitres; it might deprive us of our properties; but if the government dared to lay its hand on the Bible, then we must come to an issue. It will cover it with our bodies. My friends, will you permit your brethren to call out to you in vain? In the name of my country and my country's God, I will appeal from a British House of Commons to a British people. My countrymen would obey the laws so long as they were properly administered; but if it were sought to lay sacrilegious hands on the Bible, to tear the standard of the living God, and to raise a mutilated one in its stead, then it would be no time to halt between two opinions—then, in every hill and every valley would resound the rallying cry of 'To your tents, O Israel!'" I won't ask the Attorney-General for Ireland what he thinks of this, because this speech refers to a subject somewhat embarrassing to him; and what his opinions are upon the Education Board, it is not very easy to conjecture; but I may venture to ask the Solicitor-General, who is himself a commissioner of the Education Board, whether Daniel O'Connell, in his whole course of agitation, ever uttered a speech half so inflammatory as this? With respect to Mr. Sergeant Warren, he, I suppose, agrees in every word of it, and only laments, that, after so much sound and fury, the Recorder of Dublin is the steadfast supporter of the government, by whom all the misdeeds thus eloquently denounced have been subsequently committed. Gentlemen, I find in the *Evening Packet* of the 24th of January, 1837, an account of a great Protestant meeting which took place at the Mansion House, where all the great representatives of the Conservative interest in this country were assembled. Some very strong speeches, indeed, were made at that meeting. The Earl of Charleville said. " Well, gentlemen, you have a rebellious parliament; you have a Lord Lieutenant the slave and minion of a rebellious parliament." That speech was heard by the Right Honourable Thomas Berry Cusack Smith. Did he remonstrate against the use of language so unqualified? Not at all. He got up and made a speech, in which he stated that he was sorry to find that " Roman Catholic members of parliament paid so little regard to their oaths." When the right honourable gentleman had such impressions, I cannot feel surprised that care should have been taken to exclude every Roman Catholic from the jury-box. Let him not misapprehend me. I do not refer to his language in the spirit of resentment. Resentment is not the feeling which the conduct of the right honourable gentleman is calculated to produce. The right honourable gentleman has expressed great indignation at the references made at Mullaghmast to transactions from which the veil of oblivion ought not to be withdrawn. He said, and justly enough, that men should not grope in the annals of their country for the purpose of disinterring those events whose resuscitation can but appal and scare us. But how does the right honourable gentleman reconcile that position with his having been himself a party to a resolution passed at the meeting of which I am speaking, in which it is stated that the condition of the Protestants of Ireland is almost as alarming as it was in the year 1641, when events took place from whose recollection we ought to turn with horror and dismay. I referred you, gentlemen, to speeches. Permit me now to refer you to the great monster meetings which have taken place in assertion of the rights of the Protestants of Ireland. Mark, I do not complain of those meetings. I do not complain that 75,000 men should have assembled and moved in order of battle; but I do complain that the men who look upon those assemblages with so much indulgence, when the purposes of their own party were to be promoted, denounced, as treasonable, assemblies in which no such demonstration of organised and perfectly disciplined physical force was made. The first meeting of the monster character to which I shall refer is the great Cavan meeting, where twenty thousand men assembled under such circumstances of such deep impressiveness, as to render them equivalent in practical effect to five times that number of such a peasantry as attended the Repeal demonstration. The following incident is illustrative :—The Rev. Marcus Beresford stood up, and, after a speech in his accustomed vein, said—" I see amongst us a good and honest man from the county Monaghan, who rendered considerable service, by routing Mr. John Lawless from Ballibay—I mean Mr. Samuel Gray (cheers) ; and were I a poet I should introduce him to you by a couplet—

Here is Mr. Samuel Gray,
The Protestant Hero of Ballibay.
(Cheers and laughter.

He is a good, honest, straightforward Protestant—as glad to see the Protestants of Cavan as they are to see him."* Mr. Samuel Gray, who appears to have been transported by the reception given him by his Protestant brethren, then came forward, and was received with loud cheers. He said " he was a very humble individual, and could only claim the merit of being a sincere and consistent Protestant. He knew the Orangemen of Monaghan well—they were all prepared, and in the hour of danger would be ready to assist their brethren (cheers). As long as the spirit of the Protestants of Ulster remained unbroken—as long as they stuck together heart and hand—so long may they defy Mr. O'Connell, aided by a Whig government to put them down (cheers) Should the storm arise, a signal would be sufficient to bring him and the Orangemen of Monaghan to the assistance of their brethren." But let us now proceed to the picturesque account given of the Hillsborough meeting, celebrated in the annals of Protestant agitation, by the *Evening Mail* :—" At an early hour of the morning (some of them, indeed, over night) the great landed proprietors of the county repaired to the different points on their respective estates at which it had been previously agreed they should meet their tenants, and march then at their head to the general place of assemblage, so that the area in front of the hustings did not present a very crowded appearance, until the men arrived in large masses, each having the pride of marching, border fashion, shoulder by shoulder, beside his neighbour and brother, with whom he was ready to sacrifice life in defence of his country and religion. Shortly after eleven o'clock, a tremendous shout from the town announced the approach of the first party. They were from Moira, and were headed by the Reverend Holt Waring, who was drawn by the people. A flag the union-jack, was hoisted at Mr. E. Reilly's, as the signal of their arrival. In a few moments they were seen descending the steep hill from the town, and approaching the place of meeting in a close, dark, and dense mass, comprising certainly not less than twenty-thousand persons. Having escorted Mr. Waring to the foot of the platform they received his thanks, expressed in warm and energetic language, and having given three cheers, deployed round and took the position assigned them. * * * * Amongst those who marched at the head of the largest battalion, if we may use the expression, were the Marquisses of Londonderry and Downshire ; Lord Clanwilliam, Sir Robert Bateson, Colonel Forde, Colonel Blacker, Lord Castlereagh, and Lord Roden. The latter had fifteen thousand men in his followers. They marched from Dromore. At twelve o'clock the scene was the most imposing that fancy could conceive, or that language possesses the power of depicting. The spectacle was grand, unique, sublime. There certainly could not

* He has, since this eulogium was pronounced, been tried for murder—and sentenced to transportation for a felony one degree less heinous. — ED.

have been, upon the most moderate computation, less than seventy-five thousand persons present, exclusive of the thousands who filled the town, or thronged to absolute impediment all the adjacent roads and avenues.' From that description, gentlemen, I turn to a resolution passed by the Irish Orangemen on the 12th November, 1834, and which I find in the appendix to the report from the select committee on Orange lodges :— " And, lastly, we would beg to call the attention of the Grand Lodge, and through them return our heartfelt thanks and congratulations to our brethren through the various parts of Ireland, who, in the meetings of three thousand in Dublin, four thousand at Bandon, thirty thousand in Cavan, and seventy-five thousand at Hillsborough, by their strength of numbers, the rank, the respectability, and orderly conduct of their attendance—the manly and eloquent expression of every Christian and loyal sentiment, vindicated so nobly the character of our institution against the aspersion thrown on it, as the 'paltry remnant of a faction.' " That phrase, gentlemen, is one which Lord Stanley, in one of his wayward moods, was pleased to apply to the Orangemen of Ireland. Gentlemen, in the part of the report which I have read to you, there are some remarkable entries relating to a subject of which you have heard a good deal from the Attorney-General; and although I deviate, I am aware, from the order of topics, which I had prescribed to myself, yet, finding in the book before me matter which seems to me to be exceedingly pertinent to that topic, I shall now advert to it. Gentlemen, the entries to which I am alluding are these :—" 15th February, 1833, William Scott, 16th company Royal Sappers and Miners. That the committee would most willingly forward all document connected with the Orange system to any confidential persons in Bally, ona, as prudence would not permit the printed documents should be forwarded direct to our military brethren." " 1st January, 1834.—Resolved, that warrant 1592 be granted to Joseph Mius, of the 1st Royals." " 17th December, 1829, moved by the Rev. Charles Boyton, seconded by Edward Cottingham, that the next warrant number be issued to the 66th regiment, and that the Quebec brethren be directed to send in a correct return, in order that new warrants may be issued." Gentlemen, I refer you to these resolutions with no other view than to show you what proceedings men who conspire to establish an influence over the army naturally adopt. If it was the object of the traversers to seduce the army from their allegiance, would not expedients have been adopted very different from those imputed to the defendants? Would not repeal societies have been formed ? Would not a clandestine correspondence have taken place with the " military brethren ?" Would not money have been distributed to the soldiery ? Would not the propagators of mutiny have been located in the public-houses frequented by the soldiery ? Would not Roman Catholic priests who attend at the military hospitals, have been charged to instil repeal principles into the soldier's ear ? Does anything of this kind appear to have been done ? A letter written by the Rev. Mr. Power—a Waterford priest, who is not made a defendant —who is not to be punished for his letter—is given in evidence against my client, although he is as innocent of its composition as the foreman

U

of your jury. When that letter appeared in the *Nation* newspaper, why was not an *ex officio* information filed against the Rev. Mr. Power, whose manuscript would most certainly have been given up? But that would not have answered the purpose of the Attorney-General whose object it was to ensnare. The Attorney-General has not suggested a reason, or glanced at a pretence for not having indicted Father Power. He read his letter from the beginning to the termination. He told you that it was written by a priest—that his name was to it. He does not prosecute the priest—he does not prosecute the paper, but reserves it for the conspiracy on which his official renown is to be founded. What gentlemen, has been the course adopted by the government in those prosecutions? Sir Edward Sugden begins by dismissing some of the most respectable magistrates of the country, on account of something or other that was said in the House of Commons, and because "the meetings gave a tendency to outrage." The direct contrary has been proved by every one of the witnesses for the crown, and Mr. Ross, the clandestine sub-inspector of the Home Office, in the very last words of his examination, stated that he saw no tendency to outrage whatsoever Lord Cottenham declared in the House of Lords, that the proceeding of the Lord Chancellor was utterly unconstitutional. Let me be permitted, gentlemen, to contrast the proceedings adopted by the Lord Chancellor of Ireland with the doctrines laid down in the charge of Mr. Alderson, in his charge to the grand jury, delivered at the Monmouth summer assizes, 1839. It is reported in the 9th Carrington and Payne, page 95 :—" There is no doubt that the people of this country have a perfect right to meet for the purpose of stating what one, or even what they, consider to be their grievances; but in order to transmit that right unimpaired to posterity, it is necessary that it should be regulated by law and restrained by reason. Therefore, let them meet if they will in open day, peaceably and quietly; and they would do wisely, when they meet, to do so under the sanction of the constituted authorities of the country. To meet under irresponsible presidency is a dangerous thing. Nevertheless, if when they do meet under that irresponsible presidency they conduct themselves with peace, tranquillity, and order, they will, perhaps, lose their time, but nothing else. They will not put other people into alarm, terror and consternation. They will probably in the end come to the conclusion, that they have acted foolishly; but the constitution of this country did not, God be thanked, punish persons who mean to do that which was right, in a peaceable and orderly manner, and who are only in error in the views which they have taken on some subject of political interest." Has a single respectable gentleman of station, and rank, and living in the vicinity of the place where any of those meetings were held, been produced to state to you that they were the source of apprehension in the neighbourhood? Has any man been produced to you who stated that they had even a tendency to outrage? Not one.

(Mr. Sheil was interrupted at this period of his address by an intimation that the jury wished to retire for refreshment.)

Mr. SHEIL, when their lordships returned into court, resumed as folows:—I have already called attention to the fact that none of the gentry of the country were brought forward to state what the character of these meetings was. All the official persons examined—among whom were several of the high constables of the various districts—concurred in stating that there was no violation of the peace at any of them. Indeed, the assertion of the Attorney-General was, that the peace was kept—kept with the malevolent intention of enabling the whole population to rise at a given time, and establish a republic, of which Mr. O'Connell was to be the head. Forty-one of these meetings were held—all of the same character -- and at length a proclamation was determined on and issued for the purpose of putting a stop to the Clontarf meeting. You have heard the remarks of Mr. O'Connell, in reference to the course adopted towards that meeting, and to me they appear extremely reasonable. Notice of that meeting had been given for three weeks, yet the proclamation was not published until the day before that on which it was have taken place. Mr. O'Counell did not charge the government, when acting in this way, and delaying its measures till the last moment, with being capable of such an atrocious and destructive attempt on the lives of the people, as might have been perpetrated by sending the army amongst an unarmed populace, if the meeting had taken place. Such an event might have taken place; and it is to be regretted that a more timely warning, one that would have removed all doubt and uncertainty, was not given. I pass this consideration by, and come to another point. It is a usual practice—a rule, in fact—that when a privy council is to assemble, summonses are directed to be issued to all privy councillors being within the vicinity of the city of Dublin. On this occasion such summonses were not issued. I am given to understand that Chief Baron Brady, who is in the habit of attending at councils, was not summoned. The Right Honourable Anthony Richard Blake, a Roman Catholic gentleman, who was appointed Chief Remembrancer of the Exchequer under a Tory administration—the intimate friend of the Marquis Wellesley- -a man who had never appeared in public assemblies, or interfered in the proceedings of public meetings— a man who had never uttered an inflammatory harangue in his life— that gentleman did not receive a summons. I will make no comment on this omission of the government on this occasion, but such undoubtedly is the fact. I have told you who did not receive summonses, and I shall proceed to state who did receive them. The Recorder of the city of Dublin—by whom the jury list was to be revised—he received a summons. In his department it was that an event most untoward, as respects the traversers, befel. It was suggested in this court that the jury list possibly might have been mutilated or decimated—for decimation it was—by an accident—perhaps by a rat, as was suggested by one of the court. I am far from suggesting that there was any intentional foul play in this decimation, but that a large portion of the list was omitted is beyond a doubt. I state the fact and make no comment on it. Well, an application was made for the names of the witnesses on the back of the document, on behalf of the traversers. One of the udges declared he thought it matter of right; another of the judges intimated his opinion that it would be advisable for the crown to furnish the list within a reasonable time. From that day to this the list has never been given. The list of jurors is drawn by ballot: there are eleven Catholics upon it. They are struck off. The trial comes on. A challenge is put in to the array, upon the ground that one-tenth, or very nearly one-tenth of the jury list was suppressed. One of the court expresses an opinion that the challenge is a good one. His brethren differ from him; but when in a trial at bar, at the instance of the crown, one of the judges gives an intimation so unequivocal as to the construction of the jury list, perhaps it would have been more advisable for the crown to have discharged the order for a special jury, and to have directed the high sheriff of the city to have returned a panel. I mention these incidents, gentlemen, in order that your feeling that the traversers have been deprived of some of those contingent benefits given them by the law, should give them an equivalent for any loss which they may have sustained in your anxious performance of your sacred duty. At length, in the midst of profound silence, the Attorney-General states the case for the crown, and consumes eleven hours in doing so. I was astonished at his brevity, for the pleading on which his speech was founded is the very Behemoth of indictments, which, as you see, "upheaves its vastness" on that table. Nothing comparable in the bigness of its gigantic dimensions has ever yet been seen. The indictment in Hardy's case, whose trial lasted ten or eleven days, does not exceed three or four pages; but this indictment requires an effort of physical force to lift it up. Combined with this indictment was a tremendous bill of particulars in keeping with it. Gentlemen, the Attorney-General, as I have already observed to you at the outset of these observations, denounced the traversers at the close of almost every sentence that was uttered by him; but it struck me that it was only in reference to two of these charges that he broke forth in a burst of genuine and truly impassioned indignation. The first of those charges was —a conspiracy to diminish the business of a court of law. How well the great Lord Chatham exclaimed—I remember to have read it somewhere but I forget where—" Shake the whole constitution to the centre, and the lawyer will sit tranquil in his cabinet; but touch a single thread in the cobwebs of Westminster-hall, and the exasperated spider crawls out in its defence." The second great hit of the right honourable gentleman was made when he charged Mr. O'Connell with a deplorable ignorance of law, in stating certain prerogatives of the crown. With respect, gentlemen, to the arbitration courts, the Society of Friends are as liable to an indictment for conspiracy as the defendants. The regulations under which the Quaker arbitration system is carried on will be laid before you; and the opinions of Lord Brougham, who has always been the strenuous advocate of the arbitration system, will, I am sure, have their due weight upon you. With regard to Mr. O'Connell's alleged mistake, respecting the power of the crown to issue writs—what is it after all, but a project for swamping the House of Commons, analogous to that of Sir James Graham and my Lord Stanley for swamping the House of Lords? The plain truth is this—the

Sovereign has the abstract right to create new boroughs. But the exercise of that right might be regarded as inconsistent with the principles of the constitution. Lord Denman and one of his late Majesty's law advisers in the House of Commons distinctly asserted the right to issue writs; and although that opinion was reprehended by Sir Charles Wetherell, I believe that of its being strict law there can be little doubt. But the real question between the Attorney-General and the traversers and the only one to which you will be disposed to pay much regard, was raised by the Attorney-General when he said that there existed a dangerous conspiracy, of which the object was to prepare the great body of the people to rise at a signal and to erect a sanguinary republic, of which Daniel O'Connell should be the head. Gentlemen, how do men proceed who engage in a guilty enterprise of this kind? They bind each other by solemn oaths. They are sworn to secrecy, to silence, to deeds, or to death. · They associate superstition with atrocity, and heaven is invoked by them to ratify the covenants of hell. They fix a day, an hour, and hold their assemblages in the midst of darkness and of solitude, and verify the exclamation of the conspirator, in the language of the great observer of our nature:—

> "Oh, Conspiracy,
> Where wilt thou find a cavern dark enough
> To hide thy monstrous visage?"

How have the repeal conspirators proceeded? Every one of their assemblages have been open to the public. For a shilling, all they said, or did, or thought, were known to the government. Everything was laid bare and naked to the public eye; they stripped their minds in the public gaze. No oaths, no declaration, no initiation, no form of any kind was resorted to. They did not even act together. Mr. Duffy, proprietor of the *Nation*, did not attend a single meeting in the country. My client attended only three; Mr. Tierney, the priest, attended no more than one. It would have been more manly on the part of the Attorney-General to have indicted Dr. Higgins or Dr. Cantwell, or as he was pleased to designate them, Bishop Higgins and Bishop Cantwell. Well, why did he not catch a bishop—if not Cantwell, at all events Higgins? For three months we heard nothing but "Higgins, Higgins, Higgins." The *Times* was redolent of Higgins; sometimes he was Lord Higgins, then he was Priest Higgins, afterwards Mr. Higgins. But wherefore is not this redoubted Higgins indicted, or why did you not assail the great John of Tuam himself? He would not have shrunk from your persecution, but, with his mitre on his head and his crozier in his hand, he would have walked in his pontifical vestments into gaol, and smiled disdainfully upon you. But you did not dare to attack him, but fell on a poor Monaghan priest, who only attended one meeting, and only made one speech about the "Yellow Ford," for which you should not include him in a conspiracy, but should make him professor of rhetoric at Maynooth. Gentlemen, an enormous mass of speeches delivered by Mr. O'Connell within the last nine months has been laid before you. I think, however, you will come to the conclusion that they are nothing more than a repetition of the opinions which he

expressed in 1810 ; and when you come to conside
will, I am sure, be convinced that these speeches w
*persed with references to peace and order, with a
the law, but that there runs, through the entire m
came from the mind of Mr. O'Connell a pervading
unaffected sentiment of abhorrence for the employm
loyal, constitutional, and pacific means for the atta
He attaches fully as much importance to the mean
declares that he would not purchase the repeal of t
of one drop of blood. He announces that the mon
calls upon him to disperse his meetings, these m
persed. He does but ask " the Irish nation to b
that backing he anticipates the only success to whi
as a good citizen, and as a good Christian, he co
gentlemen, it be suggested that in popular harang
laws and submission to authority are easily simul
fearlessly assert that of the charges preserved again
the refutation. A man cannot wear the mask of l
years ; however skilfully constructed, the vizor will
and the natural truculence of the conspirator must
may have heard many references made to the ye
stanzas of a long poem have been read to you, in
on Mr. O'Connell. It was in 1798 that the celebr
to the bar, who was destined to play a part so conspi
of the world. He was in the bloom of youth—in t
the blood bounded in his veins, and in a frame full
died an equally elastic and athletic mind. He was
when men are most disposed to high and daring adve
from those rocks and mountains, of which a descri
appeared in the reports of the speeches, which hav
He had listened, as he says, to the great Atlanti
unbroken from the coast of Labrador. He carried ent
and of the impressions which great events are calct
minds like his, he was peculiarly susceptible. He
had given no hostages to the state. The conservati
tied their ligaments, tender, but indissoluble about h
at that time an enterprise on foot ; guilty, and d
but not wholly hopeless. The peaks that overhan
are dimly visible from Iveragh. What part was
adventure by this conspirator of sixty-nine ? Cur
Grattan was suspected. Both were designated as tr
but on the name of Daniel O'Connell a conjecture
can you bring yourselves to believe that the man wh
rence from the conjuration of 1798 would now, in a
himself has called not premature, engage in an in
which his own life, and the lives of those who are
himself, and the lives of hundreds of thousands
would, beyond all doubt, be sacrificed ? Can you
believe that he would blast the laurels, which it is l

won without the effusion of blood—that he would drench the land of his birth, of his affections, and of his redemption, in a deluge of profitless massacre, and that he would lay prostrate that great moral monument which he has raised so high that it is visible from the remotest region of the world? What he was in 1798 he is in 1844. Do you believe that the man who aimed at a revolution would repudiate French assistance, and denounce the present dynasty of France? Do you think that the man who aimed at revolution, would hold forth to the detestation of the world, the infamous slavery by which the great trans-Atlantic republic, to her everlasting shame, permits herself to be degraded? Or, to come nearer home, do you think that the man who aimed at revolution, would have indignantly repudiated the proffered junction with the English Chartists? Had a combination been effected between the Chartists and the Repealers it would have been more than formidable. At the head of that combination in England was Mr. Feargus O'Connor, once the associate and friend of Daniel O'Connell. The entire of the lower orders in the North of England were enrolled in a powerful organization. A league between the Repealers and the Chartists might have been at once effected. Chartism uses its utmost and most clandestine efforts to find its way into this country. O'Connell detects and crushes it. Of the charges preferred against him, am I not right when I exclaim that his life contains the refutation? To the charge that Mr. O'Connell and his son conspired to excite animosity amongst her Majesty's subjects, the last observation that I have made to you is more peculiarly applicable. Gentlemen, Mr. O'Connell and his co-religionists have been made the objects of the fiercest and the coarsest vituperation; and yet I defy the most acute and diligent scrutiny of the entire of the speeches put before you, to detect a single expression—one solitary phrase—which reflects in the remotest degree upon the Protestant religion. He has left all the contumely heaped upon the form of Christianity which he professes utterly unheeded, and the Protestant Operative Society has not provoked a retort; and every angry disputant has without any interposition on his part, been permitted to rush in " where angels fear to tread." The religion of Mr. O'Connell teaches him two things—charity towards those who dissent from him in doctrine, and forgiveness of those who do him wrong. You recollect (it is from such incidents that we are enabled to judge of the characters and feelings of men)—you remember to have heard in the course of the evidence frequent reference made to Sir Bradley King. The unfortunate man had been deprived of his office, and all compensation was denied him. He used to stand in the lobby of the House of Commons, the most desolate and hopeless looking man I ever saw. The only one of his old friends that stuck to him was Baron Lefroy. But Baron Lefroy had no interest with the government. Mr. O'Connell saw Bradley King, and took pity on him. Bradley King had been his fierce political, almost his personal antagonist. Mr. O'Connell went to Lord Althorpe, and obtained for Bradley King the compensation which had been refused him. I remembered having read a most striking letter addressed by Sir Abraham Bradley King to Mr. O'Connell, and asked him for it. He could not at first put his hand upon it ; but, while looking for it, he mentioned that soon after the death of the old Dublin alderman, an officer entered his study, and told him that he was the son-in-law of Sir Abraham, who had, a short time before his death, called him to his bedside and said —" When I shall have been buried, go to Daniel O'Connell, and tell him that the last prayer of a grateful man was offered up for him, and that I implored heaven to avert every peril from his head." Mr. O'Connell found the letter—you will allow me to read it :—

" Barrett's Hotel, Spring Gardens, 4th Aug. 1832.

" MY DEAR SIR—The anxious wish for a satisfactory termination of my cause, which your continued and unwearied efforts for it have ever indicated, is at length accomplished ; the vote of compensation passed last night.

" To Mr. Lefroy and yourself am I indebted for putting the case in the right light to my Lord Althorpe, and for his lordship's consequent candid and straightforward act, in giving me my just dues, and thus restoring myself and family to competence, ease, and happiness.

" To you, Sir, to whom I was early and long politically opposed—to you, who nobly forgetting this continued difference of opinion, and who, rejecting every idea of party feeling or party spirit, thought only of my distress, and sped to succour and support me, how can I express my gratitude ? I cannot attempt it. The reward, I feel, is to be found only in your own breast, and I assure myself that the generous feelings of a noble mind will cheer you on to that prosperity and happiness which a discriminating Providence holds out to those who protect the helpless, and sustain the falling.

" For such reward and happiness to you and yours my prayers shall be offered fervently, while the remainder of my days, passing, I trust, in tranquillity, by a complete retirement from public life, and in the bosom of my family, will constantly present to me the grateful recollection of one to whom I am mainly indebted for so desirable a closing of my life. Believe me, my dear Sir, with the greatest respect and truth, your faithful servant,

"ABRAHAM BRADLEY KING.

" To Daniel O'Connell, Esq., M.P."

You may deprive him of liberty—you may shut him out from the face of nature, you may inter him in a dungeon, to which a ray of the sun never yet descended ; but you never will take away from him the consciousness of having done a good and a noble action, and of being entitled to kneel down every night he sleeps, and to address to his Creator the divinest portion of our Redeemer's prayer. The man to whom that letter was addressed, and the son of the man to whom that letter was addressed, are not guilty of the sanguinary intents which have been ascribed to them, and of this they " put themselves upon their country." Rescue that phrase from its technicalities—let it no longer be a fictitious one ; if we have lost our representation in the parliament, let us behold it in the jury box, and that you participate in the feelings of millions of your countrymen let your verdict afford a proof. But it is not to Ireland that the aching solicitude with which the result of this trial is intently watched will be confined. There is not a great city in Europe in which, upon the day when the great intelligence shall be expected to arrive, men will not stop each other in the public way, and inquire whether twelve men upon their oaths have doomed to incarceration the man who gave liberty to Ireland? Whatever may be your adjudication he is prepared to meet it. He knows that the eyes of the world are upon him—and that posterity—whether in a gaol or out of it—will look back to him with admiration; he is almost indifferent to what may befal him, and is far more solicitous for others at this moment than for himself. But I—at the commencement of what I have said to you—I told you that I was not unmoved, and that many incidents of my political life, the strange alternations of fortune through which I have passed, had come back upon me. But now the bare possibility at which I have glanced, has, I acknowledge, almost unmanned me. Shall I, who stretch out to you in behalf of the son the hand whose fetters the father has struck off, live to cast my eyes upon that domicile of sorrow, in the vicinity of this great metropolis, and say, " 'Tis there they have immured the Liberator of Ireland with his fondest and best beloved child?" No! it shall never be! You will not consign him to the spot to which the Attorney-General invites you to surrender him. When the Spring shall have come again, and the winter shall have passed—when the spring shall have come again, it is not through the windows of a prison-house that the father of such a son, and the son of such a father, shall look upon those green hills on which the eyes of many a captive have gazed so wistfully in vain, but in their own mountain home again they shall listen to the murmurs of the great Atlantic; they shall go forth and inhale the freshness of the morning air together; " they shall be free of mountain solitudes;" they will be encompassed with the loftiest images of liberty upon every side; and if time shall have stolen its suppleness from the father's knee, or impaired the firmness of his tread, he shall lean on the child of her that watches over him from heaven, and shall look out from some high place far and wide into the island whose greatness and whose glory shall be for ever associated with his name. In your love of justice—in your love of Ireland—in your love of honesty and fair play I place my confidence. I ask you for an acquittal, not only for the sake of your country, but for your own. Upon the day when this trial shall have been brought to a termination, when, amidst the hush of public expectancy, in answer to the solemn interrogatory which shall be put to you by the officer of the court, you shall answer, " Not guilty," with what a transport will that glorious negative be welcomed! How will you be blessed, adored, worshipped; and when retiring from this scene of excitement and of passion, you shall return to your own tranquil homes, how pleasurably will you look upon your children, in the consciousness that you will have left them a patrimony of peace by impressing upon the British cabinet, that some other measure besides a state prosecution is necessary for the pacification of your country!

THE IRISH STATE TRIALS.

SPEECH IN THE HOUSE OF COMMONS, FEBRUARY 22, 1844.

I DID not rise last night at the conclusion of the speech of the Attorney-General for Ireland, for two reasons. The first was, that that speech did not terminate until nearly twelve, and I despaired of engaging the attention of the house at so late an hour; in the next place, I was anxious that the right honourable and learned gentleman should afford me an opportunity of looking at the report of the case in which I was engaged fifteen years ago, to which he has thought it judicious to advert. I wished to look at that report for the purpose of vindicating myself from what I regard as a very serious charge. I applied to the right honourable gentleman for the report, and he had the goodness at once to give it to me. This house must have been under the impression that I packed a jury, and that it was exclusively Roman Catholic. The house must have thought, that I exercised the prerogative vested in me by the crown, with the sanction of the law officers, for the purpose of placing in the jury-box twelve men, my own co-religionists, and the co-religionists of the person for whose death the prosecution was instituted. The right honourable gentleman said that he was present on that occasion; I think he will admit the truth of my assertion, that of my conduct in the course of that prosecution the attorney and counsel for the prisoner did not complain, and the regular counsel for the crown did not intimate that any fault was to be found with my conduct. In order to obtain a mixed jury, I was under the necessity, as the prisoner challenged every Catholic, to set aside Protestants, until I could obtain the religious combination which I desired to effect. It may be said that I gave the Catholics a majority of one on the jury; but when you recollect that unanimity was required for a conviction, you will at once perceive that a preponderance of one was of no consequence. If the Irish Attorney-General had followed my example in the state prosecutions, and out of the common panel had allowed five Catholics to remain on the jury, we should not have impeached his verdict. The Attorney-General has brought against me a very serious charge—he said that where a man was on his trial for his life, I acted a most censurable part. His book refutes him. I find in it a report of my speech; and in order to prove that I did not hunt down the defendant with a bloodhound sagacity, I hope I shall be forgiven if I read one or two passages, which will show the house the spirit in which the prosecution was conducted. I hope the house will listen to this self-vindication, if not with interest at least with indulgence; and I must say, that I never saw an occasion on which that feeling of the House of Commons was more strongly manifested than it had been last night, in listening to a speech of the right honourable and learned gentleman, distinguished for ability, and, let me add, for moral courage. The following is the commencement of the speech made by me in the case to which the Attorney-General refers:—

"I am counsel in a case which the gentlemen to whom the Attorney-General habitually confides the enforcement of the law have permitted me, at the instance of the persons interested in the prosecution, to conduct. I trust that I shall not abuse the licence which has been afforded me. I feel that I am invested with a triple trust. The first is that which I owe my client, for whom I do not ask for vengeance, but for that retribution for which the instincts of nature make in the bosom of a parent their strong and almost sacred call. My client is the mother of the boy for whose death the prisoner at the bar stands arraigned. I owe the next duty to Mr. Pearse himself. If I am asked in what particular I am bound to him, I answer that I cannot avoid entertaining for him that sentiment of commiseration which every well-minded man will extend to one who may be really innocent of a crime, the imputation of which is itself a misfortune ; and I do assure you (he will permit me, I hope, to extend the assurance to himself), that it is with melancholy that I raise my eyes and see him occupying the place where guilt and misery are accustomed to stand. To him I owe it as an obligation that I should not abuse the advantage of delivering a statement to which his counsel cannot reply. The scriptural injunction inscribed above that seat of justice, admonishes me that I ought not to make any appeal to your passions against a man whose mouth is closed, and to whose counsel the right of speaking, by an equally cruel and fantastic anomaly, is refused by the law. "*Aperi os tuum, muto*" is written there in golden characters, not only to suggest to your lordship the duty of a judicial interposition on behalf of the silent, but also to warn the advocate not to avail himself in any merciless spirit of his forensic prerogative against the man whom the law has stricken dumb. I shall make it superfluous on the part of his counsel to produce evidence in favour of his character—he is a man of worth and honour, and until the fatal event for which he stands indicted, has borne a reputation for peculiar kindness of heart."

After stating the facts I concluded thus :—

"At the outset of my statement I expressed myself in praise of the defendant, and, as I advance to a conclusion, I pause for an instant to reiterate my panegyric. He has been, I repeat it, up to the time of this incident, a humane and well-conducted man. Let him have the full benefit of this commendation. If it shall appear that under circumstances which constituted a necessity, and in obedience to the instinct of self-preservation he exclaimed ' fire !' then I am the very first to call on you to acquit him."

This is not the language of a man actuated by the fierce zeal of a relentless prosecutor ; I think it far less vehement than the charges of judges which we occasionally hear in Ireland. At the conclusion of the evidence, I told the judge that I thought that no case for charging the defendant with murder had been made out. I do think that the Attorney-General, in reverting to a trial which took place fifteen years ago, has not acted with ingenuousness, and I am convinced that in the opinion of the house I have freed myself from the imputation that I did not exercise the prerogative of the crown with the intent attributed to me; and if the right honourable gentleman had followed the example which I gave him on that occasion—if, in the constitution of the jury in Dublin, he had taken care that there should be five Roman Catholics and seven Protestants upon it—nay, if he had allowed even two, or one Roman Catholic on that jury, I think he would have taken not only a more merciful but a more judicious course than that which he did adopt. The jury that sat in Dublin on the late trial was composed of twelve Protestants, and the house has not yet been apprised of some circumstances connected with their selection. Eight of those jurors voted against Mr. O'Connell at the several elections at which that honourable gentleman was candidate for the city of Dublin. I do not mean to say that they had not a most perfect right to do so, or that because they had voted against him they ought of necessity to have been set aside by the crown, or that they were unfit to exercise the duties of jurors in his case; but we have first the fact of every Roman Catholic on the jury list being set aside, and then we have a jury of persons admittedly hostile to him selected. There was a controversy last night respecting Mr. Thompson. A doubt was entertained as to the fact whether he had seconded a resolution at a corporation meeting. I believe the fact is now beyond all doubt. The resolution was to this effect:—" That this meeting will support and maintain, by every means in its power, the Legislative Union between Great Britain and Ireland." There was another gentleman of more marked politics—Mr Faulkner. It will be found in *Saunders's News Letter* of the 14th o. February, 1840, that at a meeting of Protestants, convened by the Lord Mayor in pursuance of a resolution of the Common Council, and held in the King's Room at the Mansion House, a Mr. Jones is reported to have said—" I call on the meeting by every consideration to stand by their principles, and above all, to maintain the Protestant ascendancy in church and state," and then followed loud and long-continued cheering, with shouts of " no surrender," and " one cheer more." Mr. Faulkner, who was one of the jury, proposed the third resolution, and that resolution was this—" That this meeting views with deep alarm the bill introduced into parliament which proposes to interfere with the municipal corporations of Ireland, and which transfers the rights of Protestants to the Roman Catholic party in Ireland." And on another occasion, in a speech of his, reported in *Saunders's News Letter* of the 13th of April, and also in the *Evening Mail*, Mr. Faulkner called upon the meeting to uphold the Protestant ascendancy in church and state, and gave the charter toast. Some friend asked what was the charter toast? and Mr. Faulkner said, " I mean the glorious and immortal memory of the great and good King William." That gentleman ought to have been struck off. I think the house, when it considers the facts of the case—when it looks to the variety of the circumstances connected with the case, will consider these facts to be material in determining whether the jury were legitimately selected? Mr. O'Connell might have begun his speech to the jury in the words of the unfortunate Lewis: " I look for judges, but I behold none but accusers here." I turn to the circumstances connected with the prosecution: the Attorney-Gene-

-al has overlooked many incidents which he ought to have stated and which he ought to have known would not be kept back. You have obtained what you regard as a victory over the leader of the Catholic people. That victory has been obtained by you through the instrumentality of a Protestant jury. If it was fairly won, I am free to acknowledge that it is not unnaturally followed by that ministerial ovation in which the Secretary for the Colonies and the Secretary for the Home Department have not thought it indecorous to indulge; but if that victory has been unfairly won—if, while you adhere to the forms of law, you have violated the principles of justice; if a plot was concocted at the Home Office, and executed in the Queen's Bench; if, by an ostensible acquiescence in monster meetings for nine months, you have decoyed your antagonists into your toils; if foully or fortuitously (and whether fortuitously or foully the result is the same) a considerable fraction of the jury list had been suppressed; if you have tried the Liberator of the Irish Catholics with a jury of exasperated Protestants; if justice is not only suspected, but comes tainted and contaminated from her impure contact with authority—then, not only have you not a just cause for exultation, but your successes are of that sinister kind which are as fatal to the victors as to the vanquished—which will tarnish you with an ineffaceable discredit, and will be followed at last by a retribution, slow indeed, but, however tardy, inevitably sure. I have presented a double hypothesis to the house. Let us see to which of the alternatives the facts ought to be applied. I shall be permitted, in the first instance, to refer to an observation made by the Secretary for Ireland in reference to myself. The noble lord said —

" He must now advert to something which had fallen from a member of that house out of doors regarding Chief Baron Brady, and Mr. Anthony Blake. It had been observed by Mr. Sheil that an insult had been offered to the Catholics of Ireland because those gentlemen had not been summoned to a meeting of the council. He believed Chief Baron Brady was a Protestant. But let that pass. He took on himself the responsibility of not summoning those gentlemen to the council. He thought that the measure determined on was the deliberate act of government, and he did not, therefore, think it proper to ask the opinion of political opponents."

What I said was this : " A circumstance occurred connected with the proclamation which is not undeserving of note. It has always been the usage in this country (Ireland) to summon every member of the Privy Council. Upon this occasion the Chief Baron, although living in the neighbourhood of Dublin, was not summoned, and Mr. Blake, a Roman Catholic, who lives in Dublin, was not summoned. He was appointed to the office of Chief Remembrancer by a Tory government. He had been the intimate friend of Lord Wellesley, a great Conservative statesman. He had never taken any part in any violent proceedings, but he was not summoned upon this occasion, although summoned upon every other, to the Privy Council; while the Recorder of the city of Dublin, by whom the jury list was to be revised, and in whose department an accident of a most untoward kind had happened, was summoned to the council whence the proclamation went forth." That was what I said, and I take advantage of this opportunity to add, that if Mr. Blake had been at the Privy Council on Friday, he would have urged his associates not to delay the posting of the proclamation until Saturday, but would have told them, that, without any long recitals, immediate notice should be given to the people of the determination of the government. Notice of the Clontarf meeting was given for three weeks. It was to have been held upon Sunday. On the preceding Friday the council assembled. On that day the proclamation ought to have been prepared and posted. It did not appear until Saturday afternoon, and the country is indebted to Mr. O'Connell, if upon an unarmed multitude an excited soldiery was not let loose. The proclamation was obeyed. With that obedience you ought to have been contented. The monster meetings were at an end; but you had previously determined to prosecute for a conspiracy, and for that purpose you lay in wait for nine months, and that you did the proclamation itself affords a proof. The proclamation recites—

"Whereas meetings of large numbers of persons have been already held in different parts of Ireland, under the like pretence, at several of which meetings, language of a seditious and inflammatory nature has been addressed to the persons there assembled, calculated and intended to excite disaffection in the minds of her Majesty's subjects, and to bring into hatred and contempt, the government and constitution of the country, as by law established: and whereas, at some of the said meetings, such seditious and inflammatory language has been used by persons," &c.

If this statement be true, why did you not long before indict the individuals by whom those seditious speeches were delivered? Why did you not prosecute the newspapers by which inflammatory paragraphs had been almost daily published, for a period of nine months? The motive was obvious. It was your purpose—your deliberate and long meditated purpose to make Mr. O'Connell responsible for harangues which he had never spoken, and for publications which he had never read. I content myself with giving a single instance, which will afford, however, a perfect exemplification of the whole character of your proceedings. A Catholic priest published an article in the *Pilot* newspaper, upon "The Duty of a Soldier." He signed his name, James Power, to that article. He was never prosecuted—he was never threatened; he has escaped with perfect impunity; but that article was given in evidence against Daniel O'Connell, by whom it does not appear that it was even ever seen. Such a proceeding never was instituted in this country—such a proceeding, I trust in God, never will be instituted in this country—for Englishmen would not endure it; and this very discussion will tend to awaken them to a sense of the peril to which they are themselves exposed. Does not the question at once present itself to every body, if that seditious language was employed for so long a period as nine months, why did you not prosecute it before? Why did you not prosecute such an article as this which I hold in my hand, and which was published so far back as the 1st of April, 1843. You might have proceeded by criminal information or indictment, for the publication of a poem in the *Nation* newspaper, on which her Majesty's Attorney-General entered into a somewhat lengthened expatiation in addressing the jury, and declared it to be a poem of a most inflammatory character. I allude to verses entitled, "The Memory of the Dead."

"Who fears to speak of Ninety-eight?
  Who blushes at the name?
When cowards mock the patriot's fate,
  Who hangs his head for shame?
He's all a knave, or half a slave,
  Who slights his country thus;
But a *true* man, like you, man,
  Will fill your glass with us.

"We drink the memory of the brave,
  The faithful and the few—
Some lie far off beyond the wave,
  Some sleep in Ireland too;
All—all are gone—but still lives on
  The fame of those who died;
All true men, like you, men,
  Remember them with pride.

"Some on the shores of distant lands
  Their weary hearts have laid,
And by the stranger's heedless hands
  Their lonely graves were made.
But though their clay be far away
  Beyond the Atlantic foam—
In true men, like you, men,
  Their spirit's still at home.

"The dust of some is Irish earth;
  Among their own they rest;
And the same land that gave them birth
  Has caught them to her breast;
And we will pray that from their clay
  Full many a race may start
Of true men, like you, men,
  To act as brave a part.

"They rose in dark and evil days
  To right their native land;
They kindled here a living blaze
  That nothing shall withstand.
Alas! that Might can vanquish Right—
  They fell and passed away;
But true men, like you, men,
  Are plenty here to-day.

" Then here's their memory—may it be
 For us a guiding light,
To cheer our strife for liberty,
 And teach us to unite.
Through good and ill, be Ireland's still,
 Though sad as theirs your fate ;
And true men, be you, men,
 Like those of Ninety-eight."

No man in the court, who heard this poem recited by the right honourable gentleman in the most emphatic manner will deny that it produced a great effect on the jury. The Attorney-General stated, that this was but a single specimen of the entire volume, and that it very much exceeded in violence the productions of the same character in the year 1797. If the description is true, this poem having been published on the 1st of April, and a series of compositions, in prose and verse, of the same kind, having appeared for several successive months, does not every man who hears me ask, why it was that proceedings were not taken for the punishment of the persons by whom such articles were published, and for the prevention of offences to which such evil effects were attributed. My answer is this—you had determined to prosecute for a conspiracy, and you connived at meetings and publications of this class. You allowed these papers to proceed in their career, to run a race in sedition, and to establish a complete system for the excitement of the public. You did not prosecute the authors of the articles, or their publishers, at the time they were published. You afterwards joined in the defence the editors of three newspapers, and you gave in evidence against Mr. O'Connell every article published in 1843. Was that a legitimate proceeding? Has there been a precedent in this country of such a proceeding? Has there been an instance of a man indicted for a conspiracy, being joined with these editors of newspapers, and of the articles of those newspapers being given in evidence against him? You might tell me that the mode of proceeding was legitimate, if there were no other mode of punishing the editors of those newspapers. But was there no other mode? Could not those publications have been stopped? Could not the channels by which sedition as circulated through the country have been closed up? Therefore, we charge you with having stood by—(I adopt the expression of the Attorney-General) with having stood by, and with having, if not encoura ed, at least permitted very strong proceedings to be adopted by the popular party; when you thought your purpose had been obtained, you then fell on the man whom you had inclosed within your toils. I come now to the observations of the Attorney-General regarding Mr. Bond Hughes, and I confess myself to be not a little surprised at them. He said that Mr. Bond Hughes had been denounced as a perjurer, and spoke of us as if we had painted him in colours as black as those in which Roman Catholic members of parliament are occasionally held up to the public detestation ; but he kept back the fact that Mr. Bond Hughes did make two signal mistakes in his information and which he himself acknowledged to be mistakes, which before Mr. Bond Hughes was examined did produce no ordinary excitement. Not one word did the Attorney-General say in reference to a most remarkable incident in these trials. The facts stand thus :—Mr. Bond Hughes had sworn in his information that he had seen Mr. Barrett at two meetings in Dublin. It was of the utmost importance to the crown to fix Barrett, in order to implicate him with Mr. O'Connell. Mr. Bond Hughes sees Mr. Barrett at Judge Burton's chambers, and turning to Mr. Ray,* the chief clerk of the Crown Solicitor, informs Mr. Ray that he was mistaken with respect to Mr. Barrett, and that he had not seen him at the Dublin meetings. He suggests to Mr. Ray that something should be done to correct his misapprehension. Ray says nothing. Bond Hughes then applies to the Crown Solicitor himself, to Mr. Kemmis, and represents to him the painful predicament in which he is placed; Mr. Kemmis says nothing. Bond Hughes accompanies Mr. Kemmis to his house, and no rectification of that signal mistake is made. Mr. Bond Hughes stated all this at the trial, which the Attorney-General, although he went into exceedingly minute details, entirely forgot to mention. It is quite true that Mr. O'Connell at the trial acquitted Mr. Bond Hughes, but I leave it to the house to determine how far Mr. Kemmis should be relieved from blame. But lest you should think I am varnishing, or impeaching wantonly, the character of this immaculate Crown-Solicitor—you who charge us with tampering with Mr. Magrath, a man at this moment in the employment of the Recorder —I will read to you the statement of Mr. Bond Hughes, of which the Attorney-General said not a word, because, I suppose, he thought it not at all relevant Probably he supposed it to be a work of supererogation to set the public right with respect to any unfortunate misapprehension of Mr. Bond Hughes. The following is the evidence he gave :—

"Turn to Monday, the 9th of October—I mean the meeting in Abbey-street. Can you enumerate the persons present of the traversers?—There were present Mr. John O'Connell, Mr. Daniel O'Connell, Mr. Steele, the Rev. Mr. Tyrrell, Dr. Gray, Mr. Duffy, and Mr. Ray.

"Then Mr. Barrett was not amongst them?—He was not.

"Then I presume you did not see at that meeting Mr. Barrett?—No. I made a mistake in saying he was there.

"You made that mistake on a previous day, not this day?—I made the mistake on the occasion I refer to, and I corrected it as soon as I possibly could.

"Then Mr. Barrett was not present?—He did not deliver a speech upon the occasion?—He did not.

"The Solicitor-General has not asked you about a dinner at the Rotunda. Were you there in your capacity as a reporter?—I was.

"I believe then I may assume as a fact that Mr. Barrett was not at that dinner.?—No, he was not there.

* Clerk of Mr Kemmis.

" Of course he made no speech at the dinner?—No, he did not. Somebody else made a speech for him?—I was misinformed.

" You mistook some one else for Mr. Barrett on the second occasion?—I did, and I corrected the error as soon as I possibly could.

" I think you stated, in answer to a question, that in justice to yourself, you felt it your duty to correct the mistake at the earliest period you could?—Yes.

" Were you at the house of Judge Burton when the informations were to be sworn?—I was.

" Did you see Mr. Barrett there?—I did.

" Did you, on that occasion, depose to the informations?—No; I did that on a prior occasion. I had sworn to the affidavits, and I made an amended affidavit on the second occasion.

" Did I understand you to say that you corrected that mistake about Mr. Barrett on a subsequent occasion? I did not.

" Were you present at the occasion when Mr. Barrett was held to bail upon the informations previously sworn against him?—I was.

" And you saw him subscribe the recognizances?—I did.

" Did you then and there correct the mistake?—I did, on the instant.

" Oh, I mean as to the name of Barrett?—Yes; I told Mr. Ray and Mr. Kemmis.

" Were they there attending on the part of the crown?—Yes; they were.

" Did you speak to Mr. Kemmis on the subject?—No, he was engaged taking the informations, but immediately after we got out of the room I communicated it to Mr. Ray.

" Let us have no mistake here. I suppose you do not mean Mr. Ray, one of the traversers?—No; I mean Mr. Ray, the managing clerk of Mr. Kemmis.

" And did you, before you left the house of the judge, apprise these two persons of the mistake?—I did, as we were leaving the house. I said I had a doubt about Mr. Barrett.

"When did you say that?—I said it when we were leaving the judge's chamber.

" What did Mr. Kemmis say?—I spoke chiefly to Mr. Ray.

" What did Mr. Kemmis say?—I do not recollect.

" How far was it from the judge's house?—As we were going through Kildare-street.

" Before you came to Mr. Kemmis's house?—Yes.

" Cannot you recollect what Mr. Kemmis said on that occasion?—I cannot.

" Did he say it was too late to correct the mistake?—He did not.

" Did he make no observation?—I do not remember.

" And there it was left?—There it was left.

" Now you mentioned the matter to Mr. Ray. Was it in Judge Burton's chamber?—It was in the passage, as we were leaving the room.

" Mr. Barrett was then in the house?—He was. We all left about the same time.

" What did you say?—That I had been mistaken with regard to Mr. Barrett, and I doubted whether he had been at the Rotunda or Calvert's Theatre; that I had heard his name mentioned, but was mistaken as to his identity.

" What did Mr. Ray say?—I do not remember what he said.

" Very extraordinary that you should not recollect what was said on so important an occasion. Did not Mr. Ray return?—No.

" And no further steps were taken by you?—I thought when I had put them in possession of the mistake, that I had done all that was necessary. I did not think the question of identity would have been left to me.

" You had no doubt about the mistake?—I was satisfied as soon as I saw him, that he was not the person.

" How long was it after the mistake about Mr. Tierney that the mistake was corrected?—In about three days afterwards.

" That was merely a mistake about the christian name?—Yes.

" The other mistake remained uncorrected. Did you apprise Mr. Barrett of it?—No; I thought I had done all that was necessary when I had apprised the officers of the crown of it."

Great stress is laid by the Attorney-General on the sworn and unsworn statements of Mr. Kemmis. He told the Attorney-General this, and he told the Attorney-General that, but he did not rectify the errors in Mr. Bond Hughes' affidavit. Now, I think the house must wonder that a person like the Crown-Solicitor should have been guilty of a sin of omission such as I have described; and in the next place, what is more extraordinary, I think the house must be not merely surprised, but astonished, that the Attorney-General when he made it a matter of accusation against Mr. O'Connell that Bond Hughes was the subject of imputation, and had been calumniated, did not state that Bond Hughes had been mistaken, and had actually supplicated the Crown-Solicitor to rescue him from his difficulty. I wonder if Mr. Kemmis mentioned it to the Attorney-General himself? Did he so, or did he not? Oh, last night you thought, that the Attorney-General had made out a triumphant case. [Loud cheers from the opposition, met by counter cheers from the other side.] Do you consider this a fitting matter for exultation? [Conservative cheers renewed.] I must say, I cannot enter into your peculiar views, or appreciate the excellence of Tory ethics. [Loud opposition cheering.] If these things be to you "tidings of great joy," I should be loath to disturb your self-complacency. I pass from a topic upon which I have said enough. No further comments are required; but let it be remembered, that those gentlemen who charge us with the corruption of Mr. Magrath, who sought—to use a rather vulgar phrase—to turn the tables upon us by a somewhat clumsy expedient—have themselves in the transaction I have mentioned, adopted the course I have described, and respecting which it is necessary for me to say one word more. But to proceed to the other facts of the case:—The bills are found. The names of the witnesses on the back of the indictment are demanded by the defendant, that was a reasonable demand. In this country, united with Ireland—

and I hope you will extend to Ireland the same principles and habits of liberty by which you are governed—in this country the practice has uniformly been to furnish the names of the witnesses on the back of the indictment. Am I not right? The honourable and learned Attorney-General for England will do me the favour to correct me if I am mistaken. The honourable and learned gentleman intimates by gesture, that it is the practice in this country. We applied for the names of the witnesses; we received a peremptory refusal. You asked for a trial at bar, you wished to have four judges. One of those udges was Mr. Justice Perrin. When it was convenient, the right honourable and learned Attorney-General relied upon the unanimity of the court, but when they disagreed he barely glanced at it.

ATTORNEY-GENERAL (for Ireland.)—The judges were unanimous in their judgment.

Mr. SHEIL.—They allowed the Chief Justice to charge the jury; they concurred with the Chief Justice in his view of the law. But do you not think any attention is to be paid to their dissent. If from their harmony you deduce consequences so valuable, from their discord are not some inferences also to be drawn? It is the practice to give the names of the witnesses in England. Judge Perrin declared that ne thought that in Ireland also it was a matter of right to give those names. That was a solemn decision upon the point. Judge Burton, an Englishman, with some remnant left of the feeling for which his countrymen are distinguished, said, he thought that although it was not a matter of right, it would be judicious on the part of the crown to give the names. Mr. Whiteside, the eloquent counsel for Mr. O'Connell, at the conclusion of the case, made a most reasonable suggestion. The Attorney-General resisted it, on the ground that it would introduce a new practice. I think that the right honourable and learned Attorney-General, when he went into all those minute details of that part of the case yesterday, would have done right had he mentioned the opinion of Mr. Justice Burton, the decision of Mr. Justice Perrin, and the offer made by Mr. Whiteside on behalf of the defendant. Let the house bear in mind, and let the country bear in mind, that an application never resisted in this country—admitted by the honourable and learned Attorney-General for England to be always granted as a matter of right—was by her Majesty's Attorney-General for Ireland, God knows for what reason, peremptorily rejected. I admit that the right honourable and learned Attorney-General agreed to the postponement of the trial upon two grounds—the first, that time was required to prepare a proper defence, as it obviously was when it was remembered evidence had to be given regarding forty-one meetings on behalf of the crown; and on the second ground, that there were but twenty-five Catholics upon the panel for 1843, while it was perfectly manifest that much larger number of Catholic jurors ought to have been upon the special jury list. But I deny that the court refused the application. My impression, on the contrary, was that the court determined to grant the application. It was obvious that one of the judges at least was so disposed. But let me not be mistaken. I do not mean to say that that was distinctly stated by the court ; what I say is this—Judge Burton expressed his astonishment that there were only twenty-five Catholics on the jury list, and when that surprise was expressed, the Attorney-General, having against him an irresistible case, agreed to the postponement of the trial, with the view to give the parties time to prepare their defence, a course he could not avoid, and also in order that the case should not be tried before a most erroneous panel. I do not wish to deny the merit of the right honourable and learned Attorney-General but had he insisted upon going at once to trial with a panel admitted to be utterly imperfect, and denounced by the right honourable and learned Recorder himself as most imperfect, surely an imputation would then have rested upon him far stronger than that which at this moment attaches to him, and, in my opinion, not without reason. I come to the suppression of a portion of the jury list. It is right that the house should be apprised that counsel were employed on behalf of the Repeal party and on behalf of the Conservative party, when the Recorder was going through the parochial lists, and that every name was a subject of as much contention as a vote at an election. The Recorder's court became the arena of the fiercest political contention. But I will begin by declaring that in the adjudication of the parochial lists the Recorder acted with the most perfect fairness, and I have no hesitation in saying that I believe he would rather that his right hand should wither than use it in an infamous mutilation of the jury list. I entirely acquit him of impurity of motive. But, having made this statement, he will forgive me for saying that I do think it was his duty to have personally superintended the ultimate formation of the jury list, and if he had superintended it the mutilation of the jury list would not have taken place. He complained that he had been made the object of the vulgar abuse of hired counsel. He once belonged to the band of mercenaries himself, and might have spared the observation. But I do not think it either vulgar or vituperative to state that it would have been better if he had remained in Dublin after his judicial duty had terminated, and when his ministerial duty had commenced. I admit as an excuse, almost as a justification, that he had great inducement to proceed to England; for the *Evening Mail*, the recorder of great public events, did not omit to watch the movements of the right honourable gentleman, and stated, under the head of "Fashionable Intelligence," that the right honourable gentleman, having left Ingestre, proceeded to the residence of that distinguished statesman, who in all likelihood was anxious to consult the Recorder on the proposed augmentation of the grant to the Education Board. And, may I be permitted to add, parenthetically, that upon the subject of education in Ireland a judicious taciturnity has been observed by the right honourable gentleman. No one will suspect that the right honourable gentleman connived at, or had the slightest cognizance of any misdeeds which may have taken place in the transcription of the jury list. I entirely and cheerfully acquit the Attorney-General of every sort of moral imputation, but circumstances did take place in reference to this list, upon which Mr. Justice Perrin remarked in open court, that there were grounds for apprehending that something had occurred which was worse than accident. Mr. Kemmis made an affidavit in reply, but he did not contradict the fact. There never was an affidavit in reply to that of Mr. Mahony respecting the fact, although other affidavits were subsequently made, and ample opportunity for contradiction was afforded. What is the case made out against us by the other side? But the Attorney-General more than insinuates, because Mr. Magrath is a Catholic, the traversers, or some underlings connected with them, tampered with him. That is the charge made, without a possibility of sustaining it. Does the Recorder assent to this assault on the character of a person still in his employment? How frontless and how preposterous is the imputation! Does any one believe, or can any one, by the utmost stretch of credulity, bring himself to believe, that the defendants would subtract a list of one parish, containing fifteen Catholic names, in order that not one of them might be called on the jury? Yet that is the insinuation made by her Majesty's Attorney-General for Ireland. Is this a fair mode of proceeding? When the Attorney-General makes a charge of this kind he ought to invest it with plausibility; but the Attorney-General forgot that the defendants put the very charge in issue in their challenge; why did he not venture to controvert it?—We are charged with corrupting a public officer whose livelihood depended upon good faith in the performance of his duties—for what? For the purpose of removing Roman Catholics from a panel to try Roman Catholics? Is that plausible? Could such assertion be received by acclamation, except by gentlemen who had been affected by the eloquence of the right honourable and learned gentleman. The speech itself, indeed, of the right honourable and learned gentleman I was disposed to cheer, but when I found that cheers were raised for a man who was blasting the character of another, I was astonished both at the want of just feeling on the part of the Attorney-General, and that such an accusation, destitute of proof, without plausibility, should be received with acclamations by a British assembly. What took place when the discovery was made of these missing names—I do not care whether they were sixty, or twenty-four, or twenty-seven? The noble lord opposite very justly says they were balloted for, and selected by chance. That may be a good or bad principle, but the chances should be equal on both sides. The judge in Rabelais had a dice-box, and threw for the plaintiff and defendant; but he did not load the dice. You remember the old practice in the House of Commons of balloting, when the names of members were put in glasses. Suppose in such a case, the names of twenty-seven Tories were left out. Of course, honourable members, bound by their oaths, would be as incapable of doing anything unjust or improper as a Protestant jury, but what would the Tories say in such a case? Would they not say, give us a new ballot? Put the twenty-seven names back. But whether the jury list was lost, or whether it was stolen, there are two facts connected with it of no ordinary moment. When the jurors' list was applied for to the Recorder by the traversers, he expressed his anxiety to give it, if the crown would consent to his doing so. He told us that he sent the clerk of the peace to the crown solicitor, to ascertain whether the crown would consent to that which the Recorder himself thought most reasonable and just. The crown refused. The second fact is of the same character. An application was made to the sheriff for the list, and the crown refused to consent. What was the result? That till the very last moment, the traverser's attorneys had no knowledge of the state of the jurors' book. A motion is made to quash the panel. An affidavit is sworn stating that twenty-seven Catholics were omitted. The Solicitor-General makes an affidavit, and does not deny the fact. Judge Perrin declares that in his opinion, there is ground for strong suspicion that foul dealing had been practised. An offer is made by the traversers to have the names restored to the panel. The crown refused to agree. An offer is then made, and it clearly might have been done by consent, to have a new ballot, to put the omitted names into the ballot box, and that offer is also refused. The consent would have bound both parties, and that which the law contemplated would have been accomplished. The Attorney-General, notwithstanding that he professed to detail everything that had happened with the most scrupulous exactness, did not say a syllable about the challenge to the array. He talked of Pearse's case, and Lord Hawarden's case, and fifty other cases, but not a word about the challenge: and for a very good reason, that Judge Perrin declared the challenge to be good, and the panel to be void. A challenge to the array takes place, and it is alleged in the challenge, and put in issue, that sixty names had been omitted from the jury list, and that the omission was fraudulent and corrupt. That fact the crown refused to try. The following are the words of part of the challenge:—

"And the said defendant further says, that a certain paper writing, purporting to be a general list, made out from such several lists so corrected, allowed and signed as aforesaid, was illegally and fraudulently made out, for the purpose and with the intent of prejudicing the said defendant in this cause."

What reason has the Attorney-General given for not joining issue on that important allegation—an allegation sustained by Judge Perrin's previous unequivocal expression of his opinion? It might have been tried at once by the officer of the court, but a demurrer was preferred. Now mark what happens. We put at issue two facts—the loss of the names, most material—the fraud, still more. Was it not the duty of the crown, under these circumstances, to have joined issue with us? If they had joined issue, there would have been an end to our objection; and if the point had been decided against them, then, of course, the panel must have been altered, or some steps adopted. How did the court decide? Was the court unanimous? Mr. Justice Perrin, who introduced the act into Ireland, which belonged to the Reform code of the right honourable baronet opposite—Mr. Justice Perrin, who knew the object of the act—who was familiar with all its details—by whom its machinery, so to speak, had been in part altered and adapted—Mr. Justice Perrin decided that the challenge was good. But government went to trial, one of the judges having declared that the source from which justice flowed had been corrupted. A learned friend suggests to me that a demurrer always admits the fact, but I will be candid on that subject. A demurrer admits the fact, for the purpose of argument only. I did not dwell upon that point because it was in some sort a legal fiction. I went to what was much more substantial. The crown had the opportunity of ascertaining a fact of the utmost materiality; the crown shrunk from that investigation. You then went on with the case with the protest of one of the judges against you, and a verdict you have obtained, by the intervention of a jury condemned by one of the judges who sat in that court. If all of the judges were unanimous as to the abstract law, as stated by the Lord Chief Justice, they were not unanimous as to the verdict, because one of the judges condemned the panel which was the foundation of the verdict, and if the panel be shaken, the entire superstructure raised upon it, must of course fall too. I come now to another portion of this case—the striking-off of Roman Catholics from the jury. But I see I am occupying the attention of the house at too great a length; but it is a case of paramount importance. It is a case in which I was counsel, and, of course, took a very warm interest in it—it would be strange if I did not—and I believe I am, to a certain extent, better acquainted with the facts than others can be, and I conscientiously believe I have not stated anything that departs in the slightest degree from the facts. With respect to the striking-off of the Roman Catholics, it is said by Mr. Kemmis that there were ten on the list of forty-eight jurors. Now, eight of those ten I at once admit were properly struck off. I cannot for a moment pretend that eight members of the Repeal Association, or persons who were subscribers to its funds, ought to have been retained on the jury. I could no more contend for it than that you should contend that Mr. Sheriff Faulkener should have been upon the jury. But there were two names struck off who were Roman Catholics, but who were neither members of the Repeal Association, nor subscribers to the Repeal fund. Mark the affidavit of Mr. Kemmis; put it in the disjunctive—he believes that the ten persons struck off the list were either members of the Repeal Association, or had subscribed to its funds. Henrick is a Roman Catholic; what course has been taken about Henrick? The noble lord the Secretary of State for the Colonies, who appears to know more about this part of the case than the Irish Attorney-General, told us that Henrick was considered to be a Protestant, and a Conservative. Who told him so?

Lord Eliot.—Mr. Kemmis.

Mr. Sheil.—Mr. Kemmis did not swear it. It never was mentioned until this debate had commenced. You start a new case or new pretext every moment, and that new pretext is grounded on nothing better than an asseveration of his belief by the Crown-Solicitor regarding a fact, in reference to which he was most egregiously mistaken. Henrick was not a member of the Repeal Association. He never subscribed to the Repeal rent. He is a Roman Catholic. It is sworn that he is. I requested my honourable friend, the member for the county of Wexford, when this matter was in agitation, and who was acquainted with Henrick, to ask him two questions: first, whether he was a Roman Catholic and next, whether he was a member of the Repeal Association, or a subscriber to the Repeal fund? The answer was, that he was a Roman Catholic—that he was not a member of the Repeal Association, and that he had never subscribed to its fund. But you now make a new case, and say that you thought he was a Protestant, and a Conservative. Come to the case of Michael Dunne. You do not pretend that Dunne was either a member of the Repeal Association, or a subscriber to its funds. But you believed that he might have signed a requisition for a Repeal meeting, though even that allegation is not positively made. But is there no distinction between being a Repealer and being a member of the Association? Is there no distinction between being an advocate of free-trade and a member of the Anti-Corn-law League? If Mr. Cobden, and Mr. Bright, and Mr. Villiers, and the *Globe* newspaper, and the *Morning Chronicle*, were indicted to-morrow for a conspiracy, would the crown be justified in setting aside, as a juror, every man who had signed a requisition in favour of free-trade, or had signed a requisition in favour of the repeal of the Corn laws? Or suppose that in 1831 the Tories had come into office, and had indicted the Whigs for conspiring to carry Reform by intimidation, for corresponding with the Birmingham Union, and for "swamping the House of Lords," would there be no distinction made, in empanelling a jury to try those revolutionary delinquents, between an advocate of reform, and a member of that seditious association commonly called Brooks's Club, in which I had once the good fortune of hearing a most eloquent speech delivered against the Duke of Wellington by a great orator, who, mounted upon a table through whose planks he almost stamped, poured out an incendiary harangue, amidst enthusiastic acclamation and rapturous applause.— But let us go back to the jury. The panel was bad, and was so declared by the judges. You adopted the course requiring that every Roman Catholic should be struck off the list. Would it not have been wise if the crown had given its consent that some Roman Catholic should be left on the list? I deny that if the crown had consented to the formation of a new panel there would have been any objection on the part of the traversers; and in that case, if the traversers afterwards attempted to controvert the verdict, they would clearly have been stopped by their own proceedings. But suppose no consent had been given, was there not another expedient that might have been adopted? Could not the rule for the special jury have been discharged? The sheriff for the city of Dublin is a gentleman of the highest respectability—Mr. Latouche. When the Municipal Bill was passing, you took the appointment of the sheriffs from the corporation. You left that appointment to the corporations in England. You did not take the appointment from cities here; but when you came to deal with us, you took the appointment of the sheriff from cities, and vested it in the crown; because you said that if the new corporations appointed the sheriffs, they would be just as bad as the old. I do not say whether the course you took was right or wrong; but when the crown assumed the right of appointing the sheriff, they might most safely and wisely have left to the sheriff the appointment of the jury in this case. You use the words "common jury," an expression, generally speaking, which means men selected from the inferior classes. Now, the jury that tried this case were, comparatively speaking, taken from the inferior classes. There were on it Protestant grocers, Protestant piano-forte tuners, and Protestant tanners. Perhaps it would have been better if persons of a higher class had been selected; but I must admit, that there is one advantage in making the middle classes the depositaries of political power, and that the middle classes are animated with as high a sense of honour and of duty as the first patricians in the land. I should never quarrel with the jury if they had not been composed of political antagonists. An expression was used by my right honourable friend the member for the city of Edinburgh, which has strongly excited the ire of the Attorney-General for Ireland. My right honourable friend had said that if there had been a common jury the Attorney-General for Ireland would not have dared to set by the Roman Catholics, whose names might be on the list. To this the Attorney-General for Ireland has replied, "I would have dared!" and certainly no one can deny his intrepidity. But what my right honourable friend meant was this—that the crown, controlled by public opinion—controlled, if not in Ireland, at least in this country by public opinion, acting under the coercion of British sentiment, would not have ventured upon an act at once so culpable, and so imprudent, as to strike off names of the highest respectability because they were Roman Catholics. Therefore if you were sincere in the manifestation of your desire that the Roman Catholics should be capable of acting on that jury, you had a very obvious mode of carrying your purpose into effect and of realising that desire; for when you found the mistake on the panel by all the Roman Catholics being excluded, you might have got a common jury, and in that case the verdict would have been unimpeachable, and all the controversy which has taken place, and all its consequences, and all the natural and inevitable irritation, might have been avoided. Under these circumstances, is it wonderful, that in Ireland great excitement should have taken place? Is it astonishing, that the Roman Catholics of Ireland should have felt indignant to a man on the subject? Is it wonderful that great public meetings should have taken place in every district of the country, to take the subject into consideration? Were these meetings called by factious men? At the head of them stood Lord Kenmare, one of the advocates of the Union—a man of large possessions, of very ancient birth, and a man highly allied in this country. That nobleman felt that these proceedings were an insult offered to him; he, therefore, not for the purposes of partizanship, not to gratify any political passion, not from any predilection in favour of Mr. O'Connell, signs a requisition to call a public meeting to complain of the course pursued by the crown. There was another circumstance which gave an additional poignancy to the feelings of the Roman Catholics; that circumstance was this, and as the Attorney-General for Ireland thought it judicious on his part to advert to the course I pursued on a trial at Carrick-on-Suir—he will excuse me if I refer to something which concerns himself, and to an occasion on which he made himself most conspicuous in Ireland. I do not mention this for the purpose of malevolence—I bear no ill-will to the right honourable gentleman—I have no motive for ill-will—he never did me wrong; and that that right honourable gentleman should have imagined that a conspiracy was formed against him at the bar, for the purpose of wounding his feelings, and injuring his prospects, was a most unfortunate hallucination on his part. I beg, on my honour, to assure him that no such intention was ever entertained. But he is a public man, and considering that in the management of the important duties it has imposed upon him, he did not exhibit any great delicacy towards others, he must expect, that when his political antagonists scrutinize his motives and his conduct, they will ask what manner of man this must have been, and what course has he pursued? He last night alluded to my conduct at a trial which took place many years ago ; and he said, also, that he was sorry for what he had said at the meeting which he attended in 1837. As being contrite, he is to be forgiven. But when the Roman Catholics of Ireland come to compare the course pursued by the Attorney-General, at the late trial in Dublin, with the opinions he had previously expressed—it was impossible that their suspicion should not be confirmed, that unfair dealings were practised in their regard. The house is already aware of the course pursued by the right honourable gentleman upon the Education Question —a question upon which the Recorder of Dublin took care to spare his right honourable friend, when he endeavoured to escape from it. But the right honourable gentleman had distinguished himself still more upon another question. In the year 1837, a great Protestant meeting was held in Dublin—speeches and resolutions of the most violent character were made and passed at that meeting. One of the barristers who took part in those proceedings has been made Master in Chancery; two of them have been made Judges, Lefroy and Jackson and the right honourable gentleman himself has been made Attorney-General by a government which professes to govern Ireland without reference to party. At that meeting a resolution was passed declaring that the Protestants of Ireland were in as perilous a condition now, as they were in 1641, when the most frightful massacres of Protestants are said to have taken place. But what did the right honourable gentleman say at that meeting? He said that Roman Catholics in Parliament had no regard to their oaths. That declaration, censurable as it was, was more manly than if he had dealt in insidious hints and despicable insinuations. But, surely, when the public functionary by whom that language was uttered caused ten Roman Catholics to be struck off from the special jury, it was impossible not to connect that proceeding with his former conduct—it was impossible not to attribute it to the most offensive motives. Meetings took place in almost every district in Ireland, and even the Roman Catholics of England were stirred into resentment. They are, to a man, opposed to the repeal of the Union. But this outrage to the feelings of every Roman Catholic in the empire they could not endure. When the First Lord of the Treasury came into office, Lord Shrewsbury addressed a letter to Mr. O'Connell, calling on him to support the present administration. But the blood of the Talbots has caught fire—the first earl in England denounces the gross affront offered to the religion of that community of which he is an ornament. The following letter was written by Lord Shrewsbury to Lord Camoys, on the occasion of the latter noble lord presiding at a meeting of English Catholics in the metropolis:—

"Alton Towers, Feb. 6, 1844.

" MY DEAR LORD—I regret extremely that circumstances will not allow me to attend the meeting over which you are to preside to-morrow as I was anxious for an opportunity of expressing my indignation, in common with yourself and many others, at the fresh insult offered to the whole Catholic population of these kingdoms, by the conduct of the law officers of the crown in the preliminary proceedings on the interesting and important trials now taking place in Dublin. The Catholics appear to have been struck off the panel *en masse*, upon the ground that they were all Repealers; but while this fact is asserted on the one side, it is stoutly denied upon the other. In the absence of any positive evidence on the point, we are, I think, fully justified in the inference that, whether Repealers or not, no Catholic would have been allowed to sit upon that jury seeing that such determination would have been in perfect keeping with what has hitherto been the fixed policy of the present government in Ireland, to exclude Catholics from all share in the administration of public affairs, and while professing to do equal justice to all, refusing them every grace and right enjoyed by their Protestant fellow-subjects. The exceptions are too trifling even to form the shadow of an argument.

" But even presuming that the facts are upon their side, does it evince a spirit of justice in the government to discard every man who was known to be favourable to Repeal, and at the same time to leave upon the panel many who were notoriously Anti-Repealers, and who are now actually sitting in judgment upon the traversers? In either case, then, the first principles of justice have been violated, and a gross insult offered to the people of Ireland; and I am sorry that I have only been able to mark my reprobation of such conduct by signing the requisition for a meeting to express our common feelings upon the subject.

"I remain, my dear lord,
" Very truly and faithfully yours,
SHREWSBURY

" To the Lord Camoys."

Is not the fact itself a monstrous one, that in a great Catholic country, in the greatest State prosecution that has ever been instituted in that country, the Liberator of that country should be tried by an exclusive jury marshalled in antagonism against him? Strip the case of all those details upon which there has been so much controversy, look at that bare naked fact, and say whether it can be reconciled with the great principles of Catholic Emancipation? As far as trial by jury is concerned, Catholic Emancipation is repealed, and repealed in a spir?

is unjust. We are admitted to the Bench of Jus-
Justice which was adorned by a Catholic Chief
Master of the Rolls; we are admitted to the Impe-
have at this moment the honour of addressing; we
Treasury Board, to the Board of Admiralty, to the
are admitted to the Privy Council. But, admitted
admitted to the Parliament, and admitted to the
lmiralty, to the Board of Trade, and to the Privy
ren from the Jury—we are ignominiously driven
there a refuge has been supplied to that Protestant
ou have re-invested with all the most odious attri-
testable domination. And yet the noble lord the
d tells us that he is anxious for the impartial admi.
! At the last London election Mr. Baring was
ple interrogator, whether he was favourable to free
ed that he was favourable to free trade in the
n he was asked whether he would vote for the
ig scale, he said that was quite another ques-
rith the noble lord. He is favourable to impartial
:t. Ask him to admit a Roman Catholic as a juror
ition, and he exclaims, " Oh, that is quite another
wever, admit, that I believe the noble lord to have
infirmity of purpose, which, although lamentable, is
as the Yorkshire yeomanry authoritativeness, and
ticism of my Lord de Grey. There is in Dublin a
rotestant Operative Association. It exhibits in its
ts of Conservative policy in Ireland. That Associa-
dress to Lord de Grey immediately after the procla-
ued In that address it stated that " the Sacrifice
phemous fable, and that a system of idolatry unhap-
:ountry." It submits to the Lord Lieutenant that
id laws which shall have the effect of abolishing
or the suppression of the College of Maynooth; the
in keeping with another address from the same
Catholic religion is designated as a " God-disho-
pheming, and a Bible-denying superstition, whose
ry." Popery is called " the masterpiece of Satan."
idolaters upon the bench—idolaters on the judg-
conclude with a panegyric on the honourable mem-
igh, whose arrival in Dublin they announce as an
nticipated by all Irish Protestants. The other day
ributed to me; I acquit him of all blame, but that
e by me, but by a person of the same name, resi-
et, Dublin. In the *Annual Register* the speech is
stake. This Protestant Operative Association, this
your sacerdotal institutions, having addressed the
reference to the proclamation, what answer did he
unce—did he reprove contumely so wanton and so
he, as the representative of his sovereign, who

charged him when he went to Ireland to govern the country with impartiality, and expressed to him her tender solicitude for the welfare of her Irish people, express the slightest condemnation of the atrocious language which had been employed in reference to the religion of seven-eighths of the inhabitants of Ireland? No, Sir.—But in his answer to the congratulations of these conspirators against the first principles of Christian charity, he expresses his "warm acknowledgments for the honours which they have conferred upon him, in the expression of their thanks for his conduct on a late occasion." Does the First Lord of the Treasury approve of this proceeding on the part of his "Lord Deputy of Ireland?". The Secretary for the Home Department considers it as indiscreet, but as to the Secretary for the Colonies, as he, in all likelihood, sympathises with the Protestant Operative Association, I beg to hand him their address to Lord de Grey, as it will furnish admirable materials for his next "No Popery" speech. The moral effect of the verdict will not be enhanced by the conduct of Lord de Grey, or by the speeches of the Secretary for the Colonies, or the Secretary for the Home Department. That right honourable gentleman spoke of "convicted conspirators" not being able to upset the Established Church. Even if your verdict had been legitimately obtained, you should abstain from such expressions You should not give way to this inglorious exultation. You are an Englishman, and you ought not to hit a man when he is down. As to the noble lord the Secretary for the Colonies he never fails to apply a provocative to our resentments, and to verify what my friend Mr. Fonblanque says of his orations—"Every one of them is a blister of shining flies." I am surprised that the First Lord of the Treasury, knowing, as he must know, that so hot a horse is likely to bolt, allowed him to be entered for the race. He ought, at all events, if the noble lord was determined to speak, to have suggested to him, that as his government of Ireland had not been peculiarly successful, to avoid the topics which are most likely to add to the national irritation; he ought to have admonished him not make such a speech as in Canada would be likely to produce great irritation amongst the large Catholic community of that important colony. Perhaps the Prime Minister did give him some such warning, and probably, like the Irish Attorney-General, he promised to put a restraint on himself, and to extend his Conservative habits to his temper. But once on his legs, all his good resolutions were forgotten, and he could not deny himself the luxury of offering every Catholic in the house an affront in the pharisaical homily which he delivered on the oaths taken by Catholics in parliament. He read the oath—read it in italics—he read it almost as well as the Chief Justice read the speech of Daniel O'Connell. He begged of us to examine our consciences, and to consider the awful obligation which was imposed upon us. In giving us a lecture on perjury, he does not mean to offend us. Be it so; but suppose that in the spirit of retaliatory gratitude, I were to give him a lecture on an offence of far inferior culpability, on political apostacy, and were to say—"My lord, I do not mean to offend you, but I entreat you not to give way to the acrimonious feelings by which tergiversation is habitually characterised; don't play the fierce and vindictive renegade, for the sake of men with whom the partner of your conversion declared that it would be in the last degree discreditable to consort, and remember that '*sans changer*' is the motto attached to your illustrious name." I very much question whether the noble lord would consider these amiable suggestions as giving me any very peculiar title to his thanks. But there was something even more remarkable than his advice in reference to the Catholic oath in the speech of the noble lord. He was exceedingly indignant at the reflections on the Chief Justice in reference to whom delicacy forbids me saying anything, as he was "counsel on the other side," and insisted that a judge of the land ought not to be made the subject of criticism in this house; yet when he was a Whig Cabinet Minister he did not exhibit this virtuous squeamishness, but thought Baron Smith, the father of the Irish Attorney-General, would give capital sport in a committee of the House of Commons. He proposed an inquiry into the conduct of Baron Smith —an inquiry into the accuracy of the charge of Mr. Baron Smith.

Lord STANLEY.—No, I didn't.
Mr. SHEIL.—Didn't you?
Lord STANLEY.—No, I didn't.
Mr. SHEIL.—What! No vote of censure?
Lord STANLEY.—No.
Mr. SHEIL.—No motion for a committee?
Lord STANLEY.—No.
Mr. SHEIL.—Then, what was it? There was a motion I know made in this house for a committee to inquire into the conduct of Mr. Baron Smith in charging the grand jury.
Lord STANLEY.—No.
Mr. SHEIL.—Yes, but there was. The Secretary for the Home Department perhaps can tell me, because he voted against the noble lord. The Secretary for the Home Department was shocked at such a proceeding, and my Lord Monteagle, whose nerves are better now, was shocked too. Upon that occasion the noble lord (Lord Stanley), and the Secretary for the Home Department were divided; there was then only one star in Gemini. But let me turn from the noble lord, whose conduct and whose advice we hold in the estimate which they deserve, to the country to which he once said that he would give a lesson—and inquire how it is that you intend that the government of Ireland, for the future, shall be carried on. Ireland is not to be ruled by force. Indeed! It is to be ruled through Protestant jurors, and Protestant charges, and Protestant gaolers; but Protestant jurors, and Protestant charges, and Protestant gaolers, require that Protestant bayonets should sustain them, and that, with the discretion of the Home Office, the energy of the Horse Guards must be combined. But let me come to your specific measures. You have issued a landlord and tenant commission, composed exclusively of proprietors. You did not place upon it a Catholic bishop, or any other eminent ecclesiastic, having an intimate acquaintance with the sufferings of the poor. These commissioners are to fill up three or four folios of evidence, to prove to us, what every one of us already knows. The Home Secretary tells us

that he is inclined to render the landlord's remedy more compendious, but he ought to remember that Mr. Lynch, the master in Chancery, who is thoroughly acquainted with Ireland, a first-rate lawyer, and an excellent man, who has managed his own property with the most humane concern for his tenants, thought the remedy of the quarter-sessions preferable to an ejectment in the superior courts, because the costs in the superior courts are overwhelming, and the tenant purchases a little delay at a price utterly ruinous, and which deprives him of all chance of redeeming his land. The right honourable gentleman also informed us that he had a Registration Bill in his thought; I admit that the Government are entitled to large praise for having thrown the Secretary of the Colonies overboard; but why does not the right honourable gentleman inform us of his plan? He will cut down the franchise with one hand, and extend it with the other; but how will he extend it? By the Chandos' clause; that is, he will discourage the granting of long leases, and he will create a mass of vassalage in times of tranquillity, and in seasons of political excitement he will create an open revolt, by which the whole country will be distracted. But what does he mean shall be done with regard to the Catholic Church and the Protestant Church; with regard to the church with a congregation and without a revenue, nd the church with a revenue and without a congregation? Will he grant glebe leases to the Catholic clergy, will he build Catholic houses of worship, will he augment Maynooth? On these subjects the Government are silent, but it is intimated that with the revenues of the establishment no sacrilegious innovation shall be permitted to interfere, and that the Established Church shall be maintained in the plenitude of its possessions, in a country in which two-thirds of the Irish members are returned by Roman Catholics, in which Roman Catholics are masters of all the Corporations in the south of Ireland, in which every day the Catholic millions are making a wonderful progress in wealth, in industry, in intelligence, in personal self-respect, and in individual determination. And why is the church to be maintained in its superfluous temporalities? Because we are told that it is founded in Christian Protestant truth. Be it so; but permit me to inquire on which side of the Tweed in Great Britain Protestant truth is to be found? On the northern bank it is impersonated in the member for Perth—in the member for Oxford on the south. It is Calvinistic in the north, Armenian in the south; it is dressed in a black gown and a white band in the north; in the south it is episcopally enthroned, mitred, and crosiered, and arrayed in all the pomp of pontificial attire. On the north it betrays its affinity to Geneva; on the south it exhibits a strong family resemblance to that Babylonian lady, toward whom, under the auspices of Doctor Pusey, its filial affection is beginning to return. If I shall ever be disposed to recant the errors which have now continued for 1800 years, in order that, being permitted to assail the Irish Church from without, I may, as a Protestant, undermine it from within, perhaps the Secretary for the Home department, who is a borderer, will tell me on which bank of the Tweed the truth is to be discovered. But wherever it is to be found, it must be admitted that the Irish Church has not been very instrumental in its propagation. You have made no way in two centuries in Ireland, while Popery is every day, and in every way, upon the advance. The Catholic religion, indigenous to the mind of Ireland, has struck its roots profoundly and widely in the belief and the affections of the people—it has grown beneath the axe, and risen in the blast—while Protestant truth, although preserved in a magnificent conservatory, at prodigious cost, pines like a sickly exotic, to which no natural vitality can be imparted, which by every diversity of expedient you have striven to force into freshness, and warm into bloom, in vain. But you may resolve, *per fas aut nefas*, to maintain the abuses of the church, but it is right that you should know, that among the Catholics of Ireland there exists but one opinion on the subject. You heard my honourable friend the member for Kildare—he is a gentleman of fortune and of birth, highly connected, and who has again and again refused to take the Repeal pledge. He tells you that he is thoroughly convinced that an alteration in your establishment is required. A vast body of the Protestant Irish aristocracy entertain the same sentiment; and even here, the supporters of a Conservative government cannot refrain from telling you that a revision of the church cannot be long avoided. The honourable member for Wakefield, who was one of the vice-presidents, if I remember right, at the dinner given in 1838, to the First Lord of the Treasury, at the Merchant tailors'-hall, bore his important, although reluctant, testimony to the necessity of a change. That change is said to be against principle. But what an incongruity between your theory and practice: take, as an instance, the Canada clergy and reserves. The clergy reserves were appropriated by act of parliament, by one of the fundamental laws of the colony, to the maintenance of the propagation of the Protestant religion. Before the revolt in Canada (that painful instrument of political amelioration) we were told that the clergy reserves were set apart for sacred and inviolable purposes. But the Canadian insurrection produced one good result; the Archbishop of Canterbury did no more than stipulate for a change of phraseology in an act of parliament, and the Protestant clergy reserves are at this moment applied, in part, to the sustainment and the diffusion of the Catholic religion. The present Prime Minister, the Secretary for the Colonies, the Secretary for the Home Department, the Bishop of London, all agreed to this momentous alienation. The Bishop of Exeter alone stood by his colours—he implored, he adjured the House of Lords in vain—he called on the bishops to remember their oaths, he pointed out the disastrous precedent which you were about to make. He was right—the inference is irresistible, the whole appropriation question is involved in the clergy reserves. But consider whether, even in your dealings with the Irish Church, you have not acted in such a way as to render your position utterly untenable. By the Church Temporalities Act you abolished Irish Church rates. You thereby subtracted so much from the property of the church—you suppressed a certain number of bishoprics, why should you not suppress a corresponding number of benefices? You do not want so many bishops —how can so many parsons be required by you? But the Tithe Bill is a still stronger case. In 1831 the Catholic members asked nothing more than that you should apply the surplus of church property to charity and education. They never proposed to confiscate a fourth and give it to the Irish landlords. In 1835 that proposition was made by the present Secretary-at-War, then Secretary for Ireland. To the Tories the entire merit of originating that wild and Wellingtonian measure exclusively belongs. But the gallant officer, when Secretary for Ireland, proposed a bill by which one-fourth of the tithe was confiscated and put into the coffers of the landlords—you would not alienate church property—not you; but with one blow you take away one-fourth of their tithes from the church, and surrender the precious fragment to the Protestant landlords of Ireland. Your own conduct in reference to the Education Question is the strongest illustration of your own sense of the incompetence of the Irish Church to fulfil the duties of an establishment. In England, where you have an Established Church which teaches the religion of the people, you gave up the Factory Bill; you have perpetuated ignorance, and all the vices which it engenders, rather than infringe on the sacerdotal prerogative of your establishment, which claims the tutelage of the nation's mind; while in Ireland you have stripped the church of all its privileges, and declared it to be unfit for one of its most important functions—the direction of the public mind; nay, more, the Secretary for Ireland, who now thinks it politic to offer his homage to the clergy of the Established Church, with a sincerity of panegyric commensurate, I hope, with its exaggeration, denounced that clergy for their factious opposition to the Education Board. You have thus, by your own acts, pronounced a virtual condemnation of your Establishment—that monster anomaly to which nothing in Europe is to be compared. Yes; there is one analogy to be found to your sacerdotal institutions—there is one country in Europe in which your Irish policy has been faithfully copied. In a series of remarkable ukases the Emperor of all the Russias proclaims the eternal union between Poland and Russia, declares it to be the means of developing the great national advantages of Poland, expresses his surprise that the Poles should be so utterly insensible to his benevolence, reprobates the malcontents by whom fanciful grievances are got up, and establishes the Greek Church as an excellent bond of connexion between the two countries. Is there a single argument that can be urged in favour of the English Church in Ireland which does not apply to the establishment of the Greek Church in Poland? The fee-simple of Poland is now Russian. Property in Poland has been Tartarised, by very much the same process by which it has been Protestantised in Ireland. A Greek hierarchy will compensate for the absence of the nobility in Moscow and St. Petersburgh, and it will be eminently conducive to public usefulness, that a respectable Greek clergyman should be located, as a resident, in every parochial subdivision of Poland, with a living, in the inverse ratio of a congregation. Almost every year we have a debate in this house touching the wrongs of Poland, and an assurance is given by the right honourable baronet that he will use his best endeavours to procure a mitigation of the sufferings of Poland. I have sometimes thought, that in case Lord Aberdeen should venture on any vehement expostulation, which is not, however, very likely, Count Nesselrode might ask, whether Russia had not adopted the example of England towards Ireland; whether, in Ireland, torrents of blood had not been poured out by your forefathers; whether Ireland had not been put through a process of repeated confiscation; whether the laws of Russia were more detestable than your barbarous penal code; and whether, to this day, you do not persevere in maintaining an ecclesiastical institution repugnant to the interests, utterly at variance with the creed, and abhorrent to the feelings of a vast majority of the people? Such, I think, would be the just reply of a Russian statesman to my Lord Aberdeen; and, since I have named my Lord Aberdeen, I gladly avail myself of the opportunity to express my unqualified approbation of his foreign policy. When the home office plays, in reference to Ireland, so belligerent a part, and when the Secretary of the Colonies, in speaking of Ireland, " stiffens the sinews" and " summons up the blood," and, I may venture to add, imitates the action of the tiger, nothing will become my Lord Aberdeen so much as " mild behaviour and humility." Rightly did my Lord Ashburton, under his auspices, concede to America far more than America could plausibly claim.— Rightly will he relinquish the Oregon territory; rightly has he endured the intrigues of the French Cabinet in Spain; rightly did he speak of Algiers as a *fait accompli.*" Rightly will he abandon the treaties of 1831 and 1833, for the suppression of the slave trade; but, after all, this prudential complaisance may be ultimately of little avail; for who can rely upon the sincerity of that international friendship, which rests on no better basis than the interchange of royal civilities? Who can rely upon the stability of that throne of the Barricades, which has neither legitimacy for its foundation, nor freedom for its prop? And if it falls, how fearful the consequences that may grow out of its ruins! The First Lord of the Treasury will then have cause to revert to his speech of 1829, to which my honourable and learned friend the member for Worcester, so emphatically and so impressively adverted. The admonitions of the noble lord, the member for Sunderland, will then be deserving of regard. These topics are perilous; but I do not fear to touch them. It is my thorough conviction, that England would be able to put down any insurrectionary movement, with her gigantic force, even although maddened and frantic Ireland might be aided by calculating France. But at what a terrible cost of treasure and of life would reason be subdued! Well might the Duke of Wellington, although familiar with fields of death, express his horror at the contemplation of civil war. War in Ireland would be worse than civil. A demon would take possession of the nation's heart—every feeling of humanity would be extinguished—neither to sex nor to age would mercy be given. The country would be deluged with blood, and when that deluge had subsided, it would be a sorry consolation to a British statesman, when he gazed upon the spectacle of desolation which Ireland would then present to him, that he beheld the spires of your Established Church still standing secure amidst the desert with which they would be encompassed. You have adjured us, in tne name of the sworn on the Gospel of God—I adjure you, in the cept contained in that holy book—in the name of t the perfection of humanity —in the name of every c human, as you are men and Christians, to save my evils to which I point, but to avert them, and to re shall be the means of precipitating that country int will deliver its great finding against you, and that answerable to posterity, but responsible to that J sence, clothed with the blood of civil warfare, i dreadful to appear. But God forbid that these ev any other existence, except in my own affrighted those visions of disaster should be embodied in that the men to whom the destinies of England a Sovereign, may have the virtue and the wisdom to fearful ills that so darkly and so densely lower upo part, I do not despair of my country; I do not desp time when Ireland will cease to be the battle-field mutual acrimonies will be laid aside ; when our fat sacrificed to the good genius of our country. Wit have elapsed since my return to England, I have s vince me, that there exists amidst a large portion community, a sentiment of kindliness and of good land. I have seen proofs that Englishmen ha promptitude, if they have felt themselves wronge who may have done them wrong. That if English minded Englishmen, do but conjecture that injust a political antagonist, swayed by their passion for to his succour, and with an instinct of magnanim take his part. I do trust that this exalted sentimen by my countrymen as it ought to be ; and that it ma and that it may lead to a perfect national reconcili countries, instead of being bound by a mere parchu legal ligament, which an event may snap—shall be and socially identified, is the ardent desire of one who is conscious of numerous imperfections, but imperfections may be, is not reckless of the interes devotedly attached to his Sovereign ; and, so far dismemberment of this majestic empire, offers up a ever passed from the heart to the lips of any one of ness of that empire may be imperishable, and that the affluence, and that the glory, and that, above England may endure for ever.

FRANCE AND MOROCCO.

SPEECH IN THE HOUSE OF COMMONS, JULY 22 1844

lay, I informed the right honourable baronet at the head of
ty's government, that instead of moving for a committee to
w far our commercial interests were involved in the events
passing in the Barbary states, I shall content myself with
r papers, of which I have since given him notice. My first
was, that the extent to which the trade of this country has
ted by the heavy imposts which have been recently laid upon
;e of British vessels, and the products of British industry in
ts upon the coast of the Mediterranean, of which France has
elf the mistress, required a minute investigation; and that
of the ordinance, which issued on the 16th of December last,
the duties on English shipping, and of the augmentation on
n our cottons to 30 per cent., would best be proved by the
ral and documentary, which could be produced before a com-
his house; but I have heard objections raised to the form of
n, of which I had given an intimation, and in order that a
the mere form should be avoided, by which the attention of
would be in all likelihood distracted from the consideration
omentous matter, I have thought it more advisable to move
)pies of certain documents should be laid on the table of the
vhich much of the information which I seek to obtain may be
There is another motive for the adoption of this course. It
ch is least calculated to give offence to a gallant, but exceed-
:ptible people. It is not my intention (and I shall prove that
the tone with which I shall treat this important subject) to
ng by which a debate, at which France could legitimately
:e, would be produced. Nothing shall fall from me, by which
shall be afforded for imputing to me the more than reprehen-
ose of exciting a sentiment of animosity between two great
)th of which are deeply concerned in the maintenance of
whose collision would disturb the world. But while I am
need of the importance of preserving our pacific relations
ntry, whose institutions are so nobly assimilated to our own.
:onvinced that with a perfect absence from all irritating lan-
:andid statement of facts can be readily reconciled; and I
if circumstances have occurred, or are likely to occur, by
commercial interests of England may be seriously affected,
ll be gained by concealing the truth, or by turning our eyes
those objects which must sooner or later be forced upon our
ion On the 5th of March, 1830—I pass at once at the
abruptness, which is more excusable than prolixity, to the
ich I mean to advert—in 1830, on the 5th of March, Lord
wrote a despatch to an ambassador at Paris, Lord Stuart de
with regard to the great armament which France had pre-

..red for the invasion of Algiers. That despatc
most just, expressed in a most prudential and concil
the entire of the official correspondence of Lord .
remarkable for a most striking contrast between
judgment and a certain infirmity of purpose, owing
to obtain from France the assurances, of the n
appears to have been himself most fully convinc
appears to have been perfectly aware that it was c
quence to get from the French government a ple(
tion of Algiers should not be permanent, and to ha
mercial and maritime, and therefore our political i
at stake, in the events to which the French expedi
The whole correspondence is a curious specimen of
upon one hand, a plain Englishman asks that a pl(
in plain language, and, on the other hand, a Fren
and well lubricated, escapes in sinuous diplomac
Those portions of the correspondence which are ill
sent position of affairs I shall select, taking care 1
which is not appropriate and interesting. On the
Lord Aberdeen writes—

"My Lord—The extensive scale of the prepar:
dition against Algiers, and the declaration in the
Christian Majesty upon this subject, have naturall
tion of his Majesty's government. Your Excelle
of the sincere desire which his Majesty entertains
affronts which have been endured by the King
Regency of Algiers may be duly avenged, and tha
Majesty may exact the most signal reparation 1
state; but the formidable force about to be embarl
tion in the speech to which I have alluded, appear
tion of effecting the entire destruction of the Rege
infliction of chastisement. This probable change
territory so important, from its geographical position
by his Majesty's government without much inte
some explanation of the intentions of the French g(
desirable. I have communicated these sentimen
Laval, and have received from his Excellency the
ances of the entirely disinterested views of the cab
in the future disposal of the state of Algiers. 1
Excellency has promised to write to his governmer
the means of making an official communication, I l
to instruct you to bring the subject under the notic
It is probable that the French minister may be desi
the explanation we can desire. The intimate unio
ing between the two countries give us reason to
receive the full confidence of the French governmer
ing the interests of both, and which in its results m
the most important effects upon the commercial an(
of the Mediterranean states."

Prince Polignac, to whom the contents of this despatch were communicated on the 12th of March, 1830, wrote to the Duke de Laval a long despatch in which he says nothing bordering upon an understanding beyond this statement:—

"The King, whose views on this grave question are quite disinterested, will consult with his allies, in order to determine what should be the new order of things."

Lord Aberdeen saw at once that this communication was most indefinite, and was not in the least binding, and on the 23rd of March, 1830, he wrote—

"Whatever may be the means which shall be found necessary to secure the objects of the expedition, the French government ought, at least, to have no difficulty in renouncing all views of territorial possession or aggrandizement. * * * * Monsieur de Polignac is doubtless aware of the great importance of the Barbary states, and of the degree of influence which, in the hands of a more enlightened government, they could not fail to exercise over the commerce and maritime interests of the Mediterranean powers."

Lord Stuart de Rothesay made several efforts to obtain a positive assurance, but failed. On the 21st of April, 1830, Lord Aberdeen writes as follows:—

"Is it unreasonable to expect from the French government something more than a general assurance of disinterestedness, and an engagement to consult their allies, before the future fate of the regency shall be finally decided? A French army, the most numerous, it is believed, that has ever crossed the sea, is to undertake the conquest of a territory which, from its geographical position, has always been considered of the highest importance; no man can look without anxiety at the issue of an enterprise, the ultimate objects of which are so uncertain and so undefined. * * * * If we could so far forget what is due to our Sovereign and to ourselves as to rest satisfied with vague explanations in a matter so deeply affecting the interests of British commerce, as well as the political relations of the Mediterranean states, it is certain that the people of this country would not hesitate to pronounce the most unequivocal condemnation of our conduct."

How applicable are these observations to what is passing at this moment on the coast of Africa, and on the frontier of Morocco, and how justified is a member of the British Parliament in the expression of a hope that Lord Aberdeen has been more successful, in 1844, in extracting an engagement from M. Guizot, than he was in 1830 in eliciting it from the unfortunate statesman who succeeded in baffling him, and from whom no written engagement could be procured. Two months were passed in correspondence, yet nothing was attained in the form of a distinct stipulation. On the 4th of May, 1830, Lord Aberdeen wrote to Lord Stuart de Rothesay:—

"Monseiur de Polignac expresses a hope that our expectations may not be so unreasonable, as to urge him to declarations which must prove injurious to the government of his Most Christian Majesty. If the projects of the French cabinet be as pure and disinterested as is asserted by Monsieur de Polignac, he can have no real difficulty in giving us the most entire satisfaction. A concise and simple declaration could not answer the purpose better, but it would appear to be more natural than the course which your Excellency states that the French minister has been commanded by his Most Christian Majesty to adopt; to envelop in such reasoning, and to mingle considerations of national dignity and punctilio, with the statement of intentions such as I have mentioned, appears less calculated to produce conviction, and to convey the impression of sincerity and frankness."

Lord Stuart de Rothesay, of course, communicated these well-founded complaints to the French ministry; but the latter, instead of writing a plain promise, such as Lord Aberdeen asked on the 12th of May, 1830, wrote to the Duke de Laval what I perused with some amusement as a specimen of evasions, which it required some disrespect for Lord Aberdeen to have attempted. He says that the fleet was about to sail, and adds—

"His Majesty from that moment, namely, the conquest of Algiers, ought to give an assurance to his allies, that he will present himself to those deliberations, ready to furnish all explanations which they might still desire, disposed to take into consideration all rights and all interests," and so on. After this despatch had been written, a remarkable incident occurred. The Sultan had directed Tahir Pacha to proceed to Algiers, in order to adjust the differences with France. The French squadron would not permit Tahir Pacha to land, and he was forced to go to Toulon, where he was detained. Lord Stuart de Rothesay writes—" At Toulon he will be, without doubt, detained in quarantine, and if he intends coming to Paris he may possibly not reach Algiers till long after it shall be too late to take part in the negotiations which are likely to follow the capture of the place."

Algiers was taken on the 5th of July, 1830. The French general told the French that the stars mingled with the lights which they had kindled on the brow of Mount Atlas, and on the 16th of July, Lord Stuart de Rothesay wrote to Lord Aberdeen that he had waited on Prince Polignac to congratulate him, in the conviction that he would keep faith with his court. His Excellency answered, "by declaring his readiness to repeat his former assurances," and in a few days after he was a prisoner in Ham; Charles the Tenth, who could not learn anything even from the misfortunes of the Comte d'Artois, was driven from his dominions and from his country, and from the Barricades.— There arose a throne which the Duke of Wellington and Lord Aberdeen hastened to recognise as the legitimate result of the national will. But is it not wonderful that the new government was recognised by England, without any sort of stipulation in reference to Algiers? Lord Aberdeen had not obtained any specific engagement from Prince Polignac. He acknowledged himself, he was fully aware of the vast importance of the results which must follow the permanent occupation of Algiers and her three provinces by France, and yet it does not appear that when Louis Phillipe was recognised by the Tory government, they made a single observation in reference to Algiers. The Tory government remained in office for four months after the French had taken possession of Algiers, and after they had pushed their acquisitions into the adjoining territory, and yet Lord Aberdeen had no observation to make. The Whigs, finding the French army in possession of Algiers, and not being able to refer to any engagement, took no steps one way or other, and stood passively by. I pass from 1830 to 1841, avoiding any detail of the means pursued by the French to secure their conquest, and thinking it unnecessary to say anything upon the expedients by which civilisation had been extended and Christianity has been diffused by those peculiar propagators of the faith. In 1841, Lord Aberdeen had been scarce a few weeks in office, when the Count de St. Aulaire engaged him in a conversation upon Algiers, to which Lord Aberdeen attached no importance, but which the French ambassador turned very promptly to account. The King of the French introduced into his speech, made on the 15th of December, a statement that he had taken means to secure the possessions of France from all external complication; a paragraph which remained unintelligible, until M. Guizot, as a proof of the influence of France over the Tory government, stated the conversation which had taken place with Lord Aberdeen. I read the speech of M. Guizot in the journal *Des Debats*, and I inquired from the First Lord of the Treasury whether the conversation of Lord Aberdeen had been correctly reported by the Count de St. Aulaire. The right honourable gentleman said that the report was substantially correct, except that Lord Aberdeen denied that he had said that he had no objection to make. Lord Aberdeen himself stated the conversation was accidental, and on the 28th of January, 1842, wrote a despatch to Lord Cowley, in which he denied his having stated that he had no objection to the French retention of Algiers. This despatch was communicated to Monsieur de Guizot. Monsieur Guizot made no observations on the subject, but I cannot help thinking that the course subsequently adopted by the French government was influenced in no small degree by the imputed declaration of Lord Aberdeen. The French government issued an ordinance on the 16th of December, 1843, imposing a duty of four francs a ton on our shipping, and 30 per cent. on our cottons. What has been the result? I beg to call attention to the following letter, which appeared in the *Times* of July 18. It was written by their own correspondent, and is dated at Oran, July 6:—

" The commercial system lately adopted here by the government has completely shut out British commerce from this port. Formerly several British vessels came here, but no more now, except with coals, are expected. The port duties on all foreign vessels are four francs per ton. French vessels rarely pay anything. Sardinian vessels are favoured by treaty, and pay only two francs per ton. English cotton manufactures, which paid last year only 15 per cent., now pay more than 30, which amounts to exclusion."

Who is there that hears these facts who will say that the subject which I have submitted to the attention of the house is one of which the consideration ought to be avoided? The fulfilment of all Lord Aberdeen's propositions in 1830 is found in the fiscal exclusion of English manufactures. A blow has been aimed, not at the honour of England, but at her industry; and those who laugh all the idealism of national dignity to scorn, utilitarians of politics, must, in this prohibition, find a cause, not only to regret the past, but to look with solicitude to the future. The proceedings adopted with reference to Morocco cannot, in a commercial view, be regarded with indifference. They have commenced, like the expedition to Algiers. A squadron has proceeded to the Coast, which is only divided by the distance which a cannon shot could almost traverse from Gibraltar, with 12,000 men.¹ ¡The French army has invaded Morocco, and France demands not only the expulsion of the valiant Abdel-Kader, the hero of the desert, but an indemnity and a guarantee. Morocco may soon fall under the protection of France; and if it does, the results to your commerce are obvious. Mr. Macgregor, in his recent and very admirable work on the commerce of this country, has given the statistics of our trade with Morocco. We almost monopolize the market of a country inhabited by 8,000,000 of people. Are we not entitled, under these circumstances, to ask of Lord Aberdeen what course he has followed, and to call on the minister to lay on the table of the house any engagement entered into by France in reference to the state with which we are allied, and which it is so much our interest to save from the domination of a power of whose acquisitive tendencies some evidence has been afforded? To Morocco the French protective system will be beyond all doubt extended, whenever Morocco is annexed to Algiers. In this state of things it is not unnatural that we should inquire, first, what explanations have been given and demanded, and in the next place what force her Majesty's government have had the precaution to assemble in the Mediterranean? With regard to the first, as Lord Aberdeen appears not to have obtained any very satisfactory engagement in reference to Algiers, we ought to have proof afforded us that some stronger security for Morocco has been given; and with respect to the second, the government are bound to show that for any emergency which may arise, they are not unprepared. What should be the amount of our naval force? It is my good fortune to be able to refer to two very high authorities, the Duke of Wellington, and the right honourable baronet, with regard to the inexpediency of leaving England destitute of that force on which not only her strength, but her existence, depends In August, 1838, the Duke of Wellington declared that "his great object in speaking at all was to impress upon their lordships and upon the government, and upon the country, the absolute necessity of having a strong naval force in all parts of the world." What was our naval force in 1838, which the duke considered insufficient? Ships of the line, 18; frigates, 29; sloops, 39; brigs, 39; steamers, 22. In 1839, on the 11th of March, the right honourable gentleman, the First Lord of the Treasury, made a most remarkable speech on the navy estimates, in which he complained that our government had not sent a squadron to the Coast of Mexico when St. Juno de Ulloa was attacked by the French. He reproached the government with having omitted to assemble a great naval force at the points where events of signal magnitude were likely to arise. He insisted that the Whig government had permitted the naval power of England to decline, and laid it down as a rule that we should have a large fleet ready for immediate employment, and for the protection of our own shores, as well as for the exhibition of our power in remoter seas. Let us see what navn. force the right honourable gentleman thinks sufficient, when he is in office, and when events are casting shadows before them by which the Mediterranean is darkened. Here is a tabular statement of our Force in 1841 and 1844:—

Ships in Commission on 1st July, 1841, and 1st July, 1844.

1st July, 1841.		1st July, 1844.	
Ships of the Line	26	Ships of the Line	9
Frigates	36	Frigates	32
Sloops	40	Sloops	31
Brigs	39	Brigs	24
Armed Steamers	22	Armed Steamers	32
Foreign Mail Steamers	14	Foreign Mail Packets	4
Foreign Mail Brigs	22	Foreign Mail Brigs	6

Let us now look to the distribution of the force in reference to the Mediterranean in both those years:—

Distribution of Force.

Mediterranean, 1841.		Mediterranean, 1844.	
Ships of the Line	17	Ships of the Line	1
Frigates	7	Frigates	4
Sloops	4	Sloops	3
Brigs	3	Brigs	0
Armed Steamers	9	Armed Steamers	6
Mail Packets	4	Mail Packets	4
Total	44	Total	18

One ship of the line in the Mediterranean! And for this utter neglect of British interest—for this most discreditable helplessness to which we are reduced in that sea, where the fate of empires has been so often, and will be again, determined, what is the excuse? I read the statement of the First Lord of the Admiralty with astonishment, that our naval force was employed on the coast of Ireland, and could not be spared for the Mediterranean. Is not this a most lamentable admission? A man who was Lord Lieutenant of Ireland, and who is First Lord of the Admiralty, over whom the Orange flag was unfurled in one country, and to whom the honour of the union-jack is confided in the other, openly in the face of the parliament, of the country, and of the world, announces that the honour of England is to be perilled, in order that Ireland should be kept down. Do not imagine that I condemn you for having a large force in Ireland; you have made it indispensable by your misrule, and a further augmentation of that force will be, whenever you shall be at war, required—that I complain of.— What I most profoundly lament is, the policy by which you have exposed the country to the most fearful peril; when you could, by means so obvious and so easy, convert Ireland, now a source of weakness, into a monument of your strength; and in the affections of a loyal and devoted people, by common justice, raise up a bulwark of your empire infinitely better than any which Richmond Penitentiaries can afford. But let me not permit myself to depart from Algiers to Ireland, although the First Lord of the Admiralty has associated them together; let me revert to and resume the topics which will appear to be more immediately connected with the motion with which I mean to conclude I have traced the circumstances under which the French possessions in Africa were acquired; I have shown how completely our government were baffled when the expedition first landed in Algiers; I have shown the effects upon our commerce of the extension to Algiers of the principles of French colonisation; I have adverted to the aggressive proceedings adopted with regard to Morocco, and to the miserable impuissance to which our navy has been reduced; and as I began I conclude. I stated at the outset of what I said, or meant to say, that I should studiously take care not to say anything at which Frenchmen the most sensitive could reasonably complain. I hope that I have kept my promise; I was anxious to do so. I look upon the French as a most noble people. I regard the present Prime Minister of France as a man of surpassing abilities, and among men of high intellectual stature, as standing pre-eminent. The King of the French is one of the most remarkable men whom his country, fertile in greatness, has produced. He has proved that the uses of adversity are sweet, and with a diadem upon his head, has preserved that jewel which adversity is said to bear —a precious one—and finer than the brightest brilliant that glitters in his crown. But, however we may be disposed to admire the people of France, and the minister and the King of the French, we must bear in mind, that between France and England there exists, and there has always existed a feeling of competition, which should induce us to look for the proof of cordial friendship to something more substantial than mere professions of amity, however prodigally bestowed. My noble friend, the late Secretary for Foreign Affairs, was said to have alienated France; at all events, he did not lower England. But in what regard have his successors in office succeeded in obtaining from France anything beyond those phrases of diplomatic endearment which we should be taught by what is passing to appreciate at their real value. What have you got from France since you have come into office? A commercial treaty has not been signed—no single advantage for the trade of England has been secured. Your predominance in Spain is gone; the Escurial is but an appurtenance to the Tuileries; and upon the coast of Africa, whence Spain is commanded, before the armies and the armaments of France the influence of England has vanished. Talk as you will of the friendly feelings of France, and of the better understanding that prevails between the two countries than existed before you came into office, that you have gained a single point, either political or commercial, I think you will find it difficult to establish. Sir, I beg leave to move

"For copies of the ordinance of the 16th of December, imposing increased duties on our shipping and manufactures and a return of the amount of our naval force in the Mediterranean on the 1st of July, 1844."

ADJOURNMENT.

SPEECH IN THE HOUSE OF COMMONS ON THE 9TH AUGUST ON THE MOTION THAT THE HOUSE SHOULD ADJOURN TO THE 5TH OF SEPTEMBER.

INSTEAD of the customary prorogation by the Queen, the adjournment of the house is proposed by the first minister of the crown, in order that the opinions of the judges in the case of Mr. O'Connell may be delivered before the next session, and to prevent the hazard of a great injustice being done. It is felt by everybody that it would be monstrous that Mr. O'Connell should be kept in gaol for six months, and that he should afterwards be discharged upon the ground that he ought not to have been originally imprisoned. The case is conceived to be one of so much importance and so much difficulty, that a deviation from parliamentary usage is proposed by the Prime Minister, and on the 5th of September parliament is to assemble again. If the decision shall be in favour of Mr. O'Connell—if the judges shall think that the jury was improperly composed, and that the challenge to the array should have been allowed, Mr. O'Connell will be discharged. For this proceeding the government do not claim any credit, for by an opposite course the general censure of the country would be incurred. But surely the government have, by the step which they are now adopting, made the most important practical admission. They have, by an irresistible implication, acknowledged that the detention of Mr. O'Connell pending the question whether he ought to have been imprisoned at all, ought to be deeply lamented by themselves. Mr. O'Connell was imprisoned on the 30th of May. If he is discharged on the 30th of August, because the sentence was illegal—that will be the feeling of both countries—how great will be the astonishment of the one, how vehement the indignation of the other? It ought, then, to be matter of the most solemn deliberation with the government, whether instead of waiting to ascertain whether the lawyers shall have succeeded in picking the lock of the Richmond Penitentiary, it would not be far wiser to throw open the doors of the prison-house at once, and to give back his freedom to the man whom under circumstances so peculiar you have deprived of his liberty. These are facts admitted upon all sides, facts beyond dispute, almost any one of which ought to have induced the government to terminate the period of Mr. O'Connell's imprisonment. The suppression of the lists in the Recorder's Court—the refusal of the crown to join issue on the averment of fraud—the solemn opinion of one of the judges at a trial at bar that the panel was illegally and wrongfully concocted—the exclusion of every Catholic from the jury, by which the leader of a great Catholic people was tried and convicted—these are circumstances which ought to induce the government to give up a verdict thus illegitimately obtained, and to which it is the consummation of impolicy that you should so pertinaciously adhere. You have yourselves, unconscious of what you were doing, furnished in a very recent proceeding, one of the strongest arguments against your verdict which it would be possible to suggest. You have admitted, that it would be most unjust that a commission for the administration of charitable bequests should be exclusively Protestants, and that you have provided that out of the ten individuals to be selected as a committee, five at least shall be Catholics. What an inference is afforded by this special provision in your recent bill, which you represent as an act of common justice to the people of Ireland? If the charitable bequests of Ireland are not any longer to be administered by a Protestant board, is it not an outrage to common sense and common justice, that the great leader of a Catholic people should have been tried by a jury from which every one of his co-religionists was excluded by the crown, and was, in fact, composed of men who had rendered themselves conspicuous by the vehemence of their political and religious feelings? No other fact to condemn your verdict in the opinion of all impassioned men, no other fact is wanting to justify my noble friend the member for London in his deliberate declaration that Mr. O'Connell had not been fairly tried. The House of Commons has not ratified that declaration, but the present Prime Minister ought to look to something besides the House of Commons, and that for his own sake, for the sake of his fame hereafter, he ought at once to assent to the liberation of a man tried under his own Jury Act, under an act introduced by himself, and which has been converted into an instrumentality so utterly abhorrent from the purposes for which it was devised. The right honourable gentleman is one of those by whom fame is estimated at its proper value, and who can appreciate renown. You pass every day by the statue of George Canning—every day you look at Westminster Abbey—to the judgment of posterity you cannot be insensible. Of what will be hereafter said in reference to the great events which are passing, that you can be reckless, no man shall persuade me to believe. Does it not then occur to you that of your conduct in reference to your great Irish antagonist history will not approve? The time will come when your merits will not be determined by the numbers which issue from the old lobby or from the new, but by another and more impartial reckoning; and when that time shall have arrived, and when it shall be told that Daniel O'Connell at almost the outset of your political career rushed against you into the lists of political encounter—that after nearly twenty years of a fearful struggle he extorted the freedom of his country from your reluctant consciousness that it could no longer be withheld; that, finding you unwilling to complete your achievement and to carry out the lofty principle on which it was founded, he continued in antagonism to your party, and demanded that the institutions of Ireland should be remodelled and adapted to the great change which had been accomplished; that, after a long exclusion from office, you came back to power, and that instead of availing yourself of the opportunity which was afforded you of winning the hearts of millions of Irishmen, you preferred the support of a faction to the sustainment of a people; that you selected the men to whom Ireland was most antipathetic as the objects of your favour; and that when goaded by many wrongs and exasperated by affronts, your old political foe demanded the restoration of her legislature to Ireland, you empanelled a jury of twelve Protestants for his conviction; that despite the protest of one of the first judges of the land, you threw him into prison, and when an inquiry was demanded into the machinery by which your jury was manufactured, you shrank from investigation, and left your adversary in the prison-house to which, at the age of seventy, he had been consigned; do you not think—does not your own heart inform you, that history, in whose tribunal juries are not packed—history, the recorder whose lists are not lost—stern, inflexible, impartial, history, upon this series of calamitous proceedings will pronounce her condemnation? It is in your power, it is yet within your power, to give to history something nobler to tell-- to commit to it the better office of telling, that having the magnanimity to confess yourself to have been mistaken, rescuing yourself from the trammels of vindictiveness, animated by the feelings by which the minister of the greatest Sovereign and the noblest empire in the world should be inspired, you disdained the luxuries of vengeance, you did not wait for the tardy adjudication of the men by whom it is acknowledged that difficulties are entertained, but winning, by a generous action, a victory over your adversary, and over yourself, you gave back his freedom to the man to whom millions are indebted for their liberty—you acquired a title to their confidence by the only possible reparation you can make for the great injustice you have done to the Irish people. If this measure were adopted by the right honourable gentleman, if the wound could be healed by the hand which inflicted it, Ireland would be made susceptible of the ameliorations which we are assured by the government that they have in view. But Daniel O'Connell is detained in the prison to which he ought never to have been committed. What advantage have you obtained—what benefit can you expect ever to secure—from the imprisonment of Daniel O'Connell? His spirit is as much abroad as if he stood on the theatre of Mullaghmast, and tens of thousands were gathered at his call. His mind still agitates the great mass, and with the mighty millions is still blended and commingled. After the verdict (it is a remarkable fact) the Repeal rent suddenly fell, and after the execution of the sentence, it rose four-fold. You have imprisoned three proprietors of newspapers, and yet the press, undeterred by your verdict, is more exciting and more intrepid than ever. The *Nation* newspaper, distinguished by the rare eloquence with which it is written, circulates more than 11,000 copies a week—that most remarkable publication circulates in every hamlet of the country, and ministers the strongest stimulants to the high spirit of nationality which it has made it its chief object to awaken. The Catholic clergy are, almost to a man, against you. In Dublin a great and well-organized association, which no law can reach, holds its weekly meetings; and, although not elected by the people, must be admitted to be a faithful representative of the national feelings. What, then, have you gained by the imprisonment of Daniel O'Connell? what other has been the result of that rash measure, excepting the creation of a deep feeling of hostility to the English government, which, if it is any time most injudicious—it is, under the existing circumstances of the country, most perilous to provoke! There are those who tell you that Ireland is tranquil; but I, who know Ireland well—who have had a long and painful experience in Irish agitation, who have, however, near at heart the peace and security of the country, and who have taken no part, direct or indirect, in the recent excitement of that country—I, anxious only that my admonition should have the effect of inducing you to adopt a wiser course, tell you, that however ostensibly tranquil, Ireland is not safe. There can be no doubt that your competitors for the masterdom of Europe, who have begun to think that they could dispute your supremacy upon the ocean, have assumed a tone which they never would have adopted if they did not calculate upon the internal debility of England, and upon the weakness resulting from the alienation of Ireland. You have adopted a tone at last which becomes this great country, and have declared that a reparation for the outrage offered to a British subject would be required; but, having adopted this tone, it becomes you to secure yourselves against every hazard, and to marshal the people of Ireland in your cause. The higher the position you have taken, the stronger the bulwarks with which you should encompass it, and you may rest assured that you will find a muniment in the affections of the Irish people far better than the martello towers in the Bay of Bantry can supply.

INCOME TAX.

SPEECH IN THE HOUSE OF COMMONS, 19TH FEBRUARY, 1845, ON MR. ROEBUCK'S MOTION TO EXTEND IT TO IRELAND.

SIR, my honourable friend (he will permit me to reciprocate the phrase of parliamentary endearment) has often expressed his solicitude for Ireland, but as the dismal agriculturists, by whom that locality is occupied in this house, which in the vocabulary of an American may be designated as "the bench of repentance," have reason to offer up a prayer that heaven should save them from their friends, in that proverbial ejaculation Irishmen have cause to coincide. My honourable friend is determined to give us, in the form of an income tax, the benefit of British institutions—a benefit analogous to that which we derive from the English church. My honourable friend has thought it judicious to advert to many Irish members in language of exceedingly unqualified and exceedingly unprovoked condemnation. I do not agree with them in the view which they adopt, because I consider it to be wiser to attend in parliament and to do my utmost to obtain redress for the grievances of my country; but if my honourable friend will reflect a little, he will see that his censure of Mr. O'Connell and his associates is most undeserved. The case they make is this,—they insist, and with melancholy truth, that year after year they have endeavoured to obtain justice for their country, and that all their efforts have been vain; that the Irish members are swamped and overwhelmed by a great and prejudiced English majority; that Ireland has not an adequate representation in this house; that while Wales sends 33 members to parliament, with a population of 700,000, the great county of Cork, with 800,000, returns only five; that while towns in England, with a population of 2,000 or 3,000, return two members, there are towns in Ireland, Carrick-on-Suir and Thurles, for example, with a population of 12,000 each, which do not return a single representative; that the elective franchise of the two countries is not the same, and that Ireland has a miserable constituency, because you deny her a fair registration bill. This is the justification of my Irish parliamentary friends, who conceive that a bitter parliamentary experience affords a warrant for their secession. The member for Bath has often expressed a coincidence with the views of Irish members in reference to the denial of justice in these important regards, and when these men remain in their own country, he surely ought not to visit them with such unmeasured reprobation. I do not coincide in the view which they have adopted respecting the policy of staying away; but, while I state this, I cannot forbear from adding, that there is more than plausibility in the suggestion that it is better to array the people of Ireland, and form them into a vast and united mass, in order that by a pressure from without, the minister may be induced to afford redress where redress is so much required, than to deliver themselves of speeches in this house which will not be followed by any practical advantage to the country. I have thought myself bound to state thus much on behalf of men of whose love of country I have seen such proof, and I turn to the proposition of the honourable gentleman. My friend the member for Kendal, wishes the income tax to be perpetual; my friend the member for Bath wishes it to be universal. "Eternity!" cries out the one; "infinity!" exclaims the other. The member for Bath would spread the perpetual blister over the whole imperial frame. But not the whole of the blister, because while schedule D and all the other schedules are fastened upon England, he would put schedule A only upon my impoverished and emaciated country. He is in this particular singularly inconsistent. My honourable friend has adverted to a recommendation I presumed to give him. I ventured, indeed, to tell him that he might usefully avail himself of the interval which should elapse between Tuesday morning and Wednesday night, in order to peruse with attention the speech of Edmund Burke upon the conciliation of America. I do admit that in my judgment that speech might have been perused by my honourable friend with signal benefit to himself, because there are contained in it many most salutary admonitions, given by that great and prophetic statesman with an almost unparalleled eloquence. Bright as was his imagination, and although subjects the most obscure were illuminated and became transparent in the blaze of his fancy, yet his philosophy was as profound as his power of illustration was astonishing, and his wisdom was not the less oracular for the magnificent embellishment of the temple—the gorgeousness of the shrine from which his predictions were pronounced. My honourable friend has intimated that I meant more in speaking of Edmund Burke and of America than I expressed. I was sufficiently intelligible, and do not shrink from the construction which my honourable friend has put upon the reference, which he thinks it adventurous on my part to have made. But I might have referred the member for Bath to the authority of another great statesman—the distinguished advocate of Lower Canada and its Assembly in this house. Of that eminent person the member for Bath may think humbly, but everybody else must form the highest estimate of him. In the speeches of the champion of Lower Canada, principles will be found which it were well if the member for Bath were to apply practically to Ireland. He warned the government not to lay their hands on the revenue of Lower Canada—I warn him not to attempt to extort from Ireland a revenue which she cannot afford, and which we ought not to be compelled to pay. No minister by whom an income tax has ever been yet proposed ever thought it possible to extend it to Ireland. Before the Union, Mr. Pitt, although he had fatal proofs of the ignominious complaisance of the Irish Parliament, which surrendered itself at last in a moment of fatal and weak compliance, never availed himself of his influence, and of those seductive means at his disposal, to induce the Irish Parliament to impose an income tax upon Ireland. After the Union the income tax was repealed at the peace of Amiens, because it was held to be a war tax—a tax to be reserved for danger—a tax sacred to public peril, and to which, excepting in a season of great emergency, no minister as justified in resorting. The tax was, however, renewed when the ar broke out again, and the terrific struggle with Napoleon was enewed. Yet in the midst of the exigencies of England the income ix was not extended to Ireland. It was renewed by Mr. Fox, by Mr erceval, by Lord Liverpool, yet by no one of those ministers was the icome tax extended to Ireland; and when the right honourable baroet became Prime Minister, and propounded his projects of fiscal innoation, he explicitly declared that this grievous impost should not be iflicted upon the sister island. I do not rely upon the fact that there no machinery in Ireland adapted to its exaction. The imposition of a income tax upon Ireland would be unjust, and what is unfortunately ? still more importance in the estimate of public men, would be in the st degree impolitic and unsafe. The income tax in Ireland would be ost inequitable. Before the Union Ireland had a surplus revenue spended in Ireland, and the country flourished. You induced us to enter ith you into a ruinous co-partnership, of which you have had all the :ofits, while we have deeply participated in the loss. The impolicy of ngland plunged her into debt, of whose load we are compelled to bear a irt; had we remained in the enjoyment of our legislative independence, ' your ruinous expenditure we should not be the victims. It is most unfair iat you should now call on us, after all the detriment which we have ready suffered, to bear a portion of the vast cost incidental to this experient You drain us through the absentee system—an inevitable attendant) the Union—of millions of money, which, instead of circulating through eland, swell the overflowings of the deep and broad Pactolus of British)ulence. You have transferred all our public establishments to this ngle point of imperial centralization; the revenue which Ireland elds is expended not in Ireland, but here; and of this evil I cannot 'esent to you a more striking exemplification than in appealing to the ct that the crown-rents and quit-rents of Ireland have been laid out a the splendours of Windsor Castle, and the embellishment of this ist metropolis. I may parenthetically suggest to the head of the overnment, that in the quit-rents and crown-rents of Ireland he has fund at hand with which his projects in reference to education can ? readily and largely accomplished. When from Ireland you already ke so much, it would be most unjust that you should endeavour to ttract still more. But, if the proposition be most unjust, it is still/ ore unwise. If Swift, with Wood's halfpence was able to do so much,[1]

---

[1] Dr. Johnson, in his "Life of Swift," says: "He delivered Ireland from plunder and pression, and showed that wit confederated with truth, had such force as authority was able to resist. He said truly of himself, ' that Ireland was his debtor.' It was from the ne that he first began to patronise the Irish, that they may date their riches and prosrity. He taught them first to know their own interest, their weight, and their strength, d gave them spirit to assert that equality with their fellow-subjects, to which they have in ever since making vigorous advances; and to claim those rights which they have at t established. Nor can they be charged with ingratitude to their benefactor; for they ered him as a guardian, and obeyed him as a dictator."
The Author of "The Sketch of the State of Ireland, Past and Present," published in

what would not the man of whom Swift was the
achieve with the income tax? The pressure of t
cause Catholicism, Protestantism, and Calvinism to (
compact of discontent. Who can doubt that the r
the instant the income tax was extended to Irelan
Repealer, and enrol himself among the burning pa
tion Hall? In 1782 the Protestants and Catholic
the independence of the Parliament of Ireland ;
who not only hope, but believe, that before they d
that parliament in its independence may be extort
a care then how you deal rashly with Ireland. D
a small accession to the revenue, do us an injustice
ment to yourselves. There are other means of
from Ireland besides an income tax. There is
government. By doing perfect justice you can lar
is equivalent to gain. Justice is a good housew
and frugal friend, the member for Montrose, has of
tan, by adopting a sound policy in Ireland, effect a
reduce your army to a force comparatively small.
that as in Scotland 2,000 men are quite sufficient,
might be reduced in the same proportion. On Fr
honourable friend in his enthusiasm forgot his ol
forgot himself. He said nothing of retrenchme
economy of justice to Ireland. Although politi
keeping watch over the public treasure as the (
golden fleece was said of old to be guarded, m
yielded to the "magic arts" and to the eloquent
fascinating financier. But now that he is recover
trust that he will take the same view as I do
facility with which a large revenue could be obta
whose resources, through misrule, remain undev
but endeavour to adapt your institutions to Ireland
to adapt Ireland to your institutions—in that an
that a great deal of truth is condensed—if, I repe
ing Ireland to your institutions, you do but try to
tious to Ireland—if, instead of inflicting a tempor
confer a perpetual peace, you will obtain from Ii
exceeding anything which, by the torture of this

1810, says of Swift: "In this gloom one luminary arose, and I
Persian idolatry: her true patriot, her first, almost her last. S
said, he dared;—above suspicion, he was trusted;—above envy
rivalry, he was obeyed. His wisdom was practical and prophetic
warning for the future: he first taught Ireland that she might b
and that she must cease to be a despot. But he was a churchm
course, and entangled his efforts·—guiding a senate, or heading
Cromwell. As it was, he served Ireland by his courage, impro
adorned her by his letters, and exalted her by his fame.

n, it would be possible for you to obtain. Peace, true peace—peace nded upon justice, and equality, and national contentment 'as an riching, as well as a civilizing and ameliorating, attribute. Peace l pay you large import duties—peace will consume in abundance ;ar, and coffee, and tea, and every article on which a charge will nain—peace will draw from the earth twice its ordinary return, and ile it shall give you more food, will take more of your manufactures return—peace will enlarge and give security to that market which already the best you possess—peace will open a wider field to your orious industry and your commercial enterprise; and for every iefit you confer upon us, for every indulgence you shall show us, for ry gift you bestow, with an usury incalculably profitable, by peace will be repaid.

POST-OFFICE ESPIONAGE.

SPEECH IN THE HOUSE OF COMMONS, APRIL 1, 1845, ON MOVING A RE
LUTION REGARDING THE LETTERS OF JOSEPH MAZZINI, WHICH I
BEEN OPENED BY THE WARRANT OF SIR JAMES GRAHAM, ONE OF I
MAJESTY'S SECRETARIES OF STATE.

I HAVE risen in order to move the resolution of which I gave no
before the Easter recess. I submit it in the following terms:—
Resolved that this house has learned with regret, that ·wit
view to the prevention of a political movement in Italy, and m
especially in the Papal States, the letters of a foreigner, which had
relation to the maintenance of the internal tranquillity of the Uni
Kingdom, should have been opened under a warrant bearing date
1st of March, and cancelled on the 3rd of June, 1844, and that
information obtained by such means should have been communicated
a foreign power."

Let me be permitted in the first instance to correct a misconcepti
It is not my purpose to make the fatalities which happened in Calal
the grounds of imputation. I believe every word which has been sta
by Lord Aberdeen. In this country—this veracious country, in wh
the spirit of truth is pre-eminent, if a minister of the Crown, no mai
to what party he may appertain, rises in his place in either House
Parliament, and either with respect to what he has done, or what
has not done, makes a solemn asseveration, with an instinctive proi
titude he is instantaneously believed; and if in the case of every r
who is in the enjoyment of the official confidence of his Sovereign
remark holds good, how much more applicable it is to a statesman, v
honour so unimpeached, with honour so unimpeachable, as the Ear
Aberdeen. I will not deny that it has been to me the occasion of so
surprise, that with the letters of Emilio and of Attilio Bandiera bef
his eyes, letters written at Corfu, and relating to the intended desc
upon the Calabrian coast—with such means of knowledge—with
much light about him, Lord Aberdeen should have been in ignora
so complete; but his statement—the simple statement of a man
such indisputable truthfulness—outweighs every other considerati
and to any conjecture injurious to Lord Aberdeen I will not per:
myself to give way; but the actual descent upon Calabria, and the p
spective movement in the Papal States, are distinct. The scaffolds
Cosenza and of Bologna are unconnected. Lord Aberdeen has clea
himself with regard to any perfidy practised towards the Bandieras,
the Post-office intervention with regard to the movement in the eccle
astical territories has with the Calabrian catastrophe little to do. T
distinction has been lost sight of in the course of the Post-office disc
sions. Indeed, the public attention was a good deal engrossed by
parliamentary encounter between the Secretary of the Home Depa
ment and his old and valuable friend. By a singular combination
bravery and of ability, the member for Finsbury has obtained a series

successes of the most signal kind. I cannot help thinking, however, that more plausibilities may be pleaded for the opening of the letters of a member of parliament than for breaking the seals of letters written to a foreigner, who had no English confederates, who had raised no money in England, who had not made any shipment of arms, who had not enrolled any auxiliary legion, and whose letters related to transactions with which the internal tranquillity of England is wholly unconnected. The Duncombe is not as strong as the Mazzini case. What 's the case of Joseph Mazzini? He is an exile in a cause once deemed to be a most noble one. In 1814 England called on Italy to rise. The English government (it then suited their purpose) invoked the Venetian, and the Genoese, and the Tuscan, and the Roman, and the Calabrian to combine for the liberation of their country. Proclamations (I have one of them before me,) were issued, in which sentiments were expressed for which Mazzini is in exile, and for which the Bandieras died. Botta, the Italian historian, tells us that Lord William Bentinck and Sir Robert Wilson, acting by the authority of the English Government, caused a banner to be unfurled, on which was inscribed "The Independence of Italy," and two hands were represented clasped together, as a symbol of the union in which all Italians were invited by the English government to combine. How badly have we acted towards Italy! When our purpose had been served, after having administered these provocatives—after having drugged Italy with provocatives, we turned suddenly round,—we surrendered Italy to a domination worse than that of Napoleon, and transferred to Austria the iron crown. But the spirit of nationality did not expire; it remained, and a long time, dormant, but it was not dead. After the Revolution in France of 1830, and the Revolution in England in 1831, a reform of abuses—of proved abuses—was demanded in the ecclesiastical states. It was denied, and an insurrection was the consequence. It was suppressed, and Mazzini, who was engaged in it, was compelled to fly from Italy, bearing the love of Italy, the malady of exile, in his heart. Louis Blanc, in his history of the ten years, gives an account of the incidents which took place in the struggle between the Papal government and its subjects, to which I will not minutely refer, because he may not be regarded as an impartial writer; but in the appendix to the third volume of his work, a document is to be found of a most remarkable kind. Lord Palmerston had directed Sir Hamilton Seymour, who belonged to the legation at Florence, to proceed to Rome with a view, in concert with the representatives of the four great powers, to induce the Papal government to adopt such reforms as would prevent any popular outbreak, from which consequences prejudicial to the peace of Italy might be apprehended. The utmost efforts were made by Lord Palmerston not to crush the just efforts made by Italians for the reform of great abuses, but to induce the government, by a timely concession, to prevent any popular commotion. Sir Hamilton Seymour was employed by Lord Palmerston for this purpose. He writes the following letter to the delegates of the four powers, which is I think, most deserving of attention:—

Rome, September 7.

"The undersigned has the honour to inform your excellency that he has received orders from his court to quit Rome, and to return to his post at Florence. The undersigned is also instructed briefly to express to your excellency the motives which have induced the English government to send him to Rome, and also the reasons for which he is about to quit that city. The English government has no direct interest in the concerns of the Roman States, and has never thought of interfering in them. It was invited by the cabinets of France and of Austria to take part in the negotiations at Rome, and it yielded to the entreaties of both those cabinets, in the hope that their good offices, when combined, would lead to the amicable solution of the discussions between the Pope and his subjects, and thus avoid the danger of war in Europe. The ambassadors of Prussia and of Russia at Rome, having subsequently taken part in these negotiations, the ambassadors of the five powers were not long in discovering the chief vices of the Roman administration, and the remedies which they required. In May, 1831, they laid before the Papal government a memoir suggesting reforms, which they unanimously declared to be indispensable for the permanent tranquillity of the Roman States, and which the English government considered to be founded in justice and in reason. More than fourteen months have elapsed, and not one of their recommendations has been adopted or executed by the Papal government. The edicts, even, which have been prepared or published, and which announce that some of these recommendations are about to be carried into effect, differ essentially from the measures specified in the memoir The consequence of this state of things has been such as might be expected. The Papal government not having done anything to allay the popular discontent, it has augmented, and has been increased by the disappointment of the hopes which had been awakened by the negotiations at Rome. Thus the efforts made for more than a year by the five powers to re-establish tranquillity in the Roman States have been made in vain. The hope of seeing the population voluntarily submitting to the Sovereign power is not stronger than it was at the commencement of these negotiations. The court of Rome appears to rely upon the temporary presence of foreign troops, and upon the co-operation which it expects from a corps of Swiss for the maintenance of order But foreign occupation cannot be indefinitely prolonged, and it does not appear that a corps of Swiss, such as the Papal finances could support, would be sufficient to control a discontented population. Even if tranquillity could be restored by these means, it could not be expected that it would be durable, and would besides never accomplish the objects entertained by the English government in taking part in the negotiations. Under these circumstances, the undersigned has received orders from his government to declare that his government no longer entertains any hope of success, and that the presence of the undersigned at Rome no longer having any object, he has been instructed to resume his post at Florence. The undersigned is besides directed to express the regret which he profoundly feels at not having been able for a year and a half to

do anything for the re-establishment of tranquillity in Italy. The English government foresees that if there be a perseverance in the present course new troubles will break out in the Roman States of a still more serious nature, and of which the consequences will at last become dangerous to the peace of Europe. If these anticipations shall be unhappily fulfilled, England will at all events be free from all responsibility for the calamities which will be occasioned by the resistance offered to the wise and urgent counsels given by the English cabinet.
"G. H. SEYMOUR."

Such is the view taken by Sir Hamilton Seymour of the abuses existing in the Papal states. It may appear singular that I, a Roman Catholic, should think it judicious to advert to the subject. I distinguish between the Italian potentate and the spiritual head of the Catholic Church—I see in the pope, as pope, the supreme pontiff of Christendom, the successor of St. Peter in an uninterrupted apostolical lineage; —I see in the pope the supreme authority in the government of the church invested with holy prerogatives, which for the execution of his office are indispensably required. Upon questions of pure, unmixed spirituality I bow without hesitation to the decision of the pope ; but when I pass from the pontiff to the prince, I cannot be insensible to those temporal abuses, to which the dispatch of Sir Hamilton Seymour called the attention of the four powers;—abuses for which the pope himself is far less responsible than the fallible Italian ministers by whom he is surrounded. Neither will I disguise my apprehension that the Roman cabinet with a view to political purposes—with a view more especially to the conciliation of England, may be occasionally induced to recommend to his Holiness certain compliances of which a recent example has been perhaps afforded. But to return to Sir Hamilton Seymour; his dispatch reflects, I think, great honour upon Lord Palmerston ; the merit, however, is not undivided, for it belongs in part to the right honourable baronet the Secretary of State for the Home Department, himself a member of the Reform Cabinet, with whose concurrence it is indisputable that this course was adopted. When the right honourable gentleman signed a warrant for the opening of Mazzini's letters, did he revert to that document, and did he suggest to the Austrian or the Roman court the adoption of the salutary ameliorations by which alone the tranquillity of Italy can be secured ? The prediction of Sir Hamilton Seymour was fulfilled. The Romagna was in a state of almost perpetual disturbance all redress of grievances was refused ; and at length, in 1844, a conjuration for an insurrectionary movement was formed. The Austrian and Roman governments were apprised of it, and a communication was made, from what the committee call a high quarter, to the English ministry. The Secretary for the Home Department signed a warrant on the 1st of March for the opening of Mazzini's letters. The following words of Lord Aberdeen are remarkable. He said, on the 28th of February : " Your Lordships are already aware that that warrant was not issued by me or at my desire." This statement is most singular. Lord Aberdeen, the foreign minister, upon a question so grave as the exercise of such a prerogative, expressed no wish " that it should be resorted to." The matter apparently at least fell within his exclusive cognizance. He was to determine how far the peace of Europe was affected. Lord Aberdeen goes on and says : " In saying this, however, the house must not understand that I am the least prepared to censure the issue of that warrant. I am quite prepared, as well as every other member of the government, to share the full responsibility of that proceeding. I only wish the fact to be accurately stated " Now, Sir, this is clearly the language of indirect repudiation. It is true that Lord Aberdeen became an accessary after the fact, but he did not take the initiative. We all know what sharing responsibility means. Each member of the cabinet takes his quota, and in the division the burden is supposed to be lightened. But wherefore did Lord Aberdeen state that it was not at his desire that this proceeding was adopted? What had the domestic minister—the minister of the interior, to do with the subject? I have a curiosity—the noble lord the chairman of the committee will probably call it prurient—in an eminent degree the "*curiosa felicitas*" is possessed by him ; but I have a curiosity to know, why the Secretary for the Home department took on himself this very painful office? Is it that, although the temporal dominions of the pope are connected exclusively with Lord Aberdeen's department, an exceedingly interesting and agitated portion of the spiritual dominions of his Holiness is within the more immediate surveillance of the Home Secretary? But whatever was the cause regarding which the committee, who leave a good deal to the imagination, say nothing, it is certain that for three months Mazzini's letters were opened, and folded again, and resealed, and delivered to him just as if nothing at all had happened. My honourable friend the member for Finsbury brought the case before the House of Commons ; at first he was received with all the authoritativeness of office—he was surveyed by the Home Secretary with a lofty taciturnity. But the Prime Minister soon saw that public opinion ran with my honourable friend, and granted a committee. I pass over all that has been said about the constitution of the committee ; there was not a lawyer amongst them, although they were charged to inquire into the state of the law. They were not a jury of inquisitors. No, not one of them was fit to act as a commissioner on the income tax ; but it must be acknowledged that they are men of great intelligence, and of the highest worth and honour. I cannot, however, conceive how they have involved Mazzini's case in so much mystery. They tell us that they cannot tell us all. Why not? We are informed that a communication came from a "high quarter." Was it from Mr. Petre, at Rome. We are told that a communication was made to a foreign power. What foreign power? The committee state, that the information deduced from the letters—strange expression! —deduced from the letters, was communicated to a foreign power, but did not implicate any person within the reach of that foreign power. But it might have implicated some person within the reach of another foreign power to whom the information might be given at second hand. The conspirators at Bologna were not within the reach of Austria, but they were within the reach of Rome

But suppose that I abandon that suggestion, give me leave to ask how could the committee know that the information would not indirectly tend to criminate individuals? Some details must have been given; no name, but a place, a time, will suggest a name. Give a hint to a Bow-street officer, put him on the scent, and how much will be traced out by him! But what are the ablest *attachés* of the Home Office—what are the most skilful among the retinue of the right honourable gentleman, to the Bologna police? Put an Italian bloodhound on the track; let him but smell the vestage of a Liberal, and with a sanguinary instinct he will scent his victim to the death. But, whatever be the opinion of the committee, there are two facts beyond doubt; first, that the Italian newspapers boasted that Mazzini was under the peculiar surveillance of the English police; and, secondly, that six weeks after the letters were opened six men were put to death for political offences at Bologna. Of the blood shed in Calabria you are wholly innocent, and I trust that with the blood shed at Bologna the hands of no British minister are aspersed. Sir, this proceeding is without a precedent. The first minister of the crown stated that the government had only done what their predecessors had done. Which of your predecessors communicated to a foreign government the information deduced from letters? My noble friend never did so. He did, indeed, interfere in affairs of Portugal and of Spain, but never by these means. He never got information from a Miguelite or a Carlist letter, and transmitted it to Lisbon or Madrid. He sent Sir De Lacy Evans to St. Sebastian, who arrested the career of Carlist victory. He did interfere, but it was against despotism that he interposed. He interfered at Rome, but it was not with a view to the maintenance of the Conservative institutions which you have taken under your protection. Yours is the praise (the merit of originality is all your own) of having been the first to stretch the statute of Anne, founded on a statute passed during the commonwealth, into an instrumentality of this kind. You might have found in the history of the commonwealth something with regard to Italy more deserving of your imitation. At the hazard of exposing the peace of Europe, your republican forefathers made Sardinia quail, and rescued a portion of her subjects from the persecution of which they were the victims; and if all England was animated by the sentiment to which the greatest writer in your language has given an immortal expression —if 200 years ago your republican predecessors were fired by the fearless passion for religious freedom, is it fitting that their descendants should not only be insensible to the cause of civil liberty, but that they should become the auxiliaries of despotism, that they should lend an aid so sinister to crush the men who have aspired to be as you are, and that, by an instrumentality so deplorable, they should do their utmost to aid in the oppression of a country in whose freedom those who are in the enjoyment of true liberty can never be unconcerned? Where is the man who has ever looked on Italy—that beautiful Italy to whose peculiar loveliness her calamities have been so justly ascribed, in that famous sonnet of which your own Byron has composed so noble a translation; where is the man who has any acquaintance with the history of that celebrated people, and more especially with the annals of those glorious republics, by which the models of your own municipal institutions were supplied; where is the man who knows how much Italy has accomplished for the perfection of every art, and the advancement of every science—how much has been achieved by Italy, not only in the embellishment of the human mind, but in its expansion and elevation; where is he whom Galileo has ever helped to look farther into heaven; or, who has been appalled, or thrilled, or enchanted, by those masterpieces in literature, writ in the most melodious language in the world, by which the wonders of antiquity have been emulated, if, indeed, in some instances they have not been surpassed, or, to speak of objects more immediately within the cognizance of us all—where, I will venture to ask, is the man who has ever traversed the repository of art, in the centre of your own metropolis, and beheld its walls glowing with the attestations to the supremacy of Italian genius,—who has not mourned over the fall of unfortunate Italy, and for her restoration to liberty and to glory, and for her resumption of the place which she ought to occupy amongst the nations of the earth, has not offered up a prayer? You think, perhaps, that I have in a moment of excitement into which I have permitted myself to be betrayed, forgotten the facts of my case. I have not. I go back to the post-office and to the home department, and I ask what is the palliation for this proceeding? I will give it from the answer given by the prime minister to a question put by the member for Pontefract. Your extenuation is this—not that the inhabitants of Romagna have not monstrous grievances to complain of—no such thing; but this—if there be an outbreak in Romagna, the Austrian army will march into the Papal States—if the Austrian army marched into the Papal States, the French will send troops to Ancona—if the French send troops to Ancona there may be a collision—if there be a collision there may be a war between Austria and France—if there be a war between Austria and France there may be a general continental war—if there be a continental war England may be involved in it, and therefore, but not at the desire of Lord Aberdeen, you opened Mazzini's letters, and acted on the most approved principles of continental espionage. The word is strong—is it inappropriate? If you had employed a spy in the house of Mazzini, and had every word uttered in his convivial hours, at his table, or even at his bed-side, reported to you, that would be espionage. Between that case of hypothetical debasement and what has actually befallen, the best casuist in an Italian university could never distinguish. Are we, in order to avoid the hazards of war to do that which is in the last degree discreditable? You would not, in order to avoid the certainty of war, submit to dishonour. When an Englishman was wronged in a remote island in the Pacific, you announced that the insult should be repaired, or else——; and if you were prepared in that instance to incur the certainty of war, and to rush into an encounter, the shock of which would have shaken the world, should you, to avoid the hazards of war, founded on a series of suppositions, perpetrate an act of self-degradation?—There are incidents to this case which afford a warrant for that strong expression. If you had sent for Mazzini, if you had told him that you knew what he was about—if you had informed him that you were read'ng his letters—the offence would not have been so grievous; but his letters were closed again—with an ignominious dexterity they were refolded, and they were resealed, and it is not an exaggeration to say that the honour of this country was tarnished by every drop of that molten wax with which an untruth was impressed upon them. Is there any clause in the statutes of Anne, and of William, and of Victoria by which this fraud is warranted? There have been questions raised as to whether a separate warrant is requisite for every separate letter But there is no proviso in the act legalising this sleight of hand, this worse than thimble-rig proceeding. I have not entered, and I will not enter, into any legal disquisitions; it is to the policy, the dignity, the truthfulness of this transaction that my resolution is directed. It will no doubt be said that the committee—men of great worth and high integrity, and singular discrimination—have reported in favour of the government. I admit their worth, their integrity, and their discrimination, but I deny that they have reported in your favour. They avoid, cautiously avoid, finding a justification, giving an approval of your conduct. They say that they see no reason to doubt the goodness of your motives. Your motives! There is an aphorism touching good intentions to which it were a deviation from good breeding too distinctly to refer; but it is not for your good intentions that you were made a minister by the Queen, or that you are retained as a minister by the House of Commons. The question is not whether your intentions are good or bad, but whether you have acted as became the great position of an English minister, named by an English sovereign, and administering a great trust for the high-minded English people. I think that you have not; and it is because I think so, that I propose a resolution in which I have set down facts beyond doubt and beyond dispute, and with facts beyond doubt and dispute I have associated an expression of sorrow in which I trust this house will participate.

COLLEGE OF MAYNOOTH.

SPEECH MADE IN THE HOUSE OF COMMONS, APRIL 4, 1845, ON SIR ROBERT PEEL'S MOTION FOR LIBERTY TO BRING IN A BILL TO AMEND THE ACTS RELATING TO THE COLLEGE OF MAYNOOTH.

I RISE to move the adjournment [loud cries of " go on," " no, no"]. The hour is so late that I shall hardly be able to proceed [go on, go on]. I must, I see, obey the injunctions of the house, and therefore I shall go on as well as I am able. It were unjust on the part of any Irish Catholic to withhold a tribute of unqualified panegyric from the great measure proposed by the right honourable gentleman, and from the spirit in which it is propounded. He can have no motive but the honourable one of doing service to both countries; and he will, I trust, secure the gratitude of the one, and, notwithstanding a temporary clamour, his objects will, ere long, be justly estimated by the other. The grant to Maynooth is large. The substitution of a permanent legislative endowment for an annual parliamentary donation, is attended with two advantages; first, the periodical recurrence of a discussion in which religious antipathies find a vent will be avoided. Gentlemen with strong theological addictions, must henceforth seek relief in a celebrated spot of pious gathering in the Strand, and must avail themselves of that exceedingly commodious, and far more appropriate medium of evacuation. In this regard, the proposition of the right honourable gentleman is most commendable; but it is still more important that fixity of tenure should be given by an act of parliament to a great Catholic establishment. Maynooth is converted into an institution, and is placed on the same footing, as the rest of your national incorporations. You are taking a step in a right direction. You are advancing in a career of which you have left the starting-post far behind, and of which the goal, perhaps, is not far distant. You must not take the Catholic clergy into your pay, but you can take the Catholic Church under your care. You can build houses of worship, and grant glebe houses, upon a secure and irrevocable title. The perfect independence of the Catholic clergy is indispensable. A stipend at pleasure, and which the crown could call back, would be odious. An honourable relation—a relation honourable to both—may be established between the Catholic Church and the state, but you must never think of exacting from that church an ignominious complaisance. 1 am well aware that there exists in this country great objections to Maynooth, but those objections are in a great part connected with defects, of which the correction is not difficult: those defects, indeed, arise in a great degree from the niggard spirit in which you have doled out a wretched pittance to Maynooth, utterly incommensurate with its wants. I am not astonished that a Scotch volunteer should entertain an antipathy to Maynooth; but it is matter to me of some surprise that it should be an object of antipathy to an English Conservative in the true sense of a phrase often misapplied. Maynooth was founded in a great measure at the suggestion of the apostle of order, the great Edmund Burke. Let him be assured that he has made great progress in the art of governing Ireland, by whom the works of Edmund Burke are perused with admiration. That sagacious man saw that it was not the interest of Protestant England that the priesthood of Catholic Ireland should be educated in France : he thought that evils could arise from a French and Irish ecclesiastical fraternization : he did not wish that French principles should be imported into every Irish parish, and he denounced the introduction of a Gallo-Hibernian establishment into Ireland. Edmund Burke was of opinion that the Irish Catholic priesthood should be educated by the state for the state. It has been sometimes observed that the Irish priest of the old regime had, by his continental education, acquired a deportment of a superior kind. I believe this notion is, to a great degree, a mistaken one. There were, of course, several ecclesiastics of the old school, of accomplished manners ; but Farquhar the Irish dramatist, who knew his countrymen, represents Foigard as a graduate of the University of Lovain. The priests of Maynooth are not the coarse-minded men which they have been represented to be ; many of them are superior to the dignitaries of your own establishment ; but we do not want fine gentlemen for the hard services of the Irish Catholic Church. I have heard it observed that the deportment of the Irish Catholic priesthood has occasioned the alienation of the Irish Protestant proprietors. That alienation, however, has its origin in political far more than in social causes. As long as the priest was subservient at the hustings, he was welcome in the drawing-room. The separation of the gentry and the priesthood arises from a succession of political struggles—from the Catholic question, from the tithe question, from the municipal question, from the registration question—a question of which the settlement cannot be final, unless it be just. Give the Catholic priest and the Irish Protestant proprietor a common interest in maintaining the institutions of their country, and their reconciliation will be immediate and complete ; indeed, the only danger to be apprehended is, that their alliance may become too unqualified and too compact. I conceive it to be clear that the maintenance of Maynooth is matter of contract—of contract, to be explained in the spirit of legislative equity, and not of scholastic disputation. Maynooth is sustained by two statutes which preceded the Union, ratified by forty-five years of annual grant. If it be matter of contract, the question at once arises whether the sum hitherto voted is adequate to the purposes for which it is designed. That question is to be tried, by considering the extraordinary change which the country has undergone—a change to be always kept in mind by those who consider the principles upon which the government of Ireland is to be carried on. I do not know of any instance of so great a national metamorphosis. Population is doubled, but the increase of population does not afford a just measure of the astonishing moral and political transition through which the country has passed. When Maynooth was founded, there were not more than two or three Catholic barristers in Ireland. We have seen a Catholic Chief

Baron, a Catholic Master of the Rolls, and four Roman Catholics holding the high office of Attorney-General in Ireland. When Maynooth was founded, no Roman Catholic was admissible to parliament. The majority of Irish members are now returned by Roman Catholic constituencies. When Maynooth was founded, there was not a single Roman Catholic in an Irish corporation. We have now the preponderance in almost every corporation in the country. When Maynooth was founded, the great mass of the people were destitute of the elements of education, and now you can scarce meet a peasant upon a public road, who cannot read, and write, and count; and men who read, and write, and count, cannot fail to think. Under these circumstances of marvellous mutation, is the Catholic priest to remain stationary in instruction? And in the great revolution through which the country is revolving, shall not the Catholic Church be carried on with it? If it be clear that the augmented grant to Maynooth is just, it seems to me to be equally clear that it is in the highest degree expedient. It will be essentially beneficial to Ireland, and whatever is beneficial to one country must be serviceable to the other. Great ability will be allured into Maynooth—gold for genius has a magnetic power. The professorships of Maynooth will be filled by men of great talents, and great erudition. A general improvement will be the necessary result. Locate in every parish an educated Catholic priest, whose mind has undergone the process of literary refinement, and you will accomplish much in the work of national amelioration. But the advantages resulting from this measure are so obvious, that it is perhaps better that I should address myself to the objections which are pressed against it. It is said that Catholics and Protestants are to be educated together. With respect to the laity, that observation is, perhaps, a just one; but in every country in Europe, men destined for the Catholic Church are educated in ecclesiastical seminaries, and educated apart. The strictest discipline, habits of subordination almost passive, and a total abstinence from sensual indulgence of every kind are indispensable amongst those who are educated for the priesthood of the Catholic Church. Four years passed in Trinity College, Dublin, would constitute a bad apprenticeship for the confessional. The Catholic priesthood are now not only pure, but unsuspected, and where interests of such importance are at stake, no empirical experiments should be tried. It has been alleged that at Maynooth students of very humble parentage are gathered in a mass of unmixed rusticity, and each individual contributes his quota of contamination. It is a great mistake to imagine that the students of Maynooth are men of such low origin. It is to the middle classes that they generally belong, as is stated in the document read to-night by the right honourable baronet, and which emanated from the Catholic bishops of Ireland. For my part, I am not anxious to see the younger sons of the Catholic gentry enter in large numbers into the Catholic Church. The duties of a Roman Catholic priest are so severe, that men cradled in luxuries are scarcely fit for their discharge. It ought to be borne in mind that some of the greatest ornaments of the Catholic Church have always come from what I might call the Apostolic order. The Catholic

Church has a sort of ennobling influence, and the consciousness of spiritual authority often imparts dignity to those who are not highly born. How often in the olden time did the mitred plebian stand erect before the Norman baron, and in the cause of the serf and of the peasant, with the crozier turn aside the lance. It is the boast of your own Anglo-Catholic pontificate that some of the greatest of your divines have risen from the humblest gradations to the highest episcopal dignities. A man as lowly born as Wolsey may, under your reformed system, become the Archbishop of Canterbury, and take precedence of men who to the conquest of England trace back their descent.

It has been suggested that it is unreasonable to put the people of this country to the cost of educating the priesthood of Ireland; and my honourable friend the member for Sheffield has intimated an intention to postpone the additional grant to Maynooth, until a fund to be derived by some posterior arrangement, from the superfluities of the Irish Protestant Church, shall have been created. I have the utmost value for the opinions of my honourable friend, and listen to all he says, upon this or any other subject, with the most unaffected respect; but he will permit me to observe, that t would not be reasonable, to procrastinate a measure so obviously equitable, as he will be the first to admit this to be, and he ought not to insist upon the delay of what he knows to be justice to one church, until he shall have succeeded in inflicting what he considers to be injustice upon the other. Even if the sum proposed to be granted were fivefold, what the minister recommends you to concede, there is so much true economy in the results of wise legislation, that your very love of saving should induce you to act with liberality to Ireland. Are not lectures at Maynooth cheaper than state prosecutions? Are not professors less costly than Crown Solicitors? Is not a large standing army, and a great constabulary force, more expensive than the moral police with which, by the priesthood of Ireland, you can be thriftily and efficaciously supplied? The last objection to which I shall advert is the familiar one, that you ought not to become contributary to the propagation of what you take upon yourselves, with some assumption of infallibility, to be the untruth. It should be remembered by those who make this objection, that principal is entirely independent of amount. If to grant £26,000 is a mortal sin—to grant £9,000, even in the opinion of an Oxonian casuist, ought not to be considered as a venial offence. The same observation applies to all the contributions annually made for the maintenance of the Catholic Church in our colonial dependencies, and to which the First Lord of the Treasury referred with so much distinctness. But, independently of these considerations, is it not most injudicious, and what is far worse, is it not most Anti-Christian to tell seven millions of your fellow-citizens that their religion is idolatrous, and their creed is but an avenue to perdition? For my part, I hear these unchristian impunities with Christian forbearance; I do not permit my equanimity to be disturbed, by what I consider to be the bad argument, and the profane scurrilities which are directed against the Catholic religion. When I consider the grounds upon which that religion rests—when I see its doctrines coeval with the foundation of Christianity, and maintained by the authority of the fathers who have written, and the martyrs who have died for their sustainment—when I see that for so many centuries the faith of the Catholic Church has by a wonderful apostolical succession been preserved unbroken—when I see heresy after heresy decay, while the Catholic Church remains immutable and predominant, fulfilling the prediction, that no unearthly power of evil shall prevail against it—when I see it rising in providential resuscitation in those countries, in which it was supposed to have been so deeply interred, that, excepting by some interposition more than human, it could not be raised to life and to light again—when I see it making its uniform, its irresistible advances in a progress which so many circumstances concur in inducing me to believe to be mysteriously preordained—when I see it spreading itself to the remotest regions of the world, undivided, universal, and eternal—it is not with a feeling of resentment that I listen to the contumelious imputations which are cast by rash men upon the Catholic religion. I will even add, that it is with a sentiment often described as one "akin to love," that I hear well-meaning men who set up a claim to personal infallibility, indulge in denunciations of that faith, which, even upon their own admission, was professed by some of the loftiest minded and loftiest hearted Christians, by whose virtues a lustre is cast, not only upon the church in whose doctrines they believed, but upon the nature of man, which they exalted and adorned. I could retaliate if I thought it worth while or befitting to do so. I could readily refer to circumstances connected with the history of the Reformation in this country, with as much poignancy as is too frequently displayed by those who make the Catholic Church the subject of their most unjust and unreflecting vituperation. But I have no disposition to wound the sensitiveness of any man that hears me; and, indeed, so far from entertaining any hostility to the Established Church in England, I am free to acknowledge that it is in many particulars so identified with the more ancient and universal church, it has produced men so eminent for their virtue, for their eloquence, and for their sincerity, and it is distinguished, except where its revenues are concerned, by a spirit so tolerant, I will not withhold from it the humble but honest tribute of my individual commendation. While, however, I distinctly state that I feel far less anger than I feel sorrow, at the coarse invectives directed against the Catholic religion, and entertain emotions not unallied to pity towards those who are sufficiently fanatical to indulge in them; let me be permitted to add, that I think that every assault upon the character of the Catholic religion ought to be strenuously deprecated, because Christianity itself is wounded through its sides, and by those who assail the religion professed by the majority of Christians, it ought to be most seriously considered, whether they are not in reality supplying sophistications to those guilty men who labour in the propagation of infidelity, those messengers of desolation by whom hope is blasted, and whom every man who believes in revealed truth in any form, ought to concur in denouncing as the harbingers of despair, and are almost as much the enemies of man as those

> "Ministers,
> Wherever, in their sightless substances
> They tend on mortal thoughts."

I repeat it—the man who denounces the Catholic religion as an idolatry, incurs the frightful hazard of teaching other men to inquire whether the Christian religion itself is not a fable. But, even supposing the Catholic religion to be a tissue of errors, it is clear that you cannot convert us by abusing us. The Catholic Church in Ireland is "an accomplished fact;" you cannot get rid of it. You cannot uproot it; but you may give a useful direction to its branches; and if I may so say, by training them along the legalised institutions of the country, make it productive of what you yourselves would be disposed to acknowledge to be useful fruit. You must take Ireland as it is, and you must adapt your policy to the condition of the people, and not to your own peculiar religious feelings. A statesman has no right to found his legislation upon his theology; and the policy by which Ireland should be governed is entirely different from that which the antagonist of Maynooth recommended to the adoption of the first minister of the crown. What is the policy worthy of the man by whom the great office of prime minister is held, in this the greatest country in the world? In the very position which he occupies an answer to that question is to be found. How great is the height to which the chief minister of England is exalted. From that height nothing little should be discernible. Everything diminutive should vanish. Nothing but the large, the lofty, and the noble, should be seen. When from that surpassing elevation whence the British empire is disclosed to him, he turns his eyes to the island which is immediately contiguous to your own, what should he behold? Not, most assuredly, the church or the chapel, or the conventicle—not a miserable arena for scholastic controversy—not an appropriate field in which the Protestant and the Catholic, and the Calvinist should engage in a theological conflict, and trample upon every precept of the gospel, in their fierce and Anti-Christian encounter. Shall I venture to tell you what he should behold—what Bacon—what Spenser and Bacon beheld more than two centuries before him—what Pitt, what Burke, and Fox beheld in later times—one of the finest islands in the ocean, peopled by millions of men, bold, and brave, and chivalrous —whose very imperfections are akin to virtue, and who are capable of the noblest amelioration—an island blessed with a fortunate climate, a soil inexhaustibly fertile, a point of contact between the Old World and the New—an island to which Providence has been lavish in its bounty and from the development of whose incalculable resources an incalculable benefit might be conferred upon the empire; and by the statesmen whom that great work shall be accomplished an imperishable fame will be obtained. And if such be the spectacle which Ireland presents to his contemplation—in the contemplation of such a spectacle, what emotions should he experience, what desires should he derive from it, and with what aspirations should his heart be lifted up? Should he think—should he for one moment give himself leave to think—of making such a country subservient to the indulgence of any sectarian prejudice, or of any religious predilection. To assert the purposes of Providence, to carry out the designs of which wherever we turn our eyes, we behold the magnificent manifestations—to repair the misrule of centuries—to pour balm into a nation's heart—to efface pernicious recollections—to awaken salubrious hopes—to banish a splendid phantom—to substitute a glorious and attainable reality—to induce England to do justice to Ireland, and to make Ireland appreciate the justice of England, and thus to give an everlasting stability to this great and majestic empire—these are the objects to which a man should direct his whole heart and his entire soul, who feels conscious of the sacred trust reposed in him by his sovereign, and that God has given him the high capacity to fulfil it; inspired by that elevating sense of the noblest of all duties, and the high determination which he ought to bring to its performance, he should turn with a disdainful smile from the men who associate their politics with their polemics—who deduce the narrow maxims of their government from the dogmas of their presumptuous divinity—whose principles, if carried out to the conclusions to which they irresistibly tend, would lead you back to the restoration of that fatal ascendancy, of which we have already had an experience so calamitous—and he should be prepared to fling the seals of office to the winds, rather than permit himself to be stopped, or even to be retarded, in the completion of that work, of which the foundation has been laid, of which the structure has been in part erected, with which every consideration that can address itself to his heart and his understanding should induce him to proceed, and of which a perpetual honour will attend the consummation.

THE CATHOLICS OF IRELAND.

SPEECH AT PENENDEN HEATH, 24TH OCTOBER, 1828.

LET no man believe that I have come here, in order that I might enter the lists of religious controversy and engage with any of you in a scholastic disputation. In the year 1828, the Real Presence does not afford an appropriate subject for debate, and it is not by the shades of a mystery that the rights of a British citizen are to be determined. I do not know whether there are many here by whom I am regarded as an idolater, because I conscientiously adhere to the faith of your forefathers, and profess the doctrine in which I was born and bred; but if I am so accounted by you, you ought not to inflict a civil deprivation upon the accident of the cradle. You ought not to punish me for that for which I am not in reality to blame. If you do, you will make the misfortune of the Catholic the fault of the Protestant, and by inflicting a wrong upon my religion, cast a discredit upon your own. I am not the worse subject of my King, and the worse citizen of my country, because I concur in the belief of the great majority of the Christian world ; and I will venture to add, with the frankness and something of the bluntness by which Englishmen are considered to be characterised, that if I am an idolater, I have a right to be one, if I choose; my idolatry is a branch of my prerogative, and is no business of yours. But you have been told by Lord Winchelsea that the Catholic religion is the adversary of freedom. It may occur to you, perhaps, that his lordship affords a proof in his own person, that a passion for Protestantism and a love of liberty are not inseparably associated ; but without instituting too minute or embarrassing an inquiry into the services to freedom, which in the course of his political life have been conferred by my Lord Winchelsea, and putting aside all personal considerations connected with the accuser, let me proceed to the accusation. Calumniators of Catholicism, have you read the history of your country ? Of the charges against the religion of Ireland, the annals of England afford the confutation. The body of your common laws was given by the Catholic Alfred. He gave you your judges, your magistrates, your high sheriffs—(you, Sir, hold your office, and have called this great assembly, by virtue of his institutions)—your courts of justice, your elective system, and, the great bulwark of your liberties, the trial by jury. When Englishmen peruse the chronicles of their glory, their hearts beat high with exultation, their emotions are profoundly stirred, and their souls are ardently expanded. Where is the English boy, who reads the story of his great island, whose pulse does not beat at the name of Runnemede, and whose nature is not deeply thrilled at the contemplation of that great incident, when the mitred Langton, with his uplifted crosier, confronted the tyrant, whose sceptre shook in his trembling hand, and extorted what you have so justly called the Great, and what, I trust in God, you will have cause to designate as your everlasting Charter ? It was by a Catholic Pontiff that the foundation-stone in the temple of liberty was laid ; and it was at the altars of that religion, which you are accustomed to consider as the handmaid of oppression, that the architects of the constitution knelt down. Who conferred upon the people the right of self-taxation, and fixed, if he did not create, the representation of the people ? The Catholic Edward the First; while, in the reign of Edward the Third, perfection was given to the representative system, parliaments were annually called, and the statute against constructive treason was enacted. It is false, fully, infamously false, that the Catholic religion, the religion of your forefathers, the religion of seven millions of your fellow-subjects, has been the auxiliary of debasement, and that to its influences the suppression of British freedom can, in a single instance, be referred. I am loath to say that which can give you cause to take offence ; but when the faith of my country is made the object of imputation, I cannot help, I cannot refrain, from breaking into a retaliatory interrogation, and from asking whether the overthrow of the old religion of England was not effected by a tyrant, with a hand of iron and a heart of stone ? whether Henry did not trample upon freedom, while upon

Catholicism he set his foot; and whether Elizabeth herself, the virgin of the Reformation, did not inherit her despotism with her creed; whether in her reign the most barbarous atrocities were not committed; whether torture, in violation of the Catholic common law of England, was not politically inflicted, and with the shrieks of agony the Towers of Julius, in the dead of night, did not re-echo? And to pass to a more recent period, was it not on the very day on which Russell perished on the scaffold, that the Protestant University of Oxford published the declaration in favour of passive obedience, to which your Catholic ancestors would have laid down their lives rather than have submitted? These are facts taken from your own annals, with which every one of you should be made familiar; but it is not to your own annals that the recriminatory evidence, on which I am driven to rely, shall be confined. If your religion is the inseparable attendant upon liberty, how does it come to pass that Prussia, and Sweden, and Denmark, and half the German states, should be Protestants, and should be also slaves? You may suggest to me, that in the larger portion of Catholic Europe freedom does not exist; but you should bear in mind that at a period when the Catholic religion was in its most palmy state, freedom flourished in the countries in which it is now extinct. Look at Italy, not indeed as she now is, but as she was before Martin Luther was born, when literature and liberty were associated, and the arts imparted their embellishments to her free political institutions. I call up the memory of the Italian Catholic republics in the great cause which I am sufficiently adventurous to plead before you. Florence, accomplished, manufacturing, and democratic, the model of your own municipal corporations, gives a noble evidence in favour of Catholicism; and Venice, Catholic Venice, rises in the splendour of her opulence and the light of her liberty, to corroborate the testimony of her celebrated sister with a still more lofty and majestic attestation. If from Italy I shall ascend the Alps, shall I not find, in the mountains of Switzerland, the sublime memorials of liberty, and the reminiscences of those old achievements which preceded the theology of Geneva, and which were performed by men, by whom the ritual of Rome was uttered on the glaciers, and the great mystery of Catholicism was celebrated on the altars which nature had provided for that high and holy worship? But Spain, I may be told, Spain affords the proof that to the purposes of despotism her religion has always lent its impious and disastrous aid. That mistake is a signal one, for when Spain was most devotedly Catholic, Spain was comparatively free—her Cortes assumed an attitude nobler even than your own Parliament, and told the King, at the opening of every session in which they were convened, that they were greater and invested with a higher authority than himself. In the struggles made by Spaniards, within our own memory, we have seen the revival of that lofty sentiment; while amongst the descendants of Spaniards, in the provinces of South America, called into existence in some sort by yourselves, we behold no religion but the Catholic, and no government of which the principle is not founded in the supremacy of the people. Republic after republic has arisen at your bidding through that immeasurable expanse, and it is scarce an exaggeration to say (if I may allude to a noble passage in one of the greatest writers of our time), that liberty, with her "meteor standard" unfurled upon the Andes,

' Looks from her throne of clouds o'er half the world."

False, I repeat it, with all the vehemence of indignant asseveration, utterly false is the charge habitually preferred against the religion which Englishmen have laden with penalties, and have marked with degradation. I can bear with any other charge but this—to any other charge I can listen with endurance: tell me that I prostrate myself before a sculptured marble; tell me that to a canvass glowing with the imagery of heaven I bend my knee; tell me that my faith is my perdition :—and as you traverse the churchyards in which your forefathers are buried, pronounce upon those who have lain there for many hundred years a fearful and appalling sentence :—yes ; call what I regard as the truth not only an error, but a sin to which mercy shall not be extended :—all this I will bear—to all this I will submit—nay, at all this I will but smile :—but do not tell me that I am in heart and creed a slave :—that my countrymen cannot brook ; in their own bosoms they carry the high consciousness that never was imputation more foully false, or more detestably calumnious. I do not believe that with the passion for true liberty a nation was ever more enthusiastically inspired— never were men more resolved—never were men more deserving to be free than the nation in whose oppression, fatally to Ireland and to themselves, the statesmen of England have so madly persevered. What have been the results of that system which you have been this day called together to sustain ? You behold in Ireland a beautiful country, with wonderful advantages agricultural and commercial—a resting-place for trade on its way to either hemisphere; indented with havens, watered by numerous rivers ; with a fortunate climate in which fertility is raised upon a rich soil, and inhabited by a bold, intrepid, and, with all their faults, a generous and enthusiastic people. Such is Ireland as God made her—what is Ireland as you have made her? This fine country, swarming with a population the most miserable in Europe, of whose wretchedness, if you are the authors, you are beginning to be the victims—the poisoned chalice is returned in its just circulation to your lips. Harvests the most abundant are reaped by men with starvation in their faces ; all the great commercial facilities of the country are lost—the rivers that should circulate opulence, and turn the machinery of a thousand manufactures, flow to the ocean without wafting a boat or turning a wheel—the wave breaks in solitude in the silent magnificence of deserted and shipless harbours. In place of being a source of wealth and revenue to the empire, Ireland cannot defray its own expenses ; her discontent costs millions of money; she debilitates and endangers England. The great mass of her population are alienated and dissociated from the state—the influence of the constituted and legitimate authorities is gone ; a strange, anomalous, and unexampled kind of government has sprung up, and exercises a despotic sway; while the class, inferior in numbers, but accustomed to authority, and infuriated at its loss, are thrown into formidable reaction—the most ferocious passions rage from one extremity of the country to the other. Hundreds and thousands of men, arrayed with badges, gather in the south, and the smaller faction, with discipline and with arms, are marshalled in the north—the country is like one vast magazine of powder, which a spark might ignite into an explosion, and of which England would not only feel, but, perhaps, never recover from the shock. And is this state of things to be permitted to continue? It is only requisite to present the question in order that all men should answer—something must be done. What is to be done? Are you to re-enact the Penal Code? Are you to deprive Catholics of their properties, to shut up their schools, to drive them from the bar, to strip them of the elective franchise, and reduce them to Egyptian bondage? It is easy for some visionary in oppression, to imagine these things. In the drunkenness of sacerdotal debauch, men have been found to give vent to such sanguinary aspirations, and the teachers of the Gospel, the ministers of a mild and merciful Redeemer, have uttered in the midst of their ferocious wassails, the bloody orison, that their country should be turned into one vast field of massacre, and that upon the pile of carnage the genius of Orange ascendancy should be enthroned. But these men are maniacs in ferocity, whose appetites for blood you will scarcely undertake to satiate. You shrink from the extirpation of a whole people. Even suppose that, with an impunity as ignominious as it would be sanguinary, that horrible crime could be effected, then you must needs ask, what is to be done? In answering that question you will not dismiss from your recollection that the greatest statesmen who have for the last fifty years directed your councils and conducted the business of this mighty empire, concurred in the opinion, that, without a concession of the Catholic claims, nothing could be done for Ireland.— Burke, the foe to revolution—Fox, the assertor of popular right—Pitt, the prop of the prerogative, concurred. With reference to this great question their minds met in a deep confluence. See to what a conclusion you must arrive when you denounce the advocates of Emancipation. Your anathema will take in one-half of Westminster Abbey; and is not the very dust into which the tongues and hearts of Pitt, and Burke, and Fox have mouldered, better than the living hearts and tongues of those who have survived them? If you were to try the question by the authorities of the dead, and by those voices which may be said to issue from the grave, how would you decide? If, instead of counting votes in St. Stephen's, you were to count the tombs in the mausoleum beside it, how would the division of the great departed stand? There would be a majority of sepulchres inscribed with immortal names upon our side. But supposing that authority, that the coincidence of the wisest and of the best in favour of Ireland was to be held in no account, consider how the religious disqualifications must necessarily operate Can that be a wise course of government which creates not an aristocracy of opulence, and rank, and talent, but an aristocracy in religion, and places seven millions of people at the feet of a few hundred thousand? Try this fashion of government by a very obvious test, and make the case your own. If a few hundred thousand Presbyterians stood towards you in the relation in which the Irish Protestants stand towards the Catholics, would you endure it? Would you brook a system under which Episcopalians should be rendered incapable of holding seats in the House of Commons, should be excluded from sheriffships and corporate offices, and from the bench of justice, and from all the higher offices in the administration of the law; and should be tried by none but Presbyterian juries, flushed with the insolence of power and infuriated with all the ferocity of passion? How would you brook the degradation which would arise from such a system, and the scorn and contumelies which would flow from it? Would you listen with patience to men who told you that there was no grievance in all this—that your complaints were groundless, and that the very right of murmuring ought to be taken away? Are Irishmen and Roman Catholics so differently constituted from yourselves, that they are to behold nothing but blessings in a system which you would look upon as an endurable wrong? Protestants and Englishmen, however debased you may deem our country, believe me that we have enough of human nature left within us—we have enough of the spirit of manhood, all Irishmen as we are, to resent a usage of this kind. Its results are obvious. The nation is divided into two castes. The powerful and the privileged few are patricians in religion, and trample upon and despise the plebeian Christianity of the millions who are laid prostrate at their feet. Every Protestant thinks himself a Catholic's better; and every Protestant feels himself the member of a privileged corporation. Judges, sheriffs, crown counsel, crown attorneys, juries, are Protestants to a man. What confidence can a Catholic have in the administration of public justice? We have the authority of an eminent Irish judge, the late Mr. Fletcher, who declared that, in the North, the Protestants were uniformly acquitted, and the Catholics were as undeviatingly condemned. A body of armed Orangemen fall upon and put to death a defenceless Catholic; they are put upon their trial, and when they raise their eyes and look upon the jury, as they are commanded to do, they see twelve of their brethren in massacre empannelled for their trial; and, after this, I shall be told that all the evils of Catholic disqualification lie in the disappointed longing of some dozen gentlemen after the House of Commons! No; it is the bann, the opprobrium, the brand, the note and mark of dishonour, the scandalous partiality, the flagitious bias, the sacrilegious and perjured leaning, and the monstrous and hydraheaded injustice, that constitute the grand and essential evils of the country. And you think it wonderful that we should be indignant at all this. You marvel, and are amazed that we are hurried into the use of rash and vehement phrases. Have we alone forgotten the dictates of charity?—have our opponents been always distinguished by their meekness and forbearance?—have no exasperating expressions, no galling taunts, no ferocious menaces, ever escaped from them Look to the Brunswick orgies of Ireland, and behold not merely the torturers of '98, who, like retired butchers, feel the want of their old occupation, and long for the political shamuies again, but to the ministers of the Gospel, by whom their libations to the moloch of faction, in the revelries of a sanguinary ascendancy are ferociously poured out. Make allowances for the excesses into which, with much provocation, we may be hurried, and pardon us when you recollect how, under the same circumstance, you would, in all likelihood, feel yourselves. Perhaps you will say, that while you are conscious that we have much to suffer, you owe it to your own safety to exclude us from power. We have power already—the power to do mischief; give us that of doing good. Disarray us—dissolve us—break up our confederacy—take from the law (the great conspirator) its combining and organizing quality, and we shall no longer be united by the bad chain of slavery, but by the natural bonds of allegiance and contentment. You fear our possible influence in the House of Commons. Don't you dread our actual influence beyond its precincts? Catholics out of the House of Commons: we should be citizens within it. It has been sometimes insisted that we aim at the political exaltation of our church upon the ruins of the establishment—that once emancipated we should proceed to strip your clergy, and to possess ourselves of the opulence of an anti-apostolic and anti-scriptural establishment. Never was there a more unfounded imputation. The whole body of the Irish Catholics look upon a wealthy priesthood with abhorrence. They do not desire that their bishops should be invested with pontifical gorgeousness. When a bill was introduced in order to make a small, and no more than a decent provision for the Catholic clergy, did they not repudiate the offer, and prefer their honourable poverty, and the affections of the people, to the seductions of the crown? How did the people act? Although a provision for the priesthood would relieve them from a burden, did they not deprecate all connection with power? The Catholics of Ireland know that if their clergy were endowed with the wealth of the establishment, they would become a profligate corporation, pampered with luxury, swelling with sacredotal pride, and presenting in their lives a monstrous contrast with that simplicity and that poverty of which they are now as well the practisers as the teachers. They know that, in place of being, as they now are, the indefatigable instructors of the peasantry, their consolers in affliction, their resource in calamity, their preceptors and their models in religion, their visiters in sickness, and their companions at the bed of death; they would become equally insolent to the humble, and sycophantic to the great—flatterers at the noble's table and extortioners in the poor man's hovel; slaves in politics, and tyrants in demeanour, who from the porticoes of palaces would give their instructions in humility; who from the banquets of patricians would prescribe their lessons in abstinence; and from the primrose path of dalliance would point to the steep and thorny way to heaven. Monstrous as the opulence of the establishment now is, the people of Ireland would rather see the wealth of Protestant bishops increased tenfold, and another million of acres added to their episcopal territories, than behold their pure and simple priesthood degraded from their illustrious humility, to that dishonourable and anti-Christian ostentation, which,

If it were once established, would be sure to characterize their church
I speak the sentiments of the whole body of my countrymen, when I
solemnly and emphatically reiterate my asseveration that there is
nothing which the Roman Catholic body would regard with more abhorrence than the transfer of the enormous and corrupting revenues of the
establishment to a clergy who owe their virtues to their poverty, and
the attachment of the people to their dignified dependence upon the
people for their support. I should have done; and yet before I retire
from your presence, indulge me so far as to permit me to press one
remaining topic upon you. I have endeavoured to show you that you
have mistaken the character and political principles of my religion; I
have endeavoured to make you sensible of the miserable condition of
my country; to impress upon you the failure of all the means which
have been hitherto tried to tranquillize that unhappy country, and the
necessity of adopting some expedient to alleviate its evils. I have dwelt
upon the concurrence of great authorities in favour of concession
the little danger that is to be apprehended from that concession, and
the great benefit which would arise from religious peace in Ireland. I
might enlarge upon those benefits, and show you that when factions
were reconciled, when the substantial causes of animosity were removed,
the fierce passions which agitate the country would be laid at rest
that English capital would, in all likelihood, flow into Ireland; that
English habits would gradually arise; that a confidence in the administration of justice would grow up—that the people, instead of appealing
to arms for redress, would look to the public tribunals as the only arbiters of right; and that the obstacles which now stand in the way of
education would be removed—that the fierceness of polemics would be
superseded by that charity which the Christian extends to all mankind;
that a reciprocal sentiment of kindness would take place between the
two islands—that a real union, not depending upon acts of parliament,
but upon mutual interest and affection, would be permanently established
—that the empire would be consolidated, and all dangers from the enemies of Great Britain would disappear:—I might point out to you,
what is obvious enough, that if Ireland be allowed to remain as it now
is, at no distant period the natural foes of Great Britain may make
that unfortunate country the field of some formidable enterprise:—I
might draw a picture of the consequences which would arise if an enormous population were to be roused into a concurrent and simultaneous
movement:—but I forbear from pressing such considerations upon you,
because I had much rather rely upon your own lofty-mindedness, than
upon any terrible contingency:—I therefore put it to you, that independently of every consideration of expediency, it is unworthy of you
to persevere in a system of practical religious intolerance, which Roman
Catholic states, who hold to you a fine example in this regard at least,
have abandoned. I have heard it said that the Catholic religion was a
persecuting religion. It was; and so was every other religion that was
ever invested with authority. How easily I could retort on you the
charge of persecution—remind you that the early reformers, who set
up a claim to liberty of conscience for themselves, did not indulge

others in a similar luxury—tell you that Calvin, having obtained a theological masterdom in Geneva, offered up the screams of Servetus to the God of mercy and of love; that even your own Cranmer, who was himself a martyr, had first inflicted what he afterwards suffered, and that this father of your church, whose hand was indeed a guilty one, had, even in the reign of Edward the Sixth, accelerated the progress of heretics to immortality, and sent them through fire to heaven. But the truth is, that both parties have, in the paroxysms of religious frenzy, committed the most execrable crimes, and it might be difficult, if their misdeeds were to be weighed, to adjust the balance of atrocity between them. But Catholics and Protestants have changed, and with the alteration of time we ourselves have undergone a salutary reformation. Through the whole continent religious distinctions have begun to vanish, and freedom of conscience is almost universally established. It is deplorable that England should be almost the only country where such disqualifications are maintained. In France, where the religion of the state is that of Rome, all men are admissible to power, and no sort of sectarian distinction is instituted by the law. The third article of the French charter provides that every French citizen, no matter of what denomination, shall be capable of holding every office in the state. The Chamber of Deputies is filled with Protestants, who are elected by Roman Catholics; and Protestants have held places in the cabinet of France. In Hungary, in the year 1791, Protestants were placed by a Roman Catholic government on a perfect level with their fellow-citizens. In Bavaria the same principle of toleration was adopted. Thus the Catholics of Europe have given you an honourable example, and, while they have refuted the imputation of intolerance, have pronounced upon you a practical reproach. You are behind almost every nation in Europe. Protestant Prussia has emancipated her Catholic subjects, and Silesia is free. In Germany the churches are used indiscriminately by Protestants and Catholics—the Lutheran service, in happy succession, follows the Catholic mass; or the Catholic mass follows the Lutheran service. Thus in every state in Europe the spirit of religious toleration has signally advanced, while here, in this noble island, which we are wont to consider the asylum of civil liberty, the genius of persecution has found a refuge. In England, and in England only, deprivations and dishonour are inflicted upon those whose conscience inhibits their conformity with the formulas of your worship; and a vast body of Englishmen in this one of your finest counties, are called upon to offer up a gratuitous invocation to the legislature to rivet the fetters of their Catholic fellow-subjects. Do not undertake so ungenerous an office, nor interpose for the low-hearted purposes of oppression. I have heard since I came here that it is a familiar saying, that "the men of Kent have been never conquered." That you never will be vanquished in any encounter where men shall be arrayed in arms against you is my belief and my desire: but while in this regard you will always prove unconquered and unconquerable, there is one particular in which I hope that proof will be afforded that you can be subdued. Be no longer invincible, but let the victory be achieved by yourselves The worst form with which you have to contend are lodged in your own breasts — your prejudices are the most formidable of your antagonists, and to discomfit them will confer upon you a higher honour than if in the shouts of battle you put your enemies to flight. It is over your antipathies, national and religious, that a masterdom should be obtained by you, and you may rest assured that if you shall vanquish your animosities, and bring your passions into subjection, you will, in conquering yourselves, extend your dominion over that country by which you have been so long resisted, your empire over our feelings will be securely established, you will make a permanent acquisition of the affections of Irishmen, and make our hearts your own.

THE "ELECT."

DESCRIPTION OF A ROTUNDA MEETING OF "THE ELECT," IN A SPEECH AT THE CATHOLIC ASSOCIATION.

I RISE to second the resolution, "That we have read with indignation the calumnies of Mr. Butterworth upon the Catholic clergy." His assertion, that the priests gave a signal to the people at Carlow to drive their opponents from the field, is destitute of foundation. Enough of this canting bibliopolist, who would bind up the gospel of Christ and the statutes of Queen Anne together. Thank God his efforts, and those of the party whom he so fitly represents, are frustrated. A wiser spirit has begun to manifest itself in the House of Commons with regard to the education of the Irish people. Evidence has been afforded in the recent debates, and especially in the late discussion which was originated by Mr. Smith, that the Kildare-street Association will speedily be divested of that national trust, against the abuse of which we have so frequently, so vehemently, so justly, and I may now add, we have so successfully complained. Our remonstrances have been heard—a system of instruction, compatible with the ancient religion of the country, will in all likelihood, be speedily introduced. The account of the proceedings in the House of Commons, upon the presenting of a petition against the misfeasances of the Kildare-street Society, were calculated to afford a higher satisfaction in consequence of the manifestation of inveterate fanaticism, which, within these few days, has taken place in this city. I allude to the convocations which were held during the last week at the Rotunda One would be at first disposed to think that there was something inappropriate in the localities selected for those fantastic exhibitions; but the truth is, that no spot could have been more felicitously chosen for the assemblage of the fair enthusiasts, who were called together for the purpose of imbibing the holy spirit of the powerful "teachers of the Word," than the very useful asylum which is dedicated to Lucina, and sacred to the ministry of the obstetric art. How apparently distinct, but how substantially coincident are the uses to which the Rotunda is

converted! Alternately a ball-room and a conventicle—at night the
scene of waltzes, and at noon the theatre of prayers, it presents ostensibly different pictures to the imagination; but, after all, the occupations
to which it is devoted, generally lead to the same result. Mr. Bankes,
the pious and moral representative of the University of Cambridge,
intending to say that he was favourable to a particular system of religion, because it led to an intercourse between the different *sects*, happened to speak the truth by mistake, and adopted a form of phrase
which excited the risible dispositions of the house. He unconsciously
did no more than give utterance to an opinion which David Hume has
happily expressed in speaking of "the passions which so naturally insinuate themselves in the warm intimacies that arise between the devotees
of the different sexes." In this view of the matter there is nothing very
incongruous between the purposes to which the Rotunda is alternately
devoted. The sigh at a quadrille is not more impassioned than the
suspiration at a homily—the whisper of Lothario is not more perilous
than the cadences of Cantwell—and the field-preacher has fully as much
unction as the dragoon. While I am free to confess my belief, that
many of the persons who frequent the assemblies to which I have been
alluding are influenced by genuine and unadulterated enthusiasm, yet
I could not help feeling, at one of the Biblical convocations held last
week at the Rotunda, which a somewhat malicious curiosity induced me
to attend, that there is as much real worldliness, under the disguise of spirituality, at these Scriptural gatherings, as is usually exhibited in places
which are openly and avowedly dedicated to "Satan and his works."
There was at the late assemblies a more numerous muster of "The Elect"
than has for some time taken place. The pious of both sexes flocked
together from all parts of the country. An ordinary observer must
have been struck by the increase of Puritanical visages in the streets.
I was tempted, by no very sympathetic feeling, to attend at one of their
discussions; and if I saw much matter for disgust in the acrimonious,
malevolent, and unrelenting spirit which was manifested towards the
religion of the people, I could not at the same time help being amused
at the solemn foppery, the serious vanity, the spiritual coquetry, the
pious ogling, and the demure flirtation which were exhibited on the
occasion. Upon entering the assembly, I found a gentleman delivering
himself of certain conceptions, the purport of which I could not distinctly collect, except that occasionally the words "darkness and idolatry," with some references to Babylon, Anti-Christ, and the Pope,
gave a tolerable intimation of the tendency of his discourse. He was
not sufficiently frantic to be amusing—but seemed to be some dull
impostor, without any other qualification than a disastrous physiognomy
for his melancholy trade. My attention not being roused by the dismal
mediocrity of the orator, I turned to survey the congregation. It exhibited a great diversity of character. The majority of the male part of
the audience had that lurid expression—that churchyard look which
belongs to sectarian fanaticism, and is so distinct from the cheerful enthusiasm of the Catholic religion. The class I am describing appeared to
me to belong to the lower order of Protestants. There was a fierceness

about them that indicated that they had never been softened by the influences of education; for they exhibited an odious conjunction of the original savageness of their nature, with the artificial ferocity of a fanatical religion. The contrast between them and another class was striking. I allude to the glossy-faced, downy-cheeked, and ample-bellied of "the elect," who invest their lips with a perpetual simper, and cover their faces with an expression of elaborate meekness and ostentatious humility. These are your prosperous traders in the commodities of this world and of the next—fellows who are free of Dublin and of "the new Jerusalem"—drapers in linen and religion—tailors who will cut you out with the same facility a creed and a surtout—vendors of Bibles and pasquinades, and all that tribe of canting, smirking, ejaculating citizens, to whose counters the devout sympathetically resort. Intermingled with them, and with some affinity of aspect, I observed divers preachers of the gospel, of inferior note, who wisely realise the blessings of the Old Testament, by enforcing the precepts of the New. Many of them had passed the meridian of life, and seemed to think it wiser to addict themselves to some ancient maiden with "a call," than to any other more interesting, but less hopeful speculation. But a more striking, and, let me add, enviable class, were the young, the graceful, and sweet-spirited lispers of the gospel, who teach the rigid doctrines of Calvin, with the impassioned tenderness of Abelard; though they were attired in sables of the most studied simplicity of fashion, there was still a lurking foppery about them. Every proportion was brought as if carelessly and undesignedly out, and attaining the excellence of art by its disguise, they exhibited their healthful forms to the opulent and beautiful devotees, beside whom they were placed in a close and interesting contact. Whether the blush upon the faces of certain of those pious damsels arose from the heat which was produced by the compactness of the crowd, or had its origin in the holy whispers which were occasionally breathed into their ears, I will not take upon myself to aver, but I cannot avoid thinking, that many of the ardent inculcators of "gospel truth" who sat beside them, seemed to have fallen into the errors of Popery, and to be zealously and successfully engaged in the *Invocation of Saints*. It must be acknowledged, that many of the objects of their spiritual admiration would have afforded models of celestial loveliness to a painter, and assisted his conceptions of the "beau ideal" of heaven. At all events he could not have been at a loss for a Magdalen amongst them. The ecstatic look of devotion is a great heightener of expression, and a woman's eyes are never so beautiful as when they are raised to heaven. When sublunary affections intermingle themselves with devotion, the compound produces a fine physical effect, and realizes the panegyric of a Protestant bishop upon a lady, when he exclaimed, "that she was the connecting link between the female and the angelic nature." The fair votaries at the Rotunda appeared to have apportioned their attachment between the love of God and of his creatures. Their eyes were occasionally lifted in adoration, but at intervals were tenderly and surreptitiously directed to their companions of the other sex, whose exhortations were, I presume, tinctured with the phraseology of the divine pastoral of Solomon, and redolent with the spirit of high and holy love. Far be it from me to insinuate that any impurity of sentiment was mingled with those pious interchanges of the heart. True it is, that I did observe certain celebrated dames, who have occasioned " much joy in heaven," and whose charity is entitled to the full extent of Scriptural panegyric. The " Fair Penitents"—the Calistas of sixty, held a prominent place at the meeting.' I do not, however, mean to impute any remnant of their youthful addictions to those pious matrons, in whom time has approved himself a corrector of the passions; and with respect to the younger portion of the congregation, without disputing that excitement of the temperament which ill-directed enthusiasm is calculated to produce, I should be disposed to say, that no immoral results arise from the pious sympathies of the devout, and that their holy intimacies generally terminate in a permanent co-partnership of the heart. I have expatiated so much upon the fairer and more interesting portion of the congregation, that I shall not at present attempt any description of the other features in the assembly deserving of note. The lugubrious oratory of the speakers, and the spirit of Pharisaical imposture which characterised the declamation of the day, would furnish ample materials for comment. One word upon the Chairman—Lord Roden presided. We have his own authority for stating, that, like the Apostle of the Gentiles, he received a special summons from the Lord. Whether what he takes for a ray from heaven may not be some stray moon-beam that has fallen upon his mind—whether his heart has been touched, or that pulp, of which the brain is compounded, has become diseased, I shall not stop to inquire. His religion, if it were unconnected with his politics, would merely excite derision; but when we find him infusing Orangeism into Christianity, we require a large portion of that charity, of which he is so ostentatious a professor, not to look at him with a feeling of a very acrimonious kind. The hatred which is manifested in this country to the propagators of the Scriptures, arises, in a great measure from political causes. Is it wonderful that they should become the objects of our antipathy, and that our detestation for their politics should extend itself to their religion, when we find them arrayed in a systematic opposition to the liberties of our country ?—the same sentiment prevails through every gradation of rank, and from Roden to Butterworth they are the foes of Ireland. How can it be matter of surprise, that when the spirit of tyranny and of fanaticism are allied, we should hate the fanatic when we cannot but detest the tyrant ? Can we avoid looking with abhorrence upon the propagators of the Scriptures, who come to us with the Bible in one hand and with the penal code in the other ?

SPEECH IN REPLY TO MR. M'CLINTOCK.

Mr. M'CLINTOCK, a Protestant Gentleman of rank and fortune in the county of Louth, having attended a Roman Catholic Meeting, held in the chapel of Dundalk, and delivered a speech containing strictures on the Catholic religion.

Mr. SHEIL rose immediately after Mr. M'Clintock had concluded and said, The speech of Mr. M'Clintock (and a more singular exhibion of gratuitous eloquence I have never heard) calls for a prompt and immediate expression of gratitude. He has had the goodness to advise us (for he has our interests at heart) to depute certain emissaries from the new Order of Liberators to his Holiness at Rome, for the purpose of procuring a repeal of certain obnoxious canons of the Council of Lateran. If Mr. M'Clintock had not assured us that he was serious, and was not actuated by an anxiety to throw ridicule upon the religion and proceedings of those whom he has taken under his spiritual tutelage, I should have been disposed to consider him an insidious fanatic, who, under the hypocritical pretence of giving us a salutary admonition, had come here with no other end than to fling vilification upon our creed, and to throw contumely upon the persons who take the most active part in the conduct of our cause. But knowing him to be a person of high rank and large fortune, and believing him to possess the feelings as well as the station of a gentleman, I am willing to acquit him of any such unworthy purpose, and do not believe that his object in addressing us, was to offer a deliberate and premeditated insult. He did not, I am sure, (for it would be inconsistent with the character which I have ascribed to him) enter this meeting for the purpose of venting his bile into our faces, and voiding upon his auditory the foul calumnies against the religion of his countrymen, which furnish the ordinary materials of rhetoric in the Bible Societies, of which he is so renowned a member. He did not come here to talk of the Pope's golden stirrups to a mass of ignorant and unenlightened people, and to turn their belief into ridicule with his lugubrious derision. The topics which he selected were, indeed, singularly chosen, and when he talked of the Order of Liberators, I was disposed to take him for a wag.— But I raised my eyes and looked him in the face, and perceiving a person, whose countenance would furnish Cruikshank with a frontispiece to the Spiritual Quixotte, I at once acquitted him of all propensities to humour, and could not bring myself to believe it possible that Mr. M'Clintock had ever intended to be droll. At one moment I confess I was in pain for him, for I was apprehensive that the language in which he expressed himself in regard to our clergy, and the forms and attitudes of Popery, would be apt to excite the indignation of a portion of this immense auditory; but the spirit of courtesy prevailed over the feelings of the people, and so far from having been treated with disrespect, he was listened to with more than ordinary indulgence. He excited less of our anger than of our commiseration. I am upon this account rejoiced that he should have undertaken an exploit of this kind. We have given him evidence, at all events, that however intolerant the theory of our religion may appear to him, we are practically forbearing and indulgent. We allowed him to inveigh against the bridle and saddle of the Pope, without a remonstrance; we permitted him to indulge in his dismal merriment, and his melancholy ridicule, without a murmur; he will therefore have derived a useful lesson from his experiment on the public patience, and when he shall recount to his confederates the Bible Society his achievements amongst us, he will have an opportunity of telling them that we are far more tolerant of a difference o opin.on than the pious auditory which Mr. M'Clintock is in the habit of addressing. I have occasionally attended meetings of the Bible Society, and observed that whoever ventured to remonstrate against the use of the Apocalypse as a Spelling Book, incurred the indignation of the assembly. I remember to have heard it suggested, that the amatory pictures which are offered to the imagination in the Canticle of Canticles, were not exactly fitted to the private meditation of young ladies when the countenances of the fair auditors immediately assumed a expression of beautiful ferocity, and they looked like angels in a passion Henceforth, however, Mr. M'Clintock may be able to refer to the example of his Roman Catholic auditors in recommending to his pretty votaries at the Bible Society, that meekness and forbearance of which the Roman Catholic ladies have this day afforded a model. In this view the exhibition of Mr. M'Clintock may be considered as likely to be productive of some utility. But, after having thus endeavoured to convey to him an expression of the gratitude which we feel for this interposition of his advice, it is right that I should, after giving him every credit for the benevolent sincerity of his motives, examine into the details of his admonition, and endeavour to ascertain how far it is judicious upon our part to follow the course which he has taken on himself to point out; let me, however, be allowed to make one preliminary remark. On rising he informed us, that he merely obeyed the impulse of the moment and yielded to the sudden suggestions of the Spirit, in communicating his advice. I was not a little surprised that he immediately afterwards produced a series of voluminous extracts from the theological history of the Catholic Church, which, together with certain facetious references to the Cardinals, constituted the substance of his discourse. In any other man I should take this elaborate accumulation of ecclesiastical learning as evidence that he had made some preparation for a somewhat adventurous enterprise, and that he had come furnished with a panoply from the armoury of heaven. I should have supposed that he had taken some time in collecting so many weapons of celestial temper. But Mr. M'Clintock is a peculiar favourite above; he was supplied, no doubt, with these valuable notes by a preternatural means; some angelic influence must have been exercised in his favour, and a hand invisible to our profaner eyes, furnished him on the instant with those large extracts from the Canons of the Council of Lateran.

[Here Mr. M'CLINTOCK rose with some appearance of displeasure, and said that Mr. Sheil was misrepresenting him. He had stated that he had the notes for some time in his pocket.]

Mr. SHEIL—I certainly had understood that Mr. M'Clintock intimated that he had come without preparation to this meeting. I am now, however, to understand that he is not indebted for his recondite erudition to any sudden irradiation from heaven, but that he previously accumulated this mass of citations against Popery. Indeed, the external aspect of the document sustains his present allegation, for the "Sybilline leaves" which were produced by him, seemed a little sear and faded. I perceive that Mr. M'Clintock does not take the remarks which I have presumed to make in very good part. In the Evangelical Societies where he makes so conspicuous a figure, be has it all his own way. He is not much accusomed to the collisions of intellect which are incident to popular debate; it he must not expect that a person having so much veneration as have for the Pope's bridle and saddle, to which he has adverted with such a pleasant unction, should not return his compliment to my religion and give him a few hints upon his own. Mr. M'Clintock is no ordinary person. He is the uncle of Lord Roden, and the near relative of Lord Oriel; he is, besides, nearly allied to the Archbishop of Tuam of Biblical renown, and has obtained no little notoriety by his epistolary controversies with Doctor Curtis. The observations of such a man ought not to be allowed to pass without comment; I shall, therefore, proceed. Mr. M'Clintock recommends us to procure a repeal of the Canons of the Council of Lateran. I am apprehensive that Mr. M'Clintock has blinded himself with the dust of those ponderous folios which he must needs have studied, in order to exhibit such a farrago of theology as he has produced to-day. The Councils of Nice, of Constance, of Lateran, and of Trent, are as familiar to him as "household words." He has thrown them into what the lawyers call a hotch-potch together. I shall not undertake to follow him through so much dark and mysterious erudition; but, at the same time, I shall grapple with the principle upon which his reference to the Councils are founded. He tells us that we ought to procure a repeal of the denunciations against heresy before we can expect emancipation. I beg leave to suggest the propriety of putting Mr. M'Clintock into Parliament in place of his kinsman, Mr. Leslie Foster, in order to enable him to move for a repeal of the laws against witchcraft, passed by a Protestant Legislature in the reign of James I. Thus a three-fold object will be attained. We shall, in the first place, get rid of Mr. Leslie Foster; in the second place we shall reward Mr. M'Clintock for his well-meant admonitions; and in the third place we shall afford an opportunity to Mr. M'Clintock of giving the same earnest exhortations to his fellow-legislators to relieve their religion from the odium with which the enactments of superstition ought to be pursued. But let me put the language of mockery aside, and ask Mr. M'Clintock whether it be not as unjust to charge the Catholics of the nineteenth century with edicts passed some centuries ago, as it would be to impute to the Protestant religion the fanatical absurdity which dictated the statute against the "feeders of evil spirits." It is perfectly obvious that Mr. M'Clintock has conveyed a charge of intolerance in the shape of advice. He deserves a serious answer. I shall, in the first place, point out the circumstances under which any denunciations against heresy were pronounced by the assembled hierarchy of the Christian world. I shall show, in the second place, that the spirit of Protestantism was, at one period, fully as sanguinary and ferocious as that which Mr. M'Clintock has ascribed to the genius of Popery, in what he might call the night of its darkest domination. And I shall give proof to Mr. M'Clintock, in the third place, that while the faith of Roman Catholics remains unchanged, the principles by which the civil executive enforced an uniformity of creed have been long since abandoned. If, like Mr M'Clintock, I were a reader of Saint Peter without note or comment

I might refer him to the second chapter, in which
teachers who shall bring in damnable heresies;"
M'Clintock has no great relish for St. Peter, c
The Roman Catholic divines were sufficiently f
authority of the Scriptures, when the State deem
their sanction in aid of the enactments of civil p
for the writ, "*de hæretico comburendo,*" might r
Testament, both Old and New. But I thank G
a part of the faith of Roman Catholics, that the
ought to be propagated with the faggot, or that tl
ought to be dispelled with the flames of an *au*
manifest distinction between faith, which consists
religious tenets, and the practical measures by whi
to be enforced. A belief in transubstantiation is
but the punishment of heresy is matter not of bel
and cannot be said to constitute any portion of
faith. It is perfectly true, that at a period when
religion was, the only form under which Christian
system of discipline was adopted, of which the o
innovation, and it would be easy to find many
among Protestant divines in support of that rest
in religion, which, under the pretence of prese
society, were introduced by the lawgivers of a da
mate connexion between the State and the Church,
in the one, which were intended to be the props
reciprocity of corruption, they infected each ot
turned into divines, and divines into statesmen.
,ural transformation, and produced the worst r
into a comparison of the enormities committed
opposing, or the Protestants in extending, the doc
mation, perhaps it would be difficult to strike a
between them. If any excuse could be urged, (bu
it might be suggested on the part of the professor
that they were, to use a legal illustration, in poss
and opposed every casual ejector, who came to tres
sive property in heaven. The Protestants who tl
our Church, should consider the position from wh
are flung, and should remember that they live
materials. It is notorious that almost, with the
Melancthon, all the earlier Reformers were infi
After hunting Popery down, they turned like m
other. The progress of the Reformation is tra
blood. It is unnecessary to go through the details
Continent, but as Mr. M'Clintock seems to belon
department of Christianity, (I should so collect f
will pardon me for referring him to Geneva, that
doxy, for illustrations of the peaceful and forbeari
the Fathers of the Reformed Religion enforce
They tortured, they emboweled, they consumed witl

presumed to question their delegation from heaven. But let us turn to England. It is but a few days since I perused a letter by that martyr of the Reformation, the detestable Cranmer, in which he writes, that inasmuch as one Fryth did not think it necessary to believe in the corporal presence of Christ in the Sacrament, and held, in this point, much after the opinion of Œcolampadius, it was necessary to hand him over to the secular power, " where," as Cranmer says, " he Fryth, looked every day to go to the fire." Well might he exclaim, "this guilty hand;" well might the Patriarch of the Reformation, while he was himself perishing at the stake, utter that terrific cry; but he should have applied it not to the recantation of his opinions, but to the sanguinary misdeeds to which that hand had given its sanction. If the mother of Fryth had stood beside him, might she not have cried, " Your groans are like the groans of my son, and your screams remember me of his cries." But why refer to Cranmer, when I may resort to the amiable and benevolent Henry, the Father of the English Reformation. Protestants disclaim that celebrated Prince; but really they should be held responsible for his barbarities, when they impute to us every delinquency practised by the professors of our creed. Let them deny it as they will; if we trace the Protestant religion to its fountainhead, however it may have been purified in its progress, we shall find its sources stained with blood. But perhaps Mr. M'Clintock will say, that it pleased Providence to choose an unworthy instrument, in the ferocious Henry, for the accomplishment of its sacred purposes; and that when we find the cradle of their religion rocked in murder, adultery, and incest, we see an exemplification of the tendency of Heaven to deduce good from ill. It must be confessed, that Providence displayed a somewhat fantastic and capricious taste in choosing an execrable tyrant for the execution of its holy designs. It may be said, that the light only dawned in the mind of Henry—that the Spirit did not visit him in its fullest illumination—and that although the morning of the Reformation was dark and gloomy, and many a bloody cloud attended the ascending luminary, yet that in a little while the truth appeared in all its glory, and spread into the full splendour of day. Well, let me pass at once to the 27th of Elizabeth, by which it was enacted, that " every Romish Priest should be hanged until he was half dead, then should have his head taken off, and his body cut in quarters—that his bowels should be drawn out and burned, and his head fixed upon a pole in some public place." What will Mr. M'Clintock say to this? Does he think the charge of intolerance is justly confined to the religion of Rome? I will not pursue the spirit of persecution through the variety of legislative enactments in which it is exemplified. What need I do more than refer to the Penal Code enacted in this country, by which the son was incited to revolt against the father, and parricide was converted into a sort of political duty by the law. It was of this code that Sir Toby Butler said, " It is enough to make the hardest heart bleed to think on't." It would be an almost endless labour to go through all the proofs, with which history may be said to teem, of the ferocious spirit by which

sectarian power has been almost uniformly displ[
produce gibbet for gibbet against Mr. M'Clin[
difference between us would be, that Catholics
for the exercise of that unfortunate tendency
belong to the nature of man. The Protestants,
use of their time. The truth is, that both p[
and should avoid this recriminating retrospect.
wise it would be of Mr. M'Clintock, instead of
Council of Lateran, to refer his fellow-believers
events, to the universal diffusion of intelligence, an[
which the religion both of Catholics and of Protes[
The sphere of human knowledge has advanced, an[
has been carried along in the universal progressio[
same, but our system of ecclesiastical governme[
Persecution cannot be considered as an ingredient
may, indeed, be the result of his principles, but [
as of the essence of his belief. It were wiser for
look at the declarations of the Catholic Universit[
minable doctrines imputed to us—to the recent pr[
Bishops of Ireland, and to the oath which every R[
than to the moth-eaten volumes with which he l[
his mind. Let him beware of these studies—"
colour of the leaf upon which it feeds," and I kno[
than the black letter repertories of theology whi[
intellectual nourishment. But let us go beyond
and declarations, and come to facts. The liberali[
confined to mere speculation. Look at Hungary
of forty years, all distinctions between Protesta[
been abolished. Mr. M'Clintock has, *en passa[*
Charles X. and the Jesuits. Poor gentleman, he
the Jesuits as *Scrub* in the play, who rushes out i[
exclaims, "murder, robbery, the Pope and the Je[
office to defend the intellect of Charles X. I bel[
of Protestant and Catholic royalty were to be weig[
be found in a state of complete equipoise. I hardly [
would weigh the Capets to the beam, and if the he[
ness the Duke of York were to be examined by
he would, probably, find in it an equally faithful [
theory. On the head of the Duke of Cumberland,
as they are technically called, might be discovere[
Selis should be conjured to explain. But a tru[
testants complain of the intolerant spirit of the
first place the Huguenots are provided with cl[
expense. In the Rue St. Honore, in Paris, they
of worship given them by the State, and their cle[
us well, but much better, than the Roman Catholi[
receive one-third more. Let Mr. M'Clintock loo[
ter, and he will find that by the third article, 'all F[
admissible to all civil and military employments."

individual is allowed to profess his religion with an equal freedom, and obtains for his form of worship, the same protection.' But all these arguments, derived both from reason and from fact, have no weight, as long as we consider the Pope infallible. Mr. M'Clintock informs us, that no human being is exempt from frailty, and refers to King David, and the interesting story of Bathsheba. He has also quoted the uxorious propensities of his son.

Mr. M'Clintock seems well versed in the Old Testament, and appears well qualified to make elegant extracts of its more enticing incidents for the meditation of young ladies. They would make a neat volume, especially if adorned with prints; and some fair devotee well skilled in drawing should be applied to, to throw her imagination into the pencil, and furnish illustrations. A pretty subject that of David and Bathsheba, to which Mr. M'Clintock has adverted. He passed with much rapidity of transition to his holiness, and I own I expected a few anecdotes of the Borgina family, to beguile the tedium of debate. However, he confined himself to the equestrian habitudes of his holiness. I beg to apprise Mr. M'Clintock, that I for one do not consider the Pope infallible—nor is such an opinion entertained in our church Roman Catholics indeed believe that truth resides in their church, as most people believe their own to be the best religion. Mr. M'Clintock will allow me to interpret the Scriptures as I think proper. St Paul and he differ, indeed, on that head, as St. Paul condemns "private interpretation." But I meet Mr. M'Clintock on his own ground, and tell him that I find texts in Scripture which, according to my private construction, warrant a belief in the infallibility of the church. I may be wrong, but I deduce that position from the Scriptures, and the first use I make of them is, to bow down my judgment to the church. I need not repeat the text—" Thou art Peter." "Lo, I will be with you to the end of time," and so forth. I by no means insist on Mr. M'Clintock adopting my construction, but upon his own principles, he must not quarrel with the inference which I draw from the Bible. I have as much right to draw that conclusion from the Bible, as he has to believe in his election from eternity, which he derives from the same source. Why then should I be debarred of my civil rights for believing that truth must reside somewhere, and for choosing to give it a residence in the Catholic Church, instead of the bottom of a well. At all events the arguments on my side are plausible enough to have imposed on many great and good men; and I must be pardoned for following, like Mr. M'Clintock, my own vagary in religion. There is, in my mind, this difference between Mr. M'Clintock and myself. I believe the church to be infallible, and he believes himself to be so.

Mr. M'Clintock.—Not at all.

Mr. Sheil.—I shall shew Mr. M'Clintock that this conclusion is the necessary consequence of his premises. If every Protestant is entitled to draw his religion from the Bible, it follows that he must be capable so to do. If he be capable so to do, he must be enlightened by heaven, and if enlightened by heaven, as God does not lead us astray, he must be infallible. A member of the Bible Society gives the Scriptures to

his child, and desires him to make out his faith from
(he says), my sweet little divine, is the Book of Life—
what the priests and cardinals tell you, but study the
self; investigate the mystery of the Incarnation, and so
cal problems of the Apocalypse—and, my dear boy, if
want of amusement, read the pleasant story of David
and the other instructive anecdotes which you will f
in this holy book—God will preserve your imagination
fill with his divine grace every little theologian of thir
good bye, and go and play with the Gospel at 'hide
So much for divinity in its teens. But seriously spea
be not infallible, why give the Bible to the boy? It
am for corporate, and Mr. M'Clintock for individua
prefer the decrees of councils—he prefers the rhaps
ticles. I like the religion of Pascal, and Fenelon, a
Arnaud, while Mr. M'Clintock and the ladies of Dubl
lection for the new apostle of the Gentiles—Baron Mu
felto Ferdinand Mendez Pinto Wolff, formerly of λ
London, lately of the Propaganda in Rome, and now (
to the Ladies Auxiliary Bible Society, Dublin. Kirv
that the teachers of new religions were like the soldie
seamless garment of our Saviour to pieces. This cor
after selling old clothes through Germany, comes hawk
of new-fashioned christianity in Dublin. The fellow's
reminds me of Dryden's description of the fanatics—

> More haughty than the rest, the *Wolfish* race—
> Appear with belly gaunt and famished face—
> Never was so deformed a beast of grace.

I commend Mr. M'Clintock to this worthy missiona
whose infallibility and fidelity in the commemoration
ders, I presume he makes no question, and gives hii
ference to Prince Hohenloe. Good heaven! to what a
has arrived! An ignorant Israelite arrives in Dubl
doctors of the Church of Rome, in the world, to mee
tual combat, directs that answers should be inclosed f
verse to Mr. Hogan, of York-street, and is forthwith e
all the rank and beauty of Dublin. Warren, with
nothing to this; and Ingleby, "the emperor of conju
every other juggler, sinks into miserable diminution be
of celestial legerdemain. But, sir, enough of these
very foreign from those on which I had intended to ad
M'Clintock has broken in upon the ordinary course o
and has, perhaps, enlivened this meeting with some di
I hope we shall often see him amongst us, and that a
ciates of the Bible Society will do us the favour to
for, although we are greatly surpassed by them in the
extent of acquirement, grace of elocution, and power
the truth upon our side almost renders us their match.
thus much, I shall not enter into any of the subjects s

resolutions, but shall content myself with simply stating, that for the vote of thanks you have given me for my professional exertions at the election, to the success of which you are pleased to say that I contributed, I am deeply grateful.

MEATH CATHOLIC MEETING.

SPEECH AT THE MEATH CATHOLIC MEETING, HELD ON THE BANKS OF THE BOYNE, ON THE 28TH AUGUST, 1825.

This meeting was attended by the Earl of Darnley, and several other noblemen and gentlemen of high rank.

UPON the first day of July, in the year 1690, the waters of the river, on whose banks you are assembled, ran red with blood. Upon the banks of that river James and William met. The combat was long and doubtful. There was a moment when the Irish forces were upon the point of triumph. "Spare my English subjects!" exclaimed the wretched Prince, to whom the Irish language has attached his most appropriate designation; and well might his followers cry out, "Change kings and we'll fight the battle over again!" The Irish were defeated, but not overthrown. The bloody day of Aughrim succeeded. The ball that pierced St. Ruth was lodged in the breast of Ireland. Notwithstanding these disasters the Irish power was not annihilated, and the walls of Limerick still afforded the means of a permanent defence. A large body of French and Irish troops were assembled within its gates; and William, who had been formerly driven from its walls, foresaw that, if the expected succours should arrive from France, the civil war would, at all events, be protracted, and that eventually its fortune might be reversed. Under these circumstances he instructed his officers to conclude a peace with as much speed as possible. Leland, who affects to discredit the " Secret Proclamation," (as it was called) by which the Lords Justices tendered much more favourable terms than were subsequently granted, admits that William had directed Ginkle to terminate the war upon *any* conditions. It appears by a letter, written by the nephew of Lord Tyrconnell, that at one period William was willing to secure to the Catholics one-half of the churches, one-half of the offices, civil and military, and compensation for the forfeited estates. It was obviously a matter of great importance to that sagacious Prince, to put an end to intestine divisions, at a time when England was engaged in Continental warfare. As long as Limerick held out it was in the power of France to create an alarming diversion. Terms were proposed to the Irish garrison. After some negociation, in which Sir Theobald Butler, who had been Attorney-General to James the Second, took a leading part, it was stipulated, that the Irish Catholics should be secured in the undisturbed possession of their property, in the exercise of their religion, and in the rights and privileges which they had enjoyed in the reign of Charles II. In the reign of that monarch Catholics sat in Parliament, and that right was reserved as fully and effectually as if it had been distinctly specified in the contract. On the 3rd of October, in the year 1691, the Articles of Capitulation were signed. Immediately after, and before the gates had been thrown open, intelligence arrived that the sails of a foreign fleet were seen off the coast. It may readily be conjectured with what an intense emotion the news was received. Offer to yourselves an image of the scene which the city must have presented. An amnesty is proclaimed; a few days are allowed to the Irish who preferred exile to ignominy, to embark for France. They continue during that interval in possession of the fortress, whose bastions remained unbattered. The green flag, with the harp woven in gold, yet floated from the citadel. The Irish soldiers stood upon the battlements, and looked, for the last time, upon the fields of their country, upon which so many of their sons, and of their brothers, were lying dead. In the midst of that melancholy scene, in the heavy damp that hung upon their hearts, a rumour is suddenly heard, that a French fleet has been seen off the coast; a courier arrives—the flag of France has been discerned. Another messenger appears, and proclaims the arrival of twenty ships of war, under the command of Chateau-Renault, laden with ammunition, and with arms and men. It would require some portion of the powers of the eminent person who has been lately among us, and whose genius has found such admirable materials in the civil wars of his own country, to describe the effects which that intelligence must have produced among those who had but the day before set their hands to the articles of capitulation. Would he not make us thrill in the delineation of such a scene? Would he not make our hearts leap within us in painting the effects of this great but unavailing event, upon the chivalrous and gallant men who had not abandoned their Sovereign when he had deserted himself. With what a pathetic vividness would he paint the simultaneous impulse with which the weapon that hung loosely to the ground flew into the soldier's hand, as the drum beat along the ramparts, and sent forth its martial and spirit stirring call. How would he paint the rushing of men together—the earnest interrogation, the rapid utterance, the precipitous movement, the trembling and anxious lip, and vivid and flashing eye. Should we not behold the brave, the noble, the devoted, the self-immolating Sarsfield kindle with the intelligence, and starting into the warrior's attitude again. He did. The generous and gallant Sarsfield sprung up from the earth, on which he had thrown himself with despair, when the sound of France and of succour reached his ears. Every generous instinct of his nature must have been roused within him—his soul must have been at once in arms—his face must have been kindled with revenge and glory—every nerve must have been braced—every sinew must have been strung—his hand must have been placed upon that sword which had unplumed so many a helm. But it was glued to the scabbard. He could but grasp its hilt. The recollection of the treaty must have come upon him, and striking that brow which was furrowed with the casque, he must have exclaimed—" France, thou art come too late, and

Ireland is lost for ever."—You must not chide me, my lord, for presenting this picture—in these strong, and there are some who, perhaps, will deem them excessive colours. It is a theme to which it is impossible for any Catholic to revert without emotion, and I confess, for my own part, that I cannot contemplate the event to which I have referred without sympathising in the feelings of the men who were placed in a juncture so exciting, and who had still power to resist the temptation which the event I have attempted to describe must have held out to their hearts. They did resist it. In despite of the allurement which the landing of a great force had presented, the Irish Catholics, with arms in their hands, with a strong city in their possession, and while William was engaged in a foreign war, replete with embarrassment and peril, remained faithful to their compact, and, trusting to a false and perjured enemy, threw the gates open and surrendered. What part did the conquerors act? There is not in the records of mankind an example of more foul and abominable perfidy than the almost instantaneous violation of the Charter, to which justice and honour had set their seals. Where was the first announcement of the detestable purpose made? Before the altar of Almighty God! Dopping, the Bishop of Meath (he ought to have been Archbishop of Dublin) preaching before the Justices in Christ Church, the Sunday after they had returned from the camp, insisted that faith ought not to be kept with Papists. He proclaimed treachery and sacrilege as a part of his sacerdotal ethics, and Parliament soon cried "Amen!" Before their purpose was carried into execution a little mockery was deemed expedient, and a medal was struck, to use Harris's expression, "to eternize the mercy of the Sovereign!" The Queen was represented with an olive branch in her hand, as the symbol of peace—a harp was inscribed upon the reverse, with a motto which intimated a cessation of discord, in the words "*I am placidum reditura melos*," and it was further specified, that in the year 1691, "Ireland was received to mercy." A few weeks after some Catholics were deprived of their estates, and outrages were committed upon their homes and persons. These were the preliminaries to an act of more formal oppression, and in 1703 it was deemed expedient to regalize atrocity, and to incorporate villany with the law. An Act of Parliament was introduced, by which the very order of nature was inverted, and parricide was made a precept in the decalogue of the law. The atrocities of the first penal law (for the monster was mature at its birth) are described by Sir Theobald Butler with the eloquence of a man whose soul was wrung within him, and who drew his feelings not from the sources of artificial emotion, but from the deep and troubled fountains of the heart. After having conjured the House of Commons in the name of every law, human and divine, not to infringe a treaty which had been rendered sacred by the most solemn obligations by which man can be bound on earth, or should he be in awe of heaven—he that was not only the advocate of a whole people but his own, and was to be himself the victim of this parricidal law, proceeds to describe the consequences of allowing the Protestant son to tear his property from his Catholic father. And do you not, my lord, think his face must have been suffused with tears of anguish, when he said, "is not this against the laws of God and man; against the rule of reason and justice, by which all men ought to be governed? Is not this the surest way in the world to make children become undutiful, and to bring the gray head of the father to the grave with grief and tears? It would be hard from any man—but from a son, a child," (his face must have been covered with tears as he spoke)—" the fruit of my body, whom I have nursed in my bosom, and tendered more dearly than my own life, to become my plunderer, to rob me of my estate, and to take away my bread, is much more grievous than from any other, and enough to make the most flinty of hearts to bleed to think on it ;"—(alas, he was speaking to the Scots and the Jenkinsons of the day.) " For God's sake, will you consider, whether this is according to the golden rule, ' to do as you should be done unto,' and if not, you will not, nay, surely you cannot, without the most manifest injustice, take from us our birth-rights, and invest them in others before our faces." In such language did Sir Theobald Butler, who was a Catholic lawyer of the first eminence, and who had himself been a party to the treaty of Limerick, implore the Irish House of Commons to respect the law of man and of God! But it was in vain. The bill passed, and was succeeded by other enactments of the same character. Nothing was omitted that could be devised by the satanic genius of penal legislation, for the oppression and degradation of the people. Session after session new chains were forged until there was not a link left to which a fetter could be attached, and the very power of oppression had been exhausted by its accumulation. It were vain to attempt to describe the measureless villany of that system. This execrable assemblage of atrocity, in which every crime appeared to have been gathered, baffled the genius of Edmund Burke, and defied his power of expression. Its necessary results upon the national character were speedily produced. The action of servitude is reciprocal. The population was divided into thousands of tyrants and millions of slaves. The judges of the land declared that a Papist could not breathe without the connivance of the government. The common air was made a matter of indulgence. It was not until the year 1759, that the first gleam of hope began to dawn on the Roman Catholics of Ireland, and that the government first manifested some attention to the condition of the people. That first faint dawn of hope rose out of the public danger. The Duke of Bedford (the then Lord Lieutenant) stated in the House of Commons, that Mr. Secretary Pitt had apprised him, that France speculated upon the discontent of the people of Ireland. The Catholic merchants, (for like another proscribed people, the Jews, the Catholics had directed their views and their energies to commerce,) took advantage of the intimation. They proposed to address the Lord Lieutenant. The nobility and gentry, who had acquired habits of timidity, opposed it. The more democratic party prevailed. The French fleet was on the coast, and a gracious answer was returned. Mr. Mason's motion for allowing Catholics to lend money on mortgages, was lost by a majority of 188 to 151. This was the first motion in our favour. In 1772 by a great stretch of mercy, Catholics were indulged so far as to be allowed to take leases of bog not exceeding fifty acres. In 1774, America began to manifest a sense of her injuries and of her power, and the Catholics were indulged so far as to be allowed to testify their allegiance by an oath. This was the first legal recognition of their relation as subjects to the state. The air of heaven ceased to be a luxury; and their right to breathe was acknowledged by the law. In 1778, the discontents of America augmented. The Volunteers of Ireland (the dragon's teeth) were already springing up in an iron harvest. A new argument for relief was supplied, and Mr. Gardiner's bill passed by only a majority of nine in the Commons. By that bill Catholics were allowed to take leases for 999 years, and their property was made deviseable and descendible. In 1782, the resolutions of Dungannon were published. The last was in favour of the Roman Catholics, and five days after, the 21st and 22nd of Geo. III. was passed, by which Catholics were allowed to take land without limit, and certain penalties upon their clergy were removed. At length, in 1791, the French Revolution, that great event, which shook the moral world to the centre, extended its influence to Ireland, and on the 11th of February, 1791, the Catholic Committee were summoned. The aristocracy were appalled by the incidents which crowded upon mankind. They were so long habituated to a dungeon of night, that they were dazzled by the full and perfect day, and shrunk back for a moment into the obscurity to which they were accustomed. The address of the sixty-four seceders was timid, but not as it has been represented, a grovelling acquiescence in their sentence. They did not dare to petition for the elective franchise; that audacious supplication was reserved for the aspiring spirit of the Catholic traders of Dublin. Their petition was rejected by a majority of 208 to 23. But the people were not dismayed—a great national convention was summoned, and met on the 2nd of December, 1792. Here was the great root of the Catholic Association. Successive branches have been lopped off; but, thank God, the trunk is unwithered still. What was the result? It was pretended that the Catholic delegates were the greatest enemies to their own cause: and Mr. Hobart immediately afterwards moved for liberty to bring in the great Statute of 1793. On the very same night, he announced a war on the part of the French Republic against England.

The Act of 1793 gave us political power, by giving us the elective franchise; it was a moiety of Emancipation. Lord Fitzwilliam arrived with the residue of the nation's liberty in his gift; but the evil genius of the country, in the shape of a Beresford, (mark it well, freeholders of Waterford!) whispered away the freedom of Ireland, and converted the malady of the prince into the degradation of the people. In 1791, the bill to admit Catholics into parliament was lost by a majority of 155 to 84, and, on the 7th of February, 1797, the question was lost, for the last time in Ireland, by 143 to 19. The country was driven into insurrection, and hurried from rebellion to its anticipated results. The Union passed. Here let me for a moment pause, and ask of any man who reviews the progress of the Catholic question up to this great epoch, whether any thing was ever won by pusillanimous proceedings and whether the portion of liberty that was obtained by the Irish Catholics, was not wrung from the apprehensions of the minister by the determination of the people? What produced the Treaty of Limerick?—the fear of France. What produced its violation?—the base confidence in impunity. What produced the series of relaxations from 1792 to 1793?—America, Reform, and France. Was any thing ever won by sycophantic turpitude, and by crawling servility? Is it from the past that we should learn to speak in a "bondsman's key," or ask for liberty in the accents of mendicant supplication? Are we to listen to the suggestions of those who teach us, that like dogs we should "lick our wounds, and know no other cure?"—or is there anything in the past that should discourage us for the future? In 1792 there were only twenty-three members of the House of Commons in our favour. The Catholic convention assembled—victory was the vassal of France, and in 1793 a great measure was carried by an immense majority. But let me proceed, for the time which I have already occupied admonishes me to be brief. In 1801 Mr. Pitt resigned upon the ground of his alleged incapacity to fulfil his pledge. In 1805 our question was first discussed in the Imperial Parliament. It was rejected by a majority of 212. This was appalling, and yet we were not disheartened. Twenty years, (and twenty years, though a vast space in the life of an individual, constitute but a brief period in the history of a nation) have not only melted down that majority, but have produced a majority of twenty-seven in our favour, and have revolutionised the public feeling. Shall we, who were not terrified by a majority of 212 in the Commons, allow ourselves to be beaten back by 49 in the Lords? But mark the steps by which the question advanced: In 1813 there was, for the first time, a majority, on the first reading of the bill, in our favour. At that period Bonaparte was upon his throne, and the Catholic Committee was in the legal exercise of its functions. Not long after the bill, opening the Army and Navy, was passed. England was afraid her Irish officers would be driven, by the law, into the continental service. This concession furnished one argument. Strange, that in a free country the military offices should be thrown open, and the civil should be closed up! Our own dissensions afterwards impeded our advancement. Had we been united, as we now are, and as I trust we shall long continue to be—our question would, perhaps, ere this, have been carried. At length, Mr. Plunkett succeeded in bringing the bill through the House of Commons, although by an inconsiderable majority, and it was rejected in the Lords by only 39. The Catholics were allured into inertness by a false hope. The king arrived, (God knows for what purpose), and we did not even obtrude our wishes upon the royal ear. We gave our opponents reason to think that we could be reconciled to our degradation, and our petition was scouted and flung out of the Commons. We derived a useful instruction from this result of moderation. The Catholic Association sprung up. O'Connell devised and executed a noble project: A system of voluntary contribution was established. The Catholic Rent was collected. The proceedings of that great assembly fixed the attention of the empire. It was first derided, then dreaded.

and afterwards oppressed. But where is the man who will say that it achieved little for Ireland? It gave proof of the power, and the vigour of the Catholics—and shook the mind of the English nation. What was the consequence? That the prejudices against the measure have sunk among the dregs of the people. A second time it passed the Commons. It was by a great exertion that the opposition in the Lords was produced, and that opposition, be it remembered, rests upon transitory materials. Is the Duke of York immortal? Is Eldon a Tithonus, or is there any fair sorceress, any Medea, of forty who has undertaken to impart new life, heat, and vigour to the Earl of Liverpool? There is, unfortunately for the church, no "elixir vitæ" to accomplish this renovation; and if we had no other principle of hope than the calculation of an insurance-office, we should not despair. I should like to see his Royal Highness making his appearance at the Atlas-office to effect a policy, at the instance of his pious and moral associate, the Marquis of Hertford. I should like to observe the eye of inquisitorial inspection with which the appraiser of life would survey the bulky exhibit of which his Royal Highness should make proffer. But let him pass. The progress of the Catholic question depends upon the confederated energies of the Irish people. It is not enough that we should hold occasional meetings, and that strong sentiments should evaporate in steamy phrase. Something practically great and impressive must be accomplished. The resolution which was proposed by the eldest son of my Lord Gormanstown, contains a powerful recommendation. A census must be taken. Every parish must meet on the same day—and a great convention must be summoned. Let the Catholic prelates, the chief of the Catholic clergy, the nobility, the gentry, the great agriculturists, the merchants, and the members of the liberal professions meet. Let the Peers and leading Catholics be invited to unite themselves with this National Assembly. The eyes of the empire would be fixed upon its deliberations. Its sitting may be continued for fourteen•successive days. Can any man question the expediency of such a measure, if it can be accomplished; and can any man doubt the facility of its achievement who has seen what has been effected; I, for one, do not; and since I have so far spoken of myself, let me be allowed to tell you why I have come this day amongst you. It is because I feel you are engaged in no local concern, but in a cause in which we all bear a participation, and in the promotion of which it is every man's duty to engage. I knew that your meeting, from the many persons of rank who attend it, would excite no ordinary attention; and as I deemed it not improper that I should intermix my sentiments in your proceedings, and give utterance to the strenuous convictions of my mind, I came here to tell you, that I think you must relinquish all hope of achieving the freedom of Ireland, unless you adopt a bold, determined, and energetic system of action. I came here to rescue your proceedings, as far as it lies in me, from the cant of servility, which disguises itself under the name of moderation. A true and genuine moderation, I do most fervently recommend; but I as devoutly deprecate that spurious moderation, which would degenerate into inertness and which derives its origin from those habits of voluntary servitude which long continued thraldom could not fail to create. But I thank God that the sluggish and apathetic state of political feeling to which I have adverted, has undergone a most salutary change. Thank God! there is scarcely a man in the great community to which we belong, that does not feel that existence without iberty is scarcely worth keeping. Slavery not only takes away one half of its virtue from the spirit of man, but deprives life of all its value. Who can be such a sceptic in the power of an united and enthusiastic people, and in the progress of truth, of reason, and of justice, as to think it possible that when liberty is spreading its illuminations to the extremities of the world, this country, which Providence appears to have framed with " a peculiar care," should not catch a reflection of that glorious light; and that while South America is starting into freedom, Ireland should still continue enslaved? Will England withhold from the Irish Roman Catholics that freedom which England has conferred upon the 'Peruvian Creole? That this great object will be attained I entertain a strong assurance. In all likelihood almost every man that hears me will live to behold the great event which will confer peace, and wealth, and happiness upon Ireland; but if it shall be otherwise—if we are destined to descend into the earth before that great measure shall have been accomplished, it is some consolation to us to reflect, that we shall not entail our vassalage upon those who are to come after us, that if liberty shall not become vested in us, it will be derived through us; and that (where is the father who does not feel the power of that appeal?) the inheritors of our existence shall not be the heirs of our oppression, and that our children shall be free.

CONNAUGHT PROVINCIAL MEETING.

SPEECH AT THE CONNAUGHT PROVINCIAL MEETING, WHICH WAS ATTENDED BY THE DUKE DE MONTEBELLO.

I HOLD in my hand, a document of no ordinary importance. It was delivered to me by that ardent servant of his country and of his religion, the Roman Catholic Bishop of Waterford. "I give you," said that lofty-minded prelate, " the result of much labour, and much zeal. I place a document in your hands, which is signed by me, in my episcopal character, and for whose authenticity I can vouch. Take it, and let it be used for the good of Ireland, and the honour of God." He intrusted to my care what I consider to be of the utmost consequence to the promotion of our cause, and I have selected this great provincial assembly, as affording the most appropriate occasion for the statement of its contents. It is the certified census, under the sign manual of the bishop, of the comparative Protestant and Catholic population of the united dioceses of Waterford and Lismore It comprehends the returns made in their official capacity, by the parish priests of thirty-seven parishes, (returns very different from the vague computations of that strange calculator of men, Mr. Leslie Foster, who allows three Catholics and a quarter to every Protestant); and by these returns it appears that the population of the united dioceses, including the city of Waterford, amounts to ten thousand one hundred and forty-nine Protestants, and two hundred and thirty-one thousand two hundred and eighteen Roman Catholics. Yes, I repeat it, 10,149, who are not Catholics, (for Presbyterians, Quakers, Methodists, Walkerites, Rodenites, Wolffites, and nondescripts, are included under this negative denomination,) and two hundred and thirty-one thousand eight hundred and eighteen professors of that religion, which is laden with penalties, encompassed with disqualifications, and branded with dishonour by the law. Gracious God, under what a system do we live? and how justly does the world look with indignation upon those venerable institutions, which raise a handful of men into an insolent and exasperating masterdom, and throwing down a whole people to the earth, reduce us to that condition of debasing servitude, against which the understanding revolts, and the heart rebels. Ten thousand Protestants, and two hundred and thirty-one thousand Catholics—and this is the system which we are told to bear with a meek and gentle spirit—this is the condition of things, at which we are to smile, and simper, and lisp, and not imprecate and groan—this is the condition of things against which we should remonstrate in melodious murmurs, and with a graceful attitude of supplication!—This is the system against which, whoever dares to inveigh in the language that becomes a man, and gives vent to the feelings that break the nation's heart, is denounced as a savage demagogue, and a truculent declaimer. What will any man, whose mind is not blocked up by passion against all reason, all justice, all feeling, all honour, and all truth, think of such a system as this? In what light must any impartial Englishman, or any foreigner, by whom this country may chance to be visited, regard a constitution which excludes the enormous majority of its citizens, from a participation in its privileges? If—but I should not put it in by-way of hypothesis, for a French nobleman of the highest rank, the Duke de Montebello, is present in this assembly; he is accompanied by three of his countrymen, of whom two informed me, at the moment I was about to rise, that they are French Protestants, and that they consider the exclusion of the Catholics of Ireland from the full advantage of British citizenship, a reproach to the religion of the State. They told me that the whole body of French Protestants sympathise with us, and are astonished that the professors of reformed Christianity should deny to Catholics that perfect freedom of opinion, on which their own system of belief is founded. They further mentioned to me, that Monsieur de Jaucourt, and Monsieur de Portail, two members of the French government, who fill important situations in the ministry, are Protestants—and Protestants are not only legally admissible, but are actually admitted to influential offices in the State. What, then, must be the astonishment of Frenchmen, on visiting this country, to find seven millions of its inhabitants cast beyond the pale of the constitution, on account of their conscientious adherence to the national faith? The Duke of Montebello will return in a little time to France, and I have pictured to myself what he will say, when his compatriots shall inquire of him what he has seen, and heard, and felt amongst us. "I visited," he will, or might at least say, "that most important portion of the British dominions, for which, in France, much interest is felt, but, as yet, all is not known. I arrived in a country endowed by nature with its best gifts, and covered with a population of vigorous, healthy, intelligent, and generously-minded men. Yet, with all these advantages, I found an utter counteraction of the apparent designs of Providence; and where I expected a scene of national prosperity, I beheld a most miserable and degrading spectacle. The law had established an aristocracy different from that which exists in any other country, and which is not derived from rank, or birth, or public virtue, but consists in the profession of a peculiar form of religion. Protestantism is raised into a kind of nobility, and every miserable pupil of an eleemosynary school— every wretched product of a charter-house—every hard-handed mechanic—every sordid artizan, and every greasy corporator is raised into an artificial superiority over the great body of the people. The fiercest dissensions are thus nurtured by the law, and two factions are marshalled, which are halloed on by the government, and infuriated into a detestation of each other. In the North, I found a band of men called Orangemen, with arms in their hands, supported by the magistracy in their acts of outrage, and exercising that species of domination, which the consciousness of impunity naturally engenders in base and sordid minds. When I reached the metropolis, I found a Lord Lieutenant surrounded with the forms, but destitute of all the realities of power— the slave of an underling of office, set over him by Mr. Peel, and forced to submit to every slight and insult which the prevailing faction sought to put upon him. His vice-regal sceptre is a reed. He enjoys so little of the substance of authority, that he is unable to advance any liberal man to any important situation, although he should superadd the motives of personal friendship to his sense of political duty. Not long ago, he used his influence to advance a Roman Catholic barrister to the only judicial office open to the body, and utterly failed. The ascendant party feel that they are still the virtual masters, and omit no opportunity to proclaim their consciousness of superiority, and their conviction of the permanence of their dominion. The Secretary to the Lord Lieutenant is their patron, and gives a sanction, by his attendance at their atrocious festivities, to the anti-national and insulting sentiments which are announced upon these occasions. The person who is armed with most power in the local government of Ireland, makes it his business to countenance their ferocious orgies. At a recent dinner, which was adorned by his presence, a toast, reprobated by their Sovereign, was announced, amidst a yell of factious triumph, and hailed with rapturous vociferation. Thus the great mass of the people are not only oppressed, but insulted, and reminded of their degradation in every form of offence which the malignant spirit of Orange tyranny can devise. The Roman Catholics are not permitted for an instant to forget their inglorious condition. They are not only stamped with shame, but the finger of scorn is for ever pointed at the brand with which they are marked." And when he shall have said this, and much more than this, and shall have gone into all the details of contumely to which every man of us is subject—when he shall have exhibited all the multifarious varieties of degradation, and of injury, which result from this abominable system, will not some Frenchman exclaim, "And how do these seven millions bear with all this?—are they contented with their political infamy?—do they bend in meekness to the yoke?—do they prostrate themselves before their masters?—are they satisfied with this state of things?—are they so utterly base as to hug their shame, and to be fond of their degradation?" Oh, my countrymen, what answer should be given to these questions? Shall Frenchmen be told that our hearts are compounded of such base stuff? Shall it be said, by our illustrious friend, that we have reached such a meanness of spirit, and have attained such an utter corruption, and helotism of feeling, as to be contented with such a lot? Shall the son of a gallant soldier, in answering that question, say that Ireland is satisfied with her lot? Shall he say that we are such worms, that we dare not turn upon the foot that treads upon us? Will he say this? No! thank God, No! Thanks to Almighty God, he will not say so; he will speak far differently about us. He will say, that seven millions of oppressed and degraded men feel all that burning indignation that befits the complication of insult and of injury which they endure; and that they are animated by as resolved and enthusiastic a spirit as ever actuated a people in the cause of freedom. He will say that they are bound together by a single, an undivided, and inseparable sentiment; that they are as firm and as determined as they are ardent and inflamed; that every thought and feeling is fixed and concentrated in an impassioned aspiration for the liberty of their country. Let him say this, and more than this; let him add, that if ever it shall come to pass that, to the financial embarrassments of England there should be superadded, the enormous expenditure of war, and if, when stripped of her commerce—with her machinery and manufactures at a stand—with her enormous debt, hanging like an avalanche upon her head—with famine within and danger abroad—the fleets of France and of America shall unfurl their flags upon the seas, then—in that hour of tremendous peril, with an enormous population, whose bare physical power would be terrific if put into a simultaneous and gigantic action, and would be doubly terrible if there were art and skill to give it direction, order, system, and effect—then............ I have made a pause, and I feel from the silence with which you await my words, that there is something of awe in your anticipation—then............ But I shall proceed no farther. This is a subject on which much may be said, and more ought to be thought, and I shall only add—may God Almighty give that wisdom to those who are appointed by His providence to sway the destinies of empires, which shall avert those dreadful events, whose bare possibility is sufficient to appal, and from whose likelihood every good man must recoil in horror. And yet, why throw a veil upon futurity—why shu' out from contemplation what may arrive hereafter, because I may be calumniously reproached with desiring what I do but apprehend, and of endeavouring to realize what it is even dreadful to imagine. I do, in the face of heaven, solemnly protest, that I not only deprecate the political calamities to which I have adverted, but I look upon them with horror. Not only my duty as a subject, but my feelings as a man, and those instincts of humanity, of which, I trust, that I am not destitute, teach me to regard any political convulsion which may take place in this country, with a sentiment still stronger than dismay. If it should unfortunately happen that such events should take place in the course of a few years, the men, who, like myself, take the most active share in public affairs, would be the first to perish. They would be swept away in the torrent of blood by which the country would be deluged. The first blast of the trumpet would be a signal for their death, and the example of Narbis, the tyrant of Sparta, would, no doubt, be followed, who, upon an invasion in which it was expected that the Helots might gain their liberty, ordered the leaders of them to be scourged, and then beheaded, so that, as the historian tells us, the streets were red with their blood. A selfish motive, independent of every generous emotion, should teach the most active of our body to look with awe upon those awful events, of which I have but traced the shadows. But is it wise, because the contemplation of an event is attended with terrible anticipations, to clasp our hands to our eyes, and shut it out? Are dangers to be averted by being disguised?—or does he who cries "breakers a-head" drive the vessel on the rock? I hear the roaring of the billows, and see in the distance the surf breaking over the reef, and shall I not exclaim, "helm a lee!" It is to prevent, and not to hurry destruction on, that I point out the peril on which we are advancing, and drive to ruin before the wind.

O navis, referent in mare te novi,
Fluctus! oh quid agis.

I shall, then, fearlessly state what I apprehend may be the consequence of withholding their rights from seven millions of the Irish people. It will be observed, that I am not speaking of events which may take place in one, two, three, or perhaps twenty years; but any man who is not actuated by sentiments of the basest selfishness, will be as solicitous to protect his children from the evils incidental to national calamity, as to shelter himself against them. Should those claims, which are prosecuted with such an ardent pertinacity, be constantly rejected, it is to be apprehended (and such a possibility, independent of its likelihood, is surely to be averted) that the sense of their political duty may be ultimately so far weakened and impaired, that their state of exasperation, to use the language of Mr. Canning, may afford to the enemies of England an opportunity of assailing the empire in a very vulnerable point. The Secretary for Foreign Affairs has intimated this probability, and stated that the attention of the Continental powers was fixed upon this country. I, therefore, do no more than amplify and expand the sentiment of a Prime Minister—no more than he considered it consistent with official delicacy to do,

Should the anticipation of Mr. Canning come to pass, what sort of spectacle would this country present? I do verily believe that every man, who had any sort of stake in the country—every respectable Roman Catholic, would be induced to sacrifice his wrongs and his antipathies to his sense of moral and religious duty, and would adhere to his vow of allegiance. But the great body of the people would, I fear, be under the influence of very powerful temptation, and adventurers and men of desperate fortunes and aspiring minds (and they are to be found in every country) might yield to the suggestions of a wild and criminal ambition, and give a loose to their passions. In my judgment, such an enterprise would ultimately fail, because the power of England, unless she sustained very great reverses, would prevent rebellion from being ever sanctified by its result. But supposing that the event would be what every good subject and good Christian should legally and piously desire, still through what dreadful scenes the country would have to pass, before that salutary consummation could be attained. I do not deny that many would derive, from the confiscation of Catholic property, some consolatory compensations for the national misfortunes. But must not every man of ordinary feeling and humanity, no matter to what party he may belong, shudder at the thought of all the misery, both public and domestic, with which such a state of things would be attended. Some men there are, who are disposed to say, " these things may happen, but they will not happen in our time." This reminds me of the sordid selfishness of Louis the Fifteenth, who shrugged up his shoulders at the prospect of a revolution, and consoled himself by saying, " *apres moi le deluge.*" Let it, he said, rain blood, if it only falls upon my grave. The head of his son rolled upon his tomb. I have said these things before; but why should they not be reiterated? Why should not that raven cry be sounded again and again? It is not for the purposes of faction—it is not as a furious and savage alarmist that I speak thus—it is in the hope that these impassioned appeals may have some effect in awakening our antagonists to a sense of the dangers to which we are all in common exposed. Protestants of Ireland, if you have no regard for your country—if you are dead to all public considerations—if the prosperity of your native land is no object of your care, still have mercy upon your children, and unite with us in our honourable efforts to arrest the progress of those events, of which they may be the victims. Let this disastrous question be settled, and there is at once an end to all your apprehensions. Abolish the detestable remnants of the penal code—strike off the fragments of those chains that still hang upon us—place seven millions of the Irish people in their just relation to the State—make it the interest as well as the duty of every citizen to support the system of government under which he lives—fasten the great body of the people by links which shall be rivetted to their hearts—give a fair influence to the talents of the able, the rank of the titled, the affluence of the wealthy—put us, in one word, in that state which ought to make us satisfied with our condition, and in which neither our feelings shall be insulted, our pride mortified, nor our passions inflamed; and it requires but little knowledge of human nature to be convinced, that the Roman Catholics of Ireland will no yield to any class of his Majesty's subjects, in loyalty to their Sovereign attachment to his family, and allegiance to his government—fidelit to the constitution, obedience to the laws, and devotion to the interest of that great empire, of which this country forms so important, and a present so vulnerable a part.

THE ORANGEMEN OF ARMAGH.

SPEECH AT THE AGGREGATE MEETING, HELD NOVEMBER, 1826.

I, NOT very long ago, announced, at the Catholic Association, that should make some observations on the grand festival of condolence given to Colonel Verner, at Omagh. Having been prevented, by othe occupations, from attending the Association, I relinquished the idea but as I perceive that the speeches have since been published in pamphlet, and the attention of the London newspapers has bee directed to the sanguinary Christianity of Mr. Robinson, it may be a well to make some few comments upon the atrocious orgies, in whic Colonels, Parsons, and Puritans emulated each other in their maledic tions of their country. Taken as individuals, the persons assembled o the occasion deserve scorn; but they expressed the feelings of a party The lucubrations of those consecrated bacchanals, Messrs. Millei Robinson, and Company, may be considered as the catechism of faction, and deserve to be saved from immediate oblivion, upon the sam principle that a malefactor is prevented from dying of a natural death, i order to break him upon the wheel. Let us, then, proceed to the dinnei Was it not a strange notion after all! What could possess the Orange men of Armagh to bring the lugubrious triumvirate of defecte candidates together? Beaten, utterly and completely beaten—with th dust which they had been compelled to bite in their mouths, and beate the more disgracefully, because beaten by the men whom they affecte to despise—they assemble, crow, and clap their wings upon the ver dunghill of their defeat. They sung "Io triumphe," as they passe under the yoke! Mr. Robinson lamented, in his Ossianic phraseology that he of Louth was not there; all that was wanting, indeed, was, tha pleasant and vivacious senator, Mr. Leslie Foster, to complete th party; but there was he of Monaghan, and there was he of Armagh and there was he of Curraghmore. How must they have looked whei they surveyed each other in the midst of their melancholy festivities;— when he of Armagh looked upon him of Monaghan, and he o Monaghan gazed on him of Curraghmore, their faces must, like th mirrors of melancholy, (if I may so say,) have multiplied the expression of despair. The pamphlet (an authorised publication) called th meeting an assembly of "the Protestant Gentlemen of Armagh."

The Protestant gentlemen, indeed! There was scarcely a man of rank amongst them! Mr. Ensor, in his admirable commentary, has set us right on that head. We are told, indeed, that there was a great number of clergymen of the Established Church of great opulence. I doubt not that; there was many a sordid hearted parson—many a rich and rapacious ecclesiastic—many a fat and glossy vulture, gorged to the beak, and yet scenting out new carrion, and smelling a fresh feast in the ruin and misery of his country. But most of the company were a set of ferocious paupers, whose very means of life depend upon their politics, to which they may be said to owe their subsistence, for in their daily orison to the genius of Orangemen, they may appropriately cry out, "Give us this day our daily bread." In the course of his speech, Sir George Hill observed, that if they changed their principles "misery would attend them;" and I do verily believe that, without meaning it, he spoke the truth. The orators of the night may be subdivided into two great classes, the military and the ecclesiastical. There were seven parsons who made speeches, three colonels, and one general. It is only fair to give precedence to Lord George. In drinking his health, the chairman told the parsons that Lord George was put out by an intolerant priesthood. The pamphlet states, that Lord George addressed the meeting with the discrimination of a scholar, and the honesty of a soldier. With respect to his military achievements, I never heard that they extended beyond the quay of Waterford; and as to his lordship's talents, I certainly admit that the speech before me produced astonishment in my mind. The truth, I believe, is this, that Lord George hitherto concealed his abilities, lest they should be put into too active a requisition. The Africans imagine that the ourang outang has uncommon talents for eloquence, and can speak remarkably well, but that lest he should be compelled to work, the creature pretends to be dumb. So it is with Lord George. Like "the wild man of the woods," he remained in the forests of Curraghmore, and purposely concealed his genius for elocution lest it should be put to too much task. Of the rest of the military rhetoricians, Colonels Verner and Leslie, and that personification of "John Barleycorn," Colonel Blacker, it is unnecessary to say anything, for they are not worth mention. Upon some other occasion I may, perhaps, enter into some details relative to the last of them—the great supporter of the constitution and the revenue laws; but I have more important matter in hand. I proceed, therefore, to the "Soldiers in Christ," Messrs. Miller and Robinson, who may be considered in some sort as the representatives of the university. I may observe in passing, that it is not a little singular that the university of Dublin which once converted the appellation of the "Silent Sister," into an honourable designation, by refraining, it is said, through Dr. Magee's influence, from petitioning against Emancipation, should have lately manifested so angry a spirit. There were Messrs. Boyten and Stack, at Omagh. The latter gentleman stated, among other things, that he ADORED Doctor Magee. I understand that the pious gentleman conceives that the world is on the verge of dissolution, and that Doctor Magee is the prophet Enoch in disguise, "mounted on a white horse," after the manner of the Revelations. But to return to Doctor Miller—he was professor of history in Trinity College, and published his lectures in six volumes. Mr. Murray had the misfortune of putting them into type; and not long after they issued from the press, I remember to have called to Albemarle-street, and found Mr. Murray in a state of considerable exhilaration at the prospect of a great sale. Mr. Croker of the Admiralty, the great Aristarchus of Toryism, had assured him, I fancy, that he had made a great hit. Some six months after, I called again to the shop, and saw some twenty or thirty shelves, exclusively occupied with the Doctor's work. Not a copy had budged. About a year after I returned, and "The Philosophy of History" still retained its disastrous permanence. Having read the "Art of Ingeniously Tormenting," I ventured to throw out an observation on the great genius and erudition of the Doctor, who was considered in Dublin College to have thrown Hume and Gibbon into the shade, when Mr. Murray threw his eye over the immovable mass of learning with an expression of despair, and gave that sort of shrug, which none but authors understand, and which has descended from Tonson and Lintot to the eminent Bibliopolists of the present time. I had a recent occasion, however, to read the Doctor's book. The numerous assaults made by the English journals upon my sins against political sensibility, produced some solicitude of mind, and deprived me of sleep. Having passed whole nights in a state of agitated vigilance, I consulted a physician, who prescribed various medicines,

"Poppy and mandragora,
And all the drowsy syrups of the world."—

But it was in vain. At length, however, he said, "I have exhausted all my other narcotics, but I have one specific left; read "Miller's Philosophy of History," and if it does not set you to sleep, you are destined like the victim of Kahama to eternal vigilance." I accordingly provided myself with the doctor's work, and the effects were truly surprising. I had not read three lines before I felt a salutary heaviness about me. When I had gone through a dozen pages, I began to stretch and yawn in a most luxurious drowsiness, and at length I fell fast asleep. Before, however, I had completely closed my eyes, I drew a pencil along a particular passage in the book, which it may be as well that I should read, in order that you may be able to compare it with the doctor's oratory at Armagh. He is expatiating upon the miserable policy adopted towards Ireland, and says, "Such a system of conduct can be explained only, as Sir John Davies has remarked, by conceiving that those who held the government of Ireland, acted on the principle of a perpetual war, by which the English should extirpate the Irish, and possess themselves of the vacant territory. Unable, however, to execute such a plan of lawless avidity, they have only generated a national fued, which was afterwards yet more exasperated by a difference of religion, and in this state of extraordinary excitement became a powerful agent in the general combinations of the empire. The influence of this singular policy has been well illustrated by Sir John Davies in comparing the case of Ireland with that of Wales, the original laws of which were in many particulars similar to those of the former country. Edward I. as soon as he had completed the reduction of that territory, established such a modification of its laws, as in a considerable degree assimilated them to those of England; and when the insurrections of the barons, the wars of France, and the contention of the rival houses, had so withdrawn from Wales the attention of the English government, that it relapsed into its former condition. Henry VIII. perfected what had been begun by Edward, by receiving that country into an incorporating union with his kingdom, and abolishing at the same time all usages, which would have maintained its distinction. The result of this different treatment of Wales was that the country was in a short time rendered a scene of order and civilization, whereas the *feud of Ireland is still shaking our repose.*" This, I think, affords a tolerable specimen of the consistency of Doctor Miller. With what scorn we should survey him, when we contrast his mean and miserable politics at Armagh, with his published and recorded opinions upon the fatal misrule of this unfortunate country. Enough of him. I proceed to Mr. Romney Robinson, the astronomer, who, in point of sacerdotal ferocity, it must be admitted, has left the historian far behind. Mr. Robinson is now an important person, and it may gratify your curiosity to hear that he was once upon a time a poet, and published a collection of juvenile poems which made him be regarded as a blossom upon Parnassus. In order that you may form a judgment of his genius, it may not be inappropriate to read an extract from his compositions. Mr. Robinson appears to have been upon intimate terms with a certain culinary artist, commonly called a kitchen-maid, whose name was Dolly. In one instance he carried his familiarities with this vestal of the scullery to an extreme, which the damsel somewhat acrimoniously resented. He has thought it not inconsistent with his poetical dignity, to record this very interesting, but not very uncommon incident, and begins by an invocation of the Furies, to whose inspirations it must be admitted that he was not a little indebted for his own oration at Armagh.—

> "My angry lyre, Megæra string,
> In notes Tartarean battle sing;
> Instead of tears for beauty's woe,
> Let rancour burn, and discord glow—
> Tho' erst my muse has mourned with Dolly,
> My strains now sing her thoughtless folly—
> Her pots and kettles, pans and plates,
> And pokers breaking brittle pates. .
> * * * * * * *
> Once on a time when all was quiet,
> And mute the voice of brawl and riot,
> While peace was sitting by the fire,
> Then Dolly 'gan with furious ire."

You should be informed that the indignation of Dolly was produced by a liberty not necessary to be mentioned. Dolly starts up in a paroxysm of exasperation, and is compared to Mount Etna in an eruption.—

> "As when in fire Typhæus roars,
> And Etna shakes Secilia's shores,
> Thus bellowed Doll."—

This is succeeded by a passage to even in Mr. Wordsworth's Nursery of the Muses, nothing can be compared.

"She threw the poker at my head,
And deemed the blow would strike me dead.
The Poet now, with choler swell'd,
Fierce dealt a blow, and Dolly yelled."

Mr. Robinson proceeds to describe the process by which this modern Thalestris was thrown upon the ground, and when Dolly and the poet * * * * * *—but respect to my auditors prevents me from proceeding farther. Suffice it to say that Apollo suddenly appears in the kitchen, and through his celestial intervention, a reconciliation between Dolly and the poet is effected. I have read these passages from Mr. Robinson's poems, for the purpose of illustrating and justifying the claims to intellectual superiority which, in his speech at Armagh, he has claimed for the Irish Protestants Mr. Robinson became a Fellow of Trinity College; and when we consider the miracles in literature and science which have been accomplished by the Professors of that University; when we consider the illumination which they have thrown upon the whole sphere of knowledge, and the number of valuable works with which their press may be said to teem, it must be confessed that the mere fact of Mr. Robinson having once belonged to that intellectual corporation, gives him a paramount title to our respect. In the University Mr. Robinson devoted himself to the study of the stars. His familiar use of the telescope naturally led him to prefer Mr. Croker to Mr. Plunkett. During, the memorable contest between those eminent persons, Mr. Robinson consistently voted for " him of the garret." This, however, was not immaterial. Mr. Robinson and Mr. Croker are both expert at the use of the telescope; and while the one was engaged in watching the stars, Mr. Croker was occupied in observing "the transit of Venus" in the lodgings of Mrs. Clarke. But let us come to his speech. He returned thanks on behalf of the university, and enumerated some of the illustrious persons who had been produced by that college. He said nothing of Burke or Grattan, (Grattan, whose picture was removed from the great hall of the university by order of the board) nor of Curran, nor of any other advocate of freedom, whose name tends in some degree to rescue our university from shame; but he commemorated the virtues of the Calvinistic Usher, who laid down the doctrines of Geneva as the essential articles of the Irish Church, and had afterwards the meanness to sacrifice his opinion to his sovereign's will He had the folly to speak of Swift, who was deemed a dunce in our university, and who obtained his degree by special favour, which Doctor Johnson informs us, means in Dublin College, "a want of merit." Mr. Robinson also referred to Molyneux. This was an egregious mistake; for in Molyneux's celebrated book, which was burned by order of the House of Commons, principles are laid down which are far more applicable to the present case of Ireland, than they were to the times in which Molyneux poured out his argumentative vituperation. Molyneux insists that Irishmen and Englishmen have equal rights; and maintains the abominable doctrine that tyranny should be encountered with resistance, and that oppression should be beaten down by force. He menaces the British government with the consequences which may result from the indignation of the Irish people. If, then, England had any reason to apprehend any evil result from the exasperated pride of the Protestants of Ireland, (who were but a handful of men)—if Molyneux were alive, would he not exhort the English nation to consider the consequences which may arise from the Union, the confederacy, the organization, and the discontent of seven millions of the inhabitants of this country. Let Mr. Robinson then beware of referring his countrymen to the example or the principles of Mr. Molyneux, and above all, let not a Fellow of Trinity College in pronouncing an encomium upon Molyneux, call him the friend of Locke. On the part of a Fellow of Trinity College, I cannot readily conceive a more egregious mistake, than that he should have made the least reference to the great philosopher whose name he has so incautiously introduced. The University of Oxford, the seat of the Protestant religion, on the very day on which the great Lord Russell perished upon the scaffold, issued its celebrated declaration in favour of slavery, and embodied the doctrine of non-resistance with the fundamental principles of the Reformation. The University of Dublin, at the distance of more than a century, followed this glorious example; and in order to establish a perfect consistency between the principles of the English and the Irish Church, upon no other ground than that Locke's Essay upon Government justified a resistance to tyranny, excluded the work from the College course. And yet Mr. Robinson, with tnis fact staring him in the face, has the clumsy effrontery, and the awkward impertinence, to inform us, that it is to the University of Dublin, that we ought to look for the assertion and preservation of the true principles of liberty. If Mr. Robinson had merely committed those gross indiscretions, and had only offered an insult to the understanding of the public, he would not be deserving of any very vituperative comment; but the ferocity of his opinions produces a sort of counterpoise to their absurdity, and he ceases to be ridiculous only because his sentiments deserve to be abhorred. Laughter subsides in execration, and we cannot utterly despise what we so entirely detest. The sentiments expressed by Mr. Robinson are the principles of a whole faction. He has had the atrocious frankness to avow, without disguise, what others have only intimated—he has made a public profession of opinions, of which others have only given a sanguinary hint. I will not say, (for it were a vulgar and inferior phrase,) that he has let the cat out of the bag, but he has uncaged the passions of his faction, and showed the tiger crouching for its prey. In the spirit of a ferocious honesty, and with a blood-thirsty candour, he has openly acknowledged, that he and his party long for a general massacre, and aspire at an universal extirpation of the Roman Catholics of Ireland. If what he said was the mere result of a temporary excitement; if his sentiments were but the steam of drunkenness and the vapour of debauch; if his foul and nauseous opinions rose out of his mind like the reekings of a drunkard's brow, I should allow them to disperse and pass away. They should be permitted to dissipate like the stench of reveb--

which,' after a night's debauch, it is sufficient to open a window to let out. But the opinions of Mr. Robinson were not the mere evaporations of political intoxication, or the bubbles of a temporary effervescence. They were the black and putrid discharge of a foul and ulcerated heart, oozing out of a mind which should be regarded as a mass of rottenness, and which infected the whole moral atmosphere with its rank and abominable exhalations. 'Scelus anhelantem.' The phrase applied by Cicero to the teacher of massacre in his time, becomes his sacredotal savageness. Openly and avowedly, without cover, subterfuge, or modification, he proclaims a wish that a civil war may take place, which, he says, may indeed cause a national butchery, but will terminate in the achievement of much substantial Protestant good. Men with gray hairs, women and infants without the power to cry for help, are to be piled up together in one vast heap of carnage, which the genius of Orange Ascendancy is to choose for its throne. He is a chemist, a philosopher, a man who sits tranquilly in his political laboratory, and would make experiments with blood. Calmly, nobly, deliberately and savagely, he offers up a wish for the massacre of a whole people, and blends the aspirations of Caligula with the orisons of a Christian priest. For he is a priest! He too, talks of his parochial duties! Merciful Heaven! Is this man a teacher of the Gospel, and a minister of the God of mercy, of charity, and of benevolence? Is this the man who lifts up his hands from the altar—who breaks the bread of life, and distributes the commemorative cup? Is this man a priest of Christ? Oh! no, no—not of Christ; not of the divine and merciful redeemer of mankind—not of the God whose coming was announced amidst the hymns of peace, and whose last words were an adjuration of forgiveness, founded upon the frailty of mankind—not of Christ—but of that sanguinary fiend who was deified in the abominable idolatry of Phœnicia—of Moloch, the demon who was worshipped with human sacrifices, and nourished with infants' blood, would this sacrilegious priest be the appropriate minister. But let justice be done, even to him; if guilt can be diminished by its participation, then is he not entirely guilty. He has but given utterance to the detestable wish with which the hearts of Orangemen are pregnant. They pant, they burn, they sigh for another confiscation. They long for a return of the era of triangles, and the epoch of pitch caps. They would invoke the spirit of FitzGerald, and conjure the blood boultered spectre of O'Brien from the grave. They recollect, with a moral luxury, the screams of the riding-house—they remember them of the shrieks of Horish, when the torturer stood by, and presided over the feast of agony, in the ecstacy of his infernal enjoyments—when he gloated on his writhings, and refreshed himself with his groans.—But let them beware. I speak not of the government, but of the Orangemen of Ireland. If they should undertake to carry their frightful speculations into execution, they may learn by experience that they mistake their strength. We are told by their orators, that without the aid of England they could put us down. Let them take care how they indulge in that hazardous experiment. Let them beware of the sound of that trumpet which may summon seven millions to arms. It is not now as it once was. We are no longer divided and distracted as we were wont to be. We are no longer broken into fragments. We are united, confederated and combined, not by oaths and forms, for they are illegal and unnecessary, but by that spirit of moral organization which results from a sympathy in suffering, and a vast participation in wrong. Let them, then, beware how they proceed to carry their threats into performance, and remember that a whole population, rising simultaneously to protect itself against a national slaughter, will present a fearful obstacle to their projects. We will not, whatever happens, hold out our throats to the Orange yeomen—we will not stand tamely by when the ministers of our religion shall be butchered before our eyes ; when the temples of our worship shall be committed to the flames, and when the foot of murder and of rape shall bestride the threshold of our door a! This is what Mr. Robinson calls a "tropical hurricane," to be succeeded by a glorious calm ! It is a hurricane of which he may meanly expect to behold the devastations from the steeple of his church in security. Let him not forget, that in that whirlwind of the passions which he has well described, and for which he offers up his pious aspirations, the church itself may be shaken to its foundations, and they who have called up the hurricane, because they considered themselves in safety from its effects, may be the first to perish under the ruins of those institutions, of which they affect to be the main supporters, but which they are the first to put in peril. Mr. Sheil concluded his speech by declaring, that in speaking of resistance, he referred merely to the Orangemen of Ireland, and not to the English government, by which he was convinced that the atrocities of the Orange faction would not receive a sanction.

NOTICE OF A VOTE OF THANKS TO THE BISHOP OF WATERFORD.

SPEECH AT THE CATHOLIC ASSOCIATION, IN GIVING NOTICE OF A VOTE OF THANKS TO THE ROMAN CATHOLIC BISHOP OF WATERFORD

I GIVE notice that I shall, upon the first opportunity, move, that the thanks of the Association be given to the Right Rev. Dr. Kelly, the Roman Catholic Bishop of Waterford. That prelate has commenced the census. He that begins has half achieved. Dr. Kelly has conferred an incalculable obligation upon this country. Under his auspices an accurate census of the Catholic and Protestant population of his diocese has been made, and the priests of thirty-two parishes have engaged to make certified returns of the comparative numbers. In a few days an official statement of the census will be transmitted. In the interval, it may not be inapposite to communicate to you the returns of some of the parishes, which I have myself obtained from Dr. Kelly. In the parish of Ardmore, there are 7871 Catholics and 39 non-Catholics: in the parish of Susquera there are 3015 Catholics and 20 non-Catholics

In the barony of Ballynamant, there is but one Protestant. He had been a Catholic, but being appointed a collector in the excise, he was illuminated by a "special grace," and abandoned the unprofitable errors of the Church of Rome. In the parish of Carrickbeg, there are 4853 Catholics and 21 non-Catholics. In Abbeyside, 4899 Catholics and 33 non-Catholics. In Kilgobbenett, 3079 Catholics and 4 Protestants. In Ring, near Dungarvan, 2464 Catholics and 20 Protestants, and in Dungarvan, a commercial and rising town, 6952 Catholics and 168 non-Catholics. In Trinity Without, in the city of Waterford, there are 9325 Catholics and 396 non-Catholics, including the boys and girls in Killoteran Charter School. In Killea, 5929 Catholics and 376 non-Catholics. But if any person be surprised at the number of non-Catholics in this parish, it is right to apprise him that the artificial harbour of Dunmore, which has cost government an immense sum, and furnishes, of course, a means of jobbing, is situate in this parish, and of necessity, is a focus of Protestantism. The Catholics are, indeed, sent down in the diving-bell, but the Protestants, who work the apparatus, are all above water. The parish of Portlaw is upon Lord Waterford's estates, and his lordship has made great efforts to colonise his property with the professors of the hereditary creed of the house of Beresford. Accordingly he has succeeded in gathering about him 537 Protestants. But, notwithstanding all his exertions to eradicate Popery, that noxious weed still continues to flourish and spread upon his estate. There are 5567 Papists in the parish of Portlaw. I have mentioned these returns without selection, and I do believe they afford a very accurate view of the comparative population of the whole diocese. What I have stated is of great importance. But a fact remains to be communicated to you of still greater moment. It has been ascertained, in the taking of the census of Clonmel, that there are three hundred and fifty soldiers stationed in that town, and that three hundred and ten of them are professors of our damnable, idolatrous, unconstitutional, and disloyal religion. This is certified by the Rev. Dr. Flannery. Furthermore, it has been stated to me by the Rev. Mr. Sheehan (than whom there is not a more zealous, ardent, and valuable man in the city of Waterford, and who has honourably devoted himself to the independence of the county) that the garrison of Waterford (the 29th) consists of five hundred men, and although it is accounted an English regiment, and is commanded by an English baronet, out of these five hundred men there are only one hundred and seventy-seven who are not Catholics. This fact, which illustrates the condition of the British army—this great and most momentous fact, should be told with a trumpet through every country in the civilized world, and it shall be proclaimed. France and Spain, and Germany and Russia, shall hear of it. The *Etoile* shall send it forth, and stamp shame upon the men who, with exasperating exclusions, with vilifying disqualifications, with ancient wrongs, and with new insults, repay the victories that have been achieved by the feats of Irish valour, and the waste of Irish blood. Shame upon the abominable system that takes the heart-blood of Ireland and requites it thus! What will a French soldier say? What will be said by the men who survived the field of Waterloo, when they shall peruse what I am now speaking to you, (and they will peruse it) and learn that those who put their battalions to flight, and broke the spell of Napoleon's invincibility, are deemed unworthy the rights of citizens? What will they say when they shall have been told, that the arms which drove the bayonet through their ranks, are laden with heavy chackles, and that while laurels are heaped upon the brows of the captain of that great host, the soldiers who achieved that unparalleled victory are bound in chains? They will say that it is better to be unfortunate than ungrateful; and that the field of Waterloo was as disgraceful to England as it was disastrous to France; and they will say more than this—they wil' say what it is easier to imagine than it is wise to tell. But let tha· pass. I return to the census. That measure was proposed by me, and I am proud of it. There were some who doubted its feasibility. Their doubts must now be at an end, (I tell these sceptics,) and we shall hear no more of their misgivings, and their difficulties, and their paltry fears. The thing is not in the future, but in the past. It is not only resolved, but done. What will be the result of a census? It will not only teach our numbers to the legislature, but it will instruct ourselves. The clergy who can count the people can do more. They can gather the people and teach them to lift up their voices in one simultaneous call for redress. The meetings in every parish on the same day will be readily effected. Three thousand petitions will be transmitted to the tables of the legislature from the altars of God! But more than this can be accomplished. They who can count heads can count acres. The extent and value of church property, the rate of cesses, and the amount of tithes, can also be easily ascertained through the same medium. I trust that emancipation will render these investigations unnecessary, and that the ministers will see the wisdom of not arraying the people against the church. But if the measure be not accomplished in the first session of the new parliament, let it be given up, and let the axe be laid to the root. In the interval, it is well that we should know what potent means we possess to obtain justice for Ireland. If any man were to inquire of me the chief grounds upon which I rest my hopes of ultimate success, I should, without hesitation, answer, that my best hopes were grounded upon the lofty patriotism, the devoted zeal, the ardent love of liberty which characterise that pure, that pious, that enlightened, and, let me add, that powerful and influential body of unbought and unpurchaseable men—the Roman Catholic priesthood of Ireland. If we but apply, with ordinary sagacity, the great means within our power, all the obstacles in our way must be at last overcome; and the anathemas of a prince, the fears of a chancellor, the protestations of the premier, and even the late orgies at Derry, will be without avail. In referring to the city of Londonderry I can hardly avoid alluding to a gentleman who recently made a conspicuous figure among its apprentices, in return for the very delicate and forbearing manner in which, after complaining of the scoffs and ribaldry of which he was the victim, and for which he had no other consolation but his conscience and his place, he did me the honour to introduce my name. I felt it to be a condescension on the part of Mr. Dawson to appropriate so much valuable and elaborate phrase to a person for whom he appears to entertain so much compassion as myself, and I confess that I could not help feeling, on perusing the oration attributed to him, that his pity is akin to hate. Such is the interest which he takes in a person whom he affects to regard as beneath his consideration, that he has made comments upon physical imperfections, and expatiated upon the inharmonious intonations of my voice. It is not the first time that I am under obligations of this nature to the family of which Mr. Dawson is a member, and of whose passions and antipathies he may be regarded as the representative. Mr. Peel, although a minister of state, thought it not unworthy of him to make allusions from his seat in parliament to an individual of so little significance as myself. The sarcasms of the Secretary of State for the Home Department, were not, however, wholly unprovoked; for I had ventured to intimate that his language was bald, his reasoning disingenuous, his manner pragmatical, affected, and overweening; and that to his opinions more than to his talents, he was indebted for his elevation. Mr. Peel retorted; he spoke of fustian, and I talked of calico. He touched on Covent-garden, and I referred to Manchester. He alluded to Evadne, and I glanced at Spinning Jennies. He thus, as Mr. Dawson has expressed it, became my antagonist; and as if I were more than a match for the minister, he has thrown himself, with a feeling of fraternal sympathy, into the contest. I am inclined to surmise, that Mr. Dawson was induced to take a part in the conflict, by a phrase which has, I fear, given offence in a quarter where certainly none was contemplated. I spoke of the "plebeian arrogance of Mr. Peel." The shaft appears to have stuck with a deadly tenacity; but, after all, Mr. Dawson should not take this expression in such bad part. It was first suggested to me by an incident in which the public took some interest upon Mr. Dawson's own account. When evidence was given in the House of Commons relative to a couple of ex-officio informations, filed during Mr. Saurin's administration, and surprise was expressed that no intimation had been given of it to Mr. Plunkett, Mr. Peel, with more strenuousness than was called for, protested that he knew nothing whatever of a gentleman who is very nearly allied to Mr. Dawson, and whose name was introduced upon the occasion. I must confess that it struck me that this disclaimer of Mr. Dawson had a relish of that fungus kind of pride which marks a man of low origin, who is transferred, not by his own merit, but the accident of fortune, to a higher station; and I ventured to express that feeling by the phrase which has left more deep and extensive impressions than it warranted behind. By interfering in other people's concerns, and thus voluntarily taking up the cause of Mr. Dawson, I have incurred his displeasure to such a degree, that not satisfied with assailing the defects of my understanding, he has converted my tones into grave accusation, and brought an impeachment against my voice. I am free to acknowledge, that I cannot retort the charge. Of his voice in public assemblies, I can form no judgment. I have, indeed, been occasionally present at his effusions in the House of Commons, but could never hear him. Whenever he spoke, the house was seized with an universal fit of coughing. His eloquence is down to zero, and is so chilly and frozen, that his auditors immediately catch cold. The House of Commons is a far more disorderly assembly than the convivial convocations of the apprentices of Derry, and amidst the cries of order from the Speaker, and the intermingled sneezing, coughing, scraping, laughing, and expectorating of the house, it was impossible to collect a whole sentence of what he said. The only persons who seemed disposed to listen to him were Mr. Peel, Sir Thomas Lethbridge, and Mr. Butterworth. When he mentioned the name of Mr. Hamilton Rowan, and introduced the gray-headed father of one of the best officers in the navy into the debate, the face of Mr. Peel divested itself of " the conscious simper and the jealous leer," and with a savage exultation, he called upon the house to hearken to his kinsman's contumelies upon an old and venerable man. When Mr. Dawson ended a sentence with " Church and State," Sir Thomas Lethbridge awoke, and stretching his arms, yawned out "Hear," and I conclude that one of his periods must have terminated with an imprecation against his country and its religion, for Mr. Butterworth lifted up his hands and eyes to heaven, and ejaculated " Amen." I wish it to be understood that I do not pretend, for the reasons I have suggested, to give any minute description of Mr. Dawson's speeches in parliament, at the same time I may venture to assert, that he did not in the House of Commons invoke the shades of those who fell at Numantia or Londonderry. The mention of Numantia recalls to me another observation of Mr. Dawson. He has sneered at a reference made by me to Livy, and laughed at an alleged deviation on my part from the rules of Prosody. I did not use a single Latin word before the Committee. I did, indeed, refer to a passage in Livy, in answer to a question put to me by Mr. Peel, and in comparing the contests between the Patricians and Plebeians, to the struggles between the Catholics and Protestants, I pronounced the word " Plebeian," in a way which, I believe, grated upon the ear of Mr. Peel, and which he considered peculiarly discordant. I spoke it with more emphasis than sound discretion. Hereafter, however, in using the word, whether in the presence of Mr. Peel, or in reference to that gentleman, I shall endeavour to give it utterance with a less jarring intonation. So much for Mr. Dawson's charge with respect to Prosody. It is not a little ludicrous that the gentleman who brought this serious accusation against me, respecting an allusion to an ancient writer, did himself refer to that very writer for a description which is not to be found in his works. The books of Livy in which the Numantian war is detailed are lost. The next time Mr. Dawson undertakes to astonish the apprentices of Derry with his erudition, it will be judicious upon his part to quote from those books only which have been preserved. Not satisfied with the non-existent authority of Livy, he also appeals to what he calls the " plaintive lay of Horace," in his (Mr. Dawson's) lamentations upon Numantia. The *Morning Chronicle* has justly remarked that the name of Numantia occurs in a single line of Horace only, and it is introduced

without any mournful sentiment. I believe he is
ever discovered that plaintiveness was characteristi
is, in sooth, much matter of a fantastic nature in M
He complains of ribaldry, while he "spits himself a
the chair of a professor, while he manifests the m
rance, and charges his opponent with a violation of
his speech, from which Scriblerus might draw new
Sinking, he throws himself from the ruins of Numa
dyke of Londonderry. That a man so low in pa
given such a loose to his oratory, amidst the huzza
excites ridicule and contempt. But there is grav
tion. After having stated to Mr. O'Connell th
removed many prejudices from his mind, he seeks
a ground of hostility to his country; and he pr
breath, to fling a miserable sneer at Mr. Brownlow
virtue to follow his example, let him, at least, abst
tion. He charges me with a mis-statement of fac
that Hamilton Rowan had been attainted of treaso
And what are we to think of him and of Mr. Peel
an aged man by the gray hairs into the debate, a
his gallant son, cast opprobrium upon his father,
upon his name? The conduct of Mr. Peel and
the disgust of all parties in the house. The good
faction got the better of their political animosities
refrain from applauding Mr. Brougham when he
champion of old age, and trampling upon the min
the dust. Mr. Dawson is sufficiently injudicious t
shipwreck at Tramore, in relation to which Mr.
paltry a part. A ship laden with soldiers was upon
ble man plunged into the sea, and dragged eleven o
from the waves. Mr. M'Dougal applied at the
and the underling of Mr. Peel asked if he was
Dawson boasts that the question was not asked b
matter is it since it was asked by the minion of h
reflected his mind, and understood his wink? I
question without authority, it affords proof that
interrogatory in his master's office. Mr. Dawson
my cross-examination afforded a complete vindicat
so, why did Mr. Peel procure himself to be exai
very matter, and convert himself from an inqui
in order that he might give evidence on his owr
by Mr. Peel's own testimony, that the religion
made matter of comment by a Quaker, and Mr. Pe
lished a further and a most important charge agai
admits that Kirwan received no more than the w
When I stated in the committee that the governr
which Mr. Peel was placed, had given this desp
and that Mr. Peel had full cognizance of the fac
astonished. They could hardly believe, though i

that Mr. Peel could have appraised heroism at such a price. Let Mr. Peel argue the matter as he will, his web of sophistry will be without avail. He cannot get over the plain and most discreditable fact, that he paid for the lives of eleven soldiers at a less rate than £3 a head It is idle for him to allege that a certain quantity of the public money was allocated to the occasion, and that Kirwan got his share. Had he possessed one touch of generous sentiment, he would have thrown open his coffers, and flung a handful of his inglorious gold to the man whose courageous humanity was beyond all praise. Kirwan is to this day unremunerated ; and if I may venture to speak of myself, I may with justice say, that I have done more for him than Mr. Peel. I repeat it, Mr. Peel is not a high-minded, nor is he a fair-minded man. Contrast his former declarations with his present conduct. He stated in the House of Commons, that it was his anxious desire that the Catholic Question should be decided by the unbiased will of the legislature, and that, so far from endeavouring to excite, he would do all in his power to subdue the popular passions. How has he fulfilled this undertaking? He despatches his brother-in-law, his mere utensil, the creature of his smile, his political dependant, to this unfortunate country, in order that he may inflame the ferocious passions of an Orange mob. My friend, Mr. Conway, has placed his conduct in so strong a light that it is enough for me to refer to his admirable observations upon those barbarous festivities. I scarcely blame Mr. Dawson ; he is but the emissary, the apostle of Mr. Peel, and is despatched by him for the purpose of exciting discord in the country, at the hazard of producing a re-enactment o. those scenes in which the North of Ireland has been drenched with blood. It is thus that his Majesty's injunctions are obeyed by his ministers, and that the precept of peace, of charity, and of love, is exemplified by Mr. Peel

VOTE OF THANKS TO THE BISHOP OF WATERFORD.

SPEECH IN MOVING A VOTE OF THANKS TO THE ROMAN CATHOLIC BISHOP OF WATERFORD.

I RISE to move a vote of thanks to Dr. Kelly, the Catholic Bishop of Waterford. His praise may be expressed with as much brevity as force he has commenced the census of the Irish people—he has thus held out a noble example of the most useful kind of public virtue—he is an essentially practical man. There is an efficiency and an operativeness in his patriotism, which is peculiarly deserving of panegyric. The learned, pious, and energetic prelate did not allow himself to be swayed by any petty fears, or miserable solicitudes. He did not ask whether the counting of his flock was consistent with the rules of cold prudence and nice calculation. He did not stop to inquire how far the fastidious pleasure of the government should be consulted upon this momentous measure. He did not hold out a wavering balance and allow a noble opportunity to escape in its adjustment. The only question which Doctor Kelly asked was put to his own heart—he simply asked, "Will it serve my country?"—and you have the answer in the result. But it was to be expected that this great undertaking should commence with a Bishop of Waterford; and when we recollect that Hussey and Power were the predecessors of the enlightened and intrepid man to whom their crozier has been so appropriately transmitted, it will not be matter of surprise that he has acted a lofty and patriotic part. They were his models, and he has improved upon them. Dr. Hussey, the first of those remarkable men, was conspicuous at a period when great talents and great determination of character were required. He was the friend of Edmund Burke, who addressed to him one of the most admirable of his letters. The phrenetical fear of Jacobinism, which amounted to disease in the mind of Burke, did not extinguish all love of liberty in the heart of that celebrated person; and, whatever might have been his distaste for the abstract rights of man, he looked with horror upon the oppressors of that land, in place of which he had adopted what he calls his better and more comprehensive, but which, I verily believe, could not have been his dearer country. It was on the eve of the troubles of Ireland that he wrote the letter to Doctor Hussey, in which his anxiety for Emancipation is so emphatically and so unaffectedly expressed, and it was about the same period that Doctor Hussey addressed his celebrated pastoral admonition to his flock, which contains so much wise injunction and so much intrepid truth. Cumberland has given in his memoirs a sketch of the character of Doctor Hussey, with whom he was well acquainted at the court of Spain. He represents him as an able but ambitious person. The conduct of Doctor Hussey, when raised to the See of Waterford, justifies the encomium upon his talents, while it refutes the satire upon his morals—there was nothing servile, timorous, or compromising in his demeanour. He stood forward in the worst of times, with a stern and fearless aspect, and although he felt that every head on which the mitre was placed might be laid down upon the block of martyrdom, bated nothing of the loftiness of piety, and the attitude of courageous magnanimity which became a Christian pontiff. He addressed himself to the Pro-Consul of Ireland, with the boldness of an apostle, and claimed the franchises of a citizen. He it was who did not fear to proclaim that great truth, which it required more courage than inspiration to announce. He was the first to trace the progress of that mighty spirit, the rapid and headlong course of which he daringly pointed out. Well did he anticipate all the events which followed, and it may be added, that he prophesied the scenes which are passing before us, when he exclaimed—

"The rock is loosened from the mountain's brow."

Has not the rock been loosened, and is it not from the brow of the mountain? Have not the people become acquainted with their rights? Have not great passions and great desires been put into motion? Has not the rock been loosened from the mountain's brow? and is it not rolling and bounding with accelerated velocity, and sweeping every impediment before it? Where will it rest in its course, and in what gulf will it lie at last? This is an interrogatory to which no man of our time will live perhaps to give a reply. Our children, and the children of our oppressors, will read it in the history of this unfortunate land, and God grant that its pages may not be written in blood. The intrepid ecclesiastic of whom I have been speaking was succeeded by a man of a gentler mood of mind, but not a less elevated and patriotic spirit As you enter that magnificent house of worship which the Roman Catholics of Waterford have raised to the honour of God, you behold a plain marble slab, on which a beautiful inscription has been graven—the epitaph is not remarkable for any peculiar felicity of monumental expression—it is not conspicuous for any funeral epigram ; but it contains a simple and most eloquent fact, to the bare statement of which all its panegyric is confined, for it intimates that "the marble was raised to commemorate the Christian virtue of Doctor Power, by the Catholic, the Protestant, and the Presbyterian inhabitants of his diocese." The day on which the remains of that truly good and benevolent man were laid in the earth was a remarkable one—there was not a single Protestant of respectability who did not join the procession which followed his relics to the grave. That amiable and excellent person, whose life was an illustration of his precepts, was succeeded by a gentleman, of whom it is unnecessary to say more than that he was characterised by a spirit of political complaisance which arose from the imbecility of his intellect, more than from any vices of his heart. Upon his death it was found necessary to fill the See which he had left vacant. with a man of a very opposite cast of mind. The clergy of Waterford looked round for an ecclesiastic who was fitted to the time. They wanted a man of high talents and acquirements, of a firm, decided, and manly character, with a bold and inflexible spirit, and something of a republican simplicity of mind. And where did they seek him? These lovers of despotism by religion, these necessary slaves, these men who are deemed insensible to the love of liberty, and incapable of its enjoyment, these Popish priests—looked out into the democracy of America, and selected for their prelate a bishop of the United States. It was among the forests that mark the boundaries of the United States, it was in the midst of the Savannas—in the midst of poverty and of privation, and surrounded with every hardship, that Doctor Kelly had evinced the qualifications of a truly Christian pastor. He had not, when far away from his country, lost his affection for the land that gave him birth, and his anxiety to do that service to Ireland which he has proved that it is in the power of every bishop to confer, induced him to accept tne honourable tender which was made to him by the clergy of his native diocese. He came, and what more need I do than appeal for the results of his coming to the simple fact upon which I rest the resolution in which the gratitude of the Irish people is expressed? It did befit a man who lived in a free country, in a land of manly spirits and fearless minds, to put into accomplishment a measure which belongs to the spirit of genuine citizenship, and which enumerates the people for the purpose of giving assertion and extension to their rights. To such a man great praise is due, and, believe me, he will not stop here. He will teach the power and efficiency of a simultaneous but pacific assemblage of seven millions of people, and I may conjecture what he will do, by what he has already achieved. He will not be slow in adopting that fine suggestion, that the cry for liberty should be mingled with the voice of prayer, and that from the altars of God an invocation should be offered, to touch our rulers with the spirit of justice, to illuminate their minds, and awaken in them a sense of the perils of the empire. And let it not be said that it is unmeet to do so. If we call for the rain from heaven, or ask for the shining of the sun; if for grass and corn we are permitted to submit our orisons, who will say that for the great harvest of long and golden prosperity, for the maturing of those events of which the seeds have been already deeply sown—who will say that for these great objects it is unfit that we should offer up our prayers? But let me not deviate into matter which affords too wide a field for present expatiation. The office of gratitude is more pleasurable than the indulgence of even the most sanguine expectation of future good; and I shall therefore conclude by moving the following resolution:—" That the Right Rev. Doctor Kelly, the Catholic Bishop of Waterford, by commencing the Catholic census in his diocese, has conferred a great obligation upon his country, and deserves its thanks."

PRAYER FOR EMANCIPATION.

SPEECH ON MR. O'CONNELL'S MOTION, THAT A PRAYER BE OFFERED UP IN EVERY ROMAN CATHOLIC CHAPEL FOR EMANCIPATION.

I AM of opinion that a prayer for liberty should be incorporated with the liturgy of the Catholic Church. It is idle to insist that such a measure should originate with the bishops. I have no doubt that we shall have their individual assent to the proposition, although they may not deem it judicious to recommend it in their corporate capacity. It is enough that they should permit the utterance of the prayer, without enjoining its adoption. The spirit which actuates the great body of the clergy will induce them to act in conformity with our suggestion; and there is not a prelate in the land who would so far deviate from the course which has been hitherto pursued by the head of our church, as to issue an injunction against the use of so just, so reasonable, and so consistent an orison. Let us not at least anticipate any episcopal veto upon this great expedient. The Roman Catholic hierarchy are united with us in political sentiment. There is not one among them who does not personally applaud our conduct, although they do not deem it accordant with their spiritual character to take a visible and outward participation in our proceedings. The fact, that they have selected the period of our sittings for their own session affords proof of their desire that the two great assemblies which represent the wishes of the Irish people—should be convened and act together.— They are virtually in correspondence with the Association ; and have transmitted to us in an almost official shape the resolutions passed by their body. I therefore dismiss the argument pressed on the other side, that we are interfering with their legitimate province. But it is said that political matter should not be blended with religious practices, and that the call for freedom is not an object of prayer. I hold the Catholic Litany in my hand. It was given me by a Catholic priest on entering this room—let us examine the contents of the Litany as it stands, and determine how far the addition of the proposed prayer is in conformity with the character of the established supplication. I find in the first place a prayer for the preservation " of the fruits of the earth." Our physical wants have thus become the objects of our spiritual aspirations. But I may be called on to show, that political matter is already introduced into the Litany. I accept the challenge ; " vouchsafe to give peace and true concord to Christian Kings and Princes." In other words, "preserve the Holy Alliance." But I should not upon such an occasion indulge in the spirit of sarcastic jest. What follows is much better; " vouchsafe to grant peace and unity to all Christian people." This is truly a noble and exalted desire ; and its use amongst us evinces how little we are swayed by views of a narrow and sectarian character. We do not pray for peace and unity among all Catholic people. We do not limit our wishes to the benefit of those who coincide with us in our religious tenets: we implore the Almighty to grant peace and unity, (those paramount and surpassing blessings) to all the nations by whom a belief in the Divine Redeemer of mankind is professed. But, Mr. Chairman, I am arguing this question with too much minuteness and formality, and treating it as if it really stood in need of an inductive series of reasoning, when the propriety and the consistency of such a prayer are matters so obvious, that argument seems to be wasted upon them. I shall take a bolder ground, and one more fitted to the time, and becoming the closing hours of the political existence of this body. I care not whether there be a prayer in the Litany for concord or unity— I care not whether there be in the appendix to the liturgy, a prayer against earthquakes, tempests, famine, and pestilence. But abandoning all reliance upon authority, and putting form and precedent aside, I ask of this great assembly, whether it be an offence against religion to call upon the Almighty to save us or our children from the horrors of a political convulsion, to which the system pursued in its regard is precipitating this unfortunate country? I have spoken boldly and abruptly. It is not matter for hints and inuendoes. I speak without fear, because I cannot justly incur reproach ; and I am myself as much disposed as any one of those who are inclined to attribute to me motives as preposterous as they are wicked, to deprecate the frightful calamities, which, if a change of policy be not adopted, will fall at last upon this country. Let it be understood. I am not alluding to events that will happen in our time. It is not likely that they who "sow the storm" will "reap the whirlwind." I, and every man that hears me, and most of the enemies of our political rights, will, probably, be lying in the grave before the arrival of the dreadful results upon which I protest to God that I look with unaffected dismay. The case stands simply thus:—There are seven millions, or at all events, nearly that number of Roman Catholics in Ireland. Their wealth, their intelligence, their public spirit, their union, their community of purpose, and their unalterable determination to prosecute their political rights are every day on the increase. Acts of Parliament are as bonds of flax. Every effort which has been made to extinguish the desire for freedom with its hope has been utterly without effect. The denunciations of the heir to the throne have only tended to add indignation to resolve. The number of public meetings has of late exceeded all prior example of popular assemblies in Ireland—and the rank, the talent, and the energy, and the intrepid spirit manifested in these vast convocations, afford the most convincing indications of the rapid and formidable advancement of the national mind. I doubt not that this progression may go on pacifically for ten, fifteen, or perhaps for twenty or more years; but is there a man who knows any thing of human nature, who can, for a moment, indulge in the idle hope that a crisis will not at last arrive, and that this monstrous and most anomalous state of things will not generate some frightful results? Can things stand as they are? No! It is impossible. It is out of all calculation of contingency. There is hardly a man here that does not remember the horrors of 1798. The scenes of blood which were enacted in that brief period, would, in all likelihood, be greatly exceeded in atrocity in a future and better organized convulsion; but yet they were sufficiently frightful to make any man look forward with horror to their recurrence. Is it unmeet that we should implore Providence to enlighten the minds of our rulers, and instruct them in the wisdom of mercy, and the policy of toleration, which will effectually prevent the disasters of which I have drawn this black but rapid sketch? Is it unmeet to call upon Heaven to disperse the cloud that is gathering in the horizon, though years must pass before it bursts upon our heads? Is it unmeet to pray to God with all the ardour of which the heart of man is capable, to prevent a return of the scenes of which we have already had so bitter an experience? Is it unmeet for the father to clasp his offspring to his bosom and exclaim, "Merciful and Almighty God, save my children from spoliation, massacre, and shame?" Is it unmeet to implore of Heaven that torture may not be renewed? That the riding-house and the Exchange may not echo with shrieks and groans? That scaffolds may not stand in our streets, and that their channels may not be red with gore? I will frankly admit, that one among the many reasons by which I am swayed, in thus strongly enforcing this measure, is the deep community of sentiment which the utterance of a prayer for the freedom of Ireland will produce among all classes of the people. It will tend to link the clergy with us by a still stronger bond, and impart to the patriotism of the people a more exalted and enthusiastic character. Will it not be a noble spectacle to behold the brave and impetuous peasantry of Ireland kneeling, on every Sabbath, before the altar of Heaven, and lifting up their brawny arms, and their rugged and impassioned faces, in the utterance of a prayer for the liberty of Ireland?—and if any man should, after the institution of this admirable practice, by which a great political pursuit will be consecrated and made holy, be disposed to tell me that the Irish people are indifferent to their civil rights, I shall say to him— "Go into the humblest edifice dedicated to the worship of God, and when you shall have heard the prayer for emancipation pronounced from the altar, and beheld the passion and enthusiasm with which the humblest tillers of the earth will have joined in that noble supplication —when you shall have witnessed their ardent eyes and beaming countenances, and listened to the fervour of the exclamations with which they will unite their orisons with the minister of their persecuted religion, then you will not presume to tell me that seven millions of people are careless of the attainment of their political rights."

SPEECH ON THE DUKE OF YORK.

I HAVE waited until the chair had been left, and the meeting of the Association had terminated, in order to introduce a subject, which, as it is of a purely political nature, I refrained from mentioning during the discussions of the Association, lest it should give them a character of illegality, and expose me to the imputation of having violated the law. I refer to the recent observations which have been made in the London papers upon the report of a speech of mine at a public dinner. I hope that I shall not be considered guilty of an overweening egotism, in drawing the attention of the individuals who happen to be assembled here, to what may appear to relate to myself. But the topics on which I mean to address you are of public as well as of personal interest. The truculent jocularity, and the spirit of savage jest, which have been ascribed to me, in expatiating on the infirmities of an illustrious person, have been regarded as characteristic of the moral habitudes of the body to which I belong. Thus, my vindication (for I do not rise to make an apology) extends beyond myself. Yet let me be permitted to suggest, that it is most unfair to impute to a whole people the feelings or the sentiments of any single man. The Catholics of Ireland have been repeatedly held responsible for the unauthorised and unsanctioned language of individuals. Every ardent expression, every word that overflows with gall, every phrase uttered in the suddenness of unpremeditated emotion, are converted into charges against seven millions of the Irish people. It is dealing rather hardly with us, to make a loose after-dinner speech, (the mere bubble of the mind) thrown off in the heedlessness of conviviality, a matter of serious accusation against a whole community. I am not endeavouring to excuse myself upon any such plea as the Bishop of Kilmore might resort to, in extenuating his late oration in Cavan; on the contrary, I am prepared to show the circumstances, which, in my mind, gave warrant to what I said. But I deprecate the notion that the language employed either by myself, or by any other individual, should be held to represent the opinions of the Irish Catholics. It has been stated, that laughter was produced by an ebullition of disastrous merriment. I will suppose that some two or three dozen of individuals in an obscure country town, did not preserve the solemnity with which any allusion to the maladies of an illustrious person ought to have been received, yet it is wholly unjust to hold the Irish Catholics responsible for their lack of sensibility. Having said this much, in order to rescue my fellow-labourers in the cause of emancipation, from any responsibility for individual demerit, I shall proceed to state, what, in my judgment, affords a justification of the language employed upon the occasion to which I refer. I shall not deny that I entertain a solicitude upon this subject. It is affectation on the part of any man to say, that he holds the censure of the press in no account. I cannot but be sensible that I am, from my comparative want of personal importance, more exposed to the injurious consequence of such a simultaneous assault. But I do not complain; whoever intermeddles in public proceedings, must be prepared for occasional condemnation. It is one of the necessary results of notoriety, and I submit to it, as a portion of my fate. I shall not, therefore, insinuate that there is any mock sentimentality in the amiable indignation with which the writers of the Whig journals have vented their censures upon what they call the barbarous hilarity of an after-dinner harangue. I will not say, that it is easy to procure a character for high sentiment, by indulging in a paroxysm of editorial anger. Nay, I will give the gentlemen who have put so much sentiment into type, credit for sincerity, and without attempting to retaliate, without referring them to their own comments upon the illustrious immoralities of the distinguished person to whom I have alluded, I shall state the grounds of which I conceive that I have been unjustly assailed. It is right that I should at once proceed to mention exactly what took place. The chairman of the meeting in question, deviated from the ordinary usage at Roman Catholic dinners, and, in compliance with what, from his inexperience, he considered to be a sort of formula of convivial loyalty, proposed the health of a man, who is an object, to use the mildest phrase, of strong national disrelish. This, I confess, excited my indignation. I felt indignation, and where is the man who has one drop of manly blood in his heart, who would not feel indignation at being called on to offer a public homage to the individual, who "has an oath in heaven" against his country. I was tempted at first to remonstrate in the language of violent reproof against such an obnoxious toast, and I own that I felt it difficult to restrain the emotions which, in common with every Roman Catholic, I entertain towards the man, who is the avowed and devoted antagonist of Ireland. I recollected, however, that the chairman had done no more than comply with what he conceived to be a mere form, and I, therefore, preferred a mockery of the sentiment to any solemn denunciation. To the toast the expression of a hope was annexed, that with the restoration of health, his feelings towards this country should undergo an alteration. "My gorge rose" at the notion of a man, whose hereditary obstinacy has been confirmed by an adjuration of his God, becoming a valetudinarian convert to liberal opinions. The transition from anger to derision is an easy one, and I could not help indulging in the luxury of scorn (for it is not without its gratification,) and in the spirit of a gay malevolence, but not of heartless ridicule, I stated, that I did not despair of seeing a consummation of the pious aspirations in which I had been called to join, when I recollected that protestations in politics might be as fleeting as those in love, and that as "Jove laughs at lover's perjuries," I apprehended an unfortunate stability in "so help me God!" It was not unnatural that in this mood of unpremeditated mockery, I should make citations from certain celebrated epistles, where vows of everlasting attachment were succeeded by infidelities of so much infelicitous renown. The report of what I said was not full, and although I do not affect to say, that the expressions imputed to me were not used, yet they are presented to the public eye, without much concomitant matter, which would show them in, perhaps, a different light. I am sorry that the references to those celebrated letters were omitted. The following were among the passages to which I alluded, and which I think will bear me out—"How can I sufficiently express to my sweetest, my darling love, the delight which her dear, her pretty letter gave me—millions of thanks for it, my angel. Doctor O'———— delivered your letter. He wishes much to preach before royalty, and if I can put him in the way of it, I will. What a time it appears to me, my darling, since we parted, and how impatiently I look forward to next Wednesday night. God bless you, my dear love ; ah! believe me, even to my last hour, yours, and yours alone." Thus, you perceive, that his affection was sealed with as strong a vow as his antipathy. The next letter gives vent to still more impetuous emotions. "How can I express to my darling love my thanks for her dear, dear letter. Oh! my angel, do me justice, and be convinced that there never was a woman adored as you are. There are still, however, two whole nights before I shall clasp my dear angel in my arms. Clavering is mistaken, my dear, in thinking there are any new regiments to be raised. (Thereby hangs a tale.) Thanks, my love, for the handkerchiefs, which are delightful, and I need not, I trust, assure you, of the pleasure I feel in wearing them, and thinking of the dear hands who made them for me. Adieu, my sweetest love, until the day after to-morrow; and be assured, that until my last hour, I shall remain yours, and yours alone." It would be doing injustice to the celebrated writer of these exotic effusions, if I did not add that his recommendation of an Irish divine, was fully justified by the result, for the *Morning Post* mentions, that while the doctor, with the Irish Omega in his name, was preaching, the father of the illustrious individual was very attentive, and his mother and sisters were melted into tears. There is an amusement of a demi-literary kind, commonly called "*cross reading.*" I have sometimes put the "so help me God" oration, into juxta position with the ama-

tory lucubrations from which I have given a few ex
ing stood thus: "It was connected with the seriou
no more. Doctor O'—— wishes much to preac
have never seen any reason to regret or change t
took." "Oh! my angel, do me justice, and be
never was a woman adored as you are—there ar
whole nights before I can clasp my angel in my
strongly on the whole subject—" ten thousand tha
handkerchiefs, which are delightful." Here l
affected. "I have been brought up all my life in
be assured that, to my last hour, I shall ever rem
alone, 'so help me God!'" This amalgamation
his politics, in which his vices and his virtues are
sents his character in a just light. But I should la
of derision. Why have I made these references t
but for his relentless antipathies to my country,
forgotten? It is not in the spirit of wanton mal
revenge. It is for the purpose of recalling to the
myself the period at which that illustrious persor
much aversion in England, as he is in Ireland a
the purpose of branding his protestations about co
scorn which they merit; it is in order to exhibit, i
appeals to heaven; to put his morality into compari
and to tear off the mask by which the spirit of
to be disguised. Conscience, forsooth! It is en
blood boil to think on't! That he who had publi
common day, thrown off every coverlet of shame-
in the blackest stye of profligate sensuality, an avo
adulterer, whose harlot had sustained herself by th
and turned footmen into brigadiers! that he—
from the results of a foul and most disgraceful o
without sense or memory or feeling, before the eyes
with the traces of his degradation still fresh upon
upon the name of the great and eternal God, and
of sacrilegious cant, dedicate himself with an inv
the everlasting oppression of my country! This i
every Irish Catholic, on fire. This is it which rais
and exasperates! This it is that applies a torch t
it is that blows our indignation into flame. And it
eyes of men, who stand the cold spectators of our
us a fastidious sympathy in our wrongs, makes us
lent, and ferocious. This it is which makes them t
are foaming with rabid froth, and that there is poi
ness in our fangs. I will furnish our antagonists
condemnation: I will assist their vocabulary of insu
to heap contumely upon contumely, and reproach
will only answer, that if they were similarly situa
with the same poignancy, and speak with the sam

as ourselves,—I will only say, in the language of the great master of human nature—

"You should not speak of what you cannot feel."

They cannot feel our condition, or appreciate our injuries to their full extent. I cannot say the same thing of the illustrious person to whom I have alluded. He has been placed in circumstances somewhat analogous. Good God! that such a man should tell us that we labour under no privation, and are subject to no wrong! What were his own feelings —how did his heart beat when he was driven by the loud and reiterated cries of the English people, from his high office! We are told by him that an exclusion from the honours of the State is no substantive injury. Did he forget his own letter to the House of Commons, in which he offered up an act of contrition for the consequences of his impure connection, and, acknowledging that his heart was almost broken, resigned his office! Did the sacrifice cost him no pang? Did the oblation which he made to the public feeling awake no painful sensation in his mind? Did not his cheek burn, and was not his face turned into scarlet, when he took the pen with a trembling hand, (for it must have trembled,) and signed the instrument of his resignation! What a palsy must have seized his arm when he let the truncheon fall! And if in that dreadful crisis he felt a deep agony of heart, should he not make some allowance for those who, for no other cause than a conscientious adherence to the religion in which they were born and trust to die, are excluded from those honours which are accessible to every other class of British subjects? What then is the charge against me? That I have not enough of Joseph Surface in my character, to express a wish that the great obstacle to my liberty should not be removed! My crime is, that I am not a hypocrite so base, as to allow a public libation to his name to pass without a comment. It was extorted from me, and my observations were not dictated by any cold and deliberate malice toward the individual, but by the feeling of distaste which the announcement of such a toast produced in my mind. The sarcasm was directed to the sentiment and not to the man. With respect to the individual himself, I doubt not that in private life he is not destitute of good qualities. It is said that he is a person of honour, and of a kindly disposition. This I am not inclined to controvert; and it would be an injustice not to add, that in many particulars, in his official capacity, he is entitled to praise. Diligence, punctuality, and an attention to the interests of the inferior class of persons, who are placed under his superintendence, are among his merits. But what compensation does good nature afford for the denial of liberty? The mistakes of men in his condition are equivalent in their consequences to acts of deliberate criminality. Imbecility of understanding, and obstinacy of character, generate as many evil results as depravity of disposition, and, if I may employ the phrase, tyranny of heart. If I have adverted to conduct which, in a court, is called folly, but which in lower departments of society is called vice, it is not that I am anxious to exaggerate those weaknesses which exposed him to ridicule, into enormity. The absur-

ditics in love, into which he fell, should rest in ot
by talking of the pain to which the royal conscien
provoke a contrast between his life and his prote
tear open the tattered curtains of concubinage, in
ments against him from an adulterous bed. Wl
is the man who appeals to heaven? Who is the 1
house to consider the torture of conscience in w
thus placed? Who is it that lifts up his hands and (
God?" Is he a man of pure and unblemished li
bright and immaculate morality? Is he a man
fidelity to his pecuniary contracts, and who nevei
creditors to be the victims of a licentious prodign
interrogatories which this appeal to Almighty G
upon us. We are rendered astute in the detec
anxiety to find fault, and look into the life of s
microscopic scrutiny. It is much to be regretted
a solicitude to be hated by the Irish people. He
nity to gather about his name the antipathies of
ness his having accepted the office of Grand Mast
ciation of men, combined together for the oppre
countrymen, and who, perverting the word of G
massacre, employed as a motto of their sanguin
foot shall be steeped in the blood of tnine enemie
thy dog shall be red with the lapping thereof.
expected, that, for the ex-Grand Master of an Ora
entertain much tenderness and anxiety, or that an
the active part which I have, in Catholic affairs, s
when held up as an object of sympathy, to pass wi
-ive comment? I do not exult in any corporal su
endure. If he suffers pain, and it were in my p
should obey the instincts of my nature, and, di
detestations, bear him relief. But if I am asl
desire to see the misfortunes of my country prolo
liberty of Ireland is too dear." He is, it is beyor
obstacle to concession. What, then, do our oppo
If they require that excess of Christian philosoph
us to offer up our orisons for the degradation of (
too much. What would Catholic Emancipation
promote a whole people to their just level in the £
tranquillity, and open the sources of national wea
impoverished by its distractions, it would bind us
and put an end to those dissensions by which we a
by which all the charities of life are blasted; i
spirit of animosity and virulence which fills the he
worst passions, and makes them turn with an emu
each other; it would, in one word, produce a ;
national reconciliation, and fix the stability of the
i.n everlasting foundation. These would, in my
results of Catholic Emancipation; and I am only

of the whole Irish people, when I avow that I do not desire the perpetuation of the chief impediment that stands in its way, and thus obstructs a consummation which every lover of his country must most devoutly wish.

THE NEW REFORMATION

SPEECH ON THE NEW REFORMATION, SPOKEN AT AN AGGREGATE MEETING.

Mr. SHEIL said,—Peel is out—Bathurst is out—Westmorland is out—Goulburn (but he is not worth mention) is out—Wellington, the bad Irishman, (he was once a page in the castle, and acquired a habit of thinking as trailing as a Lady Lieutenant's gown) is out—and, thanks be to God, the hoary champion of every abuse—the venerable supporter of corruption in all its forms—the pious antagonist of every generous sentiment—the virtuous opponent of every liberal amelioration—the immaculate senator, who wept over the ruins of Grampound; the incorruptible judge, who declared the Princess of Wales to be innocent, the Queen of England to be guilty—Eldon, the procrastinating, canting, griping, whining, weeping, ejaculating, protesting, money-getting, and money-keeping Eldon, is out. This, after all, is something. We have got rid of that candid gentleman, who, for an abridgement of the decalogue, would abridge Ireland of her liberties. We have got rid of the gaoler who presided over the captivity of Napoleon, and was so well qualified to design what Sir Hudson Lowe was so eminently calculated to execute. We have got rid of the authoritative soldier, who has proved himself as thankless to his sovereign as he had been ungrateful to his country, and who has been put to the right about left—and, better than all—better than the presumption of Wellington, the narrow-heartedness of Bathurst, the arrogance of Westmorland, the ostentatious manliness and elaborate honesty of Mr. Peel, we have got rid of John Lord Eldon's tears. The old hypocrite! His mind is like the face of the witch in Horace, "*stercore fucata crocodili.*" Yet it were doing him wrong not to admit, that once in his life his sorrows were sincere, when, upon a recent occasion, looking the sympathetic Wetherell, and the renegade Sugden in the face, his lordship wept and blubbered a resignation. The whole empire rejoices at his fall, and by that fall much has been already gained by this country. Mr. Canning and his friends will not relinquish the determination, the moment they have acquired the power, to do us justice. I have no distrust of them; and with respect to the measure which we ought to adopt, I will say but one word, namely, that we ought not to harass and embarrass the men who are still surrounded with difficulties, and who must be allowed time to mature their good intents towards our cause. They have been long convinced that emancipation is requisite to allay our animosities, and every day affords a new illustration of its necessity. In what part of the world is religious rancour carried to such a point of detestation? Our evils were already sufficiently great, but a new and a worse calamity has lately arisen in the furious spirit of controversy which has recently broken out in Ireland. In prosecuting their favourite scheme of establishing a new reformation, (which Leslie Foster, in a paroxysm of unusual eloquence, informed the House of Commons that it would be as difficult to resist as to stop the falls of Niagara) the itinerant teachers of a new-fangled Christianity disturb the public peace, sow discord wherever they appear, and exasperate the people, by casting upon their priesthood the most contumelious invectives with which foul tongues can be supplied by still fouler and baser hearts. The new reformation! Though I should incur the anathema of the ex-secretary to Lord Lansdowne, and Dr. Bloomfield should indulge in a burlesque on the Apocalypse, I cannot but smile at this preposterous undertaking. In candour, however, I should say, that in one respect these symptoms of renovated Christianity correspond with the circumstances attending its original institution. It is among the poor, the naked, and the destitute that truth is making its way. It is among the dregs of the community that the premiums of apostacy are successfully applied. It is amidst the smoke of hovels that this new light has broken forth. It is in the exhalations of pig-styes that the holy spirit has appeared. There is no lack of Magdalens among the converts to this new reformation. This difference, however, exists between the institution of Christianity and the new reformation—neither Lord Farnham nor Lord Lorton bear any very great resemblance to the first delegates of Christ. For my part, I conceive that the real interests of religion are deeply affected by the scenes which are going on in this country, and I apprehend that if the Catholic creed be subverted, infidelity will rise out of its ruins. By teaching men to explore, you may disturb and weaken the deepest foundations of their faith. Witness the pleasant story told by Mr. Pope upon the adventures of a mouse with the eucharist. "Could a mouse run away with the Godhead?" cries Mr. Pope. "Did the author of the sun, to whose throne the eye of Galileo could not approach, perish upon a cross?" This is the impious interrogatory of the infidel, which is analogous to the pious question of Mr. Pope; and he and his confederates, by familiarising the ignorant and unthinking to the contemplation of subjects which are above their reason, and do not fall within the cognizance of the imperfect intellect of man, lend their involuntary aid to those who have set up as apostles of annihilation, and with a passion for atheism, take a disastrous pride in withering the hopes, and blasting the moral and consolatory anticipations of mankind. I confess that I look on the recent controversy which has agitated this city as likely to be injurious to the cause of genuine religion; for it has made its most sacred mysteries a subject of theological chit-chat. I do not mean to cast the least blame upon Mr. Maguire, who was actually dragged into the combat by his opponent; on the contrary, I think that Mr. Maguire acquitted himself in a manner which reflects the greatest credit upon him; for, although hitherto unknown, and wholly unpractised in public speaking, he entered the lists with the great prizefighter in polemics without dismay, and deriving a genuine eloquence from the consciousness that he spoke the truth, evinced a decided superiority over his antagonist. He was never once betrayed into anger—while his opponent, by his contumelious charges, indicated the depth to which his pride had been wounded. He looked at him with the smile with which Calvin ordered Servetus to the flames. It is by the convulsive passions that agitated the evil spirit in the disguise of an angel, that Uriel discovered the enemy of mankind—and it may be said, in the language of Milton, of this champion of the new reformation, that—

> While he spoke, each passion dimmed his face,
> Thrice changed with pale ire, envy, and despair,
> Which marred his borrowed visage, and betrayed
> Him counterfeit—
> For heavenly minds from such distempers foul
> Be ever clear

What a contrast did the poor priest, the logician of the mountains, present to this modern apostle! With the flush of rural health upon his cheek—with the benevolent expression of honest good nature upon his face—with all the evidence of sincerity impressed upon him—he replied with mildness to the charges brought against his truth and honour, and exhibited the true spirit of a Christian by holding forth a tender of amity, and begging that they should part in peace. It would be doing Mr. Pope an injustice not to say, that his good feelings got the better of his religious rancour, and he merged the animosities of the theologian in the honest emotions of the man. This was the only circumstance which could promote the cause of true religion in the whole of the six days' discussion. It was altogether a most fantastic scene. A wandering dealer in inspiration, a sort of rider to the great manufactories of religion in the metropolis, takes it into his head that he can put an end to the dispute which has agitated the world, by putting down a country priest to whom he gives a challenge. Mr. Maguire is forced into it—two seconds are chosen.—Paulus Æmilius Singer, on whose head a tongue of fire seems to have descended, and to have left its traces behind, is selected by Mr. Pope, while the philosopher of Belfast, from the spirit of genuine piety by which he is distinguished, is nominated as bottle-holder to St. Peter. The renowned commodore of the Floating Chapel, Admiral Oliver, is appointed chairman to the Protestants, while Mr. O'Connell, who was casually there, was much against his will compelled to take a joint command with the Admiral. Thus an honourable competition is established between the Navy and the Bar. God forbid that I should attempt to detail the various incidents of the theological encounter. I should not, however, omit to mention that I was greatly edified by the numerous attendance of the loyal portion of the bar, among whom were to be observed three eminent gentlemen, who had signed the Anti-Catholic petition under the influence of premature anticipations. They came to listen to Mr. Pope, in order to apply to their calamities the consolations of religion, and, indeed it was truly delightful to see, when the orator expatiated on the spiritual dangers incidental to office, how Mr. Sergeant Lefroy turned up the whites of his eyes heaven. But the person most deserving of note was Dr. Magee, w exhibited a strange alternation of feeling, for when a blow was ma by Mr. Pope at "the church without a religion," the Doctor forgot th the gentleman belonged to "a religion without a church,", while, wh the priest knocked the mitre from the head of the Establishment, t Doctor. exhibited no little uneasiness. "Had St. Paul ten thousa pounds a year?" said the priest. The Doctor gave a start. "Had t teachers of the Gospel two millions of green acres in Palestine?" The Doctor shifted his seat. "Show me an authority for the drawin room and the levee?"—the Doctor bit his nails. "Show me a text f your equipages, and your banquets, and your chariots, and your pri and your pomp, and your titles, and your tithes, and your cesses, a your church rates, and your fines, and all that system of grinding tax tion, by which the sacerdotal power and splendour are preserved. Sho me"——The priest was proceeding in this strain of formidable expo tulation, when I turned to look at his Grace, and I found that the Ar —(what shall I call him?)—the Archbishop had disappeared. I wi that Mr. Pope would take up this strain of interrogation, and th instead of trying to convince Roman Catholic peasants to adopt t tenets, he would endeavour to persuade some Protestant bishops follow the precepts of the Gospel. He ought to be tolerably well sat fied after his recent experiment, that he cannot obtain any very con derable renown by engaging in controversial contentions with our clerg In order, therefore, that he may not be left destitute of occupation beg leave to point out to him another and a better path to fame, nam the glorious enterprise of teaching certain high-priests of the Esta lishment to adopt a more apostolic fashion of life; and if he feels th there is no ordinary difficulty in the undertaking, he should rememb that his merit will be enhanced by the arduous obstacles which he w have to encounter. He has admirable qualifications for this enterpri and should take care to apply them in the most effectual and impre sive manner. I beg leave to suggest to him the following explo Having ascertained on what day a bishop gives a dinner, let him procu a copy of Hudibras, and study with precision the exact attire of a gen ine teacher of the word. I would not, however, have his hair t closely cropped, after the manner of the Roundheads, it were bett that it should stream loosely, wildly, and prophetically, as a type of l mind and his opinions. If he were to attend the theatre when M Liston performs that part of Mawworm, it might assist his fancy, thoug I must confess, that nature has done so much for him, that he hard requires any extraneous aid in order to make him look the appropria herald of the other world. When he shall have completely rigged hi self out, and put on the ghastliest aspect of inspiration, let him go for and ascend the steps of his lordship's palace, and having gained adm sion by a knock louder than a curate's tap, let him rush at once to t banquet room, and throwing open the doors, advance into the midst the episcopal festivity. Let him march, with spectral strides, and wh every eye shall have been fixed upon him, let him, with his deep a sepulchral voice, demand, whether it was after such a fashion tnat the apostles dined—whether the silver and gold, the crimson tapestry, the Asiatic carpet, the blaze of splendour, the multifarious luxury, the costly wines, the din of revelry, and tumultuous joyance, are in accordance with the lessons of poverty and self-denial prescribed by the Scriptures; and shaking his phantom hand at my lord the bishop, let him ask, how, with his pampered paunch, his bloated cheek, his swimming and voluptuous eye, he would dare to appear before that God of whom he professed himself the minister? But let not Mr. Pope stop here. After he shall have uttered his denunciations, and turned the bishop pale, let him walk forth, and proceeding to the chambers where he hears the sound of the harp and the tabor, let him rush into the centre of the dance, and after he shall have cast his lurid eyes around, when the sound of the fiddle shall have died away—when the astonished musicians shall have stood aghast and mute—when the bishop's wife shall have got into hysterics, and the bishop's daughters shall have sought refuge in the arms of their partners—then let this modern Isaiah exclaim—" Woe unto the daughters of Zion, because they are haughty, and walk with stretched-forth necks and wanton eyes, winking and mincing as they go; therefore the Lord will take away the bravery of their tinkling ornaments, and their cauls, and their round ties like the moon, the chains, and the bracelets, and the ruffles; the bonnets, and the ornaments of the legs, and the head-bands, and the tablets and the earrings, the changeable suits of apparel, and the mantles, and the wimples, and the crisping-pins, the glasses, and the fine linen, and the hoods, and the veils; and it shall come to pass, that there shall be, instead of well-set hair, baldness, and instead of a stomacher, a girdle of sackcloth, and burning instead of beauty." It will be strange if Mr. Pope does not succeed in putting waltzing, and all other importations of German attitude down. But it is not to the interior of the pontifical palace that he should confine his efforts for a genuine reformation. Let him go forth into the public streets, and with all the intrepidity that becomes his heavenly mission, denounce the anti-Christian abuses that prevail everywhere around us. Let him stand at the door of Kildare-street club, for example, and inquire of the deans, and the archdeacons, and the rectors, whether the chambers of indigent, the dungeons of the captive, the death-beds of the sinful, would not be more appropriate places of ecclesiastical resort— let him, if he sees some wealthy and luxurious dignitary rolling in his carriage with his wife and daughters to the Castle, stop the driver, and inquire whether the way to heaven is not too narrow for a coach and four. And when he sees a certain arch-priest cantering through the streets, let him seize his horse by the bridle and cry out—" Good, my lord, it was not after this fashion that Christ entered into Jerusalem on the meek and humble animal with which patience and suffering are associated." But it is not my intention that Mr. Pope should limit his spiritual achievements to this country; and after he shall have acquired the plenitude of such provincial celebrity as Ireland can confer, let him set off for London, and on one night when the minister shall have written circular summonses to

the bishops to attend, let Mr. Pope take his stat
the House of Lords, and as the lawn-sleeved succe
descend from their gilded chariots to the assembla
the powerful, and the princely of the land, let his
vaults of Westminster, and let him exclaim as th
the priests of him who said that his kingdom was

I have, I fear, pursued this topic too far, and in
levity with subjects of solemn and awful conside
cannot help regarding Mr. Pope and his fellow-
reformation with a feeling of combined censure an
every notion of religion and of common sense, the
the word of God should howl damnation in our ear
somewhat more largely and steadfastly than they d
of the Established Church, for which, at all event:
rity than for transubstantiation, passes not only
without comment! In any observations which
clergy of the Established Church, I have not refer
out rather alluded to individual cases; and I am
recently the Protestant priesthood have underg
morals, a salutary amelioration. On them I do
reflection; but I do insist, that the vast wealth po
is a crying grievance, and repugnant to every
can form, from the precepts of its Divine Auth
religion. I therefore do most strenuously blam
associates, for their invectives against the Catholi
creed of the majority of the people, when the ricl
ment, which are so unequally and disproportionatel
so much retrenchment in their extent, and so r
their allotment. A wealthy priesthood, whether C
is a glaring and hideous anomaly; yet when did we
or Captain Gordon—(that Scotch sower of diss
the thistle seed of controversy wherever he goe
hear Mathias or any one of them, deliver a single
nation of the luxurious endowment of the Establi
who can doubt that it is utterly anti-Christian, a
whole tenor and spirit of the system of creed a
inculcated in the New Testament? I protest it
drive men into utter infidelity, to hear churchmen
pits of meekness, poverty, self-denial, the cont
emembrance of death, and the worthlessness of
themselves wallowing in the enjoyments of unbou
engaged in the ardent and unremitting pursuit
pomps, and the vanities of the world. What a mo
that the church is a state engine. Gracious heav
which our Redeemer died to be employed as a
leaning fabric of government! They first put th
hands—they bid us read them over, and imbue ou
our hearts with their tenets, and then, they have t
not the height and top of presumption?) to tell us

every text in the New Testament, that the pontiffs of this poor and humble religion are to be invested with political authority, and to stand upon a level with princes and nobles, and are to have their five, their ten, their twenty thousands a-year—that the inferior clergy are in a regular gradation to be maintained at a corresponding cost—that the highest departments in the hierarchy and the priesthood are to be filled up by the sons of peers and boroughmongers, and that the whole business of religion is to be made subservient to the end of legislation, and even of court intrigue—that we should be told all this, and to make the matter worse, and more insulting to common decency and to common sense, that we should be told it by the very men who inform us that we are in damnable error, that we are misbelievers and idolaters, that our clergy are impostors, and that we are either infidels or fools—that all this should be said by the very men who bid us search the Scriptures, and call themselves the servants and the delegates of a crucified God—this, I do honestly confess, provokes indignation; makes one stamp the foot, and cry out "monstrous!" at every word! The Church of Christ, it is said, should lift up its head in the midst of courts and palaces. When did Christ himself do so? But I am wrong—He did—he stood in a court where he was hailed as king—he was clothed in purple—he held the emblem of empire in his hand, and he had a crown—but it was a diadem of thorns, which was planted in his bleeding temples, and pierced his bursting head—and it is in his name that.........But I have done—I would to heaven that the advocates for reading the Scriptures without note or comment would give a little reflection to all this. I would that they considered whether in the bosom of Protestantism itself, there are not abuses which will afford scope for their zeal, before they set up as knight-errants against Popery, and put us all at variance with each other, by dint of their wild and fanatical speculations. Let them leave the people and their religion alone, and no longer molest us with the absurd jabber and the unintelligible jargon of their fantastical theology; and if they are still determined to persevere in their oratorical vocation, let them, in place of wandering through the country for the diffusion of acrimony and the dissemination of discord, endeavour to instruct the people in the great principles of morality; let them enforce the practical injunctions, rather than contend about the mysterious tenets of religion et them inculcate habits of industry, and sobriety, and subordination; et them reconcile the higher and lower classes by habituating the ich to mercy, and the poor to patience and submission; let them bind is together in the bonds of Christian brotherhood and natural affiliation, and never let them forget the "tidings of great joy" with which he coming of Christ was told to shepherds abiding in the mountains, which, while the glory of God was celebrated, the angelic messengers roclaimed as among the results of the event which they were sent to announce from heaven, the peace, the tranquillity, and the happiness of mankind.

THE FORTY-SHILLING FREEHOLDERS.

SPEECH ON THE FORTY-SHILLING FREEHOLDERS, AT AN AGGREGATE MEETING, HELD ON THE 7TH SEPTEMBER, 1826.

THE principal object in calling this meeting, is to devise measures f the relief of the forty-shilling freeholders, and it is sufficient to st that object, in order to impress you with the importance of the occasi on which we are assembled. I rise at the very opening of the disci sion, because I have been instrumental in summoning you togeth Nothing excepting a conviction of its paramount necessity, would h induced me to exert myself for the purpose of procuring this meetir when so many of the persons who take an active share in our procee ings are absent from Dublin. But when the work of ruin and of oppr sion is going on—when the severest process of the law is in full a active operation—when from Waterford, from Louth, from Cavan, a from Westmeath, a call for succour is so earnestly made—when I f that relief, in order to be effectual, must not only be prompt, but imn diate; in one word, when the cries of the forty-shilling freeholders a in my ears, I cannot listen to any cold-hearted disquisitions upon t inexpediency of meeting at this particular season, nor do I require tl the sun should be in any particular sign of the zodiac, in order to do act of common humanity and justice. It is enough for me to kno that the high-minded peasants, who have bidden defiance to the "tyra of their fields," are under the active infliction of calamity, to make i overlook every consideration of time and place—to dismiss all le quibbles from my mind, and if I may so say, rush through every imp diment to their relief. I cannot allow common humanity to be fr trated by a forensic disputation, and obvious justice to be delayed legal sophistications. I will not take up an act of parliament, in order determine whether it is safe to be honourable, and whether human is made a misdemeanour by the law. I will not ask, whether the app cation of the rent to the succour of the freeholders may be tortur into a violation of the statute, but I will inquire of my own heart, wl ther it would not be utterly base and abominable to have excited t forty-shilling freeholders into a revolt against their superiors, and th leave the wretches, whom we have brought into acts of desperate patri ism to the compassion of the landlords and of the winds. These, S are my feelings, and I think that I may add, that there is not a man the Catholic body who does not participate in them. There is, in tru no difference of opinion, respecting the propriety of doing everything our power for the relief of the freeholders, and the only question relat to the means through which assistance ought to be afforded. I trust tl the series of resolutions which will be proposed to-day, and which have taken very great care in framing, will meet the views of the mc adverse to the application of the old Catholic rent. I am very sensit that disunion amongst ourselves is to be avoided, and if once we separa upon a single topic, it is not improbable that our differences mig excite a spirit of acrimony and contention, which would extend to all our discussions, and ultimately render us, as it did before, the scorn of our enemies, and objects of compassion to those who wish us well. An intimation has been sent from Waterford, that the old rent should remain untouched. It is somewhat remarkable that nearly at the same time a demand for £400 should have been made by Waterford, in answering which, the whole of the new rent has been exhausted. Yet, I am the first to acknowledge that the greatest respect ought to be attached to any expression of their wishes, which may come from the citizens of Waterford; and we should endeavour to accommodate ourselves as much as possible to their views. The resolutions have been drawn in that spirit. The first of them recommends, IN CASE OF NECESSITY, (but not otherwise) an application of the old rent. It distinctly limits the application to a contingency. I think, that from these observations, it is scarcely possible that any man should dissent. Let me put this plain question, in order to illustrate the propriety of the measures in contemplation: Suppose that the new rent should be inadequate to the effectual succour of the forty-shilling freeholders, and that we should be informed that a certain sum was necessary, in order to rescue them, in any particular district, from their landlords—will any man say that, rather than touch the old rent, we should abandon the freeholders? I am convinced that there is no man here with so bad a heart. If a deputation were to be sent from Monaghan to Dublin, and the delegates of the freeholders were to come forward and declare that a sum of £500 was requisite, and must be immediately advanced, what answer should be given to them? Should we say, that the old rent is inviolable; that it is the ark of our cause, and that no hand should be laid upon it? Should we answer, that the new rent was the only fund out of which an act of justice could be performed, and that the forty-shilling freeholders must wait until the public coffers shall be replenished? But, Sir, this is not mere hypothesis. There are actually in this assembly three priests from Monaghan, and two Presbyterians, who have been deputed to enforce the resolution which I propose. They will tell you, (I leave it to them who have had the ocular proof) how much calamity has been, and is still being inflicted on their county. I shall venture to illustrate my views of our situation by a comparison. What would you think if the governor of a besieged city, in which there was an old and abundant well, were to direct in a time of great exigency and drought, that the chief fountain should be sealed up, and that until a new well was complete, none of the soldiers should be allowed to drink? If the soldiers were to come hot from the thickest fire of the enemy, and exhausted by wounds and sufferings, what would you think of the governor who said, ' Go draw from the new shaft which has been sunk for water?" The soldiers might justly reply, " There is no water in it yet, and while it is sinking we shall die of thirst. Do, pray, good governor, give us a drop from the old fountain; enough only to save us from immediate death— It is all we require." Have I in this illustration presented a very unfair similitude. and are there not some amongst us who give a reply to the forty-shilling freeholders of a very analogous kind? We tell them to

resort to the new rent and to wait until it shall be collected. In
interval, their cattle are driven, they are ejected by civil bill, they
expelled from their houses, and they are reduced to starvation—
then is the proposition which I make? Dig the new well, make e
effort to render it abundant, deep and full; don't unseal the old foun
as long as there is a drop in the new source. But if the latter is exhaus
or if there be any delay in the rising of the water, then open the
fountain, and give out an adequate supply. But let me abandon the
guage of parable, and in a case which hardly requires any enforcem
refrain from resorting to these elaborate arguments in order to sa
your reason, or to awaken a just sense of duty in your minds. Ther
however, one objection to the application of the old rent, which as it
(to my surprise I confess) made an impression on some good-meaning
sons, deserves to be encountered. It is said that an aggregate mee
has no power to allocate the old rent to any such purpose. When pe
are anxious to avoid doing any particular thing, they are often a little
astute in devising reasons to justify their conduct. If no part of the
rent can be voted away, in order to assist the forty-shilling freehold
how has it happened that so much of it has been disposed of upon o
occasions, for other and very distinct purposes? How does it hap
that when salaries are to be given to public officers—when large s
are to be paid for newspaper advertisements, and other expenses
similar nature are to be defrayed, no objection is made to the plenit
of power vested in an aggregate meeting. But when an act, w
wisdom and honour concur in recommending, is to be performed,
authority of an aggregate meeting is, for the first time, disputed—
we are told that for all other purposes such an assembly is omnipot
but that the relief of the freeholders is an excepted case. Are
meetings of this description habitually designated as " the assemi
of the Catholics of Ireland;" and have they not uniformly exerc
the powers which that designation would imply? The truth is,
there cannot be any other organ of the national sentiment empio
but an assembly of this nature, and it would be wholly impossibl
carry on the public business, unless a meeting, which every individu
at liberty to attend, could act on behalf of the whole of Ireland.
not the petitions of the Catholics emanate from aggregate meetin
and are not resolutions constantly passed at these assemblies, in w
the same national authority is assumed? And what is to be do
Are the counties to be called together? What, in the mean time,
become of the forty-shilling freeholders? I shall ask another ques
which may be equally well applied to the suggestion that they sh
be relieved out of the new rent. What is to befal them if a defici
should take place? Another argument has been urged which is ref
by fact. It is said that the collection of the new rent will be imp
by the application of the old. The answer which I shall give to
suggestion appears to me to be triumphant. The county of Louth
passed a resolution in favour of the application of the old rent, if ne
sary. But I hold in my hand a series of resolutions, passed on the
of this month, at a meeting in which Sir Edward Bellew was in

chair, by which committees have been named for seven parishes, in order to raise the Catholic rent, and the priests of each parish are placed at the head of their respective committees. You thus perceive the same county calls for the application of the old rent, if necessary, and takes the most active measures in order to raise a new fund. And, observe, the money is only required by way of loan. I also received, this morning, a letter from a most respectable man, and who has a very large fortune in Louth, (Mr. Thomas Fitzgerald, of Fainvally) inclosing me a considerable subscription of the new rent, but at the same time approving strongly, in the event of necessity, of the allocation of a part of the old fund to the freeholders' relief. The deputies from Monaghan will inform you that a resolution to the effect which I have mentioned, will inspire the people of that county with the strongest confidence, and will give a fresh zeal to their exertions in the collecting of the new fund. In truth, the main object of the resolution is to impart a perfect trust to the people, and infuse into them a confidence in the integrity of those who are invested with the management of the national money. A further objection has been urged, which, if it were founded on fact, would deserve attention. It is grounded on the supposition that the persecution has ceased. This is certainly not the case. It has been stated, that in Monaghan tyranny had relaxed its energies. There cannot be a more eggregious mistake. I am authorised by the deputies from that county to state that oppression is in full activity. The series of miseries detailed to me would move the feelings of a man the least prone to sensibility. In Louth, the amiable and highly spiritualized Lord Roden has exhibited a practical exemplification of the effects of Bible reading upon his heart, and has commenced the work of retribution. It is to be wondered at, that a man whose mind should be "as smooth as the brow of Jesus," to use an expression of Jeremy Taylor, should have shown himself so susceptible to the worst passions by which our miserable nature is afflicted. I repeat it, then, the hand of oppression is yet uplifted in Louth. We must paralyse it before it descends—we must fly to the succour of the people. With respect to Waterford, the bare fact of that county having demanded £400, establishes beyond all question, that persecution is not at an end. I am assured that in Westmeath the rebellious tenantry are suffering the greatest hardships, and we are well aware of the measures of severity adopted in the county of Cavan. That election was remarkable for a disclosure of character in a person who was once notorious for his patriotism, (for he has been hurried by the impetuosity of youth into a dangerous extravagance of political virtue,) but has since given proof that a chivalrous love of country was not the domineering passion of his mind. His great wealth is the result of his own labour, and affords a proof how little intellect is required to take advantage of some fortunate accident, and to become a rich man. When he had acquired great wealth, he was told that liberalism in politics and in religion was a proof of mental superiority, and in order to pass for a philosopher, he continued patriot for some time. At length he purchased an estate in Cavan, and observed that all persons of the patrician class were addicted to the principles of ascendancy. While he remained in Dublin he had the countenance of some men of rank, as a warrant for his liberality, but in Cavan there was hardly a gentleman who was not a good Protestant. A trait of character which had not been formerly discovered at length appeared in this worthy burgher, who may be designated as the "Sir Balaam" of Merchant's-quay. He became anxious for a reputation for good breeding, and found a terrible obstacle to his ambition in his former political addictions. His efforts at patrician elegance were ineffectual. "The yellow clay still broke through the plaster of Paris." At a ball, which was not long ago given in Cavan, Lady Lucy M'Swadlum, and Miss Celestina Farintosh observed that the gestures of Mr. ——— were in a state of continual rebellion against propriety, and his limbs were insurgents against grace. Finding himself in this deplorable condition, he consulted a certain noble lictor, who is distinguished for a prodigal use of the "fasces," and inquired what in the world he should do to become genteel? "Whip me a boy or two, (said his lordship) or, at all events, turn Orangeman. It is a passport into good society, and will make as good a gentleman of you as most of us." It was with some compunction of spirit that Sir Balaam acceded to this process of transformation. His old recollections, the reminiscences of Bridge-street, and the spectres of his friends, with halters about their necks, came upon him. But at length his love of country prevailed, and he made a sort of compromise, by determining to play the patriot in Dublin, and the Orangeman in Cavan. Did any of you ever see the "Siege of Belgrade?" Do you remember Yusef? If ever Lady Lucy gets up a private play, "Sir Balaam" should perform the worthy citizen of Belgrade, who becomes Turk and Christian with such a philosophic facility of transition, by her ladyship's particular desire. When "Sir Balaam" had come to the determination to abandon his old principles, he resolved to display no ordinary alacrity in his new vocation, and saw that at the election an opportunity was offered to him for the manifestation of his zeal. He exhibited all the enthusiasm of apostacy. He was peculiarly "genteel;" in other words, in harshness towards his miserable dependants, he surpassed the more legitimate Orangemen of Cavan. "Bring up the cattle," was his familiar phrase at the hustings. "Pray, sir, what cattle?" said his agent. "The freeholders, to be sure," replied Sir Balaam, astonished at his not knowing that he referred to the useful and industrious class to which he himself originally belonged. The cattle, however, got restive, and Sir Balaam's reputation for gentility was much injured. This was a wound in the most vital point, and accordingly he has been relentless towards the wretched men who refused to sacrifice their consciences to his pleasure. But enough of him. I would not, I protest to God, for all his hoarded thousands, and ten times his estate, be capable of any of the acts of oppression with which he has taken vengeance on his unhappy tenants. I would not take the heart of such a man into my bosom for all that fifty years of accumulation has piled in his coffers. I thank God, however, that the wretches on whom he trampled were not left without succour. From whom did it come? It is with a most pleasurable sensation—it is with that feeling of thrilling admiration with which a noble action is always told and heard, that I am about to recount to you an example of lofty and spirit-stirring virtue. I pray you to attend to it, for it does good to the heart to hear such things. There are two priests in that county, the name of one of whom is Egan, and the other Reilly. They belong to that class of our clergy who fall within Goldsmith's definition of opulence, and pass for "rich with forty pounds a-year." They had out of the humble contribution of their flocks, in the lapse of many years saved a sum of about three hundred pounds each, and when they heard that "Sir Balaam" was grinding his tenants to pow, ler, these teachers of the gospel—these humble imitators of Him by whom Christianity was first propagated through the world, gathered their flocks about them and said, "you gave this money to us—you are now in want and misery—we come to give it back to you—we look for no re-payment but in heaven." "The Lord hath given, and the Lord hath taken away—blessed be the name of the Lord." I do not wonder that you hear this statement of a most honourable fact with enthusiasm; I shall not attempt to praise these humble and unostentatious ministers of God. I should travel in vain through all the language of panegyric —I should exhaust the whole repository of encomium. Glorious and lofty-minded men, you do not seek the praise of the world: you ask for no tribute of applause such as we can confer—your own hearts supply the exalted consciousness of surpassing virtue, and the eye of that God, by which those hearts are read, rests in pleasure upon two objects of his approbation as noble as ever issued from his hands. Shall we permit examples of this kind to be lost upon us? Shall we allow the poor priests to give away their miserable pittance, and to leave themselves destitute in their old age? They make no claim upon us, but shall we take advantage of the silence of benevolence, and allow them to remain unpaid. God forbid, and God forbid that we should abandon the freeholders, and permit the wretches upon whom we have entailed so much disaster, to remain without hope! For God Almighty's sake, let us not do any thing so base, so degrading, so utterly vile and bad as this! But independently of these considerations, let us remember, that even common policy requires that we should remove every feeling of distrust from the people, and that we should thoroughly convince them of a determination to give them effectual relief. If they are not saved from immediate oppression, with what face can we hereafter appeal to the spirit of patriotism, of which they have given such noble manifestations, and call upon them to perform the same part? Will they not justly say to us: "You worked upon our passions; you impelled us into rebellion against our landlords; you invoked us in the name of our country and of our religion, and you abandoned us; and, with the means of succour in your power, you refused to stretch out your hands to save us! You told us that we must wait, and that the time was not come, and that the old rent was a sacred fund; you put us off with excuses, and quibbles, and you left us with our wives and children to perish." It is therefore our interest, with a view to preserve the use of the great engine which we have obtained, to strain every nerve in the support of the peasantry. However familiar the citation of the poet's celebrated lines may be, they cannot be more appropriately applied than to the freeholders of Ireland, and we may justly say,—

"A bold yeomanry, their country's pride,
"When once destroyed, can never be supplied."

The peculiar applicability of the quotation rescues it from the triviality of common place. Never, indeed, can the spirit which has been awaked be supplied, if once we allow it to be extinguished. If the flame which has been raised through this country be once put out, every effort to rekindle it will be idle. But let it be only kept alive, and how noble and wide an illumination will it diffuse. How admirable will be the results upon the moral character of the people? With a sense of independence they will acquire that sense of dignity which is the source of virtue; and the meanest in the country—

"Will learn to venerate himself a man."

That high consciousness of their personal and political rights, which imparts so much elevation to the character of the English people, will grow up amongst them. They will no longer bow down before their landlords as if they were not compounded out of the same earth, and were not to be tried by the same God. Those exhibitions of degrading tyranny, which are so dishonourable to human nature, will no longer appear, and the aristocracy of Ireland will be themselves participators in the great national improvement. The representation of the country will be thoroughly reformed, and no man whose claims do not rest upon public virtue, will take his seat in the House of Commons. Catholic Emancipation is not the only measure which would result from this glorious liberation of the people, but a new principle would be grafted upon the government, and a fresh supply of life and vigour would be infused into the constitution. These are splendid, but not visionary projects. Their realization depends to a great extent upon the course which we ourselves adopt. Not an instant ought to be lost in affording them assistance. It would be cruel and inhuman to bid them look to the new Catholic rent, and let months pass over their heads without relief. Wait till November, indeed! Alas! their distresses are at present sufficient to excite our commiseration, without waiting for the additional incentive to compassion which would be given by the winter wind. The spectacle of calamity which is already exhibited is sufficiently moving to awaken our sensibility, and we ought not to tarry until the rain shall descend on their beds of straw, and the storm shall howl through their hovels, and their naked children shall stand shivering in groups of misery, with frozen hands and faces, at their doors. Is there a man amongst us who, with such an anticipation of calamity before his mind, and who forms even the faintest image of the wretchedness of these poor people, will hesitate for an instant to fly to their relief? ' What! shall we permit these miserable wretches and their families to be turned out of their habitations without fire, or food, or raiment? Shall we allow them to be cast forth to the mercy of the elements, and to be flung upon the public way to die? I put it to myself—I made use of every effort which I could employ to induce the peasantry to rebel against their landlords in the county of Louth. If, in the course of the succeeding winter, I should have occasion to pass through that county, and I should meet a wretched man with his family in the public road, how should I feel, if, after asking him what could have brought him to such a pass, he told me, that " he was a forty-shilling freeholder, that he had voted for the country, and that the country had left him on the road—that he did not care for himself, but that when he looked upon his children, and on the mother of them, his heart was broken, and that the Association had desired him to wait for the new rent, and to starve upon a point of law?" Let me not be accused of exaggeration. Instead of heightening the pictures of distress by any fictitious colouring, I have no pencil with which I can do justice to the melancholy reality. You will hear from the worthy clergymen who are at present in this meeting, how much has already been suffered, and how much, it is probable, must be still endured. In the name of every generous and honourable feeling—for the sake, not only of the poor freeholders, but for your own sakes, and as you value your own dignity and character, and prize the future independence of your country, come forward, and by one simultaneous exclamation, signify your assent to a measure which will not only have the effect of rescuing the peasantry from ruin, but of rescuing your own character from ignominy and disgrace. Do it in the name of justice—do it in the name of humanity—do it in the name of Ireland, and I trust I do not take his name in vain, when I say, do it in the name of God.

WEALTH OF THE ESTABLISHED CHURCH.

SPEECH ON THE WEALTH OF THE ESTABLISHED CHURCH, AT THE CATHOLIC ASSOCIATION.

I GAVE notice that I should move an humble address to the Archbishops, Bishops, Deans, Archdeacons, and other functionaries of the church, respectfully submitting to their consideration the anti-apostolic condition of the Establishment, and praying them, with a view to their own salvation, to reduce their wealth within the dimensions of Christianity and to some correspondence with the precepts of that holy book, of which they so zealously propagate the diffusion. I am not prepared to move the address to-day, for having drawn a rough draft of it, I transmitted it to a friend of mine, a curate of the Established Church, who has seventy-five pounds a-year, and a family of ten children. He ought to have slept with a copy of Malthus under his pillow, instead of taking a beautiful pauper, who is endowed with a desperate fecundity, to his arms. I really thought that this amiable gentleman would in all likelihood, see the opulence of the sacred aristocracy of the church in a strong light, and upon that account I sent him the address, in order that I might have the benefit of his poignant emendations. As I am upon my legs, it may not be inappropriate that I should mention what it was that induced me to engage in this adventurous, but not, I trust, utterly hopeless undertaking. I, not very long ago, received a letter from an old acquaintance of mine, one Anthony Pasquin, who beguiled the leisure which illness had inflicted upon him, by reading Paley's admirable book on the evidence of Christianity. Although in Anthony Pasquin's letter, subjects of a solemn nature are rather lightly treated, you will find much seriousness lurking underneath his spirit of sardonic mirth. He gives variety to a trite topic by the fantastic shape in which he presents it. We are told by Plutarch, that a banquet was once provided by a celebrated epicure, consisting of an immense variety of dishes, but that the whole was made up of pork, which had been cooked after different fashions. The church is like the pork that supplied the materials of this variegated feast, and admits of dressing in an infinite diversity of ways. God forbid, however, that I should insinuate that any of the dignitaries of the Establishment offered the comparison to my fancy, or that I should exclaim at the sight of one of them, "*Epicuri de grege porcus.*" I return to the letter of Mr. Anthony Pasquin, which is in the words following:—

"I have been lately reading Paley's celebrated work. That portion of it particularly struck me, in which he enlarges on his fundamental proposition, 'that there is satisfactory evidences that many professing to be original witnesses of the Christian miracles, passed their lives in labours, dangers, and sufferings, voluntarily undergone, in attestation of the accounts which they delivered, and solely in consequence of their belief of those accounts—and that they also submitted, from the same motives, to new rules of conduct.' The exact correspondence between the lives of the first propagators of the religion of poverty and of humility, with their precepts, is the main argument on which Paley rests his assertion, that they were firmly convinced of the truths which they were appointed to announce. It would, indeed, have been a reasonable interference that they were impostors, if, while they were inculcating the worthlessness of temporal wealth and power, they were revelling in the enjoyments of the world, which they affected to despise. Paley therefore, has laboured to establish, that their lives did not afford a practical refutation of their doctrines, and he has completely succeeded in showing that their conduct coincided with the injunctions which are conveyed in their celestial ethics. He well observes, 'I do not know that it has ever been insinuated, that the Christian mission in the hands of the Apostles, was a scheme for making a fortune or getting money.' The Christians, we are told by St. Paul, 'knew in themselves, that they had in heaven a better and an enduring substance.' It is not only in the writings of the inspired emissaries of Christianity that proofs of their scorn for gold are to be found. So late as the time of Lucian, (we are told by him) 'the Christians had a sovereign contempt for all the things of the world.' After the perusal of Paley, I took up Southey's 'Book of the Church,' the reading of which, together with his letter to Charles Butler, operated as an opiate, and put me into a profound sleep. Queen Mab was at my bedside, and wherefore should 'the midwife to the fancy' not visit me in my dreams, when she approaches more venerable personages—when 'with a tithe-pig's tail,' she comes—

'Tickling a Parson's nose, as he lies asleep—
'Then dreams he of another benefice.'

Whether she ever played these pranks with the Apostles; whether she tickled the noses of St. Peter or St. Paul, with a tithe-pig's tail, I leave it to my lords, the bishops, to conjecture. The perusal of Paley, not unnaturally, led me back to the period on which he had expatiated. I say, that this was not unnatural, but refer it to Mr. Carmichael, the partner of Mr. William Kemmis, of the crown office, and the author of a very ingenious essay upon the cause of dreams, which is published in the transactions of the Royal Irish Academy. That able metaphysician will, I hope, avail himself of the many opportunities which he has had of approaching the attorneys-general for the last twenty years, and will, in a note to the next edition of his work, apprise us, whether Mr. Saurin ever dreamed of being put out of office? Whether Lord Plunkett ever dreamed of being successor to Lord Norbury? or whether Mr. Joy—but with that gentleman's dreams I dare not meddle, but piously hope, that I am not among their objects? But let that pass—and to speak with the gravity which becomes the matter, 'in the visions of the night, when the sleep falleth upon men,' as Sergeant Lefroy would express it, I thought that I was living at the period of which I had been reading, when, some years after the death of Tiberius, Christianity was in the midst of persecution making a rapid way. I saw (here Mr. Anthony Pasquin becomes serious—for he can be so when it is meet)—I saw the inspired and lofty-minded men, to whom the great office of illuminating mankind had been committed, go forth from Palestine, and proclaim in the metropolis of the world, as the heralds of heaven, the eternal truths, of which they were the repositories. I saw them in the calm and unostentatious courage, derived from the assurance of immortality, look upon death and the torments which preceded it, without dismay. But what struck me far more than the meek heroism of endurance, was their exemplification of the divine philosophy, of which they were the professors, in the simplicity of their deportment, in the humility of their mild demeanour, in their spirit of benevolence and of mercy, in their abstinence and self-denial, in their utter contempt of riches, and in the fixedness of their regards upon those objects of everlasting interest, to which their eyes and hearts were unremittingly exalted. They did not reside in gorgeous palaces, while they instructed their followers in the wisdom of poverty and the usefulness of sorrow. Their lessons of humility were not announced from the porticoes of princes—it was not from the banquet-hall that they issued their ordinances of abstinence; nor did they, from the primrose path of luxury, point to the steep and thorny road to heaven. I saw no train of pampered minions in their retinue—I beheld no mitres upon the chariots in which they had journeyed from Jerusalem to Rome. I saw no 'bench of bishops' in the senate. I did not see their wives and daughters tripping it through the mazes of a Roman quadrille, or whirling in the arms of some brawny ensign of the Prætorian guard, through the evolutions of an Ionic waltz, and verifying Horace's description of the amusement of an Italian virgin—

> Motus doceri gaudet Ionicus
> Matura virgo, et fingitur artubus.'

I did not see the apostles and their followers turning Christianity into a domestic convenience, making the church of God a receptacle of conjugal endearment—making priests of their sons, and the wives of priests of the young ladies. Neither did I hear anything of running a bishop's life against a lease, or of a bishop executing a renewal and touching ten thousand pounds on his death-bed, when he was about to render an account of his ministry, and to stand in the dreadful sight of the living God. I heard nothing of tithes, and vestries, and cesses. I saw no ecclesiastical courts, no metropolitans, no surrogates, no ministers, no civil bills, no proctors, no distrainings, no executions, no sales of blankets, no auctions of beds of straw, 'in the name of him who died;' no trial before one priest of the corporate interests of another. I did not see the people indignant at any system of rapacity carried on under the auspices of the Divine Author of religion, and the road to heaven converted into a sort of Bagshot-heath, where the ministers of Christ claim a kind of prescriptive right to sacerdotal spoliation. There was, indeed, one individual who suggested a singular project. His name was Simon Magus. This fellow proposed to establish a mining company, declaring that he had discovered a rich vein of gold under the barren rocks of Mount Calvary. But the proposition was indignantly rejected. You are aware that dreams are proverbially capricious—

> The children of an idle brain
> Begot of nothing but vain fantasy.'

It was under this strange influence that was I suddenly transferred to a very different period. Queen Mab shifted the scene of the puppet show, which is played in a dreamer's head. I thought that all at once I posted from Rome to London—and leaped over whole tracts of centuries in a single bound. It was, perhaps, owing to my reading of Southey's 'Book of the Church,' together with Paley's Evidences, that this immense transition was instantaneously effected, and I stood at the outside of Saint Stephen's Chapel. Here a new spectacle presented itself. There came rattling down Palace-yard a series of splendid carriages, with mitres upon their panels—and which were drawn by horses superbly caparisoned, and conducted by portly charioteers, placed upon lofty seats, with laced cocked hats upon their heads, overtopping tremendous periwigs, while a profusion of golden epaulettes depended from the shoulders of these pampered slaves. When I saw them at a distance, I took these vehicles for the carriages of the great, the noble, and the princely of the land. Judge, then, of my astonishment when, as they approached, and drew up with an awful clatter at the portico of the House of Lords, I beheld the twelve apostles dressed in lawn sleeves, together with the early fathers of the church, with St. Paul at their head. 'In sooth, gentlemen,' I exclaimed, 'you are amazingly changed since I saw you last.' I was particularly struck with St. Paul—at first he looked like the picture of the apostle, in Raphael's immortal cartoon, where he is represented as announcing to the Athenians 'the unknown God.' But gradually, as Lord Byron says, in his description of a common incident in dreaming—

'I thought his face
'Faded, or altered into something new.'

And while he inquired whether he had arrived in time to vote against his old friend Lord Plunkett, and the Catholic question, as he tripped with a rapid and elastic step, and an airy and flippant deportment, in place of St. Paul, I beheld one of his successors in the venerable person of Doctor Magee." It is unnecessary that I should read any more of my friend, Anthony Pasquin's correspondence. It is enough to say, that its contents put me upon a train of thinking, by which I was induced to propose an address to the archbishops, bishops, deans, archdeacons, (*et hoc genus omne*) imploring of them to furnish the same evidences of the truth of the Christian religion, which, according to Paley, were supplied by their predecessors, and, to use the words of St. Clement, as quoted by that eminent divine, " to put before their eyes the *holy apostles*." I shall select an early opportunity of laying the address before you, and as henceforward I intend to dedicate a good deal of my attention to the spiritual improvement of the Establishment, I shall probably publish the speeches which I shall deliver on the subject, in a volume, which, in humble imitation of Mr. Southey I shall entitle " the Book of the Irish Church."

HIBERNIAN BIBLE SOCIETY.

SPEECH DELIVERED AT CORK, AT A MEETING OF THE HIBERNIAN BIBLE SOCIETY.

Mr. SHEIL asked whether he, a stranger, might be permitted to make some observations on what he had heard

The CHAIRMAN said—This, Sir, is a meeting of the Members and Friends of the Society —If you are a friend to the Society you are entitled to speak.

Mr. SHEIL said—Then, Sir, in one sense, I am a friend to the Society, and I shall evince it by an act of substantial friendship, in venturing to give you some honest, though it may possibly be mistaken advice. Mr. Sheil said, that when the former meeting was held, to which a gentleman had adverted, he was not in Cork, and upon that account he ought not to be considered as an overweening intruder upon their deliberations. They should not shrink from discussion if it was carried on in a fair and mitigated spirit. The meeting was called a private one—but it exhibited singular evidences of privacy in the numbers by which it was attended. It concerned the public; a great national question was involved in the proceedings, and it was one by which the interests of the whole community were affected. He should studiously avoid giving offence to the religious sentiments of the ardent and lovely theologians whom he saw assembled around him. We should survey the subject, than which none was more awfully important, with minds pure, unprejudiced, unimpassioned, standing as it were upon an eminence, in the unclouded atmosphere of heaven, while the mists and storms of the world were passing unheeded beneath us. He regretted that some observations had fallen from those who preceded him, which reflected upon the creed of the Irish people. At no time were controversial disputations well calculated to promote the real interests of Christianity, and they were peculiarly ill-adapted to the fair auditory whom he had risen to address. The religion of a woman ought to be an impassioned meekness, and that sweet spirit which was typified by the dove, should spread its wings upon them. While he entreated their forbearance, and that pity for human error that was akin to the love of heaven, he should take care not to abuse their indulgence. He had heard Mr. Noel with pleasure. He had given proof of high intellectual acquirements, and there was in his zeal an internal evidence of sincerity. In one sense only was he an impostor, by practising a delusion upon himself. The honourable gentleman, and his Caledonian associate, who had manifested so much anxiety for the spiritual welfare of the Irish people, and who was not only a Scotsman but a Captain, deserved much praise for the motives which had induced their religious excursion. The nautical divine had combined the enthusiasm of his profession with the characteristic sagacity of his country. Mr. Noel had pathetically lamented the moral degradation and utter wretchedness of the Irish people, and attributed both to the absence of Scriptural education. Without comparing him to an empiric, who would fain apply his own favourite remedy to every disease, he should remind him that the misery of Ireland arose from a vast variety of causes. The honourable gentleman had just come from a country whose prosperity was the accumulation of a thousand years. On the other hand, the wretchedness of Ireland was the produce of as many centuries of calamity. He who was familiar with the luxuries of the English cottage, naturally shrunk from the miseries of the Irish hovel. He (Mr. Sheil) would ask whether the vast diffusion of wealth, the extent of commerce, the number of manufactures and the equality of the people, had produced the riches and the happiness of England; or whether her unparalleled greatness was all owing to the reading of the Scriptures without note or comment? Had centuries of iniquitous misrule accomplished nothing in the work of misery, of degradation, and of guilt? If the honourable gentleman were better acquainted with Ireland, he would soon perceive that it is upon the higher classes that his religious labours ought to be bestowed This amiable itinerant would, in the course of his sacred peregrinations, soon discover that it was not in the smoke of the hovel, but in the blaze of the banquet, that the precepts of the Gospel ought to be enforced. He would endeavour to impart the practical spirit of Christianity to the barbarous aristocracy of Ireland—to civilize them into pity—to convince them that their wretched serfs are made of the same flesh and blood as themselves and belong to the great brotherhood of men. With indigration would he behold the system of merciless exaction adopted by the Irish landlord, which is so widely at variance, not only with the principles upon which the English proprietor deals with his tenant, and with the habits of his own great country, but utterly repugnant to the commiserating spirit of those holy writings, the perusal of which he strenuously inculcated. How would his honest nature be excited, when h. saw the miserable peasant cast, in a winter's night, with his famished and naked children, upon the world? How would his humanity shudder at the scenes of desolation which are daily enacted amongst us? He would then perceive that his pious adjurations ought to be directed to those very men by whom he has been infected with his opinions of our country, and that he should begin by teaching humanity to the rick before he taught polemics to the poor. In the delusion of a benevolent fanaticism, he forgets that the people are less in want of bibles than of bread. God forbid that he (Mr. Sheil) should suggest that the lower orders ought not to receive a religious education. He was of opinion that they should be instructed in the established tenets of their forefathers; that they should be taught, by means adapted to their capacities, the fixed principles of their ancient and venerable faith. Religion is peculiarly necessary to those who, while the opulent find in the pleasures of actual existence, many intense but transitory enjoyments, must look up to heaven for their only consolation. When the poor peasant rises from his bed of misery, he sees in the glories of the morning sun that heers him to his toil by day, and in the infinity of heaven's host that guides him to his home by night, the magnificent attributes of that Being whom the simple and consoling faith of his fathers teaches him to adore. The Roman Catholic faith contains a body of moral precept, as werecalculated to ensure salutary results upon society, as any modern theory in religion; and, although Mr. Noel had said that he was anxious to make Christians of the people, he (Mr. Sheil) hoped that the honourable gentleman would not consider him guilty of any very extravagant assumption, when he ventured to insinuate to him, that a Roman Catholic might, peradventure, be a Christian. Ireland was a Roman Catholic country, and Mr. Noel, if really anxious to diffuse education, would take into account the peculiar circumstances, the habits, and pre-disposition of the people, in considering the means best adapted to the attainment of that great object. The general perusal of the Bible without any interpretation, was in accordance, perhaps, with the desultory and capricious genius of the Protestant religion; but, in Ireland, there exists a ?reed utterly incompatible with that wild freedom of opinion, and which is so determinate and fixed, as to leave no field for the exercise of individual judgment in the construction of the Word of God. The Roman Catholic faith is built upon the Scriptures, as explained by the church and if the lower classes were to peruse them without that explanation upon which their religion rests, it is not unlikely that they would contract opinions inconsistent with the meaning invariably annexed by Roman Catholics to the Holy Writings. In one word, it is wholly against the principles of that church to turn the Bible into a play-thing for the fancy, and submit it to the gross vagaries and monstrous imagi nations of every loon. The whole dispute narrows itself into a question of fact. Is it, or is it not inconsistent with the spirit of Catholicism? If it be so, there is an end to argument; at least it must be admitted that Roman Catholics are justified in their strenuous opposition to any attempt to subvert their religion Now, who are the persons best qualified to determine that simple fact? One would suppose, that Roman Catholics themselves were as competent to decide the question as those gentlemen who have imported into Ireland a new assortment of curiosities in belief, and seem determined to establish in this country a manufacture of religions. Independently of the objection arising from the essential principles of Catholicism, is it not absurd to make a taskbook of the Testament, and to convert the Apocalypse into a primer? The Scriptures have been referred to, in order to show that it was the will of God that they should be universally perused. For this purpose some isolated texts have been tortured into a meaning which they do not rationally bear, while those who have poured out such a torrent of citation, forget that among the Jews, and under the old law, there were many parts of holy writ which women were never permitted to read, and which men were not allowed to peruse until they had attained the age of thirty years. When Christianity was first established it was impossible that the Scriptures could have been generally read, for the art of printing was not then known, and by no other means than that great modern discovery could an extensive distribution of the Bible be effected. A manuscript of such bulk as the Old and New Testament, must have cost a sum which a primitive Christian cannot be readily supposed to have been capable of procuring, at a period when his poverty was a literal phrase. But let us try the expediency of an indiscriminate perusal of the sacred writings by an appeal to experience. It will scarcely be contended that any great advantage can result from a multifariousness in religion; yet, it will not be denied, that if each individual is entitled to construe the Scriptures, a great variety of interpretation must be the inevitable consequence. In truth, the inventions of art do not keep equal pace with the discoveries in religion. New dogmas are every day propounded to us; they issue with a marvellous fecundity from every visionary brain; nor is it to the wise and the learned that the world is indebted for these fantastic revelations. Those mysterious intimations, which have excited the doubts and baffled the sagacity of the most illustrious of mankind, are now simplified from the summit of a sacred beer-barrel, and from the depth of a holy stall. Every difficulty vanishes before the inspired interpretation of some illuminated Crispin, and the seamless garment of our Saviour is turned inside out by some gifted tailor, who alternately cuts out a religion and a coat. Of these modern prophets one-half are impostors, and the other their own dupes; but whether they be dupes or impostors—Cantwells or Mawworms—or both, (for the union of hypocrisy and fanaticism is not unfrequent,) the consequences to religion, decency, and common sense, are disastrous. The lower classes of the Protestant community are driven into a sort of Biblical insanity by this system of excitation, and madness, now-a-days, almost invariably assumes a religious character. He would state a singular fact of the lunatics in the asylum in this city, which he had lately visited—there were a great number whose mental malady was connected with religion, and amongst those who laboured under that peculiar insanity, there was not a single Catholic. This circumstance was stated by the benevolent physician who superintends the hospital, and who seems animated by the philanthropic feelings of a Howard, in his very able work on insanity, and that gentleman himself was a strenuous Protestant. How could this fact be accounted for, but by referring it to the fanaticism which the unrestrained perusal of the holy writings had produced? An ignorant man, with a heated imagination, sits down to read the bible; he is told that he is its best interpreter, and is illuminated by a special grace —that special grace is but a lunar beam, and fills his brain with madness. His delirious dreams are taken for the visitation of the Spirit, and the images of insanity for the pictures of heaven. But the Roman Catholic has no field for his invention in belief. He has a clear, an open, and a long trodden path to follow, and plods his way to heaven without wandering through that mazy labyrinth, in which the Protestant enthusiast is left without a clue. He has an ample scope for the affections of the heart, but has little space for the excursions of the fancy. His faith is regulated and certain. He is not cast without a chart or compass upon the vague immensity which religion offers to the mind, but steers his course in a well-known track, by a steady principle—a fixed and unrevolving light. The Protestant embarks in the bible upon a voyage of discovery, while the Roman Catholic makes at once for one great haven, and by an ancient and more familiar route. He had, perhaps, pursued this train of illustration too far, and reluctantly compared the advantages of the two religions; but he thought it right to observe, that what he said was chiefly intended to apply to self-instructed innovators, and not to the members of the Established Church, whose hierarchy was as hostile as the Roman Catholic clergy to the reading of the uninterpreted Scriptures. Before he sat down he should beg leave to make one or two observations on what had fallen from Mr. Kenny, who, like the pleader in Racine's comedy, had begun his oration at the commencement of the world, but had afterwards condescendingly passed to the deluge. That gentleman had discovered in an injunction given to Abraham, a felicitous application to Ireland. Providence must have had the Ladies' Auxiliary Bible School in view in the patriarchal times. He would not attempt to pursue him in his progress from Abraham to Moses—from Moses to King David, and from David down to Timothy; but he would follow him from Jerusalem to Wexford, and beg to observe on the animadversions which he had thought proper to pronounce upon a recent and unfortunate transaction. He meant the trial at Wexford, in which he (Mr. Sheil) had been counsel. The event was deeply to be deplored, but it had been greatly misrepresented. It was utterly untrue that the parents of the child had beheld its immolation. It was sworn by the father, that the crowd was so great that he was prevented from approaching the priest, and that he did not even see what was going on. In the next place, Mr. Kenny had imputed a belief in powers of exorcism to the Roman

Catholic peasantry, as if it resulted from their religion; he (Mr. Sheil) would state a most important fact, sworn to by the principal witnesses for the crown, namely, that Protestants as well as Catholics were present at one of these deplorable instances of human folly, and that a Mrs. Winter and her daughter, both of them Protestants, knelt down, and called on God to assist Father Carroll in working the miracle. Let us not, therefore, charge upon this or upon that creed, occurrences so monstrous and so revolting; let us, rather, in the spirit of humility, grieve while we reflect, that they arise solely from the infirmity of human nature. To attribute to Roman Catholics an exclusive belief in demoniacal possession was most unjust. A Protestant bishop, the celebrated Dr. Warburton, had maintained the doctrine, and it was one for which Scriptural authority might be quoted. He would ask Mr. Kenny, whether the reading of the bible by the lower orders was calculated to remove the common superstition, that persons afflicted with epilepsy are possessed by an evil spirit? Do not the Scriptures narrate many instances of exorcism. It is now held, indeed, that the devil has been deprived of this portion of his prerogative—but surely, a peasant, reading the Scriptures, may readily think that what once was common, is at present not impossible; and besides, this very case furnishes an argument to show, that the Scriptures require a comment; for assuredly, it is necessary that the cessation of Satanic dominion should be explained to the individual who peruses the examples of its former power. So far from thinking that the Scriptures are calculated to disabuse the people of this frightful infatuation, the perusal of them, without a comment, was calculated to confirm their superstition. He regretted that Mr. Kenny had alluded to this painful incident, because, in doing so, he had expressed a detestation for the Catholic religion, which was utterly at variance with the habitual disclaimers of proselytism. If he and those who acted with him, felt so deep an abhorrence for Popery, they could not fail to exert themselves to preserve the people from so disastrous a belief. It could not be credited, that their detestations would not involuntarily ooze out. It was not possible that such a metamorphosis should take place in Mr. Kenny, as that, on one side of the poor man's threshold, he should be a strenuous hater of Popery, but the moment he had entered his habitation, to administer spiritual relief to his children, he should be transubstantiated into an impassionate lover of Catholicity. One advantage had, however, ensued from the honesty of his (Mr. Kenny's) denunciations, and indeed from the whole tone of the proceedings. It was clear, that proselytism was their substantial object, and that education was only an instrument for the accomplishment of this darling project. He begged pardon of the meeting for having so long trespassed upon them, but he was bound to say, that however great their difference of opinion, he had been heard with liberality and kindness. He should not abuse it, by entering at large into another topic, upon which, before women, it might not be delicate to dwell; he alluded to the many passages in Scripture which were written with such force, and he might say with such nakedness of diction, as rendered them unfit for indiscriminate perusal. There were

parts of the Old Testament in which images of voluptuousness were presented to the mind, on which the imagination of a youthful female ought not to be permitted to repose. To those passages he would not of course refer, or point out the forbidden fruit; but he would venture to assert, that the Odes of Anacreon did not display more luxury of imagination, or combine more sensual associations than parts of the Old Testament, the perusal of which, by women, was wisely forbidden by the Jewish Church. It was idle to say, in the language of modern cant, that the grace of God would prevent the passions from taking fire. Our daily orison contains a prayer, founded upon human frailty, that we should be preserved not only from guilt, but even from temptation; and if the passages to which he alluded were unfit for an open citation in that assembly, he could not conceive them to be the appropriate theme of a virgin's meditation. The warm fancy of a young and blooming girl could not venture into the sacred bowers of oriental poetry without peril. Besides the objection arising to the warm colouring of the pastoral of Solomon, which was a mystic representation of the conjugal union of the churches, wherewith unmarried ladies need not be made prematurely familiar, it should be recollected that the Bible contained details of atrocity at which human nature shuddered. Part of the Holy Writings consisted of history and of the narration of facts; some of those facts are of a kind, that they could not be mentioned in the presence of a virtuous woman without exciting horror. Should a woman be permitted to read in her chamber, what she would tremble to hear at her domestic board? and shall her eyes be polluted with what her ears shall not be profaned? Shall she read what she dares not hear? Shall she con over, and revolve, what she would rather die than utter? But these were painful topics—they were forced into debate by those who, in their anxiety to annihilate the religion of the country, forgot the risk to which its morality was exposed. And what good could the achievement of this object after all effect? In ceasing to be Catholics, were they certain that the people would continue Christians? Let this absurd scheme be abandoned—let the Irish peasant live and die in the religion of his forefathers, and let the propagators of modern dogmas, who send their missionaries amongst us, remember the denunciation in St. Matthew—
"Woe unto you, ye Scribes, ye Pharisees, ye hypocrites! ye compass the sea and earth to make a single proselyte, and when you have made him, he is two-fold more a child of hell than before."

PROSECUTION OF MR. O'CONNELL.

SPEECH AT THE ASSOCIATION, WHEN THE PROSECUTION OF MR. O'CONNELL, FOR SEDITIOUS LANGUAGE, PREVENTED THE INTENDED DEPUTATION TO ENGLAND.

Mr. SHEIL said, the deputation to England, would not have been without avail. The English are a wise, a generous, and lofty-minded people, and we should have appealed to their wisdom, to their justice, and to their humanity. We should have disabused them of many mistakes

—we should have demonstrated to them, that we are not unworthy of being incorporated in the great community of British citizenship—that our political ethics are much better than they had been taught to think —that there is no dogma in our religion which renders us unfit for the enjoyment of civil freedom—that our creed is the faith of their great progenitors—and that in casting contumely upon our opinions, they stamp damnation upon their father's graves. We should have told them that the Barons of Runnemede were as good citizens as the Lords of Chancery-lane, and that the sword with which Magna Charta was won, might be weighed against Lord Eldon's mace. We should have told them that the part which they have acted towards our country, reflects no credit upon them in the eyes of mankind—that having the excellence of gigantic strength, they should not use it in the spirit of gigantic domination—that liberty is like light, and is not impaired by its participation—that the disfranchisement of seven millions of British subjects cannot fail to be productive of great calamities—that we are placed in an unnatural, and therefore an injurious relation towards the empire ; and that it befits their dignity to interpose between the contending factions by which the country is torn asunder—that they had too long turned our furious contentions into sport ; and that it is unworthy of them to sit, like the spectators of a Roman theatre, at a gladiatorial exhibition of their slaves, and make a pastime of the ferocious passions with which they are arrayed against each other in all the insolence of inglorious triumph, and all the wildness of infuriated despair. We should have told them that, by a single act of magnanimous justice, they might put an end to the animosities which have cost so much English and Irish blood—that our emancipation would be an act of thrift, as well as of humanity ; and that it became their prudence, as well as the grandeur of their national character, and that it is a matter of economy as well as of honour, to make us free. "Reconcile us," we should have exclaimed," as you are wise—as you are just, redress us—and in the name of mercy rescue us from our own passions, and save us from the consequences to which your system of shame and of penalty must inevitably lead"—and what are those consequences? If they were no other than an increase of those heart-burnings and animosities, that must either rapidly augment or be instantaneously remedied by a great senative act of legislative wisdom, their anticipation, (and it requires but little of the spirit of political soothsaying to foretell results so manifest) should excite the virtue, if it does not awaken the alarm of every honest and enlightened man, and enlist the good sense and good feeling of the whole British community in our behalf. Things cannot stand as they are. Either a great national reconciliation must be effected, or hostilities must be deepened—reciprocal antipathies must be strengthened—new force and activity must be communicated to the popular passions—and if the fountain of bitterness is not sealed, it must be supplied. Are we to continue for ever in this frightful state? Are we to be everlastingly marshalled against each other by the infuriating provocations of the law? · Are we to be set with a rabid and canine fury upon each other? Are our detestations to be endowed with a dis astrous immortality? Is our hatred to be eternal? Is the corroding sentiment which consumes the bosom, and preys upon the vitals of our country, to be like "the fire that is not quenched, and the worm that dieth not?" Are we to be doomed to an everlasting execration of each other and when the present generation shall have passed away, are our children to rise out of their cradles with the same feelings with which their fathers descended into their graves? If there were no other calamity to be apprehended, this evil should be regarded as a dreadful one. But there are other results, which every wise man can foresee, and at which every good man must tremble. May God forefend that we should be instrumental in bringing events about, the thought of which sends back the blood into the heart! But is it because those events are terrible that we should clasp our hands to our eyes and hide them from ourselves? Is it because the shadows which coming events "have cast before them" are black and sinister, that we should fear to trace their dark and sombre outline? For ourselves we may be able to answer: we may vouch for our continued endurance of affliction; but can we give pledges for the prostration of those who are to come after us, and undertake that our descendants will be the heirs to our patience, as well as the inheritors of our wrongs? We cannot enter into any such recognizance. But this we can do,—we can protest that we shall omit no endeavour to prevent the feelings of anguish from being turned into a paroxysm of wild and frantic rage, and try to keep back those ebullitions of national emotion, which it is not less our interest than it is our bounden duty to restrain, and which, for a considerable period, are not likely to burst out. We have been accused (it is right that I should speak the unvarnished truth) of entertaining designs of a revolutionary tendency. The men who have adduced this charge proved it to be untrue—but there are many who may be misguided by their calumnies; and as we are the martyrs of intolerance, there are others who, in forming an estimate of our intentions, may be the victims of mistake. There are three tests by which our designs may be reasonably tried—our language, our conduct, and our personal interests—and to any one of these grounds of presumption we may fearlessly appeal. Our language has been uniformly moderate, conciliatory, and pacific in all the public documents which have issued from our body. The measures which we have adopted have been in accordance with the views of the local government, and we have omitted no means to inculcate the propriety of subordination to the law and the constituted authorities of the country: witness the resolutions passed at the last aggregate meeting, and the address of Mr. O'Connell to the people of Ireland. But there is a further and more accurate touchstone of the motives of men to be found in their obvious interest, and I will venture to assert, that he amongst us who could deliberately premeditate a political convulsion, must be insane. I do not hesitate to declare that, in my judgment, the individual who could for a moment entertain a scheme so preposterous, should be accounted a sanguinary idiot, and much fitter for an asylum than a gaol. There would not be a chance of success to redeem the crime of such an undertaking. Human life would be wasted without bounds and without avail. Carnage would be loaded with all the guilt of inutility, and flame would light the sky and massacre wet the earth, and hope could not put in its equivocal apology, or afford its dubious extenuation of outrage of dishonour and blood. I do not mean to say that if I had been born a Portuguese, I should not have enlisted under the banners of Braganza. Where is the Greek, with a heart in his bosom, who would not "take by the throat and smite the circumcised dogs?" Where is the Mexican that would not exclaim that the land of Montezuma should be free? But the efforts that were noble and just in Portugal, and in America, and in Mexico, or in Greece, derived their nobleness and their justice from the probabilities of success which consecrates and canonizes all great political undertakings. In Ireland the rebel against the law would revolt against nature. Providence appears to have pre-ordained the junction of the two countries; and without arms, without organization, without concert, with nothing but an undisciplined multitude for the accomplishment of this object, what would the leader of a rebellion expect to achieve? And where is he—where is the Cataline, or rather the Spartacus, who is to head this servile war? Is he to be found among the wealthy burghers of the metropolis? or are we to seek the great disturber among the bishops of the Association? Is the primate to convert his mitre to a casque, and his pastoral staff to a pike? or is it my Lord Kenmare, with his fifty thousand a year, who is to shake the dire dice-box in this desperate game, and commit himself to the hazard of revolutionary confisca- tion? But, perhaps, it is among the lawyers that this regenerator is to be found—

"Loud in debate, and bold in peaceful council,
But of a slow, inactive hand in war."

The lawyers! It might as well be imagined that we would pull down the dome of the Four Courts on our heads, as to subvert a government, in whose ruins we could not fail to perish. Is it not as notorious as that there is light in the heavens, that we, and every man who has raised his voice in this assembly, must be blown away on the first explo- sion of a mine, to the train of which they tell us that we are about to apply the match? Mr. O'Connell excite the people to commotion! Has he "eaten of the insane root?"—is he utterly delirious?—has he been struck with political lunacy?—is he, in a word, stark mad? Who is Mr. O'Connell? Is he a man without station, rank, or fortune? Has he nothing to lose, and everything to gain from a political convul- sion? Is he without the enjoyments that make men cling to life—make them in love with peace, and give them an endearing interest and a tender solicitude in the tranquillity of their country? Is it his ambition to drive the vessel against the rock, that, when it is breaking up, he may catch at a single plank, which he could only hold but for a moment, and which would be washed away from him by the next breaker that should burst upon his head? Gracious God! what feelings would they attribute to him? Has he no home—no character—no stay—no child? "He," says Lord Bacon, "that hath children gives hostages to the law;" and where is the man that has a single touch of the parental instincts about his heart, who would not recoil from a desperate contest into which, with his own existence, he would have to plunge the dearest portion of himself? So much for the man to whom, by the general suffrage of his country, the leadership of its people has been assigned. But are the people disposed to rebellion? The pitch cap and the triangle are formidable mnemonics. They know that the first insurrectionary movement would be followed by the re-enactment of scenes of which they have had a terrible experience. They have not forgotten the shrieks of torture, the reverberation of the whip, the bursting bowels, the scorched forehead, and the lacerated back. The spectre of Fitzgerald stalks through the land. The cries of Wright are still ringing in their ears. They hear the screams of the victim and the torturer's laugh. They still hear the groans that issued from the riding-house and the castle-yard—groans to which Castlereagh was deaf, but that were heard in heaven. There is in these recollections a terrible admonition. The people recoil from the gulf to which the Orange faction would impel them; but if the people shrink from every revolutionary enterprise, are they to suppress their complaints? Are our hearts compounded of different materials from the rest of mankind? "Hath not the Jew eyes?" says Shylock. Hath not the Catholic eyes, hands, organs, affections, senses, passions, as the Protestant hath?— Fed with the same food, hurt with the same weapons, healed by the same means, warmed and cooled by the same winter and summer, as the Protestant is? If you tickle us, shall we not laugh—if you poison us, shall we not die—if you torture us, shall we not bleed—and if you wrong us, shall we not——Revenge is Shylock's word; but I will only ask, shall we not complain?

COURSE TO BE ADOPTED BY CATHOLICS.

SPEECH, IN TRACING THE FUTURE COURSE TO BE ADOPTED BY THE CATHOLIC BODY.

I HOLD in my hand the names of sixteen gentlemen, resident in the County Galway, whom I beg to propose as members of the Association. Lord French, who has recently distinguished himself by a valuable manifestation of political zeal, is at their head, and I am assured by my friend Mr. Power, who has requested me to propose this list, that every Catholic of respectability in the county would unite with us, had not a report gone abroad that we had last week adjourned our meetings until November. In November, when the proceedings of the Association will have been resumed, our assemblies will exhibit an object as imposing as was ever presented by that body, of which we are regarded by many as the substantial image. We have already obtained a powerful hold upon public opinion, and may justly boast that the representatives of the many classes of our community have enrolled themselves in this new corporation for the benefit of Ireland. We have two archbishops at our head. You, my Lord Gormanstown, preside in that chair. My Lord Killeen stands beside you, and his noble father (noble in every sense of the word, which, when applied to him, carries a better signification than it bears in the Herald's office) has this day given us a proof of his continued devotion to that cause of which he has so long been the useful ornament. Some of the wealthiest and most influential merchants and agriculturists in Ireland are at this moment here. They who anticipate a failure of this important experiment, labour under a great delusion. The public feeling has already been declared in our favour, and if, even at this season, when Dublin is emptied of half its population, and the persons who habitually take the most active part in our proceedings, are necessarily absent, we assemble as numerously as the retainers of the minister at the close of a session of Parliament, it may be reasonably expected that in November the same zeal, force, and energy will be displayed as were formerly evinced, and that in place of dissolving in its own weakness, the new Association must perish by another and more efficient law, than the fatal enactment by which our advocates have, if I may so say, banished their clients out of court.— Thank God that they have not succeeded in paralysing the energies of the Irish people, and that the same determined spirit prevails through the whole mass of the Catholic population. Of that feeling I have had myself some noble evidences. In Wexford, the theatre of so many frightful scenes, there exists a sentiment as vivid and as intense as if its inhabitants had never been the peculiar witnesses of the disasters of their country. So far from being deterred from the performance of their political duties by those calamities in which they bore so large a part, they appear to feel that Catholic Emancipation is the only effectual preventive of their recurrence. The assembly which was held in Wexford, exhibited more enthusiasm than I have ever observed in any public meeting. It presented a most noble and admonitory spectacle, and derived from the associations with which it could not fail to be attended, an awful, and I may, perhaps, call it an appalling impressiveness. "How long," I said to myself, as I surveyed that accumulation of human visages burning with intense emotion, "how long will the cabinet of England continue to foment the passions that are raging in that vast body of bold, devoted, and enthusiastic men?" It is to be lamented, that in the midst of so much high and generous feeling, there has been an omission upon the part of the Catholics to adopt the practical means of enforcing their claims, and that by neglecting to register their freeholds, a risk has been incurred that Lord Stopford may be again returned to Parliament. I called on Cæsar Colclough, who was at the meeting which I have described, to oppose him. I invoked him by his brother's grave; the adjuration was vain. He shed tears, indeed, but refused to stand the contest. I then applied to Mr. Chichester, who, despite of his being son-in-law to my Lord Anglesea, is a friend to Ireland. Of Mr. Chichester I augur well. He professed in a manly and unaffected tone his conviction of the necessity of Emancipation, and gave intimation if he did no more, of his disposition hereafter to offer himself as a candidate. Lord Stopford may hold the county for the next session, but it is impossible that he should permanently retain it. In Waterford, a most valuable feeling has sprung up. Villiers Stuart must be returned; Lord Waterford has effectually contributed to his success. Think of the political infatuation of that feeble-minded person; notwithstanding the denunciation of Orange badges by men of all parties, Lord Waterford has recently dressed his own band in orange and blue, and exhibits his musicians, attired in that livery of insult (for such it may be called), in the most conspicuous part of the city from which his title is derived. Is not this the very wantonness of ascendancy; and is it to be wondered that the Catholic serfs of the most puissant and preposterous Marquis, should revolt from their allegiance, and obeying the dictates of their consciences and every instinct of honourable pride, should throw off the yoke of their political villainage! In Kilkenny, (for, my Lord, you will, perceive that I am retracing my progress), a corresponding spirit is universally prevalent. The Protestants of that county have conspired with the Catholics. A petition already signed by eight Protestant peers, and almost all the aristocracy, is in rapid circulation.— The Catholic meeting is attended by the chief gentry of the county, and Butler Clarke may soon have reason to recite the Penitential Psalms in the same doleful tone with which he pronounced his first parliamentary essay against the Association. The meeting at Clonmel was distinguished by the attendance of several able and eloquent ministers of our religion. The priests who delivered their sentiments upon that occasion, spoke the feelings of the whole body of our clergy; and if there be a circumstance peculiarly auspicious, it is, I think, the energetic sympathy which the priesthood have manifested in the national cause. I have, my Lord, upon former occasions, expressed my conviction, that it is principally through the instrumentality of the clergy that the rights and power of the Catholics will be presented to the English people in a just light, and, in my judgment, I cannot too frequently revert to this important topic. It is clear, that we must resort to other expedients besides those which we have hitherto adopted. In order to advance the question it is not sufficient that we should petition the legislature after our habitual fashion. Something must be done to give it an impulse, and propel it through the mind of the English people. There must not be a monotony in our call for redress; our question will go round without advancing; we shall revolve in the same dull rotation without being in the least degree progressive. Suppose that we present our usual petition in March next. The measure may pass the Commons, but the same causes which have hitherto contributed to its rejection in the Lords, will still remain in operation. The public ear will become tired by the reiterated burden of Catholic grievances, and in order to excite the popular, and I may add, the legislative interests, we must devise some measure which shall make a great and permanent impression. It is not mere novelty that I am disposed to seek—I look for some expedient which shall at once arrest the attention of the empire, and present the evils of our condition in a light which shall glare upon the public eye. Something must be done at which men will start. Seven millions of British citizens in a state of indignant exasperation; boiling with the fierce passions which shame and wrong produced; animated by a single and undivided sentiment, and moving with a common, and, I trust it will eventually prove, an irresistible impulse; this is a great object, and such a spectacle should not be presented under any ordinary view. It is not a mere annual debate in Parliament, returning in wearisome succession, and bequeathed by one expiring session to the next, which becomes a crisis like the present. What, then (I return to the interrogation), what shall be done to strike a blow upon the English mind? I think that a great instrument of political effect lies in our reach. It is no visionary scheme—no idle and fantastic speculation; we need but stretch forth our hand to grasp it. I propose, my Lord, that the secretary of this Association do forthwith insert in an official book, to be kept for the purpose, the name and the address of every parish priest in Ireland; and that a letter be addressed to each of them, requesting their co-operation in the objects which the Association have in view. Thus an individual intercourse with every parish priest in Ireland will be established, and we shall have an active and powerful agent in every parochial subdivision of the country:—we shall thus obtain a series of conductors, through which the feeling which we are solicitous to circulate, will be readily conveyed. From one extremity of the land to the other, a regular and uniform communication will be set on foot, through the Catholic priesthood, and a great national agency will be established. This being effected, a general census of the population may be taken in a week, and what is still more important, that population may be organised into supplication, and disciplined in what I may call the tactics of petitioning. Hitherto we have been desultory and irregular in our movements; one county petitioned and another did not; and there was no accordance in time or place, nor any simultaneous movement of the national mind. We must learn to kneel down together; we must learn how to perform this universal genuflection. On the same day, and at the same hour, a meeting must be held, under the direction of the parish priest, in every parish chapel in Ireland. Offer to yourselves, in anticipation, the effect of such a proceeding. If the people of Ireland meet on the first of January, 1826, in their respective houses of worship, and send a common cry for liberty from the altars of God, will not that cry reach into the cabinet—make its way to the throne—echo through the chambers of Westminster, and make—even Eldon start? Two thousand three hundred petitions, signed upon two thousand three hundred altars, and rushing at the same instant into the councils of the legislature, may not excite alarm, but cannot be treated with contempt. But I may be asked how can the Association effect all this? I answer, the Association is not to effect *all* this. We have no right to petition for the redress of grievances, but we are entitled, by a special clause, to promote education. We shall array the clergy for an end which is perfectly legal, and when they shall once have been marshalled—when once the political apparatus shall have been prepared, it will be the office of another Association, which shall sit for fourteen days, (the period allowed by law) to make use of the instruments with which they will have been provided, and to turn the means which we devise for the attainment of one object, into the achievement of another. It is for us to plant the tree of knowledge—it is for others to graft liberty upon it. We assemble the people to give them instruction. Finding them assembled, it will be for others to point out the way to freedom. This brings me to the third expedient to which I have adverted. By the law, as it stands, an association for the redress of grievances may exist for fourteen days. The law itself has given us a useful intimation. I thank Mr. Plunkett for the hint. Much may be done in fourteen days. They will afford a session to the people. Perhaps the brief duration of such a body, as the law permits, will render it still more imposing. An association may be formed which will have as great an effect upon the public mind as the former body, and the exertion necessary for its vigorous sustainment need not be so permanently vigorous. I propose the following plan: Let the hierarchy, the nobility, the chief clergy, the gentry, the great agriculturists, the leading merchants, the Catholic bar, and the members of the professions assemble on the first day of the next session of parliament. This would, indeed, be a national convention, not representing the people, but being, in some measure, the people itself, and containing the essence—the abstract—the very core of the country. It appears to me most easy of accomplishment; indeed, I see no difficulties at all in the way of its achievement. Even if there were great impediments, we should fearlessly and determinately encounter them. "*Possunt quia posse videntur*," is a maxim founded in the depth of our nature; for the confidence of success is almost success itself. When was anything great, or noble, or elevated accomplished by men who made a nice calculation of feasibility? Did the great Carthagenian, when he arrived at the foot of the Alps, draw forth his mathematical instruments to measure the height of Mount St. Bernard above the sea? He rushed at once up the mountain, and burst its rocks with the ardent spirit of his own fiery and aspiring mind. Nothing, I repeat it, great or noble was ever achieved by minute calculators of difficulty; and rightly was it observed by Voltaire, that it is not so much high faculty as determination of character that achieves political success. If there were great obstacles in our progress—though difficulties should be heaped upon each other, and "Alps on Alps arise," we should not be deterred from pursuing the steep and rugged path which should lead to liberty. But, thank God, " the way is clear and open," and we have in reality but few impediments to surmount. I have, my Lord, expressed my opinions, and perhaps at too great length, upon that question which involves so much of our interests. I thought it not inappropriate, that as I conceive the Association should adjourn until November, to sugges' what I regarded as the best plan of future action which the Catholics could adopt, distinguishing between the objects which it is legal on our part, as members of the Association, to pursue, and those ulterior ends for which we may prepare the way, and which it will be the province of a distinct association, founded upon a different principle, and of limited existence, to attain. In the prosecution of those objects the people will lend us their strenuous co-operation. Never was the popular feeling raised to a greater height—never did a nobler and more enthusiastic zeal exist among the people of Ireland. Whatever our antagonists may say, the same deep determination to seek the liberty of the country keeps its pulse in the nation's heart. From one extremity of Ireland to the other, the same pulsation beats with a strong and regular throb. It is not a mere feverish and transitory excitation, but the uniform result of the great circulation of a vital principle, and it may be justly said,

"Spiritus intus alit, totamque infusa per artus
Mens agitat molem, et magno se corpore miscet."

CATHOLIC EMANCIPATION.

SPEECH AT AN AGGREGATE MEETING, HELD IN KILKENNY.

The Honourable PIERSE SOMERSET BUTLER having moved the following resolution:—

"Resolved—That the exasperating exclusion of seven millions of British subjects from the rights and privileges of the Constitution, generates passions which arrest the progress of national improvement, impede the education of the people, prevent the diffusion of British capital, deteriorate the value of property, and render its title insecure; offer an allurement to the enemies of Great Britain, and endanger the stability of the empire."

MR. SHEIL seconded the resolution, and said—Niphon is the largest of the islands of Japan; Ximo is of inferior magnitude. If a traveller were to tell us, (the case is an imaginary one, but I shall be indulged in putting it,) that seven millions of the inhabitants of Ximo were deprived by the legislators of Niphon of the rights of citizens, because they believed in a religion more studded with mystery than the established creed of the larger island; if he told us that one-seventh of the population of Ximo, who professed the idolatry as by law established, enjoyed all the honours and emoluments of the State—that their bonzes possessed one million of acres—that they were supported with one-tenth of the produce of public labour—that their empty pagodas were built at the expense of those who rejected their worship—that the Japanese vestries excluded the infidel from all share in the ecclesiastical taxation—that deep and indignant feelings were generated by this monopoly in the seven millions of Ximoites—that the heir to the empire of Japan had declared an implacable hostility to these degraded millions. If he were, besides, to tell us that the cabinet of China, who were anxious to lower the pride of Japan, had turned their eyes to Ximo, and had calculated upon their co-operation in case a war should ensue—if he were to say that, notwithstanding the danger arising from the disaffection of the Ximoites, the legislators of Japan still obstinately persevered in their system of government, for the sake of the fat and unwieldy bonzes—if, Sir, a traveller were to tell us this, should we not ay that the government of Japan was exceedingly rash in offering outrage to so large a portion of its subjects, and that it must be composed of fatuitous and narrow-minded men? Shall that system, then, be wise in Ireland, which in Ximo would be absurd? And if an Englishman would smile at the prejudices of a constitutionalist of Japan, might we not say—

——————— Mutato nomine, de te
Fabula narratur?

The strange infatuation which presides over the councils of England, will hereafter excite astonishment, and posterity will wonder at the obdurate perseverance with which the legislators of England continued so long to inflame the minds, and administer provocation to the passions of seven millions of men. But, Sir, it is a matter of congratulation, that the prejudices which have hitherto obstructed the progress of political truth are rapidly diminishing. In England the Catholic Question has made great way, and the Protestants of Ireland begin to feel that they are embarked in the same cause as ourselves. I look round, and see almost the whole Protestant aristocracy of this county here. The High Sheriff is attended by the Grand Jury. What does this prove? That the spirit of the resolutions passed at Buckingham House is beginning to pervade the great mass of the Protestant community. The diffusion of this feeling is further evinced by the Protestant petition which is in course of signature amongst you, and to which the names of eight peers are already attached. This wise and generous anxiety for the relief of their Roman Catholic brethren is not confined to this county Among the lower orders of Protestants, it is true, that much bitterness of feeling still continues. They who have no other superiority cling, with a natural tenacity, to the prerogatives of a patrician creed—but the enlightened, the opulent, and the noble, who rest their ascendancy upon a better title, are weary of discord, and call for the pacification of Ireland. They are deeply sensible of the calamities produced by the disfranchisement of a whole people, of which an epitome is expressed in the resolution which I have risen to second. It condenses much political truth. The disqualification of seven millions of British citizens generates passions which arrest the progress of national improvement —prevent the co-operation of the several classes of the community in promoting the national good—interfere with the education of the people —impede the circulation of British capital—deteriorate the value of property, and render its title insecure—offer an allurement to the enemies of Great Britain—and endanger the security of the empire. Is not the progress of national improvement arrested by the dissensions which have been gendered by the Penal Code? The whole mind of Ireland is absorbed by this fatal question. No other topic attracts the popular attention. Arts, science, literature, are all merged in the disastrous interest attending this question. It enjoys a fatal monopoly of the public passions. This is, in itself, a great evil. Instead of co-operating for the purpose of improving the moral and physical condition of the poor—instead of devising the means of diffusing better habits and a sounder morality among them, we direct the whole energy of the country to the attainment of those civil rights, which must precede every scheme for the general melioration of Ireland. If Emancipation were passed, Catholic and Protestant intellect would be combined—we should unite together in a salutary co-operation for the national good. But at present we are kept asunder by the law; and differing on this great subject, by a necessary consequence we cannot agree on any other.— This political separation has greatly retarded the progress of education. The law raises the distinction of sect, and transfers it from religion to instruction. The spirit of party finds its way into the village schoolroom, and the fury of proselytism springs out of political discord. In the recent contests which attended the progress of Messrs. Noel and Gordon through Ireland, the effects of Catholic disqualification were conspicuous. I stood beside the former of those gentlemen, at the second meeting in Cork, and perceiving that he surveyed the great assembly before him with astonishment, and that he wondered at the vehemence of the passions which were displayed upon the question relating to the intellectual improvement of the people, I ventured to suggest to him, that the emotions which he witnessed had a political origin, and that individuals, possessing an influence over the public mind, would not interfere in matters connected with religious disputation, if their political degradation did not give an artificial intensity to their sectarian predilections. He assented to the view which I presented to him, and he afterwards, in a public meeting in England, had the manliness and candour to declare his conviction, that the Penal Code had produced all the ferment, by which his mission from the Bible Society had been accompanied. I do not mean to enter here into any consideration of the points which were then in dispute; all that I mean to suggest is, that the political disfranchisement of the Catholics arrests the progress of public improvement, by arraying the two great bodies of the community into faction, and extending their political animosities to topics which are not naturally connected with them. The resolution which I have seconded proceeds to state, that the circulation of British capital is impeded by the dissensions of the country. This is notoriously true. Irish securities fell with the hopes of Ireland. Capitalists who were prepared to advance enormous sums on mortgages of Irish estates, immediately receded from their contract. British speculation turned away from the country, when the dominion of discord was restored.— Where is the Englishman mad enough to vest his capital in a country which stands upon the verge of convulsion? It is in this view of as much importance to Protestants as to Catholics, that Ireland should be pacified. The resolution states, that the value of property is deteriorated by the dissensions of Ireland. Why should land in England sell at forty years' purchase, and in Ireland at less than twenty? Because the title to property is insecure. This is the country of confiscation, and if a political commotion should take place, what man would stamp his foot upon an acre of ground and say, "this is mine." It is better to speak at once the plain and honest truth. Mr. Canning has lately said, that the foes of Great Britain have fixed their hopes upon Ireland. Now, I ask this simple, but not seditious question: If twenty thousand Frenchmen should land upon our shores, what would be the result? Would the population of Ireland unite with the invader? If Protestants think that they would—if it be barely possible—if there be a risk of an event so terrible—if there are those who believe that in a week one hundred thousand men would start to arms—is it not actual frenzy to keep the national mind in such a state of frightful susceptibility, and to nurture the passions which may give birth to such a tremendous result? "Lead us not into temptation," is the daily prayer which I would address to the minister, and call upon him, with a vehement reiteration to deliver us from this appalling evil). I doubt not that England might succeed in crushing the foreign invader and the intestine foe; but, as defeat would be terrible, victory would be scarcely less awful; the chariot of conquest should roll over heaps of massacre, and when tranquillity was restored, it would be solitude indeed. These events may not take place until the present generation shall have passed away. But is not that a mean and selfish consolation? Do not nature and the heart of man revolt against it? May not the graves in which we shall lie low, be soaked with our children's blood, and the knife of murder, and the grasp of dishonour, be laid on those to whom we have given that life which should be incalculably more precious than our own? Mothers of Ireland, hear this admonition, and clasp your children to your hearts. I feel that I am speaking in bold and impassioned language, but that language from being impassioned is not the less true. There is sk—no one can question it—there must be, then, some sound reason for continuing to incur it. The enemies of Emancipation, they who wish to incur this dreadful chance, reply—the Church must be supported. Suppose that the Church were placed in jeopardy, (and I make the hypothesis for the sake of argument) I put the matter thus; throw the mitres of thirty bishops into one side of the scale, and in the other the liberties of seven millions of people, and which would preponderate? Is it for the sake of the Church that Ireland is to remain distracted, ferocious, poor, ignorant, and oppressed? Is all this weight of national misery to be sustained, in order that some high-priest may continue to burlesque the apostles—that some ecclesiastic parvenu may continue to insult the people with his contumelious epigrams—that he may shoot his poisoned antithesis from behind the altar, through the golden vestment of Rome, and the simple surplice of Geneva, and set off a religion without a church, against a church without a religion?—is it that he may rebuke the peers of England, as well as insult the Catholics of Ireland, and that dressed in a "brief authority," and a purple surtout, he may continue to perform his sacerdotal antics, and "make the angels weep,"—or is it that we may behold the "Castle of Indolence" turned into truth, and the voluptuous fancy of the poet embodied in a living exemplification of

---------- "A man of God
Who has a roguish twinkle in his eye—
If a tight lassie chance to trippen by,
And shines all over with ungodly dew,
Which, when observed, he sinks into his mew
And straight 'gins recollect his piety anew?"

Inhabitants of Ossory, is it for these glorious purposes that the system is to be persevered in, which is fraught with so much frightful mischief and teems with public woe? I do not mean to quarrel with the wealth of the church. It is enormous. It is a bloated and dropsical mass; but it is to the votaries of Wesley, and not of St. Peter, that the operation of tapping is reserved. Whatever aversion I have to the church arises from its being raised as an obstacle to the liberties of my country. The Attorney-General has justly remarked, that, instead of endangering the stability of the established religion, and of the gorgeous institutions by which it is attended, Roman Catholic Emancipation would contribute materially to its permanence. It is because it is now opposed as a barrier to concession that we regard it with hostility; but if once it ceased to operate as an obstruction, we should, in all likelihood, submit in apathetic acquiescence to its abuses; we should look upon it as a state engine, and if it ceased to crush us, we should not desire to interfere with its operations, or to diminish the power of the vast machine. We should not be arrayed by individual interest against its influence, and whatever might be our abstract opinion respecting its general expediency, we should not regard it as we are now forced to do, as a means of personal wrong. I doubt not, indeed, that if the Catholic question were settled, individuals of our own body might be found who would be disposed to support, as an instrument of political influence, what they are now instigated by their sense of personal suffering to condemn. But, Sir, I am deviating from the course that the resolution which I have seconded should suggest to me. Let me conclude, by stating to you with some abruptness, what, upon another occasion, I shall take an opportunity to enforce. Three great measures have, of late, been proposed, as expedients by which Emancipation may be advanced. The first is, a census of the Catholic people—the second, a meeting for fourteen successive days, in Dublin, of the prelacy, the chief clergy, the aristocracy, the merchants, and the professional members of our body—the third, and most important, is, the simultaneous assembly of the Irish people upon the same day, in their respective parishes, to petition for redress. We shall require the co-operation of the clergy, in order to achieve these great ends. I have heard it said that they should not meddle in politics. Why? Do not the parsons meddle in politics? Do not the parsons excite the religious prejudices of the English people? Does not Bloomfield meddle in politics? He was once our friend, until, finding that his head was not like Yorick's, and that a mitre might fit upon it—feeling the organ of episcopativeness in distinct and holy prominence, he betook himself to a more profitable course than the study of Greek tragedy, and set up as an orator against the Irish people. But let him pass—are not the parsons the most furious opponents of our cause? And, if they are, why should not the priests prove themselves its most strenuous advocates? Upon them rest our best hopes; they will not make an Iscariot sale of the liberties of their country to the Pharisees of the cabinet. They are unpurchased and unpurchaseable. Satisfied with the voluntary contributions of their flocks, they are contented with their primitive poverty, and from the moral elevation in which they are placed, look down with a lofty indifference upon the luxurious opulence of the Established priesthood. They will not abuse the legitimate influence which they possess, and assign it to the rulers of the land. They will not convert the temple of God into a profane and sordid mart. The blood of Christ shall not "drop for them in drachmas"—they will not make money of the mysteries of religion—convert eternal truth into a traffic—make the cross a ladder of ambition, and dig in Mount Calvary for gold.

RESOLUTION ON THE PROSECUTION OF MR. O'CONNELL

SPEECH IN MOVING A SERIES OF RESOLUTIONS RESPECTING THE PROSECUTION OF MR. O'CONNELL, BY MR. PLUNKETT.

THE prosecution of Mr. O'Connell, and the issue of the legal enterprise, in which the provincial government of Ireland had so fantastically adventured, call for an intimation of our sentiments. I rise to propose the first of a series of resolutions, which I have drawn up with a view to suggest the feelings of the Irish people, rather than give them their full expression. I move the following resolution :—

"Resolved—That the prosecution of Mr. O'Connell has excited the amazement of the English public, and is calculated to excite a stronger feeling than one of mere astonishment in the people of Ireland."

"Yes, Sir, England was amazed, and Ireland was more than astonished. If there is ground to congratulate Mr. O'Connell upon his victory, there is ground to congratulate Mr. Plunkett upon his defeat. His success would have been disastrous to his country and to himself. The blood of every honest man would have boiled in his veins at the success of this deplorable experiment. As it is, a feeling of regret is intermingled with the sentiment of displeasure. We lament that Mr. Plunkett should have given an election to his enemies, to make either a martyr of Mr. O'Connell, or a victim of himself. We survey this abortive proceeding with all its train of miserable result, "more in sorrow than in anger." We do not forget the ties of political cordiality which united Mr. Plunkett to the Roman Catholic body. We feel as if we had snatched a poniard from the grasp of an antagonist, and beholding in his face the lineaments of an early friend, instead of turning back the dagger upon his bosom, exclaim, in the accents of mingled reproach and sorrow, "Is it thus that you requite us?" God forbid that we should indulge in the language of contumelious triumph at the failure of a measure which carries with it its own retribution. The weapon which was pointed at our very existence with so deadly a level, has burst in Mr. Plunkett's hands—I hope it has not shattered them. It is enough for us that he has missed his aim—we cannot fail to recollect that there is in the detestation of our inveterate opponents, (we must not suffer ourselves to be deluded by them), a kind of redeeming virtue; and instead of co-operating in their designs, we should abstain from the manifestation of any indignant feeling, and all indulgence in any ungenerous vaunt. For the sake of the country, and for the sake of the distinguished individual who is identified with its interests, and holds so high and permanent a place in its regards, we rejoice at the failure of the preposterous prosecution. But we are not drunk with an absurd and delirious joy. In these political saturnalia, we do not forget the ignominy of our condition. We remember that there is no substantial ground of exultation. It is but an ephemeral and transitory advantage. We are still the underlings of Orange domination. Our penalties and disqualifications are still upon us; and in lifting up our arms we feel the heaviness of the fetters which we cannot long sustain in the attitude of triumph. They draw us down again, and weigh us to the earth. But we owe it, at the same time, to sound principle, and to the abstract dignity of truth, to record our condemnation of this marvellous proceeding. Gracious God! what motive could have prompted an undertaking so extravagant? When Mr. Plunkett read the words attributed to Mr. O'Connell, did he ask himself "what provocation is given to this man?—who is he?—and what am I?" ' Did he say to himself, "who am I?" Did he say, "who is William Conyngham Plunkett?" I know not whether he administered that personal interrogatory to himself; but this I know, that if he did, this should have been the answer—" I raised myself from a comparatively humble station, by the power of my own talents, to the first eminence in the State. In my profession I am without an equal—in parliament I once had no superior—I have obtained great wealth, great fame, great dignity, and great patronage. When I was out of office I kindled the popular passions—I enlisted them on my side—I was fierce, virulent, and vituperative. The minister turned pale before me. At last I have won the object of my life. I am Attorney-General for Ireland—if I had been a Catholic, instead of an enfranchised Presbyterean, what would have been my fortunes?" I can tell him:—he would have pined under the *sense* of degradation. He would have felt like a man with huge limbs where he could not stand erect—he would have felt his faculties "cribbed and cabined in," and how would he have endured his humiliation? —look at him and say! How would that lofty forehead have borne the brand of Popery? How would that high demeanour have borne the stoop of the slave? Would he have been tame, and abject, and servile, and sycophantic? No; he would have been the chief demagogue—the most angry, tumultuous, and violent tribune of the people — he would have superadded the honest gall of his own nature to the bitterness of political resentment—he would have given utterance to ardent feelings in burning words; and in all the foam of passion he would have gnawed the chain from which he could not break. And is this the man who prosecutes for words? If their condition were reversed—if Mr. O'Connell were Attorney-General, and Mr. Plunkett were the great leader of the people—if "Anthony were Brutus, and Brutus Anthony," how would the public mind have been inflamed! What exciting matter would have been flung amongst the people

What lava would have been poured out! "The very stones would rise and mutiny" Would to heaven that not only Mr. Plunkett, but every other Protestant who deplores our imprudence, in the spirit of fastidious patronage, would adopt the simple test of nature, and make our case his own, and he would confess, that if similarly situated, he would give vent to his emotions in phrases as exasperated, and participate in the feelings which agitate the great and disfranchised community, to which it would be his misfortune to belong. There is no man of ordinary candour, who will not rather intimate his wonder at the moderation, than his surprise at the imputed violence of Mr. O'Connell; with fortune, rank, and abilities of the first class—enjoying preeminence in his profession, and the confidence of his country, he is shut out from honours accessible to persons whom nature intended to place infinitely behind, and whom their religion has advanced before him. If he were to adopt, or if his country, at his suggestion, were to assume the language which is prescribed to us, the people of England would not believe that we laboured under any substantial grievances. "I do not believe you," (said a celebrated advocate of antiquity, to a citizen, who stated to him a case of enormous wrong)—"I do not believe you." "Not believe me!" "No." "What! not believe me! I tell you, that my antagonist met me in the public way—seized me by the throat—flung me to the earth, and"——"Hold," exclaimed Demosthenes, "your eye is on fire—your lip begins to quiver—your cheek is flushed with passion—your hand is clenched. I believe you now; when you first addressed me you were too calm—too cold—too measured; but now you speak, you look like one who had sustained a wrong!" And are we to speak, and act like men who had sustained no wrong? We! Six millions of—what shall I say? Citizens? No! but of men who have been flagitiously spoliated of the rights and privileges of British subjects—who are cast into utter degradation and covered with disgrace and shame—upon whom scorn is vented and contumely discharged; we, who are the victims of legislative plunder—who have been robbed, with worse than Punic perfidy, of privileges which our ancestors had purchased at Limerick with their blood—which were secured by the faith of treaties, and consecrated with all the solemnities of a great national compact—shall we speak like men who had sustained no wrongs?—We are upon our knees, but even in kneeling an attitude of dignity should be maintained. Shall we ask for the right of freemen in the language of slaves? May common sense—common feeling—common honour—may every generous principle implanted in our nature—may that God (I do not take his name in vain) may that Power that endowed us with high aspirations, and filled the soul of man with honourable emotion—who made the love of freedom an instinctive wish and unconquerable appetite—may the great Author of our being—the Creator of the human heart—may God forbid it

INCREASE OF POWER.

SPEECH ON THE INCREASE OF POWER IN THE CATHOLICS OF IRELAND.

THE Bible, with every man's comment, is now the fashion. I shall give you a text, with my own comment: "The Philistines took Samson and put out his eyes, and bound him with fetters of brass, and he did grind in the prison. Howbeit the hair of Samson began to grow after he was shaven." They put out the eyes of Ireland; they made education illicit, and declared knowledge to be contraband. They knew that slavery and ignorance were companions—they quenched the intellectual vision of the people—they bound them in penalties that cut into the mind, and corroded the heart—they set them to grind in the prison—they declared them to be incapable of all honourable occupation—they fixed a brand upon their labour, and to their industry they attached disgrace; and yet, in despite of all this, notwithstanding the detestable ingenuity of this infernal process for the debasement and demoralization of man, the innate power of the country defeated this abominable scheme. Its original and native energy were insensibly restored; war, and massacre, and slavery, and exile, could not stop the progress of population. The law of nature was stronger than the law of the land. Shorn, as Ireland was of her strength, she imperceptibly regained her gigantic vigour—"The hair of Samson began to grow upon his head." What, then, is to be done with Samson? But I do the country wrong. Unlike the strong man Ireland has recovered her sight, with the renovation of her strength. Let me drop the illustration, and appeal, not to metaphors, but to facts. The population of Ireland was reduced at one period to eight hundred thousand inhabitants. The penal code was passed—it tended to multiply them, and not to diminish the indigenous religion. The population swelled to three millions—the Volunteers arose; that which Primate Boulter pronounced to be the death of English influence was about to be effected—her junction of the Catholic and Protestant, and the merging of religion into nationality. The government flung the Catholic question into the Irish convention. Division was produced—the Protestant became alarmed, and the Catholic discontented. "Give us our liberty," exclaimed the Catholic—"preserve our ascendancy," exclaimed the Protestant. The government struck upon a middle course, and by so doing, the seeds of dissension were deposited. The Catholic purchased the soil which he had scarcely dared to tread; he acquired power with the elective franchise; a career was thrown open to the intellect of the country in the professions Popery became rich, influential, active, restless, intelligent, and aspiring The three millions rose to six. We are six millions of British subjects. Statesmen of England, what is to be done with us? What is to be done with six millions of men? You must re-enact the penal code, or make us wholly free; you must strip the lawyer of his gown, the merchant of his stock, the proprietor of his estate. The bill of discovery must be revived; filial ingratitude must again be turned into virtue, and a bounty must be set upon parricide. This might not be humane, but it would be consistent. It would be more reasonable, at all events, than the perpetuation of a system, which is at once exasperating and absurd It is not only absurd but dangerous. It is more than dangerous—it carries the seeds of destruction and the elements of ruin. England is now at the highest point of prosperity—she reposes in opulence from the fatigues and the exhaustion of a long and sanguinary war. She has, if I may say so, washed the blood and dust from her brow, and bathes herself in the warm and refreshing stream of a vast and superabundant commerce. The treasures of South America are pouring into her lap; the sun does not set upon her dominions; the fabric of her power is magnificent and immense; but is its foundation in measure with its height? Is it built upon an immutable basis? Is it placed beyond the power of all political contingency, and can it bid defiance to calculable events? The King of Babylon beheld the type of a great empire in an image with a golden head, and with feet of iron and of clay. It was shattered by a pebble. It was emblematic of a dominion which rested on frailty and oppression. The amazing wealth of England is illustrated by the symbol that surmounted the visionary form, and in the government of this unhappy, but important province, there is a combination of meanness and injustice, which is not unaptly exemplified by the hard and vile materials of which the feet of the prophetic statue were composed. It requires but little of the spirit of prophecy to foresee the hazard to which that dominion must be exposed, which, however glorious, rests upon a system at variance with the interests and with the rights of the great body of the people, which is at once paltry and grinding, despicable and cruel, and to recur to the Scriptural illustration, is made of iron and of clay. Such a system may be subverted by an accident; a stone may shatter it; literally speaking it may fall in the shifting of the wind. Let France declare war; let the English fleet be blown out of the Channel; let——But I see in the faces of many around me an expression of alarm; you think I tread upon dangerous ground; " Beware," you seem to say, "you are upon the verge of sedition—the ear of Dionysius is always open." I do not dread it; I am fearless in the integrity of my own purpose; and, knowing myself, not only from every principle of duty, but from every motive of interest, to be strenuously anxious for the pacification of my country; being little prone to political romance, never having indulged in the day-dream of Irish independence; attached, from deep conviction of its necessity, and, I will add, of its ultimate utility to the connexion with England; desiring to see my country substantially blended and consolidated with the great mass of the empire; united not merely by acts of parliament, but by a reciprocity of kindness and a mutuality of interests, I am careless of any imputation that may be flung upon my motives, either by open enemies, or by those luke-warm friends, whom we should begin to vomit. I will give utterance to the language which is dictated by my feelings, and to which my judgment gives it sanction. There are six millions of Roman Catholics in Ireland. A vast proportion of that immense body are alienated by the law. It is impossible that discontent—that disaffection should not exist. The better classes of Roman Catholics—they who have acquired, or who hope to acquire wealth—the members of professions, the opulent merchants, the extensive agriculturists, set off their interests against their feelings; and while they abhor the penal code (as which of us does not?) they have a still greater dread of a convulsion in which life and property would not only be endangered, but swept away. But there is in this country an immense mass of population, who have uniformly acted under the influence of passion, more than of reason; men who have injuries to avenge, and nothing but death, with which they are familiar, to apprehend; spirits untamed by the enjoyments of life—bound to it by no tie—cheered by no solace—having nothing but the animal instinct to attach them to existence, which their habits are calculated to surmount—men who mount the scaffold with a laugh, and leap from it with a bound. That vast body of fierce, and fearless, and desperate peasantry would be easily allured into a junction with an invader, and whatever might be the ultimate event, the immediate consequences must make every good man tremble. It is the fashion in the orgies of Orangemen to boast of the power of the Irish Protestants, and to vaunt that they would alone repel any attempt upon our shores. An accident or rather a merciful dispensation of Providence, prevented the great body of the French forces from landing at Killala. But mark what was accomplished by only a handful of men! Twelve hundred Frenchmen marched into the heart of the country and defeated six thousand of the British troops. I admit that those troops were very different from the veterans of the Peninsula—they were, like the present Irish government, formidable only to their friends. But they were as good as the Orangemen could muster, and they were discomfited almost by a band of boys. There were many difficulties in the way of the French Directory at that period There was no sympathy in religion, and the people were not prepared for their reception. But in fifteen or twenty years hence, if the system of alienation should continue, how different will be the condition of the national mind? The Bourbon family are aware of that mistake which Bonaparte committed and regretted. They turn their eyes towards Ireland—a community of religious feeling may be easily cultivated. A long peace affords opportunities of intercourse, and if, after a mature and deliberate preparation of the public sentiment, the united fleets of France and America were to appear, with twenty thousand men, and one hundred thousand stand of arms, off our coast, what would be the result? "We should beat them still," exclaims an Englishman, laying his hand with honest pride upon his sword. I trust that the national vaunt would be verified by the event! Miserable as the condition is to which we are reduced, it is better than the connexion of Ireland with a foreign power. I had rather see the streets patrolled by Scotch Highlanders than French Dragoons. There is not a man in this assembly who would not wish that such an enterprise should fail; and that it would fail I firmly believe. The patriotic aspiration of the Duke of Wellington, that his country should be re-conquered, would be realised. But I ask, in the name of common humanity, and hose instincts of universal nature, which even religious antipathies are not able wholly to subdue—I ask of the most inveterate of the faction who are leagued against the peace, as well as the freedom of Ireland, whether anything could compensate for the deluge of blood with which even victory must be bought? The events of which I speak, (and may the timely wisdom of England, and the God of heaven avert them) may not happen, and in all likelihood will not happen while we live. We shall all be gathered in the dust, blended in the great and lasting reconciliation of the grave. But shall a legislator—a British statesman—a trustee of the interests and happiness of his fellow-men, presume to say, that provided he can crawl in office to the tomb, he is indifferent about futurity. Eldon, perhaps, may say so. Let him, in his agony, clutch his money bags in one hand, and the seals in the other, and he dies contented. But can any man, with the least pretensions to elevation of character or generosity of feeling, contemplate the frightful probabilities to which I have adverted without a shudder? It is not to the philanthropist alone that we should point out this disastrous prospect. It is to the meaner advocates of ascendancy, that we should address ourselves. I do not appeal to any dignified or exalted sentiment. They cling to the bad pre-eminence which they derive from their religion. These birds of prey croak and flutter in angry tumult at the least disturbance of those foul nests which they have built upon the ruins of their country. But dead as they may be to every other sentiment, I would appeal to their self-love and throw their personal interests into the scale. A man contemplates the perpetuation of his own existence in his child; they have children, and yet, strange to say, while they manifest the utmost solicitude in the indulgence of their paternal sensibilities for the future welfare of their offspring, they entirely forget how much it must depend upon the permanent tranquillization of their country. A great Protestant proprietor sits down to draw his will—he surveys from the window of his magnificent residence, the expanse of confiscated woods and lawns with which the courageous piety of the Cromwellian forefather was rewarded. He devises his estate in strict settlement, and by a variety of complicated limitations, endeavours to escape from the laws against perpetuity, and would give, if he could, a feudal permanence to his estate, and render it unalienable. He embraces a century in the extent of his testamentary anticipations. If, at such a moment, a warning like the prophecy of Lochiel, were to be breathed upon him; if he were to be told that the time should come when his mansion should be given to the flames—when the shouts of murder and the shrieks of dishonour should ring through his halls—when his sons should be slaughtered upon his threshold, and his daughters should scream for help upon their father's grave——But I advance too far into " the field of the dead." I must pause in this dreadful picture, and yet I cannot avoid calling upon every man with a touch of the parental instincts in his heart, to awaken to the appalling likelihood of a convulsion, of which his children may be the victims. They will insure their lives for the benefit of their children; they will not insure the peace of their country. They will insure their dwellings against fire, and they will not insure the great fabric of the State against conflagration. Nay, they pile combustible matter within it, and seem almost to prepare it for an explosion. It is not to Protestants alone that I address myself. There is not a man that hears me whose offspring may not be immolated to this frightful infatuation. If ever these terrible events should arise, every class of society will be swept and sucked into the bloody vortex. There is not a parent in the land—there is not a father or a mother who does not bear a painful participation in those disastrous likelihoods. The cry of discord should sound like Alecto's trumpet; it should give a start to every mother, and make her clasp her children to her breast. I would to heaven the women of Ireland would feel the frightful possibilities of which I have given a sketch so imperfect, and, like the wives and mothers of antiquity, throw themselves between us, and holding up their children, implore us to forbear. And how easily, with what facility, and by an expedient how prompt, how obvious and simple, might our unhappy animosities be subdued for ever! How rapidly a great national reconciliation would take place! How soon the waters of bitterness would cease to run, if the fountain were sealed up! How easily our minds would mingle and coalesce together, if the law did not stand between us; how zealously should we all co-operate for the purposes of national good! Instead of waging battles about heaven, we should exemplify its precepts by good will upon earth; in place of engaging in the frenzy of polemics, we should enter into an universal alliance for the education of the people. A wholesome communication between the higher and the lower classes of society would take place; the channels of a salutary intercourse would be opened—an easy and unimpeded circulation of good feelings and of good principles would arise—English capital and English minds and habits would be diffused amongst us; and in a little time we should look back with shame and with astonishment at the rancorous feuds by which we had been divided.

VIOLENCE OF THE ASSOCIATION.

SPEECH IN VINDICATION OF THE VIOLENCE OF THE ASSOCIATION.

You are assembled upon an occasion of no ordinary moment; you meet in order to determine upon the general system which you are hereafter to adopt, and to intimate to your advocates and to your antagonists the principles upon which your proceedings are intended to be regulated, and the general course which you mean to follow. I do not exaggerate when I say, that whatever little weight may be attached to individuals, and however our opponents may affect to hold, at a cheap rate, the most active of the members of our own body, yet, that the cause itself is of such a magnitude, and upon its progress so much of the stability of parties depends, that the eyes of the country are directed to our measures, and it is a subject, both amongst our supporters and our opponents, of anxious inquiry, whether, at all hazards, we shall press the discussion of our question in the ensuing session of parliament. Although the period for discussion is yet remote, it is of consequence that it should be previously well known how far we are disposed, in order to accommodate ourselves to the conveniences of the present administration, to abstain from all "ignorant impatience" (to use the ministerial phrase) of our grievances, and to keep our question back, lest it should be a source of molestation to our supporters, and its agitation, by embroiling them with their confederates in authority, may ruffle the pillows of office. It is right that the people of Ireland should be apprised (because upon their anticipations much of their zeal and energy must depend) of the course which the managers of their question purpose to take. A decision upon this point is the more requisite, because a hope has been expressed that we should refrain from any rude and uncourteous intrusion of our sufferings upon the consideration of the ministry, and that we should leave the introduction of our cause to the discretion of our friends in the cabinet, in which, as well as in the integrity of their views and the sincerity of their support, it is said that we ought not to entertain any doubt Nobody will deny, who is at all acquainted with the character of the Irish Catholics, that by the suppression of our question the public feeling will be very considerably modified. In considering the expediency of committing the entire management of the cause to our parliamentary advocates, the result of the debate in either house of the legislature is not alone to be taken into account; we must recollect, besides, that we are acting for a sanguine, an impetuous, ardent, and impassioned multitude, to whose wishes, and I will add, to whose passions something must be conceded ; and that, while upon one hand it is of importance to consult the official conveniences of our advocates in power, it is of still greater consequence to keep alive the feeling in this country, which it has cost much labour to call up, and which may subside as rapidly to such a point of depression, that it will hereafter be difficult, if it do not become almost impossible, to raise it again to that degree of excitation which it has now usefully attained, but from which, if care be not taken, it may irremediably recede. The persons who are most active in the management of our question are often blamed for their apparent indifference to the interests of their friends, and their recklessness of all circumstance: it is alleged that we push our question into discussion when the passions of the English multitude are roused into the most vehement activity against us, and when the cabal, who derive their political existence from opposition to our claims, are enabled, by taking advantage of the prejudices which we contribute to excite, to thwart our advocates in their salutary designs, and deprive them of that power, which, to be useful, must be slowly exercised on our behalf—we are told that we should wait until Time, that great arbitrator of political differences, shall have worked a political reconciliation, and that the minister who is to emancipate us must be allowed to act on the tactics of Fabius, "*cunctando restituet rem.*" I am by no means insensible to the value of these arguments, which are greatly deserving of consideration; but I am disposed to think that the persons who press upon us are not the best acquainted with the state of public feeling in this country, and that they take but an imperfect and partial view of the case. If the effect which the bringing forward of the Catholic question is to have were to be confined to the people of England, and I will even add to the houses of parliament, the reasoning to which I have referred for the postponement of the discussion would be just. But almost all Protestants, who are prodigally liberal of their advice, have fallen into one essential mistake, by entirely overlooking the consequences with which the postponement—I should rather call it the temporary abandonment of the question—must be attended in Ireland. The plain and simple state of the case is this: the directors of Catholic politics in Ireland have two things to attend to—namely, the success of the question in parliament, and also (which our censors entirely overlook) the management of the public mind in Ireland. That we should consult the accommodation of our friends, provided it be not a serious expense of other still more important considerations, I am quite free to admit. But (and I beg to call not only your attention, but that of every liberal Protestant who may happen to disapprove of what is called the violence of the Catholic Association, to this view of the case) it should be recollected that we have to take into an account the influence which our proceedings must have upon our own body. A wise general, who, to accommodate his allies, is advised to delay an engagement with the enemy, will consider how far that delay will weaken the confidence of his own troops, and may have the effect of dissolving and disbanding those levies, which it was difficult to bring, and it is not easy to keep together. This illustration will present the policy on which we have acted in a proper light, and will show that where our own measures were apparently rash and ill-advised, they were dictated by substantially solid considerations, which were not present to the minds of those who were disposed to censure us for precipitate folly and presumptuous indiscretion. The Irish Catholics must be attended to as well as the Protestants of England. By consulting the proud prejudices and lofty caprices of the latter, the energies and enthusiasm of the former body may be gradually suspended, and by a system of perpetual subserviency to circumstances, the moral power which arises from the ardour and confederacy of an immense and vehement population, may be dissipated and wasted away. Six millions of people cannot be kept bound up in the same system of confederacy, and animated by the same ardent and unabated solicitude for the attainment of a single great object, excepting by a perpetual and unremitting appeal to their expectations. Take away hope, lethargy succeeds, and at length indifference and oblivion find their way into the public mind. This will be (it has already been—experience proves it) the consequence of not pressing the Catholic question: that the people, who had fixed their hopes upon the event of the next session, finding that their rights are not even considered worthy of deliberation, will turn away from the question altogether. The weak and the base will resign themselves to their political degradation, while the more proud and enterprising will look into futurity, and indulge in the anticipation of events, in which they may seek for vengeance as well as for redress. These are not mere idle speculations—the theory itself is sustained by probability, but facts give confirmation to the obvious suggestions of reason. The individuals who are disposed to recommend a temporising, and, to use a word which has been much abused, a conciliatory system of policy, would do well to recollect the effects which it produced in Ireland. We are often told that our violence, as it is called, and the eternal obtrusion of our question on the legislature, are equally exasperating and wearisome—that while our vehemence produces anger, our reiterated demands generate tedium, and the people of England are alternately irritated by and tired by Catholic Emancipation. This may be true; but look to the effects which are produced in Ireland by the cessation of Catholic meetings which took place in the year 1821. We virtually abandoned the question. Not only was it not debated in parliament, but in Ireland there was neither committee, nor board, nor Association. The result was, that a total stagnation of public feeling took place, and I do not exaggerate when I say that the Catholic question was nearly forgotten—all public meetings had ceased —no angry resolutions issued from public bodies—no exciting speeches appeared in the papers—the monstrous abuses of the Church establishment—the frightful evils of political monopoly—the hideous anomaly in the whole structure of our civil institutions—the unnatural ascendancy of a handful of men over an immense and powerful population—all these, and the other just and legitimate causes of public exasperation, were gradually dropping out of the national memory. The country was then in a state of comparative repose, but it was a degrading and unwholesome tranquillity. We sat down like galley slaves in a calm. A general stagnation diffused itself over the national feelings. The public pulse had stopped—the circulation of all generous sentiment had been arrested, and the country was palsied to the heart. At this period the Roman Catholics were peculiarly moderate, to use the phrase habitually employed by Catholic candidates for admission into such societies as Kildare-street Club-house, who befoul their own cause, and reviling their party, vainly hope to overcome, by their political baseness and subserviency, the objections to their exceedingly ungentlemanlike religion. I think it will be conceded to me, that it would have been difficult for the Catholics to have been more moderate. It would be hard to conjecture a condition of more complete and unqualified debasement. The "beau ideal" of political turpitude was realised, and in the full stretch of his imagination, Mr. Peel could scarcely have conceived us to be more degraded. The experiment of "moderation," which is only another expression for contented thraldom, was fully tried—and what was the result? It was two-fold. The question receded in England, and fell back from the general notice. There it was utterly forgotten, while in Ireland, the spirit and energy of the people underwent an utter relaxation, and the most vigorous efforts became necessary to repair all the moral deterioration which the whole body of the Irish Catholics had sustained. It was at length decided by those, who, whatever may be their imprudence, have never shown any want of due zeal in this great cause, that some exertion should be made. I shall give you a proof of the low ebb to which political feeling had fallen. Mr. O'Connell and myself took upon ourselves to write circular notes, which we jointly signed, to the leading Roman Catholics, entreating them to assemble together, in order to devise some means of raising the question from its low condition. These notes were treated, by the majority of persons to whom they were addressed, with indifference, and it was with great difficulty that a few individuals of any respectability were collected together. The foundations of the Catholic Association were then laid, and it must be confessed, that its first meetings afforded few indications of the importance and magnitude to which that institution was subsequently raised. The attendance was so thin, and the public appeared so insensible to the proceedings, that any men, except those who were determined not to be deterred by any obstacles, would have abandoned the enterprise in despair. The Association, in its origin, was treated with contempt, not only by the adversaries of Emancipation, but Catholics themselves spoke of it with derision, and, if I may so say, spurned at the walls of mud which their brethren had rapidly constructed, but which were afterwards to ascend into a more imposing and lofty fabric. Still we persevered, and at length the great body of the Roman Catholics were awakened from their torpor. The national lethargy was shaken off, and a considerable and gradually increasing interest was felt in our discussions. The speeches delivered in the Association were read, and whatever might have been their defects in style, and however widely they might have departed from the rules of pure and simple oratory, still they contained a powerful appeal to the feelings of the people—their degrading condition was presented in its just light. They were called upon to look upon their own shame, and were made to blush at the turpitude of their condition. Truths of a most painful and exasperating kind were told. The Catholic aristocrat was made to feel that his ancient blood, which slavery had made stagnant in his veins, was of no avail—the Catholic merchant was taught that his coffers filled with gold could not impart to him any substantial importance, when every needy corporator looked down upon him from the pedestal of his aristocratic religion—the Catholic priest was informed that he had much occasion to put the lessons of humility inculcated by the gospel, into practice, when every coxcomb minister of the Establishment could, with impunity, put some sacerdotal affront upon him. The very humblest peasant in the land was desired to look at his Protestant neighbour, and compare his condition with his own. In short, from the proudest nobleman down to the meanest serf, the whole body of Roman Catholics were rendered sensible of their inferior posture in the State. The stigma was pointed at—men became exasperated at their grievances, when they were roused to their perception—a mirror was held up to Ireland to show her her own degraded image, and when she beheld the brand upon her forehead, it began to burn. In a little time a great movement was produced through the country—the meetings of the Association became crowded—individuals of all classes gradually joined it, and insensibly its attraction became stronger every day, till it grew into one great national incorporation. The Catholic Rent was introduced by Mr. O'Connell, and established in almost every parish in the country. This was a new bond of affiliation. Every contributor considered himself as linked with the institution which he aided to support, and it may be said, that at length six or seven millions of Roman Catholics were engaged in one vast and powerful confederacy. And here let me for a moment pause, and ask whether, reviled and vilified as the Catholic demagogues have been, they still did not accomplish great things, when they thus succeeded in marshalling, and bringing the whole population of the country into array. Compare the state of the Roman Catholics in the year 1821 with their condition in the year 1825, and say at which of those periods was their attitude most imposing and imperative? Nor were the effects of the Association confined to this country. The English people had previously been taught to hold us in their contempt: but when they saw that such an immense population was actuated by one indignant sentiment, and was combined in an impassioned, but not the less effectual organization, and above all, when they perceived one thousand pounds a week pouring into our exchequer, their alarm was excited, and although their pride was wounded. they ceased to despise where they had begun to fear. At last the legislature were called upon to interfere, and all the power of the ministry was exerted in order to crush the body, which owed its very existence to the grievances which they had refused to redress. At that period an opportunity was, perhaps, afforded to carry the Catholic Question. If the friends of Emancipation who voted with the ministers had said, that relief to Ireland should be the preliminary condition to their support, the great measure would, in all probability, have been carried. But unhappily the suppressing bill was allowed to pass; nothing was done for Ireland, while the Association was attempted to be extinguished by an Act of Parliament, which has, thanks to the excited spirit of the country, been found of no effect. The Catholic Question came on almost immediately after the vote for the suppression of the Association had passed. At that time the mind of Ireland was in a glow, and that of England was almost equally excited. The result of the discussion in the House of Commons affords a tolerably just test of the general prudence of discussion. It was said on the eve of the debate, that the virulence of the Catholics had exasperated the House of Commons to such a degree, that there was no chance of the measure being carried. In his feeling even our best and most undoubted friends participated. On the very day on which Sir Francis Burdett brought the measure forward, (the incident is deserving of mention) he came, attended with several eminent persons, to a meeting of the deputies, and informed us that it was considered exceedingly hazardous to bring on the measure. We remonstrated, and pressed for a discussion. Sir Francis Burdett and his distinguished companions retired, stating that they would return to a meeting of our friends, from which they had come, and let us know their determination, and shortly after it was announced that Mr. Tierney had given his decided opinion in favour of a discussion, and that the present Master of the Mint had overcome every objection. The question was accordingly brought forward and carried in the Commons. The virulence of the Association was urged as the leading argument, but it was of no avail. On the contrary, I am convinced that the Irish people never assumed so imposing an attitude. The measure was afterwards lost in the Lords, but no candid person will attribute that loss to the Catholic Association. Its rejection was not put upon any such ground. But was the spirit of Ireland subdued or dismayed by that rejection? Certainly not; and as the best evidence of it, I may appeal to an event in the history of the country, which will not be readily forgotten, and from which very important issues may yet be expected to follow—I mean the political insurrection of the forty-shilling freeholders, which took place immediately after the failure of our question. It will be asked, perhaps, why I refer to an incident which, in its origin, did not redound much to the credit of the Catholic deputies. I admit that in offering to sacrifice the forty-shilling freeholders, a mistake—a serious, but innocent mistake was made. But while I am thus frank, let me be allowed to add, that we, who are blamed for an apparent readiness to make this sacrifice, did not know the quantity of public virtue which was to be found in rags, and that the demonstrations of humble heroism which attended the last election, resulted from the moral preparation which the minds of the peasantry had undergone, and which the Catholic Association had effected. We may be blamed for having tendered the franchises of the people, as the consideration for the national equalization, but let it not be forgotten, that if we were in fault in this particular, we had ourselves previously awakened the lower orders to that sense of their duties and of their importance, which was afterwards displayed. I have no hesitation in stating, that but for the Catholic Association the forty-shilling freeholders would never have rebelled against their proprietors. The wonders which were achieved in Waterford, in Armagh, in Monaghan, and in Louth, may be referred to that system of energy which we had previously adopted: and, with the blessing of God, and the aid of that spirit which will never, I trust, die away in our hearts, in that system of energy we will persevere. The fruits which it has already produced have been signal, and still more important consequences may yet be expected to follow. Therefore, I, for one, or I should rather say, for the thousands who sympathise with me, do declare, that never, under no circumstances—tempted by no inducements—deterred by no fears—allured by no expectations, beguiled by no promises, will we ever consent to allow a single session to pass without pressing for a discussion in Parliament. I do candidly own, that the very irritation produced by the rejection of our claims, and the exasperation of the people are amongst the most powerful inducements to urge the question on. I am for that system which will show the ministers that they never can expect to tranquillize Ireland, except by conceding our claims; I am for that system which will render our question a thorn in the sides of government, and I would drive that thorn in as deeply, and make it fester and rankle as poignantly as I am able. It is upon this principle, and because everlasting discussion forms a part of that system, that I suggest the propriety of having it known that we are determined not to suffer the ministers to slumber in their places, and that we will not yield up our liberties to their accommodation. Let us not be told that we should not disturb them in their repose, nor knock at the gates of the Legislature, lest we should awake them from the tranquillity of office, and rouse them from the golden dreams of power. We are not, after all, like the captives of Calcutta, who were allowed to perish rather than that the Rajah should be awakened from his sleep. Let not the ministers expect to slumber on undisturbed by the wrongs, and unaroused by the cries of Ireland. Ireland shall thunder at, though she may not be able to break open their doors, till the ministers shall themselves exclaim, "wake, England, with this knocking." I have Sir, stated my reasons for pressing a discussion, as part of that system on which I conceive that we should uniformly act. We must keep perpetually in view the necessity of adapting ourselves to the passions of the Irish, as well as of soothing the prejudices of the English people. This never should be lost sight of, and those who are most inclined to censure our conduct, and are sometimes at a loss to account for our "violence," as it is called, will find in this simple remark, the obvious clue to our policy. Whatever we do, men will always be found to cavil at our proceedings, and this being the inevitable consequence of whatever course we adopt, I prefer the bold and manly system to the base and servile, which will equally supply arguments against our cause. This view of our condition, and the principles on which we should act, is well put by Edmund Burke in a letter to Dr. Lawrence, recently published by the Archbishop of Cashel. Edmund Burke says—" In the Parliament of Great Britain, Lord Grenville turned the loyalty of the Catholics against themselves. He argued from the zeal and loyalty they manifested—their want of a sense of any grievance. If the people are turbulent and riotous, nothing is to be done for them on account of their evil dispositions. If they are obedient and loyal, nothing is to be done for them, because their being quiet and contented is a proof that they feel no grievance." When we are thus exposed to have either our servility or our irritation turned equally against us, and as our continued degradation is to be the premium of our loyalty, it becomes every man to make an election between the two evils, and for my own part I do not hesitate in making a choice of the alternative. If I am to be treated like a dog, I had rather be chained up as a furious hound, than beaten like a well-bred spaniel, and repaid with blows for my sycophancy and fawning. But independently of the superior manliness of taking a bold and determined course, and of calling the attention of the whole empire, and I may add, of the world, to the oppression of the Irish Catholics, which is so disgraceful to the English nation, and makes all Europe cry out "shame," the more honourable is also, I have no doubt, the wisest course. Nothing but the permanent exigency of concession will produce it. It is for us to generate that exigency. How is that to be effected? By rousing consolidating, and organising the energies of the people. Let me not be misunderstood. I am not sufficiently absurd to speak of physical force. By organization I mean no more than a moral confederacy, and a system of combined and simultaneous action in regulating all the movements of our own body. Much has been already done. But much more may still be done. We have admirable materials in our hands. In every parish in Ireland, there is a parish priest and a curate. The clergy of Ireland constitute a sort of intellectual aristocracy, and supply the place of an aristocracy of rank or wealth, in which we are deficient. I shall take an early opportunity of carrying into effect a project which I before suggested, of establishing a communication between a central committee of correspondence and every parish in Ireland. Thus simultaneous meetings through the whole country may be produced. There are difficulties in the way, but difficulties vanish before the spirit of genuine enterprise. A great exertion ought to be, and, with the blessing of God, shall be made. The whole population of Ireland shall be aroused; a fiercer ardour for liberty than ever yet was raised, shall be called up, and the tables of the legislature shall groan beneath the burden of petitions that shall be accumulated upon them. Let our English legislators learn what they have to expect from the refusal of all justice to our country. It cannot be too often and too powerfully impressed upon them. And as the number of our petitions should correspond with the vastness of the population which is affected by our grievances, so should their spirit be in union with the feelings by which we are actuated. Let there be no prostration, no debasement, in the sentiments which those petitions shall breathe; let us demand our equalization as a right, indefeasible and immutable, and show that when we ask for liberty, we are animated by the emotions of men who are deserving of freedom. There are many—aye, and in our own body—who tell us that we should approach the legislature in a base and servile attitude, as if Ireland should be fearful lest the reiteration of her complaints should weary the honourable house, and she should preface her supplications with an apology for her intrusion, and exclaim, "I hope I don't intrude." Let me not be told of the pride of the English people. If they are proud they will eventually respect us the more for adopting a little of their own character and demeanour. The tone, and the attitude of Ireland should correspond with her increasing importance and power. She should stand at the bar of the legislature erect and independent, and stretching forth her vigorous and gigantic arm, (upon which a chain should no longer be worn), she should remind her oppressors of the infraction of treaties, of the breach of contracts, of the violation of all right, of the outrage upon all honour; and having demonstrated her injuries—having disclosed all her wrongs—having torn open her bosom, if I may so say, and shown the hideous cancer of faction eating her to the heart, and corroding the life and substance of her being, she should tell them that she will be eventually as strong as she is miserable, and exclaim, "Do me justice—rescue me from wretchedness, and from distraction—give me back my liberty—raise me to the place I should maintain in the empire—give me back my spoliated rights—restore me to my violated franchises—give me back my liberty, or——I pause upon the brink of the alternative to which I had hurried, and, receding from it, leave it to you to complete the sentence. I have forborne from entering into any speculation on the probable result of the discussion in the ensuing session of Parliament, because, whatever may be our calculations as to that result, we should persevere in the system of petition. Perhaps my temperament is naturally over sanguine, but I own I am not disposed to despond in my anticipation of the fortunes of my country. The majority of the present ministry are favourable to Ireland and it is idle to suppose that our petition can put them out of office, when we recollect that there are no persons to supply their places. The opposition is now reduced to a felicitous triumvirate—to Sir Thos. Lethbridge, Mr. Peel, and his favourite prentice boy, Mr. Dawson, and even upon their permanent support, the Orange faction cannot place any very strong reliance; for Sir Thomas Lethbridge is going upon his travels, and it is to be hoped, will touch at the island of Antycira; Mr. Peel, it is believed, having discovered the royal disrelish for what the king is reported to have designated as " his genteel vulgarity," has determined to spin the remainder of his days in domestic oblivion of the solicitudes of political life—and with respect to the Right Hon. George Dawson, the friends of Emancipation apprehended that the cause will speedily lose the benefit of his opposition, and that in some foggy morning in the suicidal month of November, the hon. gentleman will be discovered in the ditchwater of the modern Numantia; for it is reported, that he has been lately seen wandering along the moat of the city of Londonderry, with a hasty step and agitated demeanour, and it is conjectured, that its dyke, covered with Orange ooze, (the appropriate emblem of his mind), may serve him a good turn, by assisting his heroic enterprise against himself. From such an opposition little is to be apprehended, and therefore no argument can be drawn from any danger to which the ministers may be exposed. With respect to the present ministry, they remain to be tried. As yet nothing has been done to induce us to look upon them with distrust; and although at first view, the appointment of Lord Anglesea, who drew an unhappily figurative phrase from his profession, seems ill-omened, yet, there is reason to think, that his lordship, whose friends said that he spoke in a " civil sense," has no notion of dragooning us into violence, or cutting us down into submission. His lordship only used the rhetorical sabre—the *tælum oratoris*, as it is called; and in justice we ought to weigh all his former votes against the ebullition of English pride into which, what he called, our violence had betrayed him. Lord Anglesea is said to be an intelligent and an ambitious man, and his good sense should teach him, that an honourable ambition would be best gratified by his being a means of effectually tranquillizing, by appeasing the discontents of Ireland. Nor can I think that Lord Lansdowne would retain the Home Department, if an Orange Lord Lieutenant were to succeed a nobleman, whose power to serve us did not correspond with his inclination. Surveying the whole frame and constitution of the ministry, I own that I am disposed to place confidence in them; and although I recollect the difference between men in and out of office—between

"Patriots, bursting with heroic rage
And placemen all tranquillity and smiles,"

still I cannot bring myself to think that the Whigs, who were so long our true and faithful advocates, will yield to the temptations of "tickling commodity," and ever substantially desert us. Suspicion is a bad and mean passion, and until I see strong reason to distrust them, I shall put a reliance in the majority of the cabinet, who profess themselves to be our supporters. But let me tell you, in whom I place a far deeper and stronger trust. I trust, it is true, in Lord Lansdowne, I trust in Mr. Tierney, I trust in Lord Goderich, and more than in Lord Goderich, and more than in Mr. Tierney, and more than in even Lord Lansdowne, and more than in the whole array of ancient Whigs and new-fangled Tories, I put my trust in the firmness, the union, the consolidation, the unconquerable energy, the unquenchable spirit, and the indomitable determination of seven millions of the Irish people.

SIMULTANEOUS MEETINGS.

SPEECH ON THE HOLDING OF SIMULTANEOUS MEETINGS.

THE Catholics of Ireland—in other words, seven millions of the inhabitants of this country, have been called on to assemble—a summons has been issued to the Irish people, to gather in simultaneous conventions. They have been enjoined to meet in the temples of their ancient creed at the same moment. The priest will appear in his stole—he will ascend the steps of the altar—he will offer the holy and mysterious sacrifice, and lift up the chalice with his consecrated hands to heaven. His fellow-believers will bow down in the performance of that solemn and venerable rite, and when the divine oblation shall have been concluded, the minister of a worship endeared by long suffering for its sake to the people, will turn round and say, "I am a citizen as well as a priest, and in my double character, and in the name of your country and of your God, I call on you to seek redress for the wrongs of the one, and to relieve from shame the religion of the other." This language, a language like this, uttered at the same instant from every altar in this country, will achieve much. I am not in the habit of making any vaunt of what I have done in this great cause—but I own that I cannot suppress an emotion of pride at having been the first to suggest a project which is not the least easy, because it is bold, and to which I look as the principal means of accomplishing the equalization of all classes of the Irish people, and through that equalization, the lasting peace and the tranquillity of the country. When once the cabinet behold the whole population completely organized and arrayed, they will not be deaf to our requisition for redress. Confiding not only in the justice, but in what is far better than the justice of our cause, and putting, as I do, my best, almost my only trust in the power and the union, and consolidation of the great community to which I belong, I shall say more:—No wise minister will dare to withold what seven millions demand, not only with an impassioned ardour and a vehement adjuration, but what is far more important—what they demand together, and call for in the name of justice at once. Lord Bacon, whose imagination was the lamp by which he threw light on his deep and vast meditations, says "that the people are like Briareus, because he was the giant of a hundred hands." Hitherto the Irish people raised up their arms irregularly and by starts—let them put forth all their power in one simultaneous supplication—let Briareus even upon his knees (for I would not allow Briareus to get up) lift up his hundred hands together, and the gigantic petitioner will not be disregarded. "Do you mean to threaten us?" some Protestant, bloated and big with the consciousness of his ascendancy, will, perhaps, exclaim—no. But I entreat him to peruse a recent treatise of the Under-Secretary of State, and he will find in the simultaneous meetings of seven millions of the Irish people, the best practical commentary upon Mr. Spring Rice's patriotic and impassioned lucubrations. What did the Under-Secretary of State declare? That which I dare not utter, but which, in his official whispers with my Lord Lansdowne, Mr. Spring Rice will not fear to intimate. Yet, to a certain extent I will speak out, and ask whether, if seven millions of the Irish people are thus marshalled, it be possible that their rights should long be kept back? Who will be sufficiently rash to answer in the affirmative? Is it wise—is it—aye—that is the word—is it safe to continue the system by which such results are generated? Was such a state of things ever yet heard of? Has it a parallel in the history of the world? Is there an instance of any government, except that of England, thus arraying and disciplining the people into alienation from the State, by a mad perseverance in a course which irritates the feelings, stimulates the passions, and exasperates the indignation of seven millions of its subjects? What but a diseased and deeply-disordered state of things could thus raise the whole population of the country into this orderly and pacific leve en masse, and bring them into phalanx? I may be asked, "if you consider this mighty gathering an evil, why do you co-operate in its production?". My reply is this:—The gathering is not the evil; in the law, which thus organises the people, lies the essence and source of calamity The assembling of the people is but the evidence of the condition of the country, and I would not deny the government the benefit of that great phenomenon. If the people can thus meet to petition—if they are so systematically organised, that at a signal of peace (for we use no other) they immediately fall into their ranks, and present an almost infinite array of supplicants, what are we to expect if we——What shall I say? If ever the prognostications of the Under-Secretary of State shall be unhappily converted from speculation to reality, and shall pass from possibility into fact. The simultaneous meetings do not produce the evil; they only serve to illustrate and place it in a conspicuous and powerful light; they throw a glare upon the penal code. These suggestions are meant for our opponents, in order that they may dispel the mist and obscurity which impede their intellectual vision, and prevent them from perceiving the brink on which they thread. I would shake, and somewhat rudely rouse these somnambulists, who dream upon a precipice, on whose verge they take their walks of visionary security. But I have another task to perform. I, what is uttered in this room did not reach beyond it, I should not waste my labour in thriftless declamation here. But that which is spoken in this assembly is heard at a great distance. The press is a speaking-trumpet—and every word I utter is carried through that great vehicle of the mind, to the remotest extremities of Ireland. I feel that every syllable that I articulate will be heard, not only by the hundreds within these walls, but by the millions without them. The press, I repeat it, is the trumpet, into which I put my spirit. I feel as if I stood upon some great eminence, and from that elevation addressed myself to congregated millions. To them, and not to you, I speak and say, " slaves —slaves, you are seven millions—know your own strength—appreciate your power—it is no longer fitting that a handful of men should lord it over you. Meet on the same day—at the same moment—meet loyally, legally and constitutionally—but meet—assemble round your altars and your priests—let the rites of your church be celebrated—let the chalice ascend and the cross be lifted up, and then raise your voices for liberty together. Raise such a call for freedom, as shall travel through every department of the State. Let the representatives of the people hearken to that burst of anguish from the people's hearts—let it reach into the lofty halls of the titled senate, and amidst the luxurious recesses of the kingly palace. Let it not be unheard. Let a shout go forth for freedom, at which England shall start—to which France shall not be deaf—at which princes shall be amazed, and cabinets shall stand appalled. Call for freedom, and call for it as your right—call for it in the name of reason—call for it in the name of justice—call for it in the name of expediency—call for it in the name of safety—call for it legally but determinedly—and above all—let seven millions call for it together.

ADJOURNMENT OF THE ASSOCIATION

SPEECH ON THE ADJOURNMENT OF THE ASSOCIATION, IN CONSEQUENCE OF MR. CANNING'S PROMOTION TO POWER.

THE time has arrived when proof should be given to England, that what the full stretch of legislative power could not effect—what an act of parliament, framed upon principles the most despotic, and constructed with all the perverse skill and malevolent nicety of legal art, could not achieve—a single measure of conciliation, or, I should rather say, the mere intimation of a more just and kindly feeling in the future government of this country, can at once and instantaneously accomplish. In order to crush the Roman Catholic Association, and carry a bill through the House of Commons for the purpose, every ministerial resource was employed—the executive influence was exercised to its utmost extent—every retainer of government, every tool of the Treasury, every expectant of office, was summoned by special requisition to the aid of the minister. The passions of the English people, their spirit of domination, their national pride, and their religious rancour, were studiously and strenuously excited, and England was persuaded, by the most vehement appeals to her ancient and inveterate animosities, to approve of an act of parliament, which afforded a fatal precedent, and struck the right of petition to the heart. Yet this obnoxious bill, which has justly received a name that suggests, if I may so say, the piracy of freedom, proved utterly unavailing, and the spirit of the Irish people appeared to derive new force and vigour from the measures of coercion which were adopted to put it down. But justice and kindness can do what severity and rigour were incapable of effecting, and the time has come, if not for the complete dissolution, for at least the temporary suspension of this assembly. In my opinion, we ought to give earnest to the government, of our disposition to assist their beneficent intentions towards this country, and of our solicitude to accommodate ourselves in every particular to their views, when we have once been convinced (as we are convinced) that a sincere disposition exists in the leading members of the administration to carry that measure upon which the happiness of Ireland mainly depends. I have not risen for the purpose of making a specific motion, because, from the peculiar circumstances in which I stand, I do not wish that a measure of adjournment should originate with myself. But I shall not be deterred by any consideration from stating what I believe to be not only the most generous and the most grateful, but also the wisest course which, under existing circumstances, we can adopt. I always thought that it beloved us, in the adverse fortunes of our country, to bear ourselves with a lofty and somewhat indignant demeanour. When I saw the spirit of perfidy presiding over the councils of the country—when I saw baseness and falsehood in the guise of candour and impartiality—when I found the faction by which Ireland has been so long insulted and oppressed, invested with despotic power, and the liberal portion of the administration utterly stripped and destitute of substantial influence, I could not but feel resentment at the monstrous imposture that was attempted to be practised upon us, and I spoke under the influence of those feelings of natural exasperation which it was impossible not to entertain, and to which it was difficult not to give vent. But now that hypocrisy and fraud have been banished from the Cabinet—now, that a man with a mind as large, and liberal, and enlightened, as was ever placed at the head of the government of these countries, has obtained that ascendancy, which has been hailed by the acclamations of the empire, and which is likely to be productive of incalculable good to Ireland- -now that there is something like honesty and fair dealing to be expected in the measures of the Cabinet, it befits us to lay aside the tone and language of acrimony and to accommodate our proceedings to the interests of those who have our benefit honestly at heart. The resolutions adopted at the aggregate meeting, not to press our petition against the desire of our advocates, appeared to me to be most judicious and expedient, and I was confirmed in that opinion, not only by the subsequent observations made by Mr. Brougham, whose attachment to our cause is not to be questioned, but still more by my Lord Eldon's wish that Catholic Emancipation should be immediately discussed. This generous aspiration of the learned and weeping lord, excited the merriment of the house. Indeed, it was ridiculous that a man who had, while in office, deprecated all consideration of the subject, should, the moment he was removed from place, urge on and endeavour to precipitate the matter into a premature discussion. Mr. Dawson, too, (the fraternal representative of Mr. Peel,) has, in a paroxysm of disappointed ambition, called for the immediate consideration of the measure. Alas! poor gentleman! his mind has been ruffled by his unexampled political adversity, and looks like the water in the old moat of Londonderry, roused from the stagnant tranquillity in which it lay covered with Orange ooze, into a storm. Mr. Peel is too cautious a man to indulge in bursts of rancour, and is anxious to preserve a character for peculiar moderation; but his brother-in-law, who was his under-secretary, and who of course imbibed his real feelings and opinions, affords an insight into the real character and motives of Mr. Peel. Our antagonists are most desirous for discussion—their solicitude to press the measure is the strongest argument that could be advanced for its suspension: and as we have wisely taken the determination not to embarrass our advocates by urging our petition, we shall only act with consistency, and follow up that judicious course of conduct by adjourning the meetings of the Association. Perhaps I shall be told that we ought not to indulge in sanguine expectations, and that we should have derived a better lesson from experience and the repeated frustration of our hopes—I answer, that we have now better grounds of confidence than we ever had since our question was first agitated in Parliament, and that it never stood in such a condition before. The circumstances of the question have changed in three material points. In the first place our most vehement opponents are out of office, the fury which they have displayed is evidence that they do not expect speedily to be restored to the luxuries of place. I cannot here refrain from making an observation relative to a recent statement made by Mr. Peel. That gentleman, who put in such extraordinary claims to manliness and honour, used to protest, when in office, that no distinction was ever made by him, in the distribution of patronage, between Catholic and Protestant. When the Catholic complained that, notwithstanding the pretended neutrality of the Cabinet, every place of emolument was given away to Orangemen, Mr. Peel used to declare. with the most solemn asseverations, that he paid no regard whatever to difference of religion, or to considerations of party in the selection of individuals for office. Mr. Goulbourn (his appropriate utensil) used to make the same declaration. What does Mr. Peel now state? He says that he adhered to the former administration because it had a Protestant Premier, and because the patronage of government, under his auspices, was exerted to support Protestant principles, and flowed in Protestant channels. So much for the ostentatious and elaborate frankness of the very manly and lofty-minded Secretary to the Home Department. The second material circumstance of change is, that a man is at the head of affairs who is devoted to our cause, and whose devotion to it is the ground upon which he has been deserted by his former colleagues. In the elevation of Mr. Canning to the highest station in the British empire, I rejoice, not only on account of my own country, but because he is the great champion of liberal opinions, and exhibits from the summit of power to which he has been raised, and from which he is beheld by all mankind, an object well worthy of their admiration. He is the author of South American freedom, and as long as liberty exists in the New World, (and it will be as eternal as the mountains from which its standard is unfurled) so long the celebrity of Mr. Canning will be transmitted from age to age in an illustrious perpetuation. In the triumph of this philosophical statesman, the cause, not only of liberty, but of intellect, has obtained a victory. The great struggle which has recently taken place, was a contest between mind and power; the grand cabal which lies defeated and shattered at the feet of this celebrated man, may be said to have been vanquished by the ascendancy of genius over all the might which the confederated oligarchy, by which the empire has been so long governed, could bring up against him. There cannot be a better evidence of the freedom of our institutions, and of the preponderance of the popular principle in our constitution, than that the eloquence of this extraordinary person prevailed not only over the power and influence of so large a portion of the aristocracy; but that the greatest captain of his time, with all his military renown, fell at once before it. It is an additional circumstance of honour to Mr. Canning that, as he himself recently stated, he is a poor man. With no other patrimony than his talents, he had almost every imaginable obstacle to contend with; yet, by the self-elevating power of intellect, he has raised himself, unaided by wealth, or aristocratic connexions, or any of the ordinary means of political ascent, to the highest point of glory to which it is possible for a subject of these countries to attain. The third circumstance of change to which I have adverted, as affording reason to change the policy on which we have hitherto wisely acted, but in which it would be injudicious to persevere, is the union between Mr. Canning and the Whigs. The opposition benches are deserted, or if they are not in utter solitude, it is only because such men as the Dawson, and Sir T. Lethbridge, that western luminary, are set, as a kind of beacon, to warn philosophy and liberality away. I am justified in saying, that a most important change, pregnant with high hopes, has taken place, and that any experience derived from past disappointment does not furnish an exact rule for our future conduct. I return, therefore, to my original advice, which is, that we suspend the meetings of the Association, with a view to smooth the way for the existing government. Independently of the other advantages which flow from this proceeding, we shall show the people of England, and the King of

England, (whose heart will, I am sure, at last prevail over any erroneous scruples suggested by my Lord Eldon's casuistry, when he was keeper of the royal conscience) that the true way to tranquillize Ireland is to treat her with kindness, and to win her affections and her gratitude. For my own part, violent and intemperate as I am deemed, there is nothing which I more sincerely and devoutly wish than to see my country at peace, to behold a reconciliation between all parties in this country, and England and Ireland inseparably bound by mutual interests, and a community of rights and privileges, together. I have always been convinced, and I never shall, I am sure, relinquish that strong persuasion, that the real happiness of Ireland can never be achieved except by an identity with England, and a complete consolidation with her empire, which never can be effected while differences of religion are made the standard of political distinction. I consider the diffusion of English habits, principles, and opinions as the greatest blessing that can befal my country. Let one act of justice be done to Ireland—let seven millions of her people be put on an equality with the rest of her inhabitants—let injurious and exasperating distinctions be abolished, and there is not a man amongst us who will not participate in the sentiment of ardent and enthusiastic loyalty, which, even in anticipation of a better system, is already growing up. The hope of witnessing the great measure of conciliation peacefully and satisfactorily carried through every branch of the legislature, has, if I may speak so much for myself, already removed every sentiment of political asperity from my mind; and, so far from indulging in any wish that the repose of England should be disturbed, that her greatness should be diminished, or her grandeur should be impaired, I trust that she will long continue to be the asylum and refuge of the genuine principles of liberty, and that the power which watches over the virtue and happiness of mankind, will, for the sake of both, render her empire equally glorious and everlasting.

VOTE OF THANKS TO MR. CONWAY.

SPEECH IN SECONDING A VOTE OF THANKS TO MR. CONWAY.

I SECOND the resolution of thanks to Mr. Conway. That gentleman, by the unremitting exercise of his distinguished abilities in the national service, has acquired a title to public gratitude, and large as the encomium is which Mr. O'Connell has pronounced upon him, it does not exceed his deserts. Mr. Conway is a Protestant; but although he does not kneel at the same altars, nor use the same formula of orison as ourselves, he derives, from the community of country, a participation in our sufferings, and gives expression to his sense of the heavy wrongs under which we labour, in language, perhaps, bolder and more strenuous than we should ourselves employ. The reason is this—the Roman

Catholic body is not wholly free from some of those bad moral results which political degradation is calculated to produce. We have been accustomed to consider ourselves an inferior class, and, until very recently, our tone and bearing were characterised by feelings which bespoke an humiliation bordering on servility. Our Protestant auxiliaries, who have not contracted the same habits, use language far more peremptory and indignant than we are wont to employ, and I need do no more than refer to the writings of Mr. Conway, in order to illustrate the justice of this remark. The merits of that gentleman are eminent indeed, and have acquired for him a high reputation, not only in Ireland, but in the sister country. He has won the applause of those whose panegyric is most valuable, as they are themselves the just objects of encomium; I may venture to state, that I myself, individually, know that Mr. Moore, who is, perhaps, the first writer of his time, looks upon Mr. Conway as a man of extraordinary abilities, and as a most useful servant of his country. The merits of Mr. Conway are obvious. His style is at once bold, vigorous, and clear; his expression is always pure, and not unfrequently highly imaginative and original. He is remarkable for the force and simplicity of his reasoning, as well as for power of diction and resources of phrase; and if the spirit of sarcasm occasionally breaks out in his compositions, and gall flows from his pen, it is against the enemies of his country that his invective, which never exceeds the fair limits of political discussion, is directed. But the chief merit of Mr. Conway—and it is a rare one in Ireland—consists in the minuteness with which he investigates elucidatory facts, and arranges the evidence by which his assertions are established. Mr. Macdonnell has well observed, that we indulge too much in abstract expatiations on our sufferings, and do not dwell sufficiently upon the specific instances of oppression, which would afford proof of the reasonableness of our complaints. Mr. Conway has not fallen into this mistake. His compositions are distinguished by the accuracy with which he goes through the details of oppression, and follows the spirit of tyranny through all its forms. Mr. Conway, in his letters to Lord Lansdowne, has displayed this, his peculiar talent, in an eminent degree. In those letters he has embraced the whole system of misgovernment which has produced the evils of this country. Although he has touched every subject with great felicity, there are two topics which he has lately treated with peculiar power and effect. He has denounced the Subletting Act, and co-operated with Mr. O'Connell in exhibiting the ruinous consequences of that most unmerciful measure. If there had been means of subsistence provided for the myriads of wretches who are to be the victims of this act of parliament, we should not complain of its effect. But every man of ordinary humanity must shudder at the idea of turning the mass of the population out of their miserable hovels, when there is no place of refuge afforded them, and they are left to perish upon the public road. If there were ships in every port ready to carry off the people to New Holland, we should, perhaps, acquiesce in this measure. But no such vent for the houseless and famishing peasantry is provided. The result, therefore, must be, that they will die in thousands upon thousands in the highway and in the streets. Even now the slaughterous consequences of this act are felt. The scythe of legislative massacre is mowing the people down, and the only consolation is, that there is a Judge in heaven before whom the framers of this measure will have to answer for this consecration of murder in the sanctuaries of legislation. The other topic to which I refer, in speaking of the services done by Mr. Conway, is the Established Church. We have too long observed a prudential silence in relation to that enormous mass of abuses—that huge accumulation of evil—that——what shall I call it? that nuisance in politics, and monstrosity in religion—the anti-Christian and anti-apostolic opulence of the Established Church. God forbid that I should attempt to insinuate that public worship, no matter in what form, should not be maintained in a manner befitting the nobleness of its object. The Church of Scotland affords a model. Its pastors are raised above indigence by the State—they are independent in circumstance, and conspicuous for their learning and their piety. The five hundred thousand Protestants of Ireland should have a respectable establishment predominant in law and in dignity; but it is insulting to reason, and it is a burlesque upon the Christian religion, that the ministers of that religion, in any shape, should roll in all the splendour of their gorgeous sinecurism, in the name of Him, who was born in a manger, and died upon a cross—what an object a bishop of the Establishment presents upon his death-bed! He grasps with his trembling hands, shaken with the tremor of agony, a renewal fine of ten thousand pounds, and then he goes to pass his account before the God of poverty in heaven. The death of a bishop! I wonder how the late bishop of Winchester looked, when his mitred spectre stood before the face of the living God—before whom, we are told by himself, that it is dreadful to appear. He died worth two hundred thousand pounds!! Bible-readers, Pope, Gordon, and the rest of you, is there warrant in the Scriptures for this? But I deviate from my subject. Mr. Conway has deserved well, by exhibiting this system in its proper light. So has Mr. Staunton, who has lately proved to demonstration, in his letters to Mr. Lamb, that the church is worth more than two millions a year! I trust that Mr. Hume will turn Mr. Staunton's admirable exposition to good account. I am sure he will. He has thanked him for the information which he has supplied, and stated that, by a perseverance in the course which Mr. Staunton has adopted, success must ultimately be achieved. To him and to Mr. Conway, for their candid co-operation in this great undertaking, we are greatly indebted. We owe large obligations to the liberal press. Almost every journal of respectability and influence in the empire are on our side. The adverse faction, indeed, in this country have newspapers which are in extensive circulation amongst them, and which are the appropriate channels by which the passions of the party find vent. There could not be a more befitting medium of evacuation for the bad and malignant feelings of the body of which those journals are the organ. It is not my habit to complain of the press. I think that every individual who, of his own accord, rushes into publicity, is a just object of comment, and, as he has made his election in betaking himself in politics, he must be prepared to submit to the strong reprehension of his antagonists, which he thus voluntarily incurs. But there are, after all, some limits to the exercise of that prerogative of vituperation, and at all events the expedient recently adopted with respect to Mr. Maguire, cannot admit of a palliation. What can be more unjustifiable, than after a public trial has taken place, to circulate hand-bills enclosed in the folds of newspapers, against a gentleman, whose only crime was, that he stood forward as the champion of his religion, which he defended with the ability of a most accomplished disputant, and the mildness which should distinguish a Christian priest. Against that individual a conspiracy of the foulest kind was formed. It was defeated But the faction have not given over their pursuit of him. They did not dare to print in their authorised journals, (which are some three or four,) any statement to his disparagement but they enclose in the folds of newspapers, libel conveying the most deadly insinuations against his character. Is this fair?—Is this consistent with the legitimate latitude of free discussion? Can the Protestants of Ireland approve of this? Is not this as ignoble as it is criminal? After having failed in their efforts to slay his character, in an open and undisguised attack, they shoot, from their dark and perfidious place of ambush, a poisoned shaft against him. Is not this the veriest treachery of malevolence? Is not this waylaying of reputation; and may it not be said of the turbulent and remorseless faction who do these things, that they would have been assassins if they had not been authors, and that they would have stabbed, if they had not written? Why should the Orangemen of Ireland put such means as these into operation, and have recourse to such unworthy stratagems against a poor, an humble, and unoffending priest? Do they want to force us into retaliation? Have we no parsons to set off against them? Do they forget? Have they so deeply drank of oblivion? Have they swallowed such large draughts of Lethe? Can they fail to remember the stigma that is branded upon the mitred forehead of their own hierarchy? Protestants of Ireland, cease, in mercy to your priesthood, to provoke us. We are your equals in invective, and we have a vantage ground in the materials of vituperation. You know ——But I will not breathe so detestable a sound. Human nature shrinks from its utterance. It would taint and pollute the moral atmosphere. Be then the name of the episcopal villain like his crime— " *inter Christians non nominandum.*"

PLATO AND DR. MAGEE.

SPEECH ON PLATO AND DR. MAGEE.

THERE is a pagan gorgeousness in the Church Establishment of Ireland, which is incompatible with the genius of Christianity, and repugnant to the first elements of our belief. Let me suppose, that some philosopher of antiquity, Plato, for example, were called up from the dead

The fancy may often be employed as a guide to [
argument be presented in an imaginative shape.
reason lights its way, may be moulded in a str
Let me then suppose (and let no severe logician q
agance of the hypothesis), that the spirit of Pl
some necromantic process of resuscitation, and tl
sited "glimpses of the moon," the task of offe
conversion to Christianity were committed to th
neck and apostolic forehead has been recently in
episcopal mitre of the metropolis. Let me be
that the ex-fellow of the University of Dublin w
early occupations from which his sacred prosperi
were intrusted with the religious education of th(
pher, and that having again become tutor, he s
his pupil. I pass by the preliminaries of introd
distinguished personages, and say nothing of the a
at the episcopal jauntiness of air and the volatile
which characterise the learned Doctor. Let m(
of Plato to have subsided at the novelty of this
which the Doctor performs so important a part,
been contented upon the other subjects of his adm
"Where are the gods of the old time? What h
Does the thunder no longer roll at his behest? '
martial maid to whom Athens had devoted her p
built that lofty shrine, whose chasteness of form '
its name with the virgin majesty of Minerva?
worship of the god of poetry and light? Has h
own adventurous boy, from the chariot of the sur
gatory the Doctor replies, "These graceful but u
idolatrous imagination of your country have retur
ness from which they rose. These splendid vapo
vanished like the illuminated mists of the mount
of Greece held their imaginary abode. These
creed have passed away, and that of which you, (
tes, in one of your noblest dialogues have given a
has been realized, in a pure and celestial system of
There came from heaven a Being whose prece
evidence of their divinity, and who, to use your
prediction, 'hath taught us to pray.' His comir
in thunder, nor was his mission illustrated with
His arrival on the earth was told in the solitude
a peaceful and lonely song to 'shepherds abidii
'Ie descended as an emissary of that Godhead of
a messenger and an emanation, in the lowliest fo
able humanity could be invested. His whole life
birth was obscure. The poor, the sorrowful, and
his companions. His only pomp consisted in the
lations, and even their sublimity was tempered by
moral inculcations; mercy dwelt for ever on his

tender attributes over all his actions. Humility was deified in his person. It was from the throne of shame and suffering that he proclaimed himself a monarch, and his last act of moral sovereignty was the pathetic cry of forgiveness, at the remembrance of which, the infidel of Geneva could not refrain from lapsing into an involuntary credulity, and exclaiming, in the spirit of the soldier who attended his agony, that if the death of Socrates was the death of a sage, the death of Jesus was that of God. His disciples participated in the divine character of their preceptor, and the twelve inspired teachers of his eternal word propagated his doctrines with the humility of him from whom they had received them. The spirit of their religion was typified by the meekness of a dove. They went forth with naked feet, and with scarce enough of raiment to shield them from the inclemency of the air. They spent their lives in the fasting and the prayer which they prescribed; they taught mankind that there was a sanctity in suffering, and a blessedness in tears; that life was a brief and miserable transition to that heaven towards which their eyes were for ever turned; and that the kingdom of Jesus was not of this world. Such were the first propagators of that sublime religion in which I have undertaken to give you instructions. I am one of the anointed representatives of those inspired, but meek and patient, men—and in me you behold a successor of the apostles." You! Plato would exclaim; and I leave you to conjecture the expression of surprise that would needs invest the features of the philosopher, in the utterance of the monosyllabic ejaculation of astonishment. The Doctor (let us suppose) proceeds to give the gospel to Plato, who peruses the holy writings and afterwards returns to his preceptor in humility. " I have read," he may be imagined to say, " I have read the wonderful book which you have placed in my hands, and I confess that all the volumes of philosophy vanish before it. It is impressed with the seal of inspiration, and its pages are the records of heaven. In my own visions of perfection, I never reached even in conjecture, to a point of moral sublimity which could be compared with the incalculable elevation of this super-human system of goodness, of mercy, and of love. But Doctor, forgive me for asking you, whether you participate in that high conviction which it is your profession to impart?" " I," cries the Doctor! " what a question to the Author of the Atonement!" "I hear, indeed," the philosopher might reply, "that you, yourself, made an atonement, but without a sacrifice. You have expiated certain deviations into liberality, into which you wandered before your advancement to the glittering top from which you super intend and overlook the religion of Jesus. Doctor, I must be candid with you: of course I cannot controvert the truth of your asseveration, but, I own, I never should have taken you to be a successor of the humble philosophers of Palestine. You remind me more of some of the spruce and acrimonious disputants, called sophists, who used of old to infest the groves of the academy. You tell me that the mildness of your master was expressed by the softness of the dove; your own spirit would find its emblem in the proud and predatory falcon. You are a preceptor of forgiveness, while your pen distils virulence in every word—your lips, that should breathe nothing but mercy, are smeared with the poison of polemics—you leave venom in your very kiss of peace: even your pastoral injunctions, that should be the effusions of tenderness and pity, overflow with bitterness and gall. You have sent an arrow, in the shape of a barbed antithesis, to rankle in the heart of your country, and not content with an insult to the living, you offer profanation to the dead. You and your brother pontiffs talk of poverty; while the yearly income which you derive from the public would, at the rate of Athenian exchange, amount to several talents. You speak of humility, while you tread on the tip-toe of importance, and haughtiness sits mitred on your brow. You prescribe the ascetic regimen of self-denial, while you quaff the richest nectar out of silver and gold. You are lapped in down, while you bid your followers make their couch of the frozen earth, and you are over-canopied with purple, while you tell them that a Christian should have no other roof but the cope of heaven above his head. From the banquet of Dives, you hold up Lazarus to imitation. Your palaces outvie the temples of the fallen Gods; and you have substituted your selves for the idols you deride. As to yourself, you are, individually, I hear, a learned and a moral man, but there are those of your fraternity who plunge headlong into the gulf of voluptuousness, and have carried their sensuality to a most foul and flagitious excess. A sordid avidity for gain rages amongst your pampered priesthood. In the complicated machinery of your exactions they grind the fruits of the peasant's industry to the husk. What, then, am I to think? Is there not a practical refutation in your inculcations? and must I not regard your injunctions of poverty, humility, and self-abnegation as a mockery of all reason, and as an insult to all common sense?" "My dear Plato," replies the Doctor, "since our last meeting you must have been infected by the factious fanaticism of some Popish priest." "I have observed, indeed," replies the philosopher, "a body of men, who claimed a succession from the primitive teachers of their religion, in whose lives I found an exemplification of their opinions, and an evidence of their high and ardent belief. Pious, humble, and abstemious, zealous in the discharge of their laborious duties, and distinguished by their pure and immaculate morality, they present an image of those disciples of their Master, whose example they practically uphold. You, Doctor, proclaim to the world, that these men constitute a church without a religion, and you tell others that they have a religion without a church; but, for my own part, I can perceive in the monstrous superstructure which has been raised in your establishment upon the simple foundation of Christianity, neither a religion nor a church." "But, Plato," replies the Doctor, "you make no allowance for the change of society and circumstances, and for the need of a conformity between the condition of mankind and the form of their worship." "I read in the sacred book which you have placed in my hands, that the spirit of evil ascended with your master to the summit of a mountain, and having bade him survey the world, offered it to his dominion. Do you think that the spectacle that was then disclosed to him offered to his contemplation a scene of magnificence inferior to the splendour of your modern earth

When Rome arose in her majesty upon the eyes of your unambitious Master, did the mistress of the world present an expanse of towers, and domes, and temples less bright and golden than the most famous of your cities? It was at a period when mankind was raised to the highest point of civilization, and in the full noon of imperial glory, that Christ appeared. Did he think it needful that his religion should be allied with the Cæsars, or that his apostles should sit mitred in the Roman senate? and if the state of mankind did not then require that Christianity should be proud, and opulent, and luxurious, why should it now be invested with attributes so abhorrent from its pure and simple nature? Take back the book which you have given me—imbue your life with its spirit, dismiss your equipages, and discard your worldly pomp, lay down your pontifical magnificence, and return the larger portion of your enormous wealth to the poor, from whom it is wrung—be meek, and gentle, and forbearing—be compassionate to the living, and be respectful to the dead; and then, resuming your functions as a teacher of the Christian religion, you may enforce the lofty maxims which it contains, not only by the acuteness of your reasoning, but by the more persuasive eloquence of your example."

THE END

www.ingramcontent.com/pod-product-compliance
Lightning Source LLC
Chambersburg PA
CBHW021426300426
44114CB00010B/662